Warren County Illinois

The Past and Present of Warren County, Illinois

Containing a History of the County--its Cities, Towns, &c....

Warren County Illinois

The Past and Present of Warren County, Illinois
Containing a History of the County--its Cities, Towns, &c....

ISBN/EAN: 9783337099657

Printed in Europe, USA, Canada, Australia, Japan

Cover: Foto ©ninafisch / pixelio.de

More available books at **www.hansebooks.com**

THE

PAST AND PRESENT

OF

WARREN COUNTY, ILLINOIS,

CONTAINING

A History of the County—Its Cities, Towns, &c., A Biographical Directory of its Citizens, War Record of its Volunteers in the late Rebellion, Portraits of Early Settlers and Prominent Men, General and Local Statistics, Map of Warren County, History of Illinois, Constitution of the United States, Miscellaneous Matters, Etc., Etc.

CHICAGO:
H. F. KETT & CO., Cor. 5th Ave. and Washington St.
1877.

HISTORY OF ILLINOIS.

The name of this beautiful Prairie State is derived from *Illini*, a Delaware word signifying Superior Men. It has a French termination, and is a symbol of how the two races—the French and the Indians—were intermixed during the early history of the country.

The appellation was no doubt well applied to the primitive inhabitants of the soil whose prowess in savage warfare long withstood the combined attacks of the fierce Iroquois on the one side, and the no less savage and relentless Sacs and Foxes on the other. The Illinois were once a powerful confederacy, occupying the most beautiful and fertile region in the great Valley of the Mississippi, which their enemies coveted and struggled long and hard to wrest from them. By the fortunes of war they were diminished in numbers, and finally destroyed. "Starved Rock," on the Illinois River, according to tradition, commemorates their last tragedy, where, it is said, the entire tribe starved rather than surrender.

EARLY DISCOVERIES.

The first European discoveries in Illinois date back over two hundred years. They are a part of that movement which, from the beginning to the middle of the seventeenth century, brought the French Canadian missionaries and fur traders into the Valley of the Mississippi, and which, at a later period, established the civil and ecclesiastical authority of France from the Gulf of St. Lawrence to the Gulf of Mexico, and from the foot-hills of the Alleghanies to the Rocky Mountains.

The great river of the West had been discovered by DeSoto, the Spanish conqueror of Florida, three quarters of a century before the French founded Quebec in 1608, but the Spanish left the country a wilderness, without further exploration or settlement within its borders, in which condition it remained until the Mississippi was discovered by the agents of the French Canadian government, Joliet and Marquette, in 1673. These renowned explorers were not the first white visitors to Illinois. In 1671—two years in advance of them—came Nicholas Perrot to Chicago. He had been sent by Talon as an agent of the Canadian government to call a great peace convention of Western Indians at Green Bay, preparatory to the movement for the discovery of the Mississippi. It was deemed a good stroke of policy to secure, as far as possible, the friendship and co-operation of the Indians, far and near, before venturing upon an enterprise which their hostility might render disastrous, and which their friendship and assistance would do so much to make successful; and to this end Perrot was sent to call together in council the tribes throughout the Northwest, and to promise them the commerce and protection of the French government. He accordingly arrived at Green Bay in 1671, and procuring an escort of Pottawattamies, proceeded in a bark canoe upon a visit to the Miamis, at Chicago. Perrot was therefore the first European to set foot upon the soil of Illinois.

Still there were others before Marquette. In 1672, the Jesuit missionaries, Fathers Claude Allouez and Claude Dablon, bore the standard of the Cross from their mission at Green Bay through western Wisconsin and northern Illinois, visiting the Foxes on Fox River, and the Masquotines and Kickapoos at the mouth of the Milwaukee. These missionaries penetrated on the route afterwards followed by Marquette as far as the Kickapoo village at the head of Lake Winnebago, where Marquette, in his journey, secured guides across the portage to the Wisconsin.

The oft-repeated story of Marquette and Joliet is well known. They were the agents employed by the Canadian government to discover the Mississippi. Marquette was a native of France, born in 1637, a Jesuit priest by education, and a man of simple faith and of great zeal and devotion in extending the Roman Catholic religion among the Indians. Arriving in Canada in 1666, he was sent as a missionary to the far Northwest, and, in 1668, founded a mission at Sault Ste. Marie. The following year he moved to La Pointe, in Lake Superior, where he instructed a branch of the Hurons till 1670, when he removed south, and founded the mission at St. Ignace, on the Straits of Mackinaw. Here he remained, devoting a portion of his time to the study of the Illinois language under a native teacher who had accompanied him to the mission from La Pointe, till he was joined by Joliet in the Spring of 1673. By the way of Green Bay and the Fox and Wisconsin Rivers, they entered the Mississippi, which they explored to the mouth of the Arkansas, and returned by the way of the Illinois and Chicago Rivers to Lake Michigan.

On his way up the Illinois, Marquette visited the great village of the Kaskaskias, near what is now Utica, in the county of LaSalle. The following year he returned and established among them the mission of the Immaculate Virgin Mary, which was the first Jesuit mission founded in Illinois and in the Mississippi Valley. The intervening winter he had spent in a hut which his companions erected on the Chicago River, a few leagues from its mouth. The founding of this mission was the last act of Marquette's life. He died in Michigan, on his way back to Green Bay, May 18, 1675.

FIRST FRENCH OCCUPATION.

The first French occupation of the territory now embraced in Illinois was effected by LaSalle in 1680, seven years after the time of Marquette and Joliet. LaSalle, having constructed a vessel, the "Griffin," above the falls of Niagara, which he sailed to Green Bay, and having passed thence in canoes to the mouth of the St. Joseph River, by which and the Kankakee he reached the Illinois, in January, 1680, erected Fort *Crevecœur*, at the lower end of Peoria Lake, where the city of Peoria is now situated. The place where this ancient fort stood may still be seen just below the outlet of Peoria Lake. It was destined, however, to a temporary existence. From this point, LaSalle determined to descend the Mississippi to its mouth, but did not accomplish this purpose till two years later—in 1682. Returning to Fort Frontenac for the purpose of getting materials with which to rig his vessel, he left the fort in charge of Touti, his lieutenant, who during his absence was driven off by the Iroquois Indians. These savages had made a raid upon the settlement of the Illinois, and had left nothing in their track but ruin and desolation. Mr. Davidson, in his History of Illinois, gives the following graphic account of the picture that met the eyes of LaSalle and his companions on their return:

"At the great town of the Illinois they were appalled at the scene which opened to their view. No hunter appeared to break its death-like silence with a salutatory whoop of welcome. The plain on which the town had stood was now strewn with charred fragments of lodges, which had so recently swarmed with savage life and hilarity. To render more hideous the picture of desolation, large numbers of skulls had been placed on the upper extremities of lodge-poles which had escaped the devouring flames. In the midst of these horrors was the rude fort of the spoilers, rendered frightful by the same ghastly relics. A near approach showed that the graves had been robbed of their bodies, and swarms of buzzards were discovered glutting their loathsome stomachs on the reeking corruption. To complete the work of destruction, the growing corn of the village had been cut down and burned, while the pits containing the products of previous years, had been rifled and their contents scattered with wanton waste. It was evident the suspected blow of the Iroquois had fallen with relentless fury."

Touti had escaped LaSalle knew not whither. Passing down the lake in search of him and his men, LaSalle discovered that the fort had been destroyed, but the vessel which he had partly constructed was still on the stocks and but slightly injured. After further fruitless search, failing to find Touti, he fastened to a tree a painting representing himself and party sitting in a canoe and bearing a pipe of peace, and to the painting attached a letter addressed to Touti.

Touti had escaped, and, after untold privations, taken shelter among the Pottawattamies near Green Bay. These were friendly to the French. One of their old chiefs used to say, "There were but three great captains in the world, himself, Touti and LaSalle."

GENIUS OF LASALLE.

We must now return to LaSalle, whose exploits stand out in such bold relief. He was born in Rouen, France, in 1643. His father was wealthy, but he renounced his patrimony on entering a college of the Jesuits, from which he separated and came to Canada a poor man in 1666. The priests of St. Sulpice, among whom he had a brother, were then the proprietors of Montreal, the nucleus of which was a seminary or convent founded by that order. The Superior granted to LaSalle a large tract of land at LaChine, where he established himself in the fur trade. He was a man of daring genius, and outstripped all his competitors in exploits of travel and commerce with the Indians. In 1669, he visited the headquarters of the great Iroquois Confederacy, at Onondaga, in the heart of New York, and, obtaining guides, explored the Ohio River to the falls at Louisville.

In order to understand the genius of LaSalle, it must be remembered that for many years prior to his time the missionaries and traders were obliged to make their way to the Northwest by the Ottawa River (of Canada) on account of the fierce hostility of the Iroquois along the lower lakes and Niagara River, which entirely closed this latter route to the Upper Lakes. They carried on their commerce chiefly by canoes, paddling them through the Ottawa to Lake Nipissing, carrying them across the portage to French River, and descending that to Lake Huron. This being the route by which they reached the Northwest, accounts for the fact that all the earliest Jesuit missions were established in the neighborhood of the Upper Lakes. LaSalle conceived the grand idea of opening the route by Niagara River and the Lower Lakes to Canadian commerce by sail vessels, connecting it with the navigation of the Mississippi, and thus opening a magnificent water communication from the Gulf of St. Lawrence to the Gulf of Mexico. This truly grand and comprehensive purpose seems to have animated him in all his wonderful achievements and the matchless difficulties and hardships he surmounted. As the first step in the accomplishment of this object he established himself on Lake Ontario, and built and garrisoned Fort Frontenac, the site of the present city of Kingston, Canada. Here he obtained a grant of land from the French crown and a body of troops by which he beat back the invading Iroquois and cleared the passage to Niagara Falls. Having by this masterly stroke made it safe to attempt a hitherto untried expedition, his next step, as we have seen, was to advance to the Falls with all his outfit for building a ship with which to sail the lakes. He was successful in this undertaking, though his ultimate purpose was defeated by a strange combination of untoward circumstances. The Jesuits evidently hated LaSalle and plotted against him, because he had abandoned them and co-operated with a rival order. The fur traders were also jealous of his superior success in opening new channels of commerce. At LaChine he had taken the trade of Lake Ontario, which but for his presence there would have gone to Quebec. While they were plodding with their bark canoes through the Ottawa he was constructing sailing vessels to command the trade of the lakes and the Mississippi. These great plans excited the jealousy and envy of the small traders, introduced treason and revolt into the ranks of his own companions, and finally led to the foul assassination by which his great achievements were prematurely ended.

In 1682, LaSalle, having completed his vessel at Peoria, descended the Mississippi to its confluence with the Gulf of Mexico. Erecting a standard on which he inscribed the arms of France, he took formal possession of the whole valley of the mighty river, in the name of Louis XIV., then reigning, in honor of whom he named the country LOUISIANA.

LaSalle then went to France, was appointed Governor, and returned with a fleet and immigrants, for the purpose of planting a colony in Illinois. They arrived in due time in the Gulf of Mexico, but failing to find the mouth of the Mississippi, up which LaSalle intended to sail, his supply ship, with the immigrants, was driven ashore and wrecked on Matagorda Bay. With the fragments of the vessel he constructed a stockade and rude huts on the shore for the protection of the immigrants, calling the post Fort St. Louis. He then made a trip into New Mexico, in search of silver mines, but, meeting with disappointment, returned to find his little colony reduced to forty souls. He then resolved to travel on foot to Illinois, and, starting with his companions, had reached the valley of the Colorado, near the mouth of Trinity river, when he was shot by one of his men. This occurred on the 19th of March, 1687.

Dr. J. W. Foster remarks of him: "Thus fell, not far from the banks of the Trinity, Robert Cavalier de la Salle, one of the grandest characters that ever figured in American history—a man capable of originating the vastest schemes, and endowed with a will and a judgment capable of carrying them to successful results. Had ample facilities been placed by the King of France at his disposal, the result of the colonization of this continent might have been far different from what we now behold."

EARLY SETTLEMENTS.

A temporary settlement was made at Fort St. Louis, or the old Kaskaskia village, on the Illinois River, in what is now LaSalle County, in 1682. In 1690, this was removed, with the mission connected with it, to Kaskaskia, on the river of that name, emptying into the lower Mississippi in St. Clair County. Cahokia was settled about the same time, or at least, both of these settlements began in the year 1690, though it is now pretty well settled that Cahokia is the older place, and ranks as the oldest permanent settlement in Illinois, as well as in the Mississippi Valley. The reason for the removal of the old Kaskaskia settlement and mission, was probably because the dangerous and difficult route by Lake Michigan and the Chicago portage had been almost abandoned, and travelers and traders passed down and up the Mississippi by the Fox and Wisconsin River route. They removed to the vicinity of the Mississippi in order to be in the line of travel from Canada to Louisiana, that is, the lower part of it, for it was all Louisiana then south of the lakes.

During the period of French rule in Louisiana, the population probably never exceeded ten thousand, including whites and blacks. Within that portion of it now included in Indiana, trading posts were established at the principal Miami villages which stood on the head waters of the Maumee, the Wea villages situated at Ouiatenon, on the Wabash, and the Piankeshaw villages at Post Vincennes; all of which were probably visited by French traders and missionaries before the close of the seventeenth century.

In the vast territory claimed by the French, many settlements of considerable importance had sprung up. Biloxi, on Mobile Bay, had been founded by D'Iberville, in 1699; Antoine de Lamotte Cadillac had founded Detroit in 1701; and New Orleans had been founded by Bienville, under the auspices of the Mississippi Company, in 1718. In Illinois also, considerable settlements had been made, so that in 1730 they embraced one hundred and forty French families, about six hundred "converted Indians," and many traders and voyageurs. In that portion of the country, on the east side of the Mississippi, there were five distinct settlements, with their respective villages, viz.: Cahokia, near the mouth of Cahokia Creek and about five miles below the present city of St. Louis; St. Philip, about forty-five miles below Cahokia, and four miles above Fort Chartres; Fort Chartres, twelve miles above Kaskaskia; Kaskaskia, situated on the Kaskaskia River, five miles above its confluence with the Mississippi; and Prairie du Rocher, near Fort Chartres. To these must be added St. Genevieve and St. Louis, on the west side of the Mississippi. These, with the exception of St. Louis, are among the oldest French towns in the Mississippi Valley. Kaskaskia, in its best days, was a town of some two or three thousand inhabitants. After it passed from the crown of France its population for many years did not exceed fifteen hundred. Under British rule, in 1773, the population had decreased to four hundred and fifty. As early as 1721, the Jesuits had established a college and a monastery in Kaskaskia.

Fort Chartres was first built under the direction of the Mississippi Company, in 1718, by M. de Boisbraint, a military officer, under command of Bienville. It stood on the east bank of the Mississippi, about eighteen miles below Kaskaskia, and was for some time the headquarters of the military commandants of the district of Illinois.

In the Centennial Oration of Dr. Fowler, delivered at Philadelphia, by appointment of Gov. Beveridge, we find some interesting facts with regard to the State of Illinois, which we appropriate in this history:

In 1682 Illinois became a possession of the French crown, a dependency of Canada, and a part of Louisiana. In 1765 the English flag was run up on old Fort Chartres, and Illinois was counted among the treasures of Great Britain.

In 1779 it was taken from the English by Col. George Rogers Clark. This man was resolute in nature, wise in council, prudent in policy, bold in action, and heroic in danger. Few men who have figured in the history of America are more deserving than this colonel. Nothing short of first-class ability could have rescued Vincens and all Illinois from the English. And it is not possible to over-estimate the influence of this achievement upon the republic. In 1779 Illinois became a part of Virginia. It was soon known as Illinois County. In 1784 Virginia ceded all this territory to the general government, to be cut into States, to be republican in form, with "the same right of sovereignty, freedom, and independence as the other States."

In 1787 it was the object of the wisest and ablest legislation found in any merely human records. No man can study the secret history of

THE "COMPACT OF 1787,"

and not feel that Providence was guiding with sleepless eye these unborn States. The ordinance that on July 13, 1787, finally became the incorporating act, has a most marvelous history. Jefferson had vainly tried to secure a system of government for the northwestern territory. He was an emancipationist of that day, and favored the exclusion of slavery from the territory Virginia had ceded to the general government; but the South voted him down as often as it came up. In 1787, as late as July 10, an organizing act without the anti-slavery clause was pending. This concession to the South was expected to carry it. Congress was in session in New York City. On July 5, Rev. Dr. Manasseh Cutler, of Massachusetts, came into New York to lobby on the northwestern territory. Everything seemed to fall into his hands. Events were ripe.

The state of the public credit, the growing of Southern prejudice, the basis of his mission, his personal character, all combined to complete one of those sudden and marvelous revolutions of public sentiment that once in five or ten centuries are seen to sweep over a country like the breath of the Almighty. Cutler was a graduate of Yale—received his A.M. from Harvard, and his D.D. from Yale. He had studied and taken degrees in the three learned professions, medicine, law, and divinity. He had thus America's best indorsement. He had published a scientific examination of the plants of New England. His name stood second only to that of Franklin as a scientist in America. He was a courtly gentleman of the old style, a man of commanding presence, and of inviting face. The Southern members said they had never seen such a gentleman in the North. He came representing a company that desired to purchase a tract of land now included in Ohio, for the purpose of planting a colony. It was a speculation. Government money was worth eighteen cents on the dollar. This Massachusetts company had collected enough to purchase 1,500.000 acres of land. Other speculators in New York made Dr. Cutler their agent (lobbyist). On the 12th he represented a demand for 5,500,000 acres. This would reduce the national debt. Jefferson and Virginia were regarded as authority concerning the land Virginia had just ceded. Jefferson's policy wanted to provide for the public credit, and this was a good opportunity to do something.

Massachusetts then owned the territory of Maine, which she was crowding on the market. She was opposed to opening the northwestern region. This fired the zeal of Virginia. The South caught the inspiration, and all exalted Dr. Cutler. The English minister invited him to dine with some of the Southern gentlemen. He was the center of interest.

The entire South rallied round him. Massachusetts could not vote against him, because many of the constituents of her members were interested personally in the western speculation. Thus Cutler, making friends with the South, and, doubtless, using all the arts of the lobby, was enabled to command the situation. True to deeper convictions, he dictated one of the most compact and finished documents of wise statesmanship that has ever adorned any human law book. He borrowed from Jefferson the term "Articles of Compact," which, preceding the federal constitution, rose into the most sacred character. He then followed very closely the constitution of Massachusetts, adopted three years before. Its most marked points were:

1. The exclusion of slavery from the territory forever.
2. Provision for public schools, giving one township for a seminary,

and every section numbered 16 in each township; that is, one-thirty-sixth of all the land, for public schools.

3. A provision prohibiting the adoption of any constitution or the enactment of any law that should nullify pre-existing contracts.

Be it forever remembered that this compact declared that "Religion, morality, and knowledge being necessary to good government and the happiness of mankind, schools and the means of education shall always be encouraged."

Dr. Cutler planted himself on this platform and would not yield. Giving his unqualified declaration that it was that or nothing—that unless they could make the land desirable they did not want it—he took his horse and buggy, and started for the constitutional convention in Philadelphia. On July 13, 1787, the bill was put upon its passage, and was unanimously adopted, every Southern member voting for it, and only one man, Mr. Yates, of New York, voting against it. But as the States voted as States, Yates lost his vote, and the compact was put beyond repeal.

Thus the great States of Ohio, Indiana, Illinois, Michigan and Wisconsin—a vast empire, the heart of the great valley—were consecrated to freedom, intelligence, and honesty. Thus the great heart of the nation was prepared for a year and a day and an hour. In the light of these eighty-nine years I affirm that this act was the salvation of the republic and the destruction of slavery. Soon the South saw their great blunder, and tried to repeal the compact. In 1803 Congress referred it to a committee of which John Randolph was chairman. He reported that this ordinance was a compact, and opposed repeal. Thus it stood a rock, in the way of the on-rushing sea of slavery.

With all this timely aid it was, after all, a most desperate and protracted struggle to keep the soil of Illinois sacred to freedom. It was the natural battle-field for the irrepressible conflict. In the southern end of the State slavery preceded the compact. It existed among the old French settlers, and was hard to eradicate. The southern part of the State was settled from the slave States, and this population brought their laws, customs, and institutions with them. A stream of population from the North poured into the northern part of the State. These sections misunderstood and hated each other perfectly. The Southerners regarded the Yankees as a skinning, tricky, penurious race of peddlers, filling the country with tinware, brass clocks, and wooden nutmegs. The Northerner thought of the Southerner as a lean, lank, lazy creature, burrowing in a hut, and rioting in whisky, dirt and ignorance. These causes aided in making the struggle long and bitter. So strong was the sympathy with slavery that, in spite of the ordinance of 1787, and in spite of the deed of cession, it was determined to allow the old French settlers to retain their slaves. Planters from the slave States might bring their slaves, if they would give them a chance to choose freedom or years of service and bondage for their children till they should become thirty years of age. If they chose freedom they must leave the State in sixty days or be sold as fugitives. Servants were whipped for offenses for which white men are fined. Each lash paid forty cents of the fine. A negro ten miles from home without a pass was whipped. These famous laws were imported from the slave States just as they imported laws for the inspection of flax and wool when there was neither in the State.

These Black Laws are now wiped out. A vigorous effort was made to protect slavery in the State Constitution of 1817. It barely failed. It was renewed in 1825, when a convention was asked to make a new constitution. After a hard fight the convention was defeated. But slaves did not disappear from the census of the State until 1850. There were mobs and murders in the interest of slavery. Lovejoy was added to the list of martyrs—a sort of first-fruits of that long life of immortal heroes who saw freedom as the one supreme desire of their souls, and were so enamored of her that they preferred to die rather than survive her.

The population of 12,282 that occupied the territory in A.D. 1800, increased to 45,000 in A.D. 1818, when the State Constitution was adopted, and Illinois took her place in the Union, with a star on the flag and two votes in the Senate.

Shadrach Bond was the first Governor, and in his first message he recommended the construction of the Illinois and Michigan Canal.

The simple economy in those days is seen in the fact that the entire bill for stationery for the first Legislature was only $13.50. Yet this simple body actually enacted a very superior code.

There was no money in the territory before the war of 1812. Deer skins and coon skins were the circulating medium. In 1821, the Legislature ordained a State Bank on the credit of the State. It issued notes in the likeness of bank bills. These notes were made a legal tender for every thing, and the bank was ordered to loan to the people $100 on personal security, and more on mortgages. They actually passed a resolution requesting the Secretary of the Treasury of the United States to receive these notes for land. The old French Lieutenant Governor, Col. Menard, put the resolution as follows: "Gentlemen of the Senate: It is moved and seconded dat de notes of dis bank be made land-office money. All in favor of dat motion say aye; all against it say no. It is decided in de affirmative. Now, gentlemen, I bet you one hundred dollar he never be land-office money!" Hard sense, like hard money, is always above par.

This old Frenchman presents a fine figure up against the dark background of most of his nation. They made no progress. They clung to their earliest and simplest implements. They never wore hats or caps.

They pulled their blankets over their heads in the winter like the Indians, with whom they freely intermingled.

Demagogism had an early development. One John Grammar (only in name), elected to the Territorial and State Legislatures of 1816 and 1836, invented the policy of opposing every new thing, saying, "If it succeeds, no one will ask who voted against it. If it proves a failure, he could quote its record." In sharp contrast with Grammar was the character of D. P. Cook, after whom the county containing Chicago was named. Such was his transparent integrity and remarkable ability that his will was almost the law of the State. In Congress, a young man, and from a poor State, he was made Chairman of the Ways and Means Committee. He was pre-eminent for standing by his committee, regardless of consequences. It was his integrity that elected John Quincy Adams to the Presidency. There were four candidates in 1824, Jackson, Clay, Crawford, and John Quincy Adams. There being no choice by the people, the election was thrown into the House. It was so balanced that it turned on his vote, and that he cast for Adams, electing him; then went home to face the wrath of the Jackson party in Illinois. It cost him all but character and greatness. It is a suggestive comment on the times, that there was no legal interest till 1830. It often reached 150 per cent., usually 50 per cent. Then it was reduced to 12, and now to 10 per cent.

PHYSICAL FEATURES OF THE PRAIRIE STATE.

In area, the State has 55,410 square miles of territory. It is about 150 miles wide and 400 miles long, stretching in latitude from Maine to North Carolina. It embraces wide variety of climate. It is tempered on the north by the great inland, saltless, tideless sea, which keeps the thermometer from either extreme. Being a table land, from 600 to 1,600 feet above the level of the sea, one is prepared to find on the health maps, prepared by the general government, an almost clean and perfect record. In freedom from fever and malarial diseases and consumptions, the three deadly enemies of the American Saxon, Illinois, as a State, stands without a superior. She furnishes one of the essential conditions of a great people—sound bodies. I suspect that this fact lies back of that old Delaware word, Illini, superior men.

The great battles of history that have been determinative of dynasties and destinies have been strategical battles, chiefly the question of position. Thermopylae has been the war-cry of freemen for twenty-four centuries. It only tells how much there may be in position. All this advantage belongs to Illinois. It is in the heart of the greatest valley in the world, the vast region between the mountains—a valley that could feed mankind for one thousand years. It is well on toward the center of the continent. It is in the great temperate belt, in which have been found nearly all the aggressive civilizations of history. It has sixty-five miles of frontage on the head of the lake. With the Mississippi forming the western and southern boundary, with the Ohio running along the southeastern line, with the Illinois River and Canal dividing the State diagonally from the lake to the Lower Mississippi, and with the Rock and Wabash Rivers furnishing altogether 2,000 miles of water-front, connecting with, and running through, in all about 12,000 miles of navigable water.

But this is not all. These waters are made most available by the fact that the lake and the State lie on the ridge running into the great valley from the east. Within cannon-shot of the lake the water runs away from the lake to the Gulf. The lake now empties at both ends, one into the Atlantic and one into the Gulf of Mexico. The lake thus seems to hang over the land. This makes the dockage most serviceable; there are no steep banks to damage it. Both lake and river are made for use.

The climate varies from Portland to Richmond; it favors every product of the continent, including the tropics, with less than half a dozen exceptions. It produces every great nutriment of the world except bananas and rice. It is hardly too much to say that it is the most productive spot known to civilization. With the soil full of bread and the earth full of minerals; with an upper surface of food and an under layer of fuel; with perfect natural drainage, and abundant springs and streams and navigable rivers; half way between the forests of the North and the fruits of the South; within a day's ride of the great deposits of iron, coal, copper, lead, and zinc; containing and controlling the great grain, cattle, pork, and lumber markets of the world, it is not strange that Illinois has the advantage of position.

This advantage has been supplemented by the character of the population. In the early days when Illinois was first admitted to the Union, her population were chiefly from Kentucky and Virginia. But, in the conflict of ideas concerning slavery, a strong tide of emigration came in from the East, and soon changed this composition. In 1870 her non-native population were from colder soils. New York furnished 133,290; Ohio gave 162,623; Pennsylvania sent on 98,352; the entire South gave us only 206,734. In all her cities, and in all her German and Scandinavian and other foreign colonies, Illinois has only about one-fifth of her people of foreign birth.

PROGRESS OF DEVELOPMENT.

One of the greatest elements in the early development of Illinois is the Illinois and Michigan Canal, connecting the Illinois and Mississippi Rivers with the lakes. It was of the utmost importance to the State. It was recommended by Gov. Bond, the first governor, in his first message. In 1821, the Legislature appropriated $10,000 for surveying the route. Two bright young engineers surveyed it, and estimated the cost at $600,000 or $700,000. It finally cost $8,000,000. In 1825, a law was passed to incorporate the Canal Company, but no stock was sold. In 1826, upon the solicitation of Cook, Congress gave 800,000 acres of land on the line of the work. In 1828, another law—commissioners appointed, and work commenced with new survey and new estimates. In 1834–35, George Farquhar made an able report on the whole matter. This was, doubtless, the ablest report ever made to a western legislature, and it became the model for subsequent reports and action. From this the work went on till it was finished in 1848. It cost the State a large amount of money; but it gave to the industries of the State an impetus that pushed it up into the first rank of greatness. It was not built as a speculation any more than a doctor is employed on a speculation. But it has paid into the Treasury of the State an average annual net sum of over $111,000.

Pending the construction of the canal, the land and town-lot fever broke out in the State, in 1834–35. It took on the malignant type in Chicago, lifting the town up into a city. The disease spread over the entire State and adjoining States. It was epidemic. It cut up men's farms without regard to locality, and cut up the purses of the purchasers without regard to consequences. It is estimated that building lots enough were sold in Indiana alone to accommodate every citizen then in the United States.

Towns and cities were exported to the Eastern market by the shipload. There was no lack of buyers. Every up-ship came freighted with speculators and their money.

This distemper seized upon the Legislature in 1836–37, and left not one to tell the tale. They enacted a system of internal improvement without a parallel in the grandeur of its conception. They ordered the construction of 1,300 miles of railroad, crossing the State in all directions. This was surpassed by the river and canal improvements. There were a few counties not touched by either railroad or river or canal, and those were to be comforted and compensated by the free distribution of $200,000 among them. To inflate this balloon beyond credence it was ordered that work should be commenced on both ends of each of these railroads and rivers, and at each river-crossing, all at the same time. The appropriations for these vast improvements were over $12,000,000, and commissioners were appointed to borrow the money on the credit of the State. Remember that all this was in the early days of railroading. when railroads were luxuries; that the State had whole counties with scarcely a cabin; and that the population of the State was less than 400,000, and you can form some idea of the vigor with which these brave men undertook the work of making a great State. In the light of history I am compelled to say that this was only a premature throb of the power that actually slumbered in the soil of the State. It was Hercules in the cradle.

At this juncture the State Bank loaned its funds largely to Godfrey Gilman & Co., and to other leading houses, for the purpose of drawing trade from St. Louis to Alton. Soon they failed, and took down the bank with them.

In 1840, all hope seemed gone. A population of 480,000 were loaded with a debt of $14,000,000. It had only six small cities, really only towns, namely: Chicago, Alton, Springfield, Quincy, Galena, Nauvoo. This debt was to be cared for when there was not a dollar in the treasury, and when the State had borrowed itself out of all credit, and when there was not good money enough in the hands of all the people to pay the interest of the debt for a single year. Yet, in the presence of all these difficulties, the young State steadily refused to repudiate. Gov. Ford took hold of the problem and solved it, bringing the State through in triumph.

Having touched lightly upon some of the more distinctive points in the history of the development of Illinois, let us next briefly consider the

MATERIAL RESOURCES OF THE STATE.

It is a garden four hundred miles long and one hundred and fifty miles wide. Its soil is chiefly a black sandy loam, from six inches to sixty feet thick. On the American bottoms it has been cultivated for one hundred and fifty years without renewal. About the old French towns it has yielded corn for a century and a half without rest or help. It produces nearly everything green in the temperate and tropical zones. She leads all other States in the number of acres actually under plow. Her products from 25,000,000 of acres are incalculable. Her mineral wealth is scarcely second to her agricultural power. She has coal, iron, lead, copper, zinc, many varieties of building stone, fire clay, cuma clay, common brick clay, sand of all kinds, gravel, mineral paint—every thing needed for a high civilization. Left to herself, she has the elements of all greatness. The single item of coal is too vast for an appreciative handling in figures. We can handle it in general terms like algebraical signs, but long before we get up into the millions and billions the human mind drops down from comprehension to mere symbolic apprehension.

When I tell you that nearly four-fifths of the entire State is underlaid with a deposit of coal more than forty feet thick on the average (now estimated, by recent surveys, at seventy feet thick), you can get some idea of its amount, as you do of the amount of the national debt. There it is! 41,000 square miles—one vast mine into which you could put any of the States; in which you could bury scores of European and ancient empires, and have room enough all round to work without knowing that they had been sepulchered there.

Put this vast coal-bed down by the other great coal deposits of the world, and its importance becomes manifest. Great Britain has 12,000 square miles of coal; Spain, 3,000; France, 1,719; Belgium, 578; Illinois about twice as many square miles as all combined. Virginia has 20,000 square miles; Pennsylvania, 16,000; Ohio, 12,000. Illinois has 41,000 square miles. One-seventh of all the known coal on this continent is in Illinois.

Could we sell the coal in this single State for one-seventh of one cent a ton it would pay the national debt. Converted into power, even with the wastage in our common engines, it would do more work than could be done by the entire race, beginning at Adam's wedding and working ten hours a day through all the centuries till the present time, and right on into the future at the same rate for the next 600,000 years.

Great Britain uses enough mechanical power to-day to give to each man, woman, and child in the kingdom the help and service of nineteen untiring servants. No wonder she has leisure and luxuries. No wonder the home of the common artisan has in it more luxuries than could be found in the palace of good old King Arthur. Think, if you can conceive of it, of the vast army of servants that slumber in the soil of Illinois, impatiently awaiting the call of Genius to come forth to minister to our comfort.

At the present rate of consumption England's coal supply will be exhausted in 250 years. When this is gone she must transfer her dominion either to the Indies, or to British America, which I would not resist; or to some other people, which I would regret as a loss to civilization.

COAL IS KING.

At the same rate of consumption (which far exceeds our own) the deposit of coal in Illinois will last 120,000 years. And her kingdom shall be an everlasting kingdom.

Let us turn now from this reserve power to the *annual products* of the State. We shall not be humiliated in this field. Here we strike the secret of our national credit. Nature provides a market in the constant appetite of the race. Men must eat, and if we can furnish the provisions we can command the treasure. All that a man hath will he give for his life.

According to the last census Illinois produced 30,000,000 of bushels of wheat. That is more wheat than was raised by any other State in the Union. She raised last year 130,000,000 of bushels of corn—twice as much as any other State, and one-sixth of all the corn raised in the United States. She harvested 2,747,000 tons of hay, nearly one-tenth of all the hay in the Republic. It is not generally appreciated, but it is true, that the hay crop of the country is worth more than the cotton crop. The hay of Illinois equals the cotton of Louisiana. Go to Charleston, S. C., and see them peddling handfuls of hay or grass, almost as a curiosity, as we regard Chinese gods or the cryolite of Greenland; drink your coffee and *condensed milk;* and walk back from the coast for many a league through the sand and burs till you get up into the better atmosphere of the mountains, without seeing a waving meadow or a grazing herd; then you will begin to appreciate the meadows of the Prairie State, where the grass often grows sixteen feet high.

The value of her farm implements is $211,000,000, and the value of her live stock is only second to the great State of New York. Last year she had 25,000,000 hogs, and packed 2,113,845, about one-half of all that were packed in the United States. This is no insignificant item. Pork is a growing demand of the old world. Since the laborers of Europe have gotten a taste of our bacon, and we have learned how to pack it dry in boxes, like dry goods, the world has become the market.

The hog is on the march into the future. His nose is ordained to uncover the secrets of dominion, and his feet shall be guided by the star of empire.

Illinois marketed $57,000,000 worth of slaughtered animals—more than any other State, and a seventh of all the States.

Be patient with me, and pardon my pride, and I will give you a list of some of the things in which Illinois excels all other States.

Depth and richness of soil; per cent. of good ground; acres of improved land; large farms—some farms contain from 40,000 to 60,000 acres of cultivated land, 40,000 acres of corn on a single farm; number of farmers; amount of wheat, corn, oats and honey produced; value of animals for slaughter; number of hogs; amount of pork; number of horses —three times as many as Kentucky, the horse State.

Illinois excels all other States in miles of railroads and in miles of postal service, and in money orders sold per annum, and in the amount of lumber sold in her markets.

Illinois is only second in many important matters. This sample list comprises a few of the more important: Permanent school fund (good for a young state); total income for educational purposes; number of publishers of books, maps, papers, etc.; value of farm products and implements, and of live stock; in tons of coal mined.

The shipping of Illinois is only second to New York. Out of one port during the business hours of the season of navigation she sends forth a vessel every ten minutes. This does not include canal boats, which go one every five minutes. No wonder she is only second in number of bankers and brokers or in physicians and surgeons.

She is third in colleges, teachers and schools; cattle, lead, hay, flax, sorghum and beeswax.

She is fourth in population, in children enrolled in public schools, in law schools, in butter, potatoes and carriages.

She is fifth in value of real and personal property, in theological seminaries and colleges exclusively for women, in milk sold, and in boots and shoes manufactured, and in book-binding.

She is only seventh in the production of wood, while she is the twelfth in area. Surely that is well done for the Prairie State. She now has much more wood and growing timber than she had thirty years ago.

A few leading industries will justify emphasis. She manufactures $205,000,000 worth of goods, which places her well up toward New York and Pennsylvania. The number of her manufacturing establishments increased from 1860 to 1870, 300 per cent.; capital employed increased 350 per cent., and the amount of product increased 400 per cent. She issued 5,500,000 copies of commercial and financial newspapers—only second to New York. She has 6,759 miles of railroad, thus leading all other States, worth $636,458,000, using 3,245 engines, and 67,712 cars, making a train long enough to cover one-tenth of the entire roads of the State. Her stations are only five miles apart. She carried last year 15,795,000 passengers, an average of 36¼ miles, or equal to taking her entire population twice across the State. More than two-thirds of her land is within five miles of a railroad, and less than two per cent. is more than fifteen miles away.

The State has a large financial interest in the Illinois Central railroad. The road was incorporated in 1850, and the State gave each alternate section for six miles on each side, and doubled the price of the remaining land, so keeping herself good. The road received 2,595,000 acres of land, and pays to the State one-seventh of the gross receipts. The State receives this year $350,000, and has received in all about $7,000,000. It is practically the people's road, and it has a most able and gentlemanly management. Add to this the annual receipts from the canal, $111,000, and a large per cent. of the State tax is provided for.

THE RELIGION AND MORALS

of the State keep step with her productions and growth. She was born of the missionary spirit. It was a minister who secured for her the ordinance of 1787, by which she has been saved from slavery, ignorance, and dishonesty. Rev. Mr. Wiley, pastor of a Scotch congregation in Randolph County, petitioned the Constitutional Convention of 1818 to recognize Jesus Christ as king, and the Scriptures as the only necessary guide and book of law. The convention did not act in the case, and the old Covenanters refused to accept citizenship. They never voted until 1824, when the slavery question was submitted to the people; then they all voted against it and cast the determining votes. Conscience has predominated whenever a great moral question has been submitted to the people.

But little mob violence has ever been felt in the State. In 1817 regulators disposed of a band of horse-thieves that infested the territory. The Mormon indignities finally awoke the same spirit. Alton was also the scene of a pro-slavery mob, in which Lovejoy was added to the list of martyrs. The moral sense of the people makes the law supreme, and gives to the State unruffled peace.

With $22,300,000 in church property, and 4,298 church organizations, the State has that divine police, the sleepless patrol of moral ideas, that alone is able to secure perfect safety. Conscience takes the knife from the assassin's hand and the bludgeon from the grasp of the highwayman. We sleep in safety, not because we are behind bolts and bars—these only fence against the innocent; not because a lone officer drowses on a distant corner of a street; not because a sheriff may call his posse from a remote part of the county; but because *conscience* guards the very portals of the air and stirs in the deepest recesses of the public mind. This spirit issues within the State 9,500,000 copies of religious papers annually, and receives still more from without. Thus the crime of the State is only one-fourth that of New York and one-half that of Pennsylvania.

Illinois never had but one duel between her own citizens. In Belleville, in 1820, Alphonso Stewart and William Bennett arranged to vindicate injured honor. The seconds agreed to make it a sham, and make them shoot blanks. Stewart was in the secret. Bennett mistrusted something, and, unobserved, slipped a bullet into his gun and killed Stewart. He then fled the State. After two years he was caught, tried, convicted, and, in spite of friends and political aid, was hung. This fixed the code of honor on a Christian basis, and terminated its use in Illinois.

The early preachers were ignorant men, who were accounted eloquent according to the strength of their voices. But they set the style for all public speakers. Lawyers and political speakers followed this rule. Gov.

Ford says: "Nevertheless, these first preachers were of incalculable benefit to the country. They inculcated justice and morality. To them are we indebted for the first Christian character of the Protestant portion of the people."

In education Illinois surpasses her material resources. The ordinance of 1787 consecrated one thirty-sixth of her soil to common schools, and the law of 1818, the first law that went upon her statutes, gave three per cent. of all the rest to

EDUCATION INSTEAD OF HIGHWAYS.

The old compact secures this interest forever, and by its yoking morality and intelligence it precludes the legal interference with the Bible in the public schools. With such a start it is natural that we should have 11,050 schools, and that our illiteracy should be less than New York or Pennsylvania, and only about one-half of Massachusetts. We are not to blame for not having more than one-half as many idiots as the great States. These public schools soon made colleges inevitable. The first college, still flourishing, was started in Lebanon in 1828, by the M. E. church, and named after Bishop McKendree. Illinois College, at Jacksonville, supported by the Presbyterians, followed in 1830. In 1832 the Baptists built Shurtleff College, at Alton. Then the Presbyterians built Knox College, at Galesburg, in 1838, and the Episcopalians built Jubilee College, at Peoria, in 1847. After these early years colleges have rained down. A settler could hardly encamp on the prairie but a college would spring up by his wagon. The State now has one very well endowed and equipped university, namely, the Northwestern University, at Evanston, with six colleges, ninety instructors, over 1,000 students, and $1,500,000 endowment.

Rev. J. M. Peck was the first educated Protestant minister in the State. He settled at Rock Spring, in St. Clair County, 1820, and left his impress on the State. Before 1837 only party papers were published, but Mr. Peck published a Gazetteer of Illinois. Soon after John Russell, of Bluffdale, published essays and tales showing genius. Judge James Hall published *The Illinois Monthly Magazine* with great ability, and an annual called *The Western Souvenir*, which gave him an enviable fame all over the United States. From these beginnings Illinois has gone on till she has more volumes in public libaaries even than Massachusetts, and of the 44,500,000 volumes in all the public libraries of the United States, she has one-thirteenth. In newspapers she stands fourth. Her increase is marvelous. In 1850 she issued 5,000,000 copies; in 1860, 27,590,000; in 1870, 113,140,000. In 1860 she had eighteen colleges and seminaries; in 1870 she had eighty. That is a grand advance for the war decade.

This brings us to a record unsurpassed in the history of any age,

THE WAR RECORD OF ILLINOIS.

I hardly know where to begin, or how to advance, or what to say. I can at best give you only a broken synopsis of her deeds, and you must put them in the order of glory for yourself. Her sons have always been foremost on fields of danger. In 1832-33, at the call of Gov. Reynolds, her sons drove Blackhawk over the Mississippi.

When the Mexican war came, in May, 1846, 8,370 men offered themselves when only 3,720 could be accepted. The fields of Buena Vista and Vera Cruz, and the storming of Cerro Gordo, will carry the glory of Illinois soldiers along after the infamy of the cause they served has been forgotten. But it was reserved till our day for her sons to find a field and cause and foemen that could fitly illustrate their spirit and heroism. Illinois put into her own regiments for the United States government 256,000 men, and into the army through other States enough to swell the number to 290,000. This far exceeds all the soldiers of the federal government in all the war of the revolution. Her total years of service were over 600,000. She enrolled men from eighteen to forty-five years of age when the law of Congress in 1864—the test time—only asked for those from twenty to forty-five. Her enrollment was otherwise excessive. Her people wanted to go, and did not take the pains to correct the enrollment. Thus the basis of fixing the quota was too great, and then the quota itself, at least in the trying time, was far above any other State.

Thus the demand on some counties, as Monroe, for example, took every able-bodied man in the county, and then did not have enough to fill the quota. Moreover, Illinois sent 20,844 men for ninety or one hundred days, for whom no credit was asked. When Mr. Lincoln's attention was called to the inequality of the quota compared with other States, he replied, "The country needs the sacrifice. We must put the whip on the free horse." In spite of all these disadvantages Illinois gave to the country 73,000 years of service above all calls. With one-thirteenth of the population of the loyal States, she sent regularly one-tenth of all the soldiers, and in the peril of the closing calls, when patriots were few and weary, she then sent one-eighth of all that were called for by her loved and honored son in the white house. Her mothers and daughters went into the fields to raise the grain and keep the children together, while the fathers and older sons went to the harvest fields of the world. I knew a father and four sons who agreed that one of them must stay at home; and they pulled straws from a stack to see who might go. The father was left. The next day he came into the camp, saying: "Mother says she can get the crops in, and I am going, too." I know large Methodist churches from which every male member went to the army. Do you want to know what these heroes from Illinois did in the field? Ask any soldier with a good record of his own, who is thus able to judge, and he will tell you that the Illinois men went in to win. It is common history that the greater victories were won in the West. When everything else looked dark Illinois was gaining victories all down the river, and dividing the confederacy. Sherman took with him on his great march forty-five regiments of Illinois infantry, three companies of artillery, and one company of cavalry. He could not avoid

GOING TO THE SEA.

If he had been killed, I doubt not the men would have gone right on. Lincoln answered all rumors of Sherman's defeat with, " It is impossible ; there is a mighty sight of fight in 100,000 Western men." Illinois soldiers brought home 300 battle-flags. The first United States flag that floated over Richmond was an Illinois flag. She sent messengers and nurses to every field and hospital, to care for her sick and wounded sons. She said, '· These suffering ones are my sons, and I will care for them."

When individuals had given all, then cities and towns came forward with their credit to the extent of many millions, to aid these men and their families.

Illinois gave the country the great general of the war—Ulysses S. Grant—since honored with two terms of the Presidency of the United States.

One other name from Illinois comes up in all minds, embalmed in all hearts, that must have the supreme place in this story of our glory and of our nation's honor ; that name is Abraham Lincoln, of Illinois.

The analysis of Mr. Lincoln's character is difficult on account of its symmetry.

In this age we look with admiration at his uncompromising honesty. And well we may, for this saved us. Thousands throughout the length and breadth of our country who knew him only as " Honest Old Abe," voted for him on that account; and wisely did they choose, for no other man could have carried us through the fearful night of the war. When his plans were too vast for our comprehension, and his faith in the cause too sublime for our participation ; when it was all night about us, and all dread before us, and all sad and desolate behind us; when not one ray shone upon our cause; when traitors were haughty and exultant at the South, and fierce and blasphemous at the North ; when the loyal men here seemed almost in the minority ; when the stoutest heart quailed, the bravest cheek paled ; when generals were defeating each other for place, and contractors were leeching out the very heart's blood of the prostrate republic: when every thing else had failed us, we looked at this calm, patient man standing like a rock in the storm, and said : " Mr. Lincoln is honest, and we can trust him still." Holding to this single point with the energy of faith and despair we held together, and, under God, he brought us through to victory.

His practical wisdom made him the wonder of all lands. With such certainty did Mr. Lincoln follow causes to their ultimate effects, that his foresight of contingencies seemed almost prophetic.

He is radiant with all the great virtues, and his memory shall shed a glory upon this age that shall fill the eyes of men as they look into history. Other men have excelled him in some point, but, taken at all points, all in all, he stands head and shoulders above every other man of 6,000 years. An administrator, he saved the nation in the perils of unparalleled civil war. A statesman, he justified his measures by their success. A philanthropist, he gave liberty to one race and salvation to another. A moralist, he bowed from the summit of human power to the foot of the Cross, and became a Christian. A mediator, he exercised mercy under the most absolute abeyance to law. A leader, he was no partisan. A commander, he was untainted with blood. A ruler in desperate times, he was unsullied with crime. A man, he has left no word of passion, no thought of malice, no trick of craft, no act of jealousy, no purpose of selfish ambition. Thus perfected, without a model, and without a peer, he was dropped into these troubled years to adorn and embellish all that is good and all that is great in our humanity, and to present to all coming time the representative of the divine idea of free government.

It is not too much to say that away down in the future, when the republic has fallen from its niche in the wall of time; when the great war itself shall have faded out in the distance like a mist on the horizon; when the Anglo-Saxon language shall be spoken only by the tongue of the stranger; then the generations looking this way shall see the great president as the supreme figure in this vortex of history

CHICAGO.

It is impossible in our brief space to give more than a meager sketch of such a city as Chicago, which is in itself the greatest marvel of the Prairie State. This mysterious, majestic, mighty city, born first of water, and next of fire; sown in weakness, and raised in power; planted among the willows of the marsh, and crowned with the glory of the mountains; sleeping on the bosom of the prairie, and rocked on the bosom of the sea; the youngest city of the world, and still the eye of the prairie, as Damascus, the oldest city of the world, is the eye of the desert. With a commerce far exceeding that of Corinth on her isthmus, in the highway to the East; with the defenses of a continent piled around her by the thousand miles, making her far safer than Rome on the banks of the Tiber;

with schools eclipsing Alexandria and Athens; with liberties more conspicuous than those of the old republics; with a heroism equal to the first Carthage, and with a sanctity scarcely second to that of Jerusalem—set your thoughts on all this, lifted into the eyes of all men by the miracle of its growth, illuminated by the flame of its fall, and transfigured by the divinity of its resurrection, and you will feel, as I do, the utter impossibility of compassing this subject as it deserves. Some impression of her importance is received from the shock her burning gave to the civilized world.

When the doubt of her calamity was removed, and the horrid fact was accepted, there went a shudder over all cities, and a quiver over all lands. There was scarcely a town in the civilized world that did not shake on the brink of this opening chasm. The flames of our homes reddened all skies. The city was set upon a hill, and could not be hid. All eyes were turned upon it. To have struggled and suffered amid the scenes of its fall is as distinguishing as to have fought at Thermopylæ, or Salamis, or Hastings, or Waterloo, or Bunker Hill.

Its calamity amazed the world, because it was felt to be the common property of mankind.

The early history of the city is full of interest, just as the early history of such a man as Washington or Lincoln becomes public property, and is cherished by every patriot.

Starting with 560 acres in 1833, it embraced and occupied 23,000 acres in 1869, and, having now a population of more than 500,000, it commands general attention.

The first settler—Jean Baptiste Pointe au Sable, a mulatto from the West Indies—came and began trade with the Indians in 1796. John Kinzie became his successor in 1804, in which year Fort Dearborn was erected.

A mere trading-post was kept here from that time till about the time of the Blackhawk war, in 1832. It was not the city. It was merely a cock crowing at midnight. The morning was not yet. In 1833 the settlement about the fort was incorporated as a town. The voters were divided on the propriety of such corporation, twelve voting for it and one against it. Four years later it was incorporated as a city, and embraced 560 acres.

The produce handled in this city is an indication of its power. Grain and flour were imported from the East till as late as 1837. The first exportation by way of experiment was in 1839. Exports exceeded imports first in 1842. The Board of Trade was organized in 1848, but it was so weak that it needed nursing till 1855. Grain was purchased by the wagon-load in the street.

I remember sitting with my father on a load of wheat, in the long line of wagons along Lake street, while the buyers came and untied the bags, and examined the grain, and made their bids. That manner of business had to cease with the day of small things. Now our elevators will hold 15,000,000 bushels of grain. The cash value of the produce handled in a year is $215,000,000, and the produce weighs 7,000,000 tons or 700,000 car loads. This handles thirteen and a half ton each minute, all the year round. One tenth of all the wheat in the United States is handled in Chicago. Even as long ago as 1853 the receipts of grain in Chicago exceeded those of the goodly city of St. Louis, and in 1854 the exports of grain from Chicago exceeded those of New York and doubled those of St. Petersburg, Archangel, or Odessa, the largest grain markets in Europe.

The manufacturing interests of the city are not contemptible. In 1873 manufactories employed 45,000 operatives; in 1876, 60,000. The manufactured product in 1875 was worth $177,000,000.

No estimate of the size and power of Chicago would be adequate that did not put large emphasis on the railroads. Before they came thundering along our streets canals were the hope of our country. But who ever thinks now of traveling by canal packets? In June, 1852, there were only forty miles of railroad connected with the city. The old Galena division of the Northwestern ran out to Elgin. But now, who can count the trains and measure the roads that seek a terminus or connection in this city? The lake stretches away to the north, gathering in to this center all the harvests that might otherwise pass to the north of us. If you will take a map and look at the adjustment of railroads, you will see, first, that Chicago is the great railroad center of the world, as New York is the commercial city of this continent; and, second, that the railroad lines form the iron spokes of a great wheel whose hub is this city. The lake furnishes the only break in the spokes, and this seems simply to have pushed a few spokes together on each shore. See the eighteen trunk lines, exclusive of eastern connections.

Pass round the circle, and view their numbers and extent. There is the great Northwestern, with all its branches, one branch creeping along the lake shore, and so reaching to the north, into the Lake Superior regions, away to the right, and on to the Northern Pacific on the left, swinging around Green Bay for iron and copper and silver, twelve months in the year, and reaching out for the wealth of the great agricultural belt and isothermal line traversed by the Northern Pacific. Another branch, not so far north, feeling for the heart of the Badger State. Another pushing lower down the Mississippi—all these make many connections, and tapping all the vast wheat regions of Minnesota, Wisconsin, Iowa, and all the regions this side of sunset. There is that elegant road, the Chicago, Burlington & Quincy, running out a goodly number of branches, and reaping the great fields this side of the Missouri River. I can only mention the Chicago, Alton & St. Louis, *our* Illinois Central, described elsewhere, and the Chicago & Rock Island. Further around we come to the lines connecting us with all the eastern cities. The Chicago, Indianapolis & St. Louis, the Pittsburgh, Fort Wayne & Chicago, the Lake Shore & Michigan Southern, and the Michigan Central and Great Western, give us many highways to the seaboard. Thus we reach the Mississippi at five points, from St. Paul to Cairo and the Gulf itself by two routes. We also reach Cincinnati and Baltimore, and Pittsburgh and Philadelphia, and New York. North and south run the water courses of the lakes and the rivers, broken just enough at this point to make a pass. Through this, from east to west, run the long lines that stretch from ocean to ocean.

This is the neck of the glass, and the golden sands of commerce must pass into our hands. Altogether we have more than 10,000 miles of railroad, directly tributary to this city, seeking to unload their wealth in our coffers. All these roads have come themselves by the infallible instinct of capital. Not a dollar was ever given by the city to secure one of them, and only a small per cent. of stock taken originally by her citizens, and that taken simply as an investment. Coming in the natural order of events, they will not be easily diverted.

There is still another showing to all this. The connection between New York and San Francisco is by the middle route. This passes inevitably through Chicago. St. Louis wants the Southern Pacific or Kansas Pacific, and pushes it out through Denver, and so on up to Cheyenne. But before the road is fairly under way, the Chicago roads shove out to Kansas City, making even the Kansas Pacific a feeder, and actually leaving St. Louis out in the cold. It is not too much to expect that Dakota, Montana, and Washington Territory will find their great market in Chicago.

But these are not all. Perhaps I had better notice here the ten or fifteen new roads that have just entered, or are just entering, our city. Their names are all that is necessary to give. Chicago & St. Paul, looking up the Red River country to the British possessions; the Chicago, Atlantic & Pacific; the Chicago, Decatur & State Line; the Baltimore & Ohio; the Chicago, Danville & Vincennes; the Chicago & LaSalle Railroad; the Chicago, Pittsburgh & Cincinnati; the Chicago and Canada Southern; the Chicago and Illinois River Railroad. These, with their connections, and with the new connections of the old roads, already in process of erection, give to Chicago not less than 10,000 miles of new tributaries from the richest land on the continent. Thus there will be added to the reserve power, to the capital within reach of this city, not less than $1,000,000,000.

Add to all this transporting power the ships that sail one every nine minutes of the business hours of the season of navigation; add, also, the canal boats that leave one every five minutes during the same time—and you will see something of the business of the city.

THE COMMERCE OF THIS CITY

has been leaping along to keep pace with the growth of the country around us. In 1852, our commerce reached the hopeful sum of $20,000,000. In 1870 it reached $400,000,000. In 1871 it was pushed up above $450,000,000. And in 1875 it touched nearly double that.

One-half of our imported goods come directly to Chicago. Grain enough is exported directly from our docks to the old world to employ a semi-weekly line of steamers of 3,000 tons capacity. This branch is not likely to be greatly developed. Even after the great Welland Canal is completed we shall have only fourteen feet of water. The great ocean vessels will continue to control the trade.

The banking capital of Chicago is $24,431,000. Total exchange in 1875, $659,000,000. Her wholesale business in 1875 was $294,000,000. The rate of taxes is less than in any other great city.

The schools of Chicago are unsurpassed in America. Out of a population of 300,000 there were only 186 persons between the ages of six and twenty-one unable to read. This is the best known record.

In 1831 the mail system was condensed into a half-breed, who went on foot to Niles, Mich., once in two weeks, and brought back what papers and news he could find. As late as 1846 there was often only one mail a week. A post-office was established in Chicago in 1833, and the postmaster nailed up old boot-legs on one side of his shop to serve as boxes for the nabobs and literary men.

It is an interesting fact in the growth of the young city that in the active life of the business men of that day the mail matter has grown to a daily average of over 6,500 pounds. It speaks equally well for the intelligence of the people and the commercial importance of the place, that the mail matter distributed to the territory immediately tributary to Chicago is seven times greater than that distributed to the territory immediately tributary to St. Louis.

The improvements that have characterized the city are as startling as the city itself. In 1831, Mark Beaubien established a ferry over the river, and put himself under bonds to carry all the citizens free for the privilege of charging strangers. Now there are twenty-four large bridges and two tunnels.

In 1833 the government expended $30,000 on the harbor. Then commenced that series of manœuvers with the river that has made it one of the world's curiosities. It used to wind around in the lower end of the town, and make its way rippling over the sand into the lake at the foot of Madison street. They took it up and put it down where it now is. It was a narrow stream, so narrow that even moderately small crafts had to go up through the willows and cat's tails to the point near Lake street bridge, and back up one of the branches to get room enough in which to turn around.

In 1844 the quagmires in the streets were first pontooned by plank roads, which acted in wet weather as public squirt-guns. Keeping you out of the mud, they compromised by squirting the mud over you. The wooden-block pavements came to Chicago in 1857. In 1840 water was delivered by peddlers in carts or by hand. Then a twenty-five horse-power engine pushed it through hollow or bored logs along the streets till 1854, when it was introduced into the houses by new works. The first fire-engine was used in 1835, and the first steam fire-engine in 1859. Gas was utilized for lighting the city in 1850. The Young Men's Christian Association was organized in 1858, and horse railroads carried them to their work in 1859. The museum was opened in 1863. The alarm telegraph adopted in 1864. The opera-house built in 1865. The city grew from 560 acres in 1833 to 23,000 in 1869. In 1834, the taxes amounted to $48.90, and the trustees of the town borrowed $60 more for opening and improving streets. In 1835, the legislature authorized a loan of $2,000, and the treasurer and street commissioners resigned rather than plunge the town into such a gulf.

Now the city embraces 36 square miles of territory, and has 30 miles of water front, besides the outside harbor of refuge, of 400 acres, inclosed by a crib sea-wall. One-third of the city has been raised up an average of eight feet, giving good pitch to the 263 miles of sewerage. The water of the city is above all competition. It is received through two tunnels extending to a crib in the lake two miles from shore. The closest analysis fails to detect any impurities, and, received 35 feet below the surface, it is always clear and cold. The first tunnel is five feet two inches in diameter and two miles long, and can deliver 50,000,000 of gallons per day. The second tunnel is seven feet in diameter and six miles long, running four miles under the city, and can deliver 100,000,000 of gallons per day. This water is distributed through 410 miles of water-mains.

The three grand engineering exploits of the city are: First, lifting the city up on jack-screws, whole squares at a time, without interrupting the business, thus giving us good drainage; second, running the tunnels under the lake, giving us the best water in the world; and third, the turning the current of the river in its own channel, delivering us from the old abominations, and making decency possible. They redound about equally to the credit of the engineering, to the energy of the people, and to the health of the city.

That which really constitutes the city, its indescribable spirit, its soul, the way it lights up in every feature in the hour of action, has not been touched. In meeting strangers, one is often surprised how some homely women marry so well. Their forms are bad, their gait uneven and awkward, their complexion is dull, their features are misshapen and mismatched, and when we see them there is no beauty that we should desire them. But when once they are aroused on some subject, they put on new proportions. They light up into great power. The real person comes out from its unseemly ambush, and captures us at will. They have power. They have ability to cause things to come to pass. We no longer wonder why they are in such high demand. So it is with our city.

There is no grand scenery except the two seas, one of water, the other of prairie. Nevertheless, there is a spirit about it, a push, a breadth, a power, that soon makes it a place never to be forsaken. One soon ceases to believe in impossibilities. Balaams are the only prophets that are disappointed. The bottom that has been on the point of falling out has been there so long that it has grown fast. It can not fall out. It has all the capital of the world itching to get inside the corporation.

The two great laws that govern the growth and size of cities are, first, the amount of territory for which they are the distributing and receiving points; second, the number of medium or moderate dealers that do this distributing. Monopolists build up themselves, not the cities. They neither eat, wear, nor live in proportion to their business. Both these laws help Chicago.

The tide of trade is eastward—not up or down the map, but across the map. The lake runs up a wingdam for 500 miles to gather in the business. Commerce can not ferry up there for seven months in the year, and the facilities for seven months can do the work for twelve. Then the great region west of us is nearly all good, productive land. Dropping south into the trail of St. Louis, you fall into vast deserts and rocky districts, useful in holding the world together. St. Louis and Cincinnati, instead of rivaling and hurting Chicago, are her greatest sureties of dominion. They are far enough away to give sea-room,—farther off than Paris is from London,—and yet they are near enough to prevent the springing up of any other great city between them.

St. Louis will be helped by the opening of the Mississippi, but also hurt. That will put New Orleans on her feet, and with a railroad running over into Texas and so West, she will tap the streams that now crawl up the Texas and Missouri road. The current is East, not North, and a seaport at New Orleans can not permanently help St. Louis.

Chicago is in the field almost alone, to handle the wealth of one-fourth of the territory of this great republic. This strip of seacoast divides its margins between Portland, Boston, New York, Philadelphia, Baltimore and Savannah, or some other great port to be created for the South in the next decade. But Chicago has a dozen empires casting their treasures into her lap. On a bed of coal that can run all the machinery of the world for 500 centuries; in a garden that can feed the race by the thousand years; at the head of the lakes that give her a temperature as a summer resort equaled by no great city in the land; with a climate that insures the health of her citizens; surrounded by all the great deposits of natural wealth in mines and forests and herds, Chicago is the wonder of to-day, and will be *the city of the future.*

MASSACRE AT FORT DEARBORN.

During the war of 1812, Fort Dearborn became the theater of stirring events. The garrison consisted of fifty-four men under command of Captain Nathan Heald, assisted by Lieutenant Helm (son-in-law of Mrs. Kinzie) and Ensign Ronan. Dr. Voorhees was surgeon. The only residents at the post at that time were the wives of Captain Heald and Lieutenant Helm, and a few of the soldiers, Mr. Kinzie and his family, and a few Canadian *voyageurs*, with their wives and children. The soldiers and Mr. Kinzie were on most friendly terms with the Pottawattamies and Winnebagos, the principal tribes around them, but they could not win them from their attachment to the British.

One evening in April, 1812, Mr. Kinzie sat playing on his violin and his children were dancing to the music, when Mrs. Kinzie came rushing into the house, pale with terror, and exclaiming: "The Indians! the Indians!" "What? Where?" eagerly inquired Mr. Kinzie. "Up at Lee's, killing and scalping," answered the frightened mother, who, when the alarm was given, was attending Mrs. Barnes (just confined) living not far off. Mr. Kinzie and his family crossed the river and took refuge in the fort, to which place Mrs. Barnes and her infant not a day old were safely conveyed. The rest of the inhabitants took shelter in the fort. This alarm was caused by a scalping party of Winnebagos, who hovered about the fort several days, when they disappeared, and for several weeks the inhabitants were undisturbed.

On the 7th of August, 1812, General Hull, at Detroit, sent orders to Captain Heald to evacuate Fort Dearborn, and to distribute all the United States property to the Indians in the neighborhood—a most insane order. The Pottawattamie chief, who brought the dispatch, had more wisdom than the commanding general. He advised Captain Heald not to make the distribution. Said he: "Leave the fort and stores as they are, and let the Indians make distribution for themselves; and while they are engaged in the business, the white people may escape to Fort Wayne."

Captain Heald held a council with the Indians on the afternoon of the 12th, in which his officers refused to join, for they had been informed that treachery was designed—that the Indians intended to murder the white people in the council, and then destroy those in the fort. Captain Heald, however, took the precaution to open a port-hole displaying a cannon pointing directly upon the council, and by that means saved his life.

Mr. Kinzie, who knew the Indians well, begged Captain Heald not to confide in their promises, nor distribute the arms and munitions among them, for it would only put power into their hands to destroy the whites. Acting upon this advice, Heald resolved to withhold the munitions of war; and on the night of the 13th, after the distribution of the other property had been made, the powder, ball and liquors were thrown into the river, the muskets broken up and destroyed.

Black Partridge, a friendly chief, came to Captain Heald, and said: "Linden birds have been singing in my ears to-day: be careful on the march you are going to take." On that dark night vigilant Indians had crept near the fort and discovered the destruction of their promised booty going on within. The next morning the powder was seen floating on the surface of the river. The savages were exasperated and made loud complaints and threats.

On the following day when preparations were making to leave the fort, and all the inmates were deeply impressed with a sense of impending danger, Capt. Wells, an uncle of Mrs. Heald, was discovered upon the Indian trail among the sand-hills on the borders of the lake, not far distant, with a band of mounted Miamis, of whose tribe he was chief, having been adopted by the famous Miami warrior, Little Turtle. When news of Hull's surrender reached Fort Wayne, he had started with this force to assist Heald in defending Fort Dearborn. He was too late. Every means for its defense had been destroyed the night before, and arrangements were made for leaving the fort on the morning of the 15th.

It was a warm bright morning in the middle of August. Indications were positive that the savages intended to murder the white people; and when they moved out of the southern gate of the fort, the march was like a funeral procession. The band, feeling the solemnity of the occasion, struck up the Dead March in Saul.

Capt. Wells, who had blackened his face with gun-powder in token of his fate, took the lead with his band of Miamis, followed by Capt. Heald, with his wife by his side on horseback. Mr. Kinzie hoped by his personal influence to avert the impending blow, and therefore accompanied them, leaving his family in a boat in charge of a friendly Indian, to be taken to his trading station at the site of Niles, Michigan, in the event of his death.

The procession moved slowly along the lake shore till they reached the sand-hills between the prairie and the beach, when the Pottawattamie escort, under the leadership of Blackbird, filed to the right, placing those hills between them and the white people. Wells, with his Miamis, had kept in the advance. They suddenly came rushing back, Wells exclaiming, "They are about to attack us; form instantly." These words were quickly followed by a storm of bullets, which came whistling over the little hills which the treacherous savages had made the covert for their murderous attack. The white troops charged upon the Indians, drove them back to the prairie, and then the battle was waged between fifty-four soldiers, twelve civilians and three or four women (the cowardly Miamis having fled at the outset) against five hundred Indian warriors. The white people, hopeless, resolved to sell their lives as dearly as possible. Ensign Ronan wielded his weapon vigorously, even after falling upon his knees weak from the loss of blood. Capt. Wells, who was by the side of his niece, Mrs. Heald, when the conflict began, behaved with the greatest coolness and courage. He said to her, "We have not the slightest chance for life. We must part to meet no more in this world. God bless you." And then he dashed forward. Seeing a young warrior, painted like a demon, climb into a wagon in which were twelve children, and tomahawk them all, he cried out, unmindful of his personal danger, "If that is your game, butchering women and children, I will kill too." He spurred his horse towards the Indian camp, where they had left their squaws and papooses, hotly pursued by swift-footed young warriors, who sent bullets whistling after him. One of these killed his horse and wounded him severely in the leg. With a yell the young braves rushed to make him their prisoner and reserve him for torture. He resolved not to be made a captive, and by the use of the most provoking epithets tried to induce them to kill him instantly. He called a fiery young chief a *squaw*, when the enraged warrior killed Wells instantly with his tomahawk, jumped upon his body, cut out his heart, and ate a portion of the warm morsel with savage delight!

In this fearful combat women bore a conspicuous part. Mrs. Heald was an excellent equestrian and an expert in the use of the rifle. She fought the savages bravely, receiving several severe wounds. Though faint from the loss of blood, she managed to keep her saddle. A savage raised his tomahawk to kill her, when she looked him full in the face, and with a sweet smile and in a gentle voice said, in his own language, "Surely you will not kill a squaw!" The arm of the savage fell, and the life of the heroic woman was saved.

Mrs. Helm, the step-daughter of Mr. Kinzie, had an encounter with a stout Indian, who attempted to tomahawk her. Springing to one side, she received the glancing blow on her shoulder, and at the same instant seized the savage round the neck with her arms and endeavored to get hold of his scalping knife, which hung in a sheath at his breast. While she was thus struggling she was dragged from her antagonist by another powerful Indian, who bore her, in spite of her struggles, to the margin of the lake and plunged her in. To her astonishment she was held by him so that she would not drown, and she soon perceived that she was in the hands of the friendly Black Partridge, who had saved her life.

The wife of Sergeant Holt, a large and powerful woman, behaved as bravely as an Amazon. She rode a fine, high-spirited horse, which the Indians coveted, and several of them attacked her with the butts of their guns, for the purpose of dismounting her; but she used the sword which she had snatched from her disabled husband so skillfully that she foiled them; and, suddenly wheeling her horse, she dashed over the prairie, followed by the savages shouting, "The brave woman! the brave woman! Don't hurt her!" They finally overtook her, and while she was fighting them in front, a powerful savage came up behind her, seized her by the neck and dragged her to the ground. Horse and woman were made captives. Mrs. Holt was a long time a captive among the Indians, but was afterwards ransomed.

In this sharp conflict two-thirds of the white people were slain and wounded, and all their horses, baggage and provision were lost. Only twenty-eight straggling men now remained to fight five hundred Indians rendered furious by the sight of blood. They succeeded in breaking through the ranks of the murderers and gaining a slight eminence on the prairie near the Oak Woods. The Indians did not pursue, but gathered on their flanks, while the chiefs held a consultation on the sand-hills, and showed signs of willingness to parley. It would have been madness on the part of the whites to renew the fight; and so Capt. Heald went forward and met Blackbird on the open prairie, where terms of surrender were soon agreed upon. It was arranged that the white people should give up their arms to Blackbird, and that the survivors should become prisoners of war, to be exchanged for ransoms as soon as practicable. With this understanding captives and captors started for the Indian camp near the fort, to which Mrs. Helm had been taken bleeding and suffering by Black Partridge, and had met her step-father and learned that her husband was safe.

A new scene of horror was now opened at the Indian camp. The wounded, not being included in the terms of surrender, as it was interpreted by the Indians, and the British general, Proctor, having offered a liberal bounty for American scalps, delivered at Malden, nearly all the wounded men were killed and scalped, and the price of the trophies was afterwards paid by the British government.

Abstract of Illinois State Laws.

BILLS OF EXCHANGE AND PROMISSORY NOTES.

No *promissory note, check, draft, bill of exchange, order, or note, negotiable instrument* payable at sight, or on demand, or on presentment, shall be entitled to *days of grace*. All other bills *of exchange, drafts or notes* are entitled to *three days of grace*. All the above mentioned paper falling due on *Sunday, New Years' Day, the Fourth of July, Christmas*, or any day appointed or recommended by the *President of the United States* or the *Governor of the State* as a day of *fast or thanksgiving*, shall be deemed as due on the day previous, and should two or more of these days come together, then such instrument shall be treated as due on the day *previous* to the first of said days. *No defense* can be made against a *negotiable instrument (assigned before due)* in the hands of the assignee without notice, *except fraud was used* in obtaining the same. To hold an *indorser*, due *diligence* must be used *by suit*, in collecting of the maker, unless suit would have been unavailing. Notes payable to *person named* or to order, in order to absolutely *transfer title*, must be indorsed by the *payee*. Notes payable to *bearer* may be *transferred by delivery*, and when so payable *every indorser* thereon is held as a *guarantor of payment* unless otherwise expressed.

In computing interest or discount on negotiable instruments, a *month* shall be considered a *calendar month or twelfth of a year*, and for less than a month, a day shall be figured a *thirtieth* part of a month. Notes *only bear interest* when so expressed, but after due they draw the legal interest, even if not stated.

INTEREST.

The *legal rate* of interest is *six per cent*. Parties *may agree in writing* on a rate not exceeding *ten per cent*. If a rate of interest greater than ten per cent. is contracted for, it works a *forfeiture of the whole of said interest*, and only the principal can be recovered.

DESCENT.

When *no will is made*, the property of a deceased person is distributed as follows:

First. To his or her *children and their descendants in equal parts;* the descendants of the deceased *child or grandchild,* taking the share of their deceased parents in equal parts among them.

Second. When there is *no child* of the intestate, *nor descendant of such child,* and *no widow* or *surviving husband,* then to the parents, brothers or sisters of the deceased, and their descendants, in equal parts among them, allowing to each of the parents, if living, a *child's part,* or to the survivor of them if one be dead, a *double portion;* and if there is no parent living, then to the brothers and sisters of the intestate, and their descendants.

Third. When there is *a widow or surviving husband, and no child or children,* or descendants of a child or children of the intestate, then (after the payment of all just debts) one-half of the real estate and the whole of the personal estate shall *descend to such widow or surviving husband* as an absolute estate forever.

Fourth. When there *is a widow or surviving husband,* and *also a child or children,* or descendants of such child or children of the intestate, *the widow or surviving husband* shall receive as his or her absolute personal estate, *one-third* of all the personal estate of the intestate.

Fifth. If there *is no child of the intestate,* or descendant of such child, and no parent, brother or sister, or descendant of such parent, brother or sister, and no widow or surviving husband, then such estate shall descend in *equal parts* to the *next of kin* to the intestate, in equal degree (computing by the rules of the civil law), and there shall be no representation among collaterals, except with the descendants of brothers and sisters of the intestate; and in no case shall there be any *distinction between the kindred of the whole and the half blood.*

Sixth. If any intestate leaves a *widow or surviving husband and no kindred,* his or her estate shall *descend to such widow or surviving husband.*

WILLS AND ESTATES OF DECEASED PERSONS.

No exact form of words are necessary in order to make a will good at law. *Every male* person of the age of *twenty-one years,* and every *female of the age of eighteen years, of sound mind and memory,* can make a valid will; it must be in *writing,* signed by the testator or by some one in his or her presence and by his or her direction, and *attested by two* or more *credible witnesses.* Care should be taken that the *witnesses are not interested* in the will. *Persons knowing themselves to have been named in the will* or appointed executor, must within *thirty days* of the death of deceased cause the will to be proved and recorded in the proper county, or present it, and *refuse to accept;* on failure to do so are *liable* to forfeit the sum of *twenty dollars per month.* Inventory to be made by executor or administrator within *three months* from date of letters testamentary or of administration. Executors' and administrators' *compensation* not to exceed six per cent. on amount of personal estate, and three per cent. on money realized from real estate, with such additional allowance as shall be reasonable for extra services. *Appraisers' compensation* $2 per day.

Notice requiring all claims to be presented against the estate shall be given by the executor or administrator *within six months* of being qualified. Any person having a claim *and not presenting it* at the time fixed by said notice is required to have summons issued notifying the executor or administrator of his having filed his claim in court; in such cases the costs have to be paid by the claimant. *Claims* should be filed within *two years* from the time *administration* is granted on an estate, as after that time they are *forever barred*, unless *other estate is found* that was not inventoried. *Married women, infants, persons insane, imprisoned* or without the United States, in the employment of the United States, or of this State, have *two years* after their disabilities are removed to file claims.

Claims are *classified* and *paid out* of the *estate* in the following manner:

First. Funeral expenses.

Second. The *widow's award*, if there is a widow; or *children* if there are children, *and no widow*.

Third. *Expenses* attending the *last illness*, not including physician's bill.

Fourth. *Debts due* the *common school* or *township fund*.

Fifth. All expenses of *proving the will* and taking out letters testamentary or administration, and settlement of the estate, and the *physician's bill* in the last illness of deceased.

Sixth. Where the *deceased* has received *money in trust* for any purpose, his executor or administrator shall pay out of his estate the amount received and not accounted for.

Seventh. *All other debts* and demands of whatsoever kind, without regard to *quality or dignity*, which shall be exhibited to the court within *two years* from the granting of letters.

Award to Widow and Children, exclusive of debts and legacies or bequests, except funeral expenses:

First. The *family pictures* and *wearing apparel, jewels* and *ornaments* of *herself* and *minor children*.

Second. *School books* and the *family library of the value of* $100.

Third. One *sewing machine*.

Fourth. *Necessary beds, bedsteads* and *bedding* for herself and family.

Fifth. The *stoves* and *pipe* used in the family, with the necessary *cooking utensils*, or in case they have none, $50 in money.

Sixth. *Household and kitchen furniture to the value of* $100.

Seventh. One *milch cow and calf for every four members of her family.*

Eighth. *Two sheep* for each member of her family, and the fleeces taken from the same, and *one horse, saddle and bridle.*
Ninth. *Provisions for herself and family for one year.*
Tenth. *Food for the stock above specified for six months.*
Eleventh. *Fuel for herself and family for three months.*
Twelfth. *One hundred dollars worth* of other property suited to her condition in life, to be *selected by the widow.*

The *widow if she elects* may have in lieu of the said award, the same personal property or money in place thereof as is or may be *exempt from execution* or attachment against the *head of a family.*

TAXES.

The owners of real and personal property, on the *first day of May* in each year, are *liable for the taxes* thereon.

Assessments should be completed before the *fourth Monday in June,* at which time the town board of review meets to examine assessments, *hear objections,* and make such *changes* as ought to be made. The county board have also power *to correct or change assessments.*

The tax books are placed in the hands of the town collector on or before the tenth day of December, who retains them until the tenth day of March following, when he is required to return them to the county treasurer, who then *collects all delinquent taxes.*

No *costs accrue* on real estate taxes *till advertised,* which takes place the first day of April, when three weeks' notice is required before judgment. Cost of advertising, twenty cents each tract of land, and ten cents each lot.

Judgment is usually obtained at *May term* of County Court. Costs six cents each tract of land, and five cents each lot. Sale takes place in June. Costs in addition to those before mentioned, twenty-eight cents each tract of land, and twenty-seven cents each town lot.

Real estate sold for taxes may be *redeemed* any time before the *expiration of two years* from the date of sale, by *payment* to the *County Clerk* of the amount for which it was sold and twenty-five per cent. thereon if redeemed within six months, fifty per cent. if between six and twelve months, if between twelve and eighteen months seventy-five per cent., and if between eighteen months and two years one hundred per cent., and in addition, all subsequent taxes paid by the purchaser, with ten per cent. interest thereon, also one dollar each tract if notice is given by the purchaser of the sale, and a fee of twenty-five cents to the clerk for his certificate.

JURISDICTION OF COURTS.

Justices have jurisdiction in all civil cases on *contracts* for the *recovery of moneys for damages for injury to real property,* or taking, detaining, or *injuring personal property; for rent;* for all cases to recover damages done real or personal property by railroad companies, in actions of *replevin*, and in actions for damages for *fraud* in the *sale, purchase,* or *exchange of personal property*, when the amount claimed as due is not over $200. They have also *jurisdiction* in all cases for *violation* of the *ordinances* of *cities, towns* or *villages*. A *justice of the peace* may *orally* order an *officer or a private person* to *arrest* any one committing or attempting to commit a *criminal offense*. *He also* upon complaint can issue his warrant for the arrest of any person *accused of having committed a crime*, and have him brought before him for examination.

COUNTY COURTS

Have jurisdiction in all *matters of probate*, settlement of estates of *deceased persons*, appointment of *guardians* and *conservators*, and settlement of their accounts; all matters relating to *apprentices;* proceedings for the *collection of taxes* and *assessments*, and in proceedings of *executions, administrators, guardians and conservators for the sale of real estate*. In law cases they have concurrent jurisdiction with Circuit Courts in all cases where Justices of Peace now have when the amount claimed shall *not exceed* $500, and in all criminal offenses where the punishment *is not imprisonment in the penitentiary or death*, but no *appeal* is allowed from Justice of the Peace to County Courts.

Circuit Courts—Have unlimited jurisdiction.

LIMITATION OF ACTION.

Accounts five years. Notes and written contracts *ten years. Judgments twenty years. Partial payments* or new promise in writing, within or after said period, will *revive the debt*. Absence from the State deducted, and when the cause of action is barred by the law of another State, it has the same effect here. *Slander and libel, one year. Personal injuries, two years. To recover* land or make entry thereon, *twenty years.* Action to foreclose mortgage or trust deed, or make a sale, *within ten years.*

All persons in *possession of land*, and *paying taxes for seven consecutive years*, with color of title, and all persons paying taxes for seven consecutive years, with color of title, on vacant land, shall be held to be the *legal owners to the extent of their paper title.*

MARRIED WOMEN

May sue and be sued. Husband and wife not liable for each other's debts, either before or after marriage, but both are liable for expenses and education of the family.

She may contract the same as if unmarried, except that in a partnership business she can not, without consent of her husband, *unless he has abandoned or deserted her*, or is idiotic or insane, or confined in penitentiary; she is entitled and can recover her own earnings, but neither husband nor wife is entitled to compensation for any services rendered for the other. At the death of the husband, in addition to widow's award, a married woman has a dower interest (one-third) in all real estate owned by her husband after their marriage, and which has not been released by her, and the husband has the same interest in the real estate of the wife at her death.

EXEMPTIONS FROM FORCED SALE.

Home worth $1,000, *and the following Personal Property:* Lot of ground and buildings thereon, occupied as a residence by the debtor, being a householder and having a family, to the value of $1,000. *Exemption continues after the death* of the householder for the benefit of widow and family, some one of them occupying the homestead until *youngest child shall become twenty-one years of age, and until death of widow.* There is *no exemption from sale for taxes*, assessments, debt or liability incurred for the *purchase or improvement of said homestead.* No release or waiver of exemption is valid, unless in writing, and subscribed by such householder and wife (if he have one), and acknowledged as conveyances of real estate are required to be acknowledged. The *following articles of personal property* owned by the debtor, are exempt from *execution, writ of attachment, and distress for rent:* The necessary *wearing apparel* of every person; *one sewing machine;* the *furniture, tools and implements necessary to carry on his trade* or business, *not exceeding* $100 in value; the implements or *library* of any *professional man*, not exceeding $100 in value; *materials* and *stock* designed and procured *for carrying on his trade* or business, and intended to be used or wrought therein, *not exceeding* $100 *in value;* and also, when the debtor is the head of a family and resides with the same, *necessary beds, bedsteads, and bedding, two stoves and pipe, necessary household furniture not exceeding in value* $100, *one cow, calf, two swine, one yoke of oxen, or two horses in lieu thereof, worth not exceeding* $200, with the harness therefor, *necessary provisions and fuel* for the use of the family *three months*, and necessary *food for the stock* hereinbefore exempted for the same time; the *bibles, school books* and *family pictures;* the *family library, cemetery lots*, and *rights of burial*, and *tombs* for the repositories of the dead; *one hundred dollars' worth of other property*, suited to his condition in life, selected by the debtor. *No personal property is exempt from sale* for the *wages of laborers or servants. Wages of a laborer* who is the head of a family can not be garnisheed, except the sum due him be in excess of $25.

ABSTRACT OF ILLINOIS STATE LAWS.

DEEDS AND MORTGAGES.

To be valid there must be a valid consideration. Special care should be taken to have them signed, sealed, delivered, and properly acknowledged, with the proper seal attached. *Witnesses* are not required. The *acknowledgement* must be made in this state, before *Master in Chancery, Notary Public, United States Commissioner, Circuit or County Clerk, Justice of Peace, or any Court of Record having a seal, or any Judge, Justice, or Clerk of any such Court.* When taken before a *Notary Public, or United States Commissioner,* the same shall be *attested* by his *official seal,* when taken before a *Court or the Clerk* thereof, the same shall be attested by the *seal* of such *Court,* and when taken before a *Justice of the Peace* residing out of the county where the real estate to be conveyed lies, there shall be added a certificate of the *County Clerk* under his seal of office, *that he was a Justice of the Peace* in the county at the time of taking the same. A deed is good without such certificate attached, but can not be used in evidence unless such a certificate is produced or other competent evidence introduced. Acknowledgements made out of the state must either be executed according to the laws of this state, or there should be attached a certificate that it is in conformity with the laws of the state or country where executed. Where this is not done the same may be proved by any other legal way. Acknowledgments where the *Homestead* rights are to be waived must state as follows: "Including the release and waiver of the right of homestead."

Notaries Public can take acknowledgements any where in the state.

Sheriffs, if authorized by the mortgagor of real or personal property in his mortgage, may sell the property mortgaged.

In the case of the *death of grantor or holder of the equity of redemption* of real estate mortgaged, or conveyed by deed of trust where equity of redemption is waived, and it contains power of sale, must be foreclosed in the same manner as a common mortgage in court.

ESTRAYS.

Horses, mules, asses, neat cattle, swine, sheep, or goats found straying at any time during the year, in counties where such animals are not allowed to run at large, or between the last day of October and the 15th day of April in other counties, *the owner thereof being unknown, may be taken up as estrays.*

No person *not a householder* in the county where estray is found *can lawfully* take up an estray, and then only *upon or about his farm* or place of residence. *Estrays should not be used before advertised,* except animals giving milk, which may be milked for their benefit.

Notices must be posted up within five (5) days in three (3) of the most public places in the town or precinct in which estray was found, giving the residence of the taker up, and a particular description of the estray, its age, color, and marks natural and artificial, and stating before what justice of the peace in such town or precinct, and at what time, not less than ten (10) nor more than fifteen (15) days from the time of posting such notices, he will apply to have the estray appraised.

A copy of such notice should be filed by the taker up with the *town clerk*, whose duty it is to enter the same at large, *in a book* kept by him for that purpose.

If the *owner* of estray shall not have appeared and *proved ownership*, and taken the same away, first paying the taker up his reasonable charges for taking up, keeping, and advertising the same, the taker up shall appear before the justice of the peace mentioned in above mentioned notice, and make an affidavit as required by law.

As the *affidavit has to be made before the justice*, and all other steps as to appraisement, etc., are before him, who is familiar therewith, they are therefore omitted here.

Any person taking up an estray at any other place than about or upon his farm or residence, or *without complying with the law, shall forfeit and pay a fine of ten dollars with costs.*

Ordinary diligence is required in *taking care of estrays*, but in case they die or get away the taker is not liable for the same.

GAME.

It is *unlawful to hunt, kill or in any manner interfere with deer, wild turkey, prairie chicken, partridge or pheasants between the first day of January and the fifteenth day of August;* or any *quail*, between the first day of *January* and the first day of *October;* or any *woodcock*, between the *first day of January and the first day of July;* or any *wild goose, duck, Wilson snipe brandt, or other water fowl, between the fifteenth day of April and the fifteenth day of August, in each and every year. Penalty:* Fine not less than $10 nor more than $25, and costs of suit, and shall stand committed to county jail until fine is paid, but not exceeding ten days.

It is unlawful to hunt with *gun, dog or net*, within the inclosed grounds or lands of another, *without permission. Penalty:* Fine not less than $3 and not exceeding $100, to be paid into school fund.

WEIGHTS AND MEASURES.

Whenever any of the following articles shall be contracted for, or sold or delivered, and no special contract or agreement shall be made to the contrary, the weight per bushel shall be as follows, to-wit:

	Pounds.		Pounds.
Stone Coal,	80	Buckwheat,	52
Unslacked Lime,	80	Coarse Salt,	50
Corn in the ear,	70	Barley,	48
Wheat,	60	Corn Meal,	48
Irish Potatoes,	60	Castor Beans,	46
White Beans,	60	Timothy Seed,	45
Clover Seed,	60	Hemp Seed,	44
Onions,	57	Malt,	38
Shelled Corn,	56	Dried Peaches,	33
Rye,	56	Oats,	32
Flax Seed,	56	Dried Apples,	24
Sweet Potatoes,	55	Bran,	20
Turnips,	55	Blue Grass Seed,	14
Fine Salt,	55	Hair (plastering),	8

Penalty for giving less than the above standard is double the amount of property wrongfully not given, and ten dollars addition thereto.

MILLERS.

The owner or occupant of every public grist mill in this state shall grind all grain brought to his mill in its turn. The *toll* for both *steam* and *water* mills, is, for grinding and bolting *wheat, rye*, or *other grain*, one *eighth part;* for grinding *Indian corn, oats, barley* and *buckwheat* not required to be *bolted*, one *seventh part;* for grinding *malt*, and *chopping* all kinds of grain, one *eighth part*. It is the duty of every miller when his mill is in repair, to *aid* and *assist* in *loading* and *unloading* all grain brought to him to be ground, and he is also required to keep an accurate *half bushel measure*, and an accurate set of *toll dishes* or *scales* for weighing the grain. The *penalty* for neglect or refusal to comply with the law is $5, to the use of any person to sue for the same, to be recovered before any justice of the peace of the county where penalty is incurred. Millers are accountable for the safe keeping of all grain left in his mill for the purpose of being ground, with bags or casks containing same (except it results from unavoidable accidents), provided that such bags or casks are distinctly marked with the initial letters of the owner's name.

MARKS AND BRANDS.

Owners of cattle, horses, hogs, sheep or goats may have *one ear mark* and one brand, but which shall be *different* from his *neighbor's*, and may be *recorded* by the county clerk of the county in which such property is kept. The *fee* for such record is fifteen cents. The *record* of such shall be *open* to examination free of charge. In cases of *disputes* as to marks or brands, such *record* is *prima facie evidence*. Owners of cattle, horses, hogs, sheep or goats that may have been branded by the *former owner*, may be re-branded in presence of one or more of his neighbors, who shall certify to the facts of the marking or branding being done, when done, and in what brand or mark they were re-branded or re-marked, which certificate may also be recorded as before stated.

ADOPTION OF CHILDREN.

Children may be adopted by any resident of this state, by filing a petition in the Circuit or County Court of the county in which he resides, asking leave to do so, and if desired may ask that the name of the child be changed. Such petition, if made by a person having a husband or wife, will not be granted, unless the husband or wife joins therein, as the adoption must be by them jointly.

The petition shall state name, sex, and age of the child, and the new name, if it is desired to change the name. Also the name and residence of the parents of the child, if known, and of the guardian, if any, and whether the parents or guardians consent to the adoption.

The court must find, before granting decree, that the *parents of the child*, or the survivors of them, have *deserted his or her family* or such child for one year next preceding the application, or if neither are living, the guardian; if no guardian, the next of kin in this state capable of giving consent, has had notice of the presentation of the petition and consents to such adoption. If the child is of the *age* of *fourteen years* or upwards, the adoption *can not* be made *without its consent.*

SURVEYORS AND SURVEYS.

There is in every county elected a surveyor known as county surveyor, who has power to appoint deputies, for whose official acts he is responsible. It is the *duty* of the *county surveyor*, either by himself or his deputy, to make *all surveys* that he may be called upon to make within his county as soon as may be after application is made. The necessary chainmen and other assistance must be employed by the person requiring the same to be done, and to be by him paid, unless otherwise agreed; but the chainmen must be disinterested persons and approved by the surveyor and sworn by him to measure justly and impartially.

The County Board in each county is required by law to provide a copy of the United States field notes and plats of their surveys of the lands in the county to be kept in the recorder's office subject to examination by the public, and the county surveyor is required to make his surveys in conformity to said notes, plats and the laws of the United States governing such matters. The surveyor is also required to keep a record of all surveys made by him, which shall be subject to inspection by any one interested, and shall be delivered up to his successor in office. A certified copy of the said surveyor's record shall be *prima facie* evidence of its contents.

The fees of county surveyors are six dollars per day. The county surveyor is also *ex officio inspector of mines*, and as such, assisted by some practical miner selected by him, shall once each year inspect all the mines in the county, for which they shall each receive such compensation as may be fixed by the County Board, not exceeding $5 a day, to be paid out of the county treasury.

ROADS.

Where practicable from the nature of the ground, persons traveling in any kind of vehicle, *must turn to the right* of the center of the road, so as to permit each carriage to pass without interfering with each other. The *penalty* for a violation of this provision is $5 for every offense, to be recovered by the *party injured;* but to recover, there must have occurred some injury to person or property resulting from the violation. The *owners* of any carriage traveling upon any road in this State for the conveyance of passengers who shall *employ* or continue in his employment as driver any person who is addicted to *drunkenness*, or the excessive use of spiritous liquors, after he has had notice of the same, *shall forfeit*, at the rate of $5 per day, and if any *driver* while actually engaged in driving any such carriage, shall be guilty of *intoxication* to such a degree as to *endanger* the safety of *passengers*, it shall be the duty of the owner, on receiving *written notice* of the fact, signed by one of the *passengers*, and *certified* by him *on oath*, forthwith to discharge such driver. If such owner shall have such driver in his *employ within three months* after such notice, he is liable for $5 per day for the time he shall keep said driver in his employment after receiving such notice.

Persons *driving* any *carriage* on any public highway are prohibited from *running their horses* upon any occasion under a *penalty* of a fine not exceeding $10, or imprisonment not exceeding sixty days, at the discretion of the court. Horses *attached* to any *carriage* used to convey *passengers* for hire must be *properly hitched* or the lines placed in the hands of some other person before the driver leaves them for any purpose. For violation of this provision each driver shall *forfeit twenty dollars*, to be recovered by action, to be commenced within six months. It is understood by the *term carriage* herein to mean any carriage or vehicle used for the transportation of passengers or goods or either of them.

The commissioners of highways in the different towns have the care and superintendence of highways and bridges therein. They have all the powers necessary to lay out, vacate, regulate and repair all roads, build and repair bridges, divide their respective towns into as many road districts as they shall think convenient. This is to be done annually, and ten days before the annual town meeting. In addition to the above, it is their duty to erect and keep in repair at the forks or crossing-place of the most important roads post and guide boards with plain inscriptions, giving directions and distances to the most noted places to which such road may lead; also to make provisions to prevent thistles, burdock, and cockle burrs, mustard, yellow dock, Indian mallow, and jessamine weed from seeding, and to extirpate the same as far as practicable, and to prevent all rank growth of vegetation on the public highways, so far as the same may obstruct public travel, and it is in their discretion to erect watering places for public use for watering teams at such points as may be deemed advisable. Every able-bodied male inhabitant, being above the age of twenty-one years, and under the age of fifty, excepting paupers, idiots, lunatics, trustees of schools and school directors, and such others as are exempt by law, is required to labor on highways in their respective road districts, not less than one or more than three days in each and every year. Three days' notice must be given by the overseer of the time and place he requires such road labor to be done. The labor must be performed in the road district in which the person resides. Any person may commute for such labor by paying at the rate of $1.50 per day, if done within the three days' notice, but after that time the rate is $2 per day.

Any person liable for work on highways who has been assessed two days or more and has not commuted, may be required to furnish team, or a cart, wagon or plow, with a pair of horses or oxen and a man to manage them, for which he will be entitled to two days for each day's work. Eight hours is a day's work on the roads, and there is a penalty of twenty-five cents an hour against any person or substitute who shall neglect or refuse to perform. Any person remaining idle, or does not work faithfully or hinders others from doing so, forfeits to the town $2.

Every person assessed *and duly notified*, who has not commuted and refuses or neglects to appear, shall forfeit to the town for *every day's* refusal or neglect, the sum of $2; if he was required to furnish a team, carriage, man or implement, and neglects or refuses to comply, he is liable to the following fines:

First. For wholly failing to comply, $4 each day.

Second. For omitting to furnish a pair of horses or oxen, $1.50 each day.

Third. For omitting to furnish a man to manage team, $2 each day.

Fourth. For omitting to furnish a wagon, cart or plow, 75 cents each day.

The Commissioners estimate and assess the highway labor and road tax. The road tax on real and personal property can not exceed forty cents on each hundred dollars' worth. The labor or road tax in villages, towns or cities, is paid over to the corporate authorities of such, for the improvement of streets, roads and bridges within their limits. Commissioners' compensation $1.50 per day. The Treasurer, who is one of their number, is entitled to 2 per cent. on all moneys he may receive and pay out.

Overseers. Their duties are to repair and keep in order the highways in their districts; to warn persons to work out their road tax at such time and place as they think proper; to collect fines and commutation money, and execute all lawful orders of the Commissioners of Highways; also make list, within sixteen days after their election, of the names of all inhabitants in his road district liable to work on highways. For refusal to perform any of his duties, he is liable to a fine of $10. The compensation of overseers is $1.50 a day, the number of days to be audited by the Highway Commissioners.

As all township and county officers are familiar with their duties, it is only intended to give the points of the law that the public should be familiar with. The manner of laying out, altering or vacating roads, etc., will not be here stated, as it would require more space than is contemplated in a work of this kind. It is sufficient to state that, the first step is by petition, addressed to the Commissioners, setting out what is prayed for, giving the names of the owners of lands if known, if not known so state, over which the road is to pass, giving the general course, its place of beginning, and where it terminates. It requires not less than twelve *freeholders* residing within three miles of the road who shall sign the petition. Public roads must not be less than fifty feet wide, nor more than sixty feet wide. Roads not exceeding two miles in length, if petitioned for, may be laid out, not less than forty feet. Private roads for private and public use, may be laid out of the width of three rods, on petition of the person directly interested; the damage occasioned thereby shall be paid by the premises benefited thereby, and before the road is opened. If not opened in two years, the order shall be considered rescinded. Commissioners in their discretion may permit persons who live on or have private roads, to work out their road tax thereon. Public roads must be opened in five days from date of filing order of location, or be deemed vacated.

DRAINAGE.

Whenever one or more owners or occupants of land *desire to construct a drain* or ditch across the land of others for *agricultural* or *sanitary purposes*, the proceedings are as follows:

1st. *File a petition* with the *clerk* of the *town board* of *auditors* in counties where there is township organization, or in counties not so organized with the clerk of the County Court, stating the necessity of the same, its starting point, route and terminus; and if it shall be deemed necessary for successful drainage that a levee or other work be constructed, a general description of the same shall be made.

2d. *After filing, two weeks'* notice must be given by posting notices in three of the most public places in such township through which the drain, ditch or other work is proposed to be constructed; and also, by publishing a copy thereof in some newspaper published in the county in which petition is filed, at least once each week for two successive weeks. The notice must state when and before what board such petition is filed, the starting point, route, terminus and description of the proposed work. On receipt of the petition by the clerk of either board as before mentioned, it is his duty to immediately give notice to the board of which he is clerk, of the fact, and that a meeting of the board will be held on a day to be fixed not later than sixty days after the filing of said petition, to consider the prayer of the same; and it is further the duty of the clerk, to publish a notice of the filing of the petition and the meeting of the board to consider it, by posting the same in the three most public places in the township or county. On the hearing, all parties may contest the matter, and if it shall appear to the board that the work contemplated is necessary, or is useful for the drainage of the land for agricultural and sanitary purposes, they shall so find and shall file their petition in the County Court, reciting the original petition and stating their finding, and pray that the costs of the improvement be assessed, and for that purpose three commissioners be appointed to lay out and construct the work. The costs of the hearing before the town board is to be paid by the petitioners. After commissioners are appointed, they organize and proceed to examine the work; and if they find the benefits greater than the cost and expense of the work, then it is their duty to have the surveyor's plans and specifications made, and when done report the same to the court, before which parties can be heard prior to confirmation. The commissioners are not confined to the route or plan of the petition, but may change the same. After report of commissioners is confirmed, then a jury assess the damages and benefits against the land damaged or benefited.

As it is only contemplated in a work of this kind to give an abstract of the laws, and as the parties who have in charge the execution of the further proceedings are likely to be familiar with the requirements of the statute, the necessary details are not here inserted.

PAUPERS.

Every poor person who shall be unable to earn a livelihood in consequence of any *bodily infirmity, idiocy, lunacy* or *unavoidable cause*, shall be supported by the father, grand-father, mother, grand-mother, children, grand-children, brothers or sisters of such poor person, if they or either of them be of sufficient ability; but if any of such dependent class shall have become so from *intemperance*, or other *bad conduct*, they shall not be entitled to support from any relation except parent or child.

The children shall first be called on to support their parents, if they are able; but if not, the parents of such poor person shall then be called on, if of sufficient ability; and if there be no parents or children able, then the brothers and sisters of such dependent person shall be called upon; and if there be no brothers or sisters of sufficient ability, the grand-children of such person shall next be called on; and if they are not able, then the grand-parents. Married females, while their husbands live, shall not be liable to contribute for the support of their poor relations except out of their separate property. It is the duty of the state's (county) attorney, to make complaint to the County Court of his county against all the relatives of such paupers in this state liable to his support and prosecute the same. In case the state's attorney neglects, or refuses, to complain in such cases, then it is the duty of the overseer of the poor to do so. The person called upon to contribute shall have at least ten days' notice of such application by summons. The court has the power to determine the kind of support, depending upon the circumstances of the parties, and may also order two or more of the different degrees to maintain such poor person, and prescribe the proportion of each, according to their ability. The court may specify the time for which the relative shall contribute—in fact has control over the entire subject matter, with power to enforce its orders. Every county (except those in which the poor are supported by the towns, and in such cases the towns are liable) is required to relieve and support all poor and indigent persons *lawfully* resident therein. Residence means the *actual* residence of the party, or the place where he was employed; or in case he was in no employment, then it shall be the place where he made his home. When any person becomes chargeable as a pauper in any county or town who did not reside at the commencement of six months immediately preceding his becoming so, but did at that time reside in some other county or town in this state, then the county or town, as the case may be, becomes liable for the expense of taking care of such person until removed, and it is the duty of the overseer to notify the proper authorities of the fact. If any person shall bring and leave any pauper in any county in this state where such pauper had no legal residence, knowing him to be such, he is liable to a fine of $100. In counties under township organization, the supervisors in each town are ex-officio overseers of the poor. The overseers of the poor act under the directions of the County Board in taking care of the poor and granting of temporary relief; also, providing for non-resident persons not paupers who may be taken sick and not able to pay their way, and in case of death cause such person to be decently buried.

FENCES.

In counties under township organization, the *town assessor* and commissioner of highways are the fence-viewers in their respective towns. In other counties the County Board appoints three in each precinct annually. *A lawful fence* is *four and one-half feet high*, in good repair, consisting of rails, timber, boards, stone, hedges, or whatever the fence-viewers of the town or precinct where the same shall lie, shall consider equivalent thereto, but in counties under township organization the annual town meeting may establish any other kind of fence as such, or the County Board in other counties may do the same. Division fences shall be made and maintained in just proportion by the adjoining owners, except when the owner shall choose to let his land lie open, but after a division fence is built by agreement or otherwise, neither party can remove his part of such fence so long as he may crop or use such land for farm purposes, or without giving the other party one year's notice in writing of his intention to remove his portion. When any person shall enclose his land upon the enclosure of another, he shall refund the owner of the adjoining lands a just proportion of the value at that time of such fence. The value of fence and the just proportion to be paid or built and maintained by each is to be ascertained by two fence-viewers in the town or precinct. Such fence-viewers have power to settle all disputes between different owners as to fences built or to be built, as well as to repairs to be made. Each party chooses one of the viewers, but if the other party neglects, after eight days' notice in writing, to make his choice, then the other party may select both. It is sufficient to notify the tenant or party in possession, when the owner is not a resident of the town or precinct. The two fence-viewers chosen, after viewing the premises, shall hear the statements of the parties, in case they can't agree, they shall select another fence-viewer to act with them, and the decision of any two of them is final. The decision must be reduced to writing, and should plainly set out description of fence and all matters settled by them, and must be filed in the office of the town clerk in counties under township organization, and in other counties with the county clerk.

Where any person is liable to contribute to the erection or the repairing of a division fence, neglects or refuses so to do, the party injured, after giving sixty days notice in writing when a fence is to be erected, or ten days when it is only repairs, may proceed to have the work done at the expense of the party whose duty it is to do it, to be recovered from him with costs of suit, and the party so neglecting shall also be liable to the party injured for all damages accruing from such neglect or refusal, to be determined by any two fence-viewers selected as before provided, the appraisement to be reduced to writing and signed.

D. Turnbull
(DECEASED)

ABSTRACT OF ILLINOIS STATE LAWS. 61

Where a person shall conclude to remove his part of a division fence, and let his land lie open, and having given the year's notice required, the adjoining owner may cause the value of said fence to be ascertained by fence-viewers as before provided, and on payment or tender of the amount of such valuation to the owner, it shall prevent the removal. A party removing a division fence without notice is liable for the damages accruing thereby.

Where a fence has been built on the land of another through mistake, the owner may enter upon such premises and remove his fence and material within six months after the division line has been ascertained. Where the material to build such a fence has been taken from the land on which it was built, then before it can be removed, the person claiming must first pay for such material to the owner of the land from which it was taken, nor shall such a fence be removed at a time when the removal will throw open or expose the crops of the other party; a reasonable time must be given beyond the six months to remove crops.

The compensation of fence-viewers is one dollar and fifty cents a day each, to be paid in the first instance by the party calling them, but in the end all expenses, including amount charged by the fence-viewers, must be paid equally by the parties, except in cases where a party neglects or refuses to make or maintain a just proportion of a division fence, when the party in default shall pay them.

DAMAGES FROM TRESPASS.

Where stock of any kind breaks into any person's enclosure, the fence being *good* and *sufficient*, the owner is liable for the damage done; but where the damage is done by stock *running at large, contrary to law*, the owner is liable where there is not such a fence. Where stock is found trespassing on the enclosure of another as aforesaid, the owner or occupier of the premises may take possession of such stock and keep the same until damages, with reasonable charges for keeping and feeding and all costs of suit, are paid. Any person taking or rescuing such stock so held without his consent, shall be liable to a fine of not less than three nor more than five dollars for each animal rescued, to be recovered by suit before a justice of the peace for the use of the school fund. Within twenty-four hours after taking such animal into his possession, the person taking it up must give notice of the fact to the owner, if known, or if unknown, notices must be posted in some public place near the premises.

LANDLORD AND TENANT.

The owner of lands, or his legal representatives, can sue for and recover rent therefor, in any of the following cases:

First. When rent is due and in arrears on a lease for life or lives,

Second. When lands are held and occupied by any person without any special agreement for rent.

Third. When possession is obtained under an agreement, written or verbal, for the purchase of the premises and before deed given, the right to possession is terminated by forfeiture on con-compliance with the agreement, and possession is wrongfully refused or neglected to be given upon demand made in writing by the party entitled thereto. Provided that all payments made by the vendee or his representatives or assigns, may be set off against the rent.

Fourth. When land has been sold upon a judgment or a decree of court, when the party to such judgment or decree, or person holding under him, wrongfully refuses, or neglects, to surrender possession of the same, after demand in writing by the person entitled to the possession.

Fifth. When the lands have been sold upon a mortgage or trust deed, and the mortgagor or grantor or person holding under him, wrongfully refuses or neglects to surrender possession of the same, after demand in writing by the person entitled to the possession.

If any tenant, or any person who shall come into possession from or under or by collusion with such tenant, shall willfully hold over any lands, etc., after the expiration the term of their lease, and *after demand made in writing* for the possession thereof, is liable to pay *double rent.* A tenancy from year to year requires sixty days notice in writing, to terminate the same at the end of the year; such notice can be given at any time within four months preceding the last sixty days of the year.

A tenancy by the month, or less than a year, where the tenant holds over without any special agreement, the landlord may terminate the tenancy, by thirty days notice in writing.

When rent is due, the landlord may serve a notice upon the tenant, stating that unless the rent is paid within not less than five days, his lease will be terminated; if the rent is not paid, the landlord may consider the lease ended. When default is made in any of the terms of a lease, it shall not be necessary to give more than ten days notice to quit or of the termination of such tenancy; and the same may be terminated on giving such notice to quit, at any time after such default in any of the terms of such lease; which notice may be substantially in the following form, viz:

To ———, You are hereby notified that, in consequence of your default in (here insert the character of the default), of the premises now occupied by you, being etc. (here describe the premises), I have elected to determine your lease, and you are hereby notified to quit and deliver up possession of the same to me within ten days of this date (dated, etc.)

The above to be signed by the lessor or his agent, and no other notice or demand of possession or termination of such tenancy is necessary.

Demand may be made, or notice served, by delivering a written or printed, or partly either, copy thereof to the tenant, or leaving the same with some person above the age of twelve years residing on or in possession of the premises; and in case no one is in the actual possession of the said premises, then by posting the same on the premises. When the tenancy is for a certain time, and the term expires by the terms of the lease, the tenant is then bound to surrender possession, and no notice to quit or demand of possession is necessary.

Distress for rent.—In all cases of distress for rent, the landlord, by himself, his agent or attorney, may seize for rent any personal property of his tenant that may be found in the county where the tenant resides; the property of any other person, even if found on the premises, is not liable.

An inventory of the property levied upon, with a statement of the amount of rent claimed, should be at once filed with some justice of the peace, if not over $200; and if above that sum, with the clerk of a court of record of competent jurisdiction. Property may be released, by the party executing a satisfactory bond for double the amount.

The landlord may distrain for rent, any time within *six months* after the expiration of the term of the lease, or when terminated.

When rent is payable wholly or in part, in specific articles of property, or products of the premises, or labor, the landlord may distrain for the value of the same.

Landlords have a lien upon the crops grown or growing upon the demised premises for the rent thereof, and also for the faithful performance of the terms of the lease.

In all cases where the premises rented shall be sub-let, or the lease assigned, the landlord shall have the same right to enforce lien against such lessee or assignee, that he has against the tenant to whom the premises were rented.

When a tenant abandons or removes from the premises or any part thereof, the landlord, or his agent or attorney, may seize upon any grain or other crops grown or growing upon the premises, or part thereof so abandoned, whether the rent is due or not. If such grain, or other crops, or any part thereof, is not fully grown or matured, the landlord, or his agent or attorney, shall cause the same to be properly cultivated, harvested or gathered, and may sell the same, and from the proceeds pay all his labor, expenses and rent. The tenant may, before the sale of such property, redeem the same by tendering the rent and reasonable compensation for work done, or he may replevy the same.

Exemption.—The same articles of personal property which are by law exempt from execution, except the crops as above stated, is also exempt from distress for rent.

LIENS.

Any person who shall by *contract*, express or implied, or partly both, with the owner of any lot or tract of land, furnish labor or material, or services as an architect or superintendent, in building, altering, repairing or ornamenting any house or other building or appurtenance thereto on such lot, or upon any street or alley, and connected with such improvements, shall have a lien upon the whole of such lot or tract of land, and upon such house or building and appurtenances, for the amount due to him for such labor, material or services. If the contract is *expressed*, and the time for the *completion* of the work is *beyond three years* from the commencement thereof; or, if the time of payment is beyond one year from the time stipulated for the completion of the work, then no lien exists. If the contract is *implied*, then no lien exists, unless the work be done or material is furnished within one year from the commencement of the work or delivery of the materials. As between different creditors having liens, no preference is given to the one whose contract was first made; but each shares pro-rata. Incumbrances existing on the lot or tract of the land at the time the contract is made, do not operate on the improvements, and are only preferred to the extent of the value of the land at the *time of making the contract*. The above lien can not be enforced *unless suit is commenced* within *six months* after the last payment for labor or materials shall have become due and payable. Sub-contractors, mechanics, workmen and other persons furnishing any material, or performing any labor for a contractor as before specified, have a lien to the extent of the amount due the contractor at the time the following notice is served upon the owner of the land who made the contract:

To ——, You are hereby notified, that I have been employed by—— (here state whether to labor or furnish material, and substantially the nature of the demand) upon your (here state in general terms description and situation of building), and that I shall hold the (building, or as the case may be), and your interest in the ground, liable for the amount that may (is or may become) due me on account thereof. Signature, —— Date, ——

If there is a contract in writing between contractor and sub-contractor, a copy of it should be served with above notice, and said notice must be served within forty days from the completion of such sub-contract, if there is one; if not, then from the time payment should have been made to the person performing the labor or furnishing the material. If the owner is not a resident of the county, or can not be found therein, then the above notice must be filed with the clerk of the Circuit Court, with his fee, fifty cents, and a copy of said notice must be published in a newspaper published in the county, for four successive weeks.

When the owner or agent is notified as above, he can retain any money due the contractor sufficient to pay such claim; if more than one claim. and not enough to pay all, they are to be paid pro rata.

The owner has the right to demand in writing, a statement of the contractor, of what he owes for labor, etc., from time to time as the work progresses, and on his failure to comply, forfeits to the owner $50 for every offense.

The liens referred to cover any and all estates, whether in fee for life, for years, or any other interest which the owner may have.

To enforce the lien of *sub-contractors*, suit must be commenced within *three months* from the time of the performance of the sub-contract, or during the work or furnishing materials.

Hotel, inn and *boarding-house keepers*, have a lien upon the baggage and other valuables of their guests or boarders, brought into such hotel, inn or boarding-house, by their guests or boarders, for the proper charges due from such guests or boarders for their accommodation, board and lodgings, and such *extras* as are furnished at their request.

Stable-keepers and other persons have a lien upon the horses, carriages and harness kept by them, for the proper charges due for the keeping thereof and expenses bestowed thereon at the request of the owner or the person having the possession of the same.

Agisters (persons who take care of cattle belonging to others), and persons keeping, yarding, feeding or pasturing domestic animals, shall have a lien upon the animals agistered, kept, yarded or fed, for the proper charges due for such service.

All persons who may furnish any railroad corporation in this state with fuel, ties, material, supplies or any other article or thing necessary for the construction, maintenance, operation or repair of its road by contract, or may perform work or labor on the same, is entitled to be paid as part of the current expenses of the road, and have a lien upon all its property. Sub-contractors or laborers have also a lien. The conditions and limitations both as to contractors and sub-contractors, are about the same as herein stated as to general liens.

DEFINITION OF COMMERCIAL TERMS.

$—— means *dollars*, being a contraction of U. S., which was formerly placed before any denomination of money, and meant, as it means now, United States Currency.

£—— means *pounds*, English money.

@ stands for *at* or *to*. ℔ for *pound*, and bbl. for *barrel;* ℔ for *per* or *by the*. Thus, Butter sells at 20@30c ℔ ℔, and Flour at $8@12 ℔ bbl.

% for *per cent* and # for *number*.

May 1.—Wheat sells at $1.20@1.25, "seller June." *Seller June* means that the person who sells the wheat has the privilege of delivering it at any time during the month of June.

Selling *short*, is contracting to deliver a certain amount of grain or stock, at a fixed price, within a certain length of time, when the seller has not the stock on hand. It is for the interest of the person selling "short," to depress the market as much as possible, in order that he may buy and fill his contract at a profit. Hence the "shorts" are termed "bears."

Buying *long*, is to contract to purchase a certain amount of grain or shares of stock at a fixed price, deliverable within a stipulated time, expecting to make a profit by the rise of prices. The "longs" are termed "bulls," as it is for their interest to "operate" so as to "toss" the prices upward as much as possible.

NOTES.

Form of note is legal, worded in the simplest way, so that the amount and time of payment are mentioned.

$100.   Chicago, Ill., Sept. 15, 1876.

Sixty days from date I promise to pay to E. F. Brown, or order, One Hundred dollars, for value received.

L. D. LOWRY.

A note to be payable in any thing else than money needs only the facts substituted for money in the above form.

ORDERS.

Orders should be worded simply, thus:

Mr. F. H. COATS: Chicago, Sept. 15, 1876.

Please pay to H. Birdsall, Twenty-five dollars, and charge to

F. D. SILVA.

RECEIPTS.

Receipts should always state when received and what for, thus:

$100.   Chicago, Sept. 15, 1876.

Received of J. W. Davis, One Hundred dollars, for services rendered in grading his lot in Fort Madison, on account.

THOMAS BRADY.

If receipt is in full it should be so stated.

BILLS OF PURCHASE.

W. N. MASON,   Salem, Illinois, Sept. 15, 1876.

Bought of A. A. GRAHAM.

4 Bushels of Seed Wheat, at $1.50	- - - -	$6.00
2 Seamless Sacks " .30	- -	.60
Received payment,		$6.60

A. A. GRAHAM.

ARTICLES OF AGREEMENT.

An agreement is where one party promises to another to do a certain thing in a certain time for a stipulated sum. Good business men always reduce an agreement to writing, which nearly always saves misunderstandings and trouble. No particular form is necessary, but the facts must be clearly and explicitly stated, and there must, to make it valid, be a reasonable consideration.

GENERAL FORM OF AGREEMENT.

THIS AGREEMENT, made the Second day of October, 1876, between John Jones, of Aurora, County of Kane, State of Illinois, of the first part, and Thomas Whiteside, of the same place, of the second part—

WITNESSETH, that the said John Jones, in consideration of the agreement of the party of the second part, hereinafter contained, contracts and agrees to and with the said Thomas Whiteside, that he will deliver, in good and marketable condition, at the Village of Batavia, Ill., during the month of November, of this year, One Hundred Tons of Prairie Hay, in the following lots, and at the following specified times; namely, twenty-five tons by the seventh of November, twenty-five tons additional by the fourteenth of the month, twenty-five tons more by the twenty-first, and the entire one hundred tons to be all delivered by the thirtieth of November.

And the said Thomas Whiteside, in consideration of the prompt fulfillment of this contract, on the part of the party of the first part, contracts to and agrees with the said John Jones, to pay for said hay five dollars per ton, for each ton as soon as delivered.

In case of failure of agreement by either of the parties hereto, it is hereby stipulated and agreed that the party so failing shall pay to the other, One Hundred Dollars, as fixed and settled damages.

In witness whereof, we have hereunto set our hands the day and year first above written. JOHN JONES,
THOMAS WHITESIDE.

AGREEMENT WITH CLERK FOR SERVICES.

THIS AGREEMENT, made the first day of May, one thousand eight hundred and seventy-six, between Reuben Stone, of Chicago, County of Cook, State of Illinois, party of the first part, and George Barclay, of Englewood, County of Cook, State of Illinois, party of the second part—

WITNESSETH, that said George Barclay agrees faithfully and diligently to work as clerk and salesman for the said Reuben Stone, for and during the space of one year from the date hereof, should both live such length of time, without absenting himself from his occupation;

during which time he, the said Barclay, in the store of said Stone, of Chicago, will carefully and honestly attend, doing and performing all duties as clerk and salesman aforesaid, in accordance and in all respects as directed and desired by the said Stone.

In consideration of which services, so to be rendered by the said Barclay, the said Stone agrees to pay to said Barclay the annual sum of one thousand dollars, payable in twelve equal monthly payments, each upon the last day of each month; provided that all dues for days of absence from business by said Barclay, shall be deducted from the sum otherwise by the agreement due and payable by the said Stone to the said Barclay.

Witness our hands.
REUBEN STONE.
GEORGE BARCLAY.

BILLS OF SALE.

A bill of sale is a written agreement to another party, for a consideration to convey his right and interest in the personal property. The purchaser must take actual possession of the property. Juries have power to determine upon the fairness or unfairness of a bill of sale.

COMMON FORM OF BILL OF SALE.

KNOW ALL MEN by this instrument, that I, Louis Clay, of Princeton, Illinois, of the first part, for and in consideration of Five Hundred and Ten dollars, to me paid by John Floyd, of the same place, of the second part, the receipt whereof is hereby acknowledged, have sold, and by this instrument do convey unto the said Floyd, party of the second part, his executors, administrators, and assigns, my undivided half of ten acres of corn, now growing on the farm of Thomas Tyrrell, in the town above mentioned; one pair of horses, sixteen sheep, and five cows, belonging to me, and in my possession at the farm aforesaid; to have and to hold the same unto the party of the second part, his executors and assigns, forever. And I do, for myself and legal representatives, agree with the said party of the second part, and his legal representatives, to warrant and defend the sale of the afore-mentioned property and chattels unto the said party of the second part, and his legal representatives, against all and every person whatsoever.

In witness whereof, I have hereunto affixed my hand, this tenth day of October, one thousand eight hundred and seventy-six.

LOUIS CLAY.

BONDS.

A bond is a written admission on the part of the maker in which he pledges a certain sum to another, at a certain time.

COMMON FORM OF BOND.

KNOW ALL MEN by this instrument, that I, George Edgerton, of Watseka, Iroquois County, State of Illinois, am firmly bound unto Peter Kirchoff, of the place aforesaid, in the sum of five hundred dollars, to be paid to the said Peter Kirchoff, or his legal representatives; to which payment, to be made, I bind myself, or my legal representatives, by this instrument.

Sealed with my seal, and dated this second day of November, one thousand eight hundred and sixty-four.

The condition of this bond is such that if I, George Edgerton, my heirs, administrators, or executors, shall promptly pay the sum of two hundred and fifty dollars in three equal annual payments from the date hereof, with annual interest, then the above obligation to be of no effect; otherwise to be in full force and valid.

Sealed and delivered in
    presence of   GEORGE EDGERTON. [L.S.]
WILLIAM TURNER.

CHATTEL MORTGAGES.

A chattel mortgage is a mortgage on personal property for payment of a certain sum of money, to hold the property against debts of other creditors. The mortgage must describe the property, and must be acknowledged before a justice of the peace in the township or precinct where the mortgagee resides, and entered upon his docket, and must be recorded in the recorder's office of the county.

GENERAL FORM OF CHATTEL MORTGAGE.

THIS INDENTURE, made and entered into this first day of January, in the year of our Lord one thousand eight hundred and seventy-five, between Theodore Lottinville, of the town of Geneseo in the County of Henry, and State of Illinois, party of the first part, and Paul Henshaw, of the same town, county, and State, party of the second part.

Witnesseth, that the said party of the first part, for and in consideration of the sum of one thousand dollars, in hand paid, the receipt whereof is hereby acknowledged, does hereby grant, sell, convey, and confirm unto the said party of the second part, his heirs and assigns forever, all and singular the following described goods and chattels, to wit:

Two three-year old roan-colored horses, one Burdett organ, No. 987, one Brussels carpet, 15x20 feet in size, one marble-top center table, one Home Comfort cooking stove, No. 8, one black walnut bureau with mirror attached, one set of parlor chairs (six in number), upholstered in green rep, with lounge corresponding with same in style and color of upholstery, now in possession of said Lottinville, at No. 4 Prairie Ave., Geneseo, Ill.;

Together with all and singular, the appurtenances thereunto belonging, or in any wise appertaining; to have and to hold the above described goods and chattels, unto the said party of the second part, his heirs and assigns, forever.

Provided, always, and these presents are upon this express condition, that if the said Theodore Lottinville, his heirs, executors, administrators, or assigns, shall, on or before the first day of January, A.D., one thousand eight hundred and seventy-six, pay, or cause to be paid, to the said Paul Ranslow, or his lawful attorney or attorneys, heirs, executors, administrators, or assigns, the sum of One Thousand dollars, together with the interest that may accrue thereon, at the rate of ten per cent. per annum, from the first day of January, A.D. one thousand eight hundred and seventy-five, until paid, according to the tenor of one promissory note bearing even date herewith for the payment of said sum of money, that then and from thenceforth, these presents, and everything herein contained, shall cease, and be null and void, anything herein contained to the contrary notwithstanding.

Provided, also, that the said Theodore Lottinville may retain the possession of and have the use of said goods and chattels until the day of payment aforesaid; and also, at his own expense, shall keep said goods and chattels; and also at the expiration of said time of payment, if said sum of money, together with the interest as aforesaid, shall not be paid, shall deliver up said goods and chattels, in good condition, to said Paul Ranslow, or his heirs, executors, administrators, or assigns.

And provided, also, that if default in payment as aforesaid, by said party of the first part, shall be made, or if said party of the second part shall at any time before said promissory note becomes due, feel himself unsafe or insecure, that then the said party of the second part, or his attorney, agent, assigns, or heirs, executors, or administrators, shall have the right to take possession of said goods and chattels, wherever they may or can be found, and sell the same at public or private sale, to the highest bidder for cash in hand, after giving ten days' notice of the time and place of said sale, together with a description of the goods and chattels to be sold, by at least four advertisements, posted up in public places in the vicinity where said sale is to take place, and proceed to make the sum of money and interest promised as aforesaid, together with all reasonable costs, charges, and expenses in so doing; and if there shall be any overplus, shall pay the same without delay to the said party of the first part, or his legal representatives.

In testimony whereof, the said party of the first part has hereunto set his hand and affixed his seal, the day and year first above written. Signed, sealed and delivered in

presence of   THEODORE LOTTINVILLE. [L.S.]
SAMUEL J. TILDEN.

LEASE OF FARM AND BUILDINGS THEREON.

THIS INDENTURE, made this second day of June, 1875, between David Patton of the Town of Bisbee, State of Illinois, of the first part, and John Doyle of the same place, of the second part,

Witnesseth, that the said David Patton, for and in consideration of the covenants hereinafter mentioned and reserved, on the part of the said John Doyle, his executors, administrators, and assigns, to be paid, kept, and performed, hath let, and by these presents doth grant, demise, and let, unto the said John Doyle, his executors, administrators, and assigns, all that parcel of land situate in Bisbee aforesaid, bounded and described as follows, to wit:

[*Here describe the land.*]

Together with all the appurtenances appertaining thereto. To have and to hold the said premises, with appurtenances thereto belonging, unto the said Doyle, his executors, administrators, and assigns, for the term of five years, from the first day of October next following, at a yearly rent of Six Hundred dollars, to be paid in equal payments, semi-annually, as long as said buildings are in good tenantable condition.

And the said Doyle, by these presents, covenants and agrees to pay all taxes and assessments, and keep in repair all hedges, ditches, rail, and other fences; (the said David Patton, his heirs, assigns and administrators, to furnish all timber, brick, tile, and other materials necessary for such repairs.)

Said Doyle further covenants and agrees to apply to said land, in a farmer-like manner, all manure and compost accumulating upon said farm, and cultivate all the arable land in a husbandlike manner, according to the usual custom among farmers in the neighborhood; he also agrees to trim the hedges at a seasonable time, preventing injury from cattle to such hedges, and to all fruit and other trees on the said premises. That he will seed down with clover and timothy seed twenty acres yearly of arable land, ploughing the same number of acres each Spring of land now in grass, and hitherto unbroken.

It is further agreed, that if the said Doyle shall fail to perform the whole or any one of the above mentioned covenants, then and in that case the said David Patton may declare this lease terminated, by giving three months' notice of the same, prior to the first of October of any year, and may distrain any part of the stock, goods, or chattels, or other property in possession of said Doyle, for sufficient to compensate for the non-performance of the above written covenants, the same to be determined, and amounts so to be paid to be determined, by three arbitrators, chosen as follows: Each of the parties to this instrument to choose one, and the two so chosen to select a third; the decision of said arbitrators to be final.

In witness whereof, we have hereto set our hands and seals.
Signed, sealed, and delivered
    in presence of   DAVID PATTON. [L.S.]
    JAMES WALDRON.   JOHN DOYLE. [L.S.]

FORM OF LEASE OF A HOUSE.

THIS INSTRUMENT, made the first day of October, 1875, witnesseth that Amos Griest of Yorkville, County of Kendall, State of Illinois, hath rented from Aaron Young of Logansport aforesaid, the dwelling and lot No. 13 Ohio Street, situated in said City of Yorkville, for five years from the above date, at the yearly rental of Three Hundred dollars, payable monthly, on the first day of each month, in advance, at the residence of said Aaron Young.

At the expiration of said above mentioned term, the said Griest agrees to give the said Young peaceable possession of the said dwelling, in as good condition as when taken, ordinary wear and casualties excepted.

In witness whereof, we place our hands and seals the day and year aforesaid.

Signed, sealed and delivered   AMOS GRIEST. [L.S.]
    in presence of
    NICKOLAS SCHUTZ,   AARON YOUNG. [L.S.]
        Notary Public.

LANDLORD'S AGREEMENT.

THIS certifies that I have let and rented, this first day of January, 1876, unto Jacob Schmidt, my house and lot, No. 15 Erie Street, in the City of Chicago, State of Illinois, and its appurtenances; he to have the free and uninterrupted occupation thereof for one year from this date, at the yearly rental of Two Hundred dollars, to be paid monthly in advance; rent to cease if destroyed by fire, or otherwise made untenantable.

                                                                       PETER FUNK.

TENANT'S AGREEMENT.

THIS certifies that I have hired and taken from Peter Funk, his house and lot, No. 15 Erie Street, in the City of Chicago, State of Illinois, with appurtenances thereto belonging, for one year, to commence this day, at a yearly rental of Two Hundred dollars, to be paid monthly in advance; unless said house becomes untenantable from fire or other causes, in which case rent ceases; and I further agree to give and yield said premises one year from this first day of January 1876, in as good condition as now, ordinary wear and damage by the elements excepted.

    Given under my hand this day.   JACOB SCHMIDT.

NOTICE TO QUIT.

To F. W. ARLEN,

Sir: Please observe that the term of one year, for which the house and land, situated at No. 6 Indiana Street, and now occupied by you, were rented to you, expired on the first day of October, 1875, and as I desire to repossess said premises, you are hereby requested and required to vacate the same. Respectfully Yours,

P. T. BARNUM.

LINCOLN, NEB., October 4, 1875.

TENANT'S NOTICE OF LEAVING.

DEAR SIR:

The premises I now occupy as your tenant, at No. 6 Indiana Street, I shall vacate on the first day of November, 1875. You will please take notice accordingly.

Dated this tenth day of October, 1875. F. W. ARLEN.

To P. T. BARNUM, ESQ.

REAL ESTATE MORTGAGE TO SECURE PAYMENT OF MONEY.

THIS INDENTURE, made this sixteenth day of May, in the year of our Lord, one thousand eight hundred and seventy-two, between William Stocker, of Peoria, County of Peoria, and State of Illinois, and Olla, his wife, party of the first part, and Edward Singer, party of the second part.

Whereas, the said party of the first part is justly indebted to the said party of the second part, in the sum of Two Thousand dollars, secured to be paid by two certain promissory notes (bearing even date herewith) the one due and payable at the Second National Bank in Peoria, Illinois, with interest, on the sixteenth day of May, in the year one thousand eight hundred and seventy-three; the other due and payable at the Second National Bank at Peoria, Ill., with interest, on the sixteenth day of May, in the year one thousand eight hundred and seventy-four.

Now, therefore, this indenture witnesseth, that the said party of the first part, for the better securing the payment of the money aforesaid, with interest thereon, according to the tenor and effect of the said two promissory notes above mentioned; and, also in consideration of the further sum of one dollar to them in hand paid by the said party of the second part, at the delivery of these presents, the receipt whereof is hereby acknowledged, have granted, bargained, sold, and conveyed, and by these presents do grant, bargain, sell, and convey, unto the said party of the second part, his heirs and assigns, forever, all that certain parcel of land, situate, etc.

[*Describing the premises.*]

To have and to hold the same, together with all and singular the Tenements, Hereditaments, Privileges and Appurtenances thereunto belonging or in any wise appertaining. And also, all the estate, interest, and claim whatsoever, in law as well as in equity which the party of the first part have in and to the premises hereby conveyed unto the said party of the second part, his heirs and assigns, and to their only proper use, benefit and behoof. And the said William Stocker, and Olla, his wife, party of the first part, hereby expressly waive, relinquish, release, and convey unto the said party of the second part, his heirs, executors, administrators, and assigns, all right, title, claim, interest, and benefit whatever, in and to the above described premises, and each and every part thereof, which is given by or results from all laws of this state pertaining to the exemption of homesteads.

Provided always, and these presents are upon this express condition, that if the said party of the first part, their heirs, executors, or administrators, shall well and truly pay, or cause to be paid, to the said party of the second part, his heirs, executors, administrators, or assigns, the aforesaid sums of money, with such interest thereon, at the time and in the manner specified in the above mentioned promissory notes, according to the true intent and meaning thereof, then in that case, these presents and every thing herein expressed, shall be absolutely null and void.

In witness whereof, the said party of the first part hereunto set their hands and seals the day and year first above written.

Signed, sealed and delivered in presence of

  JAMES WHITEHEAD,   WILLIAM STOCKER. [L.S.]
  FRED. SAMUELS.   OLLA STOCKER. [L.S.]

WARRANTY DEED WITH COVENANTS.

THIS INDENTURE, made this sixth day of April, in the year of our Lord one thousand eight hundred and seventy-two, between Henry Best of Lawrence, County of Lawrence, State of Illinois, and Belle, his wife, of the first part, and Charles Pearson of the same place, of the second part.

Witnesseth, that the said party of the first part, for and in consideration of the sum of Six Thousand dollars in hand paid by the said party of the second part, the receipt whereof is hereby acknowledged, have granted, bargained, and sold, and by these presents do grant, bargain, and sell, unto the said party of the second part, his heirs and assigns, all the following described lot, piece, or parcel of land, situated in the City of Lawrence, in the County of Lawrence, and State of Illinois, to wit:

[*Here describe the property.*]

Together with all and singular the hereditaments and appurtenances thereunto belonging or in any wise appertaining, and the reversion and reversions, remainder and remainders, rents, issues, and profits thereof; and all the estate, right, title, interest, claim, and demand whatsoever, of the said party of the first part, either in law or equity, of, in, and to the above bargained premises, with the hereditaments and appurtenances. To have and to hold the said premises above bargained and described, with the appurtenances, unto the said party of the second part, his heirs and assigns, forever. And the said Henry Best, and Belle, his wife, parties of the first part, hereby expressly waive, release, and relinquish unto the said party of the second part, his heirs, executors, administrators, and assigns, all right, title, claim, interest, and benefit whatever, in and to the above described premises, and each and every part thereof, which is given by or results from all laws of this state pertaining to the exemption of homesteads.

And the said Henry Best, and Belle, his wife, party of the first part, for themselves and their heirs, executors, and administrators, do covenant, grant, bargain, and agree, to and with the said party of the second part, his heirs and assigns, that at the time of the ensealing and delivery of these presents they were well seized of the premises above conveyed, as of a good, sure, perfect, absolute, and indefeasible estate of inheritance in law, and in fee simple, and have good right, full power, and lawful authority to grant, bargain, sell, and convey the same, in manner and form aforesaid, and that the same are free and clear from all former and other grants, bargains, sales, liens, taxes, assessments, and encumbrances of what kind or nature soever; and the above bargained premises in the quiet and peaceable possession of the said party of the second part, his heirs and assigns, against all and every person or persons lawfully claiming or to claim the whole or any part thereof, the said party of the first part shall and will warrant and forever defend.

In testimony whereof, the said parties of the first part have hereunto set their hands and seals the day and year first above written.
Signed, sealed and delivered
    in presence of   HENRY BEST, [L.S.]
    JERRY LINKLATER.   BELLE BEST. [L.S.]

QUIT-CLAIM DEED.

THIS INDENTURE, made the eighth day of June, in the year of our Lord one thousand eight hundred and seventy-four, between David Tour, of Plano, County of Kendall, State of Illinois, party of the first part, and Larry O'Brien, of the same place, party of the second part,

Witnesseth, that the said party of the first part, for and in consideration of Nine Hundred dollars in hand paid by the said party of the second part, the receipt whereof is hereby acknowledged, and the said party of the second part forever released and discharged therefrom, has remised, released, sold, conveyed, and quit-claimed, and by these presents does remise, release, sell, convey, and quit-claim, unto the said party of the second part, his heirs and assigns, forever, all the right, title, interest, claim, and demand, which the said party of the first part has in and to the following described lot, piece, or parcel of land, to wit:

[*Here describe the land.*]

To have and to hold the same, together with all and singular the appurtenances and privileges thereunto belonging, or in any wise thereunto appertaining, and all the estate, right, title, interest, and claim whatever, of the said party of the first part, either in law or equity, to the only proper use, benefit, and behoof of the said party of the second part, his heirs and assigns forever.

In witness whereof the said party of the first part hereunto set his hand and seal the day and year above written.

Signed, sealed and delivered   DAVID TOUR. [L.S.]
    in presence of
THOMAS ASHLEY.

The above forms of Deeds and Mortgage are such as have heretofore been generally used, but the following are much shorter, and are made equally valid by the laws of this state.

WARRANTY DEED.

The grantor (here insert name or names and place of residence), for and in consideration of (here insert consideration) in hand paid, conveys and warrants to (here insert the grantee's name or names) the following described real estate (here insert description), situated in the County of ——— in the State of Illinois.

Dated this ——— day of ——— A. D. 18———.

QUIT CLAIM DEED.

The grantor (here insert grantor's name or names and place of residence), for the consideration of (here insert consideration) convey and quit-claim to (here insert grantee's name or names) all interest in the following described real estate (here insert description), situated in the County of ——— in the State of Illinois.

Dated this ——— day of ——— A. D. 18———.

MORTGAGE.

The mortgagor (here insert name or names) mortgages and warrants to (here insert name or names of mortgagee or mortgagees), to secure the payment of (here recite the nature and amount of indebtedness, showing when due and the rate of interest, and whether secured by note or otherwise), the following described real estate (here insert description thereof), situated in the County of ——— in the State of Illinois.

Dated this ——— day of ——— A. D. 18———.

RELEASE.

KNOW ALL MEN by these presents, that I, Peter Ahlund, of Chicago, of the County of Cook, and State of Illinois, for and in consideration of One dollar, to me in hand paid, and for other good and valuable considera-

N. A. RANKIN ESQ.
MONMOUTH

tions, the receipt whereof is hereby confessed, do hereby grant, bargain, remise, convey, release, and quit-claim unto Joseph Carlin of Chicago, of the County of Cook, and State of Illinois, all the right, title, interest, claim, or demand whatsoever, I may have acquired in, through, or by a certain Indenture or Mortgage Deed, bearing date the second day of January, A. D. 1871, and recorded in the Recorder's office of said county, in book A of Deeds, page 46, to the premises therein described, and which said Deed was made to secure one certain promissory note, bearing even date with said deed, for the sum of Three Hundred dollars.

Witness my hand and seal, this second day of November, A. D. 1874.

PETER AHLUND. [L.S.]

State of Illinois, } ss.
Cook County.

I, George Saxton, a Notary Public in and for said county, in the state aforesaid, do hereby certify that Peter Ahlund, personally known to me as the same person whose name is subscribed to the foregoing Release, appeared before me this day in person, and acknowledged that he signed, sealed, and delivered the said instrument of writing as his free and voluntary act, for the uses and purposes therein set forth.

[NOTARIAL SEAL]

Given under my hand and seal, this second day of November, A. D. 1874.

GEORGE SAXTON, N. P.

GENERAL FORM OF WILL FOR REAL AND PERSONAL PROPERTY.

I, Charles Mansfield, of the Town of Salem, County of Jackson, State of Illinois, being aware of the uncertainty of life, and in failing health, but of sound mind and memory, do make and declare this to be my last will and testament, in manner following, to wit:

First. I give, devise and bequeath unto my oldest son, Sidney H. Mansfield, the sum of Two Thousand Dollars, of bank stock, now in the Third National Bank of Cincinnati, Ohio, and the farm owned by myself in the Town of Buskirk, consisting of one hundred and sixty acres, with all the houses, tenements, and improvements thereunto belonging; to have and to hold unto my said son, his heirs and assigns, forever.

Second. I give, devise and bequeath to each of my daughters, Anna Louise Mansfield and Ida Clara Mansfield, each Two Thousand dollars in bank stock, in the Third National Bank of Cincinnati, Ohio, and also each one quarter section of land, owned by myself, situated in the Town of Lake, Illinois, and recorded in my name in the Recorder's office in the county where such land is located. The north one hundred and sixty acres of said half section is devised to my eldest daughter, Anna Louise.

Third. I give, devise and bequeath to my son, Frank Alfred Mansfield, Five shares of Railroad stock in the Baltimore and Ohio Railroad, and my one hundred and sixty acres of land and saw mill thereon, situated in Manistee, Michigan, with all the improvements and appurtenances thereunto belonging, which said real estate is recorded in my name in the county where situated.

Fourth. I give to my wife, Victoria Elizabeth Mansfield, all my household furniture, goods, chattels, and personal property, about my home, not hitherto disposed of, including Eight Thousand dollars of bank stock in the Third National Bank of Cincinnati, Ohio, Fifteen shares in the Baltimore and Ohio Railroad, and the free and unrestricted use, possession, and benefit of the home farm, so long as she may live, in lieu of dower, to which she is entitled by law; said farm being my present place of residence.

Fifth. I bequeath to my invalid father, Elijah H. Mansfield, the income from rents of my store building at 145 Jackson Street, Chicago, Illinois, during the term of his natural life. Said building and land therewith to revert to my said sons and daughters in equal proportion, upon the demise of my said father.

Sixth. It is also my will and desire that, at the death of my wife, Victoria Elizabeth Mansfield, or at any time when she may arrange to relinquish her life interest in the above mentioned homestead, the same may revert to my above named children, or to the lawful heirs of each.

And lastly. I nominate and appoint as executors of this my last will and testament, my wife, Victoria Elizabeth Mansfield, and my eldest son, Sidney H. Mansfield.

I further direct that my debts and necessary funeral expenses shall be paid from moneys now on deposit in the Savings Bank of Salem, the residue of such moneys to revert to my wife, Victoria Elizabeth Mansfield, for her use forever.

In witness whereof, I, Charles Mansfield, to this my last will and testament, have hereunto set my hand and seal, this fourth day of April, eighteen hundred and seventy-two.

Signed, sealed, and declared by Charles Mansfield, as and for his last will and testament, in the presence of us, who, at his request, and in his presence, and in the presence of each other, have subscribed our names hereunto as witnesses thereof.

CHARLES MANSFIELD. [L.S.]

PETER A. SCHENCK, Sycamore, Ills.
FRANK E. DENT, Salem, Ills.

CODICIL.

Whereas I, Charles Mansfield, did, on the fourth day of April, one thousand eight hundred and seventy-two, make my last will and testament, I do now, by this writing, add this codicil to my said will, to be taken as a part thereof.

Whereas, by the dispensation of Providence, my daughter, Anna Louise, has deceased November fifth, eighteen hundred and seventy-three, and whereas, a son has been born to me, which son is now christened Richard Albert Mansfield, I give and bequeath unto him my gold watch, and all right, interest, and title in lands and bank stock and chattels bequeathed to my deceased daughter, Anna Louise, in the body of this will.

In witness whereof, I hereunto place my hand and seal, this tenth day of March, eighteen hundred and seventy-five.

Signed, sealed, published, and declared to us by the testator, Charles Mansfield, as and for a codicil to be annexed to his last will and testament. And we, at his request, and in his presence, and in the presence of each other, have subscribed our names as witnesses thereto, at the date hereof.

CHARLES MANSFIELD. [L.S.]

FRANK E. DENT, Salem, Ills.
JOHN C. SHAY, Salem, Ills.

CHURCH ORGANIZATIONS

May be legally made by *electing* or *appointing*, according to the *usages* or *customs* of the body of which it is a part, at any meeting held for that purpose, *two* or *more* of its *members* as trustees, wardens or vestrymen, and may adopt a *corporate* name. The chairman or secretary of such meeting shall, as soon as possible, make and file in the office of the recorder of deeds of the county, an affidavit substantially in the following form:

STATE OF ILLINOIS, } ss.
———— County.

I, ————, do solemnly swear (or affirm, as the case may be), that at a meeting of the members of the (here insert the name of the church, society or congregation as known before organization), held at (here insert place of meeting), in the County of ————, and State of Illinois, on the ———— day of ————, A.D. 18—, for that purpose, the following persons were elected (or appointed) [*here insert their names*] trustees, wardens, vestrymen, (or officers by whatever name they may choose to adopt, with powers similar to trustees) according to the rules and usages of such (church, society or congregation), and said ————

adopted as its corporate name (here insert name), and at said meeting this affiant acted as (chairman or secretary, as the case may be).

Subscribed and sworn to before me, this —— day of ——, A.D. 18—. Name of Affiant —— ——

which affidavit must be recorded by the recorder, and shall be, or a certified copy made by the recorder, received as evidence of such an incorporation.

No certificate of election after the first need be filed for record.

The term of office of the trustees and the general government of the society can be determined by the rules or by-laws adopted. Failure to elect trustees at the time provided does not work a dissolution, but the old trustees hold over. A trustee or trustees may be removed, in the same manner by the society as elections are held by a meeting called for that purpose. The property of the society vests in the corporation. The corporation may hold, or acquire by purchase or otherwise, land not exceeding ten acres, for the purpose of the society. The trustees have the care, custody and control of the property of the corporation, and can, *when directed* by the society, erect houses or improvements, and repair and alter the same, and may also when so directed by the society, mortgage, encumber, sell and convey any real or personal estate belonging to the corporation, and make all proper contracts in the name of such corporation. But they are prohibited by law from encumbering or interfering with any property so as to destroy the effect of any gift, grant, devise or bequest to the corporation; but such gifts, grants, devises or bequests, must in all cases be used so as to carry out the object intended by the persons making the same. Existing societies may organize in the manner herein set forth, and have all the advantages thereof.

SUGGESTIONS TO THOSE PURCHASING BOOKS BY SUBSCRIPTION.

The business of *publishing books by subscription* having so often been brought into disrepute by agents making representations and declarations *not authorized by the publisher;* in order to prevent that as much as possible, and that there may be more general knowledge of the relation such agents bear to their principal, and the law governing such cases, the following statement is made :

A subscription is in the *nature of a contract* of mutual promises, by which the subscriber agrees to *pay a certain sum* for the work described; the *consideration is concurrent* that the publisher shall *publish the book named,* and deliver the same, for which the subscriber is to pay the price named. *The nature and character of the work is described in the prospectus and by the sample shown.* These should be *carefully examined before subscribing,* as they are the basis and consideration of the promise to pay, and not the too *often exaggerated statements of the agent,* who is *merely employed* to *solicit subscriptions,* for which he is usually *paid a commission* for each subscriber, and has *no authority* to *change or alter* the conditions upon which the subscriptions are authorized to be made by the publisher. Should the *agent assume* to agree to make the subscription conditional or *modify or change the agreement of the publisher,* as set out by prospectus and sample, in order to *bind the principal,* the *subscriber* should see that such conditions or changes are stated *over or in connection with his signature,* so that the publisher may have notice of the same.

All persons making contracts in reference to matters of this kind, or any other business, should remember *that the law as to written contracts is,* that they can *not be varied, altered or rescinded verbally, but if done at all, must be done in writing.* It is therefore *important* that all *persons contemplating subscribing should distinctly understand that all talk before or after the subscription is made, is not admissible as evidence, and is no part of the contract.*

Persons employed to solicit subscriptions are known to the trade as canvassers. They are *agents appointed to do a particular business in a prescribed mode,* and *have no authority* to do it in any other way to the prejudice of their principal, nor can they bind their principal in any other matter. They *can not collect money,* or agree that payment may be made in *anything else but money.* They *can not extend* the time of payment *beyond the time of delivery, nor bind their principal* for the *payment of expenses* incurred in their buisness.

It would save a great deal of trouble, and often serious loss, if persons, *before signing* their names to any subscription book, or any written instrument, would *examine carefully what it is ;* if they can not read themselves, should call on some one disinterested who can.

6

INTEREST TABLE.

A Simple Rule for Accurately Computing Interest at Any Given Per Cent. for Any Length of Time.

Multiply the *principal* (amount of money at interest) by the *time reduced to days* then divide this *product* by the *quotient* obtained by dividing 360 (the number of days in the interest year) by the *per cent.* of interest, and *the quotient thus obtained* will be the required interest.

ILLUSTRATION.   *Solution.*

Require the interest of $462.50 for one month and eighteen days at 6 per cent. An interest month is 30 days; one month and eighteen days equal 48 days. $462.50 multiplied by .48 gives 222.0000; 360 divided by 6 (the per cent. of interest) gives 60, and $222.0000 divided by 60 will give you the exact interest, which is $3.70. If the rate of interest in the above example were 12 per cent., we would divide the $222.0000 by 30 (because 360 divided by 12 gives 30); if 4 per cent., we would divide by 90; if 8 per cent., by 45; and in like manner for any other per cent.

```
    $462 50
       .48
   -------
   370000
   185000
  -------
6)360
60)$222.0000($3.70
    180
    ---
    420
    420
    ---
     00
```

MISCELLANEOUS TABLE.

12 units, or things, 1 Dozen.
12 dozen, 1 Gross.
20 things, 1 Score.
196 pounds, 1 Barrel of Flour.
200 pounds, 1 Barrel of Pork.

56 pounds, 1 Firkin of Butter.
24 sheets of paper, 1 Quire.
20 quires paper 1 Ream.
4 feet wide, 4 feet high, and 8 feet long, 1 Cord of Wood.

POPULATION OF THE UNITED STATES.

States and Territories.	Total Population.
Alabama	996,992
Arkansas	484,471
California	560,247
Connecticut	537,454
Delaware	125,015
Florida	187,748
Georgia	1,184,109
Illinois	2,539,891
Indiana	1,680,637
Iowa	1,191,792
Kansas	364,399
Kentucky	1,321,011
Louisiana	726,915
Maine	626,915
Maryland	780,894
Massachusetts	1,457,351
Michigan	1,184,059
Minnesota	439,706
Mississippi	827,922
Missouri	1,721,295
Nebraska	122,993
Nevada	42,491
New Hampshire	318,300
New Jersey	906,096
New York	4,382,759
North Carolina	1,071,361
Ohio	2,665,260
Oregon	90,923
Pennsylvania	3,521,791
Rhode Island	217,353
South Carolina	705,606
Tennessee	1,258,520
Texas	818,579
Vermont	330,551
Virginia	1,225,163
West Virginia	442,014
Wisconsin	1,054,670
Total States	**38,113,253**
Arizona	9,658
Colorado	39,864
Dakota	14,181
District of Columbia	131,700
Idaho	14,999
Montana	20,595
New Mexico	91,874
Utah	86,786
Washington	23,955
Wyoming	9,118
Total Territories	**442,730**
Total United States	**38,555,983**

POPULATION OF FIFTY PRINCIPAL CITIES.

Cities.	Aggregate Population.
New York, N. Y.	942,292
Philadelphia, Pa.	674,022
Brooklyn, N. Y.	396,099
St. Louis, Mo.	310,864
Chicago, Ill.	298,877
Baltimore, Md.	267,354
Boston, Mass.	250,526
Cincinnati, Ohio	216,239
New Orleans, La.	191,418
San Francisco, Cal.	149,472
Buffalo, N. Y.	117,714
Washington, D. C.	109,199
Newark, N. J.	105,059
Louisville, Ky.	100,753
Cleveland, Ohio	92,829
Pittsburg, Pa.	86,076
Jersey City, N. J.	82,546
Detroit, Mich.	79,577
Milwaukee, Wis.	71,440
Albany, N. Y.	69,422
Providence, R. I.	68,904
Rochester, N. Y.	62,386
Allegheny, Pa.	53,180
Richmond, Va.	51,038
New Haven, Conn.	50,840
Charleston, S. C.	48,956
Indianapolis, Ind.	48,244
Troy, N. Y.	46,465
Syracuse, N. Y.	43,051
Worcester, Mass.	41,105
Lowell, Mass.	40,928
Memphis, Tenn.	40,226
Cambridge, Mass.	39,634
Hartford, Conn.	37,180
Scranton, Pa.	35,092
Reading, Pa.	33,930
Paterson, N. J.	33,579
Kansas City, Mo.	32,260
Mobile, Ala.	32,034
Toledo, Ohio	31,584
Portland, Me.	31,413
Columbus, Ohio	31,274
Wilmington, Del.	30,841
Dayton, Ohio	30,473
Lawrence, Mass.	28,921
Utica, N. Y.	28,804
Charlestown, Mass.	28,323
Savannah, Ga.	28,235
Lynn, Mass.	28,243
Fall River, Mass.	26,766

POPULATION OF THE UNITED STATES.

STATES AND TERRITORIES.	Area in square Miles.	POPULATION 1870.	POPULATION 1875.	Miles R. R. 1872.	STATES AND TERRITORIES.	Area in square Miles.	POPULATION 1870.	POPULATION 1875.	Miles R. R. 1872.
States.					*States.*				
Alabama	50,722	996,992		1,671	Pennsylvania	46,000	3,521,791		5,113
Arkansas	52,198	484,471		25	Rhode Island	1,306	217,353	258,239	136
California	188,981	560,247		1,013	South Carolina	29,385	705,606	925,145	1,201
Connecticut	4,674	537,454		820	Tennessee	45,600	1,258,520		1,520
Delaware	2,120	125,015		225	Texas	237,504	818,579		865
Florida	59,268	187,748		486	Vermont	10,212	330,551		675
Georgia	58,000	1,184,109		2,108	Virginia	40,904	1,325,163		1,490
Illinois	55,410	2,539,891		5,904	West Virginia	23,000	442,014		485
Indiana	33,809	1,680,637		3,529	Wisconsin	53,924	1,054,670	1,236,729	1,725
Iowa	55,045	1,191,792	1,350,544	3,160	Total States	1,950,171	36,113,253		59,587
Kansas	81,318	364,399	528,349	1,760	*Territories.*				
Kentucky	37,600	1,321,011		1,123	Arizona	113,916	9,658		
Louisiana	41,346	726,915	857,039	539	Colorado	104,500	39,864		392
Maine	31,776	626,915		871	Dakota	147,490	14,181		
Maryland	11,184	780,894		820	Dist. of Columbia	60	131,700		*
Massachusetts	7,800	1,457,351	1,651,912	1,606	Idaho	90,932	14,999		
Michigan*	56,451	1,184,059	1,334,031	2,235	Montana	143,776	20,595		
Minnesota	83,531	439,706	598,429	1,612	New Mexico	121,201	91,874		
Mississippi	47,156	827,922		990	Utah	80,056	86,786		375
Missouri	65,350	1,721,295		2,580	Washington	69,944	23,955		
Nebraska	75,995	123,993	246,280	828	Wyoming	93,107	9,118		498
Nevada	112,090	42,491	52,540	593	Total Territories	965,032	442,730		1,265
New Hampshire	9,280	318,300		790					
New Jersey	8,320	906,096	1,026,502	1,265					
New York	47,000	4,382,759	4,705,208	4,470					
North Carolina	50,704	1,071,361		1,190					
Ohio	39,964	2,665,260		3,740					
Oregon	95,244	90,923		159	Aggregate of U. S.	2,915,203	38,555,983		60,852

* Last Census of Michigan taken in 1874. * Included in the Railroad Mileage of Maryland.

PRINCIPAL COUNTRIES OF THE WORLD;
POPULATION AND AREA.

COUNTRIES.	Population.	Date of Census.	Area in Square Miles.	Inhabitants to Square Mile.	CAPITALS.	Population.
China	446,500,000	1871	3,741,846	119.3	Pekin	1,648,800
British Empire	226,817,108	1871	4,677,432	48.6	London	3,251,800
Russia	81,925,400	1870	8,003,778	10.2	St. Petersburg	667,000
United States with Alaska	38,925,600	1870	2,903,884	7.7	Washington	109,199
France	36,469,800	1866	204,091	178.7	Paris	1,825,300
Austria and Hungary	35,904,400	1869	240,348	149.4	Vienna	833,900
Japan	34,785,300	1871	149,399	232.8	Yeddo	1,554,900
Great Britain and Ireland	31,817,100	1871	121,315	262.3	London	3,251,800
German Empire	29,906,082	1871	160,207	187.	Berlin	825,400
Italy	27,439,921	1871	118,847	230.9	Rome	244,484
Spain	16,642,000	1867	195,775	85.	Madrid	332,000
Brazil	10,000,000		3,253,029	3.07	Rio Janeiro	420,000
Turkey	16,463,000		672,641	24.4	Constantinople	1,075,000
Mexico	9,173,000	1869	761,526		Mexico	210,300
Sweden and Norway	5,921,500	1870	292,871	20.	Stockholm	136,900
Persia	5,000,000	1870	635,964	7.8	Teheran	120,000
Belgium	5,021,300	1869	11,373	441.5	Brussels	314,100
Bavaria	4,861,400	1871	29,292	165.9	Munich	169,500
Portugal	3,995,200	1868	34,494	115.8	Lisbon	224,063
Holland	3,688,300	1870	12,680	290.9	Hague	90,100
New Grenada	3,000,000	1870	357,157	8.4	Bogota	45,000
Chili	2,000,000	1869	132,616	15.1	Santiago	115,400
Switzerland	2,669,100	1870	15,992	166.9	Berne	36,000
Peru	2,500,000	1871	471,838	5.3	Lima	160,100
Bolivia	2,000,000		497,321	4.	Chuquisaca	25,000
Argentine Republic	1,612,000	1869	871,848	2.1	Buenos Ayres	177,800
Wurtemburg	1,818,500	1871	7,533	241.4	Stuttgart	91,600
Denmark	1,784,700	1870	14,753	120.9	Copenhagen	162,012
Venezuela	1,500,000		368,238	4.2	Caraccas	47,000
Baden	1,461,400	1871	5,912	247.	Carlsruhe	38,600
Greece	1,457,900	1870	19,353	75.3	Athens	43,400
Guatemala	1,180,000	1871	40,879	28.9	Guatemala	40,000
Ecuador	1,300,000		218,928	5.9	Quito	70,000
Paraguay	1,000,000	1871	63,787	15.6	Asuncion	48,000
Hesse	823,138		2,969	277.	Darmstadt	30,000
Liberia	718,000	1871	9,576	74.9	Monrovia	3,000
San Salvador	600,000	1871	7,335	81.8	Sal Salvador	15,000
Hayti	572,000		10,205	56.	Port au Prince	20,000
Nicaragua	350,000	1871	58,171	6.	Managua	11,000
Uruguay	300,000	1871	66,722	6.5	Monte Video	44,500
Honduras	350,000	1871	47,092	7.4	Comayagua	12,000
San Domingo	200,000		17,827	7.6	San Domingo	20,000
Costa Rica	165,000	1870	21,505	7.7	San Jose	2,000
Hawaii	62,950		7,633	80.	Honolulu	7,633

POPULATION OF ILLINOIS,
By Counties.

COUNTIES.	AGGREGATE.					
	1870.	1860.	1850.	1840.	1830.	1820.
Adams	56362	41323	26508	14476	2186	
Alexander	10564	4707	2484	3313	1390	626
Bond	13152	9815	6144	5060	3124	2931
Boone	12942	11678	7624	1705		
Brown	12205	9938	7198	4183		
Bureau	32415	26426	8841	3067		
Calhoun	6562	5144	3231	1741	1090	
Carroll	16705	11733	4586	1023		
Cass	11580	11325	7253	2981		
Champaign	32737	14629	2649	1475		
Christian	20363	10492	3203	1878		
Clark	18719	14987	9532	7453	3940	931
Clay	15875	9336	4289	3228	755	
Clinton	16285	10941	5139	3718	2330	
Coles	25235	14203	9335	9616		
Cook	349966	144954	43385	10201		*23
Crawford	13889	11551	7135	4422	3117	2999
Cumberland	12223	8311	3718			
De Kalb	23265	19086	7540	1697		
De Witt	14768	10820	5002	3247		
Douglas	13484	7140				
Du Page	16685	14701	9290	3535		
Edgar	21450	16925	10692	8225	4071	
Edwards	7565	5454	3524	3070	1649	3444
Effingham	15653	7816	3799	1675		
Fayette	19638	11189	8075	6328	2704	
Ford	9103	1979				
Franklin	12652	9393	5681	3682	4083	1763
Fulton	38291	33338	22508	13142	1841	
Gallatin	11134	8055	5448	10760	7405	3155
Greene	20277	16093	12429	11951	7674	
Grundy	14938	10379	3023			
Hamilton	13014	9915	6362	3945	2616	
Hancock	35935	29061	14652	9946	483	
Hardin	5113	3759	2887	1378		
Henderson	12582	9501	4612			
Henry	35506	20660	3807	1260	41	
Iroquois	25782	12325	4149	1695		
Jackson	19634	9589	5862	3566	1828	1542
Jasper	11234	8364	3220	1472		
Jefferson	17864	12965	8109	5762	2555	691
Jersey	15054	12051	7354	4535		
Jo Daviess	27820	27325	18604	6180	2111	
Johnson	11248	9342	4114	3626	1596	843
Kane	39091	30062	16703	6501		
Kankakee	24352	15412				
Kendall	12399	13074	7730			
Knox	39522	28663	13279	7060	274	
Lake	21014	18257	14226	2634		
La Salle	60792	48332	17815	9348		
Lawrence	12533	9214	6181	7092	3668	
Lee	27171	17651	5298	2035		
Livingston	31471	11637	1553	759		
Logan	23053	14272	5128	2333		

POPULATION OF ILLINOIS—Concluded.

COUNTIES.	AGGREGATE.					
	1870.	1860.	1850.	1840.	1830.	1820.
Macon	26481	13738	3988	3039	1122	
Macoupin	32726	24602	12355	7926	1990	
Madison	44131	31251	20441	14433	6221	13550
Marion	20622	12739	6720	4742	2125	
Marshall	16950	13437	5180	1849		
Mason	16184	10931	5921			
Massac	9581	6213	4092			
McDonough	26509	20069	7616	5308	(b)	
McHenry	23762	22089	14978	2578		
McLean	53988	28772	10163	6565		
Menard	11735	9584	6349	4431		
Mercer	18769	15042	5246	2352	26	*21
Monroe	12982	12832	7679	4481	2000	1516
Montgomery	25314	13979	6277	4490	2953	
Morgan	28463	22112	16064	19547	12714	
Moultrie	10385	6385	3234			
Ogle	27492	22888	10020	3479		
Peoria	47540	36601	17547	6153	(c)	
Perry	13723	9552	5278	3222	1215	
Piatt	10953	6127	1606			
Pike	30768	27249	18819	11728	2396	
Pope	11437	6742	3975	4094	3316	2610
Pulaski	8752	3943	2265			
Putnam	6280	5587	3924	2131	d1310	
Randolph	20859	17205	11079	7944	4429	3492
Richland	12803	9711	4012			
Rock Island	29783	21005	6937	2610		
Saline	12714	9331	5588			
Sangamon	46352	32274	19228	14716	12960	
Schuyler	17419	14684	10573	6972	b2959	
Scott	10530	9069	7914	6215		
Shelby	25476	14613	7807	6659	2972	
Stark	10751	9004	3710	1573		*5
St. Clair	51068	37694	20180	13631	7078	5248
Stephenson	30608	25112	11666	2800		
Tazewell	27903	21470	12052	7221	4716	
Union	16518	11181	7615	5524	3239	2362
Vermilion	30388	19800	11492	9303	5836	
Wabash	8841	7313	4690	4240	2710	
Warren	23174	18336	8176	6739	308	
Washington	17599	13731	6953	4810	1675	1517
Wayne	19758	12223	6825	5133	2553	1114
White	16846	12403	8925	7919	6091	4828
Whitesides	27503	18737	5361	2514		
Will	43013	29321	16703	10167		
Williamson	17329	12205	7216	4457		
Winnebago	29301	24491	11773	4609		
Woodford	18956	13282	4415			
Total	2539891	1711951	851470	476183	157445	*49 55162

CONSTITUTION OF THE UNITED STATES OF AMERICA, AND ITS AMENDMENTS.

We, the people of the United States, in order to form a more perfect union, establish justice, insure domestic tranquillity, provide for the common defense, promote the general welfare, and secure the blessings of liberty to ourselves and our posterity, do ordain and establish this Constitution for the United States of America.

ARTICLE I.

SECTION 1. All legislative powers herein granted shall be vested in a Congress of the United States, which shall consist of a Senate and House of Representatives.

SEC. 2. The House of Representatives shall be composed of members chosen every second year by the people of the several states, and the electors in each state shall have the qualifications requisite for electors of the most numerous branch of the State Legislature.

No person shall be a representative who shall not have attained to the age of twenty-five years, and been seven years a citizen of the United States, and who shall not, when elected, be an inhabitant of that state in which he shall be chosen.

Representatives and direct taxes shall be apportioned among the several states which may be included within this Union, according to their respective numbers, which shall be determined by adding to the whole number of free persons, including those bound to service for a term of years, and excluding Indians not taxed, three-fifths of all other persons. The actual enumeration shall be made within three years after the first meeting of the Congress of the United States, and within every subsequent term of ten years, in such manner as they shall by law direct. The number of Representatives shall not exceed one for every thirty thousand, but each state shall have at least one Representative; and until such enumeration shall be made the State of New Hampshire shall be entitled to choose three, Massachusetts eight, Rhode Island and Providence Plantations one, Connecticut five, New York six, New Jersey four, Pennsylvania eight, Delaware one, Maryland six, Virginia ten, North Carolina five, and Georgia three.

When vacancies happen in the representation from any state, the Executive authority thereof shall issue writs of election to fill such vacancies.

The House of Representatives shall choose their Speaker and other officers, and shall have the sole power of impeachment.

SEC. 3. The Senate of the United States shall be composed of two Senators from each state, chosen by the Legislature thereof for six years; and each Senator shall have one vote.

Immediately after they shall be assembled in consequence of the first election, they shall be divided as equally as may be into three classes. The seats of the Senators of the first class shall be vacated at the expiration of the second year, of the second class at the expiration of the fourth year, and of the third class at the expiration of the sixth year, so that one-third may be chosen every second year; and if vacancies happen by resignation or otherwise, during the recess of the Legislature of any state, the Executive thereof may make temporary appointments until the next meeting of the Legislature, which shall then fill such vacancies.

No person shall be a Senator who shall not have attained to the age of thirty years and been nine years a citizen of the United States, and who shall not, when elected, be an inhabitant of that state for which he shall be chosen.

The Vice-President of the United States shall be President of the Senate, but shall have no vote unless they be equally divided.

The Senate shall choose their other officers, and also a President *pro tempore*, in the absence of the Vice-President, or when he shall exercise the office of President of the United States.

The Senate shall have the sole power to try all impeachments. When sitting for that purpose they shall be on oath or affirmation. When the President of the United States is tried the Chief Justice shall preside. And no person shall be convicted without the concurrence of two-thirds of the members present.

Judgment, in cases of impeachment, shall not extend further than to removal from office, and disqualification to hold and enjoy any office of honor, trust, or profit under the United States; but the party convicted shall nevertheless be liable and subject to indictment, trial, judgment, and punishment according to law.

SEC. 4. The times, places and manner of holding elections for Senators and Representatives shall be prescribed in each state by the Legislature thereof; but the Congress may at any time by law make or alter such regulations, except as to the places of choosing Senators.

The Congress shall assemble at least once in every year, and such meeting shall be on the first Monday in December, unless they shall by law appoint a different day.

SEC. 5. Each house shall be the judge of the election, returns, and qualifications of its own members, and a majority of each shall constitute a quorum to do business; but a smaller number may adjourn from day to day, and may be authorized to compel the attendance of absent members in such manner and under such penalties as each house may provide.

Each house may determine the rules of its proceedings, punish its members for disorderly behavior, and, with the concurrence of two-thirds, expel a member.

Each house shall keep a journal of its proceedings, and from time to time publish the same, excepting such parts as may, in their judgment, require secrecy; and the yeas and nays of the members of either house on any question shall, at the desire of one-fifth of those present, be entered on the journal.

Neither house, during the session of Congress, shall, without the consent of the other, adjourn for more than three days, nor to any other place than that in which the two houses shall be sitting.

SEC. 6. The Senators and Representatives shall receive a compensation for their services, to be ascertained by law, and paid out of the treasury of the United States. They shall in all cases, except treason, felony, and breach of the peace, be privileged from arrest during their attendance at the session of their respective houses, and in going to and returning from the same; and for any speech or debate in either house they shall not be questioned in any other place.

No Senator or Representative shall, during the time for which he was elected, be appointed to any civil office under the authority of the United States, which shall have been created, or the emoluments whereof shall have been increased during such time; and no person holding any office under the United States, shall be a member of either house during his continuance in office.

Sec. 7. All bills for raising revenue shall originate in the House of Representatives; but the Senate may propose or concur with amendments as on other bills.

Every bill which shall have passed the House of Representatives and the Senate, shall, before it becomes a law, be presented to the President of the United States; if he approve he shall sign it; but if not he shall return it, with his objections, to that house in which it shall have originated, who shall enter the objections at large on their journal, and proceed to reconsider it. If, after such reconsideration two-thirds of that house shall agree to pass the bill, it shall be sent, together with the objections, to the other house, by which it shall likewise be reconsidered, and if approved by two-thirds of that house, it shall become a law. But in all such cases the votes of both houses shall be determined by yeas and nays, and the names of the persons voting for and against the bill shall be entered on the journal of each house respectively. If any bill shall not be returned by the President within ten days (Sundays excepted), after it shall have been presented to him, the same shall be a law, in like manner as if he had signed it, unless the Congress, by their adjournment, prevent its return, in which case it shall not be a law.

Every order, resolution, or vote to which the concurrence of the Senate and House of Representatives may be necessary (except on a question of adjournment), shall be presented to the President of the United States, and before the same shall take effect shall be approved by him, or, being disapproved by him, shall be re-passed by two-thirds of the Senate and House of Representatives, according to the rules and limitations prescribed in the case of a bill.

Sec. 8. The Congress shall have power—

To lay and collect taxes, duties, imposts and excises, to pay the debts, and provide for the common defense and general welfare of the United States; but all duties, imposts, and excises shall be uniform throughout the United States;

To borrow money on the credit of the United States;

To regulate commerce with foreign nations, and among the several States, and with the Indian tribes;

To establish a uniform rule of naturalization, and uniform laws on the subject of bankruptcies throughout the United States;

To coin money, regulate the value thereof, and of foreign coin, and fix the standard of weights and measures;

To provide for the punishment of counterfeiting the securities and current coin of the United States;

To establish post offices and post roads;

To promote the progress of sciences and useful arts, by securing, for limited times, to authors and inventors, the exclusive right to their respective writings and discoveries;

To constitute tribunals inferior to the Supreme Court;

To define and punish piracies and felonies committed on the high seas, and offenses against the law of nations;

To declare war, grant letters of marque and reprisal, and make rules concerning captures on land and water;

To raise and support armies, but no appropriation of money to that use shall be for a longer term than two years;

To provide and maintain a navy;

To make rules for the government and regulation of the land and naval forces;

To provide for calling forth the militia to execute the laws of the Union, suppress insurrections, and repel invasions;

To provide for organizing, arming and disciplining the militia, and for governing such part of them as may be employed in the service of the United States, reserving to the states respectively the appointment of the officers, and the authority of training the militia according to the discipline prescribed by Congress;

To exercise legislation in all cases whatsoever over such district (not exceeding ten miles square) as may, by cession of particular states, and the acceptance of Congress, become the seat of the government of the United States, and to exercise like authority over all places purchased by the consent of the Legislature of the state in which the same shall be, for the erection of forts, magazines, arsenals, dock yards, and other needful buildings; and

To make all laws which shall be necessary and proper for carrying into execution the foregoing powers, and all other powers vested by this Constitution in the government of the United States, or in any department or officer thereof.

SEC. 9. The migration or importation of such persons as any of the states now existing shall think proper to admit, shall not be prohibited by the Congress prior to the year one thousand eight hundred and eight, but a tax or duty may be imposed on such importation, not exceeding ten dollars for each person.

The privilege of the writ of habeas corpus shall not be suspended, unless when in cases of rebellion or invasion the public safety may require it.

No bill of attainder or *ex post facto* law shall be passed.

No capitation or other direct tax shall be laid, unless in proportion to the census or enumeration hereinbefore directed to be taken.

No tax or duty shall be laid on articles exported from any state.

No preference shall be given by any regulation of commerce or revenue to the ports of one state over those of another; nor shall vessels bound to or from one state be obliged to enter, clear, or pay duties in another.

No money shall be drawn from the Treasury, but in consequence of appropriations made by law; and a regular statement and account of the receipts and expeditures of all public money shall be published from time to time.

No title of nobility shall be granted by the United States: and no person holding any office of profit or trust under them, shall, without the consent of the Congress, accept of any present, emolument, office, or title of any kind whatever, from any king, prince, or foreign state.

SEC. 10. No state shall enter into any treaty, alliance, or confederation; grant letters of marque and reprisal; coin money; emit bills of credit; make anything but gold and silver coin a tender in payment of debts; pass any bill of attainder, *ex post facto* law, or law impairing the obligation of contracts, or grant any title of nobility.

No state shall, without the consent of the Congress, lay any imposts or duties on imports or exports, except what may be absolutely necessary for executing its inspection laws, and the net produce of all duties and imposts laid by any state on imports or exports, shall be for the use of the Treasury of the United States; and all such laws shall be subject to the revision and control of the Congress.

No state shall, without the consent of Congress, lay any duty on tonnage, keep troops or ships of war in time of peace, enter into any agreement or compact with another state, or with a foreign power, or engage in war, unless actually invaded, or in such imminent danger as will not admit of delay.

ARTICLE II.

SECTION 1. The Executive power shall be vested in a President of the United States of America. He shall hold his office during the term of four years, and, together with the Vice-President chosen for the same term, be elected as follows:

Each state shall appoint, in such manner as the Legislature thereof may direct, a number of Electors, equal to the whole number of Senators and Representatives to which the state may be entitled in the Congress; but no Senator or Representative, or person holding an office of trust or profit under the United States, shall be appointed an Elector.

[* The Electors shall meet in their respective states, and vote by ballot for two persons, of whom one at least shall not be an inhabitant of the same state with themselves. And they shall make a list of all the persons voted for, and of the number of votes for each; which list they shall sign and certify, and transmit, sealed, to the seat of the government of the United States, directed to the President of the Senate. The President of the Senate shall, in the presence of the Senate and House of Representatives, open all the certificates, and the votes shall then be counted. The person having the greatest number of votes shall be the President, if such number be a majority of the whole number of Electors appointed; and if there be more than one who have such majority, and have an equal number of votes, then the House of Representatives shall immediately choose by ballot one of them for President; and if no person have a majority, then from the five highest on the list the said House shall in like manner choose the President. But in choosing the President, the vote shall be taken by states, the representation from each state having one vote; a quorum for this purpose shall consist of a member or members from two-thirds of the states, and a majority of all the states shall be necessary to a choice. In every case, after the choice of the President,

---

* This clause between brackets has been superseded and annulled by the Twelfth amendment.

the person having the greatest number of votes of the Electors shall be the Vice-President. But if there should remain two or more who have equal votes, the Senate shall choose from them by ballot the Vice-President.]

The Congress may determine the time of choosing the Electors, and the day on which they shall give their votes; which day shall be the same throughout the United States.

No person except a natural born citizen, or a citizen of the United States at the time of the adoption of this Constitution, shall be eligible to the office of President; neither shall any person be eligible to that office who shall not have attained the age of thirty-five years, and been fourteen years a resident within the United States.

In case of the removal of the President from office, or of his death, resignation, or inability to discharge the powers and duties of the said office, the same shall devolve on the Vice-President, and the Congress may by law provide for the case of removal, death, resignation, or inability, both of the President and Vice-President, declaring what officer shall then act as President, and such officer shall act accordingly, until the disability be removed, or a President shall be elected.

The President shall, at stated times, receive for his services a compensation which shall neither be increased nor diminished during the period for which he shall have been elected, and he shall not receive within that period any other emolument from the United States or any of them.

Before he enters on the execution of his office, he shall take the following oath or affirmation:

"I do solemnly swear (or affirm) that I will faithfully execute the office of President of the United States, and will, to the best of my ability, preserve, protect, and defend the Constitution of the United States."

SEC. 2. The President shall be commander in chief of the army and navy of the United States, and of the militia of the several states, when called into the actual service of the United States; he may require the opinion, in writing, of the principal officer in each of the executive departments, upon any subject relating to the duties of their respective offices, and he shall have power to grant reprieves and pardon for offenses against the United States, except in cases of impeachment.

He shall have power, by and with the advice and consent of the Senate, to make treaties, provided two-thirds of the Senators present concur; and he shall nominate, and by and with the advice of the Senate, shall appoint ambassadors, other public ministers and consuls, judges of the Supreme Court, and all other officers of the United States whose appointments are not herein otherwise provided for, and which shall be established by law; but the Congress may by law vest the appointment of such inferior officers as they think proper in the President alone, in the courts of law, or in the heads of departments.

The President shall have power to fill up all vacancies that may happen during the recess of the Senate, by granting commissions which shall expire at the end of their next session.

SEC. 3. He shall from time to time give to the Congress information of the state of the Union, and recommend to their consideration such measures as he shall judge necessary and expedient; he may on extraordinary occasions convene both houses, or either of them, and in case of disagreement between them, with respect to the time of adjournment, he may adjourn them to such time as he shall think proper; he shall receive ambassadors and other public ministers; he shall take care that the laws be faithfully executed, and shall commission all the officers of the United States.

SEC. 4. The President, Vice-President, and all civil officers of the United States, shall be removed from office on impeachment for, and conviction of, treason, bribery, or other high crimes and misdemeanors.

ARTICLE III.

SECTION I. The judicial power of the United States shall be vested in one Supreme Court, and such inferior courts as the Congress may from time to time ordain and establish. The Judges, both of the Supreme and inferior courts, shall hold their offices during good behavior, and shall, at stated times, receive for their services a compensation, which shall not be diminished during their continuance in office.

SEC. 2. The judicial power shall extend to all cases, in law and equity, arising under this Constitution, the laws of the United States, and treaties made, or which shall be made, under their authority; to all cases affecting ambassadors, other public ministers, and consuls; to all cases of admiralty and maritime jurisdiction; to controversies to which the United States shall be a party; to controversies between two or more states; between a state and citizens of another state; between citizens of different states; between citizens of the same state claiming lands under grants of different states, and between a state or the citizens thereof, and foreign states, citizens, or subjects.

In all cases affecting ambassadors, other public ministers, and consuls, and those in which a state shall be a party, the Supreme Court shall have original jurisdiction.

In all the other cases before mentioned, the Supreme Court shall have appellate jurisdiction, both as to law and fact, with such exceptions and under such regulations as the Congress shall make.

The trial of all crimes, except in cases of impeachment, shall be by jury; and such trial shall be held in the state where the said crimes shall have been committed; but when not committed within any state, the trial shall be at such place or places as the Congress may by law have directed.

SEC. 3. Treason against the United States shall consist only in levying war against them, or in adhering to their enemies, giving them aid and comfort. No person shall be convicted of treason unless on the testimony of two witnesses to the same overt act, or on confession in open court.

The Congress shall have power to declare the punishment of treason, but no attainder of treason shall work corruption of blood, or forfeiture, except during the life of the person attainted.

ARTICLE IV.

SECTION 1. Full faith and credit shall be given in each state to the public acts, records, and judicial proceedings of every other state. And

Wm Hanna

PREST. MONMOUTH NATL. BANK
AND CASHIER OF WEIR PLOW CO.

the Congress may, by general laws, prescribe the manner in which such acts, records, and proceedings shall be proved, and the effect thereof.

SEC. 2. The citizens of each state shall be entitled to all privileges and immunities of citizens in the several states.

A person charged in any state with treason, felony, or other crime, who shall flee from justice and be found in another state, shall, on demand of the executive authority of the state from which he fled, be delivered up, to be removed to the state having jurisdiction of the crime.

No person held to service or labor in one state, under the laws thereof escaping into another, shall, in consequence of any law or regulation therein, be discharged from such service or labor, but shall be delivered up on the claim of the party to whom such service or labor may be due.

SEC. 3. New states may be admitted by the Congress into this Union; but no new state shall be formed or erected within the jurisdiction of any other state; nor any state be formed by the junction of two or more states, or parts of states, without the consent of the Legislatures of the states concerned, as well as of the Congress.

The Congress shall have power to dispose of and make all needful rules and regulations respecting the territory or other property belonging to the United States; and nothing in this Constitution shall be so construed as to prejudice any claims of the United States or of any particular state.

SEC. 4. The United States shall guarantee to every state in this Union a republican form of government, and shall protect each of them against invasion, and on application of the Legislature, or of the Executive (when the Legislature can not be convened), against domestic violence.

ARTICLE V.

The Congress, whenever two-thirds of both houses shall deem it necessary, shall propose amendments to this Constitution, or, on the application of the Legislatures of two-thirds of the several states, shall call a convention for proposing amendments, which, in either case, shall be valid to all intents and purposes as part of this Constitution, when ratified by the Legislatures of three fourths of the several states, or by conventions in three-fourths thereof, as the one or the other mode of ratification may be proposed by the Congress. Provided that no amendment which may be made prior to the year one thousand eight hundred and eight shall in any manner affect the first and fourth clauses in the ninth section of the first article; and that no state, without its consent, shall be deprived of its equal suffrage in the Senate.

ARTICLE VI.

All debts contracted and engagements entered into before the adoption of this Constitution shall be as valid against the United States under this Constitution as under the Confederation.

This Constitution, and the laws of the United States which shall be made in pursuance thereof, and all treaties made, or which shall be made, under the authority of the United States, shall be the supreme law of the land; and the Judges in every state shall be bound thereby, anything in the Constitution or laws of any state to the contrary notwithstanding.

The Senators and Representatives before mentioned, and the members of the several state Legislatures, and all executive and judicial officers, both of the United States and of the several states, shall be bound by oath or affirmation to support this Constitution; but no religious test shall ever be required as a qualification to any office or public trust under the United States.

ARTICLE VII.

The ratification of the Conventions of nine states shall be sufficient for the establishment of this Constitution between the states so ratifying the same.

Done in convention by the unanimous consent of the states present, the seventeenth day of September, in the year of our Lord one thousand seven hundred and eighty-seven, and of the independence of the United States of America the twelfth. In witness whereof we have hereunto subscribed our names.

GEO. WASHINGTON,
President and Deputy from Virginia.

New Hampshire.
JOHN LANGDON,
NICHOLAS GILMAN.

Massachusetts.
NATHANIEL GORHAM,
RUFUS KING.

Connecticut.
WM. SAM'L JOHNSON,
ROGER SHERMAN.

New York.
ALEXANDER HAMILTON.

New Jersey.
WIL. LIVINGSTON,
WM. PATERSON,
DAVID BREARLEY,
JONA. DAYTON.

Pennsylvania.
B. FRANKLIN,
ROBT. MORRIS,
THOS. FITZSIMONS,
JAMES WILSON,
THOS. MIFFLIN,
GEO. CLYMER,
JARED INGERSOLL,
GOUV. MORRIS.

Delaware.
GEO. READ,
JOHN DICKINSON,
JACO. BROOM,
GUNNING BEDFORD, JR.,
RICHARD BASSETT.

Maryland.
JAMES M'HENRY,
DANL. CARROLL,
DAN. OF ST. THOS. JENIFER.

Virginia.
JOHN BLAIR,
JAMES MADISON, JR.

North Carolina.
WM. BLOUNT,
HU. WILLIAMSON,
RICH'D DOBBS SPAIGHT.

South Carolina.
J. RUTLEDGE,
CHARLES PINCKNEY,
CHAS. COTESWORTH PINCKNEY,
PIERCE BUTLER.

Georgia.
WILLIAM FEW,
ABR. BALDWIN.

WILLIAM JACKSON, *Secretary.*

ARTICLES IN ADDITION TO AND AMENDATORY OF THE CONSTITUTION OF THE UNITED STATES OF AMERICA.

Proposed by Congress and ratified by the Legislatures of the several states, pursuant to the fifth article of the original Constitution.

ARTICLE I.

Congress shall make no law respecting an establishment of religion, or prohibiting the free exercise thereof; or abridging the freedom of speech, or of the press; or the right of the people peaceably to assemble, and to petition the Government for a redress of grievances.

ARTICLE II.

A well regulated militia being necessary to the security of a free state, the right of the people to keep and bear arms shall not be infringed.

ARTICLE III.

No soldier shall, in time of peace, be quartered in any house without the consent of the owner, nor in time of war but in a manner to be prescribed by law.

ARTICLE IV.

The right of the people to be secure in their persons, houses, papers, and effects against unreasonable searches and seizures, shall not be violated; and no warrants shall issue but upon probable cause, supported by oath or affirmation, and particularly describing the place to be searched and the persons or things to be seized.

ARTICLE V.

No person shall be held to answer for a capital or otherwise infamous crime, unless on a presentment or indictment of a Grand Jury, except in cases arising in the land or naval forces, or in the militia when in actual service in time of war or public danger; nor shall any person be subject for the same offense to be twice put in jeopardy of life or limb; nor shall be compelled in any criminal case to be a witness against himself, nor be deprived of life, liberty, or property, without due process of law; nor shall private property be taken for public use, without just compensation.

ARTICLE VI.

In all criminal prosecutions, the accused shall enjoy the right to a speedy and public trial, by an impartial jury of the state and district wherein the crime shall have been committed, which district shall have been previously ascertained by law, and to be informed of the nature and cause of the accusation; to be confronted with the witnesses against him; to have compulsory process for obtaining witnesses in his favor; and to have the assistance of counsel for his defense.

ARTICLE VII.

In suits at common law, where the value in controversy shall exceed twenty dollars, the right of trial by jury shall be preserved, and no fact tried by a jury shall be otherwise re-examined in any court of the United States than according to the rules of the common law.

Article VIII.

Excessive bail shall not be required, nor excessive fines imposed, nor cruel and unusual punishments inflicted.

Article IX.

The enumeration, in the Constitution, of certain rights, shall not be construed to deny or disparage others retained by the people.

Article X.

The powers not delegated to the United States by the Constitution, nor prohibited by it to the states, are reserved to the states respectively, or to the people.

Article XI.

The judicial power of the United States shall not be construed to extend to any suit in law or equity commenced or prosecuted against one of the United States by citizens of another state, or by citizens or subjects of any foreign state.

Article XII.

The Electors shall meet in their respective states and vote by ballot for President and Vice-President, one of whom, at least, shall not be an inhabitant of the same state with themselves; they shall name in their ballots the person to be voted for as president, and in distinct ballots the person voted for as Vice-President, and they shall make distinct lists of all persons voted for as President, and of all persons voted for as Vice-President, and of the number of votes for each, which list they shall sign and certify, and transmit sealed to the seat of the government of the United States, directed to the President of the Senate. The President of the Senate shall, in presence of the Senate and House of Representatives, open all the certificates, and the votes shall then be counted. The person having the greatest number of votes for President shall be the President, if such number be a majority of the whole number of Electors appointed; and if no person have such majority, then from the persons having the highest number not exceeding three on the list of those voted for as President, the House of Representatives shall choose immediately, by ballot, the President. But in choosing the President, the votes shall be taken by States, the representation from each state having one vote; a quorum for this purpose shall consist of a member or members from two-thirds of the states, and a majority of all the states shall be necessary to a choice. And if the House of Representatives shall not choose a President whenever the right of choice shall devolve upon them, before the fourth day of March next following, then the Vice-President shall act as President, as in the case of the death or other constitutional disability of the President. The person having the greatest number of votes as Vice-President, shall be the Vice-President, if such number be the majority of the whole number of electors appointed, and if no person have a majority then from the two highest numbers on the list, the Senate shall choose the Vice-President; a quorum for the purpose shall consist of two-thirds of the whole number of Senators, and a majority of the whole number shall be necessary to a choice. But no person constitutionally ineligible to the office of President shall be eligible to that of Vice-President of the United States.

Article XIII.

Section 1. Neither slavery nor involuntary servitude, except as a punishment for crime, whereof the party shall have been duly convicted, shall exist within the United States, or any place subject to their jurisdiction.

Sec. 2. Congress shall have power to enforce this article by appropriate legislation.

Article XIV.

Section 1. All persons born or naturalized in the United States and subject to the jurisdiction thereof, are citizens of the United States, and of the state wherein they reside. No state shall make or enforce any law which shall abridge the privileges or immunities of citizens of the United States; nor shall any state deprive any person of life, liberty, or property, without due process of law, nor deny to any person within its jurisdiction the equal protection of the laws.

Sec. 2. Representatives shall be appointed among the several states according to their respective numbers, counting the whole number of persons in each state, excluding Indians not taxed; but when the right to vote at any election for the choice of Electors for President and Vice-President of the United States, Representatives in Congress, the executive and judicial officers of a state, or the members of the Legislature thereof, is denied to any of the male inhabitants of such state, being twenty-one years of age and citizens of the United States, or in any way abridged except for participation in rebellion or other crimes, the basis of representation therein shall be reduced in the proportion which the number of such male citizens shall bear to the whole number of male citizens twenty-one years of age in such state.

Sec. 3. No person shall be a Senator or Representative in Congress, or Elector of President and Vice-President, or hold any office, civil or military, under the United States, or under any state, who, having previously taken an oath as a Member of Congress, or as an officer of the United States, or as a member of any state Legislature, or as an executive or judicial officer of any state to support the Constitution of the United States, shall have engaged in insurrection or rebellion against the same, or given aid or comfort to the enemies thereof. But Congress may, by a vote of two-thirds of each house, remove such disability.

Sec. 4. The validity of the public debt of the United States authorized by law, including debts incurred for payment of pensions and bounties for services in suppressing insurrection or rebellion, shall not be questioned. But neither the United States nor any state shall pay any debt or obligation incurred in the aid of insurrection or rebellion against the United States, or any loss or emancipation of any slave, but such debts, obligations, and claims shall be held illegal and void.

100 CONSTITUTION OF THE UNITED STATES.

SEC. 5. The Congress shall have power to enforce, by appropriate legislation, the provisions of this act.

ARTICLE XV.

SECTION 1. The right of citizens of the United States to vote shall not be denied or abridged by the United States, or by any state, on account of race, color, or previous condition of servitude.

SEC. 2. Congress shall have power to enforce this article by appropriate legislation.

ELECTORS OF PRESIDENT AND VICE-PRESIDENT.

NOVEMBER 7, 1876.

COUNTIES.	Hayes and Wheeler, Republican.	Tilden and Hendricks, Democrat.	PeterCooper Greenback.	Smith, Prohibition.	Anti-Secret Societies.	COUNTIES.	Hayes and Wheeler, Republican.	Tilden and Hendricks, Democrat.	PeterCooper Greenback.	Smith, Prohibition.	Anti-Secret Societies.
Adams	4953	6308	41	17		Livingston	3550	2134	1170		3
Alexander	1219	1280				Logan	2788	2595	37		
Bond	1520	1142	17			Macon	3120	2782	268	16	
Boone	1965	963	43	2		Macoupin	3567	4076	114		
Brown	944	1495	183	1		Madison	4554	4730	39	1	
Bureau	3719	2218	145	2	11	Marion	2009	2444	209		
Calhoun	431	900				Marshall	1553	1430	135		1
Carroll	2231	918	111		3	Mason	1566	1989	86	3	
Cass	1209	1818	74	7		Massac	1231	793	20		
Champaign	4530	3103	604		1	McDonough	2932	2811	347		
Christian	2501	3287	207	1	6	McHenry	3485	1874	34		3
Clark	1814	2197	236		9	McLean	6363	4410	518	8	7
Clay	1416	1541	112			Menard	1115	1657	10		
Clinton	1329	1989	132			Mercer	2209	1428	90		3
Coles	2957	2802	102			Monroe	845	1651			
Cook	36548	39230	277			Montgomery	2486	3013	207		
Crawford	1355	1643	38			Morgan	3059	3174	109		3
Cumberland	1145	1407	129			Moultrie	1245	1679	28		
De Kalb	3679	1413	65		3	Ogle	3833	1921	104		8
DeWitt	1928	1174	746	10	3	Peoria	4665	5443	95		
Douglas	1631	1357	94			Pope	1319	800	5		
DuPage	2149	1276	25		8	Perry	1541	1383	48		
Edgar	2713	2883	161			Piatt	1807	1316	117		
Edwards	970	466	61			Pike	3055	4040	35	1	4
Effingham	1145	2265	43			Pulaski	1045	779			
Fayette	1881	2421	57			Putnam	646	459	14		
Ford	1601	712	204			Randolph	2357	2589	2		
Franklin	966	1302	391			Richland	1410	1552	55		
Fulton	4187	4669	89		1	Rock Island	3912	2838	27		
Gallatin	703	1149	282	2		Saline	980	1081	643		
Greene	1695	3160	2		9	Sangamon	4851	5847	29		
Grundy	1996	1142	108			Schuyler	1532	1804	115		
Hamilton	627	1433	770		4	Scott	910	1269	182		
Hancock	3496	4207				Shelby	2069	3553	341		
Hardin	330	611	134			Stark	1140	786	96		
Henderson	1315	1015	1			St. Clair	4708	5891	99		1
Henry	4177	1928	340		6	Stephenson	3198	2758	26		3
Iroquois	3788	2578	249	14	1	Tazewell	2850	3171	44	2	2
Jackson	2040	2071	106			Union	978	2155	3		
Jasper						Vermilion	4372	3031	268		9
Jefferson	1346	1667	647			Wabash	650	936	207		
Jersey	1345	2166		12		Warren	2795	1984	138		1
Jo Daviess	2907	2276	140	2	3	Washington	1911	1671	39		
Johnson	1307	893	61			Wayne	1570	1751	482		
Kane	5304	2854	172		5	White	1297	2066	469		4
Kankakee	2627	1363	26		2	Whiteside	3851	2131	133	8	1
Kendall	1869	524	309			Will	4770	3999	677		
Knox	5235	2632	143		1	Williamson	1672	1644	41		
Lake	2619	1647	55			Winnebago	4505	1568	70	13	2
LaSalle	6277	6001	514		15	Woodford	1733	2105	237	1	4
Lawrence	1198	1329	27								
Lee	3087	2080	100	2	6	Total	275958	257099	16951	130	157

HISTORY OF WARREN COUNTY.

TOPOGRAPHY AND GEOLOGY.

[From Geological Survey by A. H. Green.—1870.]

Warren county contains fifteen townships, or five hundred and forty square miles. The fourth principal meridian passes along its eastern border. It is intersected in the northern part, from east to west, by Main, Henderson and Cedar creeks. South of this there is South Henderson creek, rising in township 10 and running nearly west; while to the east Slug Run rises in the northern part of the same township and passing south empties into Cedar Fork, near the eastern part of the county. Cedar Fork rises near the western boundary of township 9 and runs a little to the south of east. South of this is Nigger Creek, of which Little Nigger and Swan Creek are branches. By these and smaller streams the county is well watered and its surface thoroughly drained.

Springs are not very abundant, but there are some which are large and valuable. Good wells may usually be obtained at depths varying from ten to thirty feet, but if at the latter depth water is not found, it is generally necessary to dig sixty feet or more, or through the blue clay of the drift.

The greater part of Warren county is prairie, but they are seldom large, being divided by the numerous streams. The soil is a dark vegetable loam, differing but little in its general character and appearance from that of the adjoining counties. Along the ridges that skirt the streams the soil is of less depth, lighter colored and less fertile. The subsoil is a yellow or brown clay.

Much of the land lying along the water courses was originally covered with timber. Large portions of this have been cut off. The varieties of timber here are nearly the same as in this part of Illinois—principally the common varieties of oak and hickory, with an undergrowth of hazel and sumach. Along the slopes of the hills and on the bottom lands of the streams, in addition to these, can be found red and white elm, white, blue and prickly ash, linden, sycamore, sugar and white maple, ash-leaved maple or box-elder, black walnut, butternut, buckeye, cottonwood, honey locust, American aspen, wild cherry, coffee tree, hackberry, mulberry, ironwood, wild plum, thorn, crab apple, dogwood and red bud.

The alluvial deposits of the county are not extensive, being confined to the borders of the streams, and are seldom over a half mile in width, while commonly they are less. The soil of these bottom lands is very fertile and consists of black loam, more or less mixed with sand and gravel.

The coal measures underlie nearly the whole of Warren county. Sumner and the northern part of Hale township probably embraces the entire district, or nearly so, where coal is not found. The coal measures comprise, in this county, various stratas of shales, sandstones, limestones, clays and coal, and attain a thickness in some parts of from one to two hundred feet. These stratas rest upon the Burlington limestone, and where this is found near the surface, or reached in shafting, no coal need be looked for in deeper explorations.

The upper seam is from three to three and a half feet in thickness, and has been found in few localities.

The next seam, No. 2 of the Illinois section, is from one foot, eight inches, to two feet thick in this county, elsewhere it attains a thickness of from three to five feet. Though thinner, this seam is more extensively worked than either of the others.

On sections 14 and 23, in township 10, are some valuable quarries. The rock is from six to seven feet thick at some of the localities and the whole of it is thickly bedded, so that blocks of any desirable size can be obtained. There are, however, large concretions of a *calcareo-arenaceous* rock, locally called "flint," in the sandstones. One of these was taken from the quarry of Mr. J. Worden, on section 14, that was about two and one-half feet thick, six to seven wide, and from ten to twelve feet long. This rock is very compact, hard enough to scratch glass, and in chlorohydric acid effervesces slightly. It is not considered of any value, and is so hard that when it occurs in large masses it is very expensive getting it out of the way.

In township 8 a coal seam crops out for some distance along Swan and Little Nigger creeks. At these localities mining has been carried on for years, and in places the bluffs are almost honey-combed by the entries, new and old. In some of the mines the fire-clay below the coal is varied in color, the usual tints being a light blue, though in some places it is nearly white, while in others it is yellow, or yellow and red. The coals in this county are mostly worked by drifts or tunnels driven horrizontally into the hill-sides along the outcrops of the seams, and owing to the shaley character of the roof of No. 2, considerable expense is incurred in "cribbing" to sustain the roof. The thickness of the coal is usually from twenty inches to two feet, and in driving the entries it becomes necessary to remove a portion of the roof shales, or the under-clay, in order to obtain the amount of vertical space required to take out the coal. The lower seam, No. 1, of the Illinois section, varies from two to four feet in this county. It is generally overlaid by black slate, or a dark colored, and frequently shaley limestone. This forms a very good roof and makes the working of the seam less expensive than that of No. 2, as, frequently, but little or no cribbing is required.

A little east of Monmouth is one of the most extensive mining companies in the country. Coal of a superior quality was found here, about 1871, and active preparations at once commenced to mine at this point. The seam is about twenty inches in thickness, and was found at a depth of about sixty feet. A far more valuable industry, and one which occupies the almost entire attention of the company—The Monmouth Mining and Manufacturing Company—is that of tile making. About thirty feet below the coal seam a most valuable strata of tile clay was found, and in 1875, active preparations were at once made to enter immediately upon the manufacture of this article. A stock company, representing $200,000 capital, was formed, and large buildings were erected and supplied with the

Elias Willits,
CO. JUDGE & ATTY. AT LAW
MONMOUTH ILL.

best of machinery. The buildings are so arranged and heated that the business can be carried on at all seasons of the year. Huge steam-pipes permeate the entire structure and every available foot of space is used. The company, of which the officers are: Daniel D. Parry, President; H. C. Beckwith, Secretary; and J. S. Spriggs, Treasurer, are now making all sizes of tile, from a small two inch pipe used in draining fields where the supply of water is small to the manufacture of large sewer pipes used in the drainage of cities. The utility and profit of this material to the farming community can hardly be estimated. Aside from the increase in health it brings by carrying off all surplus wat-r, it yields the richest returns for the capital invested. Fields which were once considered useless and valueless are made productive through liberal drainage; and swamps, or "sloughs," as they are called in the Western vernacular, once the source of fever and ague and all their attendant evils and discomforts, are drained of their miasmal waters, the sources of these diseases removed, and the land made to yield abundantly. Numerous instances could be given wherein one dollar invested in this article has returned to the investor many times its value ; and the intelligent reader of these pages has only to turn his attention to where the practical results are seen to verify this statement.

The tile made by this company is of an unexceptional material, and is rapidly finding its way into all parts of the West.

A few feet below the strata of clay, an excellent fire-clay was discovered. Heretofore the company was compelled to bring their fire-brick, at a heavy expense, from Ohio, but now, instead of purchasing that article, they have an abundance for sale.

THE COAL INTERESTS OF THE COUNTY.

There are reported by the county surveyor, Mr. Thos. McClanahan, twenty-nine coal mines in Warren county in operation. These employ from one to twenty men each, or one hundred and twelve in all. The average thickness of the coal vein is about thirty inches; they range from eighteen to forty inches. During the year 1875, and to March, 1876, there were mined in all 384,740 bushels ; the lowest product from any one mine being 170 bushels ; the greatest number 96,000 bushels.

The price for coal ranged from eight to twelve and one-half cents, the total amount received being $38,374.00. The depth of the mines vary from twenty to one hundred feet below the surface. The cost of opening these mines ranges from $25.00 to $5,000. The roofs of the mines are generally covered with soapstone or slate, and the bottom is principally fire-clay. The escapes are nearly always abundantly sufficient, and air in the mines pure and wholesome.

BURLINGTON LIMESTONE.—The beds of this group immediately underlie the coal measures in this county, wherever the junction of the coal with the underlying beds can be seen.

The Burlington group in Warren county consists mainly of light gray and brown limestones, chert and calcareous clay shale, and attains a thickness of from forty to fifty feet. These beds outcrop along the small streams in the southern part of township 12. Section 31, of the same township, furnishes layers of good building material sufficiently thick for all ordinary purposes. At Rockwell's mill, on Cedar Creek, the rock is quite arenaceous.

On section 1, in township 11, there are extensive quarries of limestone. Much lime is burned here, and the rock being nearly a pure corbonate of lime affords a good article. Near the middle of section 7, on Cedar Creek, and along a branch putting off to the southeast there are extensive quarries in the bluffs which supply Monmouth and the adjoining region with large quantities of excellent building material.

The Burlington limestone furnishes a good article of building stone, and is found along the southern part of township 12, and in the northern of township 11, in range 2 and 3 (See map in front part of this work). From Rockwell's Mill for several miles up Cedar Creek the outcrops of these beds form mural, or overhanging masses.

The rock is compact and dresses well, and some of the layers afford a stone susceptible of a good polish.

In section 11 the sandstone forms immense ledges, which in some places overhang the water ten or fifteen feet. "Rock House," as it is called, is in this section, and was formed in some past time, when the bed of the stream was considerably higher than at present, by the water cutting a passage through a portion of the lower strata. In the denuding process, a large pillar of sandstone was left, and now supports the outer edge of the upper strata which forms the roof.

Nearly all the outcrops of Burlington limestone will afford abundant supplies of material for lime, and being nearly pure carbonate of lime, yields an excellent article. Lime is extensively manufactured in some localities. Better facilities are being obtained for getting fuel to the kilns and the manufactured lime to market, thereby rendering this business an important source of wealth to some portions of the county.

AGRICULTURE.—Warren county contains 335,945 acres of land, valued at $8,095,104. The whole number of town lots is 4,164; their value is $1,063,688. The average value of lands is $24.10 per acre, and the average value of the lots is $255.45 each. The total value of all property in the county, including personal property, is $12,039,637. The county contains only 20,112 acres unimproved lands, and these are valued at $181,024, showing there is no worthless land.

During the year 1875, there were sown in wheat 5,879 acres; in corn, 138,870 acres—nearly one-half the area of the county—in oats, 26,180 ; in meadow, 36,316, and in other field products, 5,385 acres. There are 20,338 acres in woodland, and 3,644 acres in orchards. There were also reported to the county assessors 12,370 horses, valued at $8,564,038; 25,154 head of cattle, valued at $389,333; 4,608 sheep, valued at $9,291; 966 mules and asses, valued at $53,448; 48,368 hogs, valued at $231,737. These figures give 91,466 head of live stock, whose entire value is $1,247,847. There were also returned for taxation 4,318 carriages and wagons, worth $133,339; 2,738 clocks and watches, worth $12,720 ; 1,854 sewing machines, worth $38,701 ; 586 pianos, organs and melodeons, worth $36,186 ; there are in banks credit, money, bonds and stocks, $626,475, and in addition to this there are held $228,000 in bank stock. The entire personal property in Warren county is taxed at $2,880,845. Since the opening of the C. B. & Q. R. R., in 1855, there have been shipped from the county fifteen million bushels of grain, a million head of live stock, and several million dollars worth of manufactured machinery.

Good improved farms are worth now from $60 to $100 per acre, and the constant appearance of well-tilled farms, of comfortable homes, and all the conveniences and comforts of life are assurances of the wealth and ease with which the greater portion of the people are blessed.

The population is now, counting three times the number of persons enrolled in the late school census, under twenty-one years of age, 33,876; 22,584 of these are over age; and assuming the $12,039,637 to be the value of the property, each one of the latter class is worth $53.31.

HISTORY.

In the winter of 1822 and 1823 the Legislature of the State of Illinois laid out the "Military Tract," situated between the Illinois and Mississippi rivers, into counties, giving to each a name, and at the same time formed several other counties. At an earlier day the "Military Tract," and, indeed, all north and west of the Illinois river, including the country about Galena, was attached to and formed a part of Madison county, for judicial purposes. At that session, however, Pike county was formed, and the records of lands, patents, &c., situated on the Military Tract, were thereafter recorded at Atlas, then the county seat.

A subsequent Legislature organized Adams, Schuyler, Fulton and Peoria counties, attaching to Schuyler county the new county of McDonough, for judicial purposes. During the session of 1824-25 the county of Warren was formed, comprising all that part of the Military Tract lying west of the fourth principal meridian, extending to the Mississippi river, and including what is now Henderson county. It was named in honor of General Joseph Warren, who so gallantly defended the country at the commencement of the Revolutionary war, and who was the first officer to shed his life's blood in that struggle which gave America her independence. He was killed by a musket ball at the battle of Bunker's Hill. As every school-boy knows, the Americans were enabled to "hold the fort" while their ammunition lasted; that giving way, they slowly retreated, Gen. Warren being the last to go. As he retired he turned to look at the foe, and just at that instant received a ball in his forehead, and sank dead to the earth. He was thirty-five years of age at the time.

The Legislature met at Vandalia, then the capital of the State, and in the Act forming the county attached it to Pike county, for judicial purposes, until a sufficient number of inhabitants were within its borders to enable it to take active existence. This did not occur until June, 1830.

Late in the spring of 1827, some pioneers made their way into the county limits, and the following year the first ground was broken by a plow.

The Talbot family were the earliest settlers in Warren county. Mrs. Talbot, mother of John B. Talbot, was some eighty years of age when she came. She was born in New England, but came to Kentucky when John was born. After the death of his mother he married and removed to Oregon.

Allen G. Andrews, a nephew of Mrs. Talbot, came about the same time. He had been several years in the West Indies, and was quite a good Spanish scholar. He died some years ago on his farm, just north of Cedar creek. James B. Atwood settled on his farm in 1828. In June of that year he claimed to have broken five acres of prairie and planted it in corn. He afterwards went to Texas. Andrew Robinson settled on the farm afterwards owned by old Mr. Terpening. He located again on a farm about seven miles north-east of Monmouth, where he, in after years, died. Adam

Ritchie ("Sandy") settled near Sugar-Tree Grove in May, 1828. His son, Rev. Henderson Ritchie, born December 28, 1828, was the first white child born in Warren county. Mr. Ritchie afterwards went to Quincy, then to where Nauvoo was built, at which place he died of cholera. J. Buffum and L. P. Rockwell located where Rockwell's mill was afterwards built.

Daniel Harris, a quiet, peaceful man, erected a cabin near where the village of Ellison now stands. He was basely murdered, while eating, by a gun-shot through the window. His was the first death in the county.

It is somewhat strange that the first deaths in the region were violent. Shortly after the killing of Mr. Harris, Mr. James Moffitt went out one morning to find his cattle, which had strayed away on the unbounded prairies. Getting upon a fence surrounding some choice garden or field, he unexpectedly fell and dislocated his neck, so that death resulted soon after. Afterwards, William Martin, son of Hugh Martin, was killed by the Indians. An account of this and the trial of the murderer will be found further on in this narrative. Adam Ritchie ("Black," as he was called on account of his dark color) located here about the same date as that of his cousin Adam (called "Sandy" on account of his sandy complexion, and to distinguish him from the other), but afterwards removed to Iowa, where he was a pioneer in the organization of the first Seceder church in that State.

Dr. Isaac Galland, or Garland—the latter is probably the correct name—erected, in 1827, the first house on the site of the lower Yellow Banks, now Oquaka, Henderson county. The Dr. afterwards related that it took him nearly a week to lay up the logs of his house, eight rounds high. There were no white men to help him, save his teamster, and in the emergency he hired six or eight Indians, who were then encamped at the point of woods below. He had to pay them for each log as it was rolled to its place, and give them a drink around. As they were unused to such labor, and particularly after imbibing two or three drams of liquor, thereby becoming unsteady in their movements, they were unable to perform heavy work. Often at this stage of the labor, the logs, which were unhewn, and of the black-Jack variety, would give a lurch, and coming down on their bare arms and breasts, would tear off the skin in great flakes. They would give an ejaculatory "*ouch*," and at once quit for the day. Their love of the "fire-water" was so great, however, that they would always return on the following day, thereby repeating the process until the house was complete. A few other houses were probably built this year—1827. In 1828 and '29, quite a number of settlers came and located in different portions of the county. James and Rolla Simmons settled at Greenbush; John C. Bond shortly after, a little south of them; a family (name not now known) at the head of Swan creek; Field, Jarvis and Col. Redman at the head of Ellison creek; Samuel G. Morise, Thomas Pearce, Solomon Perkins and Shelden Lockwood near the present town of Berwick; Stephen S. Phelps at the Lower Yellow Banks; James Hodgens at Hodgens' Grove, just north-west of the present city of Monmouth; Samuel Jameson and sons, and James Ryerson south of the Yellow Banks.

Stephen S. Phelps purchased the improved claim of Dr. Garland, and removed his family to their new home in the summer of 1828. He was soon joined by the families of Beatty and Jeremiah Smith, in addition to several already mentioned. Mr. Smith erected a saw and grist mill on Smith creek, in 1829, and before a few summers had passed quite a settlement was established at this place.

In the Autumn of 1829 and spring of 1830, Elijah Davidson, Sr., William Whitman, Peter Butler and others located on the south side of Cedar creek. By this time the entire territory comprised in Warren, Henderson and Mercer counties contained only about thirty or forty families; but others were constantly coming, so that by the spring of the latter year it was thought proper to send to Peoria and secure an order for a county election from Hon. Richard M. Young, Judge of the Circuit Court, and so well known in after years throughout the State.

By the census of 1830, there were that year in the territory included within the three counties 360 inhabitants. Other reasons urged this step. They were compelled to go to Peoria for all legal purposes—for all marriage licenses—or publish a notice ten days before the event, and young people then, as now, did not at all times care to make the happy affair so public a matter; they were compelled to adopt the former course.

The citizens desired to assess and collect their own taxes, and to manage affairs their own way. Petitions to this effect were freely circulated and freely signed.

*Daniel McNeil, Jr., who then lived at Lower Yellow Banks, was appointed to go to Peoria to meet the Judge and present the petition. Judge Young was then holding court in a building sixteen by twenty feet in dimensions, situated upon the bank of the river, just where the latter leaves the lake.

It was then more than fifty miles from any part of Warren to Peoria by the most direct route. The Spoon and Kickapoo rivers were to be crossed between the two places, and they were often unfordable by reason of overflows. The Judge saw the necessity of the people, and being satisfied there were enough within the prescribed limits of the county, issued the following order:

STATE OF ILLINOIS, } set.
Fifth Judicial Circuit,

The People of the State of Illinois, To all who shall see these presents,
GREETING :

WHEREAS, By the ninth and eleventh sections of the Act entitled "An Act forming new counties out of the counties of Pike and Fulton, and the attached parts thereof," approved January 13th, 1825, it is made the duty of the presiding Judge of the Fifth Judicial Circuit of the State of Illinois, whenever it shall be made to appear to his satisfaction, that either of the counties of Hancock, Warren, Mercer, Henry, Putnam and Knox, contain three hundred and fifty inhabitants, to proceed to organize the same, and to grant an order for the election of county officers preparatory thereto : And whereas, it has been made appear to my satisfaction, that the county of Warren contains three hundred and fifty inhabitants and upwards; and inasmuch as the greater part of the qualified voters of the said county have requested, by petition, that the same should be organized with as little delay as possible, I do, therefore, in pursuance of the power vested in me, by virtue of the above recited Act, order and direct that an election be

---

* This man was more generally known than any one of the early settlers. He held almost every office in the county at one time and another, and did more to advance its interests than any one else. He was born in Hillsborough, N. H., March 24, 1792; he emigrated to Phelps, N. Y., in 1805; to Louisiana in 1810. He returned to N. Y. again in 1814, and went to Wabash county, near Vincennes, Indiana, in 1819. In 1824 he removed to Fulton county, Illinois. In 1830 he came to Warren county, where he remained until 1852, when he went to De Witt, Iowa, where he died Feb. 28, 1859, aged seventy-six years.

held in and for said county of Warren, at the house of Adam Ritchie, Jr., on Saturday, the third day of July, A. D. 1830, for the election of three county Commissioners, one Sheriff, and one Coroner, to serve, when elected and qualified, in and for the county of Warren, respectively, until they shall be superseded by persons who may be elected at the general election, to be held on the first Monday in August next; and, for the purpose of having this order carried into execution, I do hereby appoint John B. Talbot, Adam Ritchie, Jr., and Robert K. Hendricks, of said county, judges of said election, whose duty it shall be to set up written or printed advertisements or notices of said election in at least six of the most public places in said county, inclusive of the place at which the election is hereby directed to be held (having a due regard to the situation and population of the different settlements), at least ten days previous to the said election, to the end that all persons may have timely notice thereof. The election to be held *viva voce*, between the hours of nine o'clock in the forenoon and seven o'clock in the afternoon of said day, and conducted, as far as may be practicable, in conformity with the Act entitled "An Act regulating Elections," approved January 10th, 1829; and, lastly, the said judges are to certify the result of the said election to the office of the Secretary of State, as soon thereafter as may be convenient, in order that the persons who may be elected, may be commissioned and qualified with as little delay as possible, and after the election of the said county officers, I do hereby declare the said county of Warren to be organized, and entitled to the same rights and privileges as the other counties in this State.

{ L. S. } Given under my hand and seal, at Peoria, this 8th day of June, A. D. 1830, and of the Independence of the United States, the fifty-fourth.

RICHARD M. YOUNG,
Circuit Judge of the Fifth Judicial Circuit of the State of Illinois.

Mr. Ritchie lived near the centre of the population, and early on the morning of the day appointed for the election the voters assembled. Thirty-seven votes were polled, three voters being absent. The persons named in the order of Judge Young declining to serve as judges of election, the people appointed Robert K. Hendricks, Sheldon Lockwood and Peter Butler in their place, and Stephen S. Phelps and Daniel McNeil clerks. On counting the votes at the close of the balloting, John Pence, John B. Talbot and Adam ("Sandy") Ritchie were found elected Commissioners; John Rust, Sheriff, and John Ritchie, Coronor. Knox county, immediately east of Warren, and McDonough county, in the south, were each organized by order of Judge Young, on the same day, and at their elections each gave about the same number of votes as Warren.

On the Monday following the election in Warren, the Commissioners met at Lower Yellow Banks, at the house of Stephen S. Phelps, and organized as a Board of County Commissioners. They appointed Daniel McNeil their clerk, divided the county into two election precincts and two Justice's districts, the divisions being marked by the range line between three and four west. The western was called Precinct No. 1, and Yellow Banks Judge's District, the place of holding elections being the temporary courthouse. The eastern was called Precinct No. 2, and the place of holding elections was appointed at the house of Isaac Hodgens, at Hodgens' Grove, one mile north-west of the present county seat. An election was ordered to be held at these places on the first Monday in August following, that being the general election day throughout the State. It was also ordered, that in addition to the State officers elected, there should be chosen three County Commissioners, one Sheriff, one Coroner, two Justices, two Constables in each precinct; and as the District Court was expected to hold a session before this election, the Commissioners selected a Grand and Petit Jury, which took every eligible man in the county.

The county being now organized, it was necessary that the laws of the State be put into force. Judge Young issued the following order:

"STATE OF ILLINOIS, } set. :
Fifth Judicial District. }
To all whom it may concern, GREETING :

"KNOW YE, That I, Richard M. Young, Judge of the Fifth Judicial Circuit of the State of Illinois, north of the Illinois river, and presiding Judge of the Circuit Court, in and for the county of Warren, and State aforesaid, in pursuance of the power vested in me by virtue of the 10th section of the Act entitled 'An Act supplementary to an Act regulating the Supreme and Circuit Courts,' approved January 19, 1829, approved January 28, 1829, do hereby order and appoint, that Circuit Courts be held in and for the said county of Warren, at such places as may be selected and provided by the County Commissioners' Court of said county on the fourth Mondays in June and the first Mondays in October, until I shall make another order to the contrary.

"Signed, RICHARD M. YOUNG,
"*Judge of the Fifth Judicial Circuit.*"

This order was given at Galena on July 5th, preceding the general election, and on the same day the Judge gave the order for the organization of the county; he gave to Daniel McNeil the appointment of clerk, *pro tem.*, for the Circuit Court, dating it at Peoria, on October 1st, 1830, where he held court, at the house of John B. Gumner At the general election in August, votes were cast for Governor, Lieut.-Governor, Representative to the General Assembly of the State, and for the county officers, as ordered by the Commissioners. Forty-seven votes were cast, forty-three being the greatest number any one candidate received, and every voter in the county was present save three. Hon. John Reynolds received thirty-four votes for Governor, and William Kinney eleven. Hon. —— — Wright was elected Representative; and for the county offices, the following persons were chosen: John B. Talbot, Peter Butler and John Pence, Commissioners; Stephen S. Phelps, Sheriff, and John Ritchie, Coroner. At the Yellow Banks District, John Pence and Daniel McNeil, Jr., were elected Justices, and James Ryerson and William Causland, Constables. At the Hodgens' Grove District, John B. Talbot, (" Sandy ") Adam Ritchie were elected Justices, and David Findley and —— —— Constables. Daniel McNeil having been appointed Clerk of Circuit Court, the county was now in complete running order. For some reason no preparation was made for holding the Circuit Court, and the Judge met with the Clerk at the house of John B. Gunner, at Henderson's Grove, and after performing a little formulatory business, each returned to his home.

It was customary in these days to have something to "take" at all elections, and the "take" was pretty generally indulged in by all. At the election in August, already referred to, a bucket was filled with whiskey, and a sufficient number of tin cups placed therein, and all who desired could freely imbibe. The Indians were present at the time in a strong representation, and indulged in their favorite "fire-water" to their full. Approaching the successful candidates at the close of the election, they congratulated them in a series of grunts and approving gestures, using in many cases, their only English sentence expressive of their ideas—"You big chief, big chief, me little chief, so high," measuring a short distance from the ground. Or "Keokuk, big chief, big chief," measuring with extended arm as high as they could reach.

The county being now fully organized, it became necessary to have a seat of justice, and as the inhabitants residing therein could not decide upon the location, they petitioned the Legislature to select it. This the body did, by appointing three commissioners to perform the duty. They were Major Hazen Bedel, of Hancock county, John G. Sanburn, of Knox county, and John McNeil, of Fulton. The Act appointing these persons as Commissioners to locate the county seat passed the Legislature, and was approved January 27, 1831. The Act directed them to meet at the house of Stephen S. Phelps, on the first Monday of the following April, and being duly sworn by some judge or justice in the county, they were "faithfully to take into consideration the convenience of the people, the situation of the settlements with a view to the future population of said county and the eligibility of the situation, shall proceed to fix upon a place for the permanent seat of justice for said county, and give to it a name."

On the day appointed these persons met and were duly sworn before Daniel McNeil, Jr., a justice, and at once proceeded to select a location. Yellow Banks, Hodgen's Point, Center Grove and Ellison's Creek were all contestants for the place. In order to ascertain what the future population might be, the commissioners made a plat of the county and placed in each township the probable number of towns, varying from four to forty-two.

On April the 7th they completed the work assigned them, and sealing and directing a package containing their decision to the "County Commissioners Court of Warren County, Illinois," they departed to their homes.

At a called meeting of the latter court, on the 11th day of the same month, the package was opened and was found to locate the seat of justice on section 29, in township 11. The reader will find their decision given at the commencement of the history of Monmouth, in their own words.

In choosing the name of the new county seat, each commissioner selected the names; from these, three were drawn, which proved to be Isabella, Kosciusko and Monmouth. These were thrown together, and it was agreed that the one drawn should be the name. Kosciusko was drawn, when it was suggested by the commissioner who first selected it, that very few of the inhabitants could spell it correctly, and he moved a drawing of the other two names be made. This was done, and resulted in the name the city now bears.

The summer of 1831 was remarkably cold. Dark spots were plainly seen by the naked eye to cover the sun. The crops were almost a failure, and an early winter set in. Snow fell on the 4th day of October, but the skies clearing off, a fine spell of weather came in, which lasted a few weeks and enabled the settlers to gather their corn. The winter began again with a storm of rain which lasted until the prairies were covered with water. It then changed to snow, and became in a few hours bitterly cold. Within twelve hours after the change, the prairies were a complete glare of ice, and neither man or beast could move with safety. Men were known to go five miles or more to get horse-shoes and nails made, and returning home would set the shoes with a common drawing-knife and hammer. By such means only were they able to obtain fuel. The ice lasted six weeks, and about the 1st of February, 1832, a snow fell to the depth of nine inches. This lay on the ground nearly six weeks and furnished excellent sleighing, which was greatly improved by the residents in transporting any articles needed.

The spring of 1832 opened rather late, the weather was cold, and, like the previous spring, but little corn came up. The settlers had taken the precaution, however, to procure a species of Indian maize, known as "*squaw corn*," which matured much earlier than the common variety, and that season a very good crop was raised.

Their crops had hardly been planted when they were disturbed by news of an Indian war. Black Hawk and his band were becoming troublesome, and on the first of May Governor Reynolds encamped at the Yellow Banks with a large number of volunteers to aid in the subjection of this famous Indian chief. There was no one in Warren county skilled in the manual of arms, and great fears were expressed by the people least, on the Governor's absence, the savages would come from beyond the Mississippi River and destroy them. To allay these fears and give the citizens an opportunity to show their patriotism, the Governor issued the following special commission:

"CAMP AT YELLOW BANKS, }
May 4th, 1832. }

I do hereby appoint Daniel McNeil to give notice that an election for a major of militia, composing an odd battalion in Warren county, will be held at Monmouth, at some convenient time, within ten days from the date of this appointment. And I do further authorize the said McNeil to conduct said election according to law, and to give the person elected major a certificate of his election, which will authorize said major to cause elections to be held for company officers, so that said militia be organized with speed to defend their lives from Indian depredations ; and in case of necessity, the said McNeil is authorized to call on one or] more companies to range the frontier for its defense.

(Signed,) JOHN REYNOLDS.
Governor and Commander-in-Chief of the Ill. Militia."

In accordance with the above order, notice was given and an election, which resulted in the choice of Peter Butler, as major of the odd battalion, who forthwith ordered elections to be held at different points, for company officers, in certain districts of the county, and the organization of the militia was complete.

Governor Reynolds passed on to Rock River with his troops, and the citizens becoming alarmed for their safety, being without a patrol, or body of rangers, for protection, petitioned McNeil to call volunteers. He complied, and on the 31st of May issued a call, to meet at Monmouth on the 4th day of June. At this latter date a company of *thirty* men, *three* commissioned, and *five* non-commissioned officers was formed, and reported for duty at the War Department at the City of Washington and to the Governor of the State.

For the entertainment of the readers of these pages, a copy of the muster roll of this company is herewith given:

"A copy of Captain Peter Butler's company of Mounted Volunteer Rangers in the service of the United States, ordered out by Daniel McNeil,

Junior, Agent of John Reynolds, Commander-in-Chief of the Militia of the State of Illinois, from the 4th day of June, 1832, the day of its enrollment, to the 15th day of its disbandment and discharge at Fort Gumm, fifteen miles from the place of its enrollment.

"Peter Butler, Captain; James McCallon, 1st Lieut.; Solomon Perkins, 2d Lieut.; Isaac Veetrees, 1st Sergeant; Benjaman Tucker, 2d; Matthew D. Ritchie, 3d; and Adam Ritchie, 4th. The privates: John Van Atta, James C. Caldwell, John Quinm, Thomas Ritchie, Andrew Gilson, George, Gilson, William Stark, W. H. Denison, Isaiah Osborn, John Armstrong, Danas B. Cartwright, Gersham Van Atta, Elijah Hilton, James Reason, William Laswell, Paschal Pencanean, John D. Ritchie, Samuel L. Hogue, David Russell, Charles A. Smith, John Findley, Amos Williams, Gabriel Short, John McCoy, Erastus S. Denison, John Maley, Robert S. Stice, John Hendricks, William Patton and Ezra A. Allen."

These troops were disbanded in consequence of an order from the Governor calling upon the counties of McDonough and Warren to furnish a company to serve as mounted rangers until regularly discharged. This latter company was at once raised and Major Butler chosen captain and James McCullon 1st Lieutenant; many of the old company joining under these officers.

It was during the time this last company was stationed at a fort at Yellow Banks that the murder of William Martin, already referred to, occurred. This sad occurrence happened on the afternoon of a fine day while Mr. Martin was engaged in putting up hay. He was near Little York, and the two Misses McCoy saw five Indians come out from the woods near, run to Martin and shoot and scalp him. The news of the murder spread with great rapidity throughout the settlement and caused great alarm among the inhabitants. Nearly every family at once repaired to the fort for safety. A Methodist minister, who was preaching at Cedar Creek, some three miles distant, immediately on receipt of the news, in the midst of his sermon, abruptly closed his discourse, dismissed his congregation and fled with great haste to Canton.

The murderers of Mr. Martin must be found and brought to punishment. The war was over and people had returned to their homes. The grand jury, at their session in 1832, following the painful murder, found a true bill against certain Indians, names unknown, of Keokuk's band of the Sac and Fox, friendly Indians, for the murder of William Martin. This was forwarded to the Governor of the State, with a request that he would forward the same to the President of the United States, asking him to require, through the Indian Agent of said band of Indians, the murderers. The Agent, Col. Marmaduke Davenport, made the demand, and one of the murderers was delivered to the United States garrison at Rock Island and confined in Fort Armstrong. From this, however, he escaped and, crossing the Mississippi River, fled to the far West.

According to the Indian custom, the tribe at once delivered up the next of kin to the murderers. This latter fact was not, however, known to the authorities of Warren county. Peter Butler, sheriff of the county, was notified by Col. Davenport that he would be at the Lower Yellow Banks about the 20th of March, 1833, with the reputed murderer of Martin, and requested that he, Butler, would be prepared to receive the prisoners. On that day, Col. Davenport, accompanied by Pash-a-pa-ho, Wee-shaw and Keokuk, chiefs, together with quite a number of Indians, his guard and the interpreters, arrived at Yellow Banks, and delivered into the custody of Maj. Butler four young warriors, who were divested of their weapons and ornaments, and, as they expressed it, became squaws, were placed under guard and taken to Monmouth. Here they were put under the charge of Daniel McNeil, jailor, who kept them under guard until the jail, then in process of construction, was sufficiently strong for their safe keeping.

The names of the prisoners were J-o-nah, signifying, *stay here*, or *be quiet*, or *be still;* Ka-ke-mo, *he that troubles,* or *humbleth;* Wau-pe-sho-kon, *the white string;* and S-sa-pe-mo (the meaning of the latter name is not now known).

They brought with them a parcel of pipes, tobacco, dried corn, beans and a quantity of meat and tallow, sufficient to last them several days. The jailor had some of their provisions cooked for them in the Indian style, but regularly supplied them with wholesome food. One day they refused to eat until a speech had been delivered by J-o-nah, to which the others responded, and when ended, the speaker gave to the jailor a large green blanket, a pair of moccasins and a handkerchief. He was unable to understand the speech and judged the Indians wanted the blanket and handkerchief (though quite clean) washed,—the moccasins were for his wife, as a compensation for washing.

When the articles were washed and dried, the jailor took them back to the prisoners, when he discovered his error. Speeches were again made, in which the name of *Pencenean* (a French interpreter,) was often used. He was in the employ of Mr. Phelps, and a short time after, being at the jail, the Indians requested him to say to their keeper that they were shut up in prison, deprived of fishing or hunting, away from their kindred and friends and nation, and wholly dependent upon the "*French man,*" as they called the jailor, for everything they ate and drank, and that, were it not for his kindness, they would long since have starved to death; that the blanket and other articles were of no use to them now, and that they had given them to him as a token of their gratitude, and hoped that they might be so received. "Tell him," said J-o-nah, "he is my brother, and a brother of us all; and should we ever be liberated we will return to our kindred and tell them all the '*French man*' has done for us. And when he becomes old, we will fish and kill deer and buffalo, catch otter and beaver for him, and we will bring them to *Wa-wash-a-ne-quah* (S. S. Phillips, who traded much with the Indians), who will write to the '*French man*' to come down with his one-horse wagon and bring up an abundance of provisions and furs for himself, squaw, and little ones, and all our brothers shall be his brothers."

Court convened on June 14, 1833, and under a writ of habeas corpus the prisoners were brought up for trial. Col. Davenport, the Indian Agent, Mr. Le Clair, his interpreter, Keokuk, a famous chief, always friendly to the whites, Pow-a-sheite, and some fifty other chiefs and braves came up from Yellow Banks, headed by the United States flag, and encamped near the place of trial. The Indians—probably through the agent—had employed able counsel. They were Mr. Field, of Vandalia, Mr. Galewood, of Shawneetown and Mr. Hempstead, of Galena. They paid these lawyers about $500 each to defend them.

After a patient examination by the grand jury, of Keokuk and other chiefs, to identify these persons as the murderers, that body reported that "The person confined in the fort at Rock Island was the only person ever taken who was the real murderer, and that he had escaped to parts unknown." The prisoners were at once discharged, though not before Judge Young had (through the interpreter) severely reprimanded Keokuk and the other chiefs for delivering innocent persons in the room of the guilty. Keokuk replied that one guilty of the crime had been delivered up to the United States and that he had escaped, and with the four other murderers had gone beyond the Rocky Mountains. That these four prisoners were next in kin to the guilty ones, and according to their custom were given to be punished. They were all very grateful for the deliverance of their braves, and at once returned to their hunting grounds. While in the jail, the keeper had tried to learn from them where lead could be found in Iowa. They assured him there was none to be found in that State worth working, except about Dubuque. They often drew maps for him, starting at the lakes, drawing the Illinois River and its tributaries, Wisconsin, Mississippi and Missouri, embracing Turkey River, Maquoketa, Waubosepinican, Iowa and its branches and the Des Moines; and it was often spoken of by the jailor, who has transmitted these items to posterity, that it was doubtful whether anyone could, with a piece of chalk, draw on a rough board floor so good a map of these rivers and the country they traversed. A few other Indians were tried in Warren county for various crimes, one of whom, Wa-gra-sho-kon, married a daughter of the celebrated Black Hawk.

Troubles with the Indians soon, most happily, ceased. The famous Black Hawk war was closed, and emigrants came rapidly into the county. Religion and education at once took firm hold here, so that now the county contains fully as many churches and schools, according to its population, as any county in the United States.

The first sermon preached in the limits of Warren county was by Rev. Mr. Finch, a Methodist minister. The people comprising this denomination were few in number then, and lived far apart. Their first regular missionary was Rev. Barton Randall. A class was formed first at Thomas Pierce's house, and here Benton H. Cartwright, the first exhorter and licensed preacher among them, held services.

A Cumberland Presbyterian minister preached the first sermon in Monmouth, at Joel Hargrove's house. As early as 1830 or 1831, the Associate Reformed sent a missionary here, and their church formed at Henderson's Grove is the oldest religious organization in the county. The Disciples located about the same time east of Monmouth, their center being Coldbrook. The first Sunday-school in Warren was opened at Yellow Bank, in 1830, and two years after, a second school was opened in Monmouth. The first public school—supported by subscription—was opened in Monmouth by Robert Black, in 1831, and shortly after, another was started by Alpheus Russell.

Aside from Dr. Garland, the earliest physician to locate here was Dr. Ethan Cabanis. Dr. Alpheus Russell came in 1831. Both these physicians located at Monmouth.

John Wilton, the first lawyer in Warren county, located on his farm, in what is now Kelley township. He was soon followed by John H. Mitchell and Ivory Quinby.

The first recorded marriage was that of Samuel L. White to Huldah Jennings, on May 10, 1831, the ceremony being performed by John B. Talbott, Justice of the Peace.

On Saturday, June 11, 1831, the County Commissioners divided the county into three election districts, or precincts. The first of these had for its voting place the Court House, Monmouth; the second was called Yellow Banks district, and the place of voting was at the house of William Cousland; and the third was known as Ellison district, where the voters met at the house of Paris Smith. At this same time, a license was granted to William Cousland to keep an inn—the first one in Warren county—at Yellow Banks. He paid two and one-half dollars for the license, which, as in all such instruments, specified his rates for entertainment.

Stephen Phelps was also granted leave, on payment of $10, to sell merchandise at the same place. He was also collector of the taxes, and having about this time collected the sum of $208, he sent the same to Springfield by the hand of John B. Talbott, who received $5 for his services.

The county was beginning to rapidly fill with settlers, and at every meeting of the Commissioners, several petitions would be presented to grant the opening of roads throughout the county. By March, 1832, eight road districts were established, and to aid in county affairs, a tax of one-half per cent. was levied on all personal property, which at that time included several negro slaves.

It will be borne in mind by all, that at one time human slavery was allowed in Illinois, and was the cause of considerable discussion and no little trouble before it was banished from the State. There is on record in the county offices the wise and humane action of Mr. Joseph Murphy, who came into court October 2, 1834, and stated that he desired to liberate a negro man he owned, who wished to go to Liberia. He gave bonds in the sum of one thousand dollars to secure the county against any loss sustained in keeping the slave should he fail to go to Liberia or to provide for himself. Mr. Murphy allowed the man to take the name of Richard Murphy, and set him at liberty. Richard remained in Warren county, became quite wealthy, and is now one of the best citizens therein. This curse to humanity was never allowed to any extent here, and only in its mildest forms, and in many instances the slave was as well or better treated than the average hired man at the present time. The majority of persons thus held were brought here by their owners as servants from the South, and were generally considered as such.

In the autumn of 1832, Daniel McNeil was re-appointed County Clerk, and Elijah Davidson continued as County Treasurer. In order to secure warmth during the coming winter, to the county officers, a stone chimney was ordered to be built to the court-house. It might be interesting to pause here and notice the jail, which had been by this time completed. It was built of hewed logs, each one foot square, the lower story having double walls. An excavation was made in the ground two feet deep and the floor laid at the bottom of this. It was composed of two layers of oak logs hewed one foot square, the upper layer crossing the lower, thereby making a floor two feet of solid oak. The walls for seven rounds high were the same in strength and thickness, the ends of the logs being dove-tailed into each other. On the upper surface of the seventh round the upper floor was laid. This was of the same material and size as the floor beneath, save it was one thickness closely joined. In the centre a heavy trap door was made, securely fastened by a strong pad-lock. The roof was of the firmest material and well covered with good shingles. In the lower story a window or "air-hole" six by twelve inches was made, and between the logs composing the wall, iron bars one inch in thickness, were securely fastened crossing this window up and down and crossways. At the centre of one end of the upper story, a double oak plank door was placed, and a stairway leading from it to the ground built. The prisoners were conducted up these stairs into the upper story, when the trap door was raised, and they descended by a movable stairway or ladder to the cell beneath. Here they were secure. This jail was probably one of the best of the kind ever built in the west, and was the work of Jacob Rust, the lowest bidder for the contract. It was completed and accepted May 4th, 1833.

On June 29, 1840, this jail was sold to L. C. Woodworth for $62.50, he with C. L. Merrill, having secured the contract to erect the present structure for $2,831.66¾. It was accepted the following year, and has since undergone considerable repair, and will, in all probability, soon be replaced by one fully equal to any emergency.

The old log court-house was occupied about seven years. In 1835, at the March meeting of the County Commissioners, James McCallon, Elijah Davidson, and Daniel McNeil, Jr., were appointed a committee to prepare a plan for a new one. These submitted a plan for a frame structure thirty feet long, twenty feet wide, and one and a half story high. June 1st the contract for its construction was let, and Daniel McNeil appointed superintendent. The cost was to be $773.00. The old court-house was sold to James Hodgen for twenty-one dollars. The new court-house was never finished, and was used in the incomplete condition one or two years. On December 8, 1836, the county Board ordered advertisements to be inserted in the *Peoria Champion, Quincy Argus, Bounty Law Register, Sangamon Journal,* and the *Illinois Patriot,* for the best plans for a court-house, to be built of brick and stone. The present court-house was the result. It is forty by fifty feet in dimensions, two stories high, and, when constructed, had an east and south front. The latter is now closed. The contract for its construction was let to Cornelius Tunnicliff for $8,998. He commenced the work, drew the first installment of pay—$1,000—and left. His securities at once entered upon the work and completed the building. It, as well as the jail, standing immediately west, is becoming inadequate to the wants of the county, and a commodious structure will, ere long, occupy its place.

The territory now comprising Henderson county was, prior to 1841, included in Warren county. The residents of that section, especially those in the western parts, complained of the long distance to the seat of justice, and made some efforts to have it removed to a more central locality. Many of them desired it should be placed at Oquawka, on the Mississippi river, the old county seat. This would not do. To settle all matters, the western part of the county, including 164,608 acres of land, was set off into another county, and called Henderson. The county seat was located at Oquawka. Until late years this place was generally known as Yellow Banks, and as such is often spoken of in these pages. It is well to state that the latter name is simply the English translation of the Indian name the town still bears.

In 1849 the first vote on a township organization was held. It was decided in the affirmative, and the County Commissioners appointed Joseph Paddox, John C. Bond and Ira F. M. Butler a committee to divide the county into townships. This committee performed this duty, and for one or two years the county was governed accordingly. A decision of the Supreme Court, however, decided the act illegal, on account of the insufficient number of votes, and the organization was abandoned. In 1850, Mr. C. K. Smith presented a petition signed by many citizens, asking for a vote to be held at the November election. At the election the organization was defeated. Another petition was presented in 1852 by Mr. Robert Gilmore, and again defeated at the polls. On September 12, 1853, Mr. James McCoy presented a petition signed by more than fifty voters, asking that at the coming general election, in November, the vote be once more taken. This election was held on November 8th, and thirteen hundred and ninety-six votes were cast; seven hundred and sixty-eight were in favor, and the county commissioners soon after appointed John C. Bond, Samuel Hallam and Robert Gilmore a committee to divide the county into townships. This committee formed them as they now exist, save that a few of the names have since been changed.

The most prominent roads were laid out in the early settlement of the county.

These wagon roads have, in a great measure, lost their usefulness, being superceded by railroads, but are yet used as thoroughfares. In December, 1834, a road was laid out, or "viewed," as it is termed in all the records, from Monmouth to Macomb. The following year, from Monmouth to Knoxville. This same year the law requiring all able-bodied men over twenty one years of age to work two days on the roads was put in force, and had a salutary effect on the travelling facilities. Also, during the summer, the State road from Knoxville through Warren county to New Boston was viewed by Erastus Denison and Ephriam Gilmore. A route had been for some time established to Rock Island, and to other points, and after the location of the State road, the improvements in this regard were generally local.

The first railroad in the county was built in 1854, and finished to Monmouth on January 1st, 1855. The charter was obtained for a road under the title of the "Peoria and Oquawka Rail Road, but upon the refusal on the part of Oquawka to give aid to the road, Burlington raised the sum required, and in consequence the route was changed, and Burlington became what Oquawka might have been, a city of great commercial importance, and a railroad centre for all roads through Iowa. The Chicago and Quincy Rail Road was completed to Galesburg at that time, and that company leased or obtained the privilege of running their trains over the Peoria & Oquawka line to Burlington, and in a short time after purchased the entire line, when the name was changed to the Chicago & Burlington Rail Road. As soon as the Quincy branch was completed to Galesburg, 110 miles, it assumed the present title, by which it is known all over the world.

This county, when it was asked for $50,000 to aid in its construction, gave it, but the measure was strongly opposed on the ground that such a road would never pay, as the road could, it was said, take off in one day all Warren county could produce for shipment in a year. This was an argument that it would not benefit the county for the sum required, and as for the passenger traffic, it was said that a stage passed through Monmouth from Peoria three times a week, and that they were never half full. Where would the railroad get its support?

When the road was finished, there was more freight at Monmouth waiting shipment than the most sanguine had dreamed, and the result was, the county began increasing rapidly in population and improvement, until it ranks as one of the greatest shipping counties on the line of road.

In the summer of 1870, the Rockford, Rock Island and St. Louis railroad was completed through the county, giving direct communication with St. Louis on the south and Rock Island on the north. The county gave largely to assist in the construction of this road, and has derived good benefits from it. It has lately come under the control of the C. B. & Q.

The railroad company intend soon to erect a fine depot at the crossing, to take the place of the one lately destroyed by fire. This is much needed, as the travel to this point is very large.

A narrow gauge railroad is now projected from a point in Illinois, opposite Burlington, thence through Henderson, Warren, Fulton and Peoria counties, via Monmouth and Canton, to Pekin and Peoria. At Pekin connection will be made with the Rantoul and Eastern for Toledo, Ohio.

A company, with a capital stock of $1,000,000, is already formed, and received their charter on November 20, 1875. It is largely composed of the best business men of the county, and when completed will be a source of great benefit to the people along the line.

OLD SETTLERS' ORGANIZATION.

Pursuant to a call published in the Warren and Henderson county papers, many of the old settlers in the two counties met at Young America, on Saturday afternoon, January 27, 1872. The meeting was called to order by Col. S. Hutchinson, who stated the object to be the forming of a permanent organization of the old settlers of the two counties, and to make arrangements for a social re-union, to be held on the 22d day of February.

All persons who had settled in the two counties previous to the formation of Henderson county, were admitted to membership, save the editors of the papers in each of the counties, who were admitted to honorary membership. It was also decided that the officers should be a president, vice-presidents, secretary and treasurer. At the meeting held February 22d, committees were appointed to draft a constitution and by-laws and to select officers for the ensuing year. The time for the annual re-union was fixed to be on the first Wednesday in June, of each year.

On this day the first re-union was held, at which time the constitution and by-laws were approved. The re-union was held at Young America, and a most enjoyable spirit prevailed. The old settlers gave many interesting accounts of their early life, and privations endured in the settling of the counties. It was ordered to change the time of meeting until the first Wednesday in September, hereafter, which is the annual day for the re-unions.

These re-unions have been regularly held since. Nearly all the old settlers in the two counties are now members, and take an active part in sustaining the organization. The constitution is now so amended that all persons in the counties are eligible for membership who have resided therein thirty years.

The present officers are: President, Col. Samuel Hutchinson; Vice-President, James Tucker; Secretary, W. A. Grant; Corresponding Secretary, J. B. Patterson; Treasurer, Wm. Hanna.

The following is a list of the members of this association, and their date of settlements, as shown by the records of the society:

NAME.	DATE OF SETTLEMENT.	REMARKS.
E. W. Allen,	June 14, 1835,	Berwick.
B. W. Allen,	June 15, 1835,	——, Died July 10, 1872.
R. N. Allen,	June 15, 1835,	Monmouth.
James B. Allen,	May 27, 1836,	
Joseph Amey,	November 3, 1844.	Lenox Township.
Elizabeth Amey,	November 3, 1844.	Lenox Township.
T. D. Allen,	June 18, 1835,	Floyd Township.
Mrs. Fidelia Allen,	October —, 1839.	Floyd Township.
John Armstrong,	——, 1834,	Spring Grove Township.
Mrs. John Armstrong,	——, 1833,	Spring Grove Township.
Wm. H. Armsby,	——, 1840,	Denver, Col.
I. J. Brooks,	July —, 1837,	
John Birdsall,	September 23, 1838.	Ellison Township.
William Birdsall,		Ellison Township.

OLD SETTLERS ORGANIZATION.—Continued.

NAME.	DATE OF SETTLEMENT.	REMARKS.
John Barnett,	June 24, 1837,	Ellison Township.
J. W. Bond,	December 24, 1834,	Swan Township.
William C. Blake,	December 15, 1837,	
H. Balding,	May 4, 1840,	Monmouth, Ills
James R. Brent,	March 14, 1836,	Ellison Township.
Kenner Brent, Sr.,	——— 1836,	Ellison Township.
E. C. Babcock,	May 1, 1842,	Monmouth, Ills.
Draper Babcock,	October 1, 1842,	Monmouth, Ills.
Mrs. W. W. Brown,	November 26, 1841,	Monmouth, Ills.
George Babcock,	May 1, 1842,	Monmouth, Ills.
Mrs. Hiram Baldwin,	May 4, 1840,	Monmouth, Ills.
C. R. Barnett,	May 14, 1841,	Ellison Township.
Charles Baldwin,	May —, 1834,	Sumner Township.
Mrs. C. Baldwin,	October 30, 1836,	Sumner Township.
Mrs. John Barnett,	June —, 1837,	Ellison Township.
Mrs. D. G. Balching,	May —, 1834,	Ellison Township.
Mrs. Jane Barton,	October —, 1831,	Sumner.
Mrs. Martha Bell,	August 1, 1843,	
William G. Bond,	———, 1834,	Monmouth.
Jacob L. Buzan,	———, 1832,	Monmouth.
Mrs. Mary A. Bruen,	March 6, 1840,	Monmouth.
John Bruen,	July 1, 1841,	Monmouth.
John C. Bond,	December —, 1834,	Greenbush.
Ira Barnum,		Tompkins Township.
O. S. Barnum,		Monmouth, Ills.
Ebenezer Chapin,	December 1, 1839,	Henderson County.
Mrs. Catharine Chapin,	December 1, 1839,	Henderson County.
N. A. Chapin,	December 1, 1839,	Henderson County.
Mrs. O. C. Chapin,	———, 1840,	Henderson County.
John Curts,	December 20, 1835,	Henderson County.
Frederick Curts,	June 4, 1836,	Henderson County.
A. P. Carmichel,	April 10, 1836,	Tompkins Township.
John W. Caldwell,	May 4, 1830,	Monmouth Township.
Richie Campbell,	March 10, 1829,	Hale Township.
Mary S. Campbell,	September —, 1836,	Hale Township.
G. W. Chapin,	February —, 1841,	Henderson County.
Mrs. G. W. Chapin,	February —, 1841,	Henderson County.
Asa Capps,	August —, 1840,	Lenox Township.
Benjamin C. Carter,	September 3, 1843,	Swan Township.
Mrs. Phoeba Cameron,	October —, 1832,	Hale Township.
William H. Cable,	———, 1835,	Berwick Township.
John Carruthers,		
Nancy Carruthers,	October —, 1836,	
Andrew Claycomb,	November —, 1835,	Monmouth.
Mrs. H. A. Claycomb,	October —, 1830,	Monmouth.
J. W. Coghill,		Roseville.
J. W. Davidson,	May 10, 1839,	Monmouth.
Daniel T. Denman,	April 15, 1836,	Died June, ———.

OLD SETTLERS' ORGANIZATION.—Continued.

NAME.	DATE OF SETTLEMENT.	REMARKS.
Thomas H. Davidson,	November 1, 1833,	Monmouth.
Mrs. Susan Davis,	April —, 1834,	Monmouth.
Capt. D. T. Denman,	———. 1835,	Died July, 1876.
Mrs. D. T. Denman,	———, 1835,	Monmouth.
William Dilley,	March —. 1841,	Roseville.
Jacob Emrick,	March 1, 1840,	Swan.
Mrs. Abigail Emrick,	March 1, 1840,	Swan.
Truman Eldridge,	November —, 1838.	Roseville.
Mrs. Truman Eldridge,	———, 1837,	Roseville.
Andrew J. Eby,	———, 1844,	Monmouth.
David M. Findley,	———, 1835,	Henderson County.
Benjamin F. Harward,	March —, 1838,	
John H. Frantz,	———, 1835,	Spring Grove Township.
Anna M. Frantz,	———. 1835,	Spring Grove Township.
R. F. Freeman,	November —, 1838,	Floyd Township.
David Graham,	June 16, 1836,	Monmouth.
Judson Graves,	June 18, 1836,	Tompkins.
Andrew J. Gibson,	May 27, 1834,	Henderson County.
L. M. Gates,	May 3, 1836,	Died August —, 1874.
William A. Grant,	September —, 1840,	Monmouth.
L. H. Gilmore,	June 10. 1833,	Spring Grove.
L. M. Gilmore,	September 5, 1835,	Spring Grove.
Mrs. Mary Garrison,	July 8, 1833,	Late of Monmouth.
John R. Gibson,	October —, 1830,	Henderson County.
Mrs. L. H. Gilmore,	March —, 1838,	Spring Grove.
Mrs. Mary J. Graham,	April —, 1836,	Monmouth.
Mrs. Phoebe Giddings,	April —, 1840,	Floyd Township.
Robert Gibson,	February —, 1836.	Monmouth.
James T. Gilmore,	June 8, 1832,	Spring Grove Township.
M. C. Gilmore,	———, 1832.	
Loren Giddings,	October —, 1841,	Floyd Township.
Samuel Hutchinson,	June 2, 1833,	Tompkins Township.
H. S. Haskell,	June 16, 1835,	Floyd Township.
Philip Harney,	April 1, 1835,	Cold Brook Township.
W. D. Henderson,	May 5, 1835,	Monmouth.
John B. Holiday,	March —, 1834,	Henderson County.
Mrs. M. E. Holiday,	October 10, 1835,	Henderson County.
A. C. Harding,	July 4, 1838,	Died July —. 1874.
Mrs. A. C. Harding,		Monmouth.
Walter Huston,		Henderson County.
Chancey Hardin,	August —. 1840,	Monmouth.
Mrs. Chancey Hardin,	August —, 1840,	Monmouth.
William Hanna,	November 3, 1835,	Monmouth.
Sarah Hanna,	———, 1833,	Monmouth.
Mrs. H. Henry,	February —, 1837,	Monmouth.
Benjamin Hutchinson,	June —, 1833,	Henderson County.
Mrs. B. Hutchinson,	June —, 1832,	Henderson County.
Margaret G. Huston,	———, 1833,	

OLD SETTLERS' ORGANIZATION.—Continued.

NAME.	DATE OF SETTLEMENT.	REMARKS.
H. P. Holcomb,		
Hiram Ingersoll.	October —, 1835,	Kelly Township.
Mrs. Celia E. Ingersoll.	———, 1832,	Kelly Township.
Jacob Jewell,	April —, 1839,	Monmouth.
James L. Junkin,	October 10, 1835,	Hale Township.
John B. Junkin.	October 10, 1835,	Henderson County.
J. C. Jamieson,	November 27, 1829.	Henderson County.
Rebecca J. Junkin,	November 6, 1841,	Hale Township.
F. M. Jamieson,	October —, 1832,	Henderson County.
Andrew Junkin,	October 10, 1835,	Hale Township.
W. P. Jones,	October —, 1835.	Swan Township.
Moses R. Jones,	———, 1839,	Cold Brook Township.
Israel Jared,	———, 1836,	Swan Township.
Mrs. I. Jared,	———, 1838,	Swan Township.
Francis B. Kendall,	October 6, 1838,	Monmouth Township.
John Kelley,	January 3, 1840,	Deceased.
F. F. Louther,	November 6, 1841,	Tompkins Township.
Daniel Lacock,	March 22, 1840,	Ellison Township.
George C. Lamphere,	March 10, 1838.	Galesburg.
Mrs. Julia A. M. Louther,	April 1, 1841,	Tompkins Township.
James Louther,	November 6, 1841,	Tompkins Township.
William Laut,	May —, 1839,	Tompkins Township.
William Laferty,	July 4, 1840,	Died January 5, 1877.
Mrs. Sarah Louther,	November —, 1841,	Tompkins Township.
H. M. Lewis,	———. 1835,	Berwick Township.
Mrs. Sarah Laferty,	November—, 1835.	Monmouth.
Jamieson Leeper,	October —, 1839,	Monmouth Township.
Parthenia Lockwood,	May —, 1835,	
Fielding A. Lair,	October —, 1832,	Spring Grove Township.
T. J. McMahill,	October 15. 1838,	Tompkins Township.
Andrew McKemson,	April —, 1838,	
Mrs. Eleanor McKemson,	April —, 1836,	
Benjamin H. Martin,	March 30, 1836,	Biggsville, Henderson Co.
Findley Martin,	May 5, 1835.	
Mrs. B. H. Martin,	March 31, 1836,	Biggsville, Henderson Co.
John McDill,	June 7, 1837,	Henderson County.
John McKinney, Jr.,	March 26, 1832.	Keithsburg.
Preston Martin,	March 30, 1836,	Biggsville, Henderson Co.
Robert Moore,	June 15, 1836,	Tompkins Township.
Samuel McElhanney,	October 7, 1839,	Henderson County.
Isaac McCowan,	October 1, 1836,	Henderson County.
Dr. William McMillan,	January —, 1835,	Henderson County.
George W. Morey,	October 20, 1841,	Floyd Township.
James A. McCoy,	April 26, 1836,	Monmouth.
Mrs. Maria M. McMahill,	September 1, 1841.	Tompkins Township.
Mrs. Nancy McCollum,	May 3, 1840,	Monmouth.
John Martin,	November —, 1832,	Sumner Township.
Mary J. Martin,	November —, 1832,	Sumner Township.

OLD SETTLERS' ORGANIZATION.—Continued.

NAME.	DATE OF SETTLEMENT.	REMARKS.
Hugh Martin,	November —, 1832,	Sumner Township.
Mary Martin,	November —, 1832.	Sumner Township.
M. McElhanney,	September 30, 1839,	Henderson County.
Mrs. Mary A. McClure,	September 30, 1836,	Monmouth.
James H. McQnown,	September 30, 1836,	Henderson County.
William W. McCullom,	May 3, 1840,	Monmouth.
A. O. McQuinn,	———, 1842,	Henderson County.
Sarah McQuinn,	———, 1848.	Henderson County.
David McIntyre,	April —, 1834.	Monmouth, Ills.
Margaret McIntyre,	October —, 1833,	Monmouth, Ills.
D. H. McCoy,	February —, 1838,	Hale Township.
William Marshall,	June 3, 1837,	Henderson County.
David Moler,	March —. 1832,	Sumner Township.
Joseph McCoy,	May —, 1838,	Monmouth Township.
William J. Miller.	———, 1834,	Spring Grove Township.
Mrs. William Miller,	———, 1834,	Spring Grove Township.
David H McCurry,	April —, 1836,	Spring Grove Township.
Mrs. Matthew Mitchell,	November —, 1830,	Henderson County.
John McKinney, Jr.,	———, 1835,	Mercer County.
John T. Morgan,	———, 1843,	Monmouth.
John McGrew,	August —. 1844,	Alexis.
John C. McDill,	November 10, 1838,	Henderson County.
W. A. Mitchell,	October 23, 1842,	Sumner County.
Col. William I. Nevins,	October —. 1832,	Mercer County, Ills.
Mrs. Mary Ann Nevins,	October —, 1832.	Mercer County, Ills.
Mrs. Mary Nutt,	———, 1835.	Monmouth.
J. I. Nevins,	August 21, 1838,	Mercer County.
Addison Nash,	———, 1832.	Hale Township.
Hugh Nash,	———, 1832.	Monmouth, Ills.
William F. Norcross,	November —, 1843,	Monmouth.
L. S. Olmstead,	October 28, 1836,	Hale Township.
Mrs. L. S. Olmstead,	October 28, 1836,	Hale Township.
John R. Owens,	April 25, 1830,	
John A. Pence,	December 1, 1830,	Henderson County.
Mrs. J. A. Pence,	December 1, 1830,	Henderson County.
J. B. Patterson,	September 2, 1834,	Oquawka, Ills.
Mrs. J. B. Patterson,	October 6, 1836,	Oquawka, Ills.
E. H. N. Patterson,	October 6, 1836,	Oquawka, Ills.
Azra Patterson,	December 31, 1836,	Monmouth.
Joshua Porter,	November 19, 1835.	Spring Grove. Died.
S. S. Phelps,	September 10, 1828.	Oquawka, Ills.
Barzillai Parker,	June 11, 1835,	Monmouth, Ills.
Thomas M. Paxton,	October —, 1831,	Swan Township.
William E. Porter,	September 16, 1839,	Spring Grove.
Mrs. Mary Porter,	———, 1835,	Spring Grove.
Mrs. Jane Paxton,	September —, 1833,	Swan Township.
Mrs. Mary F. Perkins,	November —, 1836,	
A. B. Page,	June 5, 1840,	Monmouth.

OLD SETTLERS' ORGANIZATION.—Continued.

NAME.	DATE OF SETTLEMENT.	REMARKS.
Porter Phelps,	May —, 1836,	Lenox Township.
Mrs. Porter Phelps,	May —, 1836,	Lenox Township.
Samuel D. Phelps,	May —, 1836,	Lenox Township.
Mrs. D. Phelps,	November —, 1834,	Lenox Township.
J. F. Pollock,	June —, 1837,	Sumner Township.
William S. Paxton,	October —, 1831,	
Erastus Rise,	July 7, 1837,	Died.
David Rankin,	April 15, 1836,	Henderson County.
Mrs. C. R. Ritchie,	July —, 1833,	Henderson County.
R. W. Ritchie,	November 1, 1840,	Henderson County.
T. A. Russell,	May 1, 1831,	Henderson County.
Jesse Riggs,	July —, 1837,	Lenox Township.
Thomas H. Rice,	May 20, 1835,	Monmouth.
John Robinson,	—————, 1829,	Spring Grove.
L. D. Robinson,	April 1, 1835,	Spring Grove.
Henderson Ritchie,	December 23, 1828,	1st white child born in Co.
William C. Rice,	May 24, 1835,	Oquawka.
T. G. Ritchie,	November 7, 1840,	Oquawka.
J. Louis Bagland,	March 2, 1831,	Cold Brook Township.
James Ryason,	October —, 1828,	Henderson County.
John Riggs,	April 8, 1834,	Lenox Township.
A. D. Rockwell,	June 18, 1832,	Sumner Township.
Thomas B. Record,	October —, 1829,	Henderson County.
Mary Record,	April —, 1830,	Henderson County.
Mrs. Mary E. Rockwell,	July —, 1832,	Sumner Township.
S. W. Rodgers,	April —, 1835,	Hale Township.
James W. Robertson,	July 7, 1843,	Lenox Township.
Joseph H. Ratekin,	September —, 1835,	Swan Township.
Thomas H. Rice,		Monmouth.
Mrs. Emily Ryder,	—————, 1833,	Tompkins Township.
Moses Robinson,	—————, 1844,	Floyd Township.
Mrs. L. P. Rockwell,		Sumner Township.
Allen Salisbury,	October —, 1838,	Ellison.
Mrs. S. C. Stocton,	—————, 1838,	Henderson County.
E. M. Stocton,	—————, 1838,	Henderson County.
W. J. Smith,	August 1, 1840,	
H. Simmons,	December 26, 1839,	Swan Township.
R. K. Sirson,	June —, 1837,	Swan Township.
James Scott,	May 22, 1836,	Monmouth.
A. H. Swain,	October —, 1855,	Monmouth.
Gabriel R. Short,	October —, 1830,	Henderson County.
Francis Stuart,	May 5, 1837,	
Thomas Strathers,	—————, 1839,	Monmouth.
H. F. Sexton,	April 1, 1840,	Ellison Township.
A. B. Sisson,	June 20, 1836,	Swan Township.
S. S. Salisbury,	October 20, 1838,	Ellison.
William F. Smith,	November 12, 1835,	Monmouth.
bner Short,	October —, 1830,	Henderson County.

OLD SETTLERS' ORGANIZATION.—Concluded

NAME.	DATE OF SETTLEMENT.	REMARKS.
Margaret Statt,	May 5, 1837,	Monmouth, Ills.
H. W. Simmons,	September —, 1840,	Swan Township.
A. J. Sirson,	June 12, 1837,	Swan Township.
Mrs. Irene P. Smith,	January 8, 1843,	Spring Grove Township.
John Struthers,	———, 1832,	Monmouth Township.
John B. Shelton,	November 24, 1837,	Floyd Township
Judge L. A. Simmons,	———, 1833,	McComb.
James H. Stewart,	———, 1830,	Monmouth.
Mrs. W. Shelton,	———, 1837,	Floyd Township.
Nancy J. Sisson,	May —, 1835,	Swan Township.
William H. Shaw,	December 10, 1840,	Died.
Joseph H. Tinkham,	November 19, 1835,	Tompkins Township.
William P. Thompson,	April 26, 1835,	Ellison Township.
Rosanna Tinkham,	November 3, 1836,	Tompkins Township.
Mrs. C. A. Tinkham,	———, 1836,	Tompkins Township.
Mrs. Joseph Tinkham,	January —, 1841,	Tompkins Township.
Benjamin Tinkham, Sr.,	November 1, 1836,	Floyd Township.
Mrs. Benjamin Tinkham,	April —, 1837,	Floyd Township.
Annie L. Turnbull,	October 29, 1832,	Henderson County.
Caroline J. Tucker,	July 20, 1835,	Swan Township.
John Tucker,	June 15, 1840,	Swan Township.
Jacob Vesburg,	September 1, 1841,	Tompkins Township.
Absalom Vendevere,	———, 1836,	Swan Township.
Mrs. A. Vendevere,	———, 1837,	Swan Township.
E. E. Wallace,	October 31, 1841,	Monmouth, Ills.
Daniel Woods,	September 26, 1841,	Died May 27, 1873.
Samuel Woods,	May 28, 1838,	Monmouth, Ills.
Andrew White,	July —, 1838,	Hale Township.
Newton Woods,	October —, 1839,	Tompkins Township.
Martin H. Woods,	June —, 1837,	Tompkins Township.
J. R. Webster,	May 15, 1837,	Monmouth, Ills.
J. H. Watson,	November 27, 1836,	Ellison.
William Wood,	October —, 1839,	Tompkins.
Mrs. Andrew White,	March —, 1833,	Hale Township.
Royal Wiswell,	October 20, 1839,	Floyd Township.
John Wallace,	October 5, 1833,	Monmouth, Ills.
C. H. Warner,	November —, 1836,	Tompkins Township.
Jane E. Warner,	July —, 1835,	Tompkins Township.
Mrs. J. R. Webster,	August —, 1838,	Monmouth.
Avery Worden,	April —, 1844,	Swan Township.
Isaac A. Watson,	———, 1835,	Ellison Township.
Mrs. Maria C. Woodward,		Monmouth.
Mrs. Sarah E. Wray,	———, 1833,	Tompkins Township.
Mrs. Sarah T. Whitmark,	September 2, 1833,	Cold Brook, Township.

THE OLDEST CHURCH IN WARREN COUNTY.

The first organized church in this county was near what is called "Sugar-Tree Grove," in Hale township. It was called the "Associate Presbyterian Church of Henderson;" the latter name from its supposed proximity to the Henderson river, seven miles distant. Some persons of this denomination, it seems, had settled in this vicinity as early as 1828, from Ohio. Earlier still, persons of the same church connection had settled in the southern part of this State, and in Missouri. From some of those in the latter State, a petition for supply of gospel ordinances was sent to the Associate Synod at its meeting in May, 1825. The result was, that the Synod resolved to occupy the States of Indiana, Illinois and Missouri. From this time forward, missionaries were appointed to labor a part of each year in each of these States. In 1830, Rev. James McCarrel was appointed to what was then called the Western Mission, and in November of that year he organized Henderson congregation. This took place at the house of John Caldwell. The names of twenty-five persons are recorded, who were received as members at the organization, and are as follows: Adam Ritchie, John Ritchie, Elizabeth Ritchie, Abigail Ritchie, Martha Ritchie, Jane Campbell, John Maley, John Kendall, Elizabeth Kendall, Samuel Gibson, Elizabeth Gibson, James Junkin, Sarah Junkin, Martha Junkin, Ann Junkin, William Gibson, Matthew Ritchie, Caroline Ritchie, Adam Ritchie, Sen., John Ritchie, Jr., Sarah Junkin, David Findley, Jane Findley, Margaret Temple and John W. Caldwell. Not one of these is now a member of this church—only five are living—and these at, or near, Monmouth. The first elders were: Adam Ritchie and John Caldwell. The first pastor was Rev. James C. Bruce, from Ohio, who first began to receive support from the congregation Oct. 15, 1832, though he had preached here for some time previous as a missionary. He was installed pastor May 11, 1833, by Rev. Samuel Ingalls and Adam Ritchie, elder, who were appointed for that purpose by the Presbytery of Miami, Ohio, to which this church then belonged. This pastorate continued until Oct. 25, 1847, after which the church was without a pastor for two years. On the 25th of Oct., 1849, Rev. John Scott, D. D., was installed pastor, and continued until 1868. The leading public event which occurred during this long pastorate, was the union of the Associate Reformed and Associate churches of the United States, forming the United Presbyterian Church. The union was consummated by the synods representing these churches at Pittsburgh, Pa., May 26, 1858, and afterward unanimously approved by this congregation.

Sometime in the autumn of 1868, a call was made out for T. G. Morrow, then a licentiate, and his ordination and installation as pastor took place in April, 1869. This pastorate continued for three years. In the fall of 1873, Rev. David A. Wallace, D. D., president of Monmouth College, became pastor, and continued until failing health from many laborious duties compelled him to resign in January, 1876. The present pastor is Rev. David McDill, D. D., professor in Monmouth College.

The first house of worship in this county was built by this congregation in 1832. It was made of logs, and was 24 by 30 feet. It was used for worship until 1839, when it was far too small to accommodate the congregation. Some persons often came as far as twenty miles to attend church.

In 1837 a move was made to build a large brick church, near the first. The brick were made upon the ground near by, and heavy foundation walls of stone, three feet thick, were laid, upon which arose the spacious edifice 50 by 64 feet—a wonder for those days—which cost over $4,000. This house, too, was often filled to overflowing in those early days. It was used for worship for thirty-five years—from 1839 to 1874. The present neat and elegant structure, 40 by 60 feet, built in 1874, stands near a beautiful grove, and is hardly surpassed in its attractiveness by any edifice in the county. It cost, including fixtures and furnace, $4,252, and is all paid.

The present membership of this church is 120, and the congregation is in a prosperous condition. This church has received, since its organization, about 700 members. Many have taken certificates to aid in the formation of other churches. As an outgrowth from this "oldest church in the county," and from Cedar Creek church, there are at the present time nine United Presbyterian churches, with about 2,000 members.

The Cedar Creek church, in Sumner township, was organized July 4, 1835, as Associate Reformed, by Rev. Dr. Blakie, now of Boston, Mass. It was first called by the very appropriate name, "Sharon Church," and was the first of this denomination in this county, and probably for many contiguous counties in this region.

The following names are found upon the oldest record as the persons constituting the church at the time organized: John Giles, ruling elder; James Giles, John P. Giles, Hugh Martin, Prudence Giles, Nancy Giles, Susannah Giles, Margaret Giles, Mary L. Giles, Susan Giles, Jane Giles, John Williamson, James Campbell, Mary Findley, James Findley, Nancy Robinson, George Jay and Mary A. Jay—eighteen in all. Dr. Blakie had been sent out as a missionary of the church into the new settlements of the West, and when he found a few who had been members of churches where they had previously lived, he gathered them into a church.

Prior to his coming, Rev. John Wallace, also a missionary, from Monroe county, Va., had preached several times at the houses of some of the settlers, and was employed by the congregation, after the organization, as stated supply for a portion of his time from 1835 to 1840. The first elders were J. C. McCrery, Wm. Walker and Maj. John Brown. Rev. James C. Porter came here in 1840, and was the first pastor—installed in 1841, and continued until near the time of his death, which occurred Nov. 15, 1863. It was during this pastorate that the membership largely increased. Also, in 1858, this church joined in the union and thus became United Presbyterian.

Rev. John A. Reynolds began his work in this church in August, 1863, and remained pastor until July, 1872, nine years.

The present pastor is Rev. J. M. Atchison, who commenced his labors here Dec. 1, 1872.

This congregation has built three houses of worship. The first was of logs, built in 1836, and stood about two miles northeast from Little York. This was occupied until 1845, when a larger and better edifice was needed, and a frame structure was erected near the first, and was occupied as a house of worship over twenty years. The present commodious house was built in 1866, cost about $4,000, and stands in a beautiful grove, three miles northeast from Little York. This congregation also own a pleasant parsonage, situated one mile north of the church. Not one of the original members is now connected with this congregation; only two are known to be living—

Mrs. Wallace, widow of Rev. John Wallace, and Mrs. Jamison, now in Florida. The present membership is 140. The total contributions for last year, as reported, for all church purposes were about $2,500, averaging nearly twenty dollars per member, showing a very generous liberality. This congregation is in a growing and prosperous condition, has a flourishing Sabbath-school, averaging 110, Superintendent Zenas Hogue, and a large weekly district prayer meeting, well attended by old and young.

THE COUNTY FARM.

Until the year 1857, the poor in the county were kept by the townships. They were generally given to the "lowest bidder," as it was termed, to the one who would maintain them at the least expense to the county. In almost all cases these were the relatives of the person so kept. This method was unsatisfactory. In June of that year the county, through Porter Phelps and Hiram Norcross as its agents, purchased one hundred and twenty acres of Luther Dickson for $3,360, and on this tract a house was erected at an expense of $2,000, for this class of persons.

Soon after Albert Mitchell, Esq., was appointed Superintendent, and in 1859 the rules regulating this institution were adopted.

The institution is now in a good condition, occupying a commodious frame house. The farm is about five miles southwest of Monmouth, and at present sustains quite a number of inmates.

SCHOOL COMMISSIONERS, SCHOOL LANDS, TRUSTEES AND COUNTY SUPERINTENDENTS.

The initiatory steps in the Educational development of Warren County consisted in the election of the proper officers for disposing of school lands, the custodians of the funds raised, and the organization of districts. The first event in this direction occurred at a regular meeting of the County Commissioners' Court, held in Monmouth, Sept. 5th, 1831. This court consisted of Peter Butler and John B. Talbot, County Commissioners; Daniel McNeil, County Clerk; and James Ryerson, Sheriff. Alexis Phelps was appointed School Commissioner, and executed his bond for $12,000, with Peter Butler, John B. Talbot and Sheldon Lockwood sureties, which was approved and filed Sept. 7, 1831. At the same term of this court, Robert Kendall, James Murphy and Daniel McNeil were appointed Trustees.

These officers proceeded at once to sub-divide the school section into lots from 1 to 25 inclusive, and pursuant to public notice, said lands and lots were offered at public sale Oct. 27, 1831. The aggregate amount of lands and lots sold at auction on that day was 200 acres, ranging in price from $1.25 to $1.62½ per acre. The remainder of the section was sold at private sale, and the first annual report of the Commissioner shows, total amount received, $1,754.46; deducting expenses, net proceeds, $1,398.38.

In the spring of 1832 the following persons were appointed Trustees of Sumner Township: Hugh Martin, Anthony Cannon and James Barton. Lands were offered for sale Sept. 8, 1834. Eighty acres were sold to John G. Barton at $1.25 per acre.

In Floyd Township Trustees were appointed Dec. 2, 1833, as follows: Wm. Whitman, John G. Haley and Joseph Murphy. Land was sold Sept. 8, 1834, to Alexander Davidson, Elijah Davidson, Carter Davidson and Josiah Whitman, 80 acres each, at $1.25 per acre.

Trustees for Hale Township were appointed March 6, 1834: Wm. Nash, Adam Ritchie and James Findley. Lands sold Sept. 8, 1834, to William Nash 200 acres, David Turnbull 80 acres, each at $1.25 per acre.

Coldbrook Township Trustees, appointed June 2, 1834. Lands first offered for sale May 1, 1835.

Greenbush Trustees appointed April 21, 1834. Lands sold March 7, 1836 Berwick lands sold Dec. 7, 1835.

Tompkins sales were made March 19, 1836.

Ellison lands sold March 31, 1836, and here terminates the official records of Alexis Phelps, the first school commissioner of this county. He was succeeded by Wyat S. Berry, who sold the school lands of Swan Township for $4,070.90, Jan. 15, 1838.

The next sale of lands was the 16th Sec. of Roseville Township, July 29, 1839, for $1,029.60. Then lands of Kelly Township, Sept. 28, 1840, for $1,433.10. Samuel Wood was next appointed School Commissioner, and he sold a part of the lands of Spring Grove Township, Dec. 14, 1843. This officer was succeeded by James G. Madden, during whose term of office, by act of the Legislature, the School Commissioner became *ex-officio* Superintendent of schools.

The following comprises a list of school commissioners and *ex-officio* superintendents: W. B. Jenks, Wm. F. Smith, A. H. Tracy, V. S. Harbaugh, Willis B. Greer, F. B. Bond, Wm. H. Pierce, A. B. Cox and Ira B. Harsh, whose term of office expired in Dec. 1865. By act of the Legislature of 1865, Sec. 11 of the school law was so amended that the office of school commissioner terminated, and created the office of County Superintendent. G. I. Willson was the first elected to this office, and continued the allotted time, four years. In 1870 J. B. Donnell, the present incumbent, succeeded to this office.

SCHOOLS.

The low rate at which the school lands were sold—being in most cases not more than six per cent. of what was their real value a few years later—failed to create an endowment sufficient to establish and maintain a system of public schools. Hence schools were not "free," and while we had all the machinery of a public school system, a small per cent. only of the expense was paid from the public funds. In order, then, to maintain schools, rate-bills were established.

The first school-house built in this county was at Sugar-Tree Grove, in Hale Township, in 1832. It was made of logs, and was 14x16 ft. For windows there was one log sawed out, and small panes of glass placed in around the room. The floor was puncheon, as also were the seats and desks. This house was used for school for about eight years, when it was burned. The first teacher in the county taught this school, Miss Martha Junkin, from Ohio. People came from the distance of four and five miles, showing much interest under the difficulties experienced in early education, as in other matters.

On March 6, 1834, School District No. 1, Monmouth Township was organized, consisting of twelve sections in said township, and four sections in Hale Township. We give below a verbatim copy of the first annual reports of Trustees of Monmouth District No. 1, filed in October, 1834.

"There are in this district fifty children over five and under twenty-one years of age. There has been a school kept three months since the organization of this district. Twenty-five children have received tuition. The probable expense will be forty-five dollars.

GILBERT TURNBULL,
 JAMES McCALLON, } Trustees."

This school was "kept" in a log house with a dirt floor, and used for the common purpose of church, court house and school. It was situated on the southeast corner of Main and North streets, and afterwards used for a blacksmith shop. In 1835 a small frame school house was built on the present site of the M. E. Church, but by no means were all the educational advantages afforded the youth in those days, to be found in the public schools. In fact, they were not provided till about twenty years later. It was at best but little cheaper nor more efficient than the private or select schools. Good and efficient teachers were sometimes employed, but after serving one or two terms, it was common for them to throw off the restraints of a School Board, and set up independently. Among the earlier teachers whose names are remembered, are Messrs. McElray, Crandall, Weltman, Kellum, Randall and Gilbert Turnbull. The first female teacher was Mrs. Montgomery, who taught in her own room in a house on the present site of B. Parkes dwelling. This room was afterwards rented to Miss Paine, now Mrs. Gibson, who taught successfully for a number of terms.

Mr. Wellman, who seems to be most distinctly remembered as a pedagogue, taught in a log house, on the northeast corner of Broadway and West Avenue. Other rooms were occupied, from time to time. R. D. Hammond was the last teacher to occupy the old pioneer school house. Robert Gibson taught at the same time, on the north side of the square, where now stands J. B. Martin's market house. In 1848, the pioneer house was removed, and a more pretending edifice erected on the same ground. It had now become the duty of teachers to obtain certificates of qualification from the Commissioner, who was by law also Superintendent of Schools. In 1854, a Mr. Gray, teacher in the public school, abandoned it, "because," to use his own words, "it didn't pay." At the same time, W. B. Jenks was teaching a flourishing private school in the Presbyterian church, and Miss Julia Madden another in the Christian church. The public school was revived again by Mr. A. H. Tracy, who opened his first term with nineteen pupils, and closed with ninety-one. Mr. Tracy, assisted by his wife, taught with success for several terms. In October, 1855, all public schools were made free, by virtue of the two mill tax.

And here dates a new era in the history of schools of the county and state. The first effect of this change was to kill out the private or select schools, which had been so largely relied upon, and to more than double the number of pupils seeking instruction. Public attention was at once directed to the necessity of providing more ample accommodations; and new school houses became the order of the day. Something more than ample funds and good houses was required to meet the growing responsibilities, resulting from the new order of things, and what was true of Warren county, was equally so of the state at large. At a state convention of education, held in Chicago, in December, 1856, much interest and new life was given to the system of public instruction, resulting from its deliberations. Among those who took active part in discussions, were Newton Bateman, Wm. Bross, Simeon Wright, Supt. Wells, and Prof. Turner. At this convention it was determined to employ a state agent, for one year, to labor throughout the state in the interest of the public schools; whose salary was $1,800, to be paid by contributions. Warren county was represented in the convention by John A. Gordon, A. H. Tracy, and D. R. Stevens. Prof. Simeon Wright was selected for the work of state agent, and Warren county enjoyed his services for a number of days. The result proved all the most sanguine had hoped. Graded schools sprang up as by magic, all over the state, and public opinion took a long stride in the direction of progress and reform, and from these labors and efforts are due the present type of public instruction.

WARREN COUNTY AGRICULTURAL SOCIETY.

The Warren County Agricultural Society was organized August 7, 1852, at a public meeting held at the court house in Monmouth. The following temporary officers were then selected: Samuel Hallam, President; J. G. Madden, Secretary; G. W. Palmer, Vice President; F. B. Weakley, Treasurer. The first annual election was held September 4, 1852, resulting as follows: Samuel Hallam, President; Robt. Gibson, Vice President; J. G. Madden, Secretary; Wm. Billings, Treasurer.

The first annual Fair was held in the court house on Friday, Oct. 15, 1852. One thousand people were in attendance. The premiums consisted of certificates, no cash prizes being offered. From this small beginning the Society's annual exhibition has advanced to a position as one of the best County Fairs in the state. Over $3,000 are annually offered in premiums; the Fair is continued four days, and the total yearly attendance is about twenty-five thousand. Fair week is observed as a general holiday, and entire families flock in from all parts of Warren and adjacent counties. The Society owns extensive grounds, and suitable and commodious buildings, valued at about $12,000.

The present officers of the association are: President, John B. McGinnis; Vice President, A. H. Swain; Secretary, Geo. C. Rankin; Treasurer, Robt. M. Stevenson. Executive Committee: R. S. Patton, C. L. Buck, C. Hardin, L. D. Robinson, J. T. Richards, H. D. Harding, J. E. Alexander, E. R. Houlton, L. H. Gilmore.

The twenty-sixth annual Fair will occur September 11, 12, 13, and 14, 1877.

WARREN COUNTY LIBRARY AND READING ROOM ASSOCIATION.

This Library has resulted from a number of movements in the direction of a Public Library. The matter was considered and discussed in a variety of forms, for years before it reached a successful organization.

In 1867 the attempt was made to start a Library as a joint stock association; but the subscriptions were insufficient. The same year, the Evangelical Union of Monmouth, composed of representatives of the churches in Monmouth, took the subject under consideration, and gave it a new impulse. After consultation with many citizens, who were willing to assist, it was determined to form a corporation independent of the Evangelical Union.

It was evident that a Public Library, such as was demanded to meet the wants, common and special, of this intelligent community, would need a large amount of money given for this purpose. Accordingly, a Trust Corporation was organized, after the manner of many of the oldest and most successful institutions of the East, for benevolent and educational purposes. The Constitution and Rules were drafted by Hon. Ivory Quimby, whose sound judgment and deep interest in the project assured a good beginning in this important respect. He also provided a room, free of expense, until his death.

Twenty-five persons became responsible for the sum of twenty-five hundred dollars, for the purpose of sustaining a Reading Room during two years. These original Incorporators and Directors were the following: J. E. Alexander, F. E. Armsby, Draper Babcock, F. M. Bruner, W. G. Bone, J. S. Clark, J. L. Dryden, Chancy Hardin, Robert Holloway, A. H. Holt, J. M. Jameison, Wm. Laferty, James Long, R. C. Matthews, W. P. Pressly, D. P. Phelps, Ivory Quimby, N. A. Rankin, J. K. Ripley, T. H. Rogers, E. R. Smith, A. H. Swain, Wm. Smiley, D. A. Wallace, J. R. Webster.

A Reading Room, well supplied with papers and periodicals was opened June 1st, 1868, under the name of the Monmouth Reading Room and Library. This was sustained for two years. No books were bought, as there were no funds for that purpose.

During all this time, unknown to any one, these small beginnings were closely considered by a friend, who was only waiting to see the evidences of permanent success and usefulness. Early in the year 1870, Mr. W. P. Pressly made an offer of the gift of a Library Building, which he erected the same year. This building was given with the condition, that the net rents of the two storerooms on the first floor should be used to buy books, and the second story should be used as a Library Hall and Reading Room. He expressed the desire that the plan of the Library should be enlarged, so as to benefit the country as well as the city. The following are his published words: "Insomuch as under God we are principally indebted to the citizens of the country for the means to be used in its construction, if for no higher motive, gratitude towards them bids us now remember them as a party to be benefited, and thus made a party interested in patronizing and sustaining their own Institution." It was therefore legally incorporated as "The Warren County Library and Reading Room Association," and special provisions were made for the benefit of readers in the country.

The same year the Board of County Supervisors united in the permanent founding of the Library, by making a grant thereto "Of all rents, profits and issues hereafter accruing from the Seminary Block," and receiving the right in the Constitution of the Association to appoint one of the Trustees. Dr. Henry Tubbs has held that position ever since, by repeated appointments from the Board of Supervisors. Under his judicious supervision, the Constitution was amended, making equitable provision for the entire county.

The income from the County Grant is required to be devoted to the purchase of books, most of which must be in the Department of Agriculture and the Practical Arts. In this way, according to the Charter, any Department can be founded, bearing the name of the founder, and restricted to any special class of books.

The plan of extending the use of the Library to the country, has been eminently a success. It is used in every township in the county; and it has brought within its sphere a population sufficiently large to support and use a strong and well equipped library. For this purpose the population of the city alone is not sufficient, as the general experience of libraries has shown. The hand that gave to the Library this opportunity for extended usefulness has continued to strengthen and cherish it. It has received from him, again and again, for the purpose of printing a catalogue, for the enlargement of the lot, and for the increase of the endowment fund. This community has never received from any other citizen as large a public gift as it has from Mr. Pressly.

As the Library was founded for the benefit of all, it has been sustained and favored by all classes of citizens in town and country. The young and the old are constantly to be seen at its tables. The ladies, by various efforts, furnished the room, and none frequent it more than they. Farmers for ten or fifteen miles around use the books and magazines in their homes. Professional men and business men have given freely to its support in money, and what is equally important, in careful attention to its interests. Foremost among such should be named the late and lamented Wm. Laferty, who was for eight years its treasurer. Each year he gave it a generous gift, and he gave to it much time and affectionate attention. His practical business ability and excellent judgment have been of untold value to it during these years when its character was forming.

Much of the work which has made the Library successful has been gratuitously done by the officers, trustees, directors and various committees. The business matters have always been in the hands of careful business men in the Committees on the Building and on Finance, and on the Auditing Committee. The selection of reading matter is done by a committee representing both town and county. A committee on Book Notices calls attention through the press to the best reading. A committee of Reference give their aid in the room to readers desiring information or guidance. A cataloguing committee does the current cataloguing and prepares the bulletins.

The most approved methods of library management are in use. A printed catalogue was issued in 1874, and monthly bulletins have been printed since, showing what accessions have been made. An indicator shows what volumes or magazines are on the shelves, and what are in use. A card catalogue has just been constructed, from the bulletins, to supplement the catalogue of 1874. Special manuscript bulletins are posted up in the room from time to time, giving lists of works on subjects of present interest. Readers are urged to recommend books for purchase, with the assurance that such will be bought unless good reason exists to the contrary. New books are bought each month. The reading is fresh, popular and wholesome. The selections are made with careful fairness toward all classes of readers, and careful regard for the good of the community. That which is worthless or immoral is not bought, or is withdrawn if accidentally obtained.

The proportion of books bought in different departments is determined mainly by the reading and requests of adult readers, except where special funds are provided for some department, as is the case for works on agriculture and the useful arts. According to this rule the selections are about one-third in science, arts, philosophy and general literature; one-third in history, biography and travels; one-third in fiction and poetry.

The number of volumes in the library (April 2, 1877,) is 4,850. Of these 600 have been donated by citizens, and 4,250 purchased. For this purpose the Pressly rents produce one thousand dollars per year, and the county grant about three hundred dollars per year. About 800 volumes are added each year. One hundred and twenty magazines and papers are regularly received. Many of these are gifts from friends. The last year's circulation of books was 16,564. The daily attendance in the reading room averages about 120. About 1,000 persons use the library. The permanent funds have increased each year by donations and sale of perpetual tickets. That which is received by gift goes to the permanent upbuilding of the institution. The small charge made for the use of the library is only intended to cover current expenses, as salaries, fuel, etc. The building and books are provided without expense to readers. Many of the citizens of the county have obtained perpetual tickets, giving to their families the continual use of the library. About one-half the settled ministers of the county now have free use of the library by the kindness of friends who have purchased this right for them. This privilege is gladly extended in this way to any person or class for whom tickets are provided, either annual or perpetual. The library has one price and one rule for all. The charge is as low as it can safely be made. But there is no limit to the extent to which perpetual free tickets can be endowed by those who wish to benefit others, or their own families, in this way.

It is needful to remember that only six years have elapsed since the library was first opened for loan of books. Its plan includes many important features not yet attempted for want of sufficient means, such as a free reading room, branch libraries at other points, special departments of books not in general demand, full and frequent catalogues, endowed free tickets, and methods of extending the usefulness of the institution.

In all that has been done, this rule has been constantly followed : " Pay as you go." This principle has been impressed upon the enterprise by the prudent business men who have founded and prohibited the incurring of debts and the attempting of more than the means warrant. Thus a foundation has been laid, broad and deep, on which the future will build. Already, as a county library it has no superior, and it has obtained a high name and position among the public libraries of the West.

CIRCUIT CLERK
MONMOUTH ILLS.

THE WARREN COUNTY SUNDAY SCHOOLS.

The Warren County Sunday Schools are sixty-five in number at date of last annual report of the County S. S. Association, October, 26-7, 1876; have an attendance of seven thousand persons, about one-third of whom are adults and two-thirds children. These are not quite half the children of school age in the county. The Sunday schools are nearly all connected with the churches, and nearly every church organization has its Sunday school. *The International Series of Uniform Lessons* is in use by most of the schools.

The Sunday schools are located in the several townships as follows: Kelly, 4; Sumner, 2; Monmouth, 9; Floyd, 4; Tompkins, 5; Roseville, 5; Greenbush, 4; Point Pleasant, 1; Spring Grove, 6; Hale. 3; Coldbrook, 3; Lenox, 5; Ellison, 6; Berwick, 4; Swan, 4.

The religious denominations are represented as follows: Methodist Episcopal, 17; Baptist, (one colored), 11; United Presbyterian, (one colored), 11; "Union," 8; Christian, 7; Presbyterian, 3; United Brethren, 2; Church of God, 2; Advent Christian, 1; Methodist, 1; Congregational, 1; Evangelical Lutheran (Swede), 1.

Officers of County Sunday School Association are J. L. Dryden, Monmouth, President; C. W. Boydston, Cameron, Vice President; John A. Gordon, Roseville, Secretary; Dr. N. M. Brown, Monmouth, Treasurer.

COUNTY OFFICERS.

County Judge, Elias Willits; County Clerk, Wm. H. Sexton; Circuit Clerk, James L. Dryden; Treasurer, James H. Herdman, Sheriff, Wm.G. Bond; Coroner, R. H. McCleary; Surveyor, Thos. S. McClanahan; School Supt., J. B. Donnell.

TOWNSHIP OFFICERS, 1877.

Monmouth.—George Sickmon, Supervisor; O. S. Barnum, Asst. Sup.; F. R. Lincoln, Town Clerk; A. R. Kingsbury, Assessor; T. G. Barton. Collector; J. W. Sipher, School Trustee; W. M. Webb, C. Coats, S. McClanahan, S. G. Morris, John Lorimer, Constables; J. B. Clarke, W. D. Henderson, W. J. Walker, J. P. Foster, Avery Downer, Justices of the Peace; Amos. Burford, Commissioner of Highways; A. T. Bruner, N. P. Baymont, Alonzo Grover, H. M. Frantz, Overseers Highways.

Tompkins.—J. E. Barnes, Supervisor; J. H. Gilmore. Town Clerk; A. H. McCoy, Assessor; C. K. Brown, Collector; W. E. Drain, A. H. Walker, Justices of the Peace; Z. Daugherty, J. S. Faris, Constables; Louis Roberts, Commissioner of Highways 3 yrs.; Geo. W. Kellogg, School Trustee.

Cold Brook.—J. T. Hartman, Supervisor; Wm. Mills, Town Clerk; James Bruington, Assessor; E. C. Atchison, Collector; Geo. Bruington, Commissioner of Highways; Wm. Mills and S. T. Shelton, Justices of the Peace; Chas. Griffee and S. J. Blair; J. L. Ragland, School Trustee.

Berwick.—H. M. Lewis, Supervisor; J. V. Lewis, Town Clerk; W. D. Miller, Assessor; J. V. Lewis, Collector; J. Kirby, Commissioner of Highways; E. W. Allen and D. R. Day, Justices of the Peace; A. M. Ray and Jeff's'n. Day, Constables; John Yates, School Trustee.

Spring Grove.—L. H. Gilmore and R. W. Gerlaw received 139 votes each, and had to draw lots for the office, Supervisor. Gilmore got it. T. B. Patterson, 17 maj., Town Clerk; R. W. Lair, 8 maj., Assessor; F. A. Boggs, 26 maj., Collector; Angus McCoy, 21 maj., Commissioner of Highways; A. J. Richey, 32 maj., School Trustee; T. R. Squires, 32 maj.. J. N. Kinkaid, no opposition, Justices of the Peace; Stephen Gamble, 16 maj.. David Foust, 20 maj., Constables.

Kelly.—Nathan Cain, Supervisor; S. Beebe, Town Clerk; W. O. Hulse, Assessor; John Armstrong, Collector; D. Clary, Commissioner of Highways; O. N. Kellogg, School Trustee; S. Glass and A. Thomas, Justices of the Peace; M. Glass and James Clute, Constables.

Floyd.—J. W. Bolen, Supervisor; H. C. Higgins, Town Clerk; C. T. Cross, Assessor; D. C. Wiggins, Collector; D. C. Graham, C. T. Cross, Justices of the Peace; James Fry, Jas. Cross, Constables; S. C. Giddings, Commissioner of Highways; Benjamin Mattison, School Trustee.

Roseville.—Alphens Lewis, Supervisor; John A. Gorden, Town Clerk; Reuben Holeman, Assessor; R. L. McReynolds, Collector; Hiram T. Lape, Commissioner of Highways; Clement Pierce and J. Henry Saylor, Justices of the Peace; John Powell, Levi H. Gaunt, Constables; S. M. Eldred, School Trustee; Dist. No. 1, G. W. Gunther; 2, Henderson Ray; 3, Richard Ray; 4, Alfred Hays; 5, Nathan W. Haines; 6, Elijah Miller; 7, Thomas L. Newbern; 8, D. P. Underwood; 9, R. B. Woodward; 10, Isaac L. Pratt—Overseers of Highways.

Ellison.—E. Mitchell, Supervisor; C. Brooks, town Clerk; J. C. Morris, Assessor; A. M. Meacham, Collector; C. Brooks, Com. of Highways; J. C. Morris, J. P. Pendarvis, Justices of the Peace; John Godfrey, Jesse Hoag, Constables; A. P. Livermore, School Trustee; Dist. No. 1, John Ewing; 2, Marion Salisbury; 3, A. B. Yoho; 4, S. L. Charter; 5, A. K. Morris; 5, Andrew McLoughlin; 7, John Godfrey; 8, Jonu C. Beasley; 9, James Wright—Commissioners of Highways.

Lenox.—Lenox elects a straight, clean, clear Democratic ticket—no bull-dozing, no going behind the returns. The following are the town officers: David R. Smith, Supervisor; E. D. Lehan, Town Clerk; G. M. Saylor, Assessor; J. L. Young, Collector; Joseph Saylor, Com. of Highways; J. W. Ray, John Hodgson, Justices of the Peace; E. D. Lehan, J. R. Smith, Constables; R. A. Elliott, School Trustee.

Swan.—Geo. W. Beckner, Supervisor; Warren G. Thomas, Town Clerk; Geo. W. Beckner, Assessor; Warren G. Thomas, Collector; D. L. Crawford, School Trustee; B. A. Reed, Com. of Highways; Geo. W. Beckner, B. L. Atchison, Justices of the Peace; Isaac Davis, W. O. Kidder, Constables; Dist. No. 1, Isaac Davis; 2, John Kelsey; 3, George Stice; 4, J. H. Lippy; 5, R. A. Holeman; 6, Matthew Campbell; 7, Henry Morris; 8, Joseph Cunningham; 9, Henry VanKirk—Overseers of Highways.

Greenbush.—Supervisor, Lynn M. Greene; Town Clerk, A. L. Wingate;

Assessor, Vincent W. Butler; Collector, Orlando Dameville; Commissioners of Highways, V. W. Butler, Thomas Wilson ; Justices of the Peace, Vincent W. Butler, James F. Hartford ; Constable, C. W. Lauck ; School Treasurer, G. M. Spears ; Overseers of Highways, 1st district, T. B. Moulton ; 2d district, W. F. Smith ; 3d district, Leonard Hale ; 4th district, C. W. Lock.

Point Pleasant.—Assessor, Thomas Pennington ; Town Clerk, Jas. P. Chapman ; Assessor, Ira W. Davis ; Collector, G. W. Moore ; Commissioner of Highways, A. B. Higginson ; Justices of the Peace, J. B. O'Neall, Joseph Tucker ; Constable, Isaac Concher ; School Treasurer, W. T. Boyd. Overseers of Highways, 1st district, Eli Dixson ; 2d district, John J. Boyd ; 3d district, John Watson ; 4th district, Joseph Phillhower ; 5th district, Benjamin Sampson ; 6th district, Ira M. Davis ; 7th district, John Vankirk ; 8th district, Will Duble ; 9th district, George Torrence.

MONMOUTH.

On the 27th day of January, 1831, the Legislature appointed John G. Sanborn, Hazen Dedell, and John McNeil, commissioners, to locate the permanent seat of justice, and on the 7th of April following they, in a sealed package, directed to the county commissioners :

"Respectfully report that we have located the seat of justice for said county, on the south-west quarter of Section twenty-nine, in township Eleven North, and range Two west of the Fourth principal meridian, which said quarter section is reported and believed to be Congress land, and they have given the said seat of justice the name of MONMOUTH."

At the court, held June 12, 1831, orders for proposals to erect a court-house were issued as follows : * * * "That said proposals be received, and contracts entered into for the purpose of building a court-house of twenty by twenty-two feet on the ground, nine feet between the sleepers and joists, to be built of logs hewn down inside and out, and finished as the county commissioners shall direct, at the time and place aforesaid, and in such lot as they shall designate."

The contract for building the court-house, after the usual manner of crying it, was let to Francis Kendall for the sum of fifty-seven dollars. To this he was allowed three dollars for additional expense incurred. The Commissioners' Court had met just six days previous to this, and ordered a sale of lots in the town of Monmouth. The site had been surveyed by the surveyor, Peter Butler, for which he received twenty-one cents per lot, three hundred and twenty stakes being required. The order for sale read as follows : " The highest and best bidder to be the purchaser, provided the large or out lots be not sold, unless the bid offered shall amount to at least two dollars per acre.

"The bid on the in lots be not less than four dollars per lot, and those adjoining the public square not to be sold unless the bid offered be at least ten dollars per lot.

"The lots will be offered, with a few exceptions, alternately, and the purchaser or purchasers will receive a certificate of purchase, and required to give three separate notes of equal payments with approved security, payable in twelve, eighteen and twenty-four months, subject to a discount of twelve and a half per cent. on all moneys paid for said lots before due, calculating from the time paid; also subject to a discount of twelve and a half per cent. on the amount or price of each lot, on which a comfortable cabin or dwelling-house, store, grocery, or mechanic's shop shall be erected and finished suitable to live in, within one year from the sale of said lot."

At this sale, held on June 6th, forty-six purchases were made and recorded, aggregating in value $965.62¼.

At the Special Term of the Commissioners' Court, held July 9, 1830, it was

"On motion, ordered, That the temporary county seat of justice, or place of holding County Commissioners courts and Circuit courts, for the county of Warren, be held (until the permanent seat be located) at the upper house of Mr. Alexis Phelps, at the Yellow Banks, now Oquawka, Henderson county, on fractional section Fifteen, in town Eleven north of Range Five West."

The court-house was ready for occupancy early in the summer, and the records (what few there were) were at once taken there. During the summer and autumn but six buildings were erected, beside the court-house and jail. The former occupied the lot afterwards purchased by Capt. D. T. Denman, and on which his residence stood, while the latter was situated on the lot afterwards occupied by the wagon shop of William T. Henry.

The first settlers were Daniel McNeil, Joel Hargrove, and Elijah Davidson, of whom one, the latter, is now living.

The first mentioned of these persons opened the pioneer store of Monmouth; Daniel McNeil, the second; Stapp and Berry, the third, and the fourth by McCallon and Gibson.

To open a grocery at that time, it was necessary to obtain a town license, in which generally was specified the prices to be charged for articles used in the keeping of customers. It appears that these trades people were accustomed to often combine the privilege of entertaining travelers with the grocery business, as there is on record in the county office many items like the following:

"For each meal victuals, - - - 25 cents.
"For each night's lodging, - - - 6¼ cents.
"For horse kept over night, - - - 25 cents.
"For horse feed. - - - 12½ cents.
"For ½ pint whiskey, gin, rum, wine or cordial, 12½ cents.
"For ½ pint peach, French or apple brandy, 25 cents."

The above "scale of prices" was granted on November 25, 1835, when Warren county contained, according to a census taken then, 2,623 inhabitants, and was twenty-six miles broad and thirty-six miles long; and when Monmouth contained but seven houses, according to some authorities, and about eighty inhabitants, although, by the close of the year 1837, there were eighty houses and 400 inhabitants.

At the December term of the County Commissioners Court, in 1834, the first license to keep a tavern in Monmouth was granted to James M. Garrison, who gave a bond of $200, and paid for this license $5.00. The following were the rates fixed in the license:

"Each meal of victuals, - - - - 25 cents.
"Lodging per night, - - - - - 12½ cents.
"Or if single bed be demanded, - - 6¼ cents.
"Keeping horse per night, - - - 25 cents.

"Single feed for horse, - - - - - 12½ cents.
"Each half pint of wine, rum, gin or brandy of any kind, 25 cents.
"(Less quantity in same proportion.)
"Each half pint of whiskey, - - - - 12½ cents.
"Each gill of whiskey, - - - - - 6¼ cents."

The licenses for opening stores were generally from seven to ten dollars, and were renewable each year. S. Phelps & Co. were granted one at the June term, 1835, for $8.00. Elijah Davidson, the first grocery man, was given his license December 5, 1831. for $2.50. He was appointed county treasurer in the spring of 1832, and held the office several years. Martin McCowen was granted license to open a grocery in 1834, and, as in all grocery licenses, the rates of charges were also given. W. B. Stapp and W. S. Berry were granted license to "vend merchandise" in the summer of 1835, and paid $11 license fee. At the same time Ferdinand Vandyke and William Tracy received their permits for the same purpose. James P. Hogue, James McCallon and W. F. Smith's permits were given at the same time, and from that time, names of the old merchants often appear on the old records, showing that Monmouth was increasing rapidly in business and population. During these five years it had only been a village, but the citizens were actively discussing the feasibility of forming a town government, and enjoying a town's privileges. James McCallon, Daniel McNeil, Jr., and others, were the most energetic in this move, and finally in compliance with the general demand, posted notices in the most conspicuous places in town, said notices informing the "legally qualified voters of the town of Monmouth" that a meeting to determine this question would be held at the school house on November 29, 1836. The proceedings to incorporate Monmouth as a town, as recorded, were commenced at this date. These proceedings were under the general law of the State in force at that time, being the act approved February 12, 1831, entitled "an act to incorporate the inhabitants of such towns as may wish to be incorporated." Ten days prior to November 29th, a notice had been publicly posted up in compliance to law, and in pursuance of this call "the male citizens of the town of Monmouth" met at the school house at this date, and having organized by calling Elijah Davidson to he chair, and Harry Jennings as clerk, "the object of the meeting was fully set forth" and voting for and against the incorporation of the town commenced. Twenty-three votes were cast in favor of the incorporation and none against.

The voters were: Wm. F. Smith, Daniel McNeil, Jr., R. W. McMillen, Mordecai McBride, B. F. Berry, Yost Huffman, J. J. Caldwell, G. W. Vaugan, J. P. Hogue, Samuel Brazelton, Geo. H. Wright, Alex. Hogue, F. Vandyke, James McCallon, S. T. McBride, Thos. Butler, Andrew Robinson, Frank Kendell, Peter I. Dodge, Thos. G. Hogue, Elijah Davidson, Harry Jennings and Alex. Ritchie.

It was at once ordered that an election be held on December 5th following, for five trustees to serve twelve months, or until their successors were qualified. At this time Elijah Davidson, Daniel McNeil, Jr., James McCallon, Alex. Ritchie and George H. Wright were duly elected, and at once qualified.

Daniel McNeil, Jr., was chosen President of this Board of Trustees and Harry Jennings, Clerk and Treasurer. The first official act of this Board was the passing of the following ordinance, at their meeting held on December 26, at the house of James McCallon:

"ORDINANCE 1ST.—Be it ordained by the President and Trustees of the Town of Monmouth, in council convened, that the corporation and jurisdiction of the officers of the Town of Monmouth be one-half mile east, one-half mile west, one-half mile south and one-half mile north from the center of the Public Square, containing one mile square."

Other ordinances were also passed for the government of the town, for the regulation of public houses and groceries, the punishment of offenders, regulating the running at large of stock and any and all affairs pertaining to the welfare of a town.

Under this form of government the town was controlled, with several changes in the rulers, until 1852, when the General Assembly passed the following Act, approved June 21st, of that year:

"SECTION 1.—Be it enacted by the people of the State of Illinois, represented in the General Assembly, That the inhabitants of the Town of Monmouth, in the county of Warren and State of Illinois, be, and are hereby constituted a body politic and corporate, by the name and style of 'The City of Monmouth,' and by that name shall have perpetual succession, and may have and use a common seal, which they may change and alter at pleasure."

Section second fixes the boundaries at one mile from the center of the Public Square, each way, and section third provides for the division of the city into two wards.

From that time forward the government has remained unchanged, save that the increase in population has made more wards and an increased number of councilmen, there being two from each ward. The first election for mayor and other officers, under this act, was held on Saturday, October 23, 1852. Samuel Wood was elected to that office, and four aldermen, from the two wards, who convened for the transaction of business on November 3d, and fairly launched the city under the new government.

Until the advent of the C., B. & Q. Railroad, in 1854, the growth of Monmouth was slow. That year, however, the town sprang into active life, and improvements of every kind began to be made. The next year the college, whose history appears elsewhere, was located, and gave an additional impetus to persons looking for an intellectual home. A few years after, the library was founded, and made another prominent attraction. Good hotels were built, fine stores appeared, and the Union Hall, one of the largest in this part of the State, was erected.

A fire company is now sustained, and but little danger is apprehended from that dread element.

There are three good banks, two excellent weekly papers, and a monthly, issued in the interests of the college.

Eleven churches are sustained, whose membership will aggregate over two thousand.

The city is divided into four wards, in each of which a good school is maintained.

THE POST-OFFICE.—Daniel McNeil was the earliest postmaster appointed in the county. On September 10, 1830, he, acting as county clerk, advised the Postmaster General at Washington City, that the county of Warren was now established according to law, and that the county seat was established at Lower Yellow Banks, on the Mississippi River, on the 9th of July, preceding. This place being about half way between Des Moines River and Rock River rapids, did "request the Postmaster General to establish the post-office, to be called the 'Warren Court House Post-Office,' and further request him to forward the mail immediately to said office from Fulton county, Schuyler county, or from Venus, Hancock county." This request was complied with, and Mr. McNeil appointed to the office. As soon as the Indian hostilities commenced, he was compelled to remove from Yellow Banks to a place of safety. He came to Monmouth, but there being no house there, he repaired to an old camp, about a mile northeast. This he repaired and occupied some time, and here, during the first week, his wife killed two large rattlesnakes in the house. He carried the letters generally in his *hat*, and when meeting any one for whom he had mail, would hail them, take off his hat and deliver them their letters. On one occasion, on removing his portable post-office, the mail was blown away by a fierce wind prevailing at the time. It occasioned him no little trouble to find it.

The postage at that time was from ten to twenty-five cents on each letter, and money being scarce, the recipient of the letter would often be compelled to forego the pleasure of reading it for several days until he could get the money to pay the postage. Then, letters were carried without being prepaid, but could remain but a few weeks in the office, when they were forwarded to the Dead-Letter Office. As soon as the town of Monmouth was established an office was made there. It now does a large business, ranking as a second-class office. Its report for 1876 shows that there were sold, 352,127 stamps, stamped envelopes and postal cards. For these $7,611.36 were received. There were 2,626 money orders issued, which amounted to $31,055.41 in value; 1,920 orders were paid, amounting to $33,354.82; 605 letters were registered, and 756 of this kind were received; 999 letters were sent to the Dead-Letter Office. This report shows that the office handled $72,021.59 during the year.

The first bank established in the county was by Ivory Quinby. His was a private institution, and in it he was soon succeeded by the firm of Gregg & Hubbard.

Afterwards a bank was opened by E. L. Chapman, which in the early part of 1862 was merged into the present First National Bank. This latter institution is one of the oldest in the United States, being the eighty-fifth established. In 1872 a private bank was opened by C. Jones & Co., which was also, on November 1, 1870, merged into a National bank, being the present Monmouth National.

The Second National Bank was established in the early part of 1875.

All these banks are in excellent condition and stand high in the mercantile world.

MANUFACTORIES.

The first two-horse cultivator for corn and the first two-horse planter were invented and made in this county. These enable one man to do the work of nearly six, and have been a saving of many millions of dollars heretofore paid for labor. These agricultural implements are now largely used in the Southern States in the cultivation of cotton.

In 1859, W. S. Weir began experimenting with a corn plow, as the old methods of cultivating corn required so much labor, resulting in a plow for which a patent was first issued in December, 1862.

In 1863, after thoroughly trying the invention, arrangements were made for manufacturing on a larger scale. The first shop was built in the northwest part of the city, 24x36 feet, joined by a blacksmith shop 24x30 feet. During the year, with the assistance of nine men, 400 plows were made. In the winter of 1864-5, 500 were manufactured and found a ready sale.

The demand for these cultivators, at this time, necessitated a still further enlargement. A location was selected on Wood street, near the C., B. & Q. Railroad, where buildings were erected for wood work and foundry, the dimensions of which were 100x36 feet. A capital stock of $35,000 was represented, and the force of men increased to twenty-five.

For the season of 1866, 800 cultivators were made. Arrangements for the completion of a larger number were made, the following season, and the work was carried on with vigor. On the morning of January 20, 1867, by some unexplained accident, the entire works, with contiguous buildings, were destroyed by fire, entailing a loss of $35,000, including 1,200 cultivators stored in the building. Of this amount, $10,000 was covered by insurance.

By the first of March, a main building 34x36 feet, two stories high, was ready for business, together with a blacksmith shop 24x70, and a foundry 40x70 feet. Fifty men were employed, and 1,500 cultivators were in readiness for the spring trade.

In the fall of 1867, the Weir Plow Company was organized with a capital of $50,000.

Three thousand cultivators were made in 1868; 4,000 in 1869; 6,500 in 1870. In the fall of this year the working force was increased to sixty men, and 10,000 cultivators were placed upon the market.

The company has again increased the number of its employes, until they now give employment to over 300.

In 1871 they erected their present shops, whose combined floors cover more than three acres. The capital invested is over $600,000, and about $5,000 worth of agricultural implements are made daily.

The Pattee brothers, manufacturers of the "New Departure," tongueless cultivator, obtained their patent in 1872, and commenced to manufacture at Buda, Bureau county. Two years after they erected shops here and commenced at once the manufacture. They have a large foundry, machine and blacksmith shops, and make the cultivator from the crude material. They are daily in receipt of sufficient orders to exhaust all their manufactured stock. During 1876, 4,000 cultivators were sold in addition to those sold from Buda and Roseville. They are also made at this latter place.

Mr. W. S. Hopper is also engaged extensively in the manufacture of a cultivator which finds a ready sale, more than 3,000 being now in use. His establishment is directly north of the C., B. & Q. depot. He purchased the buildings in 1869, and in company with Mr. Palmer, began the making of his plows. His trade has grown steadily and is chiefly in the western and southwestern states.

Aside from the principal shops of the city, Monmouth contains one or two flouring mills, a good carriage and wagon factory, and a large number of shops of various kinds.

The city enjoys a large trade with the surrounding country. As fine stores can be seen here as in any city west of Chicago, and many persons come from the farthest parts of the county to trade here.

It has been shown elsewhere in these pages that the greater part of the business of the residents of Warren county were engaged in agriculture and in stock raising. As an evidence of this and the amount of business done at Monmouth station, the following is given :

"During the year ending with December, the shipments on the C., B. & Q. from Monmouth, included 215 cars of hogs, 12,160 head ; eight cars of sheep, 682 head; 208 cars of cattle, 3,366 head; 105 cars of corn, 42,000 bushels ; 33 cars of oats, 16,300 bushels ; 18 cars of rye, 7,200 bushels ; 3 cars of barley, 1,200 bushels."

THE SCHOOLS.

The educational advantages of Monmouth have always maintained a high standard. In 1831 a private school was opened by Robert Black. He was shortly followed by Alpheus Russell, both finding their support in subscriptions. No public provision was made until 1834, when at the meeting of the County Commissioners, on May 6th, the petition of Jacob Rust and others to establish the boundaries of school district No. 1 was granted. This included Monmouth, and on the site of the present Methodist Episcopal Church a frame school house, about eighteen feet square, was erected. This was a very comfortable structure, and was often used for other purposes, such as town meetings, religious services, or any public gathering. It was here, on the 29th of November, 1836, the election for the town organization was held. On October 2d, 1834 the trustees of the Monmouth district made their first report to the County Commissioners. It reads as follows :

"There are in this district fifty children between the ages of five and twenty-one years. There has been a school kept three months since the organization of the district. There have twenty-five children received tuition. The probable expense will be $45."

This report is signed by Gilbert Turnbull and James McCallon, and appears to record the first public school in Monmouth.

This small building was occupied several years. About the year 1840 it was sold and converted into a dwelling. On its site a much larger structure was erected to accommodate the increasing school population. Ere long it was found to be insufficient, and several private schools were opened. The basement of the Presbyterian Church and the Christian Church were rented and occupied. This occurred about the year 1852 or '3. The schools were under the control of the town and city councils, but no active part seems to have been taken by either board until the year 1855, when at a meeting of the city council, in June, it was ordered that the sum of $2,500 be appropriated to erect the East Ward school house. This same autumn school was opened in the school house already in use, in the Christian Church, and in the basement of the Presbyterian Church. The council employed Mr. W. B. Jenks to occupy the school house, who was to receive as compensation for his services three dollars per scholar in all common branches, and four dollars from each of those who pursued the higher studies. They employed Mr. A. H. Tracy for the Christian Church at the same terms.

The East Ward house was completed and occupied during the years 1855-6, and gave ample room until 1858-9, when the school population had so increased that the West Ward school house was erected to accommodate them. It was found that the city council could not give the necessary attention to the schools they demanded, and the city charter was amended February 21, 1863, placing the care of the schools under a board of three directors. These were elected March 3d. They were John S. Spriggs, A. Young Graham and Nathaniel A. Rankin. For the years 1863-4 S. A. Hammer was by them elected principal, and also eleven teachers, six in the East Ward and five in the West. For the next year two principals were chosen, and the school term extended to six months. The same year the contract for the South school house was let. In 1867 the North Ward house was built, and the school year made nine months. The following year the South school house was enlarged. In 1869 the board of directors was increased to five, and each principal of a ward was made superintendent of that building, and under this plan the city schools are still conducted. The secretary of the board acts as city superintendent, though he takes no part in the instruction. The schools are in an excellent condition, and give employment to twenty-two teachers, whose aggreggate monthly salaries are over $1,200.

CHURCHES.

The First United Presbyterian Church. This congregation was organized by Rev. Robert Ross, May 9, 1853, more than twenty-three years ago, as an Associate Reformed church.

Nineteen persons united, whose names were as follows: John, Ann, Isabella and James S. Gowdy, Isabella Young, James G. and Martha E. Madden, T. W. Smiley, John and Mary J. Saville, John E. Clark, Mrs. Clark, Robert A. Kendall, James E. McNair, Edward Kirk, Isabella Wallace, Julia A., Maria S. and Susan Madden. The first communion service was held June 11th, following, when thirty-four persons sat down to the communion table, ten of whom now remain in the congregation. This church has received into her fellowship over fourteen hundred persons, and now has a membership of four hundred.

The congregation worshipped in the court-house from the organization until the close of 1856, when the old college chapel was finished and services were conducted there. The chapel becoming too small for the increasing congregation, it was decided to erect a church edifice. During the last week of June, 1857, $6,000 were subscribed for that purpose, and building at once commenced. This structure (the present building) was completed in the early part of the summer of 1848, and the first services held therein on July 4th of that year.

From an anniversary sermon preached in May, 1876, by the pastor, Rev. J. G. Barnes, the following extracts relating to history of this denomination in Monmouth are taken: "The first Associate Reformed minister who preached in Monmouth was Rev. J. C. Porter, in the winter of 1847-'48. After the death of Rev. Willson, pastor of the Presbyterian Church, he preached for them at the request of the session, until they could obtain supplies of their own. He and other supplies preached in the court-house, generally to small audiences, until November, 1854, when a call was extended to Rev. S. F. Vannate, who afterwards lost his life by a shell on board a vessel on the Mississippi river, during the late war. An academy having been established here by the Second Associate Presbytery of Illinois, it was thought best to find some one to take charge of both church and school. Dr. David A. Wallace, of East Boston, Mass., was called, who came, and on the second Sabbath of February, 1856, preached twice in the

Baptist and once in the Presbyterian church. On the first Sabbath of October, 1856, he entered upon his duties, and remained in charge of both church and school till August, 1860, when he resigned his care of the former to give his entire attention to the latter. In the fall of 1858, the Theological Seminary of this denomination was removed from Oxford, Ohio, to Monmouth, and Dr. Young acted as pastor of the congregation until December 31, 1862. In 1863, in April, a call was sent to Rev. David G. Bradford, now pastor of the Presbyterian Church at Princeton, Bureau county, which he accepted and remained in this relation until August, 1867. Rev. R. B. Ewing was the next pastor, coming in the spring of 1868, and remaining until January 1, 1870. In May, of that year, the present pastor, Rev. Barnes, was called."

The first officers of this church were James Gowdy and T. W. Smiley, elders, (still living), James C. Crawford, John P. Giles and Robert B. Davidson. The first Sabbath-school superintendent was Nathan Brown, Sr. There were five teachers and twenty-five scholars. There are now nearly two hundred scholars.

On November 20, 1862, twenty-one members withdrew to form the Second United Presbyterian Church of Monmouth. The third church and the one at Kirkwood were also formerly part of this church.

The Second United Presbyterian Church was organized at the house of Mr. A. Y. Graham, in Monmouth, October 25, 1862. The members were, prior to this time, communicants in the First United Presbyterian Church; but that becoming large and the membership somewhat scattered, it was desirous to form another congregation. The constituent members were: M. A. Campbell, Catharine Graham, Mary C. Wolf, Esther J. Campbell, W. C. Brown, A. Y. Graham, M. D. Campbell, J. D. Wolf, James Findley, Lizzie Campbell, Prof. J. C. Willson, Prof. J. C. Hutchinson, R. M. Campbell, Lizzie W. Willson, Lizzie Hutchinson, J. F. McCreary, James Strain, Elizabeth McCreary, and Nancy Strain—19. Until the year 1866, they worshipped in the college chapel, when by this time they had so increased in numbers that a church edifice was deemed necessary. This was erected a little south of the college buildings, and cost the congregation about $10,000. When the church was organized the Revs. A. Young and Dr. D. A. Wallace were called as associate pastors, also being connected with the college. December 31, 1868, Dr. Wallace resigned to devote his entire time to the latter institution, and Dr. Young assumed the entire duties of pastor, continuing until June 11, 1871. On August 11, 1872, Rev. D. M. Ure was called. He continued to fill the pulpit till August 4, 1874, when he resigned. The present pastor, Rev. W. T. Campbell, was installed February 25, 1875.

From a membership of nineteen, the church has grown to three hundred and seventy-five, and sustain a Sabbath-school of nearly or quite two hundred scholars.

The Third U. P. Church was organized in January, 1867, in the South Ward school house, with forty members. A convenient house of worship was built soon after, and Rev. J. M. Henderson was the first pastor, from 1868 to 1873. Rev. D. R. Inches then succeeded to the pastorate, and continued until the fall of 1876. Present number of members about forty. In Sabbath school seventy. No pastor at present.

Swedish Lutheran Church. Was organized in March, 1868, with twenty-five members. The meetings for divine worship were held in a building owned by Mr. John Beck, one of the principal constituent members. The presiding minister was Rev. — Dalstien, of Galesburg, who labored here as his time and circumstances would allow, for some time. They met in this room and in the court-house until the year 1870, when they erected their present house of worship, costing about $1,400. They now number one hundred and twenty-five members, and control a Sunday-school of fifty scholars. The pastor is Rev. E. Peterson.

The Methodist Episcopal Church was organized over Daniel McNeil's store in 1840. The trustees elected at the organization were: L. C. Woodworth, Charles Cummings, Asa D. West, Alford Allen and Daniel McNeil. Two years before this time the persons professing this belief had met for divine worship in the same place, and as a result had gathered enough adherents to form the society. Rev. N. G. Bergman was presiding elder at the organization, and occasionally preached for them afterwards. In 1840, they erected a house of worship. This was used until about the year 1857. It was always known as the "Monmouth Chapel," being used for many public meetings of various kinds. About this time, becoming too small for the increasing congregation, it was removed and the present commodious edifice erected upon its site. The following is a partial list of the ministers of this church: Revs. C. Rowley, A. C. Price, J. P. Brooks, C. Springer, J. S. Cummings, E. Wasmuth, A. Magee, P. Warner, J. G. Evans, Wm. Underwood, L. Janes, and the present pastor, J. D. Smith. The membership is now 275, and the attendance at Sunday-school 200.

The Baptist Church. This congregation occupy a very comfortable house of worship, heated by furnaces and supplied with stained glass windows. Several other churches in Monmouth have introduced these improvements, which aid much in the convenience and appearance of the buildings.

This congregation was organized in 1844 at the house of Benj. C. Ward, with the following constituent members: Wm. F. Smith, Mrs. Geo. C. Lamphere, Mr. and Mrs. John Howard, Mr. and Mrs. Benj. C. Ward, and Mrs. Fry.

Their earliest meetings were held in the present court house, under the ministry of Elder Bartlett, of Knoxville. For some time the services were held in private houses, principally in a room over the store of Deacon E. C. Babcock and in a room belonging to Wm. F. Smith, on the southeast corner of the Square. In 1848 the first house of worship was built upon the present site, under the supervision of Elder Joseph Elliott and John Babcock, at a cost of $3,300. In 1868 it was remodeled and improved, at an expense of $3,000, making the aggregate cost of the present structure $6,300. The present membership of the society is 175. The church maintains a Sabbath school of 150 members and a Sunday school library of 250 volumes. The following are the names of the various pastors who have served this church, in the order of their pastorates: Eld. Bartlett, Eld. Wilbur, Eld. Hovey, Eld. Monroe, Eld. Levisee, Eld. Western, Eld. Joseph Elliott, Eld. Brimhall, Eld. Erastus Minor, Eld. Newton, Eld. Anson Tucker, Eld. Northrop, Eld. Tolman, Eld J. C. Miller, Eld. Wm. Bolton, Eld. H. B. Foskett, and then the present incumbent Eld. Harry Taylor.

The First Presbyterian church of Warren county was organized in 1836, by Rev. Cyrus Riggs, and reported to the presbytery of Schuyler, in session at Macomb, in that year. This was the church that afterwards took the name of "Fall Creek," and was dissolved by the presbytery and with their own consent, August 26, 1873. Its membership had run down to seven or eight, and it was impossible to revive it.

The Presbyterian church of Monmouth was organized by Rev. L. G. Bell, September 2d, 1837. At its organization there were sixteen members, all of whom being members of the First Church of Warren county, were dismissed to enter the new church. The new church had only occasional supplies of preaching until September, 1839, when its first pastor was settled. In the meantime services were held by Revs. L. G. Bell, Michael Hamer, James Stafford, Joseph J. Craig and W. K. Stewart, all of whom are dead except Mr. Hammer and Mr. Craig. Rev. Bell moved to Iowa, and in that new territory spent his time in organizing and fostering new churches, until his death, some years ago. His remains were brought to Monmouth for interment. Rev. Stewart, another pioneer of the church, died in Macomb, where he had been pastor for many years.

In October, 1839, Rev. Samuel Wilson, then laboring at Rushville, was called to become pastor of the united churches of Monmouth and Fall Creek, and he was installed by the presbytery then in session in this place. This relation continued till August 15, 1847, when it was closed by his death. At that time the church numbered sixty-seven members.

Until 1842 or 1843 the church had no house, but worshipped in various places; sometimes in a store-room on the corner of Broadway and the Square, now occupied by the Monmouth National Bank building; sometimes in a room in the old American House, that stood where Claycomb's brick block now stands. J. P. Hogue, one of the elders of the church, was proprietor of the hotel. Sometimes the meetings were held in the court house, and it was at one of the meetings in the court house that Rev. Wilson was installed pastor.

On the 17th of April, 1842, Theodore Coburn and his wife deeded to the church the lot on which the present building stands. On the lot a small brick building was erected soon after the deed was given, and, becoming insecure, was taken down in 1851.

In 1852 the present church building was erected, and some years ago was enlarged to accommodate the growing congregation.

In the fall of 1851 Rev. R. C. Matthews, having left the theological seminary, prepared to preach, visited Burlington, Iowa, where he chanced to become acquainted with a member of the church in Monmouth, and was invited to come over the river and preach, the church having no minister at that time. He came, and on the 20th of December, of that year, he preached his first sermon in the court house. The old brick church had been taken down and the new one was not finished, which was the reason for the meeting being held in the court house of Monmouth. The next day a congregational meeting was held, and the Doctor was invited to stay and preach three months, which he accepted, and divided his time between Monmouth, Fall Creek and North Henderson. On the 20th of March, 1852, he was called to become pastor of the church, by the acting elders, Robert Grant, James Dickson, Porter Phelps, A. C. Gregg and Hiram Norcross. In December, 1852, he was regularly installed pastor, and continued as such, respected and beloved by his congregation and the entire community.

During his ministry he has welcomed into the church seven hundred and eighteen members.

The Sunday school. In the fall of 1838 the pastor organized the Sunday school and remained superintendent until 1840, when he was succeeded by

Rev. Sam'l. Wilson, who occupied both positions until about 1846. The number of scholars was from fifteen to twenty, requiring the services of four or five teachers. One of these latter, Mr. John Leeper, remained as teacher about twenty-five years.

In the autumn of 1861 the board of instruction organized under the constitution of the First Presbyterian church, and elected their officers. That year 95 scholars attended one day during the last quarter of the year, being the greatest number of any one day. Twenty teachers were present. During 1862-3 and '4,—especially during 1863,—the school and church enjoyed a great season of revival and largely increased ; 214 scholars and 29 teachers are reported. On August 2d the school assembled for the first time in the basement of the church. For the year ending January 21st, 1866, 375 were reported enrolled. The lessons were prepared by Dr. Matthews.

This school has steadily maintained a good growth. It has largely contributed of its members to the church, 225 of the scholars uniting therewith since 1852. It has helped sustain a mission school, given freely to other causes, and now is large and very prosperous. Four of its members have gone out as ministers, two as elders, six as superintendents and forty as teachers in the Sunday schools.

The Christian Church. The earliest meetings of this congregation were held in the school house and in various halls in the (then) village.

On March 31st, 1839, they were organized into a church by Elders Pliny Hatchett, Levi Hatchett and James R. Ross. Elijah Davidson was chosen clerk of this meeting and the following persons united : Elijah and Nancy Davidson, Hezekiah and Eleanor Davidson, Alex. and Rachel Davidson, Wm. C. and Mrs. M. Hall, Wm. C. Butler and his wife Rebecca, James Hodgson, Jacob L. and Nancy Buzan, Amelia Ann Davidson, Solomon S. Davidson, Wm. B. Davidson, Elizabeth Davidson and Thos. H. Davidson, eighteen in all, of whom none are now members ; nearly all have died or removed. In 1840 they built their first house of worship, which occupied a lot immediately north of the present Baldwin House. This church was taken away after doing good service as a house of worship and as school house, and, in the spring of 1861, the present building erected. It is a very comfortable structure and cost $5,000. The number of members is now 125, and the Sunday school approaching the same number.

Resident ministers engaged in Christian Church since the organization in 1839 : Alexander Davidson, James E. Gaston, T. J. Mattock, J. W. Butler, L. S. Wallace, John Errett, A. P. Aten, F. M. Bruner, T. V. Berry, John Lagrange, J. M. Williams, Alex. Davidson, A. J. Cane, J. W. Errett, S. S. Wallace and J. W. Butler are some of the pastors who have labored here. The present occupant of the pulpit is Rev. F. M. Bruner.

African M. E. Church. Was organized in a hall on Main street about ten years ago. There were twelve members, of whom Charles Knight, Frances Price, Zachariah Price, Harriet Lee and A. H. Knight, who acted as class leaders, were the principal ones. In 1870 they erected a church costing about $800, which they yet occupy. There are now twenty-two members and an attendance of fifteen scholars at the Sunday school.

African Baptist Church. Was organized at the residence of Mrs. Miller, September 10th, 1866. There were but few members, the principal ones being Henry McCord and wife, and B. Granger and wife.

A church was erected at the corner of East and Cherry streets, at an expense of $1,500. It is still used. Their first pastor was Rev. J. C. Graves. Since then they have been ministered to by Rev. J. H. Bandy and others.

They have at present thirty-one members and a Sunday school of forty scholars.

THE PRESS.

The Monmouth *Atlas* is the oldest newspaper published in this section of the country. It was started in the year 1845 by C. K. Smith. E. S. Byron and F. K. Smith were for a short time associated with him in its management. but through his labor and perseverance the paper became a valuable contributor to the development of the country and its steady and prosperous growth. The present senior proprietor, Jno. S. Clark, purchased the establishment of Mr. Smith in 1857. In the fall of 1865 he sold an interest to J. H. Reed, who assisted in its management until May, 1869, when Mr. R. was succeeded by Samuel S. Clark, and with an unimportant exception, the business has since been conducted by Jno. S. Clark & Son. In their hands the establishment has increased to several times its dimensions when purchased by Mr. Clark, more than twenty years ago, and the circulation of the paper has kept pace with the increase of population. Mr. Geo. Rankin is now connected with the paper. The *Atlas* is recognized as one of the leading and most prosperous Republican newspapers of the State.

The *Review* was established in 1855 by the present editor and proprietor, Mr. A. H. Swain, who has been a practical printer since 1845, learning his trade in Pennsylvania. He commenced the publication of the *Review*, bringing his material with him, in an old brick building on Main street, where he remained one year. At the expiration of that time he removed his presses to Patterson's block on East street, where he published the paper four years. He then returned to Main street to a room in Carr's block, where he published the paper until 1876, when he removed the office to its present location in Kingsbury's block on Broadway. Mr. Swain publishes the official Democratic paper of the county, and since its commencement has never missed a number.

THE MONMOUTH COLLEGE,

Originated with the members of the Second Associate Reformed Presbytery of Illinois, in a desire to provide means for affording a Christian education to the youth of the church in the West, and to raise up properly qualified candidates for the ministry. Hence this Presbytery organized an academy at Monmouth. In 1855, it determined to raise it to the rank of a college, and appointed a board of trustees, who elected a president and two professors, and arranged for the opening of the college in September, 1856. In this movement Rev. J. C. Porter and Rev. R. Ross were among the most active. At the date fixed for opening, the building then in process of erection not being ready, the college was opened in the public school house, which is now occupied as a residence by Mr. Cowen, and stands on West avenue, east side, the third house from Broadway.

At a meeting of the Associate Reformed Synod of Illinois, held in Keokuk, Iowa, October, 1856, the college was transferred to that Synod by the Presbytery. The Synod, in a series of resolutions, affirmed the principles according to which it intended the college to be conducted, and appointed trustees. After the consummation of the union constituting the United Presbyterian Church, the care and supervision of the college passed to the Synod of Illinois of that body. In 1868, the Synod of Iowa united with the Synod of Illinois in the maintenance and control of the college. When the Synod of Kansas was organized out of the Synod of Illinois, it continued to share with the Synod of Illinois its responsibilities to the college. In 1874 a plan of union was agreed upon by the synods above named with the Second Synod of the West, in accordance with which it also became a part of the constituency of the college. The synods now comprised in this union are the Second Synod of the West, and the Synods of Illinois, Iowa and Kansas. These synods contain 244 ministers, 317 churches, and over 20,000 communicants.

The original act of incorporation was approved Feb. 16, 1857. It created the board of trustees, a body corporate and politic by the name and style of "The Monmouth College," and gave them customary powers. It vested in the Associate Reformed Synod of Illinois the power of appointing three-fourths of the trustees, and in the trustees themselves one-fourth. An act was signed Feb. 18, 1859, so amending the original act as to give to the "United" Presbyterian Synod of Illinois the powers before vested in the Associate Reformed Synod. The charter was further amended in 1869, after the union of the Synod of Iowa with the Synod of Illinois in the management of the college. The charter, as amended, adjusted the government of the college to its new relations, and provided for the admission of other bodies to its constituency.

The first college building was erected on the block of land donated by Hon. A. C. Harding, located in the northwest section of the city of Monmouth. It was about 40x60 feet, two stories, and contained a chapel and eight rooms. In 1860, Messrs. A. Y. and D. Graham donated to the college ten acres situated on Broadway, in the eastern part of the city, together with one-sixth of the remainder of the quarter of which it was a part. The board immediately took measures to erect on the proffered site a new building suited to the growing wants of the college. The work commenced in 1861, and on the 12th day of May, 1863, the professors and students took possession of the building. It is 50x80 feet, three stories high above the basement, and contains eighteen rooms. It cost, including furniture and fences, about $20,000. In 1875 it was found that this building was too small for the wants of the college, and steps were taken for the erection of an addition, 50x60, on the north side of the old building, at a cost of about $14,000. It is now finished. It is three stories high above the basement, of the same style of architecture as the old, and will contain a chapel and eight other rooms in addition to those in the basement. The enlarged structure will furnish ample accommodations for the wants of the college.

The preparatory classes below the sub-Freshman are heard in the original college building known as the academy.

The first attempt to endow the college was made on the Scholarship system. The original scholarship entitled the purchaser to the perpetual tuition of one student. It cost $100. The purchaser could pay cash for it or give his note bearing 6 per cent. interest per annum. Afterwards the sale of this class of scholarships was stopped, and a new one offered, entitling to 20 years tuition, for $100 in cash, or for a note bearing interst at the rate of ten per cent. per annum. Subsequently it was determined to sell

W. G. Bond
SHERIFF, WARREN COUNTY ILLS.

no more scholarships at this rate. In lieu thereof, for every one hundred dollars, scrip was issued entitling to tuition, at current rates, to the amount of $200, payable one-tenth annually. Again this plan was modified by giving scrip for the sum donated, dollar for dollar, entitling to tuition to the amount of the face of it, at the rates current at the time of the sale. Many thousands of dollars were thus secured. Finally, however, all these schemes were abandoned, because the education promised by the college cost it more than the principal and interest of the money paid for the scholarship amounted to. Endowment on this principle was found to be impossible. In 1871, it was determined to solicit donations, without any tuition in turn, for the Endowment fund. On this plan over $75,000 have been secured, which is being collected and invested in bonds secured by mortgage or real estate, and bearing interest at the rate of ten per cent. per annum. A few thousand dollars have also been secured by the sale of a perpetual scholarship for $1,000.

The first President of the College was Rev. David A. Wallace, who still holds the place. The following have been connected with it as Professors and Instructors:

Rev. M. Morrison, } Original Professors.
Rev. J. R. Brown, }
J. B. McCartnay, M. D.
Miss M. J. Hutchison,
Rev. A. Young,*
Rev. R. Ross,
Rev. J. C. Hutchison,*
John H. Wilson,*
George Norcross,
Rev. A. M. Black,
Rev. J. C. Webber,
Thos. H. Rodgers,*
Mrs. T. H. Rogers,
Miss Eliza B. Wallace,*
Miss Mary Pressly,
Miss E. J. Young,
Rev. J. A. P. McGow,

Miss Agnes Strong,*
John A. Gordon,*
Alex. Rule,
Miss Rebecca S. Killough,
Rev. J. R. Doig,
S. H. Price,*
Miss Armenia Watt,
Mrs. L. A. Smeallie,
Miss E. Caldwell,
T. A. Blair,
S. K. Crawford,*
Thos. S. McClenohan,*
Miss M. E. Cleland,
Ed. F. Reid,*
G. I. Gordon,*
Miss C. M. White.*

The number of students in all departments, each year from the begining, has been as follows:

1856 & 7,	99	1861 & 2,	191	1866 & 7,	367	1871 & 2,	372
1857 & 8,	151	1862 & 3,	159	1867 & 8,	380	1872 & 3,	377
1858 & 9,	172	1863 & 4,	225	1868 & 9,	368	1873 & 4,	378
1859 & 60,	182	1864 & 5,	276	1869 & 70,	370	1874 & 5,	447
1860 & 1,	220	1865 & 6,	360	1870 & 1,	368	1875 & 6,	397

Of these, 155 are in the college proper.

The number of graduates each year from the beginning has been as follows:

YEAR.	CLASSICALS.	SCIENTIFICS.	YEAR.	CLASSICALS.	SCIENTIFICS.
1858,	2	2	1868,	11	17
1859,	3	7	1869,	21	18
1860,	5	7	1870,	21	12

Those at present connected with the college are marked (*).

YEAR.	CLASSICALS.	SCIENTIFICS.	YEAR.	CLASSICALS.	SCIENTIFICS.
1861,	5	2	1871,	17	8
1862,	13	8	1872,	29	16
1863,	2	5	1873,	15	13
1864,	11	10	1874,	22	18
1865,	12	10	1875,	17	17
1866,	11	13	1876,	22	13
1867,	15	10			

The whole number of graduates, classical and scientific, has been 460; 254 classicals, and 206 scientifics. Of the classicals, 19 were ladies, and of the scientifics, 136. The Honorary Degree of A. M. has been conferred on 4 persons; of D. D., on 32; of LL. D., on 1. Of the 235 gentlemen who graduated from the classical course, 134 were candidates of the ministry, and of the scientifics. 5. Three gentlemen and two ladies are missionaries in the foreign field.

LODGES.

Monmouth Lodge, No. 37, A. F. and A. M.—Officers: M. Holliday, W. M.; A. Wilson, S. W.; A. C. Russell, J. W.; D. D. Diffenbaugh, Treas.; W. S. Holliday, Sec'y. Meets at Monmouth, first and third Tuesday evenings.

Trinity Lodge. No. 561, A. F. and A. M.—Officers: E. C. Johnson, W. M.; W. A. Grant. S. W.; A. T. Walker, J. W.; J. Mornington, Treas.; W. W. Brown, Sec'y. Meets at Monmouth, second and fourth Thursdays of the month.

Warren Lodge, No. 160, I. O. O. F.—Officers: M. S. Baldwin, N. G., John Harvey. V. G.; John Walker, R. Sec'y; James Neise. Treas.; M. L. Holliday, P. Sec'y. Meets at Monmouth, each Monday evening.

Monmouth Lodge, No. 577, I. O. O. F.—Officers: N. J. Nelson; N. G.; James Bolack, V. G.; Isaac Marks, R. S.; L. S. Hollen, P. S.; R. Lahann, Treas. Meets at Monmouth, every Tuesday evening.

Monmouth Council, No. 14, R. and S. Masters.—Officers: D. D. Durkle. T. I. G. M.; L. D. Robinson, Dep'ty G M.; Ransom Dorney, P. C. of W.; Wm. Holliday, Capt. of G.; R. L. Russell, C. of C.; W. W. Brown, Rec.; T. Rosenzweig, Steward; E. C. Johnson, Treas.; James Marshal, Sentinel. Meets at Monmouth, first Monday of each month.

Warren Chapter, No —, R. A. M.—Officers: D. D. Dunkle, H. P.; Dr. R. B. McGeary, King; L. D. Robinson. Scribe; Ranson Doney, C. H.; Martin Holliday, R. A. C.; D. D. Duffenbaugh, Treas.; D. H. Morey, Sec'y.

City Government.

City Election, first Monday in April.
Council meets first Monday in each month.
The following is a complete list of the City Officers from the organization of Monmouth as a city, in 1852:

1852.—Samuel Wood, Mayor ; N. A. Rankin, Wm. E. Rodgers, James Thompson and E. S. Swinney, Aldermen ; B. F. Corwin, Clerk ; G. W. Savage, Attorney ; James Finney, Marshal.

1853.—Geo. W. Palmer, Mayor ; Samuel Webster, Wm. Y. Henry, Wm. E. Rodgers, and James Mekemson, Aldermen ; B. F. Corwin, Clerk ; James Finney, Marshal.

1854.—E. S. Swinney, Mayor ; Wm. E. Rodgers, Hiram Norcross, Wm. Billings, and Wm. Cowan, Aldermen ; B. F. Corwin, Clerk ; Reuben Grimes, Marshal.

1855.—Robert Grant, Mayor ; R. S. Joss, J. C. McKamy, Samuel Wood, and William Cowan, Aldermen ; W. B. Jenks, Clerk ; F. A. Earp, Marshal.

1856.—W. H. Young, Mayor ; Jas. Hill, A. S. Gilbert, Wm. Billings, and H. Smith, Aldermen ; W. B. Jenks, Clerk ; A. White, Marshal.

1857.—I. Quimby, Mayor ; H. F. Henry, C. Hardin, T. Cornell, and James Neis, Aldermen ; A. E. Arnold, Clerk ; R. Grames, Marshal.

1858.—J. H. Holt, Mayor ; A. C. Gregg, Wm. Cowan, H. McAdams, and R. H. Grames, Aldermen ; W. B. Jenks, Clerk ; J. A. Boynton, Marshal.

1859.—N. A. Rankin, Mayor ; J. W. Scott, Jas. Neis, Jas. Shoemaker, Thos. Pearse, and R. H. Grames, Aldermen ; V. G. Harbaugh, Clerk ; Stephen McBride, Marshal ; Albert Bonker, Sexton. (He filled this office till 1874.)

1860.—N. A. Rankin, Mayor ; H. G. Hardin, J. Findley, C. W. Palmer, and J. W. Collins, Sr., Aldermen ; J. W. Collins, Jr., Clerk ; W. A. Grant, Treasurer ; J. D. Wolfe, Attorney ; E. A. Paine, Marshal.

1861.—H. G. Hardin, Mayor ; D. Babcock, William M. Gregg, Wm. Gowdy, and Samuel Wood, Aldermen ; A. O. France, Clerk ; W. A. Grant, Treasurer ; Seth Smith, Marshal ; P. E. Reed, Attorney.

1862.—H. G. Hardin, Mayor ; D. R. Sevens, W. Coman, Geo. D. Woods, and R. C. Rowley, Aldermen ; W. M. Gregg, Clerk ; W. A. Grant, Treasurer ; J. Lorimer, Marshal.

1863.—S. Wood, Mayor ; D. Babcock, W. P. Smith, W. Cowan, and M. R. Williams, Aldermen ; W. M. Gregg, Clerk ; W. A. Grant, Treasurer, J. Lorimer, Marshal.

1864.—Wm. Cowan, Mayor ; Geo. Babcock, W. Gettemy, Wm. F. Smith, and Seth Smith, Aldermen ; J. K. Ripley, Clerk ; W. A. Grant, Treasurer ; A. P. Carmichael, Marshal.

1865.—W. Cowan, Mayor ; Chas. Corwin, Wm. Cannon, Francis Fowler, and Carlos Gambell, Aldermen; J. K. Ripley, Clerk; W. A. Grant, Treasurer; Wm. F. Davis, Marshal.

1866.—Geo. Babcock, Mayor; Jos. K. Russell, J. Cunningham, D. C. Brady, and B. J. Beecher, Aldermen; J. W. Berger, Clerk; Chas. Jamison, Attorney; W. A. Grant, Treasurer; P. F. Smith, Marshal.

1867.—Jno. M. Turnbull, Mayor; Jos. H. Blackburn, H. Baldwin, J. N. Reece, Rob't Y. Frew, and C. A. Dunn, Aldermen; D. D. Parry, Clerk; Wm. Marshall, Attorney; N. A. Scott, Treasurer; Seth Smith, Marshal.

1868.—Sam'l Wood, Mayor; C. A. Dunn, J. Stevenson, W. A. Grant, S. Graham, N. G. Harding, and C. W. Palmer, Aldermen; S. S. Findley, Clerk; Jno. Porter, Attorney; W. Corwin, Marshal.

1869.—J. A. Templeton, Mayor; D. Graham, C. L. Buck, J. A. Bates, H. H. Roberts, J. M. Henderson, and G. Chapin, Aldermen; W. H. Sexton, Clerk; Wm. Marshal, Attorney; J. A. Boynton, Marshal.

1869.—J. A. Templeton, Mayor; D. Graham, C. L. Buck, J. A. Bates, H. H. Roberts, J. M. Henderson, and G. Chapin, aldermen; W. H. Sexton, clerk; Wm. Marshall, attorney; J. A. Boynton, marshal.

1870.—S. Douglas, Mayor; D. Graham, A. H. Tracy, J. Garvin, D. S. Hayden, N. G. Harding, and W. C. Norcross, aldermen; M. L. Stansbury, clerk; A. Kidder, attorney; J. Martin, marshal; A. Bunker, Sexton.

1871.—W. B. Boyd, Mayor; D Graham, W. L. Hopper, I. P. Pillsbury, J. S. Spriggs, N. G. Harding and Geo. Chapin, aldermen; W. Townley, clerk; J. Porter, attorney; J. W. Graham, marshal.

1872.—W. M. Buffington, Mayor; R. M. Campbell, D. D. Diffenbaugh, J. B. Eilenberger, H. C. Robson, R. C. Rowley, and H. B. Young, aldermen; C. K. Smith, clerk; Wm. Marshall, attorney; O. D. Wilcox, marshal.

1873.—D. Babcock, Mayor; D. Graham, C. Gambell, N. G. Harding, W. H. Merridith, I. P. Pillsbury, and D. R. Stevens, aldermen; C. K. Smith, clerk; I. M. Kirkpatrick, attorney; W. S. Emert, marshal.

1874.—Jacob Holt, Mayor; D. Graham, C. Gambell, W. H. Merridith, D. R. Stevens, A. V. T. Gilbert, J. H. Spiggs, aldermen; J. R. Berry, Clerk; B. T. O. Hubbard, treas; O. D. Wilcox, Marshal.

1875.—Jacob H. Holt, Mayor; W. A. Grant, clerk; Wm. H. Merideth, John Turnbull, Carlos Gambell, J. H. Spriggs, C. Coates, T. C. Hardin, aldermen; Charles M. Skinner, Marshal.

1876.—J. S. Dryden, Mayor; Geo. C. Runkin, Clerk; Draper Babcock, James Cunningham, D. Graham, C. Gambell, T. E. Harding, J. W. Sipher, aldermen; A. R. Bay, Marshal.

1877.—Jacob H. Holt, Mayor; J. H. Spriggs, N. S. Horne, John Turnbull, C. L. Buck, F. A. Earp and Geo. Sickmon.

ROSEVILLE.

Truman Eldridge, who now occupies one of the most inviting farms and homes within the Corporation, came, in 1836, from Hancock, Mass., and took 240 acres, a part of which is embraced in the northwest portion of the village. Shortly after he returned to his home and spent two years, and in 1838 returned, and in 1839 built a home and commenced the improvement of his land. In 1848 he took up, at the government price, 80 acres more, directly north, and in 1850 bought 160 acres more, embracing the northeast portion of the Corporation. The southeast quarter section was bought thirty-four years ago by Solomon Sovereign, and thirty years ago the southwest by John Reeves. The Corporation, one mile square, laid out in streets at right angles, embraces equal portions of these four quarter sections.

The first store was opened on a small scale by John Adams, in 1856, a little south of where it now stands, on the southwest corner of Penn avenue and Main street. The brick building owned by E. Pierce occupies its original site. Soon N. W. Baker succeeded John Adams, and not long after, Dally and Arter, and these were succeeded by E. P. Emans, who now owns and occupies a two story frame on the northwest corner.

The first township meeting was held in the old Union Church, on April 4, 1854. Truman Eldridge presided at the meeting, and at its close the first township officers were chosen.

Until the advent of the C. B. & Q. Railroad, almost all the produce was taken to Oquawka, there to be shipped to St. Louis by the Mississippi River. When the railroad was completed trade was changed to Monmouth, and a local trade was started in Roseville.

New Lancaster and Elliston, a few miles west, were enjoying quite a local trade, which continued until 1870. During the summer of this year, the Rockford, Rock Island & St. Louis Railroad was completed through the county. This was the beginning of the prosperity of Roseville. It was now properly platted and the plat recorded by John A. Gordon, in the name of Mr. Eldridge and others of the most active residents, and an active trade at once opened.

The stores and shops at New Lancaster were moved here, and the town from being a "corners," as it was commonly called, rapidly arose to a "town," with its attendant privileges. Mr. John A. Gordon opened the depot and held the position several years.

Mr. Eldridge gave several lots to those who would erect shops or stores thereon, not a few of which liberal offers were accepted.

On May 8, 1874, the town had attained a population of 514 inhabitants, and was incorporated. Since then the population has increased to nearly 900. In 1856, Mr. James G. Reed located at the school house, about a mile east of the village. Here he commenced work as a blacksmith. Shortly after, he removed his shop to Roseville, where he added to his small shop a room about sixteen by twenty-four feet.

He soon purchased an engine to aid him in his rapidly growing trade, and increased the number of his employes. About a year ago the present firm was organized, and a still further increase in the buildings and machinery made. Their speciality is windmills, plows and tongueless cultivators. Quite a number of shops are maintained, good stores, one bank and an excellent flouring mill.

THE SCHOOLS.

The earliest attempts to educate the youth of this community was made in a small log school house, about one mile south of the site of the village. The frame school house east of town was next built. At its location there was a shop and small store, and the residents entertained some hopes of securing a town here. School was maintained here until a few years ago, when it was removed to town and the present edifice constructed. It is a two story building, capable of accommodating two hundred scholars; 156 are now in attendance. Three teachers are employed.

THE CHURCHES.

The Congregationalist Church was organized November 15, 1851, by President Blanchard, then of Galesburg, and consisted of eleven members, whose names were Stephen and Phœbe Delley, William and Mary Delley, David and Elizabeth Tuttle, Mrs. Elizabeth Axtell, and Miss Eunice Robinson. Four years after the organization they erected the present church building, at an expense of $3,000 dollars. The lumber was brought from Oquawka. Some time after, they erected the parsonage, worth $2,000. Rev. Asa Martin commenced his labors here, at a salary of $120 per year, in 1851, and remained one year. He was succeeded by Rev. J. A. Rodgers, the first installed pastor, who remained until 1858. He is now president of Berean College, Kentucky. Rev. A. R. Mitchell was called to succeed him, and occupied the pulpit until 1861. He was followed by Rev. Alfred Morse, who remained three years and was succeeded by Rev. Cyrus H. Eaton, from 1864 to 1867. Then Rev. Arthur E. Arnold filled the pulpit until 1868. From that date until the early part of 1877 the pulpit was occupied by Rev. J. D. Wykoff. The present pastor, Rev. R. A. Wood, has just lately been installed.

The membership is now 100, the attendance at Sunday-school 75.

The Baptist Church was organized in 1852 by Rev. S. G. Miner. It now numbers 175 members and 100 Sunday-school scholars. The organization was perfected in a school house, about one mile east of the present site of the town, with about 25 members. When the school house was erected in town, they used it for divine worship until they erected their present church. It cost about $2,000 dollars.

The following have been some of the pastors of this church: Elders Joseph Elliott, ——— Morse and J. D. Kent. The present pastor is E. C. Cady.

The Methodist Episcopal Church is the outgrowth of a class of some half dozen members organized in 1839, who were Solomon Sovereign and wife, John Jared, Sr. and wife, Mrs. Sisson, Mrs. Welty, Mrs. Kirkpatrick. They held their first meetings in Jared's school house, about three miles southeast of Roseville. In the fall of 1841, and until the spring of 1842, the meetings were held in Josiah Kirkpatrick's house, about two and a half miles south of Roseville. They were then held at Solomon Sovereign's house, now used for a hotel by Eli Gilbert, opposite the depot. The meetings were held in this house until the first school house was built. This served as a sanctuary until the present church and parsonage were built in 1867, at a cost of $5,500. This class, in its infancy, formed one of the appointments on the Aquawka circuit, which included all of what is now

Henderson and Warren counties, Monmouth, Kirkwood and other places of importance now were appointed on the circuit. Among the first ministers who broke the bread of life were the venerable Henry Summers, W. M. Clark, Richard Haney, William Haney and Benjamin Applebee. These men are all yet living and are members of the Central Illinois Conference. Though all are on the superannuated list except R. Haney and B. Applebee. J. Kern was appointed pastor in 1856, W. J. Beck in 1857, A. C. Higgins in 1858, W. B. Morse in 1859, R. Morey in 1860 and '1, B. C. Swarts in 1862 and '3, J. A. Windsor in 1864, G. C. Woodruff in 1865, W. B. Carithers in 1866, Thomas Watson in 1867 and '8, J. W. Coe in 1869 and '70, R. Beeler in 1871, C. B. Couch in 1872 and '73, J. W. Coe in 1874 and '5. J. S. Cummings is the present very efficient presiding elder on the district, and N. T. Allen the present energetic pastor under whose labors the past winter seventy-five members have been added to the church, making the present membership one hundred and seventy-seven, with a Sabbath school of one hundred scholars.

The Christian Church was organized in 1859, or 1860, with about 25 members. There are now more than double that number, and a Sunday-school of nearly 50 scholars. In 1871 they erected a comfortable church, costing about $1,500. Their parsonage is worth about $800. The Rev. George L. Brackan is the present pastor.

The Lutheran Church, composed mostly of Swedes, comprises a membership of 35. They were organized into a body ecclesiastic February 26, 1876, with 26 members, and on October 29, following, dedicated their present house of worship. Rev. G. Wiberg occupies the pulpit, ministering part of his time in other places. The Sunday-school numbers about 25 scholars.

The Union Baptist Church was organized in 1844 or '5 in an old school house. It was used for some time for both purposes, and in it the first township meetings were held.

The members had belonged to the Berwick Church and organized here, this being a more central location.

They have now a very comfortable church and sustain a regular meeting.

Talbott's Creek Christian Church was organized about 1838-9, and for some time included the Cameron and Alexis members.

Joseph Murphy and L. S. Wallace were among the first elders. John E. Murphy, Thos. Wallace, Wm. Wallace, Wm. Murphy and Wm. Hopper, with their families, were among the constituent members. John E. Murphy was the pioneer preacher among them. Thos. Griffith and Henry Bruner, father of the present pastor of Monmouth Church, were also early members. Their present church was erected near David Warren, an old member, and one who helped the church in its early trials. They occupied this building until 1855 or '6, when a house of worship was erected at an expense of $2,000, which they still occupy. They have a membership of about one hundred, and sustain a Sunday school of about the same number. Rev. D. D. Miller, pastor at Cameron, preaches here. This congregation has sent out several colonies, which are now large and growing churches.

THE PRESS.—Two weekly papers are sustained here. *Wilson's Weekly*, the younger, was started about eight months since by the Wilson brothers, two quite young men, and is already enjoying a good circulation. It is a good local paper, and a very creditable enterprise.

The Roseville *Gazette*, an independent family newspaper, by G. G. McCosh. Terms, $1.50 per annum in advance. It is published every Wednesday, and each issue contains twenty-eight columns of matter. It has a large and rapidly increasing circulation, chiefly in Warren and Henderson counties. Advertisements inserted at reasonable rates. Terms made known on application. A branch office is located at Monmouth, Ill., cor. Main street and Public Square, fitted up with the most modern and improved styles of type and machinery, is capable of turning out first-class job printing at lowest living rates. All orders for printing and all communications, to receive prompt attention, should be addressed to the publisher at Monmouth, Ill.

ROSEVILLE VILLAGE.

The Board of Trustees for the ensuing year will be as follows : James G. Reed, George W. Cochler, Thomas Bell, Frank W. Meacham, David S. Carnahan and John Huggett. Austin Fuller, Village Clerk. I. A. Gordon, Policeman.

Roseville Lodge, No. 284 *I. O. of G. T.*—Officers : W. H. Buckley, W. C.; Miss Mattie Noakes, V. C.; J. L. Woodmansee, R. Secy.; George Davenport, P. Secy.; Miss Jennie Hielman, Treas. Meets at Roseville every Monday evening.

Roseville Lodge, No. 537, *I. O. O. F.*—Officers : G. W. Cockler, N. G.; J. Hartley, V. G.; C. L. Rose, Secy.; J. W. Conlee, Treas.; J. W. Conlee, P. Deputy. Meets at Roseville every Wednesday evening.

Roseville Lodge, No. 519, *A. F. and A. M.*—Officers : J. W. Conlee, W. M.; J. C. V. Kelley, S. W.; Eli Dixon, J. W.; D. M. Taliferro. Treas.; G. W. Cockler, Secy. Meets at Rossville first and Third Fridays of each month.

KIRKWOOD

Is pleasantly located on the C., B. & Q. R. R. twenty-one miles east from Burlington, Ia. In the year 1836 five families had located in this township, as follows : Samuel Hanna, Z. M. Davis, James Gibson, R. Tinkham, Benjamin Tompkins, after whom the township was named. Prior to the building of the railroad through this county, settlement was slowly made in this region, but on the completion of the road, in 1855, new life was infused and business sprang up as if by magic. In the year 1854 David Irvine laid out the original village of Kirkwood to which two additions have been made, called Quinby's additions.

For many years a brisk trade has been carried on here, especially in grain, which has hardly been surpassed by any town on any railroad leading to Chicago. The village was incorporated in 1865, and the following were the first Trustees : O. Lanphere, J. L. Batcheler, J. K. Cummings, A. Carmichael and J. B. Sofield. The present board is, T. F. Lowther, Geo. Kellogg, A. C. Van Riper, L. Rapalee, Wm. McCoy, W. K. and J. H. Gilmore, Clerk.

BUSINESS INTERESTS.

The first store here was opened by Knowles, Ray & Chapin in 1855. The First National Bank is one of the solid institutions of this county, and

Theo. Bradley M. D.
ROSEVILLE

is ably managed by Dr. Henry Tubbs, President, and Willard C. Tubbs, Cashier. Chapin, Houlton & Davis have a large private banking business; also an extensive mercantile trade. There are at the present time five general stores, four grocery houses, four drug stores, two hardware stores and agricultural implements, two boot and shoe stores, two bakeries, one bookstore and news room, one jeweler, two blacksmith shops, two shoe shops, two wagon shops, one lumber yard and two elevators.

SCHOOLS.

The graded schools of this village are the just pride of all her people. There are two neat and commodious school houses—six rooms—in which schools are maintained nine months of the year. The number of children enumerated by the census of 1876 is 482 in the village and in the township 975.

CHURCHES.

The Presbyterian Church of Kirkwood was organized in 1856, and was first called South Henderson Church. Meetings were first held in a school house about two miles southwest of town. A committee had been appointed by Schuyler Presbytery to assist in the formation of the church. This committee was Rev. J. H. Nevins, R. C. Matthews, D. D., and Elders Hiram Norcross and James Boggs. At the organization there were twenty-six members, "of whom many have fallen to sleep, but a few remain unto this day." The first elders were Jacob Ackerman, Alex. M. Hervey and Nathan Carr. Of these, Fathers Carr and Ackerman yet live, having more than fulfilled their four score years. The first stated preaching was by Rev. J. H. Nevins for one year. Then Rev. W. L. Lyons for three and a half years. From July, 1863, to April, 1865, was a vacancy, with occasional preaching by Dr. J. M. Jamison and others. At this latter date Rev. J. W. Ash began his labors here, and was the regular supply for two years. Then Rev. J. W. Allen was here for two years, and during his administration a new and commodious church was built, 40 by 65 feet, and cost $11,000. In 1870 Rev. G. N. Johnson supplied for six months. Then Rev. J. H. Marshall was stated supply for two and a half years. The present minister, Rev. E. W. Thompson, is the only installed pastor the church has ever had. He began his labors here in 1874. The first house of worship built by this Church was a small frame structure, 20 by 30 feet, in the south part of town, in 1858. For two or three years it was occupied by the M. E. congregation on alternate Sabbaths. This was afterwards sold to the Roman Catholics and moved off the lot. In 1868 the present church was erected, and is an elegant gothic structure. It was thoroughly refitted in 1875. The present membership is 125. An interesting Sabbath school is maintained throughout the year, with an attendance of 125. E. P. Clauson is superintendent. The church is in a prosperous condition.

The United Presbyterian Church of Kirkwood, Ill., was organized in 1858 at Center Grove school house with about eighteen members, among whom were David Irvine and wife, Dr. J. Biddle and wife, John Woods and wife and I. H. Martin and wife. The meetings were first held at the above named school house, also at Mr. Edward Wray's hall. Their church was built in 1863 at a cost of $2,800. The pastors who have served at this church are Rev. I. B. Foster three years, Rev. W. J. McSurely two years,

Rev. I. B. Waddle seven years. The present membership is one hundred and fifty-seven. Average Sabbath school attendance eighty.

The Young America Church was organized August 12th, 1855, with ten members. Their present house of worship was built in 1858 at a cost of $877.50. Rev. I. B. Fuller presides. There are at present seventy members and forty Sabbath school scholars.

The Universalist Church was organized in 1860 at Rap's Hall. Thirteen members were received, among whom were N. A. Chapin and Geo. Williams. For some time services were held at Rap's Hall, where they remained until the completion of their church, which was dedicated in 1866, its cost being $4,000. The church was rebuilt in 1869 at an additional cost of $3,000. Rev. C. L. Walsh preached two years. Rev. A. Clayton one year, Rev. A. Tibbitts two years, Rev. Hibbard eighteen months, L. H. Tabor three years. The present number of members thirty, with the same number of Sabbath school scholars.

The M. E. Church was organized in 1856 at the Young America Hotel. The first sermon was preached by Rev. O. Swartz January 5th, 1856, in hotel. Afterward meetings were held at the Presbyterian church on alternate Sabbaths. The members of the first class were John Ramsdell, leader, Elizabeth Ramsdell, Mary E. Youmans, Daniel and Matilda Tinker, Oliver and Rachel Hall, William L. and Margaret Roberts. The pastors in charge have been as follows: Rev. James Tubbs, three years; Rev. C. Springer, two years; Rev. B. C. Couch, two years; Rev. M. Spurlock, one year; Rev. J. J. Fleharty, two years; Rev. Samuel Fisher two years; Rev. Jesse Smith, two years, and the present pastor, Rev. C. H. Brace, who began his work in September, 1876. The first trustee election was held in the old Presbyterian house, March 20th, 1865, and the following were elected: Henry Tubbs, Alex. Youmans, B. Logan, E. H. Randall and T. W. Beers. The house of worship was built in 1865 at a cost, including grounds and parsonage, of $8,300. Dedication services were conducted by Dr. Eddy, from Chicago. Preacher in charge, Rev. James Tubbs, to whose labors may be largely attributed the origin and completion of the work free of debt.

The present pastor is Rev. Charles H. Brace. The present membership about 250. The Sabbath School numbers 125. Superintendent, Rev. C. H. Brace. This charge is in a prosperous condition.

VILLAGE BOARD OF TRUSTEES.

A. C. Van Riper, W. K. Gamble, L. Rapalee, J. B. Gregory, H. W. Allen, R. R. Davison. J. H. Gilmore, Clerk.

A. Lincoln Lodge No. 518.—Geo. N. Carr, W. M.; Frank Farrel, S. W.; Geo. Carlin, J. W.; W. J. Scofield, Sec'y; C. K. Brown, Treas. Meets second and fourth Tuesdays of each month.

DENNY.

This is one of the earliest settled locations in this county. L. P. Rockwell and Jonathan Buffum came here on a prospecting tour in 1830 from Ashtabula county, Ohio, and found Adam Ritchie located in a small block house on the hill. This had been built by Ritchie in the previous year.

Rockwell and Buffun bought his claim of 160 acres, having upon it a mill site on Cedar Creek. They remained here during the winter of 1830 and '31, and engaged in building a saw-mill, the first in the county.

They returned in the fall to Ohio, and in April, 1832, they set sail with their families and some others on a raft down the Ohio river. They started from Warren county, Pa., and were four weeks on the raft in reaching Cincinnati. Here, after much delay, they took passage on a steamboat for St. Louis, and on arriving there found the same boat was going to Beardstown, and so continued their journey to this point. From this latter place they went by ox teams to Canton, and then to their new homes on Cedar Creek. They added another block house near the first and built a stockade for fort. The nearest mill or postoffice was about seventy miles distant. Soon, however, the postoffice was established at this point and was first called Cedar Creek Postoffice, and in 1851 the name was changed to Denny at Washington. In the spring of 1832 Rockwell and Buffun rented their saw-mill to Chester Potter, who was also from Ashtabula county, Ohio. He added a small pair of burrs for grinding wheat and corn. These millstones were only twelve and a half inches in diameter, but did the grinding for a large scope of country. They were made by Potter from a Granite Boulder or "Nigger-head" found on the prairie in this county. Potter, however, continued here only one year, when he moved to Kelly Tp. and set up a mill for himself on Henderson Creek. Buffun sold out his interest to Rockwell September 21st, 1832, and went to Fulton county, afterwards to Rock Island. On the 8th of August, 1835, L. P. Rockwell and D. G. Baldwin entered into agreement to build a large flouring mill, which resulted in the erection of the present Rockwell Mills. The first P. M. here was J. Buffun, one year; then L. P. Rockwell for about twenty years. He died in 1860. The first school was in 1834—teacher, Miss Betsy Hopper. There is not a more pleasant location in this county than Denny.

LITTLE YORK.

This vicinity was first settled in 1829, and was among the earliest in this county.

Among those who first came here were: Matthew D. Ritchie, Otho W. Craig, William McCoy, Hugh Martin, Sr., and others. Much fear and some trouble was experienced from the Indians by the early settlers. A roving band of those desperadoes were skulking along the timber on Cedar Creek, on the 9th day of August, 1832, when five of their number rushed out, shot and scalped William Martin, who was at work alone putting up hay. A block house had been built as a kind of fort, where persons and families resorted in time of supposed danger. Several women and children were at the fort at this time, and heard the shots, saw Martin fall, and the Indians run to him, shoot again, and scalp him. The news spread rapidly, and caused great alarm among the inhabitants. Martin had been at the fort but a short time previous, was cautioned by the women about working alone, though it was not known that any Indians were in the vicinity. He returned to his work singing a favorite tune.

The block house stood a few rods east from where now stands the pleasant residence of Hugh Martin, brother of William, and he was killed about eighty miles north. His body was not recovered until the next morning, and when examined, it was found that the last shot was made so near as to burn his clothing.

A company of Rangers followed the trail of the Indians as far as New Boston, where they were just in time to see them in their canoes, nearly across the Mississippi river. They fired upon them, but did not avail to stop them.

An account of the trial of these murderers is given in another part of this work.

The village of Little Rock was laid out in 1835 by William McCoy and M. D. Ritchie. James Kendall opened the first store in this vicinity, at the block house in 1833, and after his death, in the next year, his widow moved the goods to a building on the site of the village, and continued in the trade. This she sold to Arthur McFarland, who soon sold to J. F. Pollock, and he had a prosperous trade there for many years. He was the first P. M. for nearly twenty years. The first school was in 1837, taught by Peter Turpening. At the present time there is a good school house and a good bell, with pleasant grounds ornamented with trees.

The principal merchants are Messrs. Wallace & Morrison, general merchandise. There are two harness shops, three blacksmith shops, one wagon shop, and a boot and shoe shop.

This village is located in a thriving and industrious farming community, and is in Sumner Township, twelve miles northwest from Monmouth.

The U. P. Church of Little York was organized April 19th, 1863, by Rev. John Scott, D. D., of the Presbytery of Monmouth. At the formation of this church there were forty-one members from the U. P. churches of Cedar Creek and Henderson. The first pastor was Rev. Wm. H. McMillan, ordained and installed Oct. 4, 1864, who continued his labors for six years. The next pastor was Rev. W. T. Campbell, ordained and installed June 13, 1871, and continued four years. The present pastor is Rev. David Anderson, who began his work here in October, 1875. This congregation own a pleasant and commodious house of worship, which cost $4,000, and a convenient parsonage, recently built at a cost of $2,000. The present number of members is 130.

ALEXIS

This village, though bearing the same name as the royal prince, is *not* a Russian Town. It was first called Alexandria and recently abbreviated to its present name for convenience. It is situated twelve miles north and east from Monmouth, and was laid out in Nov., 1870, by Robert Holloway and J. E. Alexander upon land owned by them. The first house was moved to the Town site Nov. 20, 1870, and upon the first train North on the Rockford, Rock Island and St. Louis R. R., J. E. Alexander moved his goods, and established the station. He has held the office of Station and Express Agent since the opening of the Railroad. The books of the Co. show that from this point there has been shipped 500 cars of stock in a year, and, sometimes 140 cars of grain per month. The growth of the town has been rapid, and although a sweeping fire in Jan., 1877, destroyed nine business houses, new buildings are rising to take their place, showing the confidence there is in the stability of the town.

There are four general stores, five groceries, two drug stores, two hardware and agricultural implements, one book and stationery store, two blacksmith shops, one flouring mill, one machine shop, two lumber yards and two hotels.

A fine two story school house was built in 1874, cost $2,600, and the schools are well graded, Superintendent, C. Galloway. The number of children by examination of Sept., 1876, was 384.

The first village Trustees came into office July 28, 1873, and their names are as follows: John C. Blaney, Prest.; A. G. Talbot, O. E. Bugbee, O. G. Chapman, James Loveridge, Daniel Churchill; John Douglas, Clerk, Chas. E. Johnson, Treasurer.—The present Board is Peter Bogue, Prest.; Daniel Churchill, Hiram Ingersoll, James H. Shaw, Robert Knox, W. W. Graham; Thos. B. Patterson, Clerk; Chas. E. Johnson Treas., and W. H. Brown Police Magistrate. The total population is about 700.

PRESS.

Mr. James Everett started the *Alexis Journal* at this place in 1874. He had originally intended to make it an eight column, four page paper; but from some cause cut it down to seven columns, four pages, in which form the first number appeared, on February 13, 1874, and was continued until the close of volume three, in 1877. Mr. Everett retired from its management in August, 1876, having sold the office to Dr. Chaffee. At the close of volume three, the prospect of its future seemed very gloomy, and it was decided to discontinue its publication. A few weeks later, having received sufficient encouragement, the Dr. concluded to resume, but decided to make a change in the name and style of the paper; accordingly the name was changed to *The Alexis Index*, and the size of the sheet enlarged to a five column, eight pages, a change which the proprietor feels assured was fully warranted, and is duly appreciated by the people. Its circulation and influence is steadily increasing, although its local advertising patronage has been materially cut down by the recent fire, and stringency of the times; still, the office is doing a fair business, remunerative to its owner, and much of its loss of local advertising is compensated for by its Monmouth patronage.

CHURCHES.

The United Presbyterian church was organized April 4, 1871, by Rev. J. M. Henderson. Meetings were first held at a school house some two miles distant. At the time of the organization there were thirty-one members, among whom are the following: Wm. A. Elder, Mrs. Jennie Elder, R. J. Lawhead and wife, Samuel Lawhead and wife. C. C. Graham and wife, Dr. J. F. McCutcheon and wife, J. C. Graham and wife and others.

The stated supplies for this congregation have been, Rev. J. M. Henderson, A. M. Black, D. D., and James I. Doig, D. D. This church has now its first regular pastor, Rev. M. F. McKirchan, who was ordained and installed May 30, 1876. The present number of members is fifty-three. Attendance at Sabbath school, seventy-six, J. C. Graham, Supt. A pleasant house of worship was built in 1873, at a cost of $3,100.

The United Brethren in Christ. The first meetings of this church were held in the Mohler school house, four miles S. W. of the town. At this place, the church was organized in the winter of 1859, with forty members. The following are a few of the names first received: A. J. Ritchey, Mary Ritchey, David Swiler, Catherine Swiler, John Line, Mary Line, and others.

The first pastor was Rev. D. F. Bair. Then followed Rev. J. R. Hommond, Rev. Ezra Hall, Rev. Daniel Ross, Rev. J. Slutts, Rev. St. Clair Ross, Rev. A. Norman, Rev. O. F. Smith, Rev. A. Worman, Rev. P. R. Adams Rev. J. P. Worman, and the present pastor, Rev. G. H. Varce.

A church edifice was built in 1872, at a cost $2,250. The present membership is 36. Sabbath school averages 50 pupils.

The Baptist church was organized July 4, 1868, at Spring Grove school house, afterwards moved to Alexis. Among those who were first members, are the names of Thomas Dunn, Mrs. Hannah Dunn, Miss Jennie A. Dunn, Miss Josephine E. Dunn, L. A. Palmer and others. The ministers who have supplied this church are as follows: Rev.——Welcher, Rev. E. L. Moore, Rev. O. Tompkins, Rev.——Lewis, Rev.——Shirley. A neat church was built in 1875 at a cost of $3,000. The present number of members is twenty-six. Attendance at Sabbath school averages twenty-five, M. M. Palmer, Superintendent.

M. E. Church. The first meetings were held in a grove in 1871. Afterward met in a hall. Among the pastors who have labored here are Revs. C. Atherton, P. A. Cool, A. Keller and C. E. Rowe, present pastor. Services are held on alternate Sabbaths in the Baptist Church. Present membership ninety-five. Attendance at Sabbath school eighty. Supt., Thomas Anderson.

Catholic. This organization is just completing a commodious structure, which will cost with improvements in contemplation about $3,000.

VILLAGE OFFICERS.

Trustees: A. G. Talbot, J. E. Lafferty, J. C. Blaney, John Oswalt, George B. Dodge, Dr. J. W. McClanahan. Clerk: Thos. B. Patterson. Police Magistrate: W. H. Brown.

LODGES.

Alexandria Lodge, No. 702, A. F. and A. M., at Alexis: John E. Alexander, W. M.; J. H. Wright, S. W.; P. H. Gregory, J. W.; T. R. Squires, Secy.; Steven Gamble, Treas.; M. D. Scott, S. D.; F. E. Wray, J. D.; J. H. Shaw, Tyler. Meets Friday evenings on or before full moon.

Alexis Lodge, No. 526, I. O. O. F.: Allen Laird, N. G.; George Santee, V. G.; W. H. Brown, R. Secy.; Chas. E. Johnson, P. Secy.; Robert T. Wray, Treas. Meets every Tuesday evening.

SPRING GROVE CHURCH.

The United Presbyterian Church of Spring Grove was organized June 22, 1855, by Rev. Matthew Bigger of the Presbytery of Monmouth, with fifty-one members. The first pastor was Rev. James C. McKnight, who was ordained June 11, 1856, and remained over four years. Rev. Wm. Graham was next pastor and continued this relation until his death, in the Fall of 1863. Rev. Thomas P. Patterson was ordained Oct. 27, 1864, and was pastor until April, 1868. Rev. David Inches began his labors with this church in June, 1869, and continued his work for five years. The present pastor is the Rev. Rufus Johnson, who began June 15, 1876. The present number of members is about seventy. This congregation own a large hosue of worship costing about $4,000 and a good parsonage with three acres of ground.

The Church of God is located in southeast quarter of Sec. 10, Spring Grove township. It was organized in 1865 by Rev. Rudolph White, and the earliest meetings were held in the school house in district No. 4. Among the original members were John Bailey and wife, D. C. Swiller, wife and three children, John Cannon and wife, and others. The church was built in 1867 and cost $1,600. The present pastor is Rev. Thos. De-Shiria. Membership about twenty-five and Sabbath school the same; John Simcox, Superintendent.

LENOX

Was laid out by C. C. Dixon in 1872, who owned the farm on which the village is platted. He had settled here in 1834, at a time when there was but one house between his and Monmouth, then containing but four or five houses.

No village was thought of until the Rockford, Rock Island and St. Louis railroad was contemplated. The company guaranteed the location of a depot to some ten or twelve residents who were active in securing the right of way through the township. Foremost among them was C. C. Dixon and J. W. Bridenthal. These located the station on the present site and Mr. Dixon at once took steps to lay out the town. The village plat and farm were afterwards purchased by Mr. Bridenthal, the present owner. Mr. T. H. Norwood opened the first store and the post office in the dwelling of Henry Redout. Shortly after John Hodgen and John Young erected the present store room occupied by Mr. Young and Graham. One or two additional stores have been opened and a good carriage and wagon shop is now in operation.

A large quantity of grain is shipped from this point. For the year 1876 331 car loads of grain were shipped. In addition to this, 70 car loads of live stock were sent to market.

The town and post office were given the name of *Lenox*. As there was a Station North of Monmouth by that name. Until it was discontinued, the village and office was called Lenox Station.

SCHOOLS.

One of the oldest district schools in the township is located here. As soon as the school population of the community warranted the erection of a house, a small structure was built. This was used with an occasional enlargement and repair, until 1876, when the present structure, one of the best in the township, was erected.

The attendance is now about forty scholars, which require the services of one teacher.

CHURCHES.

For several years past a Presbyterian church was maintained. About twelve years since through the effort of Mr. Dixon, who donated a lot, a comfortable house of worship was erected, and at one time quite a congregation had grown up, and regular preaching was sustained. Owing to removals and other causes has so diminished the church that the organization was disbanded, the remaining members going to Monmouth or to other churches. The Methodists now occupy the church but as yet have no organization.

GERLAW.

This village has a pleasant location. It was laid out as a town site May 2, 1871, on land owned by R. W. Gerlaw, after whom it bears its name. It is situated in the N. W. quarter of Section 34, Spring Grove township, and is on the Rockford, Rock Island R. R. six miles north from Monmouth.

A. A. Elder opened the first store in Sept., 1871. James Webster sometime after, built a large store, with a fine hall in second story. A brisk trade has been carried on here, considering its nearness to the county seat. The books of the R. R. Co. show that the shipment of stock has reached more than 200 cars in a single year. Very little grain is shipped from this point, as all is needed by feeders of stock.

The Christian church was organized in 1858, by Rev. L. S. Wallace, and a house of worship was built about about two miles north east from the town at a cost of $950. This building was moved to the town site in 1874, and was thoroughly repaired. Among the first members were J. T. Gilmore and wife, R. W. Lair and wife, B. F. Gardner and wife and others. The present membership is about forty. No pastor.

CAMERON

Was laid out by Robert Cameron, Feb. 22, 1854, and was for some time known as Cameronville. His plat included the south west part of the town lying south of the railroad. Charles Waste laid out a portion directly east of this, and north and west of this, across the railroad in Coldbrook township. Quinby's addition was soon after made.

A. B. Hawkins was the first merchant in town. His store stood directly east of Isaac Wilson's shop in a now vacant lot.

Owen C. Waste and Smith & Skinner of Galesburg opened stores soon after, and for some time a fine trade was engaged. Mr. Hawkins had previously kept a store in Coldbrook, but as soon as the C. B. & Q. R. R. was completed and Cameron platted he removed his store and goods to that place. Nearly all the business of Cold Brook was brought to Cameron at this and latter dates.

The town has always been small, but a good trade is steadily maintained. A good number of stores and shops are now in successful operation, and enjoying a good patronage.

SCHOOLS.

The first district school house was built south of the railroad, and was the first house erected on the village plat. There being two districts, (the railroad being the dividing line between the township of Cold Brook and Floyd,) in 1871, these were consolidated into one, and the present two story building erected.

It will accommodate 100 pupils, the attendance being now eighty-five.

COUNTY TREASURER

CHRISTIAN CHURCH.

This is the oldest congregation of this denomination. It was organized in 1831. Their earliest meetings were held in private houses and in the school house. At this time they were at Cold Brook.

Some of their Elders were John G. Haley, Elijah Davidson and Wm. Whitman. Levi Hatchett, John E. Murphy and L. S. Wallace were some of the earliest ministers.

A house of worship was built in Cold Brook in 1839. The congregation continued to meet here until 1854 or '5 when they removed to Cameron and there erected their present church, costing about $3,000. A portion of the congregation went near the present town of Alexis, where they have now a strong church. About 1851 or '2 Elder R. R. Haley and Deacon John E. Murphey, with some thirty members went to Monmouth, Oregon, where they formed the nucleus of a large and flourishing congregation. Josiah Whitman, S. T. Sheton and Henry E. Haley were chosen to fill the offices made vacant by those removing to Oregon.

The Cameron congregation have now about 125 members and sustain a Sunday school of 70 scholars. Rev. D. D. Miller is the present pastor.

THE M. E. CHURCH.

In the fall of 1856, ministers of this denomination commenced services in the school house, and soon thereafter organized the church.

Some twelve or fifteen persons united. Among them were Mr. and Mrs. Watt, Mr. and Mrs. Porterfield, Frank Morey, Benj. Tinkham, Mrs. Fox, Mrs. Gay and Mary Gay. Rev. Fisher presided at the organization.

In 1857, they erected their present church edifice, which is now inadequate to the wants of the congregation and will soon be replaced by a commodious house.

The growth of the congregation has been slow, and at no time has the membership been large. The number now is about forty.

The First Baptist Church at this place was organized June 30th, 1866, and its first meetings were held in the district school house with an original membership of nine persons, which has increased to sixty-five, and a Sunday school of sixty.

The present church was built in 1869 at a cost of $3,200. The pastors have been the Revs. Wm. Whitehead, Jno. Bolton, W. R. Welch, E. L. Corfield and J. R. Pennington. Their present pastor is Rev G. D. Kent.

SWAN CREEK.

The settlement in this locality dates back to about 1837. A post-office has been maintained here since that date.

As soon as the railroad was completed, steps were taken to establish a depot here, but although the company would stop their trains, they would not build a switch or erect the necessary buildings until the residents had raised $1,000. This was secured mainly through the efforts of Mr. George Worden, one of the earliest residents and who had keep a store since December, 1856, in a building opposite his dwelling. It is now used as a dwelling and harness shop. Mr. Worden laid out the town April 15, 1871, and soon after Rev. W. C. Romine opened a store. He is now in Roseville. B. Ragin and Aaron Burr, opened stores about this time and have steadily upheld their trade. There are now three or four good stores, the same number of shops, a good mill and elevator.

A large amount of shipping is done from this point. Before the completion of the railroad in 1870, this was taken to Oquawka and to Prairie City, where nearly all trading at this time was done.

Now the produce is shipped to Chicago and St. Louis.

SCHOOLS.

A good school has always been held here. In 1876, a large comfortable house was erected, which is a credit to the town. About fifty scholars are daily in attendance.

CHURCHES.

The Methodist Episcopal Church was organized in 1872 and '3. The earliest meetings were held in the school house, a little north of the village. Those who took part in these meetings were Austin A. Cornell, Andrew J. Sisson, Nancy J. Sisson, Rufus K. Sisson, Mary E. Sisson, Burwell Booth, Anna M. Phillips. These had been members of the M. E. Church at Pleasant Mound, six miles southeast of Swan Creek, except Burwell Booth who had been a member of the M. E. Church at Point Pleasant. In 1873 a church was built at a cost of $2,000. Rev. C. B. Conch served from 1872 till September, 1874. He was followed by Rev. J. W. Coe, who served till September, 1876. Their present pastor, Rev. N. T. Allen, was appointed September, 1876. Twenty-six members have been added to the church the past winter, the result of a revival under the leadership of the present pastor and the earnest efforts of the members. There are now sixty-one members and a thriving Sabbath school of eighty scholars.

YOUNGSTOWN

Was laid out by the Kidder family and others in the spring of 1872.

The first store was opened by H. V. Simmons in a building erected by C. W. Mapes. The building is now occupied by Wm. Miner. One or two other stores have since been erected. One or two shops are now in operation.

The town plat was, until 1872, the farm of the Kidder family, and when the plat was surveyed and a station established, before one was allowed at Swan Creek, as the railroad company objected to two depots so closely together. This latter objection was, however, overruled by the energy of the citizens along the line.

Youngstown supports a good local trade, and is the shipping point for all farm produce from this locality.

SCHOOLS.

Schools has been held in the district school house many years. An effort is now being made to add an additional room and grade the school. This will promptly be carried out in a year or so.

CHURCHES.

About 1870, the members of the Baptist denomination met in the school house for divine worship and in 1873, were organized into a church. It is known at the Swan Creek Baptist church. Soon after the name was changed to correspond with the town and as such is now known.

The membership at first was small but now is largely increased, and sustain a minister one half the time, he devoting the other Sabbath to the Pleasant Baptist church.

Rev. Joel Pennington now occupies the pulpit.

Youngstown Lodge, No. 387, A. F. and A. M.—Officers: W. W. Shoop, W. M.; R. B. Predmore, S. W.; H. H. Kidder, J. W.; H. V. Simmons, Secy.; P. P. Smith, Treas. Meets at Youngstown on the second and fourth Saturdays of each month.

KELLY TOWNSHIP.

CHURCHES.

The M. E. Church was organized in 1837, its first meetings being held in private houses and school houses. In 1872 their present church building was erected, on Sec. 04, at a cost of $2,300.

The pastors and their respective terms of service have been as follows: Rev. Mr. Atherton, 1870 and 1871; Rev. Henry Brink, Jr., 1871 to 1873; Rev. C. W. Swartz, 1873 to 1874; Rev. A. Keller, 1874 to 1876. M. W. Smith assisted Mr. Keller one year, and the present pastor is Rev. C. E. Rowe.

SHANGHAI.

The "Second Advent Church" was organized about 1857, the principal original members being Samuel Black and wife, A. N. Yarde and wife, H. Richardson and wife, Spencer Ryner and wife, J. Pine and wife, B. Watson and wife.

The earliest meetings were held in the school house. Their present church, at Ionia, was built in 1867 at a cost of about $2,700. The first minister was Guy Rathbone, who preached three years, from 1856 to 1859. From this time until the church was built the pulpit was filled by "supplies" when Wm. McCullock and H. McCullock took charge from 1867 to 1869. Geo. Hurd followed until 1871, then Wm. McCullock in 1872, after him Marshall McCullock from 1872 to 1875, when the present incumbent, Geo. Hurd, took charge.

The Sunday school, in summer, numbers about forty-five scholars, with a church membership of about one hundred.

The great tornado in May, 1868, completely destroyed their church, but was immediately rebuilt at an additional cost of over $1,400.

POINT PLEASANT TOWNSHIP.

CHURCHES.

The Cumberland Presbyterian Church was organized at Boothe school house September, 1863, with about seventeen members, viz: Josiah Kirkpatrick, Lucinda Hindman, Mary Hughens, Eliza Hindman, Amanda Johnson, W. R. Hindman, John B. O'Neal, Mary E. Dixon, Mary Dixon, Mary E. Boyd, Elizabeth Hughens, Susan F. Dean, Esther Hughens, J. M. O'Neal, Malony O'Neal, Elizabeth O'Neal, Elizabeth Curtis, Mary Lester, Emma J. Boyd. The church was bought from the M. E. society for $500. Their first pastor, John Crawford, served ten years. Rev. J. D. Foster is the present pastor. The membership is fifteen. No Sabbath school at present.

COLFAX.

The Methodist Episcopal Church was organized at Center school house in the spring of 1875. The first meetings were held at this place. The members were David Vangilder, Jennie Vangilder, E. F. Dehart, L. A. Dehart, J. A. Williams, J. Chapman, M. Chapman, C. Gunn, Cath. Gunn, M. B. Torrance, Mary Conklin, Rhoda Chapman, Eliza J. Altman, W. H. Dehart, John R. Conklin, C. B. Torrance, Sarah J. Morey. Their church was built in the spring of 1875, at a cost of $1,700. Rev. J. W. Coe served six months. He was followed by Rev. P. S. Garrettson, who took charge September, '75, and is the present pastor. There are at present thirty-five members and a Sabbath school of thirty-five scholars.

NEW HOPE.

The Predestinarian Baptist Church was organized in 1836, at the house of Caleb Hedges. The earliest meetings were held at this house, also the Downie School-house. Among the original members were Joseph Rogers and wife, John Murphy, B. Lewis, and John Riggs. All the original members are supposed to be dead, except John Riggs.

This Church has had three pastors, namely, Rev. Charles Vandiveer, who served several years, Rev. George Tracy, and Rev. I. N. Vanmeter, their present pastor. The clerks were Wm. Gunter, R. M. Simmons, and Alfred W. Simmons. The present deacons are John Vandiveer, and Andrew W. Simmons. Elder, R. W. Simmons. There are now thirty-nine members.

Berwick Lodge, No. 619, A. F. & A. M.—Officers: R. H. Shelton W. M.; J. M. Norris, S. W.; Leander Giddings, J. W.; E. A. Hearkness, Secy.; Geo. Berrington, Tres. Meets at Cameron every second and fourth Thursday evenings.

Official Vote of Warren County, November, 1876.

Townships.	For President.			For Governor.			Lieut. Governor.			Secretary of State.			Auditor Pub. Accts	
	Hayes, Rep.	Tilden, Dem.	Cooper, Ind.	Cullom, Rep.	Stewart, Dem. & Ind	Shuman, Rep.	Glenn, Dem.	Pickrell, Ind.	Harlow, Rep.	Thornton, Dem.	Hooton, Ind.	Needles, Rep.	Hise, Dem. & Ind
Greenbush,	82	129	19	83	147	82	132	16	82	132	16	82	148
Berwick,	68	108	4	67	112	68	112		67	112		68	111
Floyd,	135	62	14	135	71	135	62	9	135	62	9	135	71
Coldbrook,	82	126	11	83	136	83	130	6	83	130	6	83	136
Kelly,	129	84	21	129	105	129	103	2	129	103	2	129	105
Swan,	93	144	22	95	164	93	151	15	93	151	15	93	166
Roseville,	220	152	7	221	159	220	155	5	220	155	5	220	156
Lenox,	93	89	10	93	99	93	90	9	93	90	9	93	99
Monmouth,	877	478	6	883	474	882	476	2	879	479	3	879	482
Spring Grove,	65	48	3	65	51	65	47	4	65	47	4	65	51
Alexis Precinct,	79	97	10	79	107	79	99	8	79	99	8	79	106
Point Pleasant,	100	104	2	100	106	100	106		100	106		100	106
Ellison,	147	104		147	104	147	104		147	104		147	104
Tompkins,	308	150	8	309	157	308	153	5	308	153	5	308	158
Hale,	150	65		150	65	150	65		150	65		150	65
Sumner,	167	44	1	167	45	167	45		167	45		167	45
Total	2795 1984	1984	138	2806 2102	2102	2301 2030	2030	81	2797 2033	2033	82	2798 2109	2109
Majorities,	811			704		771			764			689	

Townships.	State Treasurer.			Attorney General.			Congress 10th District.			Board of Equaliz'n		State's Attorney.	
	Rutz, Rep.	Gundlach, Dem.	Aspern, Ind.	Edsall, Rep.	Lynch, Dem.	Coy, Ind.	Marsh, Rep.	Hungate, Dem.	Christie, Ind.	Boice, Rep.	Caheen, Dem. & Ind	Snyder, Rep.	Norcross, Dem. & Ind
Greenbush,	82	132	16	82	132	16	83	144	3	82	148	76	153
Berwick,	67	111		68	111		68	110	1	68	111	67	112
Floyd,	135	62	9	135	62		134	77		134	67	129	81
Coldbrook,	83	130	6	83	130	6	81	130	1	82	136	77	139
Kelly,	129	103	2	129	103	2	129	103	1	129	105	129	103
Swan,	93	151	15	93	151	15	93	152	14	93	166	71	175
Roseville,	220	155	5	220	156	5	220	155	5	221	159	210	156
Lenox,	93	90	9	93	90	9	94	90	7	93	99	94	90
Monmouth,	878	480	3	878	480	3	879	476	1	874	483	848	498
Spring Grove,	65	47	4	65	47	4	65	51		65	51	65	50
Alexis Precinct,	79	99	8	79	99	8	79	106		79	106	79	106
Point Pleasant,	100	106		100	106		100	106		100	106	91	109
Ellison,	147	104		147	104		146	105		147	104	143	104
Tompkins,	308	152	6	309	151	6	305	160	1	308	158	309	155
Hale,	150	65		150	65		149	66		150	65	143	71
Sumner,	167	45		167	45		164	47		165	46	154	50
Total,	2796 2032	2032	83	2798 2032	2032	74	2789 2084	2084	34	2790 2110	2110	2685 2152	2152
Majorities	794			766			705			680		533	

Official Vote of Warren County.—Concluded.

Townships.	For Representatives. 23d District.				Circuit Clerk.		For Sheriff.		For Coroner.	
	Boydston, Rep.	Westfall, Rep.	Whitaker, Dem.	Epperson, Ind.	Dryden.	Barhour.	Bond.	Vanderveer.	McCleary.	Holliday.
Greenbush	123	123	161½	427½	75	155	79	143	82	145
Berwick,	105	102	151½	178½	68	111	69	110	67	111
Floyd,	335½	74	70½	149	135	75	130	81	133	76
Coldbrook,	117	129	75	331½	84	135	72	146	83	136
Kelly,	193½	193½	17	292½	129	103	129	103	129	103
Swan,	141	141	219	273	87	163	77	168	95	154
Roseville,	330	330	336	153	225	150	207	165	220	155
Lenox,	136½	136½	133½	160	98	91	100	88	95	90
Monmouth,	1328½	1314	706	691	864	490	799	491	873	477
Spring Grove,	97½	97½	15	138	65	50	65	50	65	50
Alexis Precinct,	117	117		321	86	105	79	107	79	106
Point Pleasant,	150	150	114	201	99	107	99	105	100	106
Ellison,	220½	222	154½	156	149	102	147	104	147	104
Tompkins,	402	400½	220½	244½	319	146	312	149	302	162
Hale,	225	225	97½	97½	149	65	133	70	149	66
Summer,	249	249	66	66	169	42	150	48	167	44
Total,	4330	4064	2401½	3880	2801 2090	2090	2647 2128	2128	2786 2085	2085
Majorities,					711		519		701	

WARREN COUNTY WAR RECORD.

ABBREVIATIONS.

Adjt............Adjutant.	e............enlisted.
Art............Artillery.	excd............exchanged.
Col............Colonel.	inf............infantry.
Capt............Captain.	kld............killed.
Corpl............Corporal.	m. o............mustered out.
Comsy............Commissary.	prmtd............promoted.
comd............commissioned.	prisr............prisoner.
cav............cavalry.	Regt............Regiment.
captd............captured.	Sergt............Sergeant.
disd............discharged.	wd............wounded.

EIGHTY-THIRD INFANTRY.

The Eighty-Third Infantry Illinois Volunteers was organized at Monmouth, Ills., in August, 1862, by Col. A. C. Harding, and mustered in August 21. Moved from camp August 25, via Burlington and St. Louis to Cairo, arriving 29th, and reporting to Brigadier General Tuttle, commanding post. Sept. 3d moved to Fort Henry and on the 5th, leaving two companies at Fort Heiman and three at Fort Henry, moved to Fort Donelson, where the headquarters of the regiment remained during the year; Colonel W. W. Lowe, 5th Iowa Calvary, commanding Brigade.

The companies from Forts Henry and Heiman subsequently rejoined the regiment, and it remained at Fort Donelson until Sept. 20, 1863, when the right wing moved to Clarksville. The regiment had heavy guard duty to perform, and as the whole country, especially the banks of the Tennessee and Cumberland Rivers, were infested with guerrillas, had daily skirmishes with the enemy, some of them quite severe as at Waverly (Tennessee) and at Garretsburg (Kentucky) where the lamented General Ransom, then colonel of the Eleventh Illinois, had command.

On the 3d Feb. 1863, at Fort Donelson, nine companies of the Eighty-third with Company C, Second Illinois Light Artillery, successfuly resisted the attack of Forrest and Wheeler, with eight thousand men, the battle lasted from 1:30 p. m. until 8:30 p. m. when the enemy were compelled to retire with a loss of eight hundred killed and wounded. The loss of the Regiment was 13 killed and 51 wounded. Colonel Harding was promoted to Brigadier General for gallant conduct on this occasion and Lieutenant Colonel A. A. Smith to Colonel. While at Clarksville, the Regiment was engaged in several expeditions under Major General L. H. Roseau, in pursuit of Forrest and Wheeler who were attempting the destruction of General Sherman's communications.

During the year 1864, the Regiment had some two hundred miles of communications to guard, and much heavy patrol duty. During the winter of 1864-5 the Eighty-third was on provost duty at Nashville, Tennessee. On the 26th June, 1865, was mustered out at Nashville and moved for Chicago, Ills., Brevet Brigadier General Arthur A. Smith commanding, where it received final pay and discharge.

ROSTER OF THE REGIMENT.

Colonel, Abner C. Harding, rank Aug. 21, 1862. Mustered Aug. 21, 1862. Promoted Brig. Gen. Vols. May 23, 1863.
Colonel, Arthur A. Smith, rank March 11, 1863. Mustered June 4, 1863. Promoted Brevet Brig. Gen. March 13, 1865. Mustered out June 26, 1865.
Lieut. Colonel, Arthur A. Smith, rank Aug. 21, 1862. Mustered Aug. 21, 1862. Promoted.
Lieut. Colonel, Elijah C. Brott, rank March 11, 1863. Mustered June 4, 1863. Mustered out June 26, 1865.
Major, Elijah C. Brott, rank Sept. 30, 1862. Mustered Sept. 30, 1862. Promoted.
Major, Wm. G. Bund, rank March 11, 1863. Mustered June 4, 1863. Mustered out June 26, 1865.
Adjutant, Wesley B. Casey, rank Aug. 21, 1862. Mustered Aug. 21, 1862. Resigned Aug. 5, 1864.
Adjutant, John W. Green, rank Aug. 5, 1864. Mustered Sept. 1, 1864. Mustered out June 26, 1865.
Quartermaster, Jno. B. Colton, rank Aug. 21, 1862. Mustered Aug. 21, 1862. Promoted Brigade Quartermaster.
Quartermaster, Harmon D. Bissell, rank Jan. 6, 1863. Died Feb. 3, 1863.
Quartermaster, Geo. Snyder, rank Feb. 3, 1863. Mustered March 6, 1863. Resigned Feb. 7, 1864.
Quartermaster, Wm. H. Sexton, rank Feb. 7, 1864. Mustered March 1, 1864. Mustered out June 26, 1865.
Surgeon, Esaias S. Cooper, rank Nov. 14, 1862. Mustered Nov. 14, 1862. Mustered out June 26, 1865.
First Assistant Surgeon, J. P. McClanahan, rank Aug. 21, 1862. Mustered Oct. 1, 1862. Resigned March 30, 1854.
First Assistant Surgeon, Wm. L. Cuthbert, rank May 5, 1865. Absent on duty at muster out of regiment.
Second Assistant Surgeon, Richard Morris, rank Sept. 30, 1862. Mustered Sept. 30, 1862. Promoted Surgeon 103d Regiment.
Second Assistant Surgeon, Wm. L. Cuthbert, Jan. 1, 1863. Mustered Jan. 2, 1863. Promoted.
Second Assistant Surgeon, Edwin H. Cooper, rank May 5, 1865. Mustered May 19, 1865. Mustered out June 26, 1865.
Chaplain, Adam C. Higgins, rank, Aug. 21, 1862. Mustered Aug. 21, 1862. Mustered out June 26, 1865.
Sergeant Major, Theo. H. Hurd, enlisted 1862. Discharged Feb. 3, 1863, disabled.
Sergeant Major, Thomas J. Baugh, enlisted 1862. Discharged Feb. 3, 1863, disability.
Sergeant, John W. Green, enlisted 1862. Promoted Adjutant, Sept. 1, 1864.
Sergeant Major, Wm. P. Speakman, enlisted 1862. Mustered out June 26, 1865.
Quartermaster Sergeant, Harmon D. Bissell. Killed at Fort Donelson, Feb. 3, 1863
Quartermaster Sergeant, Geo. W. Snyder, enlisted 1862. Promoted R. Q. M. March 6, 1865.
Quartermaster Sergeant, Wm. H. Sexton, enlisted 1862. Promoted R. Q. M. March 1, 1864.
Quartermaster Sergeant, Wm. M. Buffington, enlisted 1862. Mustered out June 26, 1865.
Commissary Sergeant, Wm. Shores, enlisted 1862. Promoted First Lieut. Co. H.
Commissary Sergeant, Harlow B. Norton, enlisted 1862. Discharged for promotion in U. S. C. Artillery.
Commissary Sergeant, Samuel C. Hogue, enlisted 1862. Mustered out June 26, 1865.
Hospital Steward, Marcellus M. Rowley, enlisted 1862. Discharged Jan. 10, 1863, disability.
Hospital Steward, Hiram S. Roberts, enlisted 1862. Mustered out June 26, 1865.
Principal Musician, Weston S. Livermore, enlisted 1862. Mustered out June 26, 1865.
Principal Musician, Nathaniel Coleman, enlisted 1862. Mustered out June 26, 1865.

Company A.

Captain Philo C. Reed, rank Aug. 21, 1862, mustered Aug. 21, 1862. Killed Feb. 3, 1863.
Captain Geo H. Palmer, rank Feb. 3, 1863, mustered March 6, 1863. Mustered out June 26, 1865.
First Lieutenant Geo. H. Palmer, rank Aug. 21, 1862, mustered Aug 21, 1862. Promoted.
First Lieutenant Davis M. Clark, rank Feb. 3, 1863, mustered Mch. 6, 1863. Mustered out June 26, 1865
Second Lieutenant Davis M. Clark, rank Aug. 21, 1862, mustered Aug. 21, 1862. Promoted.
Second Lieutenant Cyrus Bute, rank Feb. 3 1863, mustered Mch. 6, 1863. Mustered out June 26, 1865.
First Sergeant Wm. P. Speakman, e. Aug. 2, 1862. Promoted Sergeant Major.
Sergeant James L. Stain, e. July 30, 1862. Mustered out June 26, 1865 as First Sergeant.
Sergeant Cyrus Bute. e. Aug. 5, 1862. Prmt. 2d. Lieut.
Sergeant Wm. H. McCool, e. Aug. 5, 1862. Mustered out June 26, 1865.
Sergeant N. A Scott, e. July 24, 1862. Mustered out June 26, 1865 as Private.
Corporal Holmes Clayton, e. July 18, 1862. Mustered out June 26, 1865 as Sergeant.
Corporal Samuel G. Morris, e. Aug. 4, 1862. Mustered out June 26, 1865 as Private.
Corporal Seymour J. Nutt, e. Aug. 5, 1862. Mustered out June 26, 1865.
Corporal M. V. T. Burns, e. Aug. 2, 1862. Mustered out June 26, 1865 as Sergeant.
Corporal Wm. M. Buffington, e. Aug. 2, 1862. Promoted Q. M. Sergeant,
Corporal C. D. Shoemaker, e. Aug. 5, 1862. Mustered out June 26, 1865.
Corporal W. G. Strain, e. Aug. 2, 1862. Discharged Jan. 10, 1865 as private, disabled.
Corporal James H. Bowman, e. Aug. 5, 1862. Mustered out June 26, 1865, as Private.
Musician J, A. Wallace, e. Aug. 2, 1862. Mustered out June 26, 1865.
Musician H. A. Smith, e. Aug. 5, 1862. Mustered out June 26, 1865.
Wagoner C. D. Anderson, e. Aug. 5, 1862. Mustered out June 26, 1865.

PRIVATES.

Anthony A. W. e. Aug. 5, 1862, m. o. June 26, 1865.
Ames J. V. e. Aug. 4, 1862 disd. Nov. 15, 1862, disab.
Abby Grant, e. Aug, 5, 1862, killed May 13, 1865.
Abby George, e. Aug. 5, 1862, m. o. June 26, 1865.
Arter Daniel, e. Aug. 5. 1862, disd. Jan 24, 1863, disab.
Babcock Noyes, e. Aug. 1, 1862 m. o. June 26, 1865.
Bay A. R. e. Aug. 2, 1862 disd. Jan 24, 1863, disab.
Burdick J. T. e. Aug, 2, 1862, killed Oct. 28, 1863.
Borton C. W. e. Aug. 2, 1862, m. o. June 26, 1865.
Brown W. e. Aug. 5, 1862, m. o. June 26, 1865.
Burns Wm. e. Aug. 5, 1862, m. o. June 26, 1865.
Bryan A. e. Aug. 5, 1862, disd. Feb 17, 1863, wounded.
Baker J. R. e. Aug. 6, 1862, m. o. June 26, 1865.
Balding F. H. e. Aug. 5, 1862, disd. Feb. 3, 1863, disab.
Bramhall J. H. e. Aug. 5, 1862, disd. Jan. 24, '63, disab.
Brooks Wm. H. e. Aug. 5, 1862, killed Feb. 3, 1863.
Culbertson J. W. e. Aug. 1, 1862, m. o. June 26, 1865.
Cox G. W. e. Aug. 2, 1862, killed Oct. 23, 1862.
Claycomb Wm. O. e. Aug. 4, 1862, m. o. June 26, 1865.
Clark C. e. Aug. 5, 1862, m. o. June 26, 1865.
Chicken Wm. e. Aug. 5, 1862, m. o. June 26, 1865.
Campbell James, e. Aug. 5, 1862, m. o. June 26, 1865.
Campbell Jno. e. Aug. 5, 1862, died May 27, 1864.
Clark Joel, e. Aug. 5, 1862, m. o. June 26, 1865.
Clark Merrett, e. Aug 5, 1862, m. o. June 26, 1865.
Clyborne Wm. L. e. Aug. 5. 1862, m. o. June 26, 1865.
Dickson Luther, e. July 18. 1862, disd, July 9, '63, disab.
Dickson, S. R. e. Aug. 5, 1862, killed Jan. 2, 1863.
Dillon M. L. e. Aug. 5, 1862, m. o. June 26, 1865.
Dally Frank, e. Aug. 5, 1862, died Dec. 17, 1862
Fulton James M. e. Aug. 5, 1862, m. o. June 26, 1865.
Francis H. e. Aug. 5, 1862, m. o. June 26, 1865.
Findley J. T. e. Aug. 5, 1862, m. o. June 26, 1865.
Gordon Aaron, e. Aug. 5, 1862, m. o. June 26, 1865.
Godfrey D. C. e. Aug. 5, 1862, m. o. June 26, 1865.
Goddard James, e. Aug 5, 1862, m. o. June 26, 1865.
Gouldin H. R. e. Aug. 5, 1862, disd. April 10, '63, wds.
Holloway W. e. Aug. 2, 1862, died Feb. 3, 1863.
Humbsh P. e. Aug. 4, 1862, m. o. June 26, 1865.
Hoag, W. e. Aug. 6, 1862, m. o. June 26, 1865.
Hoerner. J. A. e. Aug. 5, 1862, m. o. June 26, 1865.
Harris M. V. e. Aug. 6, 1862, died April 24, 1863.
Haynes J. P. e. Aug. 5, 1862, died June 28, 1863.
Ingwood G. e. Aug. 5, 1862 m. o. June 26, 1865.
Joss C. H. e. Aug. 2, 1862, disd. June 9, 1863, disab.
Jones O. e. Aug. 5, 1862, m. o. June 26, 1865.
Lowrey J. E. e. Aug. 2, 1862, disd. May 29, 1863 disab.
Leeper J. e. Aug. 5, 1862, disd. Jan. 12, 1863, disab.
Metzger G. e. Aug. 4, 1862, m. o. June 26, 1865.
Matthews J. J. e. Aug 5, 1862. m. o. June 26, 1865.
Martin W. J. e. Aug. 5, 1862, m. o. June 26, 1865.
Nelson N. J. e. Aug. 5, 1862, m. o. June 26, 1865.
Norton H. B. e. Aug. 5, 1862, prmt. Commissary Sergt.
Payton James, e. Aug. 2, 1862, disd. May 29, '65, disab.
Prevost, C. C. e. Aug. 1, 1862, m. o. June 26, 1865.
Prevost F. C. e. Aug. 2, 1862, m. o. June 26, 1865.
Pears N. L. e. Aug. 5, 1862, m. o. June 26, 1865.
Palmer M E. e. Aug. 5, 1862, m. o. june 26, 1865.
Post Sheldon, e. Aug. 5, 1862, disd. April 18, '63, disab.
Ripley J. R. e. Aug. 1, 1862, disd. March 17, '63, disab.
Rowley M. M. e. Aug. 1, 1862, disd. Jan. 10, '63, disab.
Reed T. J. e. Aug. 5, 1862, m. o. June 26, 1865.
Reeves Jno. e. Aug. 5, 1862, m. o. June 26, 1865.
Seeton T. M. e. Aug. 2, 1862, m. o. June 26, 1865.
Speakman H. C. e. Aug 2, 1862, m. o. June 26, 1865, as Corporal.
Sterrett D. S. e. Aug. 5, 1862, m. o. June 26, 1865.
Shaffer J. A. e. Aug. 4, 1862, m. o. June 26, 1865.
Sanford C. L. e. Aug. 5, 1862, disd. Jan. 5, 1864, disab.
Turner G. W. e. Aug. 5, 1862, trans. to navy May 18, '64.
Tinkum I. A. e. Aug. 5, 1862, m. o. June 26, 1865.
Tinkum J. H. e. Aug 5, 1862. m. o. June 26, 1865.
Todd, C. S. e. Aug. 6, 1862, m. o. June 26, 1865.
Vertrus J. R. e. Aug. 2, 1862, m. o. June 26, 1865.
Williams Perry, e. Aug. 4. 1862, deserted Sept. 30, 1863.
Wilde J. H. e. Aug. 4, 1862, m. o. June 26, 1865.
Whitman W. e. Aug. 4, 1862, m. o. June 26, 1865.
Wagetaff R. e. Aug. 5, 1862, m. o. June 26, 1865.
Wedlin Gustus, e. Aug. 5, 1862, disd. Jan. 24, '63, disab.
Winebright G. e. Aug. 5, 1862, m. o. June 26, 1865.
Wells Wm, J. e. Aug. 5, 1862, m. o. June 26, 1865.

RECRUITS.

Burns Jesse, e. Mch. 3, '65, trans. to Co. E 61st Ill. Inf.
Corcoran R. e. Mch. 3, '65, trans. to Co .E 61st Ill. Inf.
Coppersmidt Andrew, e. March 3, 1865, trans. to Co. E, 61st Ill. Inf.
Foster M. e. April 4, 1865, trans. to Co. E 61st Ill. Inf.
Hahn M. e. Jan. 28, '64, trans. to Co. E. 61st Ill. Vol. Inf.
Hudson G. W. e. April 4, 1865, drowned March 7, 1865.
Monroe G. W. e. Mch. 28, '65, trans. to Co. E 61st Ill. Inf.
Nichols Geo. e. Mch. 3, '65, trans. to Co. E 61st Ill. Inf.
Palmer Allen, e. Mch. 31, '64, trans to Co. E 61st Ill. Inf.
Russel Wm. e. Mch. 3, '65, trans. to Co. E. 61st Ill. Inf.
Snapp E. e. April 4, '65, trans. to Co, E 61st Ill. Inf.
Talby W. F. e. Mch. 6, '65, trans. to Co. E 61st Ill. Inf.
Wells A. B. e. Mch. 7, '65, trans. to Co. E 61st Ill. Inf.
Worden Linden, e. Mch. 30, '65, trans. to Co. E 61st Ill. Inf.
Williams J. A. e. Mch. 17, '65, trans to Co E 61st Ill. Inf.
Wilson C. C. e. Mch. 14, '65, trans. to Co. E. 61st Ill. Inf.

Company B.

Captain Jno. McClanahan, rank Aug. 21, 1862, mustered Aug. 21, 1862. Died of wds. Feb. 23, 1864.
Captain Wm. W. Turnbull, rank Feb. 3, 1863, mustered July 1, 1863. Killed Aug. 20, 1864.
Captain Jas. Moore, rank Aug. 20, 1864, mustered Sept. 30, 1864. Mustered out June 26. 1865.
First Lieutenant Jas. Moore, rank Aug. 21, 1862, mus. tered Aug. 21, 1862. Promoted
First Lieutenant Jas. H. Herdman, rank Aug 20, 1864, mustered Oct. 5, 1864. Mustered out June 26. 1865.
Second Lieutenant Wm. W. Turnbull, rank Aug. 21, 1862, mustered Aug. 21, 1862. Promoted.
Second Lieutenant Jas. H. Herdman, rank Feb. 3, 1863, mustered March 6, 1863. Promoted.
Second Lieutenant Wm. S. Struthers, rank March 20, 1865, mustered April 2, 1865. Mustered out June 26, 1865.
First Sergeant James H. Herdman, e. July 26, 1862. Promoted 2d Lieutenant.
Sergeant Josiah Martin, e. Aug. 2, 1862. Disd. Feb. 16, 1863, disab.
Sergeant Wm. S. Struthers, e. July 21, 1862. Promoted 2d Lieutenant.
Sergeant Robt. H. Thompson, e. July 21, 1862. Disd. Feb. 10 1863, disab.

WARREN COUNTY WAR RECORD.   183

Sergeant Geo. N. Sansom, e. July 14, 1862. Disd. July 17, 1864, for Pro. in U. S. C. H. Arty.
Corporal James Cowan, e. Aug. 5. 1862. Disd. Feb. 10, 1863. disab.
Corporal Murdock McKinzie, e. Aug. 6, 1862. Mustered out Jan. 26, 1865, as Sergeant.
Corporal Jno A. Wright, e. Aug. 2, 1862. Mustered out Jan. 26, 1865, as Sergeant.
Corporal J. H. Giles, e. Aug. 2, 1862. Died Dec. 10. '62.
Corporal M. A. Thompson, e. Aug. 7, 1862. Killed Aug. 20, 1861.
Corporal Samuel C. Hogue, e. July 27, 1862. Promt. Com. Sergt.
Corporal Robt. Gowdy, e. Aug. 5, 1862. Mustered out June 26, 1865.
Corporal James C. Moore, e. Aug. 6, 1862. Disd. Feb. 10, 1863. disab.
Musician Jno. A. Patterson, e. July 18, 1862. Mustered out June 26, 1865.
Musician J. Pattison, e. Aug. 11, 1862. Kld Aug. 20, '64.
Wagoner Wm. Chalmers, e. July 26, 1862. Mustered out June 26, 1865.

PRIVATES.

Arnold J. W. e. Aug. 6, 1862, m. o. June 26, 1865.
Armstrong J. e. Aug. 11, 1862, m. o. June 26, 1865.
Baldwin G. e. Aug. 6, 1862, m. o. June 26, '65 as Corpl.
Baldwin C. e. Aug. 6, 1862, disd. Jan. 8, 1863, disab.
Brewer James, e, Aug. 2, 1862, disd. Dec. 22, '63. disab.
Brown James, e. July 19, 1862, m. o. June 26, 1865.
Prownler H. e. Aug. 6, 1862, disd. Oct. 12, 1864, disab.
Butterfield R. V. e. Aug. 6, 1862, m. o. June 26. 1865.
Butterfield A. Z. e. Aug. 11, 1862, m. o. June 26, 1865.
Cannon W. A. e. July 25, 1862, m. o. June 26, 1865.
Cline D. O. e. Aug. 11, 1862, m. o. June 26, 1865.
Copeland C. R. e. Aug. 7, 1862, m. o. June 26, 1865.
Cowan R. e. July 23, 1862, m. o. June 26, 1865.
Cowan T. e. Aug. 23, 1862, m. o. June 26, 1865.
Clark Francis, e. July 23, 1862, m. o. June 26, 1865.
Elder D. C. e. Aug. 11, 1862, m. o. June 26, 1865.
Elliott J. J. e. Aug. 1, 1862, m. o. June 26, 1865.
Elliott R. H. e. July 20, 1862, m. o. June 26, 1865.
Ellis Wm. e. July 26, 1862, m. o. June 26, 1865.
Finley W. W. e. July 26, 1862, kld Aug. 20, 1864.
Foster S. A. e. Aug. 6, 1862, kld. Aug. 20, 1864.
Galloway J. S. e, July 24, 1862, disd. Mch 13, '63, disab.
Garside Jos. e. Aug. 12, 1862, disd. April 25, '64, disab.
Gilleland W. T. e. Aug. 5, 1862, m. o. June 26, 1865.
Glover Wm. M. e. Aug. 2, 1862, m. o. June 26, 1865.
Gowdy D. C. e. Aug. 5, '62, m. o. June 26, '62, as Sergt.
Hays R. e. Aug. 2, '62, m. o. June 26, '65, as Corpl.
Hogue I. C. e. Aug. 1, 1862, disd. Feb. 1863, disab.
Hogue Wm. A. e. Aug. 2, 1862, m. o. June 26, 1865.
Hogue F. C. e. Aug. 5, 1862, m. o. June 26, 1865.
Hogue J. H. e. July 26, 1862, m. o. June 26, 1865.
Hull M. Deroy e. Aug. 2, '62, disd. Oct. 18, '63, disab.
Johnson N. e. July 30, 1862, m. o. June 20, 1865.
McColton D. C. e. July 22, '62, disd. Mch. 31, '65, disab.
McCulley M. e. Aug. 6, 1862, m. o. June 26, 1865.
McMillen Jno. e. Aug. 2, '62, disd. Feb. 2, '63, disab.
McCreary G. B. e. Aug. 2, 1862, m. o. June 26, 1865.
McClelland R. e. Aug. 2, '62, m. o. June 26, '65 as Corpl.
Martin J. M. e. Aug. 2, '62, m. o. June 26, '65 as Corpl.
McKelvie M. e. Aug. 6, 1862, m. o. June 26, 1865.
Moore L. A. e. Aug. 6, 1862, died Nov. 3, 1862.
Moore R. C. e. Aug. 2, 1862, disd. Jan. 24, 1863, disab.
Moley I. H. e. Aug. 11, 1862, disd. April 4, 1863, disab.
Morrison Robt. P. e. Aug. 5, 1862, m. o. June 26, 1865.
Muilnix R. F. e. Aug. 6, 1862, m. o. June 26, 1865.
Neely James, e. Aug. 2, 1862, m. o. June 26, 1865.
Nelson Alexander, e, July 26, 1862, died Nov. 19, 1862.
Olmsted A. F. e. Aug. 6, 1862, m. o. June 26, 1865.
Paine W. N. e. Aug. 5, 1862, m. o. June 26, 1865.
Pollock T. G. e. Aug. 11, 1862, disd Feb. 12, '63, disab.
Paine J. E. e. July 26, 1862, m. o. June 26, 1865.
Parsons Austin, e. Aug. 6, 1862, m. o. June 26, 1865.
Pense A. L. e. Aug. 2, 1862, m. o. June 26, 1865.
Preston J. A. e. Aug. 11, 1862, disd. Feb. 12, '63, disab.
Preston J. M. e. July 26, 1862, m. o. June 26, 1865.
Paul Wm. e. Aug. 11, 1862, disd. Jan. 8, 1863, disab.
Pyles A. B. e. Aug. 11, 1862, m. o. June 26, 1865.
Rockwell E. W. e. July 14, 1862, died Feb. 27, 1863.
Rogers A. A. e. July 22, 1862, di-d. April 20, '65, disab.
Rogers N. e. July 26, 1862, disd. Feb. 10, 1863, disab.
Ross D. W. e. Aug. 6, 1862, m. o. June 26, 1865.
Sample J. R. e. Aug. 6, 1862, disd. Mch. 7, 1864, disab.
Sansom J. L. e. July 19, 1862, disd. Oct. 28, 1862, disab.
Scott R. e. Aug. 4, 1862, m. o. June 26, 1865.
Scott Wm. P. e. Aug. 4, 1862, disd. Nov. 18, '62, disab.

Shnidaler Jno. e. July 26, '62, disd. Sept. 19, '63, disab.
Smith O. W. e. Aug. 6, 1862, m. o. June 26, 1865.
Smith S. R. e. July 26, 1862, m. o. June 26, 1865.
Sterrett S. E. e. Aug. 11, 1862, m. o. June 26 1865.
Sansom J. B. e. Aug. 11, 1862, disd. for pro. as 2d Lieut. 8th U. S. C. H. Art.
Stevenson R. M. e. Aug. 2, 1862, m. o. June 26, 1865.
Struthers J. A. e. July 26, 1862, m. o. June 26, 1865.
Teas Wm. P. Aug. 11, 1862, m. o. June 26, 1865.
Turnbull D. A. e. July 26, 1862, m. o. June 26, 1865 as Corporal.
Weeks T. C. e. Aug. 5, 1862, m. o. June 26, 1864.
Wilson W. C. e. July 19, 1862, m. o. June 26, 1865.
Wilson J. G. e. Aug. 2, '62, m. o. June 26, '65 as Sergt.
Wood J. W. e. Aug. 2, 1862, died April 2, 1865.
Wood W. e. Aug. 5, 1862, deserted Oct. 21, 1863.
Warwick A. M. e. Aug. 11, 1862, m. o. June 26, 1865.

RECRUITS.

Alexander C. L. e. March 20, 1865, trans. to Co. E 61st Ill. Inf.
Baird J. S. e. Nov. 20, '63, trans. to Co. E 61st Ill. Inf.
Black A. e. Feb. 25, 1864, trans. to Co. E. 61st Ill. Inf.
Dougherty O. J. e. March 20, 1865, trans. to Co. E 61st Ill. Inf.
Glen J. H. e. Nov. 20, 1863, died March 3, 1865.
Hogue J. W. e. Nov. 13, 1863, kld. Aug. 20, 1864.
Harper J. A. e. Feb. 25, '64, trans to Co. E 61st Ill. Inf.
Looby Patrick, e. Feb. 17, 1865, trans. to Co. F. 61st Ill. Inf.
Morrison M. M. e. Feb. 25, 1864, trans. Co. E 61st Ill. Inf.
Moore J. A. e. Dec. 24, '63 trans. Co. E 61st Ill. Inf.
Michaels W. N. e. Jan. 13, '64, trans. Co. E 61st Ill. Inf.
McCay P. e. Jan. 20, 1864, trans Co. E. 61st Ill. Inf.
McGeary E. e. Feb. 17, 1865, trans. Co. E. 61st Ill. Inf.
McCoy T. M. e. Feb. 17, 1865, trans. Co. E. 61st Ill. Inf.
McCrary M. R. e. Feb. 12, '65, trans. Co. E 61st Ill. Inf.
Martin W. F. e. Dec. 24, 1863, kld. Aug. 20, 1864.
Monre F. M. e. Jan. 28, 1864, disd. April 4, 1865, disab.
Nickol A. M. e. Feb. 17, 1865, trans. Co. E 61st Ill. Inf.
Thompson W. N. e. Nov. 13, 1863, trans. Co. E 61st Ill. Inf.
Thompson W. M. e. Feb. 17, 1865, trans. Co. E 61st Ill. Inf.
Waller G. W. e. Feb. 17, '65, trans. Co. E. 61st Ill. Inf.
Cobb Milton, e. Oct. 13, 1863, deserted Jan. 18, 1864.
Ferguson E. e. Oct. 10, 1863, died March 16, 1864.

Company C.

Captain Lyman B. Cutler, rank Aug. 11, 1862, mustered Aug. 21, 1862. Mustered out June 26, 1865.
First Lieutenant John C. Gamble, rank Aug. 11. 1862, mustered Aug. 21, 1862. Mustered out June 26, 1865.
Second Lieutenant S. L. Stephenson, rank Aug. 11, 1862, mustered Aug. 21, 1862. Mustered out June 26, 1865.
First Sergeant J. S. Campbell, e. July 21, 1862, killed Feb. 3, 1863.
Sergeant John R. Leslie e July 21, 1862, mustered out June 26, 1865, as First Sergeant.
Sergeant A. B. Chaffee, e. July 31, 1862, mustered out June 26, 1865, as private.
Sergeant J. W. Beard, e. July 19, 1862, discharged June 10, 1863 disability.
Sergeant L. Peal, e. July 22. 1862, absent at muster out.
Corporal J. H. Montgomery, e. July 21, 1862, discharged July 2, 1864, to accept Chaplaincy 16th U. S. C. I.
Corporal E. H. Brittan, e. July 24, 1862, mustered out June 26, 1865, as private.
Corporal A. Caskey, e. July 22, 1862, discharged Sept. 28, 1864, to accept position as Adjutant 101st U. S. C. I.
Corporal A. B. Hawkins, e. Aug. 2, 1862, discharged May 7, 1865, as private disabled.
Corporal S. S. Patton, e. July 21, 1862, mustered out June 26, 1865, as Sergeant.
Corporal G. W. Robinson, e. Aug. 2, 1862, mustered out June 26, 1865, as private.
Musician W. T. Livermore, e. Aug. 2, 1862. Promoted principal musician.
Musician, A. West, e. July 28, 1862, m. o June 26, 1865.
Wagoner J. M. Strong, e. Aug. 2, 1862, mustered out June 26, 1865.

PRIVATES.

Allen B. B. e, Aug. 1, 1862, died Feb. 11, 1863 wds.

Augst J. e. Aug. 2, 1862. Died.
Anderson J. e. July 29, 1862, m. o. June 26, 1865.
Anderson G. W. e. July 18, 1862, disd. Jan. 10, 1863 disab.
Amey H. e. Aug. 4, 1862, m. o. June 25, 1865.
Bunker A. M. e. July 18, 1862, m. o. June 26, 1865.
Barrett G. L. e. July 30, 1862, disd. Jan. 24, 1863 disab.
Benkert E. G. e. July 19, 1862, m. o. June 26, 1865.
Bailey H. J. e. Aug. 2, 1862, m. o. June 26, 1865.
Brown C. M. e. Aug. 2, 1862, disd. Feb. 18, 1863 disab.
Butler Ira. e. July 31, 1862, murdered Jan. 30, 1864.
Coleman D. E. e. Aug 11, 1862, m. o. June 26, 1865.
Caldwell J. M. e. Aug. 2, 1862, m. o. June 26, 1865 as Corpl.
Chapman G. D. e. Aug. 2, 1862, m. o. June 26, 1865.
Crozier M. e. Aug. 2, 1862, m. o. June 26, 1865.
Crandall E. H. e. July 26, 1862, disd. Jan. 10, 1863 disab.
Crosby W. e. Aug. 11, 1862, m. o. June 26, 1865.
Dively J. e. Aug. 4, 1862, m. o. June 26, 1865.
Edwards W. L. e. July 30, 1862, m. o. June 26, 1865.
Frazier L. B. e. Aug. 2, 1862, m. o. June 26, 1865.
Falsom Geo. W. e. Aug. 2, 1862, kld. Feb. 3, 1863.
Gowdy Thomas, e. July 31, 1862, m. o. July 26, 1865.
Grubbs J. W. e. Aug. 4, 1862, m. o. June 26, 1865.
Godfrey J. e. Aug. 2, 1862, m. o. June 26, 1865.
Griffin H. M. e. Aug. 2, 1862, m. o. June 26, 1865 as Corpl.
Griffin W. e. Aug. 5, 1862, m. o. June 26, 1865.
Hill B. F. e. Aug. 2, 1862, died in Ky. Apr. 22, 1863.
Horner M. e. July 29, 1862, disd. Dec. 22, 1862 disah.
Higgison F. M. e. Aug. 2, 1862, disd. Nov. 17, 1862.
Henry G. T. e. Aug. 2, 1862, m. o. June 26, 1865.
Jones John, e. Aug. 1, 1862, m. o. June 26, 1865.
Jones J. H. e. Aug. 11, 1862, m. o. june 26, 1865.
Lusk L. M. e. July 18, 1862, m. o. June 26, 1865.
Lawhead R. J. e. Aug. 6, 1862, m. o. June 26, 1865.
McReynolds R. L. e. July 30, 1862, m. o. June 26, 1865.
Morris C. L. e. July 19, 1862, m. o. June 26, 1865.
Mitchell J. F. e. Aug. 11, 1862, died Aug. 10, 1864.
Mitchell G. L. e. July 25, 1862, m. o. June 26, 1865 as Corpl.
Murdock Jonas, e. Aug. 4, 1862, m. o. June 26, 1865 as Corpl.
Matteson A. e. July 31, 1862, disd. Mch. 31, 1863 disab.
McWilliams S. T. e. July 30, 1862, m. o. June 26, 1865.
McWilliams T. T. e. July 30, 1862, m. o. June 26, 1865.
McCombs, e. Aug. 2, 1862, disd. Dec. 10, 1862, disab.
McIntyre Wm. e. July 25, 1862, m. o. June 26, 1865.
McKown J. B. e. July 22, 1862, m. o. June 26, 1865.
Nichols J. R. e. Aug. 2, 1862, disd. Dec. 12, 1862 disab.
Pherman Jos. e. July 24, 1862, disd. Dec. 17, 1862 disab.
Pike S. M. e. July 24, 1862, m. o. June 26, 1865.
Peal Geo. F. e. July 30, 1862, died Nov. 10, 1862.
Robinson B. F. e. July 31, 1862, died Feb. 19, 1863.
Rouse N. B. e. Aug. 5, 1862, m. o. June 26, 1865.
Rice H. e. Aug. 4, 1862, m. o. June 26, 1865.
Smith E. e. Aug. 11, 1862, m. o. June 26, 1865.
Smith J. e. Aug. 11, 1862, m. o. June 26, 1865.
Sellman A. e. Aug. 8, 1862, m. o. May 20, 1865.
Shirley S. L. e. July 31, 1862, m. o. June 26, 1865.
Stewart L. T. e. Aug. 2, 1862, disd. May 1, 1865 disab.
Stewart J. E. e. Aug. 2, 1862, died Feb. 13, 1863.
Speaks J. B. e. Aug. 2, 1862, disd. May 6, 1863 wd.
Shirwin J. C. e. Aug. 2, 1862, m. o. June 26, 1865.
Salisbury S. e. Aug. 2, 1862, m. o. June 26, 1865.
Salisbury M. e. July 31, 1862, m. o. June 26, 1865 as Corpl.
Talbot J. B. e. Aug. 11, 1862, disd. Dec. 5, 1863 disab.
Worman J. T. e. Aug. 2, 1862, m. o. June 26, 1865.
Wiggins C. e. July 31, 1862, m. o. June 26, 1865 as Corpl.
Wagoner J. A. e. July 31, 1862, died Dec. 1, 1862.
Weaver J. W. e. July 29, 1862, m. o. June 26, 1865.
Walker D. e. Aug. 2, 1862, m. o. June 26, 1865.
Wright W. M. e. July 25, 1862, m. o. June 26, 1865.
Wilcox Levi, e. Aug 2, 1862, m. o. June 26, 1865.
Wilkinson W. R. e. Aug. 2, 1862, kld. Feb. 3, 1863.
Yates J. e. July 31, 1862, m. o. June 26, 1865 as Corpl.

RECRUITS.

Butler C. H. trans. Co. D 61st Ill. Inf.
Bailey D. B. e. Feb. 17, 1865, trans. Co. E 61st Ill. Inf.
Bruce M. H. e. Feb. 17, 1865, trans. Co. H 61st Ill. Inf.
Barrett Wm. H. e. Mch. 3, 1865, trans. Co. E 61st Ill. Inf.
Crosier G. R. e. Oct. 30, 1863, trans. Co. E 61st Ill. Inf.
Derensey D. e. Mch. 10, 1865, trans. Co E 61st Ill. Inf.
Graham B. F. e. Feb. 29, 1864, trans. Co. E. 61st Ill. Inf.
Hammond J. e. Feb. 25, 1864, trans. Co. E 61st Ill. Inf.
Marston F. e. Feb. 25, 1864, trans. Co. D 61st Ill. Inf.
McWilliams J. T. e. Feb. 22, 1865, trans. Co. D 61st Ill. Inf.
Wallace H. F. e. Feb. 25, 1864, trans. Co. D. 61st Ill. Inf.

Wallace S. S. e. Feb. 25, 1864, trans. Co. D 61st Ill. Inf.
Wheeler C. W. e. Nov. 30, 1863, trans. Co. D 61st Ill. Inf.
Wells H. T. e. Mch. 10, 1865, trans. Co. D 61st Ill. Inf.
Wells G. W. e. Apr. 7, 1865, trans. Co. D 61st Ill. Inf.
Galson S. e. Sept. 19, 1863, m. o. June 26, 1865.
Martin W. e. Sept. 19, 1863, m. o. June 26, 1865.

Company F.

Captain Jno. Morgan, rank Aug. 21 1862, mustered Aug. 21, 1862. Mustered out June 26, 1865.
First Lieutenant Jos. A. Boyington, rank Aug. 21, 1862, mustered Aug. 21, 1862. Resigned Mch. 15, 1863.
First Lieutenant Jas. W. Morgan, rank Mch. 25, 1863, mustered Mch. 15, 1863. Mustered out June 26, '65.
Second Lieutenant Jas. W. Morgan, rank Aug. 21, 1862, mustered Aug. 21, 1862. Promoted.
Second Lieutenant Wm. A. Peffer, rank Mch. 25, 1863, mustered May 15. 1863. Mustered out June 26, '65.
First Sergeant J. W. Milligan e. Aug. 11, 1862, died Oct. 3, 1863.
Sergeant S. Buffington e. Aug. 12, 1862, dis. May 5, 1863, disab.
Sergeant J. M. Crosier e. Aug. 6, 1862, m. o. June 26, 1865.
Sergeant I. Leeper e. Aug. 6, 1862, dis. Dec. 26, 1862, disab.
Sergeant Wm. A. Peffer e. Aug. 6, 1862. Promoted Second Lieutenant.
Corporal A. Hallem e. Aug. 6, 1862, mustered out June 26, 1865.
Corporal J. H. Boynton, e. Aug. 11, 1862, mustered June 26, 1865, as private.
Corporal W. H. Clark, e. Aug. 13, 1862, promoted Capt. 16th U. S. C. I. June 26, 1864.
Corporal W. S. Green, e. Aug. 7, 1862, mustered out June 26, 1865, as private.
Corporal J. A. Marsha, e. Aug. 11, 1862, mustered out June 26, 1865, as private.
Corporal Geo. Mannon, e. Aug. 13, 1862, mustered out June 26, 1865, as Sergeant.
Corporal W. R. Tubbs, e. Aug. 11, 1862, killed Feb. 3, 1863.
Corporal J. L. Romans, e. Aug. 7, 1862, mustered out June 26, 1865, as private.
Musician L. Sovereign, e. Aug. 13, 1862, mustered out June 26, 1865.
Musician M. F. Sharp, e. Aug. 15, 1862, discharged Jan. 12, 1863, disabled.

PRIVATES.

Abbott H. e. Aug. 11, 1862, m. o. June 26, 1865.
Aholts D. W. e. Aug. 9, 1862, m. o. June 26, 1865.
Allison H. M. e. Aug. 13, 1862, m. o. June 26, 1865, as Corpl.
Barnes M. e. Aug. 13, 1862, m. o. June 26, 1865.
Barnes I. M. e. Aug. 13, 1862, dis. Apr. 10, 1863, disab.
Barnum C. L. e. Aug. 8, 1862, m. o. June 26. 1865.
Barnum G. A. e. Aug. 8, 1862, m. o. June 26, 1865.
Baugh T. J. e. Aug. 11, 1862, pro. Sergt. Major.
Black W. J. e. Aug. 12, 1862, m. o. June 26, 1865.
Brownhall, G. D. e. Aug. 12, 1862, m. o. June 26, 1865.
Bone C. C. e. Aug. 13, 1862, m. o. June 26, 1865 as Corpl.
Clark Henry, e. Aug. 13, 1862, m. o. June 26, 1865.
Clark A. H. e. Aug. 11, 1862, m. o. June 26, 1865.
Clem A. J. e. Aug. 11, 1862, m. o. June 26, 1865.
Crosier Charles, e. Aug. 11, 1862.
Duncan J. W. e. Aug. 12, 1862, m. o. June 26, 1865, as Sergt.
Davis F. B. e. Aug. 13, 1862, m. o. June 26, 1865, as Co. pl.
Diehl Simon, e. Aug. 6, 1862, dis. Mch. 12, 1864, disab.
Drennen A. H. e. Aug. 13, 1862, m. o. June 26, 1865.
Evans W. A. e. Aug. 11, 1862, dis. Feb. 3, 1864.
Gerris J. B. e. Aug. 7, 1862, m. o. June 26, 1865.
Gibson R. S. e. Aug. 8, 1862, m. o. June 26, 1865.
Gilland D. J. e. Aug. 11, 1862, dis. Apr. 10, '63, disab.
Grayham J. C. e. Aug. 15, 1862, m. o. June 26, 1865.
Hardenbrook R. L. e. Aug. 9, 1862, m. o. June 26, '65.
Hill J. e. Aug. 13, 1862, m. o. June 26, 1865.
Hass D. S. e. Aug. 6, 1862, dis. May 5, 1863, disab.
Homer I. C. e. Aug. 9, 1862, m. o. June 26, 1865.
Kerns, D. P. e. Aug. 8, 1862, m. o. June 26, 1865.
Lape J. D. e. Aug. 13, 1862, dis. Feb. 25, '63, disability.
Lamphere O. e. Aug. 8, 1862, m. o. June 26, 1865.
Larson Ole, e. Aug. 12, 1862, m. o. June 26, 1865.
Mathew J. H. e. Aug. 13, 1862, died Feb. 23, '63, wds.

McComb J. R. e. Aug. 11, 1862, m. o. June 26, 1865.
McCune J. e. Aug. 11, 1862, m. o. June 26, 1865.
Medhurst W. e. Aug. 13, 1862, m. o. June 26, 1865.
Medhurst J. B. e. Aug. 13, 1862, m. o. June 26, 1865.
Migher D. e. Aug. 12, 1862, dis. Mch. 8, 1865, disab.
Moore J. E. e. Aug. 6, 1862, died Feb. 6, 1863.
Mohler L. e. Aug. 13, 1862, trans. V. R. C.
Mohler Wm. H. e. Aug. 13, 1862, died Oct. 21, 1862.
Machy H. e. Aug. 13, 1862, m. o. June 26, 1865.
Osborn J. M. e. Aug. 12, 1862, died Aug. 16, 1863.
Palmer M. M. e. Aug. 8, 1862, m. o. June 26, 1865.
Patterson T. R. e. Aug. 13, '62, dis. Jan. 24, '63, disab.
Perrin Wm. Jr. e. Aug. 6, 1862, m. o. June 26, 1865.
Potter T. e. Aug. 7, 1862, m. o. June 26, 1865.
Pruden Peter W. e. Aug. 11, 1862, m. o. June 26, 1865.
Ramsey J. S. e. Aug. 12, 1862, m. o. June 26, 1865.
Reighter T. F. e. Aug. 6, 1862, m. o. June 26, 1865, as Sergt.
Reynold M. e. Aug. 9, 1862, m. o. June 26, 1865.
Rice W. F. e. Aug. 9, 1862, dis. Feb. 6, 1863, disab.
Richey W. H. e. Aug. 15, 1862, m. o. June 26, 1865.
Richter P. e. Aug. 9, 1862, dis. Jan. 24, 1863, disab.
Rhodenbaugh N. e. Aug. 13, 1862.
Roney S. W. e. Aug. 11, 1862, m. o. June 26, 1865.
Rusk M. D. e. Aug. 8, 1862, m. o. June 26, 1865.
Sawtell J. E. e. Aug. 9, 1862, m. o. June 26, 1865.
Shallenberger Wm. H. e. Aug. 9, 1862, dis. Jan. 12, 1863, disab.
Smilie Wm. B. e. Aug. 6, 1862, m. o. June 26, 1865.
Short F. e. Aug. 13, 1862, died Dec. 26, 1862.
Shoemaker L. G. e. Aug. 13, 1862, dis. July 17, 1863.
Smith J. W. e. Aug. 11, 1862, m. o. June 26, 1866.
Spencer F. H. e. Aug. 11, 1862, m. o. June 26, 1865.
Steeth L. M. e. Aug. 7, 1862, died Oct. 30, 1862.
Struter Wm. e. Aug. 9, 1862, m. o. June 26, 1865.
Thomas A. e. Aug. 9, 1862, die. Aug. 31, 1863, disab.
Van Lewen J. B. e. Aug. 9, 1862, m. o. June 26, 1865.
Weir J. B. e. Aug. 12, 1862, m. o. June 26, 1865.
Wickham Geo. e. Aug. 11, 1862, died Nov. 3, 1862.
Wilton W. e. Aug. 8, 1862, m. o. June 26, 1865.
Yargus Wm. e. Aug. 7, 1862, m. o. June 26, 1865.

RECRUITS.

Allen Henry, e. Jan. 5, 1864, trans. Co I 61st Ill. Inf.
Clark James, e. Feb. 4, 1864, trans. Co. I 61st Ill. Inf.
Clark John, e. Feb. 4, 1864, trans. Co. I 61st Ill. Inf.
Dement W. M. e. April 7, 1865, deserted June 18, 1865.
Futhey L. e. April 7, 1865, trans. Co. I 61st Ill. Inf.
Gevins James, e. April 20, '64, trans. Co. I 61st Ill. Inf.
Hogue W. H. e. Nov. 20, '63, trans. Co. I 61st Ill. Inf.
Kerns S. T. e. April 7, 1865, trans. Co. G 61st Ill. Inf.
Kirkpatrick R. ———, dis. May 8, 1863, disab.
Lusk T. W. e. June 11, 1863, trans. Co. G 61st Ill. Inf.
McCune J. H. e. Nov. 20, 1862, trans. Co. G 61st Ill. Inf.
Reed O. L. ———, m. o. June 26, 1865.
Sloan Thomas, ———, m. o. June 26, 1865.

Company H.

Captain Wm. G. Bond, rank Aug. 21, 1862, mustered Aug. 21, 1862. Promoted Major.
Captain Giles Crissey, rank Mch. 11, 1863, mustered June 6, 1863. Mustered out June 26, 1865.
First Lieutenant Walter N. Bond, rank Aug. 21, 1862, mustered Aug. 21, 1862. Resigned Mch. 25, 1863.
First Lieutenant Wm. Shores, rank Mch. 25, 1863, mustered May 16, 1863. Mustered out June 26, 1865.
Second Lieutenant James C. Johnson, rank Aug. 21, '62, mustered Aug. 21, 1862. Resigned Mch. 14, '63.
Second Lieutenant Francis M. Nance, rank Mch. 14, 1863, mustered May 16, 1863. Mustered out June 26, 1865.
First Sergeant Giles C. e. Aug. 4, 1862. Promoted Captain.
Sergeant F. M. Nance, e. Aug. 9, 1862. Promoted Second Lieutenant.
Sergeant J. Hartford, e. Aug. 6, 1862, discharged Feb. 25, 1863.
Sergeant L. Booth, e. Aug. 9, 1862, mustered out June 26, 1865.
Sergeant Wm. Thatcher, e. Aug. 9, 1862, deserted June 30, 1863.
Corporal B. F. or R. Ostrander, e. Aug. 1, 1862, mustered out June 26, 1865 as First Sergeant.
Corporal DeKalb Morris, e. Aug. 7, 1862, mustered out June 26, 1865.
Corporal Daniel Perdue, e. Aug. 9, 1862, discharged April 10, 1863.

Corporal J. C. Morris, e. Aug. 9, 1862, mustered out June 26, 1865.
Corporal G. T. Sheffield, e. Aug. 1, 1862, died Sept. 29, 1863.
Corporal J. L. Dorris, e. Aug. 9, 1862, mustered out June 26, 1865 as Sergeant.
Corporal P. H. Woods, e. Aug. 4, 1862, mustered out June 26, 1865 as Sergeant.
Corporal S. T. McBride, e. Aug. 11, 1862, died Nov. 23, 1862.
Wagoner Wiley Clayton, e. Aug. 11, 1862, discharged Jan. 12, 1863.

PRIVATES.

Almond J. W. e. Aug. 9, 1862. Died of wds.
Bostwick S. E. e. July 26, 1862, kld. Apr. 28, 1865.
Brown Perry, e. Aug. 6, 1862, m. o. June 26, 1865.
Bostwick G. L. e. Aug. 1, 1862, m. o. June 26, 1865.
Beam J. e. Aug. 6, 1862, m. o. June 26, 1865.
Boydston W. T. e. Aug. 7, 1862, m. o. June 26, 1865.
Coursan John, e. Aug. 2, 1862, m. o. June 26, 1865.
Coursan S. e. July 26, 1862, disd. Jan. 10, 1863.
Claycomb F. e. Aug. 2, 1862, m. o. June 26, 1865.
Charls A. e. Aug. 9, 1862, m. o. June 26, 1865.
Curtis J. e. Aug. 11, 1862, disd. Apr. 15, 1863.
Curtis T. B. e. Aug. 11, 1862, m. o. June 26, 1865.
Cunningham H. e. Aug. 6, 1862, m. o. June 26, 1865.
Damitz Wm. e. Aug. 6, 1862, m. o. June 26, 1865.
Davis J. K. P. e. Aug. 6, 1862, m. o. June 26, 1865.
Edie I. e. July 26, 1862, m. o. June 26, 1865.
Enfield John, e. Aug. 9, 1862, disd. May 4, 1863.
Gillett O. F. e. Aug. 4, 1862, disd. Jan. 6, 1863.
Gregg R. A. e. Aug. 4, 1862, died Oct. 4, 1862.
Gillham W. e. Aug. 5, 1862, disd. June 4, 1865.
Gillett R. G. e. Aug. 7, 1862, m. o. June 26, 1865.
Geoghegan Wm. B. e. Aug. 7, 1862, disd. June 9, 1863.
Gorden J. e. Aug. 9, 1862, m. o. June 26, 1865.
George I. H. Aug. 9, 1862, m. o. June 26, 1865.
Howell W. H. e. Aug. 11, 1862, m. o. June 26, 1865.
Hammond H. H. e. Aug. 5, 1862, m. o. June 26, 1865.
Johnson R. M. Aug. 4, 1862, died June 19, 1863.
Johnson S. C. e. Aug. 6, 1862, m. o. June 26, 1865.
Jones Andrew, e. Aug. 9, 1862, m. o. June 26, 1865.
Kerries Jacob, e. Aug. 9, 1862, disd. Jan. 6, 1864.
Long J. e. Aug. 11, 1862, m. o. June 26, 1865.
McBride A. e. July 29, 1862, disd. Feb. 20, 1865.
Mabry C. e. Aug. 1, 1862, m. o. June 26, 1865.
Murrill W. e. Aug. 1, 1862, m. o. June 26, 1865.
May Quincy, e. Aug. 6, 1862, disd May 8, 1865.
Maeras F. e. Aug. 6, 1862, deserted Dec. 31, 1864.
Moulton T. e. Aug. 6, 1862, m. o. June 26, 1865.
Means G. H. e. Aug. 7, 1862, m. o. June 26, 1865.
Moier L. e. Aug. 8, 1862, drowned Aug. 4, 1863.
Mackey J. e. Aug. 9, 1862, m. o. June 26, 1865.
Patterson S. e. Aug. 9, 1862, m. o. June 26, 1865.
Parks W. e. Aug. 9, 1862, m. o. June 26, 1865 as Corpl.
Perdue C. C. e. Aug. 9, 1862, m. o. June 26, 1865, as Corpl.
Park W. B. e. Aug. 9, 1862, m. o. June 26, 1865.
Porter Lewis, e. Aug. 12, 1862, m. o. June 26, 1865.
Palmer F. R. e. Aug. 12, 1862, died Nov. 25, 1862.
Robinson I. e. Aug. 9, 1862, m. o. June 26, 1865.
Regan J. e. Aug. 9, 1862, m. o. June 26, 1865.
Roberts R. e. Aug. 6, 1862, m. o. June 26, 1865.
Saffer S. W. e. Aug. 5, 1862, disd. Oct 2, 1862.
Spencer T. J. e. Aug. 7, 1862, m. o. June 26, 1865.
Sheppard G. W. e. Aug. 7, 1862, m. o. June 20, 1865.
Swartz L. W. e. Aug. 7, 1862, m. o. June 26, 1865.
Sargent T. B. e. Aug. 9, 1862, disd. Oct. 30, 1862.
Sappington O. F. e. Aug. 11, 1862, m. o. June 26, 1865.
Sharp T. J. e. Aug. 9, 1862, m. o. June 26, 1865.
Tinder I. R. e. Aug. 1, 1862, m. o. June 26, 1865.
Tate J. e. Aug. 11, 1862.
Wicks J. J. e. Aug. 12, 1862, m. o. June 26, 1865.
Walker J. K. e. July 26, 1862, m. o. June 26, 1865.
Wright A. e. Aug. 4, 1862, m. o. June 26, 1865.
Young H. e. Aug. 1, 1862, disd. Oct. 1, 1864.
Young J. K. P. e. Aug. 6, 1862, m. o. June 26, 1865.

RECRUITS.

Allard A. C. m. o. June 26, 1865.
Bostwick T. H. e. Jan. 28, 1864, trans. Co. I 61st Ill. Inf.
Butler A. e. Mch. 10, 1865, trans. Co. I 61st Ill. Inf.
Barber R. P. e. Mch. 10, 1865, trans. Co. I 61st Ill. Inf.
Cunningham T. e. Mch. 10, 1865, trans. Co. I 61st Ill. Inf.
Carothers W. G. m. o. June 26, 1865.
Davis J. S. disd. May 19, 1865.
George S. A. e. Feb. 22, 1865, trans. Co. I 61st Ill. Inf.
Houts J. B. e. Mch. 10, 1865, trans. Co. I 61st Ill. Inf.

Houts H. e. Mch. 15, 1865, trans. Co. I 61st Ill. Inf.
Heanderburg I. H. e. Mch. 10, 1865, trans. Co. I 61st Ill. Inf.
Hitchcock Niles, e. Mch. 17, 1865, trans. Co. I 61st Ill. Inf.
Hitchcock C. P. e. Mch. 17, 1865, trans. Co. I 61st Ill. Inf.
Hills J. A. m. o. June 26, 1865, as musician.
Jomel J. M. e. Mch. 15, 1865, trans. Co. I 61st Ill. Inf.
Kelley W. e. Mch. 10, 1865, trans. Co. I 61st Ill. Inf.
Laprey D. e. Mch. 15, 1865, trans. Co. I 61st Ill. Inf.
Landaker P. e. Mch. 16, 1865, trans. Co. I 61st Ill. Inf.
Latze, D. disd. Jan, 9, 1863
Landon M. m. o. June 26. 1865, as Corp.
McClure H. B. e. Mch. 6, 1865, trans. Co. I 61st Ill. Inf.
Miller S. e. Mch. 6, 1865, tran-. Co I 61st Ill. Inf.
Moore G. W. c. Mch. 6, 1865, trans. Co. I 61st Ill. Inf.
Morris M. e. Mch. 10, 1865, trans. Co. I 61st Ill. Inf.
McGowan A. e. Mch. 30, 1865, trans. Co. I 61st Ill. Inf.
Ostrander C. A. e. Mch. 6, 1865, trans. Co. I 61st Ill. Inf.
Owens J. e. Mch. 3, 1865, trans. Co. I 61st Ill. Inf.
Osborn A. e. Mch. 3, 1865, trans. Co. I 61st Ill. Inf.
Peck A. e. Mch. 10, 1865, trans. Co. I 61st Ill. Inf.
Parkins W. H. e. Mch. 10, 1865, trans. Co. I 61st Ill. Inf.
Saylor J. H. e. Jan. 10, 1864, trans. Co. I 61st Ill. Inf.
Stockton T. e. Mch. 10, 1864, trans. Co. I 61st Ill. Inf.
Sheppard J. m. o. June 26, 1865.
Slocum W. T. disd. Oct. 30, 1862.
Shores W. Promoted Com. Sergt.
Tuttle S. H. e. Mch. 6, 1865, trans. Co. I 61st Ill. Inf.
Taylor Wm. B. e. Mch. 6, 1865, trans. Co. I 61st Ill. Inf.
Vanvelzer Francis, e. Mch. 16, 1865, trans. Co. I 61st Ill. Inf.
Watson H. e. Mch. 4, 1864, trans. Co. I 61st Ill. Inf.
Welch N. e. Mch. 10, 1865, trans. Co. I 61st Ill. Inf.

Company I.

Baker N. W, e. Aug. 14, 1862, m. o. June 26, 1865, as Corpl.
Endicott J. e. Aug. 14, 1862, m. o. June 26, 1866.
Eilenberger D. B. e. Aug. 20, 1862, died July 29, 1864.
Knapp J. L. e. Aug. 18, 1862, m. o. June 26, 1865.
Murphy S. S. e. Aug. 18, 1862, m. o. June 26, 1865.
Page W. E. e. Aug. 14, 1862, m. o. June 26, 1865.
Smith J. T. e. Aug. 8, 1862, disd. Jan. 24, 1863, disah.
Thompson W. H. e. Aug. 14, 1862, disd. Mch. 7, 1863, disab.
Thomas E. W. e Aug. 14, 1862, m. o. June 26, 1865.
Courson James, e. Apr. 11, 1865, trans. Co. I 61st Ill. Inf.

Company K.

Dorris W. H. e. Aug. 15, 1862, m. o. June 26, 1865.
Ross G. H. e. Aug. 6, 1862, m. o. June 26, 1865.

Unassigned Recruits.

Bradshaw D. Deserted from 89th Ill. returned.
Jones Riley, e. Mch. 3, 1865.
Yargus J. A. e. Nov. 27, 1863, died Feb. 4, 1864.

138th (100 days) INFANTRY.

The One Hundred and Thirty-Eighth Illinois Infantry Volunteers was organized at Camp Wood, Quincy, Ills., by Colonel Jno. W. Goodwin and mustered in June 21, 1864 for 100 days. On 26th July the Regiment moved to Fort Leavenworth, Kansas, and was assigned to garrison duty, Colonel Goodwin commanding post. Major Tunison with Companies C and F occupied the post of Weston, Missouri, from July 7 to Aug. 3. Brigadier General Thomas A. Davis commanding District of North Kansas, and Major General Curtis commanding Department Kansas.

The Regiment was mustered out of service of the United States at Springfield, Ills., Oct. 14, 1864.

ROSTER OF REGIMENT.

Colonel, Jno. W. Goodwin, rank June 21, 1864. Mustered June 21, 1864. Mustered out Oct. 14, 1864.
Lieut. Colonel, Alex. H. Holt, rank June 21, 1864. Mustered June 21, 1864. Mustered out Oct. 14, 1864.
Major, Jno. Tunison, rank June 21, 1864. Mustered June 21, 1864. Mustered out Oct. 14, 1864.
Adjutant, Jno. H. Johnson, rank June 21, 1864. Mustered June 21, 1864. Mustered out Oct. 14, 1864.
Quartermaster, Jn. H. Elward, rank May 17, 1864. Mustered May 17, 1864. Mustered out Oct. 14, 1864.
Surgeon, Jas. J. Rowe, rank June 21, 1864. Mustered June 21, 1864. Mustered out Oct. 14, 1864.
First Assistant Surgeon, David P. Bigger, rank June 21, 1864. Mustered June 21, 1864. Mustered out Oct. 14, 1864.
Second Assistant Surgeon, Smith T. Ferguson, rank June 21, 1864. Mustered June 21, 1864. Mustered out Oct. 14, 1864
Chaplain, Benj. F. Ha-kin, rank June 21, 1864. Mustered June 21, 1864. Mustered out Oct. 14, 1864.
Sergeant Major, J. Strawn, enlisted May 10, 1864. Mustered out Oct. 14, 1864.
Q. M. Sergeant, D. Harding, enlisted May 2, 1864. Mustered out Oct. 14, 1864.
Commissary Sergeant, J. S. Porter, enlisted, May 6, 1864. Mustered out Oct. 14, 1864.
Hospital Steward, J O. Patterson, enlisted, May 16, 1864. Mustered out Oct. 14, 1864.
Principal Musician, G. B. Hunt, enlisted May 3, 1864. Mustered out Oct. 14, 1864.
Principal Musician, S. M. Brunner, enlisted May 17, 1864. Mustered out Oct. 14, 1864.

Company A.

Capt. Wm. L. S. McClanahan, rank June 21, 1864, mustered June 21, 1864. Mustered out Oct. 14, 1864.
First Lieutenant Guy Stapp, rank June 21, 1864, mus. tered June 21, 1864. Mustered out Oct. 14, 1864.
Second Lieutenant John A. Finley, rank June 21, 1864, mustered June 21, '64. Mustered out Oct. 14, 1864.
First Sergeant O. G. Given, e. May 2 1864, mustered out Oct. 14, 1864.
Sergeant W. A. Abrams, e. May 2, 1864, mustered out Oct. 14, 1864.
Sergeant C. M. Stevenson, e. May 2, 1864, mustered out Oct. 14, 1864.
Sergeant E. P. Burroughs, e. May 7, 1864, mustered out Oct. 14, 1864.
Sergeant A. B. Struthers, e. May 2, 1864, mustered out Oct. 14, 1864.
Corporal J. C. Leslie, e. May 9, 1864, mustered out Oct. 14, 1864.
Corporal D. S. Hardan, e. May 2, 1864, mustered out Oct. 14, 1864.
Corporal J. F. Ridlon, e. May 2, 1864, mustered out Oct. 14, 1864.
Corporal R. McConnell, e. May 9, 1864, mustered out Oct. 14, 18'4.
Corporal S. J. Stewart, e. May 4, 1864, mustered out Oct. 14, 1864.
Corporal J. W. Brook, e. May 2, 1864, mustered out Oct. 14, 1864.
Corporal D. J. Cathcart, e. May 9, 1864, mustered out Oct. 14, 1864.
Corporal J. A. Gettermey, e. May 2, 1864, mustered out Oct. 14, 1864.
Musician C. F. Davis, e. May 3, 1864, mustered out Oct. 14, 1864.
Musician R. Fraul, e. May 6, 1864, mustered out Oct. 14, 1864.
Wagoner T. M. Marshall e. May 7, '64, died July 30, '64.

PRIVATES.

Acheson Jos. e. May 9, 1864, m. o. Oct. 14, 1864.
Allen J. T. e. May 2, 1864, m. o. Oct. 14, 1864.
Alfred F. e. May 6, 1864, m. o. Oct. 14, 1864.
Anderson J. O. e. May 6, 1864, m. o. Oct 14, 1864.
Avenell C. P. e. May 2, 1864, m. o. Oct. 14. 1864.
Babcock J. W. e. May 2, 1864, m. o. Oct. 14, 1864.
Bailey D. B. e. May 3, 1864, m. o. Oct. 14, 1864.
Barrett W. H. e. May 3, 1864, m. o. Oct. 14, 1864.
Bassett F. L. e. May 6, 1864, m. o. Oct. 14, 1864.
Beveredge A. e. May 2, 1864, m. o. Oct. 14, 1864.
Bickett A. H. e. May 3, 1864, m. o. Oct. 14, 1864.
Boyd Geo. S. e. May 4, 1864, m. o. Oct. 14, 1864.
Brown Wm. e. May 2, 1864, m. o. Oct. 14, 1864.
Caldwell A. F. e. May 7, 1864, m. o. Oct. 14, 1864.
Campbell J. M. e. May 6, 1864, m. o. Oct. 14, 1864.
Carson F. M. e. May 7, 1864, m. o. Oct. 14, 1864.
Claycomb S. e. May 2, 1864, m. o. Oct. 14, 1864.
Cooper W. e. May 3, 1864, m. o. Oct. 14, 1864.
Crawford J. S. e. May 2, 1864, m. o. Oct. 14, 1864.
Davis A. A. e. May 4, 1864 m. o. Oct. 14, 1864.
Duncan B. A. e. May 5, 1864, m. o. Oct. 14, 1864.
Earp D. D. e. May 7, 1864, m. o. Oct. 14, 1864.
Findley S. S. e. May 2, 1864, m. o. Oct. 14, 1864.
Foster M. L. e. May 2, 1864, m. o. Oct. 14, 1864.
Frasier G. e. May 6, 1864, m. o. Oct. 14, 1864.
Frisbee E. e. May 2, 1864, m. o. Oct. 14, 1864.
Gettemy J. e. May 2, 1864, m. o. Oct. 14, 1864.
Gibson D. S. e. May 7, 1864, m. o. Oct. 14, 1864.
Giles J. R. e. May 2, 1864 m. o. Oct. 24, 1864.
Graham S. L. e. May 7, 1864, m. o. Oct. 14, 1864.
Hall E. E. e. May 2, 1864, m. o. Oct. 14, 1864.
Henderson C. E. e. May 5, 1864, m. o. Oct. 14, 1864.
Herdman P. A. e. May 2, 1864, m. o. Oct. 14, 1864.
Johnson W. F. e. May 2, 1864, m. o. Oct. 14, 1864.
Jones T. e. May 16, 1864, m. o. Oct. 14, 1864.
Kennedy P. e. May 15, 1864, m. o. Oct. 14, 1864.
Killian W. P. e. May 2, 1864. m. o. Oct. 14, 1864.
Kerr S. F. e. May 2, 1864, m. o. Oct. 14, 1864.
Knapp H. H. e. May 15, 1864, m. o. Oct. 14, 1864.
Leighty J. e. May 3, 1864, m. o. Oct. 14, 1864.
Liggott J. B. e. May 3, 1864, m. o. Oct. 14, 1864.
Lusk J. W. e. May 7, 1864, m. o. Oct. 14, 1864.
Madden J. B. e. May 11, 1864, m. o. Oct. 14, 1864.
Mannon S. E. e. May 5, 1864, m. o. Oct. 14, 1864.
Mathews J. W. e. May 30, 1864, m. o. Oct. 14, 1864.
Mitchell W. R. e. May 9, 1864, m. o. Oct. 14, 1864.
McAdams G. e. May 4, 1864, m. q. Oct. 14, 1864.
McAdams F. e. May 2, 1864, m. o. Oct. 14, 1864.
McClanahan M. R. e. May 30, 1864, m. o. Oct. 14, 1864.
McIntire D. e. May 11, 1864, m. o. Oct. 14, 1864.
McKinney W. e. May 6, 1864, m. o. Oc. 14, 1864.
McLean J. e. May 2, 1864, m. o. Oct. 14, 1864.
McReynolds D. e. May 2, 1864, m. o. Oct. 14 1864.
Nelson S. B. e. May 16, 1864, m. o. Oct. 14, 1864.
Newbanks R. e. May 4, 1864, m. o. Oct. 14, 1864.
Paine B. W. e. May 6, 1864, m. o. Oct. 14, 1864.
Ramp W. F. e. May 16, 1864, m. o. Oct. 14, 1864.
Renwick A. e. May 30, 1864, m. o. Oct. 14, 1864.
Rood J. B. e. May 2, 1864, m. o. Oct. 14, 1864.
Runge J. C. e. May 9, 1864, m. o. Oct. 14, 1864.
Schussler J. B. e. May 2, 1864, m. o. Oct. 14, 1864.
Scott W. e. Mav 17, 1864, m. o. Oct. 14, 1864.
Wallace D. M. e. May 2, 1864 m. o. Oct. 14, 1864.
Woods W. S. e. May 22, 1864, m. o. Oct. 14, 1864.
Woods R. P. e. May 30, 1864, m. o. Oct. 14, 1864.

RECRUITS.

De Cook H, e. May 9, 1864, m. o. Oct. 14, 1864.
Graham W. F. e. May 10, 1864, m. o. Oct. 14, 1864.
Henderson J. T. e. May 2, 1864, m. o. Oct. 14, 1864.
McDill J. A. e. May 9, 1864. m. o. Oct. 14, 1864.
Reed D. e. May 14, 1864, m. o. Oct. 14, 1864.
Secrist C. C. e. May 2, 1864, m. o. Oct. 14, 1864.
Selleck C. G. e. May 3, 1864, m. o. Oct. 14, 1864.
Smith J. D. e. May 30, 1864, m. o. Oct. 14, 1864.
Stevenson R. E. e. May 9, 1864, m. o. Oct. 14, 1864.
Stewart S. T. e. May 11, 1864, m. o. Oct. 14, 1864.
Stockton S. e. May 16, 1864, m. o. Oct. 14, 1864.
Taylor J. e. May 9, 1864, m. o. Oct. 14, 1864.
Walker W. J. e. May 2, 1864, m. o. Oct. 14, 1864.
Watson B. e. May 16, 1864, m. o. Oct. 14, 1864.
Young W. B. e. May 2, 1864, m. o. Oct. 14, 1864.

Company B.

Reed Daniel e. May 14, 1864, died Aug. 9, 1864.
Smith J. D. e. May 30, 1864, m. o. Oct. 14, 1864.

Company C.

Captain Jasper N. Reece, rank June 21, 1864, mustered June 21, 1864. Mustered out Oct. 14, 1864.
First Lieutenant Wm. B. Morse, rank June. 21, 1864. mustered June 21, 1864. Mustered out Oct. 14, 1864.
First Sergeant, D. Knight, e. May 2, 1864, m. o. Oct. 14, 1864.
Sergeant H. L. Hosington, e. May 5, 1864, mustered out Oct. 14, 1864.
Sergeant A. Reitchy, e. May 2, 1864, mustered out Oct. 14, 1864.
Sergeant I. S. Smith, e. May 3, 1864, mustered out Oct. 14, 1864.
Corporal L. Hoyden, e. May 2, 1864, mustered out Oct. 14, 1864.
Corporal J. Snapp, e. May 7, 1861, mustered out Oct. 14, 1864.
Corporal B. Fluharty, e. May 3, 1864, mustered out Oct 14, 1864.
Corporal G. A. Johnson, e. May 7, 1864, mustered out Oct. 14, 1864.
Corporal J. Jenkins, e. May 2, 1864, mustered out Oct. 14, 1864.
Corporal H. Reddout, e. May 3, 1864, mustered out Oct. 14, 1864.
Corporal T. Butler, e. May 2, 1864, mustered out Oct. 14, 1864.
Wagoner B. F. Worden, e. May 7, 1864, mustered out Oct. 14, 1864.

PRIVATES.

Allingham Chas. A. e. May 16, 1864, m. o. Oct. 14, '64.
Booth B. e. May 7, 1864, m. o. Oct. 14, 1864.
Bowen J. G. e. May 2, 1864, m. o. Oct. 14, 1864.
Baker B. R. e. May 11, 1864, died. July 30, 1864.
Cowick Lee B. e. May 9, 1864, m. o. Oct. 14, 1864.
Crissy H. e. May 7, 1864, m. o. Oct. 14, 1864.
Clyborn F. S. e. May 2, 1864, m. o. Oct. 14, 1864.
Dunbar T. J. e. May 17, 1864, m. o. Oct. 14, 1864.
Dickson H. M. e. May 30, 1864, m. o. Oct. 14, 1864.
Evans J. H. e. May 9, 1864, m. o. Oct. 14, 1864.
Fairchild A. e. May 3, 1864, died Sept. 25, 1864.
Foster T. J. e. May 7, 1864, m. o. Oct. 14, 1864.
Foster L. e. May 7, 1864, m. o. Oct. 14, 1864.
Giddings J. W. e. May 12, 1864, m. o. Oct. 14, 1864.
Giddings L. e. May 3, 1864, m. o. Oct. 14, 1864.
Giddings T. W. e. May 3, 1864, m. o. Oct. 14, 1864.
Gilham C. e. May 7, 1864, m. o. Oct. 14, 1864.
Hatfield A. e. May 4, 1864, absent sick at muster out.
Hanis J. B. e. May 16, 1864, m. o. Oct. 14, 1864.
Hall C e. May 2, 1864, disd. Sept. 1, 1864, to re-enlist.
Heston W. H. e. May 9, 1864, m. o. Oct. 14, 1864.
Hahn J. e. May 9, 1864, m. o. Oct. 14, 1864.
Jewell Wm. H. e. May 3, 1864, m. o. Oct. 14, 1864.
Kidder N. e. May 7, 1864, m. o. Oct. 14, 1864.
Lewis J. B. e. May 3, '64, disd. Sept. 1, '64, to re-enlist.
Lapray D. e. May 7, 1864, m. o. Oct. 14, 1864.
McMahill W. e. May 7, 1864, m. o. Oct. 14, 1864.
Meadows W. H. e. May 9, 1864, m. o. Oct. 14, 1864.
Miner L. e. May 9, 1864, m. o. Oct. 14, 1864.
Perry J. C. e. May 7, 1864, m. o. Oct. 14, 1864.
Pierce A. e. May 7, 1864, m. o. Oct. 14, 1864.
Randall O. T. e. May 3, 1864, m. o. Oct. 14, 1864.
Richardson A. e. May 7, 1864, disd. Aug. 31, 1864 to re-enlist.
Rayson A. e. May 7, 1864, m. o. Oct. 14, 1864.
Roberts G. e. May 7, 1864, m. o. Oct. 14, 1864.
Shelton D. R. e. May 3, 1864, disd. Aug. 31, 1864, to re-enlist.
Shelton F. B. e. May 7, 1864, m. o. Oct. 14, 1864.
Smith W. P. e. May 3, '64, disd. Sept. 1, '64 to re-enlist.
Smith C. R. e. May 7, 1864, m. o. Oct. 14, 1864.
Shepard G. W. e. May 17, 1864, m. o. Oct. 14, 1864.
Shepard J. C. e. May 17, 1864, m. o. Oct. 14, 1864.
Wilson T. e. May 3, 1864, m. o. Oct. 14, 1864.
Wilson J. M. e. May 9, 1864, m. o. Oct. 14, 1864.
Wiswell M. M. e. May 9, 1864, m. o. Oct. 14, 1864.

Company D.

PRIVATES.

De Cook H. e. May 9, 1864, m. o. Oct. 14, 1864.
Graham W. F. e. May 10, 1864, m. o. Oct. 14, 1864.
Henderson J. T. e. May 2, 1864, m. o. Oct. 14, 1864.
McDill J. A. e. May 9, 1864, m. o. Oct. 14, 1864.
Secrist C. C. e. May 2, 1864, m. o. Oct. 14, 1864.

Selleck C. G. e. May 3, 1864, m. o. Oct. 14, 1864.
Stevenson R. E. e. May 9, 1864, m. o. Oct. 14, 1864.
Stewart S. T. e. May 11, 1864, m. o. Oct. 14, 1864.
Stockton S. c. May 16, 1864, m. o. Oct. 14, 1864.
Taylor J. e. May 9, 1864, m. o. Oct. 14, 1864.
Walker W. J. e. May 2, 1864, m. o. Oct. 14, 1864.
Watson B. e. May 16, 1864, m. o. Oct. 14, 1864.
Young W. B. e. May 2, 1864, m. o. Oct. 16, 1864.

Company E.

Captain Geo. D. Sofield, rank June 21, 1864, mustered June 21, 1864. Mustered out Oct. 14, 1864.
Second Lieutenant Benj. C. Davis, rank June 21, 1864, mustered June 21, 1864. Mustered out Oct. 14, '64.
Sergeant J. J. Bonner, e. May 3, 1864, mustered out Oct. 14, 1864.
Sergeant A. L. Pease, e. April 27, 1864, mustered out Oct. 14, 1864.
Corporal M. L. Smith, e. April 27, 1864, mustered out Oct. 14, 1864.
Corporal J. D. Gordon, e. May 14, 1864, mustered out Oct. 14, 1864.
Musician S. Livermore, e. May 6, 1864, mustered out Oct. 14, 1864.
Wagoner J. C. Montgomery, e. May 27, 1864, mustered out Oct. 14, 1864.

PRIVATES.

Adams A. J. e. April 27, 1864, m. o. Oct. 14, 1864.
Brent J. K. e. May 14, 1864, m. o. Oct. 14, 1864.
Carr G. N. e. May 14, 1864, m. o. Oct. 14, 1864.
Chase Luman e. May 14, 1864, m. o. Oct. 14, 1864.
Dram A. H. e. May 4, 1864, m. o. Oct. 14, 1864.
Dunn A. e. May 14, 1864, m. o. Oct. 14, 1864.
Gregg W. e. May 7, 1864, m. o. Oct. 14, 1864.
Hogue J. e. April 27, 1864, m. o. Oct. 14, 1864.
Haynes E. M. e. May 14, 1864, m. o. Oct. 14, 1864.
Hogue J. D. e. May 6, 1864, m. o. Oct. 14, 1864.
Irvine J. M. e. May 14, 1864, m. o. Oct. 14, 1864.
Irvine E. E. e. April 27, 1864, m. o. Oct. 14, 1864.
Johnson T. F. e. April 27, 1864, m. o. Oct. 14, 1864.
Kaiser G. A. e. April 27, 1864, m. o. Oct. 14, 1864.
Kindle J. H. e. May 6, 1864, m. o. Oct. 14, 1864.
Lehman I. e. May 7, 1864. died Sept. 9, 1864.
Montgomery W. J. e. May 14, 1864, disd. Sept. 1, 1864 to re-enlist.
Montgomery W. E. e. April 27, '64, m. o. Oct. 14, '64.
Pinckney D. e. May 14, 1864, deserted. June 22, 1864.
Pease R. B. e. April 27, 1864, m. o. Oct. 14, 1864.
Rhea C. M. e. May 5, 1864, m. o. Oct. 14, 1864.
Rankin S. P. e. April 27, 1864, m. o. Oct. 14, 1864.
Ramsdell E. E. e. May 14, 1864, m. o. Oct. 14, 1864.
Stourmant W. S. e. May 14, 1864, m. o. Oct. 14, 1864.
Tompkins Milan L. e. April 27, 1864, m. o. Oct. 14, '64.
Tompkins Matthew L. e. May 14, '64, m. o. Oct. 14, '64.
Todd E. e. April 27, 1864, m. o. Oct. 14, 1864.
Vandenburg, e. May 5, 1864, m. o. Oct. 14, 1864.

102nd INFANTRY.

Surgeon, David B Rice, rank Sept. 30, 1862. Mustered Dec. 18, 1862. Resigned July 12, 1863.
Principal Musician, J. W. Ames. Mustered out June 6, 1865.

Company A.

Captain Robert W. Colligan, rank Jan. 7, 1863, mustered April 4, 1863. Resigned July 12, 1863.
First Lieutenant John Morrison, rank July 15, 1864, died of wounds July 3, 1864.
Second Lieutenant John Morrison, rank July 12, 1863. Promoted.
First Sergeant R. W. Callaghan, e. Aug. 10, 1862. Promoted Captain.
Sergeant J. Morrison, e. Aug. 10, 1862, died July 31, 1864, wounds.
Corporal W. H. Black, e. Aug. 6, 1862, dis. Feb. 17, 1863, priv. disab.
Corporal A. Talbot, e. Aug. 10, 1862, mustered out June 7, 1865.
Corporal N. Daggett, e. Aug. 10, 1862, dis. Sept. 30, 1864, priv. wounds.
Corporal G. W. Miller, e. Aug. 6, 1862, mustered out June 6, 1865, as Sergeant.

PRIVATES.

Anderson W. F. e. Aug. 14, 1862, dis. Mch. 16, 1863, disab.
Blake A. D. e. Aug. 10, 1862, dis. Jan. 16, 1863, disab.
Crosby G. W. e. Aug. 6, 1862, m. o. June 6, 1865, as Corpl.
Crandall W. H. e. Aug. 10, '62, dis. Mch. 12, '63, disab.
Daggett E. e. Aug. 10, 1862, died Jan. 22, 1863.
Foster Richard, e. Aug. 10, 1862, m. o. June 6, 1865.
Gentry E. W. e. Aug. 6, 1862, m. o. June 6, 1865.
Glass H. M. e. Aug. 13, 1862, m. o. June 6, 1865.
Miller J. A. e. Aug. 6, 1862, dis. Jan. 16, 1863, disab.
Murdock J. e. Aug. 13, 1862, m. o. June 6, 1865.
Nast L. e. Aug. 10, 1862, killed May 15, 1864.
Olson, S. H. e. Aug. 10, 1862, m. o. June 6, 1865.
Pearson A. e. Aug. 13, 1862, m. o. June 6, 1865.
Routh, J. C. e. Aug. 6, 1862, dis. Oct. 28, 1864, disab.
Richardson D. e. Aug. 13, 1862, m. o. June 6, 1865.
Richerson Asa, e. Aug. 13, 1862, dis. Jan. 29, '63, disab.
Vestal E. M. e. Aug. 13, 1862, died Dec. 23, 1862.

Company B.

Captain Elisha C. Atchison, rank Sept. 2, 1862, mustered Sept. 2, 1862. Resigned April 9, 1863.
Captain Wm. Armstrong, rank April 8, 1863, mustered May 7, 1863. Honorably disd. May 15, 1865.
First Lieutenant Wm. Armstrong, rank Sept. 2, 1862, mustered Sept. 2, 1862. Promoted.
First Lieutenant Jas. C. Beswick, rank April 8, 1863, mustered May 6, 1863. Resigned Jan. 14, 1864.
First Lieutenant Ambrose Stegall, rank Jan. 14, 1864, mustered April 12, 1864. Mustered out June 6, '65.
Second Lieutenant Jas. C. Beswick, rank Sept. 2, 1862, mustered Sept. 2, 1862. Promoted.
Second Lieutenant Ambrose Stegall. rank April 8, 1862, mustered May 6, 1863. Promoted.
Sergeant A. Stegall, e. Aug. 6, 1862, promoted First Sergeant, then Second Lieutenant.
Sergeant David Hocker, e. Aug. 9, 1862, died Nov. 4, 1862.
Sergeant J. W. Terpinning, e. Aug. 9, 1862, mustered out June 6, 1865, as First Sergeant.
Corporal J. M. Kellogg, e. Aug. 7, 1862, killed May 15, 1864.
Corporal L. A. Woods, e. Aug. 6, 1862, mustered out June 6 1865, as private.
Corporal J. J. Armstrong, e. Aug. 8, 1862, Sergeant absent at mustering out.
Corporal A. Beswick, e. Aug. 5, 1862, Sergeant absent at mustering out.
Corporal M. S. Re-s, e. Aug. 7, 1862, mustered out June 6, 1865, as Sergeant.
Music an D. Ingersoll, e. Aug 9, 1862, dis. June 25, 1863, disab.
Wagoner S. R. Curtis, e. Aug. 9, 1862, mustered out June 6, 1865

PRIVATES.

Armstrong W. B. e. Aug 9, 1862, m. o. June 6, 1865.
Artless David, e. Aug. 9, 1862, m. o. June 24, 1865, disr. of war.
Bugbee E. D. e. Aug. 9, '62, m. o. Jun 6, '65, as Corpl.

WARREN COUNTY WAR RECORD. 189

Brown J. W. e. Aug. 9, 1862, dis. Feb. 21, 1863, disab.
Boyd D. R. e. Aug. 9, 1862, m. o. June 6, 1865.
Black J. M. e. Aug. 22, 1862, m. o. June 6, '65, as Corpl.
Beswick O, e. Aug. 22, 1862, m. . . June 6, 1865.
Corning D. e. Aug. 22, 1862, m. o. June 6, 1865.
Church S. e. Aug. 8, 1862, m. o. June 6, 1865.
Chapin W. S. e. Aug. 9, 1862, m. o. June 22, 1865, prisr. of war.
Cussins S. e. Aug. 8. 1862, kld. May 15, 1864.
Dunn J. B. e. Aug. 9, 1862, dis. Jan. 25, 1863, disab.
Dewitt J. E. e. Aug. 18, 1862, m. o. June 6, 1865.
Dewitt L. e. Aug. 13, 1862, m. o. June 6, 1865.
Dunn G. W, e. Aug. 11, 1862, m. o. June 6, 1865.
Davis S. C. e. Aug. 22, 1862, deserted Sept. 10, 1862.
Fort C. W. e. Aug. 9, 1862, died Nov. 15, 1864.
Fe ris E. K. e. Aug. 9, 1862, dis. Jan. 3, 1863, disab.
Graham W. D. e. Aug. 6, 1862, m. o. June 6, 1865.
Harsh L. e. Aug. 9, 1862, drown d July 2, 1863.
Hemson Jno. e. Aug. 7, 1862, died July 10, 1864.
Heflin S. G. e. Aug. 6, 1862, m. o. June 6, 1865.
Holenbeck C. e. Aug. 15, 1862, died Mch. 23, 1864.
Kiser A. e. Aug. 9, 1862, m. o. June 6, 1865.
Mi es J. M. e. Aug. 7, 1862, dis. Jan. 16, 1863, disab.
Parson. C. B. e. A g. 11, 1862, m. o. June 6, 1865, as Corpl.
Pet rson A. e. Aug. 8, 1862, dis. Feb. 23, 1864, disab.
Porter T. e. Aug. 22, 1862, dis. Feb. 15, 1863, disab.
Rees W. H. e. Aug. 7, 1862, m. o. June 6, 1865.
Russell G. D. e. Aug. 9, 1862, absent at m. o. wounded.
Russell E. E. e. Aug. 6, 1862, m. o. June 6, 1865, as Corpl.
Snyder T. M. e. Aug. 11, 1862, dis. May 26, '65, wds.
Snyder J W. e, Aug. 11, 1862, m. o. June 6, 1865.
Sherman G. e. Aug. 11, 1862, m o June 6, 1865.
St. George R. e. Aug. 9, 1862, dis. May 1, 1863, disab.
Snavely J. e. Aug. 21, 1862, died April 28, 1863, wds.
Sallee W, G. e. Aug. 15, 1862, dis. Jan. 15, 1863, disab.
Terpenning S. e. Aug. 14, 1862, m. o. June 6, 1865.
Walton James. e. Aug. 6, 1862, m. . , June 6, 1865.
Wimmer W. R. e. Aug. 6, 1862, m. n. June 6, 1865.
Weiser D. S. e. Aug. 22, 1862, dis. Feb. 6, 1863, disab.

RECRUITS.

Chapin L. D. e. Nov. 20, 1864, m. o. June 6, 1865.
Donnelly J. e. Feb. 5, 1864, dis. Oct. 7, 1864, disab.
St. G orge T. e. March. 9, 1864, trans. Co. C 16th Ill. Infantry.
Walton J. e. Nov. 20, 1863, trans. Co. C. 16th Ill. Inf.

Company D.

Corporal Rowley Page, e. Aug. 6, 1862, mustered out June 6, 1865, as Sergeant.
Corporal J. E. Ragland, e. Aug. 22, 1862, dis. Oct. 13, 1864, disab.
Musician J. W. Ames, e. Aug. 5, 1862. Promoted Principal Musician.

PRIVATES.

Bing W. J. e. Aug. 6, 1862, m. o. June 6, 1865.
Barnhisel F. L. e. Aug. 7, 1862, m. o. June 6, 1865.
Cone W. M. e. Aug. 9, 1862, m. o. June 6, 1865, as Corpl.
Drake H. A. e. Aug. 6, 1862, m. o. June 6, 1865.
Huestis C. L. e. Aug. 6, 1862, m. o. July 12, 1865, prisr. of war.
Lester J. E. e. Aug. 8, 1862, m. o. June 6, 1865.
I age Daniel F. e. Aug. 7, 1862, m. o. June 6, 1865.
Page Timothy, e, Aug. 10, 1862, died Mch. 13, 1863, disab.
Pugh E. M. e. Aug. 6, 1862, m. o. July 15, 1865, pris.
Rhykert J. H. e. Aug. 9, 1862, absent at m. o. of Regt.

Company E.

Langheard J. e. Aug. 9, 1861, m. n. June 6, 1865.
Simpson D. R. e. Aug. 9, 1862, m. o. June 6, 1865.
Wiley J. H. e. Aug. 9, 1862, m. o. June 6, 1865.
Wiley R. e. Aug. 9, 1862, absent, wd., at m. o. of Regt.

FOURTEENTH INFANTRY (Reorganized).

Company H.

Captain Leonard B. Peck, rank March 9, 1865, mustered March 9, 1865. Mustered out Sept. 16, 1865.
Second Lieutenant Solomon Grace, rank March 9. 1865, mustered Mch. 9, 1865. Mustered out Sept. 16, 1865.
Sergeant W. H. Black, e. Feb. 17, 1865. Deserted twice, reduced to ranks.
Sergeant W. Beswick, e. Feb. 20, 1865.
Corporal J. H. Landon, e. Feb. 17, 1865. Mustered out Sept. 16, 1865 as Sergeant.
Corporal W. H. Newkirk, e. Feb. 18, 1865. Pro. Sergt.
Corporal E. Hart, e. Feb. 18, 1865. Mustered out Sept. 16, 1865.
Corporal P. Richardson, e. Feb. 18, 1865. Pro. Sergt. Mustered out Sept. 16, 1865.
Musician W. H. Brown, e. Feb. 17, 1865. Mustered out Sept. 16, 1865.
Musician E. H. Stilson, e. Feb. 17, 1865. Mustered out Sept. 16, 1865.

PRIVATES.

Alexander Jno. e. Feb. 24, 1865, m. o. Sept. 16, 1865, as Corpl.
Carter L. e. Feb. 17, 1865, m. o. June 10, 1865.
Church H. e. Feb. 17, 1865, m. o. Sept. 16, 1865.
Clifton J. H. e. Feb. 18, 1865, deserted July 29, 1865.
Deilere J. e. Feb. 18, 1865, absent sick at m. o.

Forquer J. M. e. Feb. 17, 1865, deserted twice.
Grace S. e. Feb. 17, 1865, m. o. March 8, 1865 for prom.
Hendricks C. e. Feb. 20, 1865, deserted Feb. 20, 1865.
Hickson H. e. Feb. 17, 1865, m. o. Sept. 16, 1865.
Hartgrove R. e. Feb. 17, 1865. Leg broke at hospital at m. o.
Heston C. e. Feb. 18, 1865, m. o. Sept. 16, 1865.
Hall S. T. e. Feb. 18, 1865, m. o. June 10, 1865.
Hopper R. A. e. Feb. 17, 1867, deserted twice.
Lyons W. e. Feb. 20, 1865, m. o. Sept. 16, 1865.
Meyer E. e. Feb. 17, 1865, m. o. May 29, 1865.
Premer W. e. Feb. 18, 1865, m. o. May 29, 1865.
Pool A. e. Feb. 18, 1865, m. o. May 11, 1865.
Parks J. e. Feb. 17, 1865, deserted Feb. 18, 18'5.
Richardson J. e. Feb. 18, 1865, deserted June 27, 1865.
Ryner W. e. Feb 17, 1865, m. o. Sept. 16, 1865.
Robbins E. Feb. 18, 1865, m. o. Sept. 16, 1865.
Randies A. J. e. Feb. 17, 1865, m. o. Sept. 16, 1865.
Savage W. e. Feb. 18, 1865, sick at muster out
Samuels W. H. e. Feb. 17, 1865, deserted July 3, 1865.
Smith J. M. e. Feb. 18, 1865, sick at muster out.
Shutts D. C. e. Feb. 17, 1865, deserted June 25, 1865.
Terpenning D. e. Feb. 17, 1865, m. o. July 11, 1865.
Trible I. M. e. Feb. 17, 1865, m. o. June 20, 1865.
Tulman J. e. Feb. 24, 1865, m. o. Sept. 16, 1865.
Thomas H. e. Feb. 17, 1865, m. o. Sept. 16, 1865.
Williams S. e. Feb. 17, 1865, m. o. June 13, 1865.
Yocum W. M. e. Feb. 17, 1865, m, o. June 26, 1865.

FORTY-SEVENTH INFANTRY (Reorganized).

Company H.

Captain Wm. F. Gowdy, rank March 9, 1865, mustered March 9, 1865. Mustered out Jan. 21, 1866.
First Lieutenant Jno. A. Finley, rank March 9, 1865, mustered March , 9, 1865. Mustered out Jan. 21, '66.

Second Lieutenant Jas. B. Brent, rank March 9, 1865, mustered March 9, 1865. Mustered out Jan. 21, '66.
First Sergeant Jos. E. Whitenack, e. Feb. 22, 1865, mustered out Jan. 21, 1866.
Sergeant Albert D. Sturgess, e. Feb. 13, 65, mustered out Jan. 21, 1866.

Sergeant John A. Kennedy, e. Feb. 13, 1865, mustered out Jan. 13, 1868.
Sergeant John R. Guiless, e. Feb 14, 1865, mustered out Jan. 21, 1866.
Sergeant K F. Powell, e. Feb. 18, 1865, mustered out Jan. 21, 1866.
Corporal Jno. A. McDill, e. Feb. 21, 1865, mustered out Jan. 21, 1866.
Corporal Jas. B. Charlton, e. Feb. 24, 1865, mustered out Jan. 21, 1866 as Private.
Corporal Geo. S. Boyd, e. Feb. 13, 1865, mustered out Jan. 21, 1866.
Corporal C E. Henderson, e. Feb. 21, 1865, mustered out Jan 21, 1866.
Corporal J. L. Kelshaw, e. Feb. 14, 1865, mustered out Jan. 21, 1866.
Corporal M. C. Thompson, e. Feb. 14, 1865, mustered out Jan. 21, 1866.
Corporal Jno. P. McClung, e. Feb. 13, 1865. Died.
Corporal Jas. A. Wanrick, e. Feb. 14, 1865, mustered out Jan 21, 1866.
Musician Jno. W. Matthews, e. Feb. 18, 1865, discharged Aug. 19, 1866.
Wagoner Andrew A. Davis, e. Feb. 13, 1865, mustered out Jan. 21, 1866.

PRIVATES.

Allard Wm. C, e. Feb, 14, 1865. Died.
Burton Jno. M e. Feb. 14, 1865, m. o. Jan. 21, 1866.
Brazelton Jos. F. e. Feb. 14, 1 65, m. o. Jan. 21, 1866.
Brent Geo. W. e. Feb. 14, 1865, m. o. Jan. 21, 1866 as Corporal.
Butler Wm. e. Feb. 14, 1865, m. o. Jan. 21, 1866.
Brown Josiah J. e. Feb. 14, 1865, m. o. Jan. 21, 1866.
Brown Jno. J. e. Feb. 13, 1865. Died.
Brown Chas H. e. Feb. 14, 1865, m. o. Jan. 21, 1866.
Burk Oliver O. e. Feb. 14, 1865, m. o. Jan. 21, 1866.
Brent Homer J. e. Feb. 14, 1865, m. o. Jan. 21, 1866.
Belleville Jas. M. e. Feb. 21, 1865, m. o. Jan. 21, 1866.
Caldwell J. M. e. Feb. 13, 1865, m. o. Jan. 21, 1866.
Camel Jno. M. e Feb. 20, 1865, m. o. Jan. 21, 1866.
Chewning Wm. e. March 1, 1865, m. o. June 24, 1865.
Delaney Wm. T. e. Feb. 14, 1865, m. o. Jan. 21, 1866.
Daniels Chas. M. e. Feb. 14, 1865, m. o. Jan. 21, 1866.
Enfield Richard F. e. Feb. 14, 1865, m. o. Jan. 21, 1866.

Graham Geo. R. e. Feb. 21, 1865, m. o. Jan. 21, 1866.
Godfrey Clark, e. Feb. 14, 1865, m. o. Jan. 21, 1866.
Hall Edward E. e. Feb. 13, 1865, m. o. Jan. 21, 1866.
Hohenadle George, e. Feb. 20, 1865, m. o. Jan. 21, 1866.
Henderson Jas. M. e. Feb. 14, 1865, m. o. Jan. 21, 1866.
Jones Jno. M. e. Feb. 18, 1865, m. o. Jan. 21, 1866.
Johnson Wm. F. e. Feb. 21, 1865, m. o. Jan. 21, 1866.
Killian Wm. E. e. Feb. 13, 1865, m. o Jan. 21, 1866.
Absent without leave.
Kennedy Patrick, e. Feb. 14, 1865, m. o. Nov, 8, 1865.
Lusk Jno. W. e. Feb. 20, 1865, m. o. Jan, 21, 1866.
Lars, Son Niles, e. Feb. 13, 1865, m. o. Jan. 21, 1866,
Lynaur or Lyman David, e. Feb. 13, 1865, m. o. Jan. 21, 1866.
McLellan Wylie, e. Feb, 13, 1865, m. o. Jan. 21, 1866.
Mannon Adrian A. e. Feb. 14, 1865, m, o. Jan. 21, 1866.
Absent sick.
McAdams Fred. e. Feb. 18, 1865, m. o. Jan. 21, 1866.
Merrill Harding, e. Feb 18, 1865, m. o. Jan. 21, 1866.
Murphy Wm. M. e. Feb. 14, 1865, m. o. Jan. 21, 1866.
Miller Thos H. e. March 1, 1865. Died.
McGee Jno. A. e. Feb. 21, 1865, m. o. Jan. 21, 1866.
McGee Benj. W. e. Feb. 21, 1865, m., o. Jan. 21, 1866.
Nash Wm, A. e. Feb. 13, 1865, m. o. Jan. 21, 1866.
Pulse Lewis A. e. Feb. 21, 1865, m. o. Jan. 21, 1866.
Page Isaac, e. Feb. 14, 1865, m. o. Jan. 21, '66 as Corpl.
Purce Peterson, e. March 1, 1865, m. o. Jan 21, 1866.
Pinkney Chauncey, e. Feb. 14, 1865, m. o. Jan. 21, 1866.
Runge Jno. C. e. Feb. 18, 1865, m. o. Jan. 21, 1866.
Rodgers Robert, e. Feb. 14, 1865, m. o. Aug. 15, 1865.
Russell Wm. W. e. Feb. 20, 1865, m. o. Jan. 21, 1866.
Strater Jno. S. e. Feb. 18, 1865, m. o. Jan. 21, 1866.
Salesbury Warren, e. Feb. 14, 1865, m. o. Jan. 21, 1866.
Smith Emory W. e. Feb. 21, 1865, m. o. Jan. 21, 1866.
Sturgess Seldon, e. Feb. 13. 1865, m. o. Jan. 21, 1866.
Strow Jno. N. e. Feb. 14, 1865, m. o. Jan. 21, 1866.
Sturgess Jno. F. e. Feb. 13. 1865, m. o. Jan. 21, 1866.
Sample Jas. H. e. Feb. 13, 1865, m. o. Jan. 21, 1866.
Thorn Jno. S. e. Feb. 14, 1865, m. o. Jan. 21, 1866.
Thompson Jas. C. e. Feb. 14, 1865, m. o. Jan. 21, 1866.
Thompson Thos. S. e. Feb. 21, 1865, m. o. Jan. 21, '66.
Walker Albert N. e. Feb. 17, 1865, m. o. Jan. 21, 1866.
Wilson Jno. H. e. Feb. 21, 1865, m. o. Jan. 21, 1866.
Walker Jno. H. or A. e. Feb. 14, '65, m. o. Jan. 21, '66.
Wright Simeon B. e. Feb. 13, 1865, m. o. Jan. 21, 1866.
Shaw Jas. H. e. Feb. 21, 1865, m. o. Jan. 21, 1866.

SEVENTEENTH INFANTRY.

Company F.

First Lieutenant Jno. R. Chartor, rank April 20, 1861, mustered May 25, 1861. Resigned Sept. 3, 1862.
First Lieutenant Chas C. Williams, rank Sept. 3, 1862. Term expired June, 1864.
Second Lieutenant Chas. C. Williams, rank April 20, 1861, mustered May 25, 1861. Promoted.
Second Lieutenant Wm. S. M. McClanahan, rank Sept. 3, 1862. Resigned July 24, 1863.
First Sergeant W. S. McClanahan, e. May 25, 1861.
Sergeant J. B. Stephenson, e. May 25, 1861, kld. May 28, 1863.
Sergeant T. W. Scott, e. May 25, '61, disd. Nov. 23, '62.
Sergeant R. L. Duncan, e. May 25, 1861.
Sergeant M. C. Hubbard, e. May 25, 1861.
Corporal D. C. Brady, e. May 25, 1861.
Corporal J. B. Clark, e. May 25, 1861.
Corporal R. M. Campbell, e. May 25, 1861.
Corporal J. A. Smith, e. May 25, 1861.
Corporal C. C. Brown, e. May 25, 1861.
Corporal S. B. Fuller, e. May 25, 1861.
Corporal H. K. Pressly, e. May 25, '61, kld. June 4, '63.
Corporal C. F. Gillett, e. May 25, 1861, trans. to gunboat service Feb. 3, 1862.
Musician J. L. Shaw, e. May 25, 1861.
Musician W. L. Sweezy, e. May 25, 1861.

PRIVATES.

Alexander E. L. e. May 25, 1861, disd. April 24, 1862.
Alexander W. e. May 25, 1861, kld. May 22, 1863.
Buffington T. S. e. May 25, 1861, disd. April 24, 1862.

Brown W. e. May 25, 1861.
Clark H. e. May 25, 1861, disd. April 16, 1862.
Clark D. M. e. May 25, 1861, disd. April 3, 1862.
Cannon E. N. e. May 25, 1861.
Carmichael C. A. e. May 25, 1861.
Claycomb M. e. May 25, 1861, dishonorably disd. April 2, 1862.
Carpenter G. W. e. May 25, 1861, died Feb. 18, 1862.
Dryden J. W. e. May 25, 1861, died March 14, 1862.
Deckert J. A. e. May 25, 1861.
Eulenberger M. L. e. May 25, 1861.
Earp J. C. e. May 25, 1861, disd. Mch. 22, 1863, disab.
Furr C. e. May 25, 1861, re-enlisted as veteran.
Fort J. P. e. May 25, 1861.
Graham W. W. e. May 25, 1861.
Gibson T. W. e. May 25, 1861.
Hobbs K. e. May 25, 1861.
Haflin A. T. e. May 25, 1861.
Harper H. P. e. May 25, 1861, disd. April 30, 1862.
Herbert J. S. e. M-y 25, 1861.
Higgins L. e. May 25, 1861, disd. Nov. 5, 1862.
Herbert H. J. e. May 25, 1861.
Harrington R. C. e. May 25, 1861.
Harper R. A. e. May 25, 1861, died May 31, 1862.
Johnson E. e. May 25, 1861.
Kendall C. W. e. May 25, 1861, kld. Feb. 15, 1862.
Kinkle R. C. e. May 25, 1861, trans. gunb't Feb. 3, '62.
Kennedy M. B. e. May 25, 1861.
Kepler J. D. e. May 25, 1861, re-enlisted as veteran.
Kimmerer N. e. May 25, 1861, disd. Mch. 31, '62, disab.
Latshaw C. e. May 25, 1861.
Langdon W. W. e. May 25, '61, disd. Apr. 15, '63, disab.
Liby S. e. May 25, 1861.

Moses Nusbaum
MERCHANT, MONMOUTH

Miller J. B. e. May 25, 1861.
McKelvy, c. May 25, 1861.
Moore E. G. e. May 25, 1861.
Martin G. e. May 25, 1861.
Myers G. A. e. May 25, 1861, disd. Aug. 25, 1862.
McIntyre G. e. May 25, 1861, re-enlisted as veteran
McCampbell W. e. May 25, 1861.
Matchell G. B. e. May 25, 1861, disd. Aug. 14, 1862.
Mahan J. R. e. May 25, 1861, re-enlisted as veteran.
Morey D. H. e. May 25, 1861.
Nelson S. C. e. May 25, 1861, disd. Dec. 22, 1862.
Olert F. e. May 25, 1861, kld. April 6, 1862.
Osborn R. S. e. May 25, 1861, disd. Mch. 22, '63, disab.
Palmer A. S. e. May 25. 1861.
Russell J. e. May 25. 1861.
Rupp W. W. e. May 25, 1861.
Rogers R. W. e. May 25, 1861.
Robinson T. S. e. May 25, 1861.
Russell H. A. e. May 25, 1861.
Shaw M. e. May 25, 1861.
Stone W. e. May 25, 1861, disd. April 30, 1862.
Strahl J. P. e. May 25, 1861.
Suggs J. L. e. May 25, 1861, disd. April 22, 1861.
Shindollar R. e. May 25, 1861, re-enlisted as veteran.
Stephenson T. e. May 25, 1861, disd. April 5, 1862.
Smith G. O. e. May 25, 1861.
Shelly J. e. May 25, 1861.
Scott W. L. e. May 25, 1861, re-enlisted as veteran.
Tubbs R. F. e. May 25, 1861, dis. April 5, 1862.
Taylor, A. J. e. May 25, 1861, dis. Dec. 14, 1861.
Thume F. e. May 25, 1861, k'ld April 6, 1862.
Voris W. M. e. May 25, 1861.
Woode N. R. e. May 25, 1861.
Walling E. B. e May 25, 1861.
Waddle W. e. May 25, 1871, dis May 15, 1864.
Walsh J. e. May 25, 1861.
Wright J. A. e. May 25, 1861, dis. April 24, 1862.
Warren S. B. e. May 25, 1861, m. o. May 11, 1865.
Wilcox C. S. e. May 25, 1861, trans. reg'l band May 25, 1861.

RECRUITS.

Crawford J. W. e. July 15, 1861, trans. Co. D 8th Ill. Inf.
Clawson J. e. Sept. 20, 1861, died Nov. 17, 1861.
Cowan S. e. April 20, 1861, re-enlisted as veteran.
Dungan D. M. e. April 20, 1861, dis. May 13, 1862.
Liby A. e. Aug. 8, 1862, trans. Co. I 8th Ill. Inf.
Mitchell, W. M. e. Feb. 26, 1862, re-enlisted as vetr'n.
Moore E. G. e. April 20, 1861, dis. July 26, 1862.
Nelson T. M. e. Aug. 7, 1862, kld. May 22, 1863.
Smith S. e. April 20, 1861.
Stutger J. e. Sept. 20, 1861, trans. Co. I 8th Ill. Inf.
Smith G. D. e. Sept. 1, 1862, trans. Co. I 8th Ill. Inf.
Turner J. R. e. April 20, 1862.

VETERANS.

Cowan S. e. Dec. 23, 1863, trans. Co. E 8th Ill. Inf.
Furr C. e. Dec. 23, 1863, trans. Co. D 8th Ill. Inf.
Kepley J. D. e. Dec. 23, '63, trans. Co. E 8th Ill. Inf.
Mahan J. R. e. Mch. 8, '64, trans. Co. E 8th Ill. Inf.
McIntyre Geo. e. Mch. 8, '64, trans. Co. E 8th Ill. Inf.
Mitchell W. M e. Mch. 8, '64, trans. Co. E 8th Ill. Inf.
Scott W. L. e. Dec. 23, 1863, trans. Co. E 8th Ill. Inf.
Shindoler R. e. Dec. 14, '63, trans. Co. E 8th Ill. Inf.

Company I.

Anthony M. H. e. May 25, 1861, kld. April 6, 1862.
Bard W. F. e. May 25, 1861, dis. June 17, 1862.
Findlay J. e. May 25, 1861.
Gaston J. e. May 25, 1861.
Gould S. e. May 25, 1861.
Furling G. e. June 15, 1861, dis. Oct. 20, 1861.
Reynolds J. M. e. May 25, 1861, dis. April 26, 1862.
Sanders T. J. e. May 25, 1861.
Williams S. D. e. May 25, 1861, dis. July 1, 1862.

VETERANS.

Findley J. e. Nov. 18, 1862, trans Co. E 8th Ill. Inf.
Fuller J. e. Dec. 11, 1862, trans. Co. E 8th Ill. Inf.

THIRTY-SIXTH INFANTRY.

Company B.

Second Lieutenant Geo. Berger, rank Oct. 8, 1865, not mustered. Mustered out (as Sergeant) Oct. 8, '65.
Sergeant F. Brownlee, e. Aug. 5, '61, died Dec. 25, '63.

PRIVATES.

Berger G. e. Sept. 1, 1861, re-enlisted as veteran.
Boyd T. e. Sept. 1, 1861, deserted March 11, 1863.
Brownlee O. F. e. Sept. 1, 1861, disd. Sept. 22, 1864, term expired.
Campbell A. R. e. Sept. 1, 1861, m. o. Sept. 29, 1864.
Campbell J. B. e. Sept. 1, 1861, disd. Sept. 22, 1864, term expired.
Campbell S. e. Sept. 1, '61, disd. Sept. 22, 64, term ex.
Campbell W. L. e. Sept. 1, 1861, disd. Sept. 22, 1864 as Corporal, term expired.
Clark T. e. Sept. 17, 1861, m. o. Oct. 8, 1865 as Corpl.
Cowan T. e. Sept. 1, 1861, disd. Feb. 7, 1862, disab.
Donnell T. e. Sept. 1, 1861, disd. March 23, 1863.
Donnell D. C. e. Sept. 1, 1861, disd. June 14, 1863, wds.
Galloway L. e. Sept. 1, 1861, deserted Sept. 10, 1862.
Hogue D. T. e. Sept. 1, '61, disd. Sept. 22, '64, term ex.
McClorg D. e. Sept. 1, 1861, Sgt. kld. Dec. 31, 1862.
McConnell T. H. e. Sept. 1, 1861, disd. March 19, 1862, disability.
McCutcheon N. P. e. Sept. 1, 1861, missing.

Company C.

Captain Elias B. Baldwin, rank Aug. 20, 1861, mustered Sept. 23, 1861. Promoted Lieutenant Colonel 8th Missouri Cavalry Nov. 6, 1862.
Captain Jas. B. McNeal, rank Sept. 15, 1862, mustered March 12, 1863. Died of wds. Sept. 3, 1864.
Captain Jas. J. Wilson, rank Sept. 3, 1864, mustered Nov. 2, 1864. Mustered out Oct. 8, 1865.

First Lieutenant Jos. B. McNeal, rank Aug. 20, 1861 mustered Sept. 23, 1861. Promoted.
First Lieutenant Jno. M. Turnbull, rank Sept. 15, '62, mustered March 12, 1863. Resigned Nov. 4, 1864.
First Lieutenant Jno. A. Porter, rank March 13, 1865, mustered Mch. 21, '65. Mustered out Oct. 8, 1865.
Second Lieutenant Jno. M. Turnbull, rank Aug. 20, 1861, mustered Sept. 23, 1861. Promoted.
Second Lieutenant Jacob Sands, rank Sept. 15, 1862, mustered March 12, 1863. Resigned Feb. 17, 1865.
Second Lieutenant Wm. A. Mitchell, rank Oct. 8, 1865, not mustered. Mustered out (as Sergt) Oct. 8, '65.
First Sergeant J. Sands, e. April 19, 1861. Promoted Second Lieutenant.
Sergeant J. A. Porter, e. April 19, 1861. Promoted Second Lieutenant from First Sergeant.
Sergeant E. A. Crawford, e. April 19, 1861, died Feb. 9, 1863.
Sergeant S. Brownlee, e. April 19, 1861, dis. Sept. 23, 1864, as private, term ex.
Sergeant D. S. Irvin, e. April 19, 1861, killed Dec. 16, 1864.
Corporal R. Gilmore, e. Aug. 1, 1861, dis. Sept. 23, 1864, as private, term ex.
Corporal J. J. Wilson, e. April 23, 1861, re-enlisted as veteran.
Corporal J. A. Pearce, e. Aug. 1, 1861, Sergeant, killed Nov. 25, 1863.
Corporal W. Ward, e. Aug. 1, 1861, mustered out April 1, 1865, as private, prisoner of war.
Corporal W. Kingsland, e. April 23, 1861, dis. Sept. 23, 1864, as private, term ex.
Corporal G. N. Mercer, e. May 1, 1861, Sergeant, died Oct. 23, 1864, wds.
Corporal D. B. Brownlee, e. April 23, 1861, private, died Nov. 24, 1861.
Musician J. L. Dryden, e. Aug. 15, 1861, mustered out Oct. 26, 1864, wounded.
Musician J. F. Young, e. April 23, 1861, dis. Sept. 23, 1864, term ex.

PRIVATES.

Atkins E. L. e. Aug. 1, 1861, capt'd Sept. 20, '63, died.
Allen W. S. e. Aug. 13, 1861, Corpl., kld. Sept. 20, '63.
Angles V. e. July 2, 1861, died April 19, 1862.
Arthurs J. W. e. Aug. 4, '61, m. o. Oct. 8, '65, as Sergt.
Arthurs W. T. e. Aug. 4, 1861, kld. Dec. 31, 1862.
Azdell W. C. e. Aug. 24, 1861, dis. Aug. 28, '62, disab.
Armstrong J. e. Aug. 26, 1861, dis. Aug. 10, 1862, disab.
Bailey C. B. e. Aug. 1, 1861, dis. Sept. 23, '64, term ex.
Butt L. e. May 1, 1861, kld. Sept. 20, 1863.
Baxter J. e. Aug. 12, 1861, kld. Dec. 31, 1862.
Baird N. T. e. Aug. 12, 1861, dis. Dec. 3, '62, disability.
Baldwin D. P. e. May 1, 1861, kld. May 14, 1864.
Barton T. G. e. May 1, 1861, dis. July 31, '62, disab'ty.
Beck F. e. April 25, 1861, died June 30, 1862.
Baughman I. e. Sept. 1, '61, m. o. Oct. 18, '65, as Corpl.
Cavis J. G. e. Aug. 26, 1861, kld. Sept. 20, 1863.
Carson I. e. Aug. 10, 1861, m. o. Oct. 8, 1865.
Criswell W. P. e. Aug. 12, 1861, m. o. Oct. 8, 1865.
Carey I. N. e. Aug. 12, 1861, dis. April 2, 1863, disab.
Constant F. e. Aug. 18, 1861, m. o. Jan. 24, 1865.
Dowell G. e. Aug. 1, 1861, dis. Sept. 23, '64, term ex.
Donnell H. P. e. Aug. 10, 1861, dis. June 2, 1865, as Corpl., wds.
Davis J. e. Aug. 10, 1861, kld. May 17, 1864.
Eckelson A. e. May 1, 1861, dis. Sept. 23, 1864.
Elder J. e. May 1, 1861, kld. Dec. 31, 1862.
Edgar J. B. e. May 1, 1861, dis. Aug. 19, 1863, disab'ty.
Fisher W. e. May 1, 1861, died Sept. 1, 1863.
Godfrey R. e. Aug. 1, 1861, died May 16, 1862.
Graham J. Q. e. Aug. 1, 1861, m. o. Oct. 8, 1865.
Gibson Wm. M. e. Aug. 1, '61, dis. April 14, '62, wds.
Gilmore R. e. Aug. 15, 1861.
Harper H. W. e. Aug. 15, 1861, trans. V. R. C.
Hayes O. e. May 1, 1861, m. o. June 2, 1865, prisr. of war.
Haitzell W. e. May 10, 1861, dis. Sept. 23, '64, term ex.
Henderson J. F. e. May 1, 1861, died Oct. 10, '62, wds.
Hercher F. e. April 20, 1861, dis. Oct. 9, '63, disability.
Harris J. H. e. Aug. 1, 1861, kld. Mch. 7, 1862.
Henderson H. e. May 1, 1861, m. o. Oct. 8, 1865.
Kintzey W. e. Aug. 10, 1861, m. o. Oct. 8, 1865.
Leggett T. e. Aug. 10, 1861, trans. veteran reserve.
Lord H. H. e. May 1, 1861, m. o. O t. 8, 1865.
Monroe G. e. May 1, 1861, m. o. Feb. 18, 1865, pr'sr. war.
McCoy J. W. e. May 1, 1861, m. o. Oct. 6, 1864, as Sergt.
Mattison S. W. e. Aug. 10, 1861, m. o. Oct. 8, 1865.
McClanahan F. e. May 1, 1861, trans. to vet. reserve.
McPherrin J. C. e. May 1, 1861, trans. to marine brig St. Louis.
McGregor J. e. May 1, 1861.
McMullen J. K. e. May 1, 1861, dis. Sept. 25, 1863, disability.
McElroy W. C. e. Aug. 10, 1861, trans. Battery G 1st Mo. Art.
Mitchell W. A. e. Aug. 1, 1861. m. o. Oct. 8, 1865.
Moss J. W. e. Aug. 26, 1861, kld. June 19, 1864.
Munson E. E. e. Aug. 26, 1861, dis. Sept. 23, 1864, term ex.
Nelson G. e. Aug. 10. 1861, died June 23, 1862.
Nichols G. W. May 1, 1861, dis. Sept. 23, '64, term ex.
Paxton S. e. Aug. 14, 1861, m. o. Oct. 8, 1865, as Sergt.
Pike L. M. e. Aug. 26, 1861, kld. Nov. 25, 1863.
Patterson W. e. Aug. 26, 1861, died Jan. 5, 1864.
Ralston J. e. Aug. 12, 1861, died Sept. 23, '65, wds.
Spickerman O. A. e. Aug. 24, 1861, dis. Sept. 23, 1864.
Stewart J. e. Aug. 14, 1861, died Dec. 1, 1863.
Shook J. e. Aug. 12, 1861. died Jan. 17, 1863, wds.
Sawins B. W. e. May 1, 1861, died Sept. 28, 1864.
Shearer W. e. Aug. 10, 1861, died Dec. 1, 1861.
Shearer H. e. Aug. 10, 1861, died Dec. 10, 1861.
Smith J. H. e. April 20, 1861, died Jan. 15, 1863, wds.
Schotts F. e. Aug. 15, 1861, d ed Dec. 1, 1863, wds.

Stewart A. e. May 1, 1861, dis. Sept. 23, 1864, term ex.
Stewart I. e. May 1, 1861, m. o. Sept. 20, 1864.
Toll W. R. e. April 20, 1861, dis. Sept. 23, '65, as Sergt.
Tice J. P. e. Aug. 15, 1861, died Nov. 30, 1861.
Thompson G. W. e. May 1, 1861, m. o. Mch. 15, 1865, prisr. of war.
Way-taff H. e. Aug. 8, 1861, died Nov. 14, 1861.
Ward J. H. e. July 28, '61, m. o. Sept. 13, '64, wnded.
Wilson S. N. e. May 4, 1861, died Aug. 25, 1864.
Wilson J. e. Aug. 14, 1861, dis. July 2, 1865, as Corpl., wds.
Wimmer E. e. May 17, 1861, died Dec. 17, 1864, wds.
Wright S. G. e. May 17, 1861, dis. May 19, '63, disab.

RECRUITS.

Arthurs J. C. e. Feb. 16, 1864, m. o. Oct. 8, 1865.
Arthurs A. Y. e. Feb. 16, 1864, m. o. Oct. 8, 1865.
Allen J. A. e. Aug. 6, 1862, died Jan. 8, 1863.
Baird T. F. e. Aug. 13, 1861, dis. June 3, 1862, di ab.
Barten J. P. e. Feb. 25, '64, m. o. Oct. 8, '65, as Corpl.
Black J. M. e. Mch. 5, 1864, trans. V. R. C. Mch. 15, 1865.
Carson S. e. Aug. 26, 1864, m. o. June 15, 1865.
Gormley T. B. e. Aug. 1, 1861, died Sept. 28, 1863.
Henderson R. A. e. Mch. 4, 1864, m. o. Oct. 8, 1865.
Hayes J. H. e. Aug. 31, 1862, m. o. June 14, 1865.
Kitchen J. W. e. Feb. 16, 1864, m. o. Oct. 8, 1865.
Knox G. H. e. Aug. 14, 1862, died Aug. 7, 1864.
Lukes J. M. e. Mch. 7, 1864, m. o. Oct. 8, 1865.
Mitchell F. T. e. Feb. 25, 1864, m. o. Oct. 8, 1865.
Pollock J. A. e. Aug. 25, 1862, trans. U. S. Engs. Sept., 1864.
Rodgers W. A. e. Feb. 18, 1864, dis. Feb. 3, '65, wds.
Sm th W. H. e. Feb. 29, 1864, died Sept. 28, 1864.
Sawins F. J. e. Aug. 18, 1862, m. o. June 15, 1865.
Stewart W. E. e. Aug. 5, 1862, died Sept 23, 1863.
Snodgrass A. e. Aug. 9, 1862, died July 17, 1864, wds.
Wright J. C. e. Feb. 18, 1864, m. o. June 19, 1865, as Corpl.

Company K.

Second Lieutenant John H. Johnson, rank — 8, 1865, not mustered. Mustered out, as Sergt. Oct. 8, '65, 1865.
Corporal W. B. Giles, rank Aug. 12, 1861, killed Oct. 8, 1862.

PRIVATES.

Birdsall S. e. Aug. 20, 1861, kld. June 27, 1864.
Honey B. e. Aug. 20, 1861, trans. V. R. C.
Hogue J. M. e. Aug. 20, '61, m. o. Oct. 8, '65, as Sergt.
Hogue J. H. e. Aug. 20, 1861, died Feb. 11, 1864.
Hogue J. H. e. Aug. 20, 1861, m. o. Oct. 17, '64, wndd.
Hall W. C. e. Aug. 20, 1861, m. o. Oct. 17, 1864.
Johnson J. H. e. Aug. 20, 1861, m. o. Oct. 8, 1865.
Long A. e. Aug. 20, 1861, Corpl., kld. Sept. 2, 1864.
McCartney S. H. e. Aug. 20, 1861, dis. July 2, 1864.
Pollock G. R. e. Aug. 20, 1861, kld. "B" Stone River.
Sype H. P. e. Aug. 20, 1861, kld. June 27, 1864.
Stevenson J. e. Aug. 20, 1861, dis. Aug. 16, 1862.
Underwood C. W. e. Aug. 20, 1861, m. o. Oct. 8, 1865.
Underwood J. H. e. Aug. 20, 1861, kld. Oct. 8, 1862.
Weekes J. F. e. Aug. 20, 1861, dis. Sept. 22, 1864, as Sergt., term ex.

VETERANS.

Hammond D. P. e. Jan. 1, 1864, m. o. Oct. 8, 1855, as Sergt.
Poll J. e. Jan. 1, 1864, trans. U. S. V. V. Engineers.

RECRUITS.

Hogue Z. E. e. Feb. 25, '64, m. o. Oct. 8, '65, as Corpl.
Moore R. C. e. Feb. 20, 1864, m. o. Oct. 8, 1865, Corpl.
Underwood G. A. e. Feb. 23, 1864, kld. Dec. 16, 1864.

SIXTY-FIRST INFANTRY.

Company D.

RECRUITS—transferred from 83rd Ill. Vol. Inf.

McWilliams J. F. e. Feb. 3, 1865, m. o. Sept. 8, 1865.
Ross R. J. e. Jan. 5, 1864, m. o. Sept. 8, 1865.
Stewart Wm. e. Feb. 2, 1864, m. o. Sept. 8, 1865.
Wallace H. F. e. Feb. 25, 1864, m. o. Sept. 8, 1865.
Wallace S. F. e. Feb. 26, 1864, m. o. Sept. 8, 1865.
Wells H. T. e. Mch. 10, 1865, m. o. Sept. 8, 1865.
Wells G. W. e. Mch. 10, 1865, m. o. Sept. 8, 1865.
Wheeler C. W. e. Oct. 30, 1863, m. o. Sept. 8, 1865.
Williams Jas. A. e. Aug. 16, 1864, m. o. Sept. 8, 1865.

Company E.

RECRUITS—Transferred from 83d Ill. Vol. Inf.

Alexander C. L. e. Mch. 20, 1865, m. o. Sept. 8, 1865.
Black A. e. Feb. 25, 1864, m. o. Sept. 8, 1865.
Burns Jesse, e. Mch. 3, 1865, m. o. Sept. 8, 1865.
Barrett W. H. e. Mch. 3, 1865, m. o. Sept. 8, 1865.
Bailey D. B. e. Feb. 17, 1865, m. o. Sept. 8, 1865.
Crosier G. R. e. Oct. 30,1863, m.o. Sept. 8,1865 as Sergt.
Coppersmith A. e. Apr. 11, 1865, m. o. Sept. 8, 1865.
Dougherty O. J. e. Mch. 20, 1865, m. o. Sept. 8, 1865.
Foster Minard, e. April 4, 1865, m. o. Sept. 8, 1865.
Graham B. F. e. Feb. 29. 1864, m. o. Sept. 8, 1865.
Gardner A. e. Mch. 14, 1865, m. o. Sept. 8, 1865.
Guillings J. F. e. Mch. 14, 1865, m. o. Sept. 8, 1865.
Harper J. A. e. Feb. 25, 1864, m. o. Sept. 8, 1865.
Hammond J. C. e. Feb. 25, 1864, m. o. Sept. 8, 1865.
Kline H. R. e. Mch. 10, 1865, m. o. Sept. 8, 1865.
Looby P. e. Feb. 17, 1865, m. o. Sept. 8, 1865.
Monroe G. N. e. Mch. 28, 1865, m. o. Sept. 8, 1865.
Morrison M. e. Feb. 26, 1864, m. o. Sept. 8, 1865.
McCoy P. e. Jan. 20, 1864, m. o. Sept. 8, 1865.
McGeary J. e. Feb. 17, 1865, m. o. Sept. 8, 1865.
McCoy T. M. e. Feb. 17, 1865, m. o. Sept. 8, 1865.
McCrary M. R., m. o. Sept. 8, 1865.
Nichols A. M. e. Feb. 17, 1865, m. o. Sept. 8, 1865.
Russell Wm. e. Mch. 3, 1865, m. o. Sept. 8, 1865.
Snapp E. e. Apr. 4, 1865, m. o. Sept. 8, 1865.
Thompson W. N. e. Feb. 17, 1865, m. o. Sept. 8, 1865.
Worden Linder, e. Mch. 30, 1865, m. o. Sept. 8, 1865.
Wilson C. e. Mch. 16, 1865, m. o. Sept. 8, 1865.
Walter G. M. e. Feb. 17, 1865, m. o. Sept. 8, 1865.

Company H.

RECRUITS—Transferred from 83rd Ill, Vol, Inf,

Bruce N. or M. H. e. Feb. 17, 1865, m. o. Sept. 8, '65.
Hohn W. M. e. Jan. 28, 1864, m. o. Sept. 8, 1865.
Palmer Allen, e. Mch. 3, 1864, m. o. Sept. 8, 1865.

Company I.

RECRUITS—Transferred from 83rd Ill. Inf.

Bostwick T. H. e. Jan. 28, 1865, m. o. Sept. 8, 1865 as Corpl.
Butler A. e. Mch. 10, 1865, m. o. Sept. 8, 1865.
Barber R. B. e. Mch. 10, 1865, m. o. Sept. 8, 1865.
Courson J. e. Apr. 11, 1865, m. o. Sept. 8, 1865.
Cunningham T. e. Mch. 10, 1865, m. o. Sept. 8, 1865.
Futhey L. e. Apr. 7, 1865, m. o. Sept. 8, 1865.
George S. A. e. Feb. 22, 1865, m. o. Sept. 8, 1865.
Hogue J. D. e. Feb. 22, 1865, m. o. Sept. 8, 1865.
Hogue W. H. e. Nov. 20, 1863, m. o. Sept. 8, 1865.
Houts J. B. e. Mch. 10, 1865, m. o. Sept. 8, 1865.
Houts H. e. Mch. 15, 1865, m. o. Sept. 8, 1865.
Hitchcock M. e. Mch. 12, 1865, m. o. Sept. 8, 1865.
Hitchcock C. e. Mch. 17, 1865, m.o. Sept. 8, 1865 as Corpl.
Hudiurgh I. H. e. Mch. 10, 1865, m. o. Sept. 8, 1865.
Imnul J. e. Mch. 10, 1865, m. o. Sept. 8, 1865.
Kelley W. e. Mch. 10, 1865, m. o. Sept. 8, 1865.
Lepray D. e. Mch. 15, 1865, m. o. Sept. 8, 1865.
Laundaker P. e. Mch. 17, 1865, m. o. Sept. 8, 1865.
McClure H. B. e. Mch. 6, 1865, m. o. Sept. 8, 1865.
Morris M. e. Mch. 10, 1865, m. o. Sept. 8, 1865.
Miller S. e. Mch. 6, 1865, m. o. Sept. 8, 1865.
Moor G. W. e. Mch. 6, 1865, m. o. Sept. 8, 1865 as Corpl.
McGowan A. e. Mch. 17, 1865, m. o. Sept. 8, 1865.
Ostrander C. A. e. Mch. 6, 1865, m. o. Sept. 8, 1865.
Osborn A. or J. E. Mch. 3, 1865, m. o. Sept. 8, 1865.
Peck A. e. Mch. 10, 1865, m. o. Sept. 8, 1865.
Sailer J. H. e. Jan. 23, 1864, m. o. Sept. 8, 1865.
Stacker T. e. Mch. 10, 1865, m. o. Sept. 8, 1865.
Tuttle S. H. e. Mch. 6, 1865, m. o. Sept. 8, 1865.
Taylor W. B. e. Mch. 6, 1865, m. o. Sept. 8, 1865.
Vanvelzer F. e. Mch. 16, 1865, m. o. Sept. 8, 1865.
Welsh W. e. Mch. 7, 1865, m. o. Sept. 8, 1865.

FIFTIETH INFANTRY.

Company I.

Captain Jos. D. Wolf, rank Sept. 15, 1861, mustered Sept. 12, 1861. Mustered out June 19, 1862.
Captain Francis J. Dunn, rank Nov. 22, 1862, mustered Feb. 28, 1863. Mustered out Oct. 24, 1864.
Captain John T. Cuzzins, rank June 14, 1865, mustered June 25, 1865. Mustered out July 13, 1865.
First Lieutenant George W. Elliot, rank May 19, 1862. Resigned Nov. 15, 1862.
First Lieutenant John T. Cuzzins, rank July 18, 1864, mustered Oct. 12, 1864. Promoted.
First Lieutenant John S. Winbigler, rank June 14, 1865, mustered July 2, 1865. Mustered out July 13, 1865.
Second Lieutenant George W. Elliott, rank Sept. 15, 1861, mustered Sept. 12, 1861. Promoted.
Second Lieutenant Philip S. Douglas, rank Nov. 15, '62, mustered Feb. 28, '63. Resigned Oct. 28, '64.
Second Lieutenant Wm. Brownell, rank July 10, 1865, not mustered. Mustered out (as serg't) July 13, '65.
Sergeant F. J. Dunn, e. Sept. 16, 1861. Promoted First Sergeant, then Captain.
Sergeant A. Austin, e. Sept. 16, 1861.
Corporal J. T. Lukins, e. Sept. 16, 1861, disd. Oct. 15, 1862.
Corporal W. H. H. Roney, e. Sept. 16, 1861.
Corporal R. C. Smith, e. Sept. 16, 1861, disd. July 12, 1862.
Corporal B. S. Davis, e. Sept. 16, 1861, m. o. Sept. 27, 1864.
Corporal H. Swiler, e. Sept. 16, 1861, re-enlisted as veteran.
Musician H. M. Shepherd, e. Sept. 16, 1861, re-enlisted as veteran.
Wagoner J. S. Jones, e. Sept. 16, 1861, disd. Sept. 24, 1862.

PRIVATES.

Black S. R. e. Sept. 16, 1861.
Boggs F. M. e. Sept. 16, 1861, kld. Apr. 6, 1862.
Colter J. W. e. Sept. 16, 1861, died Apr. 27, 1862.
Cuzzins J. T. e. Sept. 16, 1861, re-enlisted as vet.
Conville A. e. Sept. 16, 1861, disd. in 1862.
Carle J. e. Sept. 16, 1861, re-enlisted as vet.
Douglas P. S. e. Sept. 16, 1861, pro. Sergt. then Lieut.
Dodd A. e. Sept. 16, 1861, m. o. Sept. 27, 1864.
Farris J. S. e. Sept. 16, 1861, disd.
Greenlee J. J. e. Sept. 16, 1861, re-enlisted as vet.
Harris E. H. e. Sept. 16, 1861, deserted May 7, 1864 Second desertion.
Hogue S. A. e. Sept. 16, 1861, re-enlisted as vet.
Hess J. e. Sept. 16, 1861, re-enlisted as vet.
Harendon B. J. e. Sept. 16, 1861, deserted May 29, 1862.
Hall J. B. e. Sept. 16, 1861, disd. June 24, 1862.
Johnson C. V. e. Sept. 16, 1861, re-enlisted as vet.
Kibby M. e. Sept. 16, 1861, disd. Aug. 9, 1862.
Kitchen J. W. e. Sept. 16, 1861, disd. May 13, 1862.
Logan G. W. e. Sept. 16, 1861, disd. Aug. 9, 1862.
Logan G. R. e. Sept. 16, 1861, re-enlisted as vet.
Line H. e. Sept. 16, 1861, re-enlisted as vet.
Mark J. M. e. Sept. 16, 1861, re-enlisted as vet.
Mohler G. W. e. Sept. 16, 1861, re-enlisted as vet.
Mahaffey J. C. e. Sept. 16, 1861, disd. Sept. 25, 1862.
Miller S. e. Sept. 16, 1861, wd. Feb. 12, 1862.
Myers D. J. e. Sept. 16, 1861, disd. May 21, 1862.
Nelson W. B. e. Sept. 16, 1861, disd. Apr. 27, 1862.
Pike S. M. e. Sept. 16, 1861, re-enlisted as vet.
Quinn Elias, e. Sept. 16, 1861, disd. June 10, 1862.
Quinn P. C. e. Sept. 16, 1861, re-enlisted as vet.
Rusk O. A. e. Sept. 16, 1861, re-enlisted as vet.
Rainard W. H. e. Sept. 16, 1861, died 1863.
Sterritt J. M. e. Sept. 16, 1861, died April 25, 1862 wds.
Sterling D. e. Sept. 16, 1861, died May 5, 1862.
Stephens J. M. e. Sept. 16, 1861.
Staley J. W. e. Sept. 16, 1861, re-enlisted as vet.
Smith J. e. Sept. 16, 1861, re-enlisted as vet.
Thompson A. M. e. Sept. 16, 1861, re-enlisted as vet.
Underwood D. J. e. Sept. 16, 1861, re-enlisted as vet.
Ware E. e. Sept. 16, 1861.

Winbigler J. S. e. Sept. 16, 1861, re-enlisted as vet.
Wood, M. e. Sept. 16, 1861, disd. Aug. 13, 1862.

VETERANS.

G. R. Logan, e. Dec. 30, 1863, m. o. July 13, 1865 as Sergt.
Brenner C. e. Jan. 21, 1864, m. o. July 13, 1865.
Beeyly E. W. e. Jan. 1, 1864, m. o. July 13, 1865.
Blind C. e. Jan. 1, 1864, m. o. July 13, 1865.
Brownlee W. e. Jan. 1, 1864, m. o. July 13, 1865, as Sergt.
Carl J. e. Jan. 1, 1864, m. o. July 13, 1865.
Cuzzins J. T. e. Jan. 1, 1864. Promoted First Sergt., then First Lieut.
Greenlee J. J. e. Jan. 1, 1864, m. o. July 13, 1865.
Hess J. e. Jan. 1, 1864, m. o. July 13, 1865.
Hogue S. A. e. Jan. 1, 1864, m. o. July 13, 1865.
Johnson C. V. e. Jan. 1, 1864. Corpl., captured Feb. 25, 1865, in S. C., not heard from since.
Laird J. e. Jan. 1, 1864, m. o. July 13, 1865.
Line H. e. Jan. 1, 1864, m. o. July 13, 1865 as Corpl.
Mark J. M. e. Jan. 1, 1864, m. o. July 13, 1865.
Mohler G. W. e. Jan. 1, 1864, m. o. July 13, 1865.
McGee D. C. e. Jan. 1, 1864, m. o. July 13, 1865.
Mouldin A. e. Jan. 1, 1864, trans. V. R. C.
Pike S. M. e. Jan. 1, 1864, kld. Oct. 5, 1864.
Quinn P. e. Jan. 1, 1864, m. o. July 13, 1865 as Corpl.
Rusk O. A. e. Jan. 1, 1864, m. o. July 13, 1865 as Corpl.
Staley J. W. e. Jan. 1, 1864, m. o. July 13, 1865.
Smith J. e. Jan. 1, 1864, m. o. July 13, 1865.

Swiler H. e. Jan. 1, 1864, m. o. July 13, 1865.
Thomas A. e. Jan. 1, 1864, m. o. July 13, 1865 as Corpl.
Thompson A. M. e. Jan. 1, 1864, m. o. July 13, 1865 as Sergt.
Underwood D. J. e. Jan. 1, 1864, m. o. July 13, 1865 as Corp.
Winbigler J. S. e. Jan. 1, 1864, pro. Sergt., First Sergt., then First Lieut.

RECRUITS.

Appleby W. e. Feb. 25, 1864, m. o. July 13, 1865.
Arnold W. e. Feb. 25, 1864, disd. Oct. 22, 1864 disab.
Brownlee e. Feb. 25, 1864, re-enlisted as vet.
Coulter O. H. e. Feb. 25, 1864, m. o. July 13, 1865.
Clements J. B. e. Feb. 25, 1864, m. o. July 13, 1865.
Ent Geo. O. e. Feb. 4, 1864, m. o. July 13, 1865.
Gallion J. e. Feb. 25, 1864, m. o. July 13, 1865.
Hogue R. J. e. Feb. 25, 1864, m. o. July 13, 1865.
Leggett R. S. e. Feb. 25, 1864, m. o. July 13, 1865.
Mohler e. Feb. 24, 1864, m. o. July 13, 1865.
Monroe J. e. Feb. 25, 1864, m. o. July 13, 1865.
Martin W. S. e. Feb. 25, 1864, m. o. July 13, 1865.
McGregor J. G. e. Feb. 4, 1864, m. o. July 13, 1865.
Mahaffey J. H. e. Feb. 25, 1864, m. o. July 5, 1865.
Ralston A. e. Feb. 25, 1864, m. o. July 13, 1865.
Stinemater L. e. Feb. 25, 1864, m. o. July 13, 1865.
Spencer C. T. e. Feb. 25, 1864, m. o. July 13, 1865.
Taylor D. e. Jan. 4, 1864, m. o. July 13, 1865.
Wageman Geo. e. Feb. 25, 1864, trans. V.R.C. May 1, 1865.

FIFTY-NINTH INFANTRY.

Company B.

Captain Hendrick E. Paine, rank July 17, 1861. Resigned April 3, 1863.
Captain Jas. Johnson, rank April 3, 1863, mustered April 18, 1863. Mustered out Dec. 8, 1865.
First Lieutenant Jno. H. Johnson, rank July 17, 1861. Resigned Dec. 22, 1862.
First Lieutenant Jas. Johnson, rank Dec. 22, 1862. Promoted.
Second Lieutenant Andrew R. Johnson, rank Aug. 6, 1861. Killed at battle of Perryville, Ky.
Second Lieutenant Jas. Johnson, rank Oct. 8, 1862. Promoted.
Second Lieutenant Robt. D. Irvine, rank April 3, 1863, mustered April 18, 1863. Mustered out Dec. 8, '65.
First Sergeant A. R. Johnson, e. July 17, 1861. Promoted Second Lieutenant.
Sergeant R. D. Irwin, e. July 17, 1861. Promoted Second Lieutenant.
Sergeant H. M. Rowe, e. July 17, 1861. Priv. Tr. to Miss. M. Brig. Feb. 11, 1863.
Sergeant H. W. Sawyer, e. July 17, 1861, disd. May 20, 1862.
Corporal J. D. Callaghan, e. July 17, 1861, disd. Aug. 1, 1861, disab.
Corporal J. Johnson, e. July 17, 1861. Promoted Second Lieutenant.
Corporal J. C. Jones, e. July 17, '61, m. o. July 15, '65.
Musician F. M. Haines, e July 17, 1861. Promoted Prin. Musician.
Wagoner E. H. French, e. July 17, '61, died Mch. 26, '64.

PRIVATES.

Ackerman S. G. e. July 17, 1861, disd. Dec. 14, 1863, as Sergt. disab.
Anderson J. e. July 17, 1861, disd, Sept. 30, '61, disab.
Adams W. B. e. July 17, 1861, deserted Feb. 5, 1865.
Birdsell C. E. e. July 17, 1861, m. o. Dec. 8, 1865, as Sergt.
Bonner J. e. July 17, 1861, disd. Aug. 5, 1861, disab.
Brown W. e. July 17, 1861, re-enlisted as veteran.
Bundy W. E. e. July 17, 1861, m. o. Sept. 19, 1864.
Brazelton G. A. e. July 17, 1861, m. o. Dec. 8, 1865.
Birdsell H. A. e. July 17, 1861, disd. Aug. 5, 1861, disab.
Caldwell F. M. e. July 17, 1861, died July 5, '64, Sergt.

Chapman J. e. July 17 1861, disd. Sept. 20, 1861, wds.
Cecil E. e. July 17, 1861, disd. Aug. 5, 1861, disab.
Daugherty L. C. e. July 17, 1861, m. o. Dec. 8, 1865, as Corporal.
Dennis J. R. e. July 17, 1861, wounded and missing.
Daggett C. N. e. July 17, 1861, m. o. Dec. 8, 1865
Earnist R. e. July 17, 1861, died May 8, 1862, wds.
Finch G. H. B. e. July 17, 1861, kld. Mch. 7, 1862.
Grant Thos. e. July 17, 1861, trans. to Miss. M. Brig. Feb. 11, 1863.
Gibson J. A. e. July 17, 1861, m. o. Dec. 8, 1865.
Haseltine E. G. e. July 17, '61, trans. Miss. Feb. 11, '62.
Haskins F. H. e. July 17, 1861, deserted Sept. 10, 1862.
Hunnycutt G. H. e. July 17, '61, disd. Apr. 7, '62, disab.
Herring Geo. e. July 17, 1861, deserted Aug. 9, 1865.
Higgerson B. R. e. July 17, 1861, m. o. Dec. 8, 1865.
Hough Jos. e. July 17, 1861, m. o. Dec. 8, 1865.
Mitchell R. e. July 17, 1861, disd. Apr. 24, 1863, disab.
Nowles J. W. e. July 17, 1861, m. o. Dec. 8, 1865.
Rider H. e. July 17, 1861, died Sept 16, 1861.
Rehm F. e. July 17, 1861, m. o. Dec. 8, 1865.
Richez H. D. e. July 17, 1861, disd. Aug. 5, '61, disab.
Reck A. M. e. July 17, 1861, deserted Sept. 10, 1862.
Siston T. M. e. July 17, 1861, died Sept. 5, 1861.
Sandy W. H. e. July 17, 1861, re-enlisted as veteran.
Stephens E. C. e. July 17, '61, disd. Jan. 16, 63, disab.
Shindeler P. e. July 17, 1861, died July 10, 1862.
St. George W. H. e. July 17, 1861, died Dec. 12, 1861.
Terpenning H. e. July 17, 1861, m. o. Sept. 19, 1864.
Upright A. F. e. July 17, '61, disd. May 20, '62, disab.
Vandenburg J. e. July 17, '61, disd. Dec. 15 '61, disab.
Vandewerker E. e. July 17, '61, disd. Dec. 15, '61, disab.
Wingo C. W. e. July 17, 1861, deserted Oct. 8, 1865.
Warner J. e. July 17, 1861, dsid. Jan. 16, 1863, wds.

RECRUITS.

Beard W. H. m. o. Dec. 8, 1865, as Corporal.
Caldwell G. B. e. Feb. 22, 1864, disd. May 9, 1865, wds.
Carson J. A. e. Mch. 10, 1864, m. o. Jan. 22, 1863.
Ferrington W. C. kld. Dec. 15, 1864.
Lanstrom A. J. e. April 12, 1865, m. o. Dec. 8, 1865.
Nelson N. P. e. Mch. 10, 1864, died Feb. 9, 1865, wds.
Nolan J. e. Feb. 22, 1864, died July 15, 1865.
Slater James, e. Mch. 5, 1864, m. o. Dec. 8, 1865.
Smith W. A. disd. Sept. 15, 1862, disab.

FIFTY-EIGHTH INFANTRY

Second Assistant Surgeon Alex. G. Leslie, rank May 5, 1865, mustered May 27, 1865. Mustered out April 1, 1866.

Company G.

First Lieutenant Chas. Rowe, rank Mch. 30, 1865, mustered Mch. 30, 1865. Resigned Jan. 27, 1866.
Corporal W. Jackson, e. Mch. 7, 1865, mustered out Mch. 16, 1866.
Corporal A. Fletcher, e. Mch. 7, 1865, mustered out Mch. 6, 1866.
Corporal G. W. Lunt, e. Mch. 7, 1865, mustered out Mch. 21, 1865.
Wagoner R. Montgomery, e. Mch. 7, 1865, mustered out Mch. 6, 1866.

PRIVATES.

Enderlin A. e. Mch. 11, 1865, m. o. Mch. 10, 1866.
Finke J. H. e. Mch. 11, 1865, m. o. Mch. 10, 1866.
Fletcher A. e. Mch. 24, 1865, m. o. Mch. 23, 1866.
Fry A. e. Mch. 7, 1865, m. o. Mch. 6, 1866.
Fry Geo. e. Mch. 7, 1865, m. o. Mch. 6, 1866.
Gowland J. e. Mch. 22, 1865, died July 9, 1865.
Kunzelman F. e. Mch. 11, 1865, m. o. Mch. 10, 1866.
Noakes W. e. Mch. 24, 1865, died Aug. 10, 1865.
Nuessl J. e. Mch. 11, 1865, m. o. Mch. 10, 1866.
Rampley J. e. Mch. 7, 1865, m. o. Nov. 21, 1866.
Rowe C. e. Mch. 7, 1865, prmt. First Lieut.
Seevers S. A. e. Mch. 7, 1865, m. o. Mch. 6, 1866.
Smith J. H. e. Mch. 7, 1865, died Mch. 30, 1865.

Company I.

Corporal R. M. Trimble, e. Mch. 13, 1865, m. o. Mch. 12, 1866.
Anderson Jno. S. e. Mch. 3, 1865, m. o. Mch. 3, 1866, as Sergt.
Stewart W. H. e. Mch. 1, 1865, m. o. Mch. 1, 1866.
Streeter J. S. e. Feb. 18, 1865, deserted April 1, 1865.
Thomas G. W. e. Mch. 22, 1865, m. o. Mch. 24, 1866.

MISCELLANEOUS INFANTRY

FROM 8th, 9th, 12th, 16th, 20th, 30th, 32nd, 33rd, 37th, 39th, 43d, 51st, 53rd, 55th, 57th, 62nd, 71st, 84th, 91st, 118th, and 151st REGIMENTS.

Brown M. G. e. Sept. 28, 1864, m. o. Sept. 27, 1865.
Fenwick J. M. e. Jan. 5, 1864, m. o. May 4, 1866.
Savage E. e. Jan. 18, 1864, died Nov. 1, 1864.
Thomas James, e. Sept. 28, 1864, m. o. Sept. 27, 1865.
Louiver P. e. Jan. 5, 1864, m. o. May 4, 1866.
Reynolds J. R. e. Jan. 18, 1864, dis. Feb. 26, 1865.
Furr Churchill, e. Dec. 23, 1863, m. o. Feb. 2, 1865.
Cowan S. e. Dec. 23, 1863, m. o. May 4, 1866.
Fuller J. e. Dec. 11, 1863, m. o. May 4, 1866. Promoted Sergt.
Cooley Sam'l, e. Sept. 20, 1864, killed April 9, 1865.
Conley P. e. Sept. 28, 1864, m. o. Sept. 27, 1865.
Findley J. W. e. Nov. 18, 1863, supposed drowned April 26, 1866.
McIntire G. e. March, 8, 1864, m. o. May 4, 1866.
Mitchell W. N. e. March 8, 1864, m. o. May 4, 1866.
Mahan J. R. e. March 8, 1864, disd. Nov. 27, 1865.
Scott W. L. e. Dec. 23, 1863, m. o. May 4, 1866.
Shindollar R. e. Dec. 18, 1863, never reported.
Liby A. e. Aug. 8, 1862, m. o. Aug. 7, 1865.
Smith G. D. e. Sept. 1, 1862, m. o. Aug. 31, 1865.
Slutzer J. e. Sept. 20, 1861, disd. Sept. 20, 1864.
Reynolds C. L. e. Dec. 11, 1863, m. o. May 4, 1866.
Surgeon Samuel M. Hamilton, rank July 26, 1861, mustered July 26, 1861. Promoted.
Bruner G. W. e. July 26, 1861.
Livingston J. H. disd. April 23, 1862.
Getty James, disd. July 11, 1862, wds.
Courson W. e. Oct. 18 1864, m. o. June 20, 1865.
Chapin L. D. e. Nov. 20, 1863, m. o. July 8, 1865.
St. George T. e. March 1, 1864, m. o. July 8, 1865.
Walton J. Nov. 20, 1863, m. o. July 8, 1865.
Blemi C. H. e. May 24, 1861.
Coones N. N. e. May 24, 1861, re-enlisted as Veteran.
Carr W. H. e. May 24, 1861, disd, March 10, 1862.
Earnest D. e. May 24, '61, trans. 60th Ill. Inf. Jan. 1, '64.
Gay A. e. May 24, 1861, died Sept. 14, 1862.
Paine E. e. May 24, 1861, re-enlisted as Veteran.
Marlow J. E. e. Jan. 1, 1864, m. o. July 8, 1865.
Underwood U. e. Nov. 2, 1864.
Payton M., disd. Oct. 24, 1862, wds.
First Sergeant A. J. Reid, e. Sept. 30, 1861, disd. Nov. 21, 1863, disabled.
Morrison G. W. e. Sept. 30, 1861, m. o. July 17, 1865.
Maxwell W. J. e. Oct. 18, 1864, m. o. June 22, 1865.
Dixon J. W. e. Oct. 18, 1864, m. o. July 21, 1865.
Lomax E. e. Oct. 18, 1864, never reported to Co.
Porter J. N. e. Aug. 23, 1861, m. o. Nov. 24, 1865.
Smith J. T. e. Aug. 26, 1861.
Hills A. e. March 8, 1862.
Jennings J. e. March 9, 1865, died Oct. 19, 1865.
Taylor J. M. e. March 28, 1862, disd. Dec. 5, '63, disab.
Lieurance P. e. March 10, 1865, m. o. Nov. 25, 1865.
Lieurance H. e. March 10, 1865, m. o. Nov. 25, 1865.
Vaughn J. T. e. March 10, 1865, m. o. Nov. 24, 1865.
Anderson A. A. e. Sept. 19, 1861, m. o. Nov. 24, 1865.
Ball N. e. Sept. 19, 1861, disd. Feb. 19, 1863, as Corpl., disab.
Brewster C. H. e. Sept. 19, 1861.
Fletcher C. J. e. Sept. 19, '61, m. o. Nov. 24, '65, Corpl.
Laird D. e. Sept. 19, 1861.
Richardson A. e. Sept. 19, 1861, deserted Apr. 4, 1862.
Smith I. S. e. Sept. 19, '61, disd. Sept. 3, '62, disab'ty.
Bay J. M. e. Jan. 1, 1864, m. o. Nov. 24, 1865.
Hamilton N. B. e. Jan. 1, 1864, m. o. Nov. 24, 1865.
Amey A. e. Oct. 12, 1861, m. o. Nov. 24, 1862.
Hamilton N. B. e. Oct. 7, 1861, re-enlisted as Veteran.
Haynes C. e. Oct. 7, 1861, died Nov. 7, 1862.
Jones F. A. e. March 5, 1864, prisr. of war, since trans.
Corporal T. J. Allison, e. Aug. 15, 1861. Mustered out Sept. 29, 1864, as Sergeant.
Deck J. C. e. Sept. 11, '61, m. o. May 15, '66, as Serg't.
Murphy D. e. Feb. 10, 1864, deserted Feb. 20, 1866.
Henderson R. e. Sept. 23, 1861, 1st Sergeant. Re-enlisted as Veteran.
Conrod A. e. March 22, 1865.
Gorton C. or S. e. Mch. 22, 1865.
Myers T. M. e. Mch. 22, 1865.
Peterson J. e. Dec. 23, 1865.
Second Lieutenant Nils Peterson, rank March 3, 1865. Resigned Sept. 30, 1865. Mustered Mch. 17, 1865.
Allen John, e. Jan. 1, 1862.
Gamble Hugh, e. Jan. 1, 1862.
Burns M. P. e. April 4, 1865, m. o. July 22, 1865.
Brazelton J. H. e. Oct. 16, 1862, re-enlisted as veteran.
Gamble Hugh, e. Oct. 18, 1861.
Miller S. L. e. Oct. 18, 1861.
Murray A. e. Oct. 23, 1861, m. o. Aug. 14, 1865.
March J. e. Oct. 4, 1861, reported deserted.
Peterson M. C. e. Sept. 25, 1861, m. o. Oct. 31, 1864 as orporal.
Puntney J. e. Oct. 18, 1861, m. o. Oct. 31, 1864.
Peterson A. e. Oct. 18, 1861, m. o. Oct. 31, 1864.
Swartslander C. e. Aug. 23, '61, disd. Jan. 20, '63, wds.
Garegan P. e. Jan. 2, 1861, m. o. Aug. 14, 1865.
Baines J. A. e. Nov. 4, 1861, died July 23, 1864, wds.

Herring C. W. e. Nov. 1, 1861.
Umgetter G. e. Nov. 28, 1861.
Davis M. e. Feb. 13, 1864, m. o. July 7, 1865.
Heflin L. H. e. Feb. 10, 1864, absent sick at m. o.
Hendricks W. F. e. Feb. 27, 1864, m. o. July 7, 1865.
Miles J. M. e. Feb. 10, 1864, m. o. July 7, 1865.
McAllister J. e. Feb. 10, 1864, m. o. July 7, 1865.
Fleet W. e. Dec. 16, 1861.
Wheeler Chas. e. Dec. 16, 1861, deserted Feb. 6, 1862.
Belleville J. D. e. Feb. 1, 1862, re-enlisted as veteran.
Palmer L. e. Feb. 1, 1862, re-enlisted as veteran.
Scott G. H. e. Feb. 1, 1862, re-enlisted as veteran.
Stevens E. W. e. Feb. 1, 1862, disd. Dec. 7, 1863.
Wilson J. e. Feb. 1, 1862, deserted Oct., 1864.
Buckingham W. e. Feb. 18, 1865, sub. trans. to Co. G. as consolidated.
Ervolt B. R. e. July 18, 1862.
Edwards J. e. July 14, 1862.
Harp G. e. July 19, 1862.
Hall J. e. July 14, 1862.
Jopling G. W. e. July 14, 1862.
Neis A. e. July 14, 1862.
Smith W. H. e. July 14, 1862.

Thomas W. e. July 14, 1862.
First Lieutenant Alex. P. Nelson, rank Sept. 1, 1862, mustered Sept. 1, 1862. Resigned Oct. 26, 1863.
Kelley Michael, e. Jan. 5, '64, trans. Co. F, 21st Ill. Inf.
Sergeant Edward W. Davis, e. Aug. 8. 1862, m. o. July 12, 1865.
Booth H. L. e. Aug. 8, 1862, m. o. July 12, 1865.
Carter P. S. e. Aug 11, 1862, disd. Dec. 1, 1862, disab.
Coon C. H. Aug. 14, 1862, disd. May 13, 1865.
Ramey N. C. e. Feb. 29, 1864, trans. to Co. K, 28th Ill. Inf.
Copsacker Wm. e. Feb. 22, 1865, m. o. Oct. 1, 1865.
Clampit T. e. Feb. 22, '65, absent, sick at m. o. of Rgt.
Dalton Jos. m. o. Oct. 1, 1865.
Hill M. F. m. o. Oct. 1, 1865.
Larme J. L. m. o. Oct. 1, 1865.
Starks W. m. o. Oct. 1, 1865.
Cord T. C. e. Feb. 20, 1865, trans. to Co. C.
Cummings Jas. e. Feb. 18, 1865, deserted Feb., 1865.
Golden J. e. Feb. 18, 1865, m. o. Jan. 24, 1866, as wagr.
Harrison T. E. e. Feb. 20, 1865, m. o. Jan. 24, 1866.
Nixson J. F. e. Feb. 20, 1865, m. o. Jan. 24, 1866.

FIRST CAVALRY.

Company G.

Captain Geo. W. Palmer, rank July 5, 1861. Mustered out July 14, 1862.
First Lieutenant Samuel Douglas, rank July 5, 1861. Resigned June 23, 1862.
Second Lieutenant Alex. H. Holt, rank July 5, 1861. Mustered out July 14, 1862.
First Sergeant W. K. Trabue, e. April 24, 1861. Promoted Captain Co. G.
Q. M. Sergeant R. H. Gosslie, e. April 24, 1861. Mustered out July 14, 1862 as private.
Sergeant J. M. Thomas, e. April 24, 1861. Disd. Feb., 1862, wds.
Sergeant W. L. Davies, e. April 24, 1861. Promoted Q. M. Sergeant 2d battalion.
Sergeant J. McFarland, e. April 24, 1861. Promoted Second Lieutenant Co. K, 11th cavalry.
Sergeant T. L. Manson, e. April 24, 1861. Disd. March 18, 1862, disab.
Corporal E. M. Dean, e. April 24, '61, m. o. July 14,'62.
Corporal J. M. Weakley, e. April 24, 1861. Disd. Oct. 9, 1861.
Corporal B. Lightner, Jr. e. April 24, 1861. Disd. Oct. 9, 1861.
Corporal D. S. Leighty, e. April 24, 1861. Trans. to Co. K, 11th Ill. Cav.
Corporal R. H. Bartlett, e. April 24, 1861. Mustered out July 14, 1862.
Corporal A. J. Eby, e. April 24, 1861. Mustered out July 14, 1862.
Corporal W. Oliver, e. April 24, 1861. Mustered out July 14, 1862 as private.
Corporal W. C. Fleming, e. April 24, 1861. Disd. Oct. 9, 1861.
Bugler G. H. Palmer, e. April 24, 1861. Disd. Oct. 9, 1861.
Bugler J. A. Daly, e. April 24, 1861. Disd. Oct. 9, 1861, wds.
Blacksmiths P. Florida, e. April 24, 1861. Disd, Oct. 9, 1861.
Blacksmith M. L. Goodwin, e. April 24, 1861. Disd. Oct. 9, 1861.
Saddler J. Dennison, e. April 24, '61, m. o. July 14, '62.

PRIVATES.

Anderson J. P. e. April 24, 1861, m. o. July 14, 1862.
Austin M. e. April 24, 1861, m. o. July 14, 1862, Serg't.
Bales W. S. e. April 24, 1861, disd. Oct. 9, 1861.
Baker W. e. April 24, 1861, disd. Oct. 9, 1861.
Carter W. A. A. e. April 24, 1861, disd. Oct. 9, 1861.
Carter H. e. April 24, 1861, disd. Oct. 9, 1861.
Caldwell S. L. e. April 24, 1861, disd. Oct. 9, 1861.
Chaplin W. R. e. April 24, 1861, disd. Oct. 9, 1861.
Chaffee W. N. e. April 24, 1861, m. o. July 14, 1862.

Chaffee A. B. e. April 24, 1861, m. o. July 14, 1862.
Clark E. e. April 24, 1861, m. o. July 14, 1862.
Countryman C. e. April 24, 1861, m. o. July 14, 1862.
Cowan R. e. April 24, 1861, m. o. July 14, 1862.
Cole G. O. e. April 24, 1861, disd. Oct. 9, 1861.
Cross A. e. April 24, 1861, disd. Oct. 9, 1861.
Demmer C. e. April 24, 1861, m. o. July 14, '62, Serg't.
Edie I. e. April 24, 1861, disd. Oct. 9, 1861.
Florida M. e. April 24, 1861, disd. Oct. 9, 1861.
Frans S. P. e. April 24, 1861, disd. Oct. 9, 1861.
George E. e. April 21, 1861, disd. Oct. 9, 1861.
Griffin A. e. April 24, 1861, disd. Oct. 9, 1861.
Howk R. e. April 24, 1861, disd. Oct. 9, 1861.
Huntley W. A. e. April 24, 1861, disd. Oct. 9, 1861.
Hubbard H. R. e. April 24, 1861, prmt. Segeant Major 2d Battalion.
Hume J. e. April 24, 1861, disd. Oct. 9, 1861.
Hughson P. E. e. April 24, 1861, m. o. July 14, 1862.
Jones J. G. e. April 24, 1861, m. o. July 14, 1862.
Lawson O. E. e. April 24, 1861, m. o. July 14, 1862.
Merrifield G. e. April 24, 1861, m. o. July 14, 1862.
Mehaffey J. e. April 24, 1861, m. o. July 14, 1862.
Melloy G. W. e. April 24, 1861, disd. Oct. 9, 1861.
Mills H. e. April 24, 1861, disd. Oct. 9, 1861.
Maxson H. e. April 24, 1864, disd. Oct. 9, 1861.
McClellan W. e. April 24, 1861, m. o. July 14, 1862.
McCoy Jos. e. April 14, 1861, m. o. July 14, 1862.
McComb R. e. April 24, 1861, m. o. July 14, 1862.
McMillen A. e. April 24, 1861, m. o. July 14, 1862.
Noyes C. e. April 24, 1861, disd. Oct. 9, 1861.
Patterson J. e. April 24, 1861, m. o. July 14, 1862.
Pauley W. M. e. April 24, 1861, m. o. July 14, 1862.
Paul T. e. April 24, 1861, disd. Oct. 9, 1861.
Peebles R. e. April 24, 1861, disd. Oct. 9, 1861.
Peters P. E. e. April 24, 1861, kld. Sept. 19, 1861.
Post H. L. e. April 24, 1861, disd. Oct. 9, 1861.
Prescott A. V. e. April 24, 1861, trans. to Co. K, 11th Ill. Cav., since kld.
Rector J. H. e. April 24, 1861, m. o. July 14, 1862.
Rodenbough H. e. April 24, 1861, m. o. July 14, 1862.
Robinson J. C. e. April 24, 1861, disd. Oct. 9, 1861.
Robertson H. e. April 24, 1861, disd. Oct. 9, 1861.
Rose F. e. April 24, 1861, disd. Oct. 9, 1861.
Romans J. L. e. April 24, 1861, m. o. July 14, 1862.
Russell F. e. April 24, 1861, m. o. July 14, 1862.
Sharpe F. M. e. April 24, 1861, disd. Oct. 9, 1861.
Shumway A. e. April 24, 1861, kld. while in 30th Ill.
Smith P. F. e. April 24, 1861, disd. Oct. 9, 1861.
Sproull J. M. e. April 24, 1861, disd. Oct. 9, 1861.
Stanley J. S. e. April 24, 1861, disd. Oct. 9, 1861.
Taylor L. e. April 24, 1861, disd. Oct. 9, 1861.
Taylor D. e. April 24, 1861, disd. Oct. 9, 1861.
Taylor A. J. e. April 24, 1861, disd. Oct. 9, 1861.
Talbott T. e. April 24, 1861, disd. Oct. 9, 1861.
Talcott A. e. April 24, 1861, m. o. July 14, 1862.
Tucker D. e. April 24, 1861, died Sept. 22, 1862.

WARREN COUNTY WAR RECORD. 199

Van Zandt B. e. April 24, 1861, disd. Oct. 9, 1861.
Waldron J. M. e. April 24, 1861, m. o, July 14, 1862.
Watt S. J. e. April 24, 1861, m. o, July 14, 1862.
Williams S. L. e. April 24, 1861, m. o. July 14, 1862.
Woods H. C, e. April 24, 1861, disd. Oct. 9, 1861.
Woertendyke F. e. April 24, 1861, disd. Oct. 9, 1861.

RECRUITS.

Anderson J. e. Jan. 2, 1862, m. o. July 14, 1862.
Angel H. W. e. Jan. 27, 1862, m. o. July 14, 1862.
Arnold J. W. e. March 1, 1862, m. o. July 14, 1862.
Baumgardner J. e. Feb. 24, 1862, m. o. July 14, 1862.
Boston N. M. e. Feb. 27, 1862, m. o. July 14, 1862.
Boston P. e. Feb. 26, 1862, m. o. July 14, 1862.
Brogdon T. e. Jan. 27, 1862, m. o. July 14, 1862.
Barnes P. e. Feb. 5, 1862, m. o. July 14, 1862.
Barnes R. B. e. Feb. 28, 1862, m. o. July 14, 1862.
Clayton S. T. e. Feb. 27, 1862, m. o. July 14, 1862.
Chapman W. e. Jan. 30, 1862, m. o. July 14, 1862.
Cannon J. O. e. Feb. 26, 1862, m. o. July 14, 1862.
Cannon C. W. e. Feb 26, 1862, m. o. July 14, 1862.
Cattrell A. A. e. April 24, 1861, disd. Oct. 9, 1861.
Davidson J. e. Feb. 23, 1862, m. o. July 14, 1862.
Doll S. H. e. April 1, 1862, m. o. July 14, 1862.
Dicus W. H. e. Feb. 24, 1862, m. o. July 14, 1862.
Dicus J. e. March 24, 1862, m. o. July 14, 1862.
Everns H. e. Feb. 27, 1862, m. o. July 14, 1862.
Frazell M. e. March 1, 1862, m. o. July 14, 1862.
Finnry L. e. Feb. 23, 1862, m. o. July 14, 1862.
Glenphere A. e. Feb. 7, 1862 m. o. July 14, 1862.
Haller M. e. Feb. 14, 1862, m. o. July 14, 1862.
Hammond R. F. e. March 1, 1862, m. o. July 14, 1862.
Hindsman C. e. Feb. 24, 1862, m. o. July 14, 1862.
Hindsman W. e. Feb. 24, 1862, m. o. July 14, 1862.
Hutchison W. April 24, 1861, m. o. July 14, 1862.
Hodges R. A. e. Jan. 1, 1862, m. o. July 14, 1862.
Houghy R. e. Feb. 27, 1861, m. o. July 14, 1862.
Haley C. e. Feb. 21, 1862, m. o. July 14, 1862.
Hughes C. e. Jan. 13, 1862, m. o. July 14, 1862.
Hampton T. P. e. March 27, 1862, m. o. July 14, 1862.
Jenks J. K. e. March 1, 1862, m. o. July 14, 1862.

Knight D. C. e. March 21, 1862, m. o. July 14, 1862.
Lockard Jns. e. Feb. 27, 1862, m. o. July 14, 1862.
Lumoy J. L. e. Feb. 1, 1862, m. o. July 14, 1862.
Leslie B. e. Jan. 27, 1862, m. o. July 14, 1862.
Lottus J. e. Jan. 27, 1862, m. o. July 14, 1862.
Libby I. e. Feb. 1, 1862, m. o. July 14, 1862.
Moore W. e. March 27, 1862, m. o. July 14, 1862.
Martin D. P. e. Feb. 27, 1862, m. o. July 14, 1862.
Mead W. e. Jan. 18, 1862, m. o. July 14, 1862.
Morgan R. e. Jan 24, 1862, m. o. July 14, 1862.
McGregor J. e. Feb. 6, 1862, m. o. July 14, 1862.
Mumford C. C. e. Feb. 27, 1862, m. o. July 14, 1862.
McIntyre A. e. Jan. 24, 1862, m. o. July 14, 1862.
McGuire P. e. March 1, 1862, m. o. July 14, 1862.
McGehe W. e. March 1, 1862, m. o. July 14, 1862.
Morris S. J. e. April 24, 1861, disd. Oct. 9, 1861.
Odear J. e. Feb. 12, 1862, m. o. July 14, 1862, as Corpl.
Ostrander R. Feb. 13, 1862, m. o. July 14, 1862.
Palmer C. M. e. Dec. 1, 1861, m. o. July 14, 1862.
Paully R. e. Jan. 27, 1862, m. o. July 14, 1862.
Puler R. e. Feb. 7, 1862, m. o. July 14, 1862.
Palmer C. P. e. Feb. 27, 1862, m. o. July 14, 1862.
Pierce H. e. Feb. 28, 1862, m. o. July 14, 1862.
Quaite J. M. e. April 24, 1861, m. o. July 14, 1862.
Quimby C. e. April 24, 1861, m. o. July 14, 1862.
Remis T. e. Feb. 14, 1862, m. o. July 14, 1862.
Reynolds W. H. e. March 1, 1862, m. o. July 14, 1862.
Rusk M. D. e. April 1, 1862, m. o. July 14, 1862.
Smith D. e. Feb. 1, 1862, m. o. July 14, 1862.
Schrum S. e. Jan. 25, 1862, m. o. July 14, 1862.
Snyder J. W. e. Feb. 1, 1862, m. o. July 14, 1862.
Toole P. e. March 1, 1862, m. o. July 14, 1862, as Sergt.
Tenbrooke T. C. e. Jan. 23, 1862, m. o. July 14, 1862.
Turner H. e. March 27, 1862, m. o. July 14, 1862.
Thomas A. e. March 27, 1862, m. o. July 14, 1862.
Warnom C. T. e. Jan. 1, '62, m. o. July 14, '62, Corpl.
Watt H. e. Feb. 17, 1862, m. o. July 14, 1862.
Westfall B. e. Jan. 20, 1862, m. o. July 14, 1862.
Williams W. C. e. March 30, 1862, m. o. July 14, 1862.
White J. K. P. e. April 9, 1862, m. o. July 14, 1862.
Younger T. e. Jan. 27, 1862, m. o. July 14, 1862.

ELEVENTH CAVALRY.

Adjutant Eli Mundorff, rank July 18, 1865, mustered July 27, 1865. Mustered out Sept. 30, 1865.

Company A.

McKelney M. e. Feb. 27, 1865, m. o. Sept. 30, 1865, as Sergt.
Wilson H. e. Mch. 31, 1865, trans. Co. E 5th Ill. Cav.

Company E.

Barge W. e. April 8, 1865, trans. Co. G Ill. Cav.
Beldin J. A. e. April 12, 1865, trans. Co. K. 5th Ill. Cav.
Humas A. e. June 1, 1862, disd. April 11, 1864.
Crumpton W. D. e. April 12, 1865, trans. Co. E 5th Ill. Cav.
Shelton J. P. e. Mch. 31, 1865, trans. C o. G 5th Ill. Cav

Company F.

Bradley J. e. April 11, 1865, trans. Co. G 5th Ill. Cav
Bon W. H. e. April 8, 1865, trans. Co. G 5th Ill. Cav.
Claycomb M. e. April 8, 1865, trans. Co. G 5th Ill. Cav

Company H.

Second Lieutenant, Tennis Vreeland, rank Mch. 28, 1865 mustered April 11, 1865. Mustered out Sept. 30, 1865.
Corporal Tennis Vreeland, e. Nov. 27, 1861. Promoted Sergeant, then Lieut.

PRIVATES.

Cooper S. O. e. Nov. 27, 1861, disd. Dec. 22, 1864.
Montgomery F. W. e. Nov. 27, 1861, m. o. Sept. 30, '65.
Montgomery P. J. e. Nov. 27, 1861, m. o. Sept. 30, 1865.

VETERANS.

Glover J. S. e. Dec. 30, 1863, m. o. Sept. 30, 1865.
Rose W. e. Mch. 9, 1864, m. o. Sept. 30, 1865.
Vreeland M. e. Feb. 5, 1864, m. o. Sept. 30, 1865.

RECRUITS.

Ackerman J. A. e. Feb. 22, 1865, m. o. Sept. 30, 1865.
Bell J. A. e. Dec. 12, 1863, m. o. Sept. 30, 1865.
Cooper H. C. e. Feb. 21, 1864, m. o. Sept. 30, 1865.
Edwards A. e. Dec. 12, 1863, m. o. Sept. 30, 1865.
Edwards A, H. e. Feb. 17, 1864, m. o. Sept. 30, 1865.
Galloup D. e. April 11, 1865, trans. Co. G 5th Ill. Cav.
Glover J. S. e. Dec. 28, 1862, re-enlisted as veteran.
Ingram A. e. Feb. 21, 1864, m. o. Sept. 30, 1865.
Mundorf Z. P. e. Feb. 21, 1864, m. o. Sept. 30, 1865.
Marshall D. e. Mch. 31, 1864, trans. Co. E 5th Ill. Cav.
McCraw W. C. e. Dec. 14, 1863, died July 8, 1865.
Polk C. H. e. Mch. 31, 1865, trans. Co. K 5th Ill. Cav.
Rankin S. P. e. Mch. 9, 1863, m. o. Sept. 30, 1865.
Riggle C. e. Mch. 31, 1865, trans. Co. E 5th Ill. Cav.
Staley Z. T. e. Feb. 21, 1864, m. o. Sept. 30, 1865.
Stockton S. J. e. Mch. 31, 1865, m. o. Sept. 30, 1865.
Vreeland M. e. Jan. 18, 1862, re-enlisted as veteran.
Wray F. M. e. April 23, 1864, m. o. Sept. 30, 1865.

Company I.

Captain Jno. J. Worden, rank Dec. 20, 1861, mustered Dec. 20, 1861. Resigned April 18, 1862.
Captain Jno. A. Davis, rank June 6, 1866, mustered July 2, 1865. Mustered out Sept. 30, 1865.
First Lieutenant David S. Scott, rank Sept. 23, 1862, mustered Sept. 23, 1862. Resigned Sept. 20, 1863.
First Lieutenant Jno. A. Davis, rank Sept. 29, 1863, mustered Sept. 3, 1864. Promoted.
Second Lieutenant David S. Scott, rank Apr. 18, 1862, Promoted.
First Sergeant J. H. Rowland, e. Oct. 15, 1861, m. o. Sept. 30, 1865.
Q. M. Sergeant D. S. Scott, e. Oct. 9, 1861. Promoted Second Lieutenant.
Sergeant J. K. Spradling, e. Oct. 17, 1861. Sick at muster out.

Sergeant J. A. Davis, e. Oc. 7, 1861. Prmt. Sergt., then First Lieutenant.
Corporal J. Titus, e. Oct. 17, 1861, disd. Oct. 24, 1862.
Corporal H. C. Howell, e. Nov. 10, 1861, kld. March 13, 1863.
Corporal H. C. Fuller, e. Oct. 17, 1861, prmt. Sergt., then Second Lieutenant.
Corporal L. Perry, e. Oct. 17, 1861, kld. Jan. 14, 1863.
Corporal W.C. Griffin, e. Nov. 10,'61, m.o. Sept. 30,'65.

PRIVATES.

Anson S. e. Nov. 7, 1861.
Eblesisor G. F. e. Oct. 15, 1861, deserted June 1, 1862.
Edie H. e. Nov, 7, 1861, disd. Aug. 21, 1862.
Fuller J. e. Nov. 10, 1861, m. o. Sept. 30, 1865.
Griffon J. D. e. Nov. 10, 1861, died Jun: 26, 1862.
Griffin W. C. e. Dec. 30, 1863, m. o. Sept. 30, 1865.
Henry R. D. e. Nov. 12, 1861, disd. Jan. 26, 1862.
Jewett J. W. e. Oct. 17, 1861, died July 28, 1 62.
Kinney, E. S. e. Nov. 17, 1861, m. o. Sept. 30, 1865.
Landin I. e. Nov. 17, 1861, absent in hospital.
Means J. H. e. Oct. 7, 1861.
Patterson T. J. e. Oct. 15, 1861, disd. Jan, 3, 1863.
Nevens L. e. Oct, 15, 1861, m. o. Sept. 30, 1865.
Simmons L. W. e. Oct. 15, 1861, disd. Aug. 21, 1862.
Simmons A. J. e. Nov. 7, 1861.
Simelroth P. e. Nov. 10, 1861, disd. Jan. 26, 1862.
Simelroth W. B. e. Nov. 10, 1861, m. o. Sept. 30, 1865.
Sheppard J. e. Nov. 10. 1861, m. o. Sept. 30, 1865.
White J. R. e. Oct. 7, 1861, deserted Dec. 24, 1862.
Wides N. e. Nov. 7, 1861, m. o. Sept. 30, 1865.
White A. P. e. Nov. 10.

RECRUITS.

Anson J. e. Mch. 11, 1865, m. o. Sept. 30, 1865.
Bond N. W. e. Mch. 11, 1865, m. o. Sept. 30, 1865.
Blue A. J. e. Oct. 12, 1861, disd. Aug. 21, 1862.
Blue H. e. Oct, 12, 1861, deserted Jan. 1, 1862.
Courson S. e. Mch. 31, 1864, m. o. Sept. 30, 1865.
Cable C. H. e. March 26, 1864, m. o. Sept. 30, 1865.
Crabb T. W. e. Mch. 11, 1865, m. o. Sept. 30, 1865.
Gilham G. e. Mch. 22, 1865, m. o. Sept. 30, 1865.
Kelsey S. e. Mch. 11, 1865, m. o. Sept. 30, 1865.
Mareil J. E. e. Mch. 11, 1865, m. o. Sept. 30, 1865.
Ratekin J. R. e. Feb. 22, 1865, m. o. Sept. 30, 1865.
Slocum W. e. Feb. 22, 1865, m. o. Sept. 30, 1865.
Semmelroth P. e. March 11, 1865, m. o. Sept. 30, 1865.
Whitcomb W. R. e. Aug. 25, 1864, m. o. Sept. 30, 1865.
Wade W. J. e. Mch. 4, 1865, m. o. Sept. 30, 1865.
Worden F. M. e. Nov. 7, 1861, deserted Dec. 1, 1861.
Wilson S. T. e. April 28, 1864, m. o. Sept. 30, 1865.

Company K.

Captain John McFarland, rank Dec. 19, 1864. Mustered out Sept. 30, 1865.
First Lieutenant Richard A. Howk, rank Dec. 20, 1861, mustered Dec. 20, 1861. Resigned July 8, 1862.
First Lieutenant Jno. McFarland, rank July 9, 1862, mustered Dec. 25, 1862. Promoted.
First Lieutenant Thomas Paul, rank March 28, 1865, mustered April 11, '65. Mustered out Sept. 30, '65.
Second Lieutenant Jno. McFarland, rank Dec. 20, 1861, mustered Dec. 20, 1861. Promoted.
Second Lieutenant Gustavus A. Cole, rank July 31, '62, mustered Feb. 6, 1663. Promoted Capt. Co. L.
First Sergeant Frank Rose, e. Nov. 1, 1861. Disd. July 1, 1862, disab.
Com. Sergeant A. J. Ebey, e. Nov. 6, 1861. Transferred to 1st. Illinois Cavalry.
Sergeant D. Leighty, e. Nov. 6, 1861. Died Jan. 5, '64.
Sergeant C. Countryman, e. Nov. 6, 1861. Transferred to 1st. Illinois Cavalry.
Sergeant W. S. Bales, e. Nov. 6, 1861.
Sergeant R. P. Prescott, e. Nov. 6, 1861. Killed June 18, 1862.
Corporal A. J. Taylor, died Dec. 1, 1864.
Corporal T. Paul, e. Nov. 1, 1861. Promoted Sergeant, then First Lieutenant.
Corporal Wm. Baker, e. Nov. 1, 1861. Mustered out Sept. 30, 1865.
Corporal P. F. Smith, e. Nov. 1, 1861.
Corporal E. A. Hayford, e. Nov. 6, 1861. Discharged Nov. 19, 1862, disab.
Bugler A. C. Bemus, e. Nov. 1, 1861. Transferred to Co. E, Jan. 10, 1862.
Bugler J. Sullivan, e. Nov. 1, 1861. Discharged Oct. 19, 1862, disab.
Saddler F. Wortendike, e. Nov. 6, 1861. Mustered out Sept. 30, 1865.

Farrier H. C. Hammond, e. Nov. 1, 1861. Discharged, drummed out Jan. 1862.
Blacksmith W. Murphy, e. Nov, 6, 1861.
Wagoner J. Keller, e. Nov. 1, 1861. Discharged Nov. 14, 1862, disab.

PRIVATES.

Armstrong W. e. Nov. 6, 1861, deserted Aug. 23, 1863.
Alley A. e. Nov. 25, 1861, deserted Oct. 7, 1862.
Allred L. O. e. Nov. 1, 1861, m. o. Sept. 30, 1865.
Allred A. J. e. Nov. 1, 1861, disd. May 25, 1862, disab.
Baker W. e. Dec. 30, 1863, m. o. Sept. 30, 1865.
Cecil E. e. Nov. 1, 1861, m. Sept. 30, 1865.
Clifford J. W. e. Nov. 20, 1861, m. o. Sept. 30, 1865.
Countryman F. e. Nov. 1, 1851, m. o. Sept. 30, 1865.
Davis J. e. Nov. 1, 1861, m. o. Sept. 30, 1865.
Dixon J. T. e. Nov. 6, disd. Feb. 12, 1862.
Elmore G. W. e. Nov. 1, 1861, died Aug. 8, 1862.
Erp L. D. e. Nov. 1, 1861, disd. Dec. 19, 1864.
Gossett C. T. e. Nov. 1, 1861, disd. June 13, '62, disab.
George E. e. Nov. 1, 1861, disd. Sept. 3, 18'2, disab.
Kennedy M.G. e. Nov. 1, '61, m. o. Sept.30, 65,as Sergt.
Kill A. e. Nov. 1, 1861, deserted Dec. 1, 1872.
Libby J. e. Nov. 6, 1861, disd. Dec. 19, 1864.
Leighly J. W. e. Nov. 6, 1861, disd. July 3, 1862.
McCollum J. A. e. Nov. 6, 1861, m. o. Sept. 30, '65, as Corporal.
Nelson H. B. e. Nov. 6, 1861, m. o. Sept. 30, 1865.
Romans P. F. e. Nov. 1, 1861, m. o. Sept. 30, 1865.
Romans J. L. e. Nov. 1, 1861, trans. 1st Ill Cav.
Randal C. L. e. Nov. 1, 1861, killed July 20, 1865.
Stowler S.
Suggs J. D. e. Nov. 26, '61, m.o. Sept. 30, '65, as Sergt.
Suggs Jno. e. Nov. 6, 1861, returnd to 17th Ill. Inf. as deserter from that Regt., Jan. 1, 1862.
Smith C. K. e. Nov. 1, 1861, disd. Dec. 19, 1864.
Wilson W. T. e. Nov. 6, 1861, disd. June 13, 1862.

RECRUITS.

Anderson G. P. e. Dec. 28, 1861, re-enlisted as veteran.
Bell John, e. March 31, 1864, m. o. Sept. 30, 1865.
Burch F. J. e. March 9, 1865, m. o. Sept. 29, 1865.
Boston N. M. e. Aug. 17, 1862, m. o. July 28, 1865.
Harrett J. W. e. Aug. 19, 1862, deserted Feb. 1, 1863.
Coon D. e. Feb. 21, 1864, m. o. Sept. 30, 1865.
Cunningham J. H. e. Feb. 7, 1864, m. o. Sept. 20, 1865.
Clark J. K. F. e. Feb. 27, 1865, m. o. Sept. 29, 1865.
Call H. D. e. Feb. 27, 1865, m. o. Sept. 30, 1865.
Collins S. e. Feb. 27, 1865, m. o. Sept. 30, 1865.
Cole G. O. e. Dec. 31, '61, prmt. Sergt. then 2d Lieut.
Carter H. e. Dec. 30, 1861, re-enlisted as Veteran.
Davies W. L. e. March 9, 1865, m. o. Sept. 29, 1865.
Dennis J. M. e. Jan. 28, 1864, m. o. Sept. 30, 1865.
Delong S. e. Aug. 26, 1862, m. o. June 9, 1865.
Duncan J. M. e. Dec. 30, 1861, re-enlisted as Veteran.
Duncan W. e. Dec. 3, 1863, died Aug. 27, 1864.
Haley H. F. e. Feb. 27, 1865, m. o. Sept. 30, 1865.
House A. e. April 12, 1865, trans. Co. E, 5th Ill. Cav.
Johnson J. K. e. Feb. 27, 1865, m. o. Sept. 26, 1865.
Jones E. T. e. Nov. 1, 1861, re-enlisted as Veteran.
Johnson W. N. Dec. 30, 1861, re enlisted as Veteran.
Johnson G. e. Jan. 16, 1862, re-enlisted as Veteran.
Little R. J. e. Dec. 12, 1863, m. o. Sept. 30, 1865.
Liby Isaac, e. Feb. 25, 1864, m. o. Sept. 30, 1865.
Long P. e. April 11, 1865, trans. 5th Ill. Cav.
McKelvy D. e. Jan., ——, m. o. Sept. 30, 1865.
Mackey W. F. e. March 30, 1865, m. o. Sept. 30, 1865.
Meadows W. H. e. Feb. 27, 1865, m. o. Oct. 2, 1865.
Meller W. H. e. Apr. 13, '65, trans.Co. K,5th Ill. Cav.
Montgomery J. A. e. Feb. 17, 1864.
Oiler L. e. April 8, 1865, trans. to 5th Ill. Cav.
Porter G. R. e. March 9, 1865, m. o. Sept. 30, 1865.
Prevost H. C. e. Dec. 13, 1863, m. o. Sept. 30, 1865.
Schrum S. e. March 3, 1865, m. o. Sept. 30, 1865.
Stence Benj. e. Feb. 25, 1864, m. o. Sept. 30, 1865.
Staller W. e. March 9, 1865, m. o. Sept. 30, 1865.
Sheppard H. C. e. Nov. 15, 1861, died Dec. 1, 1861.
Thompson J. P. e. Feb. 27, 1865, m. o. Sept. 29, 1865.
Ulmer J. E. e. March 10, 1865, m. o. Sept. 30, 1865.
Vantine C. e. March 9, 1865, m. o. Sept. 30, 1865.
Whisler D. e. Feb. 25, 1864, m. o. Sept. 30, 1865.
Whisler W. e. Dec. 1, 1861, re-enlisted as Veteran.

Company L.

Captain Gustavus A. Cole, rank March 28, 1865. Mustered April 12, 1865. Mustered out Sept. 30, 1865

Unassigned Recruit.

Wood R. G. e, March 29, 1864.

TWELFTH CAVALRY,

Company L.

Captain Richard A. Howk, rank Jan. 12, 1864. Mustered Jan. 12, 1864. See Co. G, consolidated.
First Lieutenant Carlton F. Cossett, rank Jan. 12,1864. Mustered Jan. 12, 1864. See Co. G consolidated.
Second Lieutenant Jas. P. Dickson, rank Jan. 12, 1864. Mustered Jan 12, 1864. Died of disease, at Naperville, Ill., July 19, 1864.

PRIVATES.

Anderson G. W. e. Nov. 20,'63, trans. Co. G as cons'd.
Bunker L. e. Nov. 20, 1863, trans. Co. G. as cons'd.
Bissell G. e. Nov. 20, 1863, trans. Co. G as cons'd.
Bute Jno. e. Nov. 20, 1863, trans. Co. G as cons'd
Barnes J. W. e. Nov. 13, 1863, trans. Co.G as cons'd.
Burnes Jas. e. Dec. 19, 1863, trans. Co. G as cons'd.
Crosby Jno. e. Dec. 20, 1863, died Sept. 12, 1864.
Clark A. W. e. Dec. 20, 1863, trans. Co. G as cons'd.
Cavis J. H. e. Nov. 13, 1863, trans Co. G as cons'd.
Culbertson J. H. e. Dec. 17, '63, trans.Co. G as cons'd.
Dillon W. H. e. Nov. 30, 1863, trans. Co. G. as cuns'd.
Davis J. e. Nov. 30, 1863, trans. Co. G as cons'd.
Diehl G. W. e. Nov. 30, 1863, trans. Co. G as cons'd.
Dickson J. P. e. Dec. 3, 1863, prmt. 2d Lieut.
Ddrenzy Jno. e. Dec. 19, 1863, trans. Co. G as cons'd.
Elliott G. e. Dec. 7, 1863, died Sept. 26, 1864.
Frazell S. e. Nov. 6, 1863, trans. Co. G as cons'd.
Frazell W. e. Nov. 6, 1863, trans. Co. G as cons'd.
Frazell M. M. e. Dec. 26, 1863, trans. Co. G as cons'd.
Fulton J. e. Nov. 13, 1863, trans. Co. G as cons'd.
Forbes W. T. e. Dec. 17, 1863, trans. Co. G as cons'd.
Griffin J. e. Dec. 3, 1863, trans. Co. G as cons'd.
Gardner W. H. e. Nov. 13, 1863, trans.Co. G as cons'd.
Goodenough E. e. Dec. 28, 1863, trans. Co. G cons'd.
Henderson T. L. e. Nov. 13, 1863,trans. Co.G as cons'd.
Hall J. B. e. Nov. 23, 1863, trans. Co. G as cons'd.
Hargraves J. S. e. Dec. 26, 1863, trans. Co. G as cons'd.
Henry E. R. e. Dec. 28, 1863, trans. Co. G as cons'd.
Hoerner M. e. Nov. 13, 1863, trans. Co. G as cons'd.
Hoerner D. G. e. Nov. 13, 1863, trans. Co. G as cons'd.
Haggerty W. e. Dec. 18, 1863, disd. June 18, '64, disab.
Leighty J. e. Nov. 20, 1863, trans. Co. G as cons'd.
Larebee T. E. e. Nov. 13, 1863, trans. Co. G as cons'd.
Luster C. e. Dec. 19, 1863, trans. Co. G as cons'd.
Myers G. A. e. Nov. 23, 1863, trans. Co. G as cons'd.
Marks S. S. e. Dec. 1, 1863, died Feb. 1, 1864.
Perry M. F. e. Nov. 1, 1863, died Aug. 14, 1864.
Reynolds E. M. e. Nov. 6, 1863, trans. Co. G as cons'd.
Stewart C. e. Nov. 20, 1863, trans. Co. G. as cons'd.
Steele C. e. Dec. 3, 1863, trans. Co. G as cons'd.
Ritchie S. P. e. Nov. 6, 1863, trans. Co. G as cons'd.
Stevens G. W. e. Nov. 6, 1863.
Strickland S. e. Nov. 6, 1863, died Aug. 26, 1864.
Strickler S. A. e. Nov. 6, 1863, trans. Co. G as cons'd.
Steward J. C. e. Nov. 20, 1863, trans. Co. G as cons'd.
Scott D. W. e. Dec. 10, 1863, trans. Co. G as cons'd.
Sheppardson A. e. Nov. 20, '63, trans. Co. G as cons'd.
Thomas G. W. e. Nov. 20, 1863, trans. Co. G as cons'd.
Terpering G. A. e. Dec. 17, '63, trans. Co. G as cons'd.
Terpering C. W. e. Dec. 17,'63, trans. Co. G as cons'd.
Van Nortwick G. e. Nov 20, '63, trans. Co. G as cons'd.
William W. S. e. Nov. 23, 1863, trans. Co. G as cons'd.
Winbigler G. e. Nov. 6, 1863, trans Co. G as cons'd.
Wornom C. T. e. Nov. 20, 1863, trans. Co. G as cons'd.
Waldrom J. M. e. Dec. 17, 1863, trans. Co. G. as cons'd.
Walsh J. B. e. Dec. 29, 1863, trans. Co. G. as cons'd.
Wilcox C, S, e. Dec. 28, 1863, trans. Co. G. as cons'd.

RECRUITS.

Clark C. e. Dec. 30, 1863, trans. Co. G, as cons'd.
Dennis F. e. Dec. 30, 1863, trans. Co. G, as cons'd.
Loftus J. H. e. Dec. 30, 1863, trans. Co. G as cons'd.

Company G (consolidated).

Captain Richard A. Howk, rank Jan. 12, 1864, mustered Jan. 12 1864. Mustered out.
First Lieutenant Carlton T. Gossett, rank Jan. 12, 1864, mustered Jan. 12, 1864. Mustered out.

Company K (consolidated).

First Lieutenant Benj. M. Gardner, rank March 28, 1865, mustered April '10, 65. Resigned June 23, '65.

NINTH CAVALRY,

Company L.

First Lieutenant Sam'l S. Summers, rank Oct. 10, 1865. Resigned (as Second Lieutenant) Aug. 29, '65.
Second Lieutenant Sam'l S. Summers, rank Mch. 28, 1865. Mustered April 27, 1865. Promoted.

PRIVATES.

Robb Crawford, e. Nov. 1, 1861.
Severance C. E. e. Oct, 1, 1861.
Summers Sam'l S. e. Nov. 1, 1861.
Clovis Wm. A. e. Nov. 20, 1861, m. o. Nov. 11, 1864.
Clayton Wm. H. e. March 31, 1864, m. o. May 17, '65.
Davidson Jno. C. e. Jan. 5, 1864, m. o. Oct. 31, 1865.
Finney Sam'l A. e. Oct. 3, 1862.
Foster E. R. e. Oct. 20, 1862.
Haley Clay. e. Nov. 3, 1862, m. o. Oct. 31, 1865.
Morey Moses D. e. Dec. 1, died at Helena, Ark., Sept. 23, 1862.
Miner Henry. e. Oct. 3, 1862, m. o. Oct. 31, 1865.
Mills Wm. e. Feb. 29, '64, m. o. Oct. 31, '65, as Sergt.
Parrish Little Berry, e. Dec. 18, '63, absent, sick at m. o. of Regt.
Suggs Jno. e. Oct. 8, 1862, m. o. Oct. 31, 1865.
Sutne Benj. e. Nov, 25, missing in action since Battle of Guntown, Miss., June 11, 1864.,

SEVENTH CAVALRY,

Company D.

Second Lieutenant Sam'l M. Reynolds, rank Oct. 15, 1864. Mustered Mch. 16, 1865, m. o. Nov. 5, 1865.
Sergeant David W. Bradshaw, e. Aug. 10, 1861. Promoted Second Lieutenant.
Corporal Samuel M. Reynolds, e. Aug. 10, 1861. Re-enlisted as Veteran.
Corporal A. H. L. Giffin, e. Aug. 10, 1861. Re-enlisted as Veteran.
Corporal Jas. P. Reed, e. Aug. 10, 1861. Re-enlisted as Veteran.

PRIVATES.

Boue Wallace G. e. Aug. 10, '61, disd. Mch. 3, '63,wds.
Dagget Nealy, e. Aug. 10, '61, disd. Apr. 25, '62,disab.
Meadow Jacob, e. Aug. 10, 1861, deserted Feb. 14, '62.
Reynold Leonard J.e.Aug. 10,'61,re-enlisted as vet'rn.
Ritchey Anthony,e. Aug. 10, '61, disd.Oct. 24.'62, disab.
Staley Abraham, e. Aug. 10, 1861, m. o. Oct. 15, 1864.
Day David K. e. Mch. 8, 1865, m. o. Nov. 4, 1865, as Corporal.
Jenkins Jno. e. March 1, 1865, m. o. Nov. 4, 1865.
Rose Silas M. e. March 24, 1865, m. o. Nov. 4, 1865.

Company G.

Cook Christopher, e. March 8, 1865, m. o. Nov. 4, '65.
Howard Chas. T. e. March 8, 1865, m. o. Nov. 4, 1865.

Company K.

Butler Erastus E. e. April 1, 1865, m. o. Nov. 4, 1865.
Peterson Andrew, e. April 1, 1865, m. o. Nov. 4, 1865.

Company L.

Hardenbrock Wm. G. e. Apr. 1, '65, m. o. Nov. 4, '65.
Jeffrey Wm. M. e. April 11, 1865, m. o. Sept. 23, 1865.

Unassigned Recruits.

Jeffrey David I. e. April 1, 1865, m. o. May 25, 1865.
Peterson Anderson, e. April 11, 1865.
White Asa I. e. Mch. 8, '65, died at Camp Butler, Ill. April 16, 1865.

MISCELLANEOUS CAVALRY.

Bowels Geo. e. Aug. 6, '61, disd. Aug. 14, '62, disab.
Bond L. M. e. Mch. 29, 1864. Deserted Sept. 12, 1865.
Brookner F. e. Mch. 29, 1864, m. o. Nov. 22, 1865.
Hoisington Geo. e. Aug. 6, 1861, disd. Aug. 11, 1864.
Hoisington Lee, e. Aug. 6, '61, disd. May 14, '62, disab.
Higgins Robt. e. Aug. 8, 1862, m. o. June 11, 1865.
Harris, F. J. e. Aug. 8, 1862, m. o. June 11, 1865.
Kidder Henry H. e. Aug. 6, 1861, disd. Aug. 11, 1864.
Crawford Jno. S. e. Aug. 8, 1862, re-enlisted as vet'rn.
Kidder Benj. H. e. Aug. 8, 1862, m. o. June 11, 1865, Co. Q. M. Sergt.
Loveridge A. G. e. Aug. 8, '62, re-enlisted as veteran.
Quaite Ephraim, e. Mch. 29, '64, disd. Oct.4,'64, disab.
Smock Sam'l H. e. Aug. 8, 1862, re-enlisted as vet'rn.
Stem Seth P. e. Aug. 8, 1862, m. o. June 11, 1865.
Stem F. T. P. e. Aug. 8, 1862, killed in action at Sabine Cross Roads, La., Apr. 8, 1864.
Wilson Geo. H. e. Aug. 8, 1862, m. o. June 11, 1865.
Anthony Chas. e. April 11, 1865. Deserted July 6, '65.
Brown Saml. e. Feb. 15, 1864, m. o. Oct. 27, 1864.
Cochrane S. e. April 11, 1865, m. o. Oct. 27, 1865.
Crumpton W. B. e. April 12. 1865, absent, sick, at m. o. of Regt.
House Adolphus, e. Apr. 12, 1865, deserted July 6, '65.
Marshall David, e. March 31, 1865, m. o. Oct. 27, '65.
Polk Chas. e. March 31, 1865, m. o. Oct. 27, 1865.
Pickering Wm. e. March 31, 1865, m. o. Sept. 30, 1865.
Riggle Clark, e. March 31, 1865, m. o. Oct. 27, 1865.
Wilson Benj. F, e. March 31, 1865, m. o. Oct. 27, 1865.
Burge Wm. e. April 8, 1865, m. o. Oct. 27. 1865.
Bradley Jonathan, e. April 11, 1865, m. o. Oct. 27, '65.
Byers Rudolph, e. April 13, 1865, m. o. Oct. 27, 1865.

Bon Wm. N. e. April 8, 1865, deserted July 3, 1865.
Bugler H. C. Beckwith, e. Dec. 21, 1861. Deserted.
Ball J. e. Dec. 2, 1861.
Brown H. S. e. Jan. 22, 1862.
Judson H. C. e. Dec. 21, 1861, Corporal, deserted.
Johnson P. e. Dec. 2, 1861, trans. to Co. A as consld.
Martin S. M. e. Jan. 29, 1862.
Allen J. L. trans. to Co. B as consolidated.
Badenbaugh H. e. Dec. 12, 1861, trans. to Co. B. consld.
Brown H. F. e. Nov. 15, 1861, disd. in 1862.
Beck R. A. e. Nov. 18, 1861, disd. Oct. 9, 1862.
Gibson A. O. e. Nov. 4, 1861, disd. in 1862.
Gibson T. A. e. Nov. 12, 1861. disd. in 1862.
Kavanaugh H. E. e. Oct. 4, 1861, disd, in 1862, disab.
Lowe A. e. Dec. 12, 1861.
Lane G. W. e. Dec. 3. 1861, disd. Oct. 6, 1862, disab.
Linn Jos. e. Nov. 1, 1861, trans. to Co. B as consld.
Linn M. e. Nov. 1, 1861.
Smith C. A. e. Nov. 20, 1861, trans. to Co. B as consld.
Shehi H. e. Nov. 12, 1861, disd. in 1862.
Snuggs J. e. Nov. 12, 1861.
Strickland A. e. Dec. 3, 1861, died in 1862.
Barnes G.
McIntyre S. trans. to Co. B as consolidated.
Newell C.
Allen J. L. e. Jan. 3, 1864, trans. to Co. M.
Linn Jos. e. Jan. 3, 1864, trans. to Co. M.
McIntyre S. e. Jan. 3, 1864, trans. to Co. M.
Smith C. A. e. Jan. 3, 1864, trans. to Co. M.
Second Lieutenant Wm. K. Trabue, rank Dec. 31, 1861. Mustered out Aug. 9, 1862.

ERRATA.

"Augus McCoy," Spring Grove tp., page 314, should be Angus McCoy.

"David Foust," in Business Directory, Alexis, page 318, should be in Gerlaw.

"Miss Agnes Strong," in History of Monmouth College, page 157, should be Miss Agnes Strang.

"TOO LATES."

TOMPKINS TOWNSHIP.

ABBEY HENRY M. Proprietor of Tremont House, Kirkwood; born in Yates Co., N. Y., March 12, 1834; came to this Co. in 1861; Rep; Presb; Hotel valued at $6,000; has owned and kept the "Tremont" last seven years; married Martha Clark, Nov. 1, 1868; four children.

REED GEO. W. Farmer; Kirkwood; born in this Co., July 30, 1846; Rep; Lib; owns house and lot, valued at $800; enlisted in Co. H, I. V. I., Feb. 14, 1865; served to close of war; disabled by exposure so that his health is very poor; married Miss Luella Perkins, of Warren Co., Dec. 4, 1871; one son, Albert Marsh, born Jan. 3, 1874.

Biographical Directory.

ABBREVIATIONS.

Adv	Adventist
Bapt	Baptist
Co	company or county
Cath	Catholic
Cong	Congregational
Ch	Church
dem	democrat
Epis	Episcopal
Evang	Evangelist
Ind	Independent
I. V. I	Illinois Volunteer Infantry
I. V. C	Illinois Volunteer Cavalry
I. V. A	Illinois Volunteer Artillery
lab	laborer
Luth	Lutheran
Meth	Methodist
mkr	maker
P. O.	Post Office
Presb	Presbyterian
prop	proprietor
rep	republican
Rev	Reverend
sec	section or secretary
Spir	Spiritualist
supt	superintendent
treas	treasurer
Univ	Universalist
Unit	Unitarian
U. P.	United Presbyterian
U. B.	United Brethren

MONMOUTH CITY.

ABBOTT MRS. AMY, widow.

Acheson Martha, widow; U. P.; from Ohio.

Adams G. W. farmer; dem; from England.

Adams M. W. carpenter; dem; from Va.

Ahlstrand Fred, employee in Weir Plow Works; from Sweden.

Ainsworth L. H. boarding house; ind; from Massachusetts.

Alger Mrs. M. widow; Chris; from Ohio.

Allen Robert, employee, Weir Plow Co.; rep; Meth.

Allen Charles, engineer; dem; from New York.

Allen Fred A. fence artist, bds. at Baldwin House; dem; from Massachusetts.

Allen George H. clerk; ind; born Illinois.

Allen J. H. farmer; rep; U. P.; from Ohio.

Allen Laura, Presb; from New York.

Allen N. prop. hotel Union; dem; from O.

Allen R. N. retired; rep; from New York.

Allen Wm. stone cutter; rep; Meth; born Illinois.

Anderson Charles, employed in Weir Plow Works; from Sweden.

Anderson N. shoemaker; dem; Luth; from Sweden.

Anderson Peter, lumberman; rep; Luth; from Sweden.

Armsby Geo. E. retired; dem; from Mass.

Appleby Geo. laborer; rep; U. P.; from Pennsylvania.

Apsey Geo. laborer; rep; Epis; from Eng.

Arendt Ambrose, blacksmith; rep; Meth; from Pennsylvania.

Arendt George, policeman; rep; Meth; from Pennsylvania.

Arendt John, laborer; rep; Luth; from Pa.

Arms J. D. grocer; rep; Presb; from Mass.

Armsby Fred E. farmer, bds. at Baldwin House; dem; owns 1,330 acres.

Arnold A. E. bookkeeper; bds. Baldwin House; rep; from Connecticut.

Atchinson N. trav. agt.; U. P.; from Ohio.

Atkins Seth, moulder; dem; from Conn.

BABCOCK E. C. retired; rep; Bapt; from Massachusetts.

BABCOCK DRAPER, Merchant; Monmouth; born in Wales, N. Y., Dec. 1, 1827; came to this Co. in 1842, and was engaged with his father in general merchandising in the same location he now occupies; has held office of Co. Treasurer three successive terms; was Deputy U. S. Collector from the passage of the law appointing Collector until the consolidation; was one of the organizers of the First National Bank, and has been a Director ever since; has also held office of Mayor, and a Trustee of Monmouth College; he married Mary E. Elliott in 1852; she was a daughter of Rev. Joseph Elliott, and was born in New York in 1830; has four children.

Baber Louis, laborer; rep; Meth; from Kentucky.

Bailey J. W. travelling agent Weir Plow Works; rep; from Maine.

Bain Samuel, retired; rep; U. P.; from North Carolina.

Baine George, employee Weir Plow Co.; rep; from Indiana.

Baine R. laborer; rep; Meth; from Va.

Bake W. C. clerk; dem; Presb; born Ill.

Baker Jno. R. blacksmith; rep; Meth; from Virginia.

Baldwin George W. of Baldwin House; rep; from Pennsylvania.

BALDWIN HIRAM, Proprietor of Baldwin House, Monmouth; born in Chester Co., Penn., Dec. 9, 1808; came to this Co. in 1840; Rep; hotel value, $20,000; the Baldwin House is one of the oldest hotels in the city; Mr. Baldwin married Miss Maria Mackey, March 29, 1831, who was born in Lancaster Co., Penn., Aug. 18, 1808; have two sons, James W. and George W., who are associated with their father in running the hotel, under the firm name of Baldwin & Sons.

Baldwin James W. of Baldwin House; rep; from Pennsylvania.

Baldwin John H. plasterer; rep; from Pa.]

Baldwin M. S. grocer; rep; Presb; from Pennsylvania.

Baldridge Samuel, farmer; rep; U. P.; from Ohio.

Barbour George R. bookkeeper Weir Plow Works; dem; from Connecticut.

Barnes Rev. J. G. pastor First U.P. Church; rep; from Pennsylvania.

BARNUM ORLANDO S. Merchant and Farmer; Monmouth; born in Oswego Co., N. Y., Feb. 7, 1830; Rep; Bapt; owns 260 acres; he came to this State and Co. in 1844; holds office of Supervisor; married Harriet E. Allen in 1856; she was born in New York.

Barrett George, laborer; dem; Luth; from Germany.

Barton J. B. carpenter; rep; U. P.; from New York.

Barton T. S. clerk agricultural implements; dem; Meth; from Pennsylvania.

Baskerville Emanuel, feather renovator; rep; from England.

Bates Henry H. grocer; rep; Meth; from O.

Bates J. A. grocer; rep; Meth; Maryland.

Bates L. A. clerk; rep; from Ohio.

Beaumont Sarah; Meth; from Pennsylvania.

Beaumont Walter, laborer; dem; Meth; born Illinois.

Bay Albert, city marshal; rep.

Bay Mrs. Maria, widow; Meth.

Boynton Ira, farmer; dem; born Illinois.

Boynton J. A. grocer; dem; from Maine.

Beachum Wm. brick layer; dem; Lib.

Beck Jno. boots and shoes; rep; Luth; from Denmark.

Becker A. N. merchant; ind; Bapt; from New York.

Beckwith B. retired; rep; Bapt; from Conn.

BECKWITH HENRY C. Secretary of the Monmouth Mining and Manufacturing Co.; born in Ashtabula Co., O., Nov. 29, 1844; came to this Co. in 1846; Rep; Bapt; owns 100 acres, Sec. 28; he served two years in the 13th I. V. C. in the late war; was one of the organizers of the Monmouth Mining and Manufacturing Co.; married Alice P. Bower, Aug. 25, 1869; she was born in Ohio; has two children.

Beedee E. C. clerk; Ind; from Maine.

Beistrup Geo. employe Weir Plow Works; Luth; from Denmark.

Bell Fred. carpenter; Ind; from England.

Bell Thos. carpenter; dem.

Benson Oliff, laborer; from Sweden.

Benson Thos. coal digger; from England.

Berry John, local editor *Review*; boards at Baldwin House; rep; from Pennsylvania.

Best Mrs. Lizzie; widow; from New York.

Bickmond Robt. dyer; dem; from Scotland.

Billings Mrs. Sarah, widow.

Bivens Isabella; U. P.; from Tennessee.

Black Jno. retired; rep; U. P.; from Ireland.

BLACKBURN CHAS. E. Dealer in Harness and Saddlery Hardware; Monmouth; born in Indiana, Sept. 19, 1847; Rep; Pres; he came to this Co. in 1853; enlisted in the 151st I. V. I., and served till close of the war; married Miss Olive Jewell, Nov. 2, 1871; she was born in Warren Co., April 29, 1849.

Blackburn Mrs. K. G., widow; Meth; from Ohio.

Blanchard Ed. collar manufacturer, wholesale and retail; from Kentucky.

Blair Simon, laborer; rep; from Tennessee.

Blosser John, employee C. L. Buck.

Boggess Mrs. Jas. B.; Meth.

Boluck Joseph, employee in mills; dem; from Canada.

BOND WM. G. Sheriff; Monmouth; came to this Co. in 1834; has held office of Collector and Supervisor previous to his election as Sheriff; was mustered in the service of the late war as Captain; was promoted to Major; served three years; first wife was Elizabeth Donner; had four children; second wife was Irene J. Pennington; third wife was Mary E. Moore.

Boss Arthur, painter; rep.

Bosserman A. B. merchant; boards at Baldwin House; dem; from Pennsylvania.

Boozan Rich. laborer; dem; Cath; from Ireland.

Bower James, stock dealer; rep; from Ohio.

Bower Z. B. book keeper; rep; from Ohio.
Bowman C. E. billiards; rep; from Penn.
Boyce Mrs. Eli; Meth; from Ohio.
Boyce Wm. W. painter; dem; Ohio.
Boyd J. N. student; rep; Presb; from Penn.
Boyd R. H. farmer; rep; Presb; from Penn.
Boyd W. B. Weir Plow Works; rep; Presb; from New York.
Bradshaw J. H. harness maker; dem; from New York.
Brady Rev. E. A. local minister Methodist church; rep; from Pennsylvania.
Branch Martin, laborer; rep; Meth; from Alabama.
Bramhall Frank, wagon maker; dem; from New York.

BREED G. H., M. D. Homeopathic Physician; Monmouth; born in Buffalo, N. Y., March 10, 1851; came to this Co. in 1868; has been engaged in the practice of his profession since 1873; married Miss Frances L. Cornell in 1875; she was born in Warren Co.

Brewer J. T. merchant; rep; Univ; from Virginia.
Brewer, J. W. physician; dem; from Penn.
Brewer Jno. E. druggist; from Penn.
Brewer Wm. T. clerk; rep; U. P.; from New York.

BRISTOL C. B. Local Shipping-Clerk of Weir Plow Works; born in Va., Feb. 18, 1840; came to this Co. in 1868; Rep; Presb; owns house and lot, value $2,000; enlisted in Co. B, 65th Regt. I. (veteran) V. I., 1862; remained in the service until Aug. 3, 1865; mustered out with rank of Sergt.-Maj.; married S. J. McFarland, of Indiana Co., Penn., May, 1867.

Broderick Wm. laborer; dem; Cath; from Ireland.
Brooks Eliza, U. P.; from Ohio.
Brooks W. W. coal-digger; rep; Presb; born Illinois.
Brown Chas. brick-layer and plasterer; Ind; from New York.
Brown Chas. mason; rep; from New York.
Brown John, banker; from Penn.
Brown Joseph, farmer, works for C. Hardin.
Brown Mrs. Mary H. widow; M. E.; from Pennsylvania.
Brown Thomas, laborer; rep; U. P.; from Virginia.
Brown W. W. restaurant; dem; from New York.
Brownlee Emily, U. P.; from Ohio.

BROWNLEE MRS. JOANNA, born in Washington Co., Pa., July 11, 1826; came to this Co. in 1850; U. P.; Mrs. Brownlee is widow of French Brownlee, who came to this State in 1833; he enlisted in the 36th I. V. I.; left home Sept. 3, 1861, and was sworn into service at Aurora, Sept. 12; died in hospital at Chattanooga, Dec. 25, 1863, after a lingering illness; Surgeon Lytle said of him after his decease: "He was one of the faithful, not only to his country, but to his God;" he was buried at Little York; was born in Washington Co., Penn., Aug. 28, 1823; held the offices of Supervisor and Justice of the Peace for several years; four daughters, Teresa K., Sylvia L., Irena F. and Epha M.

Bruner Rev. F. M. pastor Christian Church.
Bruen John, farmer; dem; from New Jersey.
Bruen Miss Mary L., Presb; from New Jersey.
Buck C. L. stock dealer; rep; from Vt.
Buckholz Chas. harness-maker; rep; born Illinois.
Buffington Thos. farmer; rep; Quaker; from Pennsylvania.
Buffington Wm. M. Asst.-Postmaster; rep; from Pennsylvania.
Bullis W. laborer; dem.
Bunker Albert, laborer; rep; from New York.
Bunker Geo. laborer; rep; from Ohio.
Bunker Mrs. J. M. dress-making; from Ohio.
Bunker Zack, laborer; rep; born Illinois.
Burlingim H. merchant; rep; from New York.
Burnett Wm. H. farmer; dem.
Burns Peter, engineer; dem; from Canada.
Burrell Daniel, carpenter; rep; U. P.; from Pennsylvania.
Burrell J. G. carpenter; rep; U. P.; from Pennsylvania.
Burrell Samuel, gardener; rep; U. P.; from Pennsylvania.
Burrell Wm. gardener; rep; U. P.; from Pennsylvania.
Burnside Robt. retired farmer.
Butler J. H. cooper; dem; born Illinois.
Buzan Jacob L. farmer; dem; from Ky.
Byers Jacob, farmer; rep; Meth; from Penn.
Byers Solomon, farmer; rep; from Penn.

CABLE CHANCEY M. farmer; rep; Bapt, from New York.
Cable Henry, farmer; Meth; from New York.
Call Harry, mail-carrier; rep; from Ohio.
Callow John, superintendent Harding estate; rep; from Isle of Man.
Campbell A. T. postal-clerk; rep; from Pennsylvania.
Campbell Jno. M. grain dealer; rep; from Pennsylvania.
Campbell Jno. M. clerk; rep; from Ohio.
Campbell M. D. grain dealer; rep; U. P.; from Pennsylvania.

Campbell Thos. retired; rep; U. P.; from Ohio.
Campbell Wm. gardener; dem; from Penn.
Campbell Rev. W. T. pastor Second U. P Church; rep; from Ohio.

CANNON A. R. Mechanic; born in Warren Co., Ill., March 8, 1835; Rep; owns house and lot, valued at $1,000; Mr. Cannon has been a resident of this Co. since his birth; married Catherine S. Johnson, of Seneca Co., N. Y., Dec., 1862; six children, Eva I., Nina L., Emma E., Nellie B., Archie M. and Willie (deceased).

Cannon James, cook; rep; from Georgia.
Cannon John, mason; dem; from Kentucky.
Cannon Louis, mason; dem; from Missouri.
Cannon Stephen, laborer; Cath; Ireland.
Cannon Wm. laborer; born Illinois.
Card Henry M. laborer; rep; Bapt; from Virginia.
Carland James, laborer; rep; from Ohio.
Carling Samuel, laborer; dem; from New Jersey.
Carr Judson, carriage maker; dem; born Illinois.
Carr Jno. carriage dealer; dem; Bapt; from New York.
Carr Jno. carriage maker; dem; Bapt; from New York.
Carr Nathan, retired; dem; from New York.
Carrell John, employee Weir plow works; rep; Bapt; from Indiana.
Carringer A. S. blacksmith; rep; from Penn.
Carrigan M. J. painter; rep; from Mass.
Cassel Mons. farmer; rep; Luth; from Sweden.
Catlin R. B. barber; rep; from Penn.
Catlin S. carpenter; rep; Meth; from N. Y
Cecil N. hotel; dem; from Maryland.
Chaffee J. A. hardware; dem; from Vt.
Chapin Frank, painter; rep; from Ohio.
Chapin Geo. carpenter; rep; from Ohio.
Chapin Warren, carpenter; rep; Prot.
Chapin Will W. carpenter; from New York.
Chapman Thompson, laborer; dem; from Kentucky.
Chapman W. L. laborer; dem; born Illinois.
Chase J. H. livery; rep; from New York.
Chesher H. J. traveling agent plow works; rep; from Ohio.
Cheviton Edwin, laborer; rep; from Isle of Wight.
Childs Wm. A. retired; rep; from Mass.
Church W. W. wagon maker; dem; born Illinois.
Churchill G. Franklin, farmer; dem; born Illinois.
Churchill Jas. H. laborer; dem; born Ill.
Churchill N. farmer; dem; from New York.
Churchill T. M. carpenter; dem; born Ill.
Clark Curtis, employee coal yard; rep; from Ohio.
Clark G. W. retired; rep; from Ohio.
Clark John, collier; dem; Cath; Ireland.

CLARK JOHN S. Editor and Proprietor of Monmouth *Atlas;* Monmouth; born in Hudson, N. Y., 1819; came to this Co. in 1857; Rep; Presb; Mr. Clark purchased the Monmouth *Atlas* Sept., 1857; and has since that time been its editor.

Clark James, drayman; dem; from Ky.
Clark J. Q. employee Plow Co; rep; Ohio.
Clark Mary, dress maker; from New York.
Clark Mrs. O. S. dress maker; Chris; from Ohio.
Clark Samuel, associate editor *Atlas;* rep; Bapt; born Illinois.
Cloter Samuel, carpenter; rep; Prot; Ohio.
Claycomb Geo. teamster; rep; born Illinois.
Claycomb H. D. teamster; rep; born Ill.
Claycomb Samuel, clerk; rep; born Illinois.
Claytor Geo. L. employee Weir Plow Co.; rep; from Ohio.
Claytor Samuel, carpenter; rep; from Va.
Cleland Robert, teamster; dem; Meth; from Pennsylvania.
Clendenin Geo. S. druggist; ind; Bapt; from Pennsylvania.
Clippinger J. C. carpenter; rep; Meth; from Ohio.
Coates C. constable; rep; Lib; from Penn.
Cole James, moulder; from Missouri.
Colville B. P. painter; rep; from Ohio.
Colville James, butcher; rep; from Ohio.
Colville Joseph; painter; rep; Chris; Ohio.
Commins James, laborer; from Ireland.
Conrad G. P. billiards; dem; from Germany.
Conrad Wm. billiards; dem; from Penn.
Conrad Wm. clerk; boards Baldwin House; rep; from Germany.
Cook Wm. carpenter; rep; from New York.
Cooper Mrs. H. M.; U. P.; from Ohio.
Cooper Jas. retired; rep; from Ireland.
Copeland Caleb, carpenter; rep; from New York.
Copeland David, painter; rep; from New York.
Copeland Thos. blacksmith; rep; U. P; from Ireland.
Corey Jas. employe agricultural shops; born America.
Cornell J. E. proprietor Baldwin House omnibus line; rep; born Illinois.
Cornell R. H. painter; rep; born Illinois.

CORNELL MRS. SARAH, Widow; Monmouth; born in Middletown, Orange Co., N. Y., Aug. 30, 1821; came to this State in 1847; she married Theodore Cor-

nell in 1847; he was born in New Jersey, July 17, 1815, and died Sept. 26, 1866; has five children living; two deceased.
Conner C. painter; Lib; from Germany.
Costello James; laborer; dem; Cath; from Ireland.
Costello John, machinist; dem; Cath; from England.
Costello Thos. laborer; Cath; from Ireland.
Cotes F. H. miller.
Cowan Wm. blacksmith; rep; from Penn.
Cox J. M. barber; from Michigan.
Crandall A. carpenter; Ind; from New York.
Crandall Geo. D. carpenter; from New York.
Cretchville David, laborer; rep; Meth; from Tennessee.
Crow Mrs. Ella; from New York.
Culberson Jas. W. milkman; rep; Presb.
Cumming Rev. J. S. elder Meth. church; rep.
Cunningham David; dem; Cath; Ireland.
Cunningham Jas. farmer; rep; from Ohio.
Curley Jas. laborer; Ind; from Ireland.

DAGGETT T. G. carpenter; rep; from New York.
Danley Mrs. Elizabeth; widow; U. P.; born Illinois.
Danley John, retired; rep; U. P.; from Penn.
Darr Wm. carpenter; Meth; from Penn.
Davidson Caroline; U. P.; from New York.
DAVIDSON JAMES, Livery, Feed, and Sale Stable; Monmouth; born in Belmont Co., Ohio, April 27, 1848; he came to this Co. in 1869; has been engaged in the livery business six years; married Miss Anna E. Drury, 1871; she was born in Washington Co., Pa.
Davidson J. W. lawyer; dem; from Ky.
Davidson Robt. retired; rep; U. P.; from Ohio.
Davidson T. H. gunsmith; dem; from Ky.
Davis A. T. painter; rep; from New York.
Davis Joseph, plasterer; rep; U. P.; from Kentucky.
Davis Joseph, carpenter; rep; born Illinois.
Deabeny Jacob, carpenter; rep; from Ohio.
De Hague J. farmer; rep; born Illinois.
De Long Sandford, hardware clerk; rep; Bapt; from New York.
Denman Geo. B. merchant tailor; dem; born Illinois.
Denman Mrs. M.; Bapt; from New Jersey.
Dennis Edward, employee Pottery Works; rep; from England.
Dennis G. H. harness maker; dem; born Illinois.
Derenzy D. laborer; dem; from Penn.
Dev—n F. farmer; from France.
Dial Thos. laborer; dem; Cath; from Irel'd;

Dickinson J. C. freight and ticket agent, C. B. & Q.; rep; from Ohio.
Diffenbaugh D. D. grocer; rep; Meth; from Pennsylvania.
DIFFENBAUGH SAMUEL, Confectioner, Notions, etc.; born in Lancaster Co., Pa., March, 1828; came to Co. in 1864; married Miss Fannie Groff in 1854; she was born in Pennsylvania; has five children; lost two.
Dixon Henry, shoemaker; rep; Chris; from Pennsylvania.
Dixon Martha; Presb; from New York.
Dober Nelson, laborer; rep; from Tennessee.
Donaho Mrs. J. B. washerwoman; from Pennsylvania.
Doney Ransom, mason; rep; from Kentucky.
DONNELL JAS. B. County Superintendent of Schools; Monmouth; born in Pennsylvania, August, 1833; came to this Co. in 1854; Rep; U. P.; he was engaged in teaching 17½ years previous to his election as County Superintendent, which office he has held eight years; he married Catharine G. Douglass, Nov. 1, 1864; she was born in West Newton, Pa.
Doolittle George, gardener; rep; from New York.
Downer Harvey, blacksmith; rep.
Dredge Henry W. painter; rep; from Ohio.
Drennin P. H. books and stationery; rep; U. P.; from Pennsylvania.
DRYDEN JAMES L. Clerk Circuit Court; born in Miami Co., O., July 30, 1840; Rep; Presb; came to this State in 1846, and to this Co. in 1864; has resided here thirteen years; was in the army, Co. C, 36th Regt. I. V. I.; was severely wounded at Chicamauga, by which he lost use of his left arm; has held office of Mayor of City, and was Clerk of Circuit Court for eight years; married Miss Frances E. Hill, Oct. 12, 1871; she was born in this city, July 26, 1850.
Dryden Mary, U. P.; from Kentucky.
Dryden Sarah E. U. P.; from Ohio.
Dryden W. A. salesman; rep; Presb; from Ohio.
Duer Harry T. farmer; rep; from Ohio.
Duer John S. stone mason; rep; from Penn.
Duer Thos E. farmer; rep; from Ohio.
Dull Benj. cooper; dem; Presb; from Ohio.
Dunbar J. C. druggist; rep; U. P.; from Scotland.
Dunbar Mrs. Jane, widow; Presb; from Pennsylvania.
Duncan Mrs. Agnes, U. P.; from Penn.
Dungan D. M. undertaker; dem; from Ohio.
Dunkle D. D. moulder; dem; Presb; from Pennsylvania.
Dunn C. A. planing-mill; rep; from Penn.
Dunn O. B. retired; rep; from Penn.

Dunn J. D. teamster; dem; from Penn.

DUNN BROTHERS. Proprietors City Marble Works; they are dealers in American and foreign marble, and handle rough stone, and are prepared to execute orders for monuments, mantels, tops for tables, etc., and guarantee satisfaction in workmanship and price.

Dwight Ed. blacksmith; rep; born Ill.
Dwight L. W. blacksmith; rep; born Ill.
Dwight S. H. foreman Weir Plow Co.; rep; from New York.

EARP F. A. drover; rep; from Ky.

Earp Geo. B. clerk; rep; Chris; born Ill.
Earp J. J. gardener; dem; from Kentucky.
Earp Jas. express driver; rep; from Ky.
Earp L. D. livery; rep; from Kentucky.
Eaton H. F. clerk; dem; from Conn.
Eby A. J. carpenter; rep; Meth; from Penn.
Eby Theodore, farmer; rep; born Illinois.
Eckles Emand, carpenter; rep; from Md.
Eckles Locksley, farmer; rep; from Ohio.
Edens W. B. blacksmith; rep; from Tenn.
Edwards Chas. laborer; rep; Chris; born Illinois.
Edwards F. blacksmith; dem; Meth; from New Jersey.
Edwards T. B. blacksmith; rep; Meth; from New Jersey.
Eilenberger Benj. baker; rep; from N. J.
Eilenberger Eli; rep; from New Jersey.
Eilenberger Jacob, blacksmith; rep; from Pennsylvania.
Eilenberger Milton, painter; rep; from New Jersey.
Eklund A. S. carpenter; dem; from Sweden.
Elder J. C. barber; rep; Bapt.
Embleton T. W. employee pottery; rep; U. P.; from England.
Embree W. W. retired real estate dealer; dem; from Kentucky.
Emert Wm. carpenter; rep; born Illinois.
Endriss John, carpenter; dem; Cath; from Germany.
Endriss John, tobacconist; dem; Cath; from Germany.
Ephlin James, machinist; rep; from Penn.
Ernest Henry, brewer; dem; Cath; from Germany.
Errickson H. farmer; from Sweden.
Erskine Mrs. Jane, U. P.; from Penn.

ERWIN & LEINS, Merchant Tailors; came to this Co. Oct., 1866; carry a stock of from $8,000 to $12,000; this house was established in 1866, and has steadily grown in public favor until it enjoys a reputation second to none in its line west of Chicago.

Ewing Henry J. salesman; dem; Presb; from Pennsylvania.
Ewing John, physician; dem; from Penn.
Ezell Joseph, teamster; rep; from Ky.
Ezelle Wm. laborer; rep; born Illinois.

FARQUAR JNO. stock dealer; rep; U. P.; from Ohio.

Farquar Mrs. Mary, U. P.; from Ohio.
Farrier Geo. O. cigar-maker; rep; from Germany.
Fay G. H. sewing-machines; rep; from Massachusetts.
Feldt N. blacksmith; from Sweden.
Felt Nels, blacksmith; from Sweden.
Ferrander Mrs. A. widow; Chris; from New York.
Ferrington W. C. farmer; rep; from Ohio.
Ferrington Warren, carpet-weaver; rep; born Illinois.
Fields J. W. physician; dem; from N. H.
Fields Wm. T. painter; Ind; from Vermont.
Fieroved Simon, farmer; dem; Meth; from Pennsylvania.

FINDLEY DAVID E. Grocer and Baker; born in Muskingum Co., O., 1840; Rep; U. P.; he came to this Co. in 1856; married Miss Mary E. Gettemy, 1864; she was born in Penn.; has six children, three sons and three daughters.

Findley James, prop. fruit vineyard; rep; U. P.; from Ohio.
Findley Mrs. Martha, widow.
Finley Mrs. C.; Cath; from Ireland.
Finley Jeremiah, laborer; dem; Cath; from Ireland.
Finley Leander, farmer; rep; U. P.; from Ohio.
Fleharty Jacob, molder; dem; from Ohio.
Fleharty John, molder; rep; from Wisconsin.
Fleharty Robert, teamster; rep; from Canada.
Fleming Mary E. mantau-maker; Presb; from Pennsylvania.
Floyd Clark, laborer; rep; Bapt; from Ky.
Frazell Warren, painter; rep; from Ohio.
Free John, section boss; Luth; Sweden.
Frozier J. A.; U. P.; from Ohio.
Fry James, agent; rep; from Pennsylvania.
Frymire Arthur, butcher; dem; born Ill.
Foote B. F. molder; rep; born Illinois.
Foot B. F. teaming; dem; from New York.
Ford James, brick mason; rep; from New York.
Ford John C. queensware; rep; from Ohio.
Forney James, employee Weir Plow Works.
Fort Mark, works at Baldwin House; rep; from Tennessee.
Foster H. W. photographer; rep; from Ind.

FOSTER J. C. Photographer; Mon-

EDITOR OF "REVIEW"

mouth; born in Ohio in 1841; came to this Co. in 1865; has been in business during that time, excepting one year; married Miss Sarah M. Hess in 1867; she was born in Indiana; has three children.

Foster J. P. justice of the peace; rep; U. P.; from South Carolina.

Foster Robt. teamster; dem; from Penn.

Foster T. C. grocer; rep; U. P.; from Ohio.

Foster Will M. farmer; born South Carolina.

Fought Peter, shoe and boot maker; rep; from Pennsylvania.

Fox Paul, barber; boards at Baldwin House; from Germany.

Fuller Geo. agent; rep; Lib.

Furr J. C. farmer; rep; Bapt; from Virginia.

GALBREATH W. M. bookkeeper; rep; U. P. from Pennsylvania.

Galloway Charles, farmer; rep; from Ohio.

Galloway John, hedge trimmer; rep; U. P.; from Ohio.

Galloway J. A. sewing machine agent; dem; from Ohio.

Galloway W. H. laborer; dem; U. P.; from Ohio.

GAMBELL GEO. H. Merchant; Monmouth; born in Worcester Co., Mass., July 3, 1836; he came to this Co. in 1870; married Miss Mary Harvey in 1871; she was born in Pennsylvania; has two children, Carlos and Florence.

Gambell John, blacksmith; dem; born Ill.

Gambell O. W. blacksmith; rep; from Mass.

Gardner Mrs. Hannah, widow.

Garvin Margaret; U. P.; from Virginia.

GAYER F. Brewer; Monmouth; born in Germany, Feb. 15, 1836; owns 119½ acres in this Co.; came to this country in in 1854, and to this Co. in 1857; married Augusta N. Fowler in 1862; she was born in Germany; has five children, Bertha, Frank, Frederick, Anthony and Oscar.

Gayer John, farmer; dem; Luth; Germany.

Gettem J. A. clerk; rep; U. P.; from Ohio.

Gettemy John A. teamster; rep; U. P.; from Ohio.

Getts Adam, cigar maker; rep; Luth; from Iowa.

Gibson Benjamin, shoemaker; ind; from Pennsylvania.

Gibson Mrs. Martha, widow; Bapt; from O.

GIBSON ROBERT A. Farmer; Monmouth; born in Green Co., Ohio, Nov. 6, 1815; came to this Co. in 1831; Dem; U. P.; 172¾ acres, value $16,000; has lived in this Co. forty-six years; is one of the early settlers; married Maria Davidge in 1843, who was from Trimble Co., Ky., and died in 1846; one daughter, Sarah D.; married the second time Amanda Paine, Jan. 17, 1861.

GIBSON SAMUEL. Farmer; Sec. 30; P. O. Monmouth; born in Blount Co., Tenn., Sept. 3, 1804; came to this Co. in fall of 1830; Dem; U. P.; 134½ acres, value $18,000; has lived on the same place forty-one years; is one of the early settlers of this Co.; married Elizabeth Pierce, Aug. 3, 1826, who was born in Bourbon Co., Ky.; seven children, one deceased.

Gibson Wm. M. boots and shoes; rep; born Illinois.

Gilbert A. V. T. druggist and physician; rep; Presb; from New York.

Gilbert Charles W. druggist; rep; born Ill.

Gilbert Frank P. clerk; dem; Meth; from Virginia.

Gilbert Stephen, clerk; rep; from Virginia.

Gillett John, moulder; rep; from New York.

Gilliland W. T. restaurant; rep; U. P.; from Ohio.

Gilman Mrs. B.; Cath; from Ireland.

Glendenning Wm. grocer; dem; Presb; from Pennsylvania.

Glenn Agnes, U. P.; from South Carolina.

Glenn David, laborer; dem; from Penn.

Glenn Isabella, U. P.; from South Carolina.

GLENN & KIRKPATRICK. Attorneys; Monmouth; the former was born in Ohio, and the latter was born in Penn., and came to this State in 1852.

Glogaski Jacob, clothier; dem; Prussia.

GOOD P. D. Clothing Dealer; Monmouth; born in Penn. in 1850; came to this Co. in 1867; married Miss Aguilla Kressby, Oct. 5, 1876; she was born in Penn. in 1855.

Gordon Mrs. E.; U. P.; from Ireland.

Gordon Mrs. E. A.; U. P.; from Ohio.

Gordon Prof. George I. professor in College; rep; U. P.; from Ohio.

GORDON LEVANT J. Harness Maker; Monmouth; born in New York, June 12, 1822; Dem; Prot; he came to this State and Co. in 1850; married Martha A. Kill in 1852; she was born in New York; has five children, three sons and two daughters; lost one.

Gossett Cornelia, washing; Epis; from Ky.

Gowdy Mrs. E. T., U. P.; from Ohio.

Gowdy Jos. teacher; rep; U. P.; from Ohio.

Gowdy Thos. retired; rep; U. P.; from Ohio.

GRAHAM ALPHEUS P. Merchant; Monmouth; born in Penn., Dec. 12, 1823; Rep; Presb; he came to this State 1854; lived ten years in Iowa; has held office of School Director; married Ann F. Gregg, 1855; she was born in Cumberland Co., Penn., and came to this State 1846; has two sons, William P. and Alexander G.

Graham David, merchant; rep; U. P.; from South Carolina.

Graham Ed. Y. dry goods merchant; rep; U. P.; from Ohio.
Graham Mrs. Eliza, widow; U. P.; from Ohio.
Graham Jamieson, carpenter; rep; from Ohio.
Graham M. G. laborer; rep; from Ohio.
Graham M. M. photographer; rep; from Ohio.
Graham Samuel, retired; rep; U. P.; from Pennsylvania.
Graham T. W. grocer; rep; U. P.; from Kentucky.
Graham Thomas, lumber dealer; rep; U.P.; from Pennsylvania.
Grames Frank, telegraph operator; dem; born Illinois.
Grames R. H. carriage maker and house painter; from New York.
Granger Benj. laborer; rep; from Kentucky.
Grant Wm. A. grocery clerk; rep; born Ill.
Gray Anne V., U. P.; from Indiana.
Gray J. B. carpenter; rep; Luth; from Penn.
Gray Jane, U. P.; from Indiana.
Gray Susan, U. P.; from Indiana.
Green Jas. C. moulder; Lib; from Maryland.
Green S. D. W. blacksmith, foreman W. P. W.; rep; from Pennsylvania.
Greer Robert, attorney; boards at Baldwin House; rep; from Ohio.
Gregg A. C. retired; rep; Presb; from Penn.
Griggs J. H. grocer; dem; from Ohio.
Griggs Wm. W. railroad baggage master; rep; from Massachusetts.
Grove John, employee Weir Plow Co.; rep; Presb; from Pennsylvania.
Gustason Jno. Luth; from Sweden.

HAAS E. L. carpenter; rep; from Pennsylvania.
Harchelrode Christian, laborer; rep; from Pennsylvania.
Haines Thos. H. barber; rep; Bapt; from Tennessee.
HALE ALFRED, Monmouth; born in Washington Co., Tenn., 1816; Rep; Meth; he lived in Tennessee seventeen years, and removed to Shreveport, La., in 1837, and lived there thirty-one years, and came to this State and Co. in 1868; he married Vinne Willde in 1857; she was born in Tenn.
Haley Clay, teamster; rep.
Hall D. A. grocer; rep; Meth; from Del.
Hall J. T. laborer; ind; Chris; from Penn.
Hallam Gilbert, policeman; rep; Chris; born Illinois.
Hallam Samuel, retired; rep; Chris; from Pennsylvania.
Halliday Alex. farmer; dem; Meth; from Ohio.

Halliday Jos. farmer; dem; Meth; from O.
Halliday M. H. grocer; rep; Presb; from Ohio.
Halliday W. S. physician; dem; Bapt; from Ohio.
Hamilton A. student; rep. U. P.; from Penn.
HAMILTON S. M. Physician; Monmouth; born in Penn., Oct. 23, 1828; came to this Co. in 1858; he was mustered in the service of the late war as Surgeon of the 9th I. V. I.; served one year, and two years Division Surgeon; he married Eliza Starritt, 1856; she was born in Augusta, Maine.
Hammerstein John, employee agricultural shops; from Germany.
Hamsher T. O. carpenter; dem; Meth; from Pennsylvania.
Hanna J. R. student; dem; born Illinois.
HANNA WM. Banker; Monmouth; born in Fayette Co., Ind., June 19, 1827; Dem; Univ; he came to this Co. in 1825; he is President of the Monmouth National Bank, Treasurer of the Weir Plow Co., and President of the Burlington, Monmouth & Illinois River R. R.; married Sarah Findley, 1851; she was born in Indiana; has two children; lost one.
Harbaugh V. G. proprietor boarding house; ind; from Pennsylvania.
Harden A. S. butcher; rep; from Ohio.
HARDIN CHAUNCEY, Banker; Monmouth; born in New York, Jan. 15, 1815; came to this Co. 1840; owns 4,000 acres of land in Warren Co., 2,100 acres in Mason Co., 10,500 acres in Iowa, and 2,400 acres of improved land in Minn.; was engaged in merchandising two years; held office of Deputy Sheriff; farmed seven years; he built 50 miles of the Peoria & Oquawka R. R., now C., B. & Q. R. R.; was in the hardware business seven years; was Vice Prest. Monmouth Nat. Bank, and is now Prest. of the 2d Nat. Bank, Monmouth; has a Bank at Waseca, Minn., one at Dodge Centre, Minn., and one at Eldora, Iowa; he married Harriet A. Gordan in 1840; she was born in New York; has five children; lost one.
Hardin H. G. banker; rep; from New York.
HARDING ABNER C. deceased, whose portrait appears in this work, was born at East Hampton, Conn., Feb. 10, 1807; received an academical education; studied law; removed to Monmouth, Warren Co., Ill., June, 1838, where he engaged in the practice of his profession, in extensive farming operations, and in railroad management; was a member of the Constitutional Convention of Illinois in 1848; was a member of the State Legislature of Illinois in 1848, 1849, 1850; enlisted as private in the 83d Reg. of I. V. I., and was commissioned as Colonel; was promoted to Brigadier-General for his gallant and

brave defense of "Fort Donelson," Feb. 3, 1864, where, with a force of only 800 men, he held at bay a force of over 8,000 men and 13 pieces of artillery, under Gens. Wheeler, Foster and Wharton, and after six hours' fighting compelled them to withdraw, thus leaving reinforcements and supplies which were coming up the river for Gen. Rosecrans, free to reach their destination. The dead, wounded and prisoners of the rebels exceeded the entire command of Col. Harding; he lost about 100 men. Gen. Harding was elected to the Thirty-ninth Congress, and re-elected to the Fortieth Congress; married Susan A. Ickes, from Perry Co., Penn., June 30, 1855; had two children by former marriage, Geo. F. and Mary R.; Mr. H. died July 19, 1874, aged 67 years.

Harding Charles B. student; rep; from N.Y.

Harding F. W. cashier 2d National Bank; rep; from New York.

Harding N. G. farmer; rep; from New York.

Harkless Thos. employee Weir Plow Co.; rep; born Illinois.

Harper P. B. carpenter; rep; U. P.; from Virginia.

Hartaugh Peter, teamster; dem; Adv.

Hartman A. cigar maker; dem; Cath; from Germany.

Harvey D. hardware; rep; Meth; from Ohio.

Harvey J. M. druggist; dem; from Ohio.

Harvey John, merchant; Meth; from Ohio.

Harvey W. teller in bank; rep; Meth; from Ohio.

HARVEY & SHULTZ, Druggists and Chemists; Monmouth; this house was established in 1862, by Brewer & McGrew; they give careful attention to physicians' prescriptions, and are dealers in drugs, medicines, window glass and surgical appliances.

Hawkins Jos. driller; dem; born Illinois.

Hawkins Orrin, grocer; rep; Bapt; from New York.

Haydn David, gun smith; rep; from Ohio.

Haydn Lewis, rep; from Ohio.

Haynes Jamison L. dem; born Illinois.

Hays Mrs. Anne, Presb; from England.

Hays Charles, moulder; rep; from Mich.

Hays Mrs. E. F. widow; U. P.; from Ohio.

Hays M. music dealer; rep; from Penn.

Hays Mrs. Rhoda, widow; U. P.; from Ohio.

Hays S. D. C. student; rep; U. P.; born Illinois.

Hays S. P. laborer; rep; Meth; from Tenn.

Hays W. G. M. student; rep; U. P.; born Illinois.

Heffner Howard D. clerk; boards at Baldwin House; dem; from Pennsylvania.

Henderson Rev. G. D. teaches in college; rep; U. P.; from Pennsylvania.

Henderson W. D. miller; rep; U. P.; from South Carolina.

Henry Charles, carriage maker; ind; Lib; from Vermont.

Henry Geo. painter; rep; from Vermont.

Henry Horatio, lumberman; rep; Bapt; from Massachusetts.

Henry Hugh, carriage maker; rep; from Vermont.

Henry K. W. painter; ind; from Michigan.

Herbert J. B. physician; rep; Bapt; from Ohio.

Herbert Jno. J. grain dealer; rep; Bapt; from District Columbia.

HENDERSON JAMES H. County Treasurer; Monmouth; born in Washington Co., Penn., Oct. 17, 1833; Rep; U. P.; He came to this State 1854, and to this Co. in 1855; enlisted in 83d Ill. Inf., and served three years, until close of the war; previously held office of Township Collector; married Emma J. Mitchell, 1860; she was born in Ohio; has seven children, four sons and three daughters.

Hern John, farmer; dem; from Penn.

Hern A. employe shops.

HERSHEY J. M. Botanic Physician; Monmouth; born in Pennsylvania, in 1819; came to this Co. in 1850; he treats all chronic diseases, no matter of how long standing; he also applies magnetic treatment, and if patients come and see him after consultation, no cure, no pay; he can refer to almost numberless cases of most astonishing cures, after given up by other treatment.

Hershey Samuel, carpenter; rep; Meth; from Pennsylvania.

Hewett Geo. merchant; rep; from England.

Higgins John, laborer; dem; Cath; from Ireland.

Higgins Thomas, laborer; dem; Cath; from Ohio.

Hill Clinton, laborer; dem; from Ohio.

Hill Frank, teamster; dem; from Ohio.

Hill Geo. clerk; rep; born Ill.

Hill J. W. agricultural implements; rep; from Pennsylvania.

Hill Jos. carpenter; dem; Luth; from Penn.

Hocum Swan, employe Weir Plow Co.; rep; Luth; from Sweden.

Hoerner Henry, retired; rep; Luth; from Pennsylvania.

Hohenadel F. baker; dem; from Germany.

Hohenadel F. A. baker; Lib; born Illinois.

Holcomb Amelia, dressmaker; born Illinois.

Holcomb Nels. laborer; rep; Luth; Sweden.

Hollinsworth Levi, retired; rep; Meth; from Ohio.

Holloway Edmund, son of Robt. Holloway; dem; born Illinois.

HOLLOWAY ROBERT, Attorney; Monmouth; born in Kentucky, in 1829; came to this Co. in 1851; Dem; Presb; owns 2,500 acres of land in this Co.; he was one of the founders of the town of Alexis, in Spring Grove tp.; was Presidential Elector in 1856; he married Miss Catharine Thompson, 1854; she was born in Pennsylvania; has four children.

Holly Wm. sewing machines; dem; from O.

Holmberg John, tailor; from Sweden.

Holmes John, laborer; dem; from Penn.

Holt A. H., U. S. treasury clerk; rep; Bapt; from New York.

Holt Jacob H. retired; dem; from New York.

Holton A. J. painter; rep; born Illinois.

Hood E. E. grocer, wholesale and retail; rep; U. P.; from Pennsylvania.

Hood John, butcher; rep; U. P.; from Ind.

Hood Samuel, retired; rep; U. P.; from Pennsylvania.

Hood Thomas, teamster; rep; U. P.; from Pennsylvania.

Hood Thomas A. butcher; rep; U. P.; from Indiana.

Hood Wm. farmer; rep; U. P.; from Ind.

Hopper Wm. L. manf. of plows; rep; Chris; from Kentucky.

Horn Elijah, carpenter; rep; from Ohio.

Horne John, drug clerk; rep; U. P. from Indiana.

Horne W. S. retired; U. P.; from Scotland.

Hotaline L. G. clerk National Hotel; rep; from New York.

Howk R. A. butcher; rep; from New York.

HUBBARD B. T. O. Cashier of the First National Bank of Monmouth; born in Otsego Co., N. Y., Jan. 8, 1833; came to this Co. in 1857; has held position of Cashier of the First National Bank since Jan. 1, 1867; he married Miss Frances R. Fay in Oct., 1859; she was born in Massachusetts; has one child.

Hubbard M. P. laborer; rep; from New York.

Huey J. D. insurance agent; rep; Presb; from Pennsylvania.

Humble Jos. machinist; dem; Meth; from Wisconsin.

Humphrey B. T. farmer; from Ohio.

Hunt George, teamster; dem.

Hunt Mrs. S. J.; widow; from Virginia.

Hutchinson A. P. attorney; dem; born Ill.

Hutchinson J. C. prof. Monmouth College; rep; U. P.; from Ohio.

Hutton Joseph, miner; rep; Meth; from England.

INCHES REV. DAVID, U. P. minister; from Scotland.

Irwin J. C. merchant; rep; from Penn.

Irwin W. H. merchant; rep; from Ohio.

JACKSON PETER, whitewasher; rep; from Kentucky.

Jackson Peter, laborer; rep; from Kentucky.

James Isaac, laborer; rep; Bapt; from Va.

Jamieson J. B. retired; dem; Presb.

Jamieson Rev. J. M. Presb. minister; dem; from Pennsylvania.

Jamison Miss Susie; Presb; from Iowa.

Jamison Wm. retired; rep; U. P.; from Scotland.

Janes R. K. dentist; rep; Meth; from New York.

Jarvis M. L. apiarian; lib; Spir; from New. York.

Jefferson L. F. carpenter; rep; from N. Y.

Jewell Jacob, farmer; rep; from New York.

Johnson H. A. jeweller; dem.

Johnson Mrs. H. W.; from New York.

Johnson Henry, carpenter and painter; rep; U. P.; from Ohio.

Johnson Jno. mason; Luth; from Sweden.

Johnson J.F. horse dealer; dem; New York.

Johnson Mrs. Kate, widow; Luth; from Sweden.

Johnson Louis J. laborer; from Sweden.

Johnson Nils, tailor; rep; Luth; Sweden.

Johnson Ole, tailor; dem; Luth; Norway.

Johnson Thomas, Sr. insurance agent; rep; U. P.; from Virginia.

Johnson Tom, employed by Weir Plow Co.; rep; Luth; from Norway.

Johnson T. H. engineer; rep; Chris; from Ohio.

Johnson W. K. R. R. employee; ind; Meth; from New York.

Johnson Thomas, Jr. insurance agent; rep; Presb; from Virginia.

Jones A. C. telegrapher; rep; from Wales.

Jones J. H. employed by Weir Plow Co.; ind; from Ohio.

Jones Jerry, employed by Weir Plow Co.; dem; from Indiana.

Jones Moses, farmer; dem; from Indiana.

Jones Thomas, telegraph operator; rep; Bapt; from England.

Jordan George, painter; rep; from Maine.

Joss S. E. clerk; rep; Presb; born Illinois.

Joss R. S. wool manufacturer; rep; Presb; from Pennsylvania.

KEEDLE JOHN, baker; dem; from England.

Keedle Thomas, farmer; dem; from Eng.

Kegan Peter, works on railroad; dem; Cath; from Ireland.

Kelly Barnard, laborer; dem; Cath; from Ireland.

Kerr Robert L. carriage trimmer; rep; U.P.; from Scotland.

Kettering A. F. laborer; dem; born Illinois.
Kettering Benjamin T. farmer; rep; Chris; from Pennsylvania.
Kettering Ellen, Meth; from Pennsylvania.
Kettering Mrs. Mary, Meth; from Penn.
KIDDER ALMON, Attorney; Monmouth; born in Warren Co., July, 1837; Rep; Presb; has practiced law for fifteen years; married Anna C. Jacobs, May 30, 1865; she was born in Penn.; has one child, Nina B.; lost one.
Kilgore J. C., M.D. firm Webster & Kilgore; rep; U. P.; from Ohio.
Kimball John, harness maker.
Kingsbury A.R. contractor and builder; rep; Bapt; from Vermont.
Kinkead Mrs. B. widow; U. P.; from Ohio.
Kliner A. shoe merchant; from Prussia.
Kobler G. J. butcher; rep; Luth; from Germany.
Kobler John, cabinet maker; rep; Germany.
Koffroth Mrs. L. E. dressmaker; Chris; from Pennsylvania.
Krothman Jacob, undertaker; dem; from Germany.
KYLER THOS. S. Proprietor Exchange Hotel, Monmouth; born in Penn., March 19, 1823; came to this Co. in 1863; married Clarinda B. Lowry, March 30, 1854; she was born in Armstrong Co., Penn.; has five children; lost two.

LACY JOHN, laborer; rep; from Pennsylvania.
Lacy Moses, clerk; rep; from Ohio.
Lafferty Mrs. Sarah, widow; from New York.
Lahm R. L. cigar manufacturer; rep; from Germany.
Lambert Decatur, laborer; rep; from New York.
Langdon Mrs. S. M. widow; U. P.; from England.
Layman T. G. agent; dem; from Kentucky.
Lee J. R. merchant; rep; from Ohio.
Lee Mrs. M. J.; U. P.; from Pennsylvania.
Lee Mrs. Susan.
LEEPER JAMISON, Farmer; Sec. 35; Monmouth; born in Union Co., Ind., May 9, 1811; came to this Co. in 1839; Dem; Chris; owns 300 acres of land, val. at $18,000; has held offices of Supervisor of Town and School Director for three years; married Eliza Sankey, Jan., 1830, from Butler Co., Ohio.
Leeper John, blacksmith; rep; Presb; from Kentucky.
Leighty Jacob, harness maker; rep; born Illinois.
Leins Adam, merchant tailor; rep; from Germany.
Lemon Wm., R. R. employee; dem; Meth; from West Virginia.

Liby Isaac, laborer; rep; from Pennsylvania.
Liby Samuel, groceryman; Ind; from Penn.
Lillgadhall Amel, employed in Weir Plow Works; from Sweden.
Lincoln F. R. physician and teacher; rep; Presb; from Massachusetts.
Lindsey James, painter; rep; born Illinois.
Lindstrum S. J. tailor; rep; Luth; from Sweden.
Little James R. foreman Weir Plow Works; dem; Presb; born Illinois.
Little Leoman, employed by Weir Plow Co.; dem; born Illinois.
Little S. A. carpenter; rep; born Illinois.
Lofgren Oscar, moulder; rep; from Sweden.
Logan John M. carpenter; rep; U. P.; from Pennsylvania.
Lorimer John, auctioneer; rep; from Ohio.
Lorimer Samuel, clerk; rep; from Ohio.
Loveland Mrs. H. G., from Massachusetts.
Lucas Charles, laborer; dem; born Illinois.
Lucas C. clerk; dem; from Kentucky.
Lucas Matthew, employed by Weir Plow Co.; rep; from New Jersey.
Luft A. music teacher; Chris; from Germany.
Lundeen A. F. stone mason; from Sweden.
Lundgren Charles, shoemaker; rep; Luth; from Sweden.
Lusk L. M. printer; dem; from Penn.
Lusk Wilson, jeweller; dem; from Penn.

McBRIDE A. laborer; dem; from Pennsylvania.
McBroom Mrs. Sarah, widow; U. P.; from Pennsylvania.
McCallum Wm. pedlar; dem; from South Carolina.
McCartney J. W. painter; rep; Delaware.
McCartney Samuel, painter; rep; born Ill.
McCashin Wm. E. farmer; rep; U. P.; from Pennsylvania.
McClanahan Samuel, ditcher; rep; U. P.; from Ohio.
McCleary R. B. physician; rep; born Ill.
McClenahan J. teacher; rep; Presb; from Ohio.
McConnell R. business manager commercial house; dem; born Illinois.
McCormick Geo. dealer in grain and agl. impts.; dem; from Ohio.
McCoy D. H. farmer; dem; born Illinois.
McCOSH G. G. Printer; born in Penn., March 31, 1846; came to this Co. in 1873; Ind Rep; Prot; served in Co. G, 6th U. S. Cav. during the war; married Cora Coates, April 14, 1875, of Warren Co., Ill.; one daughter, Nettie H.
McCready Nancy, Presb; from Ireland.
McCullough J. B. hardware; rep; Presb; from Ohio.

McCullough W. W. book-keeper; rep; Presb; from Indiana.

McCUTCHEON JOHN M. Retired; born in Steubenville, O., Oct. 13, 1830; he came to this State in 1845; he lived in Randolph Co. twenty-six years previous to his removal to this Co. in 1871; he married Miss Fannie W. Bruen in 1869; she was born in N. J.

McDill David, D. D., Prof. Monmouth College; rep; U. P.

McDowell A. G. carriage-maker; rep; Meth; from New Jersey.

McDowell J. F. printer; ind; Meth; from Indiana.

McDowell Rev. N. minister; rep; U. P.; from Pennsylvania.

McFadden Chas. fireman; rep; from Ohio.

McFarland Alex. teacher; from New York.

McFarland Daniel, retired; dem; from New York.

McFarland Jas. retired; dem; U. P.; from New York.

McGaw T. G. apiary; rep; U. P.; from Ohio.

McGrew Jerry, music dealer; dem; Bapt; from Indiana.

McGuire, painter; rep; from Penn.

McGuire E. F. boarding-house; U. P.; from Pennsylvania.

McGuire Miss Elizabeth, boarding-house; U. P.

McGuire J. boarding-house; U. P.; from Pennsylvania.

McGuire Miss Jane, boarding-house; U. P.

McIntosh Roderick, stone-cutter; rep; U. P.; from Scotland.

McKinley Milton, moulder; dem; from Wisconsin.

McLaughlin Wm. shoemaker; ind; U. B.; from Virginia.

McMillan Jas. janitor; rep; U. P.; from Scotland.

McMillan Jno. musician; rep; from Rhode Island.

McNally Wm. teamster; from Ireland.

McNeal Mrs. Catherine, widow; U. P.; from Pennsylvania.

McNeil C. carpenter; dem; from Penn.

McQuiston Wm. H. stationery and news dealer; rep; U. P.; from Ohio.

Mackey Elis, U. P.; from Pennsylvania.

Mackey Jonathan, teamster; dem; from Pennsylvania.

Malanthy Michael, R. R. employee; dem; Cath; from Ireland.

Mannon Jas. A. merchant; rep; from Ohio.

Mannon John, farmer; rep; U. P.; from Ohio.

Mark H. C. clerk; dem; from Indiana.

Marks Isaac, miller; rep; from England.

Marshall Dr. Hugh, physician; from South Carolina.

Marshall Jas. miner; Ind; from Ireland.

MARSHALL JAMES R. Foreman Monmouth Mining and Mnfg. Co.; born in Belfast Co., Antrim, Ireland, in 1838; came to this Co. in 1871, and has been employed at the same works since that time; married Susan Orr in 1865; she was born in Banbridge, Down Co., Ireland; has two children, named Louise R. and John R.

Marshall J. W. trader; rep; from Ireland.

Marshal Wm. laborer; rep; from Ireland.

MARTIN JOSEPH. Capitalist; born in Ireland, in 1816; came to this Country in 1864, and to this Co. in 1869; he lived in Galena twenty-five years, and was engaged in lead mining; he was one of the organizers of the First National Bank, and has been a director from its organization; his first wife was Jane Groves; she was born in Ireland, and died Oct. 19, 1869; his second wife was Mrs. Jennie Patton, daughter of Judge Lee, of Ohio.

Martin J. B. butcher; dem; Presb; from Pennsylvania.

Mason S. Y. retired; dem; from Ohio.

MATTHEWS R. C., D. D. Pastor of the First Presb. Church; born in Jefferson Co., Va., 1822; he became Pastor of this church in Jan., 1852, and it is the second largest pastorate in this denomination in the State.

Matson Swan, employee Weir Plow Co.; rep; Luth; from Sweden.

Matthus W. works at Monmouth Mining and Mnfg. Co.

Matthews Jas. laborer; rep; from Ohio.

MATTHEWS JOHN W. Attorney and Master in Chancery; Rep; Presb; was born in Miss., July 7, 1848; came to this Co. when very young; enlisted in the 47th I. V. I. in the late war; married Miss May G. Stevens, Feb. 8, 1876; she was born in New York.

Matthews Nancy H. Presb; from Ky.

Matthews Wm. laborer; rep; Epis; from England.

Melton John, grinder Wier Plow Co.; dem; from Indiana.

Mercer M. P. grocer; dem; from Indiana.

Merideth W. merchant; rep; Presb; from Ohio.

Merril J. M. mnfr. Washing Machine; rep; Meth; from Vermont.

Morningstar Jacob, brick-maker; dem; from Ohio.

Meyer Fred. brick-moulder; rep; from Germany.

MILLEN WM. M. Teacher; born in Indiana, July 20, 1847; Rep; U. P.; came to this State in 1849, and to this Co. in 1856; was educated at Monmouth College;

has been engaged in teaching seven years, the last year as Principal of the East Ward School.

Miller C. C. retired; dem; from Kentucky.

Miller C. laundry; rep; U. P.; from Ky.

Miller Gilbert, miner; from Scotland.

Miller Hiram C. employed by Weir Plow Co.; rep; from Virginia.

Miller John, clothier; dem; Jew; from Prussia.

Miller John, cigar maker; dem; Luth; from Germany.

Miller Jacob, laborer, works for C. Hardin.

Miller Wm. C. laborer; dem; from Ohio.

Miller Wm. W. farmer; rep; U. P.; from Ohio.

Mills E. B. blacksmith; dem; from Ohio.

Mills Eli, blacksmith; dem; from Ohio.

Mills John, travelling agent; dem; born Ill.

Miner George, farmer; rep; born Illinois.

Mitchell Mrs. A. L. T. teacher in public school; Presb; from Indiana.

Mitchel Esau, bill poster; rep; Bapt; from Tennessee.

Mitchell George L. local editor; rep; from Indiana.

Mitchell Parmelia, Meth; from Ohio.

Mitchell Wm. physician; rep; U. P.; from Pennsylvania.

Mitchell Wm. M. postal clerk; rep; from Indiana.

Moisen Joseph, laborer; rep; from Canada.

Monnon James A. dry goods; rep; from O.

Montgomery John S. hardware; dem; born Illinois.

Montgomery Jos., painter; rep; from Pa.

Montgomery Samuel, laborer; rep; U. P.; from Pennsylvania.

Moore Charles, painter; rep; from Penn.

Moore Ed. printer; dem; born Illinois.

Moore Mrs. Elizabeth; U. P.; from Penn.

Moore F. M. laborer; rep; Meth; from Indiana.

Moore James H. farmer; rep; U. P.; from Pennsylvania.

Moore J. Hutch, overseer Weir Plow Works; rep; born Illinois.

Moore John, clerk; rep; from Pennsylvania.

Moore John, clerk; rep; from Pennsylvania.

Moore J. G. stock dealer; rep; U. P.; from Ohio.

MOORE MRS. S. J. Hotel Keeper; Monmouth; born in Warren Co., Ill., Mar. 18, 1845; owns hotel, valued at $1,500; Mrs. Moore has kept the Railroad Eating House for the last year; has four children, Freddie, Bertie, Amanda F. F. H. E. and Kit.

Moore S. R. carpenter; dem; Meth; from Pennsylvania.

Moore W. S. hotel depot; rep; from Penn.

Moose Albert, cigar maker; from Germany.

Morehead Louis, drayman; rep; from Ky.

Moreland John, machinest; dem; from Virginia.

Morey D. H. travelling agent; dem; Presb; from New York.

Morey George, crockery dealer; dem; born Illinois.

Morey H. T. doctor; dem; from New York.

Morgan David, wagon maker; from Ky.

Morgan D. J. wagon maker; rep.

MORGAN JOHN T. Attorney; Monmouth; born in Erie Co., N. Y., Nov. 25, 1831; Rep; Prot; came to this State in 1843; served three years in the Army as Capt. of Co. F., 83rd Ill. Inf.; in 1870 was elected to the 27th General Assembly of Ill., and served two years; in 1874 was elected State Senator for the 23rd District; he married Maria Harroun, Nov. 8, 1858; she was born in Penn.; has four children.

Morrel C. H. polisher; rep; from Iowa.

Morris Eugene, retired; rep; Bapt; from O

Morris S. G. butcher; rep; from Ohio.

Morrison D. McD. student; rep; U. P.; from Ohio.

Morrison James, farmer; rep; U. P.; from Ohio.

Morrison William, grocer; rep; U. P.; from Ohio.

Morton Andrew, clerk; rep; from Indiana.

Morton George, retired; rep; U. P.; from Scotland.

Morton William A. rep; from Indiana.

Mosha Ira G. Attorney; rep; from New York.

Munson Mrs. John, widow; Bapt; from Ky.

Murphy John, stone mason; dem; Cath; from Ireland.

Murphy J. A. laborer; dem; Cath; from Ireland.

Murray Barney, laborer; dem; Cath; from Ireland.

NASELUND JONAS, tailor; dem; Luth; from Sweden.

NASH HUGH, Farmer and Stock Raiser; Monmouth; born in Green Co., O., June 5, 1824; came to this Co. in Fall of 1832; Rep; U. P.; 207 acres, value $12,500; his father, William Nash, was among the early settlers of Hale tp., and died in Oct., 1867; Mr. Nash married Mary J. McKinney, June 18, 1845; five children; married the second time, Elizabeth Henderson, May 5, 1859; four children.

Naylor Jacob, laborer; rep; from Penn.

Neely George, carpenter; dem; from Penn.

Nelson Andrew, carpenter; rep; Luth; from Sweden.

Nelson Carl, carpenter; rep; Luth; from Denmark.
Nelson Edgar, mason; rep; Luth; Sweden.
Nelson Mrs. H. widow; Luth; from Sweden.
Nelson Louis, laborer; rep; from Sweden.
Nelson N. J. shoemaker; rep; from Sweden.
Nerftrun P. laborer; from Sweden.
Nesbit Mrs. J. widow; U. P.; from South Carolina.
Nesbit James, painter; rep; U. P.
Ness George W. employed in Weir Plow Works; rep; Chris; from Indiana.
Nichols Jackson, laborer; rep; Bapt; from Missouri.
Nichols J. W. clerk in commercial house; rep; from New Jersey.
Nichols Mrs. Rachel; widow; Meth; from Ohio.
Niebuhr Henry, tailor; dem; from Germany.
Niess James, carpenter; rep; Meth; from Pennsylvania.
Nolan Daniel, laborer; dem; Cath; from Ireland.
Norcross J. G. provision dealer; dem; from Pennsylvania.
Norcross Wm. provision store; Chris; from Pennsylvania.
NORCROSS WM. C. Attorney; Monmouth; born in Erie Co., Penn., Aug. 22, 1842; Dem; Presb; he came to this Co. in 1844; has practiced law for ten years; has held offices of School Director and city Alderman; married Miss Isabel B. Henry, Sept. 3, 1868; she was born in Washington Co., Penn.; has one child.
NORCROSS WM. F. Retired Farmer; Monmouth; born in Erie Co., Penn., Feb. 14, 1812; dem; Presb; owns 60 acres; he came to this State and Co. in 1843; has held offices of Assessor and School Director; married Maria L. Dickson in 1840; she died in 1857; married Maria S. Judson in 1863; has five children, four sons and one daughter.
Norman H. laborer; rep; from England.
Norman Mrs. Rebecca, from England.
Norse Wm. brick mason; rep; from N. Y.
NORTON MRS. ALMIRA C. Widow; Monmouth; born in Cornwall, Conn., Dec. 13, 1809; came to this Co. in 1863; Bapt; owns house and five acres, value $4,000; Mrs. Norton's maiden name was Almira C. Tupper; she married Elisha B. Norton, March 16, 1829; he was born in Hartland, Conn., Feb. 7, 1807, and died Oct. 13, 1876; her son, H. B. Norton, enlisted in 83rd I. V. I., in Aug., 1863, as private, and was promoted through all grades, to Captain in 1864; he died Jan. 4, 1871; has three daughters living; Aurelia R., married C. P. Norton; Fannie P. married Dr. Wm. R. Hamilton, and Melicent H. married Rev. Ralph E. Wilkin.

Norton Mrs. E. B.; widow.
Nott L. C. painter; rep; from New York.
Nottleman Hans, cigar manufacturer; dem; from Germany.
Numbers L. F. laborer; rep; from Ohio.
NUSBAUM MOSES, Merchant; Monmouth; born in Bavaria, 1834; he came to this country in 1845, and to this Co. in 1861; married Miss Mary Stein in 1861; she was born in Pottsville, Pa.; has three children, one son and two daughters.
Nutt Frank, farmer; dem; from Indiana.
Nutt L. B. teamster; dem; from Ohio.
Nutt S. J. wagon manufacturer; rep; from Indiana.
Nye Chas. E. laborer; dem; born Illinois.
Nye Charley, laborer; rep; from Mass.
Nye Elisha, furniture; dem; Lib; from Mass.

OBERG LOUIS, tailor; rep; from Sweden.
O'Farrell Rev. T. parish priest; from Ireland.
Oliver O. F. mechanic; rep; from New York.
Olsen A. clerk; Luth; born Illinois.
Olsen Matt. laborer; from Sweden.
Ovenstein Jacob, employee Weir Plow Works dem; from Germany.
Owens Ed. laborer; dem; Cath; from Irel'd.

PAGE TIM. employee Weir Plow Co.; rep; from New York.
Paine Hendrick E. retired; rep; from Ohio.
Palmer C. P. carpenter; rep; Meth; born Illinois.
Palmer Isaac, farmer; from Pennsylvania.
Palmer M. S. engineer; born Knox Co.
PALMER WM. Proprietor Commercial House; Monmouth; born in Conn., March 1, 1808; came to this State 1858, and to this Co., 1873; married Julien Soper, 1835; she was born in Conn.; has three children; lost one.
Parker Burr, retired; rep; from Maryland.
Parker Burr, Jr., teacher; rep; born Illinois.
Parker Mrs. Susan A.; widow; Presb; from Kentucky.
PARKINSON EDWARD, Teacher; Monmouth; born in Ohio, Dec., 1844; came to this Co. in 1854; Rep; U. P.; has been engaged in teaching seven years, four years as teacher of the South Ward school, this city; he married Miss Mary B. Miller, in June, 1874; she was born in Missouri, in 1855.
Parrot David, baggage-master, C. B. & Q. R. R.; dem; U. B.; from Virginia.
Parry D. D. Pres. Tile Manufactory; rep; U. P.; from Ohio.
Parry D. S. horse buyer; rep; U. P.; from Ohio.
Parry Walter, retired; rep; U. P.; from Wales.

Parsons Mrs. Hannah; widow; from Engl'd.
Pattee H. H. agricultural implements; dem; from New Hampshire.
Pattee J. H. agricultural implements; dem; from New Hampshire.
Patterson Azro, retired; dem; Ind; from Vermont.
Patterson David, commission merchant; dem; from Pennsylvania.
Patterson Mrs. Elis.; U. P.; from Ohio.
Patterson John, farmer; rep; U. P.; from Pennsylvania.
Patterson Mrs. Sarah A., widow; U. P.; from Ohio.

PATTEN JAS. C. salesman; Monmouth; born in Ohio, Oct. 29, 1844; he came to this State, 1847, and to this Co., 1875; engaged in the clothing business; married Miss Belle Streater, 1873; she was born in Illinois; has one child, Minnie Belle.

Paul Frank, laborer; rep; from Florida.
Paxton W. S. wagon maker; rep; U. P.; from Virginia.
Peacock M. I.; U. P.; from Ohio.

PEACOCK THEO. G. Attorney; Monmouth; born in Knox Co., O., 1846; Rep; U. P.; he came to this State in 1875; holds office of Justice of the Peace.

Pease Alfred, barber; rep; from Penn.
Pebbles F. H. farmer; rep; from Mass.
Penland Geo. painter; rep; from Ohio.
Pennington Alfred, carpenter; dem; Meth; from Kentucky.
Penix Geo. laundry; rep; U. P.; from Ky.
Parrine Thos. laborer; rep; from Ohio.
Perrin Wm. retired; rep; from England.
Perrot Mrs. Anna; Epis; from Ireland.
Peters Geo. laborer; rep; U. B.; born Ill.
Peterson Charley, teamster; rep; Luth; from Sweden.
Peterson Jonas, laborer; rep; Luth; from Sweden.
Peterson John, laborer; from Sweden.
Peterson S. D. railroad employee; Luth; from Sweden.
Pettit W. S. jeweller; rep; from New York.
Pressly Wm. P. merchant; Presb; from South Carolina.
Price S. H. music dealer; dem; born Illinois.
Price Zachariah, janitor schools; rep; Meth; from Missouri.
Phelps Delos P. attorney; dem; born Ill.

PHELPS S. S. Livery, Feed and Boarding Stable; Monmouth; born in Henderson Co., June 10, 1849; Rep; Lib; has been engaged previously to present business in dealing in stock; married Mary Cowan in 1869; she was born in Henderson Co.; has one child.

Phillips M. whitewasher; rep; Bapt; from South Carolina.
Pierce A. G. postal clerk, C. B. & Q. R. R.; rep; born Illinois.
Pinkerton Wm. hardware merchant; rep; U. P.; from Ohio.
Pillsbury I. P. agricultural implements; dem; from New York.
Pettenger Andrew; retired; rep; Meth; from Pennsylvania.
Pleasanton Peter, clerk; from Germany.
Plummer Mrs. Francis; widow; U. P.; born Illinois.
Pollock Thos. G. laborer; rep; U. P.; from Ohio.

PORTER JOHN. Attorney; Monmouth; born in Pennsylvania, April 27, 1824; Rep; Presb; owns 260 acres, valued at $40 per acre; came to this Co, in 1851; has held office of County Judge two terms; was member of 26th General Assembly; married Mary E. Robb, in 1847; she was born in Pennsylvania; has seven children; lost one.

PORTER JNO. A. Teacher and Principal of the North Ward School; Monmouth; born in Ohio, 1838; Rep; U. P.; he came to this State in 1840; was educated at Monmouth College; he entered the army as a private in the 36th I. V. I., in Aug., 1861; was wounded at Resaca, Ga., May 15, 1864, and again at Nashville, Tenn., Dec. 16, 1864; was mustered out as First Lieutenant, Oct. 8, 1865; has been engaged in teaching 16 years; the past six years as principal of the city schools; married Miss Fannie E. McClure, April 30, 1868; she was born in Indiana; has two sons.

Porter J. H. clerk; rep; Bapt; from Iowa.
Porter J. Knox, hardware; rep; Presb; born Illinois.
Porter Mrs. S. E.; widow; U. P.; from Penn.
Porter Wm. laborer; rep; U. P.; from Irel'd
Potter Jas. C. clothier; rep; from Ohio.
Powers Mike, railroad employee.

QUINBY MARY E. Methodist; from Ohio.
Quinn James, railroad employee; dem; Cath; from Ireland.
Quinn P. C. employed by plow works; rep; U. P.; from Ohio.
Quirk Michael, works on railroad; dem; Cath; from Ireland.

RADMACHER JACOB, brick maker; dem; Meth; from Germany.
Raines Harvey, laborer; rep; Meth; from Missouri.
Ramsey Mrs. Martha, widow; U. P.; from Ohio.
Ramsey W. T. carpenter; rep; U. P.; from O.
Randall Mrs. D. A. widow; from New York.

Randall E. A. baker; rep; born Illinois.
Randall Mrs. —. widow; Cath; from Ireland.
RANKIN GEORGE C. Local Editor Monmouth *Atlas;* born in Warren Co., Ill., Aug. 29, 1850; Rep; holds office of City Clerk; Secretary of Warren Co. Agricultural Society; Secretary of Monmouth Driving Park Association.
RANKIN N. A. Was born in Henderson, Ky., Feb. 1, 1809; married Martha Halloway, Dec. 25, 1834; had ten children, seven of whom are living; removed to Springfield, Ill., in 1834, and to Shelbyville, Ill., in 1843; came to Monmouth in Sept., 1845, and for fifteen years was one of the most prominent business men in the city and county; was a member of Monmouth's first City Council, being elected an Alderman in 1852; was elected Mayor of Monmouth in 1859 and 1860; was Asst. U. S. Assessor of Internal Revenue in 1863, and for several years; was the first President of the Warren Co. Library and Reading Room; was President of the Warren Co. Agricultural Society in 1864, also in 1865; was elected a member of the Co. Board of Supervisors in 1869 and 1870; has served several years as School Director, Justice of the Peace, etc.; has been an Elder in the Christian Church for many years; politically is a Rep.
Rankin Wm. H. furniture; dem; from Ky.
Rathmaw Crist. cigar maker; ind; from Germany.
Raymond A. F. carpenter; rep; from Ohio.
Raymond E. H. carpenter; rep; from Ohio.
Reed Geo B. moulder; dem; from Ohio.
Reed Mrs. L. M. widow; Bapt; from Mass.
Reed Omic, carpenter; rep; Meth; from Ohio.
Reed Robert, laborer; rep; Prot; from Pennsylvania.
Reed Samuel, carpenter; rep; from Penn.
Redmon John, laborer; from Ireland.
Regnier Felix, harness maker; dem; from Ohio.
Reid Edward, carpenter; rep; Meth.
Reid Prof. E. F. college professor; rep; U. P.; from Ireland.
Reid Geo. employed in agricultural shops.
Reichard J. T. merchant; dem; from Md.
Reimer Jacob, laborer; rep; from Denmark.
Rice T. H. retired; rep; Presb; from Ky.
Rice Wm. A. clerk 1st Nat. Bank; rep; Presb; born Illinois.
Richardson Mark S. blacksmith; rep; Bapt.
Rickel Mary, Meth; from Ohio.
Rickstar G. L. employed by Plow Co.; rep; from Pennsylvania.
Riggs John P. laborer; dem; born Illinois.
Ritchey John H. brick mason; dem; Presb; from Pennsylvania.

Roadhouse Colan, engineer; rep; from Canada.
Roadhouse L. machinist; rep; from Canada.
Roberts Peyton, insurance agt.; rep; Meth; born Illinois.
Robertson W. A. salesman; rep; from New York.
Robinson Hugh, engineer Weir Plow Co.; rep; from Kentucky.
Robinson John, carpenter; rep; U. P.; from Ohio.
Robinson L. D. farmer; rep; from Virginia.
Robinson Moses, farmer; dem; from Ky.
Robinson W. A. carpenter; rep; U. P.; from Kentucky.
Rock Alex. M. blacksmith; rep; from Ohio.
Rogers Geo. W. teacher; rep; born Illinois.
Rogers John, painter; rep; Presb; from Virginia.
Rogers Prof. T. H. college professor; rep; Presb; from Indiana.
Romig W. A. tinner; Presb; rep; from Pennsylvania.
Root William, artist; boards at Baldwin House; rep; born Illinois.
Rosenzweig F. butcher; rep; Luth; from Germany.
Ross Mrs. Robt. widow; U. P.; from Ohio.
Ruebert Wm. tinker.
Rugh J. C. engineer; rep; from Penn.
Rulon D. G. painter; rep; Meth; from Ind.
Rulon H. M. engineer; dem; Meth; from Indiana.
Rulon J. F. painter; rep; Meth; from Ind.
Rupp Wm. P. city clerk and weigh master; rep; Epis; from Pennsylvania.
Russel A. C. coal miner; rep; Presb; from Scotland.
RUSSELL DAVID, Superintendent at the Monmouth Manufacturing and Mining Co.; Monmouth; born in Scotland, 1820; came to this country in 1849; and to this Co. in 1871; married Miss A. Watson in 1869; she was born in Scotland.
Russel R. L. clerk; rep; Presb; from Scotland.

Salline N. shoemaker; rep; Luth; from Sweden.
Saltzman John, tobacconist; rep; Epis; from Germany.
Samson Geo. A. carpenter; rep; Meth; from England.
Sandine August, laborer; rep; Luth; from Sweden.
Sanstron Nilson, carpenter; rep; Luth; from Sweden.
Savage Charles S. teamster; rep; from Iowa.
Savage Ed. clerk for Babcock; boards at Baldwin House; rep; from Maryland.

Savage Henry, retired; rep; U. P.; from Pennsylvania.
Savage Henry S. student; rep; from Iowa.
Saville Chas. W. painter; rep; U. P.; from Ohio.
Saville John, blacksmith; rep; U. P.; from Virginia.
Saville J. F. musician; rep; U. P.; born Illinois.
Schall W. P. restaurant; rep; U. P.; from Pennsylvania.
Schussler Geo. farmer; rep; from Penn.
Scott David, blacksmith; rep; from Penn.
Scott Frank, employed by Plow Co.; dem; from Pennsylvania.
Scott Geo. painter; rep; from Pennsylvania.
Scott James, merchant; rep; Presb; from Virginia.
Scott James A. merchant; rep; Presb; born Illinois.
Scott J. W. grocer; dem; from New York.
Scott John, D.D., professor Monmouth College; rep; U. P.; from Scotland.
Scott Mrs Mary, Presb; from Pennsylvania.
Scott N. A. wholesale grocer; rep; born Ills.
Scott Robt. F. merchant; rep; Presb; born Illinois.
Scott Wm. P. laborer; dem; from Indiana.
Scott Washington, painter; rep; from Penn.
Scott Wm. painter; rep; from Penn.
Scott Walter B. merchant; rep; Presb; born Illinois.
See Aaron, employee Plow Works; dem; from New York.
Seerist Mrs. M. B. widow; Presb; from Penn.
Sexton John, laborer, works at Pottery; dem; Cath; from Ireland.

SEXTON W. H. County Clerk; born in Penn., June, 1837; Rep; he came to this State in 1857, and to this Co. 1866; enlisted in the 83d I. V. I., and served three years; has held offices of City Clerk, Deputy Circuit Clerk, and Deputy County Clerk, previous to his election to office of County Clerk; married Marian Burlingame, in 1873; she was born in New York; has two children, one son and one daughter.

Shaw Alex. grocer; dem; from Virginia.
Shaw Mrs. A. J. widow; Presb; from Ohio.
Sheldon F. M. laborer; rep; from Wis.
Shellenbarger Wm. H. carpenter; dem; Meth; from Pennsylvania.
Sheibel Morris, barber; rep; from Germany.
Sheridan Geo. painter; rep.
Shehi John N. teamster; rep; from Ky.
Shields John, blacksmith; rep; U. P.; from Pennsylvania.
Shields Wm. laborer; dem; Cath; from Ireland.

Shields Wm. blacksmith; rep; from Penn.
Shippy L. M. tailor; dem; from Ohio.
Shippy Mack, baker; dem; from Ohio.

SHOEMAKER C. D. Mechanic; born in Chemung, N. Y., Nov. 15, 1828; came to this Co. in 1851; Rep; enlisted Aug. 5, 1862, Co. A, 83d Regt. I. V. I.; remained in service till July 5, 1865; married Sophia Hoerner, Dec. 28, 1854; three children, William H., Charles Jay and Effie Sophia.

Shoemaker Elis, Meth; from Penn.
Shoemaker Jas. carpenter; dem; from Penn.
Shoemaker Samuel, carpenter; dem; Presb; from Penn.
Shores Wm. farmer; dem; from Ohio.
Shultz August, employee Weir Plow Works; from Germany.
Shultz Fred. employee Weir Plow Co.; dem; from Germany.
Shultz R. H. retired; dem; from Ky.
Shultz Wm. M. druggist and physician; dem; from Kentucky.
Sickman Geo. stock raiser; rep; Chris; from New York.
Signor Geo. salesman; rep; born Illinois.
Sinnickson Henry, plow-maker; Luth; from Denmark.
Sipher J. W. lumberman; rep; from New York.
Sipher Moses, carpenter; rep; Meth; from New York.
Sistrom Chas. cigar-maker; rep; Sweden.
Skinner E. laborer; rep; Bapt; born Ill.
Skinner Moses, farmer; rep; U. P.; from Tennessee.
Skinner Pleasant, farmer; rep; Bapt; from Tennessee.
Skinner Samuel, barber; rep; Meth.
Sloan Geo. P. farmer; dem; from Tenn.
Sloats Joseph, cattle dealer; dem; from Ohio.
Slocumb Lewis, painter; bds. Baldwin House; rep; from New York.
Smalley Geo. employee brick yard; dem; born Illinois.
Smilie D. B. laborer; dem; Meth; from Pennsylvania.
Smilie David H. student; born Illinois.
Smilie Geo. W. laborer; dem; Meth; born Illinois.
Smilie Jo. G. laborer; dem; from Penn.
Smiley John, laborer; dem; born Illinois.
Smiley Wm. B. carpenter; dem; from Penn.
Smith Amanda J. Meth; from Ohio.
Smith Chas. T. cook at Baldwin House; rep; from New Hampshire.
Smith Clayborn, laborer; rep; Bapt; from Tennessee.
Smith Mrs. Elizabeth, widow; from Ohio.

Smith Geo. laborer; rep.
Smith Geo. laborer; rep; from Tennessee.
Smith Geo. A. employee Wier Plow Co.; rep; from New Hampshire.
Smith Rev. J. D. pastor M. E. Ch.; Ind; from New Jersey.
Smith J. W. baggage-master R. R.; rep; Presb; from New Hampshire.
Smith James, carpenter; rep; born Ill.
Smith Jas. H. painter; dem; Meth; from Ohio.
Smith Jno. laborer; dem; from Ireland.
Smith Joshua, carpenter; rep; from New York.
Smith Lee H. painter; dem; Meth; born Ill.
Smith Munson, carpenter; rep; from New York.
Smith Peter, blacksmith; rep; Luth; from Denmark.
Smith Samuel, farmer; rep; from Ky.
Smith Samuel, Wier Plow Works; rep; born Illinois.
Smith S. W. printer; dem; Lib; from Ohio.
Smith Wm. drug merchant; rep; born Ill.
Smith W. laborer; dem; from Penn.
Smith Wm. F. druggist; rep; Bapt; from Kentucky.
SMITH WILLIS P. Dentist; born in Otsego Co., N. Y., Aug. 31, 1821; he came to this State in 1861; has held office of Alderman; married Miss Harmony Hubbard, 1846; she was born in N. Y.; has two children; lost one.
SMITH & DUNBAR, Druggists and Chemists; this house was established in 1835, by W. F. Smith, being the first in this line in the Co.; they are dealers in drugs, medicines, paints, oils, glass, etc.
Snyder Geo. W. attorney and notary public; Rep; from Pennsylvania.
Sobey Wm. blacksmith; dem; from Engl'd.
Soderstrom Jacob, boot and shoemaker; ind; Luth; from Sweden.
Solomon Gus. clerk A. Kliner; from Prussia.
Soule M. C. lumber-dealer; rep; Meth; from New York.
Spiegel Hermann, cigar-maker; from Iowa.
Spriggs J. A. book-keeper; rep; Presb; from Pennsylvania.
Spriggs G. H. druggist; rep; Presb; from Pennsylvania.
Spriggs J. S., M. D. druggist; rep; Presb; from Pennsylvania.
Spriggs J. W. druggist; rep; from Penn.
SPRIGGS & BROTHER, Druggists; came to this Co. 1857; have been established in business twenty years.
Stack John, R. R. employee; dem; Cath; from Ireland.

Stapp Frank, farmer; dem; from France.
Stapp Guy, clerk Scott & Sons; rep; Bapt; born Illinois.
Stark Gust, employee Wier Plow Co.; rep; Luth; from Sweden.
Steen J. W. student; rep; Presb; from Ohio.
Steen Miss M. R.; U. P.; from Penn.
Stedman Nelson, foreman Wier Plow Works; rep; from Michigan.
Stedman N. painter; rep; from New York.
Stein John, cigar-maker; rep; from Sweden.
Stephens John, laborer; Ind; born Ill.
Stephens Mrs. Martha, widow; Chris; from Kentucky.
Stephenson Mrs. M. L. widow; from Penn.
Stephenson Sam'l, retired; rep; U. P.; from Kentucky.
Sternberger John, cigar-maker; rep; from Pennsylvania.
Sterett Margaret D.; U. P.; from Virginia.
Stevens Chas. painter; rep; Bapt; from New Hampshire.
Stevens David R. contractor and builder; rep; from New York.
Stevens Eugene W. carriage painter; rep; Bapt; from Massachusetts.
Stevenson John, farmer; rep; from Illinois.
Stevenson Joseph, banker; rep; U. P.; from Ohio.
Stevenson J. H. restaurant; from Ohio.
Stevenson Robert M. bookkeeper in First National Bank; rep; U. P.; from Ohio.
Stevenson Rob. teller in First National Bank.
Stevenson Robt. E., employed in Weir Plow Works; rep; from Pennsylvania.
Stewart Mrs. Elizabeth, widow; Chris; from Maryland.
Stewart Isaac, clerk for Baldwin & Hawkins.
Stewart James H. attorney; dem; Presb; from Kentucky.
Stewart Mrs. S. M.; U. P.; from Ohio.
Stimson F. agent American Express Co.; rep; from New York.
Stitt Miss I. milliner; U. P.; from Ireland.
Stoddard H. G. painter; dem; from Ohio.
Stokes Hiram, laborer; rep; Bapt; from Virginia.
Strang Mrs. Janet, widow; U. P.; from N. Y.
Streeter Albert, laborer; rep; Bapt; from New York.
Streeter D. carpenter; rep; from New York.
Streeter William, carpenter; rep; from New York.
Strickler Samuel, carpenter; rep; Meth; from Pennsylvania.
Strimmell Thomas W. carpenter; rep; from Pennsylvania.
Struthers John, coach-maker; rep; U. P.; from Virginia.

Sullivan George, tinner; dem; Cath; from New York.

Sullivan Jeremiah, hardware; dem; from Maryland.

Sullivan Wm. H. grinder at Weir Plow Works; dem; from Vermont.

Surdberg Peter, employee Weir Plow Works; from Sweden.

SWAIN A. H. Editor and Proprietor of Monmouth *Review;* Monmouth; born in Fayette Co., Penn., Oct. 13, 1828; came to this Co. in 1855; Dem; Prot; owns house and lot, with paper, valued at $5,000; Mr. S. established the *Review* in 1855, and has issued it regularly each week for the last twenty-two years; married Miss Mary L. Brewer, June, 1856; one daughter, Mary.

Swanson Andrew, tailor and cutter; rep; from Sweden.

Swanson Nels, organs and musical instruments; rep; Luth; from Sweden.

Swanson S. musical instructor; rep; Luth; from Sweden.

Swiler C. farmer; rep; from Pennsylvania.

Swiler Daniel, plasterer; rep; Ch. of God; from Pennsylvania.

Swinney D. G. clerk; born Illinois.

Swinney Ephriam S. retired; dem; from Ohio.

Swinney E. S. ex-Co. Clerk; dem; from O.

Swinney J. Milt. clerk; dem; born Illinois.

TAYLOR REV. HARRY, pastor First Bapt. church; rep; from Virginia.

Taylor W. M. druggist; rep; born Illinois.

Taylor Wm. R. employed in Weir Plow Works; dem; born Illinois.

Templeton D. C. travelling agent of Weir Plow Co.; rep; U. P.; born Illinois.

Templeton Jno. A. travelling agent of Weir Plow Co; rep; U. P.; from Pennsylvania.

Tharp Joseph, teacher; rep; Meth; from O.

Thomas George, farmer; rep; from New York.

Thomas John, teamster; rep; U. P.; from Tennessee.

Thomas Thaddeus, laborer; rep; from Va.

Thompson John G. mason; rep; from Ohio.

Thomson Mrs. W. J., widow; U. P.; from Ohio.

Thomson Wm. C. farmer; rep; from Penn.

THUSON MARTIN, Livery and Feed Stable; Monmouth; born in Denmark, Dec. 24, 1847; came to this Co. in 1869; rep; Luth; always well supplied with good teams; charges reasonable.

Timonson T. laborer; rep; Luth; Sweden.

Toal Edward, laborer; dem; Cath; from Ireland.

Todd Dennis, painter; rep; Bapt; from Iowa.

Todd Miles, cooper; rep; Bapt; from Ohio.

Torman John W. switchman; rep; born Illinois.

Tourly, John, laborer; dem; Presb; from Germany.

Torley John, employee brick yard; dem; from Germany.

Townley Mrs. Eliza B.; U. P; from New Jersey.

TRACY A. H. Teacher; Monmouth; born in Erie, Pa., June 18, 1821; came to this Co. in April, 1854; Rep; Presb; commenced teaching as a profession at the age of twenty-two years; after three years' service, he was elected as Examiner and Superintendent in Erie Co., Pa., which office he held for five years; then came to this State and settled in Monmouth; began his work of teaching here in Public Schools, May 8, 1854; six years of successful labor followed; served one term as School Commissioner of this Co.; married Miss Harriet E. Shirwin, March 11, 1852; have six children.

TRESHAM W. D. Dealer in Boots and Shoes; Monmouth; born in Virginia, April, 1845; came to this Co. in 1867; has been engaged in the boot and shoe trade ten years; married Anna M. Swinney in 1871; she was born in Warren Co.; has two children.

Trulson Nels, laborer; rep; Luth; from Sweden.

Tucker Mrs. E. J.; National Hotel; Presb; from Indiana.

Tuckey Richard, laborer; dem; Meth; from England.

TURNBULL DAVID, deceased; Farmer; born in Green Co., Ohio, Oct. 18, 1809; came to this Co. in 1833; Rep; U. P.; married Miss Nancy Mitchell, 1831, who was born in Pennsylvania; they had twelve children, of whom John M., Ann E., Sarah I., Mary A., William W., David A., Thomas B. and Nannie J. were spared to assume for themselves the duties of life; Mr. Turnbull was all his life an active citizen, a zealous worker, both in Church and State, and while he could not be called an office seeker, held almost continuously some needful but unprofitable office, from 1835 until near his death, which occurred May 10, 1871; he served two terms as Sheriff of the Co.; was several years Chairman of the Board of Supervisors, and acted as Assistant Provost Marshal most of the years of the late war; having lived in Warren Co. from the time he came West in 1833, he was known by most of the citizens of the Co., and died enjoying their respect as fully as a positive, independent citizen could do.

Turnbull John, merchant; dem; U. P.; from Ohio.

TURNBULL JOHN M. Postmaster; Monmouth; born in Ohio, July 23, 1833; Rep; U. P.; he came to this Co., Oct.,

1853; enlisted in the 36th I. V. I., and was wounded and lost a leg before Atlanta; has held office of Postmaster since 1865; married Anna P. Orr, of Washington Co., Iowa, in Oct., 1854; has four children.

Turner James M. farmer; rep; Chris; from Massachusetts.

Turtellotte L. O. Dep. Co. clerk; rep; Univ; from Massachusetts.

URE REV. D. M., U. P. minister; rep; from Scotland.

VAN HOOREBEKE A. G. importer; from Belgium.

Van Coorebeke L. M. horse dealer; from France.

Vantill Charles, painter; rep; from New Jersey.

Vanskyke Henry, brick maker; rep; from Ohio.

Vantine Charles, painter; rep; from New Jersey.

Vantyne Peter, painter; rep; from N. J.

Varwick J. W. painter; dem; from Iowa.

Vine James, farmer; rep; Presb; from New York.

Volander Joseph, teamster; dem; Germany.

WALLBER D. W. boot and shoemaker; ind; Luth; from Switzerland.

Wakefield Mrs. May; widow; Presb; from Pennsylvania.

Walker Miss Ellen; U. P.; from Ohio.

Walker Thos. W. attorney; dem; born Ill.

Walker Wm. physician; dem; Presb; from Virginia.

Walker Wm. attorney; rep; born Illinois.

WALKER WM. J. & A. T. Attorneys; born in Spring Grove tp., Warren Co.; they give careful and prompt attention to business entrusted to their care. W. J. Walker is also a Justice of the Peace.

Wallace Daniel, plasterer; rep; from Ky.

WALLACE DAVID A., D. D. President of Monmouth College; born in Guernsey Co., O., June 16, 1826; came to this Co. in 1856; rep; U. P.; graduated at Miami University, Ohio, Aug. 13, 1846; licensed to preach in the A. R. (now U. P.), April, 1849; ordained in Fall River, Mass., in June, 1851; moved to Boston in Feb., 1853, and to Monmouth, Sept., 1856, and became President of the College; was for a time Pastor, both of the First and Second U. P. Churches of Monmouth, and of the Henderson Church; married Martha J. Findly, Aug. 27, 1851, of New Concord, O.; five children.

Wallace David, clerk; rep; from Ohio.

Wallace E. E. hardware; rep; born Ill.

Wallace Geo. laborer; rep; from Tenn.

Wallace G. G. student; rep; U. P.; from Ohio.

WALLACE JAMES H. Physician; born in Penn., Nov. 16, 1834; lived in Ohio twenty-two years; came to this State in 1876; is associated with Dr. Crawford in the practice of his profession; married Miss S. J. Troutman in 1862; she was born in Wayne Co., O.; has six children.

Wallace J. C. restaurant; rep; from Ohio.

WALLACE JOHN F. Books and Picture Frames; Monmouth; born in Massachusetts; came to this State in 1856; he married Miss Sadie E. Ulmer in 1871; she was born in Penn.; has two children.

Wallace Jno. F. engineer; rep; U. P.; from Massachusetts.

Wallace Mrs. Mary; U. P.; from Ohio.

Wallace Thos. R. student; rep; U. P.; from Ohio.

Walters David, teamster; dem; from Penn.

Ward Enos, carpenter; rep; U. P.; from Kentucky.

Warren Mrs. L. A.; Meth; from New York.

WATKINS JOHN, Employee of the Monmouth Manufacturing and Mining Co.; born in Ohio, Sept., 1844; Rep; Lib; he came to this Co. in 1872, and has been in the employ of this Company since that time.

Watt A. C. teacher; rep; Presb; from Penn.

Watt John, photographer; rep; U. P.; from Pennsylvania.

WAUGH O. K. Veterinary Surgeon; Monmouth; born in New York, March 14, 1818; came to this State in 1836, and to this Co. in 1866; has practiced his profession for 16 years; his wife was Miss A. D. Beckstead, and was born in Canada; has nine children.

Webb V. C. plasterer; rep; from Ohio.

Webb Wm. M. police constable; rep; Bapt; from Pennsylvania.

Webster H. A. butcher; rep; from Penn.

WEBSTER J. R. Physician; born in Penn., 1835; came to this Co. in 1837; has been practicing the past 20 years; he married Miss S. Nye in 1869; she was born in Massachusetts; has two children.

Webster W. H. carpenter.

Webster W. L. merchant; rep; Meth; from Ohio.

Wedlein Gus, shoemaker; rep; Luth; from Sweden.

Weede N. R. physician; rep; U. P.; from Pennsylvania.

Weeks Thos. C. farmer; rep; U. P.; from Ohio.

Weir F. M. book-keeper; rep; U. P.; born Illinois.

Weir Frances, U. P.; from Kentucky.

Weir Jas. B. moulder; rep; from Ohio.

Weir Paulina M., U. P.; from Ohio.
Weir W. S. Weir Plow Co.; rep; U.P.; from Ohio.
Welch P. railroad employee; dem; Cath; from Ireland.
Wells G. V. salesman; dem; born Illinois.
Welsan P. tailor; rep; from Sweden.
Westine F. harness maker; rep; from Iowa.
Westerfield Geo. W. blacksmith; dem; born Illinois.
Westerfield Isaac, wagon maker; rep; born Illinois.
Westerfield James, wagon maker; rep; Presb; from Ohio.
Whisler John R. farmer; dem; from Penn.
Whitcomb Jno. farmer; rep; from New York.
White Alfred, drayman; dem; from Ky.
Whitenack Wm. insurance agt.; rep; Meth; from Kentucky.
Whitney Moses P. railroading; rep; from Virginia.
Whitten Jno. clerk; rep; U.P.; from Ireland.
Wicken Thos. farmer; rep; U. P.; from England.
Wiencker W. employee Weir Plow Co.; from Germany.
Wilcott W. carriage maker; dem; from Ohio.
Wilcox Chas. carpenter; dem; from N. Y.
Wilcox O. D. stone mason; dem; from New York.
Wiley James A. student; rep; U. P.; from Ohio.
Wiley John, carpenter; rep; U. P.; from Kentucky.
WILEY MISS MAGGIE L. teacher; Monmouth; born in Ohio; came to this Co. in 1869; has been engaged in teaching nine years, the past four years as Principal of the West Ward School.
Wiley Wm. T. musician; rep; U. P.; from Ohio.
Wilder Charles A. pattern-maker; rep; from Ohio.
Williams Benj. employed in Weir Plow Works; dem; born Illinois.
Williams D. H. painter; rep; Meth; born New York.
Williams Mrs. E. J.; Chris; from Ohio.
Williams James, cook; rep; Meth; from District Columbia.
Williams James H. boots and shoes; rep; from Canada.
Williams Miss M. J. dressmaker; Presb; from Virginia.
WILLETS ELIAS, Attorney; Monmouth; born in Wayne Co., Ind., Aug. 12,
1826; rep; Prot.; he came to this State in 1851, and to this Co. in 1862; holds office of Judge of the Co. Court; married Elizabeth Fish in 1850; she was born in Baltimore, Md.; has three children; lost four.
Willson Mrs. Jane, widow; Bapt; born Ill.
Willson James, clerk in grocery; born Ill.
Wilson George, laborer; rep; from Iowa.
Wilson Prof. J. H. college professor; rep; U. P.; from Indiana.
Wilson James H. mason; Ind; from Ky.
Wilson Jane, dressmaker; Meth; from Ohio.
WILSON ROBERT A. Bookseller; Monmouth; born in Ohio, March 14, 1850; came to this Co. in 1871; Rep; U. P.; established himself in business in 1875, and is a dealer in books, wall paper, picture frames, etc.
Winbigler Miss Julia, U. P.; from Indiana.
Wise James, expressman; rep; Bapt.
Wise Levi H. laborer; rep; from Indiana.
Witt Geo. R. butcher; dem; born Illinois.
Witt H. laborer; dem; from Tennessee.
Wolfe W G, book-keeper; rep; Presb; from Pennsylvania.
Wonder Jacob, retired; rep; Meth; from Pennsylvania.
Wonder John, merchant; rep; from Penn.
Woods Geo. D. farmer; rep; from Penn.
Woods Mrs. Jane P. widow; Presb; from Pennsylvania.
Wood S. retired; rep; from Maine.
Woodward Dr. N. S. physician; dem; from Pennsylvania.
Worrell Milton, machinist; rep; Cong; from Pennsylvania.

YATES MRS. A. W. widow; Bapt; from Tennessee.
Yoder Chas. tinner; rep; from Penn.
Young Eliza, Chris; from Pennsylvania.
Young Mrs. Isabella, U. P.; from Ohio.
Young J. P. huckster; dem; from Sweden.
Young Warren, harness-maker; Ind; from New York.
Young W. B. cashier Monmouth National Bank; rep; from Ohio.
Young Wm. H. carpenter; dem; from Penn.
Young W. W. author; dem; born Illinois.

ZIGLER A. hostler; rep; from South Carolina.
Zimmerman Oscar, barber; bds. at Baldwin House; rep; from Germany.
Zimmington Ed. laborer; rep; from Iowa.
Zoeller Peter, brewer; rep; Cath; from Germany.

MONMOUTH CITY BUSINESS DIRECTORY.

Babcock Draper, Wholesale and Retail Dealer in Dry Goods and Carpets, Fancy Goods, Notions, &c.

Baldwin & Sons, Proprietors "Baldwin House."

Barnum O. S. Wholesale and Retail Dealer in Hardware and Cutlery, Leather and Rubber Belting, Farming Tools, Pumps, Plows, Cultivators, Reapers, Mowers, Threshing Machines, Wood Spouting, Wagons, Buggies, and Carriages.

Blackburn C. E. Manufacturer and Retail Dealer in Harness and Harness Hardware.

Breed G. H., M. D., Homœopathic Physician.

Clark Jno. S, Editor and Proprietor Monmouth *Atlas.* George C. Rankin, Local Editor.

Davidson Jas. Livery, Feed and Sale Stables; first-class rigs on short notice; Carriages for Funerals, Receptions, etc.

Diffenbaugh S. Confectioner; Home-made Candies, Notions, etc.

Dunn Bros., Proprietors City Marble Works; Dealers in American and Foreign Marble.

First National Bank, Organized in 1863; Capital $75,000; Surplus $50,000.

Findley David E. Grocer and Baker.

Foster J. C. Photographer.

Gibson & Tresham, Dealers in Fine Boots and Shoes; Ladies' and Gents' Boots and Shoes made to order.

Gayer F. Brewer.

Glenn & Kirkpatrick, Attorneys at Law.

Graham & Clark, (successors to H. D. Wood & Co.) Fashionable Hatters, and Dealers in Gentlemen's Furnishing Goods.

Good P. D. Clothing Dealer.

Hamilton S. M., M. D., Physician.

Harvey & Schultz, Druggists and Apothecaries; Pure Drugs, Patent Medicines, Imported Perfumeries; Pure Wines and Liquors for Medicinal Use, Fancy and Toilet Articles, etc.; Prescriptions Compounded.

Hershey J. M. Botanic Physician.

Hollaway Robert, Attorney.

Irwin & Leins, Merchant Tailors.

Kidder Almon, Attorney at Law.

Kyler Thos. S. Proprietor Exchange Hotel.

Monmouth Mining and Manufacturing Co. Daniel D. Parry, Prest.; H. C. Beckwith, Secy.; J. S. Spriggs, Treas.; Miners of Coal and Clay, and Manufacturers of Stone Sewer Pipe from 3 to 24 inches in diameter; all sizes of Elbows, Branches and Traps; also Paving and Drain Tile.

Monmouth National Bank. Capital $100,000; Surplus $20,000; Wm. Hanna, Prest.; Almon Kidder, V. Prest.; W. B. Young, Cashier.

Matthews John W. Attorney at Law, and Master in Chancery; office in Smith's new building.

Moore Mrs. S. J. Proprietor Railroad Eating House, crossing of C., B. & Q. and R., R. I. & St. L. Railroads; R., R. I. & St. L. Passenger Trains stop 20 minutes for Meals at this House; Good Beds and Airy Rooms. N. B.—Travelers can secure Tickets and have Baggage transferred to the C., B. & Q. R. R, at this crossing, and avoid 'Bus transportation.

Morgan Jno. T. Attorney.

O. J. Barnum
HARDWARE & IMPLEMENTS
MONMOUTH ILL.

Norcross J. G. & Bro. Dealers in Farm Machinery, Seeds, Flour, Lime, Cement, etc.
Norcross Wm. C. Attorney.
Nusbaum Moses, Clothing Dealer.
Palmer Wm. Proprietor Commercial House.
Peacock Theo. G. Attorney.
Phelps S. S. Jr., Livery, Feed and Sale Stable.
Porter Jno. Attorney.
Smith W. P. Dentist.
Smith & Dunbar. Druggists and Chemists.
Spriggs & Bro., Dealers in Drugs, Medicines, Chemicals, Dye Stuffs, Paints, Oils, Glass, Putty, Perfumery and Fancy Articles, Patent Medicines, etc.

Swain A. H. Editor and Proprietor Monmouth *Review.*
Second National Bank of Monmouth, Chauncy Hardin, Prest.
Thuson Martin, Livery and Feed Stable.
Walker Wm. J. & A. T. Attorneys at Law.
Wallace J. H., M. D., Physician.
Wallace John F. (successor to Drennen & Wallace,) Books, Stationery and Wall Paper; Main St.
Waugh O. K. Veterinary Surgeon.
Webster J. R. Physician.
Willets Elias, Attorney.
Wilson R. A. Dealer in Books, Wall Paper, Picture Frames, Bibles, Albums, Pocket Books, etc.

MONMOUTH TOWNSHIP.

ALEXANDER CHARLES L. farmer, lives with his mother; Sec. 9; rep; U. P.
Alexander T. W. farmer, lives with his mother; Sec. 9; rep; U. P.
Alexander John W. farmer, lives with his mother; Sec. 9; rep; U. P.
ALEXANDER ELIZABETH D. Farming; Sec. 9; P.O. Monmouth; born in Chester District, S. C., Aug. 8, 1820; came to this Co. in 1854; U. P.; owns 160 acres, value $8,000; married John W. Alexander, Dec. 1, 1842; he was born in Blount Co., Tenn.; he died Nov. 21, 1863; has six children, four sons and two daughters; lost two.
ALLISON MATTHEW E. Farmer; Sec. 27; P. O. Monmouth; born in Washington Co., Penn., Oct. 31, 1818; Rep; U. P.; owns 160 acres, value $11,200; he came to this State in 1855, and to Warren Co. in 1865; married Miss Diana Miller in 1849; she was born in Washington Co., Penn.; has four children, Thomas, Mary M., Omie and Alpheus.
Anderson H. A. miller; Sec. 6; P. O. Monmouth; rep; Cong.
Andrews Talbot, farmer; Sec. 6; P. O. Monmouth; rep; Lib; born Warren Co.
Avenell C. P. farmer; Sec. 6; P. O. Monmouth; rep; U. P.

Avenell Thomas, farmer; Sec. 6; P. O. Monmouth; rep; U. P.; from England.
BARNES E. V. A. farmer; Sec. 28; P. O. Monmouth; rep; Presb.
Baymount James, farmer; Sec. 8; P.O. Monmouth; rep; Presb.
Baymount Nathan P. farmer; Sec. 8; P. O. Monmouth; rep; Presb.
Beach George, farmer; Sec. 30; P. O. Monmouth; rep.
Beach Mrs. L. C. widow; farmer; Sec. 30; P. O. Monmouth.
Berry George, farmer; Sec. 17; P. O. Monmouth; rep.
BERTSCHEY F. E. Farmer; Sec. 1; P. O. Gerlaw; born in Germany, March 16, 1848; Dem; Lib; rents 120 acres of J. H. Denison; he came to this country in 1852, and to this Co. in 1865; married Ella J. Lair in Nov., 1870; she was born in Warren Co.; has two children.
BOAL ELIJAH, Carpenter; Sec. 25; P. O. Monmouth; born in York Co., Pa., March 8, 1816; Dem; Luth; came to this Co. in 1854; has held office of School Director; married Susan Spidel, June 13, 1839; she was born in Cumberland Co., Penn., Nov. 2, 1816; has six children,

Catharine, Jacob, John, Mary, Emanuel O. and Fred.

Boal Emanuel O. farmer, rents of J. B. Meginnis; Sec. 25; P.O. Monmouth; dem.

BOAL JACOB, Farmer; Sec. 25; P.O. Monmouth; born in Cumberland Co., Pa., Nov. 4, 1841; came to this Co. in 1854; Dem; Luth; rents of J. B. Meginnis; came with his parents to this Co. when 13 years of age; married Emaline McKenny, June 29, 1868; she was born in Virginia; has two children, Ella and James C.

BOSWORTH ADISON, Farmer; Sec. 35; P. O. Monmouth; born in Trumbull Co., O., Feb. 24, 1827; Rep; Chris; owns 120 acres, value $8,400; he came to this State and Co. in 1850; married Miss Margaret Whitman in 1854; she was born in Warren Co.; has six children, Horace W., Lena M., Lizzie, Grace, Florence and Leonard; lost three.

Boyd R.H. retired; Sec. 28; P.O. Monmouth; rep; U. P.

Boulby R. D. plasterer; Sec. 32; P. O. Monmouth; rep.

Brewster Isaac, laborer for R. Wallace; Sec. 36; dem; Meth.

BRIGGS JOHN F. Farmer; Sec. 6; P. O. Monmouth; born in Penn. in 1827; Rep; Lib; rents 160 acres of J.T. Morgan; he came to this Co. in 1868; he enlisted in the 51st Ohio Inf. and served three years; he married Susanna Cotland in 1854; she was born in Ohio in 1838, and died April 4, 1877; has six children, William, George, Mary, Sanclot, Jessie and Chace; lost two.

BROOKS CHAPMAN V. Farmer and Stock Raiser; Sec. 26; P. O. Monmouth; born in Jefferson Co., N. Y., Nov. 22, 1822; Rep; Presb; owns 400 acres, value $28,000; he came to this State and Co. in 1850; has held offices of Supervisor and School Director; married Jane M. Weakley in 1850; she was born in Cumberland Co., Penn.; has six children, Joseph W., Priscilla F., Willis J., Chapman V., Albert R. and Milton S.

Brown Joseph, works for C. Hardin; Sec. 28; P. O. Monmouth.

Brown Oliver P. farmer, rents of F. Gayer; Sec. 9; P. O. Monmouth; dem; Presb.

BRUNER ISAAC, Farmer; Sec 11; P. O. Monmouth; born in Tenn. Nov. 30, 1818; Dem; Meth; owns 81 acres, value $4,000; he came to Ill. in 1829, lived in Sangamon Co. 12 years, and Knox Co. 23 years; came to this Co. in 1864; married Sarah J. Ragland in 1846; she was born in Ky; has four children, two sons and two daughters; lost one.

BRUNER PETER, Farmer; Sec. 17; P. O. Monmouth; born in Breckenridge Co., Ky., May 10, 1814; Rep; Lib; owns 240 acres, value $14,500; he came to this State and Co. in 1836; has held office of School Director; married Sallie Claycomb, Sept. 20, 1838; she was born in Breckenridge Co., Ky., June 11, 1817; has ten children, seven sons and three daughters; lost two.

Bruner W. H. farmer; Sec. 1; P. O. Monmouth; rep; Lib.

Burford Ames, farmer; Sec. 4; P. O. Monmouth; rep; U. P.; from Pennsylvania.

BUTLER P. FRANK & RALPH O. Farmers; Sec. 36; P. O. Monmouth; Dem; Meth; own 120 acres, value $7,200; their parents moved from Warren Co., Ky., in 1829, and settled in Warren Co., Ill., where both were born.

CALDWELL JOHN F. farmer, lives with his father; P. O. Monmouth; rep; U.P.

CALDWELL JOHN W. Farmer and Stock Raiser; Sec. 19; P. O. Monmouth; born in Muskingum Co., Ohio, June 4, 1813; Rep; U. P.; owns 190 acres, value 19,000; he came to this State and Co. May 4, 1830, and is one of the oldest settlers; married Sarah A. Conner in 1837; she was born in Rockbridge Co., Va., 1817; has one son, John F. Caldwell.

CAMERON JOHN, Farmer; Sec. 7; P. O. Monmouth; born in Co. Tyrone, Ireland; Rep; U. P.; owns 48 acres, value $2,400; came to this country in 1836; served ten years in the ordinance department of the Regular Army; was in the Mexican War, and in 13 general engagements; married Phœbe Higgins in 1852; has six children, three sons and three daughters; lost two.

Cargill David E. farmer and renter; Sec. 36; P. O. Cameron; dem; Chris.

Carson John W. farmer and teacher; Sec. 3; P. O. Gerlaw; rep; Chris; from Ohio.

CARSON SAMUEL, Farmer; Sec. 19; P. O. Monmouth; born in Ireland in 1851; rents 200 acres of Mrs. Garwin; came to this country in 1869, and to this Co. in 1872; married Nancy Hamilton in 1873; she was born in Ireland; has one child, Thomas Barnes.

Coulter O. H. farmer; Sec. 21; P. O. Monmouth; rep; Presb.

CHICKEN WM. Farmer and Miner; Sec. 15; P. O. Monmouth; born in England, June 4, 1822; Rep; Meth; owns 50 acres, value $2,500; he came to this country in 1849; lived seven years in Mo.; came to Ill. in 1856; enlisted in 83rd Ill. Inf.; served three years; held office of School Director; married Sarah Scott in 1852; she was born in England; has five children, Sarah, Ann, Emma, Vilitia and Mabel.

CLIPPINGER ANTHONY, Farmer; Sec. 22; P. O. Monmouth; born in Franklin Co., Penn., June 6, 1820; Rep; Ch. of God; owns 570 acres, valued at $23,000; he came to this State and Co. in 1850; lived thirty years in Penn.; has held office of School Director; married Susanna Cobel in 1849; she was born in Franklin Co., Penn.

Cooper Wm. mason; Sec. 8; P. O. Monmouth; dem; from Ireland.

COULTER DAVID, Gardener; Sec. 32; P.O. Monmouth; born in Penn., Nov. 14, 1825; came to this Co. in 1858; Rep; Presb; married Elizabeth J. Harris, in 1846; she was born in Penn.; has eight children; the eldest, O. H. Coulter, enlisted in the 50th Ill. Infantry, in 1863, and served until close of the war.

Crandall R. gardener; Sec. 32; P. O. Monmouth; rep; Meth.

CURRAN JAMES, Farmer; Sec. 4; P. O. Monmouth; born in Juniata Co., Penn., Feb. 24, 1806; Rep; U. P.; owns 180 acres, value $9,000; lived in Ohio 18 years; came to this Co. in 1858; has held office of School Director; married Mary Thompson in 1833; she was born in Penn.; has six children, four sons and two daughters.

Downer A. farmer; Sec. 30; P. O. Monmouth; rep; Bapt.

Davis J. R. farmer; Sec. 20; P. O. Monmouth; dem; Lib; from Indiana.

Dennison J. H. farmer; Sec. 2; P.O. Gerlaw; rep; Lib; from New York.

Douglass S. retired farmer; Monmouth; rep; Chris; from Ireland.

Dunbar John, carpenter; Sec. 21; P. O. Monmouth; rep; Presb.

Eaton James, laborer; P. O. Monmouth; dem; Meth.

Fairburn Clarence W. farmer, lives with father; P. O. Monmouth; rep.

FAIRBURN JAMES A. Farmer; Sec. 36; P. O. Monmouth; born in Virginia in 1816; Rep; Meth; rents 115 acres of J. B. Meginnis; came to Warren Co., Ill., in 1865; married Miss Elizabeth Tole in 1836; she was born in Va.; has eight children, two sons and six daughters.

FINDLEY JAMES I. Farmer; Sec. 10; P. O. Monmouth; born in Ohio, 1837; Rep; U. P.; rents 160 acres of A. C. Kirkpatrick; he came to this State 1854, to this Co. 1858; holds office of School Director; married Miss Sarah R. Walker, 1860; she was born in Ohio; has five children, three sons and two daughters.

FLACK WM. Farmer and Stock Dealer; Sec. 8; P. O. Monmouth; born in England, May 13, 1832; Rep; Presb; owns 270 acres, value $15,500; came to this country 1855; lived one year in Ohio and one year in Michigan; came to Warren Co. 1857; has held office of School Director for many years; married Nancy McCreedy in 1859; she was born in North of Ireland; has four children, William, Fannie, Charles and Albert; lost four.

Fowler Francis, farmer; Sec. 16; P. O. Monmouth; ind; Lib; from Germany.

FRANTZ HIRAM M. Farmer; Sec. 26; P. O. Monmouth; born in Md., March 7, 1844; came to this Co. 1868; Rep; Chris; lived in Perry Co., Ohio, 21 years; enlisted in the 31st Ohio Inf., Co. D, and served from April 16, 1861, till August, 1865, and never missed an engagement or a day's duty during the time; married Flora T. Murphy in 1870; she was born in Warren Co.; has one child, named Talma J.; owns 151 acres, value $9,000.

Frantz Isaac, farmer, rents of G. Sickman; Sec. 33, P. O. Monmouth.

Frantz Soloman, farmer; Sec. 26; P. O. Monmouth; rep; Meth; from Pennsylvania.

FRANTZ W. H. Farmer, Stock Raiser and Stock Dealer; P. O. Monmouth; born in Penn., April 10, 1829; Rep; Lib; owns 640 acres, value $38,000; lived three years in Ohio; came to this Co. 1851; has held office of School Director; married Miss May Lucas, April 10, 1857; she was born in Warren Co., 1838; has six children, Delevan C., Katie, Lina, Pearlie, Ella J. and Mary L.

Frederick John, farmer; Sec. 32; P. O. Monmouth; from Germany.

FRYMIRE BARNEY, Farmer; Sec. 12; P. O. Monmouth; born in Warren Co., April, 1847; Dem; Chris; owns 70 acres, value $4,500; has held office of School Director; married Theresa Barner, 1869; she was born in Knox Co.; lost one child.

FRYMIRE HARDIN D. Farmer; Sec. 13; P. O. Monmouth; born in Warren Co., Oct. 23, 1842; Dem; Chris; owns 120 acres, value $6,000; married Miss Eliza Cannon; she was born in York Co., Penn.; has seven children, four sons and three daughters; lost one.

FRYMIRE JOHN H. Farmer; Sec. 14; P. O. Monmouth; born in Breckinridge Co., Ky., Oct. 4, 1828; came to this Co. 1837; Dem; Chris; owns 226 acres, value $9,000; has held office of Treasurer Masonic Lodge No. 37 one year, and City Treasurer of Monmouth one year; sold goods four years in Monmouth; married Mary Griffie in 1849; she was born in Kentucky; has eight children, four sons and four daughters.

FRYMIRE WM. Farmer; Sec. 12; P. O. Monmouth; born in Breckinridge Co., Ky., Nov. 15, 1806; Dem; Chris; owns 230 acres, value $11,500; came to this State and Co. 1837; has held office of School Director; married Pollie Bruner 1827; she was born in Breckinridge Co., Ky.; has seven children, five sons and two daughters; lost three.

Funk Jacob, farmer; Sec. 31; P. O. Monmouth; rep; from Pennsylvania.

Funk Jacob, farmer; Sec. 31; 91 acres.

GARLINGER J. farmer; Sec. 30; P. O. Monmouth; rep; U. P.

GIBSON JOHN, Farmer; Sec. 30; P. O. Monmouth; born in this Co., Aug. 24, 1849; Dem; has always lived in this Co.; married Belle Patterson, Nov. 18, 1875, who was born in this Co.; have one child, Edgar A.

Gibson Wm. farmer and stock raiser; Sec. 30 and 31; P. O. Monmouth; dem; U. P.

Graham James H. farmer; Sec. 36; P. O. Monmouth; from Ireland.

Gray Edward, farmer; Sec. 7; P. O. Monmouth; rep; Bapt.

Grier Daniel M. farmer; lives with his father; Sec. 28; rep; U. P.

GRIER ROBERT C. Farmer; Sec. 28; P. O. Monmouth; born County Donegal, North of Ireland, Dec., 1812; Rep; U. P.; owns 110 acres, value $11,000; came to this country 1838; lived in Penn. seventeen years, and in McLean Co., Ill., nine years, and came to Warren Co. 1864; married Margaret McAyeal in 1844; she was born in Penn., 1823; has three sons, James A., Robert J. and David M.

Grover Alonzo, farmer; Sec. 33; P. O. Monmouth; rep.

Grover B. H. farmer; Sec. 33; P. O. Monmouth; rep.

HAINES JAMISON L. farmer; Sec. 35; P. O. Monmouth; dem; Chris; born Ill.

Hallam David M. farmer; Sec. 26; P. O. Monmouth; rep; Chris; from Ohio.

Hamilton Daniel R. farmer; Sec. 7; P. O. Monmouth; rep; Presb; from Virginia.

Harding H. D. farmer; Sec. 28; P. O. Monmouth; rep; from New York.

HARDISTY JEROME, Farmer; Sec. 18; P. O. Monmouth; born Ky., Nov. 16, 1825; Dem; Cath; rents of O. S. Barnum; came to this State in 1839, and settled in Randolph Co.; came to Warren Co. in 1853; married Mary J. Mudd, 1847; she died in 1848; married Julia Ann Johnson, 1857; she was born in Ind.; has eight children, Harriet A., George H., John H., William J., Thomas S., Francis M., Mary M. and Katie L.

Harper James M. farmer, rents of H. D. Harding; Sec. 22; P. O. Monmouth; rep.

HARTZELL JOHN H. Farmer; Sec. 11; P. O. Monmouth; born in Ohio, Feb. 21, 1853; Dem; Meth; owns 80 acres, value $5,000; he came to this State and Co. in 1872; married Miss Emma L. Shaw, Dec. 24, 1875; she was born in Warren Co. Feb. 21, 1854; has one child, Oscar M.

Haver Wm. O. farmer, works for Mrs. Shaw; Sec. 11; rep.

HOLSAPPLE E. T. Miller; Sec. 6; P. O. Monmouth; born in Ind., 1841; Ind; Chris; owns 19 acres and the Pearl Mill, value $7,000; lived in Iowa seven years, and in Rock Island Co. fourteen years; married Albina Bryan, 1865; she was born in Rock Island Co.; has three children, one son and two daughters.

Henderson John F. laborer for J. P. Stevenson; Sec. 6; rep; U. P.

Henderson Rev. G. D. Sec. 28; P. O. Monmouth; rep; U. P.

Hengstler Anthony, farmer; Sec. 7; P. O. Monmouth; dem; Cath; from Germany.

Hentsman Henry C. farmer for Mrs. A. C. Sykes; P. O. Monmouth; rep; Meth.

HODGENS ISAAC C. Farmer and Stock Raiser; Sec. 18; P. O. Monmouth; born in Washington Co., Penn., Jan. 20, 1843; Dem; Pres; owns 192 acres, value $9,600; came to this Co. in 1867; married Miss Rachel Davidson in March, 1860, who was born in Belmont Co., Ohio; has two children, Harry and Robert D.

Houser, W. farmer, teamster; Sec. 36; dem.

HONSMAN DAVID, Farmer; Sec. 15; P. O. Monmouth; born Lancaster, Pa., Nov. 5, 1820; Rep; Meth; came to this State and County in 1865; has lived here twelve years; has held office of School Director; married Barbara Lucas, in Sept. 1841; she was born in Cumberland Co., Penn., 1822; has four children, named Samuel, Henry, David, and Anna N.; owns 80 acres, valued at $5,200.

Hubbard Thos. miner; Sec. 36; P. O. Monmouth; Meth; from England.

JONES VIDNEY, farmer, lives with W. Frymire; Sec. 12; P. O. Monmouth; dem.

JOSS GEO. L. Farmer; Sec. 26; P. O. Monmouth; born in Warren Co., July 18, 1848; Rep; Meth; rents 85 acres of Henry Hoerner; his parents have lived in Warren Co. between thirty and forty years; he married Agnes C. Swifler, June 18, 1868; she was born in Cumberland Co., Pa.; has two children, names John W. and Eva B.

KENDALL D. M. farmer, lives with his father; Sec. 4; rep; U. P.

KENDALL FRANCIS B. Farmer; Sec. 16; P. O. Monmouth; born in Warren Co., Oct. 6, 1838; Dem; U. P.; owns 150 acres, valued at $9,000; his father was one of the earliest settlers, coming to this County in 1830, married Sarah Gardner, in 1858, who was born in Kentucky, and died Nov. 6, 1875; has three children, named John P., Alice A. and Clara M.; lost two, one of them, Rollin A., a musical prodigy, died on his 12th birthday; married Miss Agnes Patterson, March 8, 1877; she was born in Warren Co. in 1854.

KENDALL ROBT. Farmer; Sec. 4; P. O. Monmouth; born in Bedford Co. Pa., 1800; Rep; U. P.; owns 370 acres, value about $19,000; came to this Co. in 1853; married Anna R. McNair, 1829;

she was born in Penn., and died in 1870; has three children, two sons and one daughter, the wife of A. Burford; lost three sons.

Kildow John, quarryman; Sec. 7; P. O. Monmouth; dem; Meth; from Ohio.

Kittering Jacob, farmer; Sec. 27; P. O. Monmouth; rep; Lib; from Pennsylvania.

LARSON H. farmer; Sec. 19; P. O. Monmouth; rep; Luth; from Denmark.

LARSON LOIS, Farmer; Sec. 19; P. O. Monmouth; born in Sweden in 1849; Rep; Luth; rents of G. Harding; came to this Co. in 1868; married Mary Felt, 1875; she was born in Sweden; has one child, Fred. L.

LAW JAS. Farmer and Stock Raiser; Sec. 17; P. O. Monmouth; born Washington Co., Pa., 1809; Dem; U. P.; owns 180 acres, value $14,400; 160 acres Iowa, value $1,600; came to this State and Co. in 1848; has lived here 28 years; has held office of School Director for many years; married Mary Skinner, March 14, 1844; she was born in Ohio; children are named Helen V., Robert, Mary, Samuel, Sarah, William Charles and Marcia; lost two.

LEEPER JAMISON, Farmer; Sec. 35; P. O. Monmouth; born in Union Co., Ind., May 9, 1811; Dem; Chris; owns 300 acres, value $18,000; came to Illinois in 1839; lived in Indiana 28 years; has held offices of Supervisor and School Director for many years; married Miss Eliza Sankey in 1830; she was born in Hamilton Co., Ohio, March, 1810.

McCOY JOSEPH, farmer; Sec. 34; P. O. Monmouth; rep; Lib.

McCULLEY THOMAS B. Farmer; Sec. 22; P. O. Monmouth; born in Guernsey Co., Ohio, May 22, 1850; Dem; U. P.; rents 168 acres of R. A. Gibson; came to this State in 1864; married Mary Graham in 1872; she was born in Warren Co.; has two children, named Laura M., and Alerie Eugene.

McCullough T. H. gardener; P. O. Monmouth; rep; U. P.

McKnight Thomas, S. farmer; Sec. 5; P. O. Monmouth; rep; U. P.

McLean Roderick, farmer; Sec. 27; P. O. Monmouth.

Mackey Wm. farmer; Sec. 22; P. O. Monmouth; rep.

Mahoney John, farmer, renter; Sec. 10; P. O. Monmouth; Cath; from Ireland.

MEGINNIS JAS. Farmer; Sec. 26; P. O. Monmouth; born in Pennsylvania, Dec. 21, 1839; Dem; Meth; rents 400 acres of his father; came to this State and Co. in 1852; has held office of School Director; married Miss Priscilla F. Brooks, Feb. 1, 1872; she was born in Warren Co., April 5, 1853; has four children, named Jane M., Maggie B., Anna M., Priscilla C.

Meginnis J. B. retired farmer; Monmouth.

MERWIN JACOB, Farmer; Sec. 10; P. O. Gerlaw; born in Pennsylvania, Aug. 19, 1820; Rep; Luth; owns 97 acres, value $4,400; he came to this State and Co. in 1862; has held office of School Director; married Amanda D. Smith; she was born in Ohio in 1820; has two children, named Sylvester P. and Ernest E; lost one.

MILLER BARNEY, Farmer; Sec. 11; P. O. Monmouth; born in Ohio, April 23, 1847; Rep; Lib; came to this State and Co. in 1854; married Miss Etta Shaw, 1872; she was born in Warren Co.; has one child, Harry E.

Miller Jacob, works for C. Hardin; Sec. 28; P. O. Monmouth.

Morgan Jas. W. farmer; Sec. 32; P. O. Monmouth; rep; Prot.

Morrison G. W. farmer, works for A. Rankin.

Morrison John, farmer, rents of T. S. McKnight; Sec. 5.

MORROW'S D. heirs, Farmers; Sec. 12; P. O. Monmouth; Dem; Chris; own 160 acres, value $8,000; also a saw mill; D. Morrow was born in South Carolina; he came to this Co. in 1837; married Isabelle Read, who was born in Kentucky; he died in Sept. 1857; he left eight children, six sons and two daughters; two since deceased.

Morrow E. M. farmer; Sec. 12; P. O. Monmouth; dem; Chris; born Illinois.

Morrow I. K. farmer; Sec. 12; P. O. Monmouth; born Alabama; came to Ill. 1837.

Morrow T. A. farmer; Sec. 12; P. O. Monmouth; born in Alabama.

Morrow Wm. farmer; Sec. 12; P. O. Monmouth; dem; Chris; from Alabama.

Myers D. J. farmer; Sec. 16; P. O. Monmouth; rep; Prot; from Indiana.

NILES OSCAR G. farmer; lives with B. Miller; Sec. 11; rep; Lib.

NELSON ALFRED, Farmer; Sec. 3; P. O. Gerlaw; born in Sweden, 1848; Luth; rents 120 acres of G. Hardin; came to America in 1874; married Emma Peterson, 1874; she was born in Sweden; has one child, John E.

NICHOL JOHN, Farmer; Sec. 18; P. O. Monmouth; born in Belmont Co., O., Jan. 24, 1820; Rep; U. P.; owns 160 acres, value $9,600; he lived in Ohio 34 years, and came to this Co. in 1854; has held office of School Director for many years; married Mary J. Pollock, in 1853; she was born in Green Co., O.; has seven children, Ruth C., Morrison O., John B. P., William F., M. E. Dayton, Fannie A. and Chester V.

Noe A. W. gardener; Sec. 21; P. O. Monmouth; dem.

OSTROM GEO. farmer; Sec. 16; P. O. Monmouth; rep; Univ; from N. Y.

OSWALD PETER, Farmer; Sec. 9; P. O. Monmouth; born in Prussia, 1834; Dem; Lib; owns 80 acres, value $3,600; came to this country in 1856, and to this State and Co. in 1858; has held office of School Director; married Anna E. Patterson in 1862; she was born in Cumberland Co., Pa., 1844; has three children, John F., Frank W., and Ellen.

OWENS J. F. Farmer; Sec. 2; P. O. Gerlaw; born in Cincinnati, May 8, 1829; Rep; Chris; owns 260 acres, value $19,500; lived in Davenport, Iowa, 17 years; came to this Co. in 1855; has held offices of Supervisor and School Director; married May T. Hopper, 1855; she was born in Todd Co., Ky.; has six children, one son and five daughters.

Ozenbaugh Frank, farm hand, works for Mr. Kendall.

PAGE A. B. farmer; Sec. 14; P. O. Monmouth; rep; Bapt; from N. H.

PARKER HENRY C. Farmer; Sec. 8; P. O. Monmouth; born in Warren Co., Nov. 10, 1844; his parents came to the State in 1835; married Miss Margery Grames, Dec. 30, 1875; she was born in Steuben Co., N. Y., Nov. 11, 1852; rents of his father.

Patterson John; Sec. 22; P. O. Monmouth; rep; Meth; from Ohio.

Patton N. T. tile manufacturer; Sec. 26; P. O. Monmouth.

Peal Thornton, nurseryman; Sec. 21; rep; from England.

PEARSON HIRAM, Farmer; Sec. 13; P. O. Monmouth; born in Canada, Oct. 12, 1829; Rep; Ch. of God; owns 40 acres, value $2,800; he came to this State and Co. in 1869; married Miss Maria Ashton, 1853; she was born in Canada; has three children, Martha M., Almea C., and Sarah S.; lost one.

Penny Alex. farmer, rents of W. H. Frantz; Sec. 23; P. O. Monmouth.

PETERSON CHAS. G. Farmer; Sec. 19; P. O. Monmouth; born in Sweden, Nov. 3, 1847; Rep; Luth; rents of G. Harding; came to this country in 1869, and to this Co. in 1870; married Betsey Johnson, in 1875; she was born in Sweden; has one child, Hattie Amanda.

Peterson George R. sexton of the cemetery; Sec. 20; P. O. Monmouth; rep.

Pringle John, miner; Sec. 23; P. O. Monmouth; from Scotland.

QUEEN D. H. farmer; Sec. 10; P. O. Gerlaw; rep; U. P. from Ohio.

QUINN ELIAS, Farmer; Sec. 8; P. O. Monmouth; born in Ohio, Jan. 18, 1834; Rep; U. P.; owns 72 acres of land, value $36,000; he came to this Co. in 1850; he enlisted in the 50th I. V. I.; served ten months, and was discharged on account of ill health; has held office of School Director; married Ann E. Nelson in 1870; she was born in Philadelphia, 1830; has one child, named Clarence E.

RANKIN ALEX. Sec. 5; P. O. Monmouth; rep; U. P.; came to Ill. 1836

Roberts Mrs. D. M. farmer, rents of Dr. Regner; Sec. 33; P. O. Monmouth.

Robertson Jas. farmer; Sec. 27; P. O. Monmouth; U. P.

Robertson Wm. farmer, rents of J. B. Meginnis; Sec. 35; P. O. Monmouth; U. P.

RUGH OLIVER P. Farmer; Sec. 27; P. O. Monmouth; born in Perry Co., O., Aug. 18, 1818; Rep; Meth; lived in Ohio nineteen years, and in Indiana eighteen years; came to Warren Co. 1855; married Hannah Dull, Feb. 8, 1848; she was born in Washington Co., Penn.; has one child, named John D.; lost four.

RUSE HENRY, Farmer; Sec. 26; P. O. Monmouth; born Suffolk Co., England, Feb. 15, 1835; Rep; Presb; came to this Co. in 1855; lived in England twenty-one years; married Sarah McCreedy, Jan., 1862; she was born in County Down, north of Ireland, Nov. 14, 1845; has four children, named Effie I., Katie L., Harry and Carl H.

RYNER RACHEL, Farmer; Sec. 1; P. O. Gerlaw; born in Penn., 1798; owns 80 acres, value $4,500; she married Jacob Ryner, in 1815; he was born Penn., and lived in N. Y., Ohio, and came to this State in 1839; he died in 1863; had eight children, six sons and two daughters.

SICKMAN C. farmer; Sec. 36; P. O. Cameron; rep; Meth; from New York.

Sierer Lewis, farmer, lives with father; Sec. 36; P. O. Monmouth; dem; Luth.

SHARP FRANCIS M. Miner; Sec. 15; P. O. Monmouth; born in Penn., Aug. 9, 1842; Dem; Meth; came to this Co. in 1855; married Mary E. Ferry, March 31, 1863; she was born in France; has five children, named Hugh M., Laura T., Francis M., John W. and Anna M.

SIERER WM. Farmer; Sec. 36; P. O. Monmouth; born Cumberland Co., Penn., April 20, 1823; Dem; Luth; owns 240 acres, value $14,400; came to this Co. in 1864; married Eliza Miller, March 18, 1847; she was born in York Co., Penn., June 17, 1829; has eight children, named Wm. M., Lewis, Riley, Mary, Ellsworth, Fulmer, Oliver and Ann Margaret; lost three.

Sierer Wm. M. lives with his father; dem; Luth.

Smith Jno. farmer, rents; Sec. 3; P. O. Gerlaw; dem; Prot.

WARREN COUNTY : MONMOUTH TOWNSHIP.   235

Smith R. G. farmer; Sec. 2; P. O. Gerlaw; dem; Lib; from Ohio.

SMITH RYAN G. Farmer; Sec. 4; P. O. Gerlaw; born in Greene Co., O., Sept. 4, 1819; Ind; Meth; owns 204 acres, value $12,200; came to this Co. in 1846; is one of the old settlers; has held office of School Director many years; married Elizabeth Buck, in 1849; she was born in Erie Co., O., 1831; has six children, named Cornelia, Abigail, Adaline, Fanny M., Oriett, George Wm.; lost two.

Swiler Jacob B. farmer; Sec. 27; P. O. Monmouth; rep; Ch. of God; from Penn.

Snooks Elisha, rents; Sec. 10; P. O Monmouth; dem; Meth; from Iowa.

Speakman Jacob, farmer; Sec. 31; P. O. Monmouth; rep; Lib; from Pennsylvania.

Speakman W. P. farmer; Sec. 31; P. O. Monmouth; rep; Lib; from Pennsylvania.

Stack Jno., R. R. employee; Sec. 31; P. O. Monmouth; dem; Ireland.

Steiner A. B. farmer; Sec. 28; P. O. Monmouth; rep.

Stevenson Jno. P. farmer; Sec. 17; P. O. Monmouth; rep; from Pennsylvania.

Stone Wm. teamster; Sec. 24; P. O. Monmouth; rep; Meth.

SHAW MRS. LOUISA J. Farming; Sec. 11; P. O. Monmouth; born in Crawford Co., Ind., May 8, 1833; owns 100 acres, valued $7,000; came with her parents to this State and Co. in 1835; married Canfield Shaw in 1853; he was born in Genesee Co., N. Y., in 1830, and died Oct. 8, 1865; has two children, named Emma L. and Effie; lost one.

STRUTHERS JAMES H. Farmer; Sec. 10; P. O. Monmouth; born in Warren Co., 1847; Rep; U. P.; owns 100 acres, value $5,000; he married Miss Mary J. Findley, in Aug., 1871; she was born in Miss.

STRUTHERS JOHN A. Farmer; Sec. 8; P. O. Monmouth; born in Warren Co., Oct. 1, 1841; Rep; U. P.; owns 115 acres, value $6,900; he enlisted in 83d I. V. I., and served three years; married Mary Fee, 1870; she was born in Ind.; has two children, Effie B. and Alice R.

STRUTHERS THOMAS, Farmer; Sec. 10; P. O. Gerlaw; born in Greene Co., O., 1821; Rep; U. P.; owns 100 acres, value $5,000; he came to this State and Co. in 1832; has held office of School Director for many years; married Mary Humphrey, Feb. 12, 1846; she was born in Ohio, 1815; has four children, one son and three daughters; lost one.

Stull Ben. farmer, rents of H. E. Root; Sec. 23; P. O. Monmouth; rep; Lib.

STULL MARTIN. Farmer; Sec. 8; P. O. Monmouth; born in Ohio, 1828; Dem; Meth; owns 45 acres, value $3,000; came to this Co. 1852; has held office of School Director; married Sidney Weaver, 1854; she was born in Penn.; has four children, three sons and one daughter.

SYKES MRS. A. C. Farming; Sec. 9; P. O. Monmouth; born in Lancaster Co., Penn., Aug. 25, 1819; came to this Co. in 1838; Presb; owns 240 acres, value $19,000; married W. P. Sykes in 1836; he was born in Philadelphia, Oct. 11, 1805; died Dec. 13, 1875; lost two children.

TAYLOR WM. farmer, rents of J. Leeper; Sec. 34; P. O. Monmouth.

WALLACE JAS. farmer; Sec. 24; P. O. Monmouth; dem; Meth; 80 acres.

WALLACE JOHN, Farmer; Sec. 13; P. O. Monmouth; born in Ky., Feb. 11, 1827; Dem; Chris; owns 120 acres, value $7,200; he came to this State and Co. in 1832; has lived near the place he now resides the whole time; has held the office of School Director for many years; married Sarah McFarline, Oct. 23, 1851; she was born in Warren Co., 1834; has three children, named Nettie, Almy and Addie.

WALLACE ROBERT. Farmer; Sec. 36; P. O. Monmouth; Dem; Chris; owns 83 acres, value $4,150; he was born in this Co., 1843; married Emma Johnson, 1869; she was born in this Co.; died April 5, 1872; had two children, named John Hardin and Clarence; married Miss Mary Hart, Nov., 1874; she was born in Ill.; has one child, name Charles Lewis.

Wallace Wm. farmer; Sec. 12; P. O. Monmouth; dem; Chris; from Kentucky.

Watson B. T. farmer; Sec. 28; P. O. Monmouth; rep.

Watson T. farmer; Sec. 28; P. O. Monmouth; Bapt; from England.

Wells Henry P. farmer, rents; Sec. 17; P. O. Monmouth; dem; Meth.

Wells J. M. farmer, lives with mother; Sec. 34; dem; Meth.

WELLS MRS. MATILDA, Farmer; Sec. 16; P. O. Monmouth; born in N. Y., 1823; Meth; owns 12 acres, value $600; lived in Ind. twelve years; came to this State 1848; married Wm. Wells, 1842; he was born in Ky., 1812; he died Jan. 15, 1874; has seven children, five sons and two daughters; lost three children.

WELSH THOMAS, Miner; Sec. 24; P. O. Monmouth; born in Scotland, 1811; Rep; Bapt; owns 30 acres, value $1,000; came to this country in 1853; lived one year in Maryland, in Ohio five years, in Penn. three years, and came to this State in 1862; married Agnes Young, in 1834; she was born in Scotland; has five children, two sons and three daughters; lost five.

Welsh Andrew, miner; Sec. 24; P. O. Monmouth; rep; Ch. of God; from Scotland.

Welsh William, miner; Sec. 24; P. O. Monmouth; rep; Chris; from Scotland.

Wheeler Chas. quarryman; Sec. 6; P. O. Monmouth; rep; Lib.

WHITE J. M. Farmer; Sec. 27; P. O. Monmouth; born in Chester Co., Pa., April 12, 1835; Rep; Meth; owns 181¼ acres, value $16,000; he lived in Pennsylvania 24 years; came to this Co. in 1859; married Miss Sarah J. Rankin, March 18, 1858; she was born in Fayette Co., Pa.; has two children, Thomas and Lucian; lost one.

Whistler Wm. farmer; Sec. 7; P. O. Monmouth; dem; Luth; from Pennsylvania.

Williams Mrs. Persia M.; Sec. 1; from New York; came here in 1837.

Wilson Henry, fruit grower; Sec. 27; P. O. Monmouth; ind; Spir.

WILSON JNO. G. Farmer and Stock Raiser; Sec. 20; P. O. Monmouth, born in Perry Co., Ohio, Nov. 5, 1824; came to this Co. in 1851; Dem; U. P.; owns 130 acres, value $13,000; has lived in this Co. 26 years; has been largely identified with the interests of the Co. has held offices of Supervisor and County Commissioner; married Eliza Fowler, 1846; she was born in Ohio; died, 1853; has two children, Hamar F. and Maria J.; married Melvilla A. Skinner, 1854; she was born in Ohio; has four children, James J., Samuel A., Carrie A. and Robert L.

Wilson Wm. W. farmer; Sec. 16; P. O. Monmouth; dem; Lib; born Ohio.

Wortendyke F. farmer; Sec. 16; P. O. Monmouth; dem; Meth; from New York.

YOUNG JOHN, Farmer and Miner; Sec. 15; P. O. Monmouth; born in Scotland, Dec. 24, 1823; Dem; Meth; owns 235 acres, value $12,000; came to this country in 1849; lived seven years in Missouri; came to Warren Co,. 1856; has held office of School Director; married Mary Wilson, 1849; she was born in Scotland; thirteen children, nine sons and four daughters; lost two.

SUMNER TOWNSHIP.

ADAMS JAMES, farm laborer; Sec. 32; P. O. Little York; dem; from Iowa.

Allen Andrew, retired; P. O. Little York; rep; U. P.; born in 1801; here 1830.

Allen James B. farmer; Sec. 15; P. O. Little York; rep.

Allen Theodore, farmer, works for George Gibson; P. O. Little York; rep.

Allen Wm. A. farmer; Sec. 4; P. O. Duck Creek; rep; U. P.; 80 acres; from Ohio.

Amberson B. C. carpenter; Denny; rep; U. P.; from Pennsylvania.

Anderson Rev. David, pastor U. P. Church; Little York; rep; from Philadelphia, Pa.

Arendt John, farm laborer; P. O. Denny; rep; Prot.

Armstrong David, farmer, renter; P. O. Little York; rep; from West Virginia.

ARMSTRONG H. M, Farmer and Stock Raiser; Sec. 9 and 10; P. O. Little York; born in West Va., May 4, 1833; came to this Co. in 1856; Rep; 200 acres, value $12,000, personal $2,000; married Miss Mary Holmes in Feb., 1861; they have eight children, Lenna, Sarah J., Kate, Mary, Fannie N., Frank, George and Chester; two sons deceased.

Armstrong W. H. farm laborer; P. O. Little York; rep; from West Virginia.

ARTHURS J. F. Farmer; Sec. 15; P. O. Little York; born in North Carolina, Dec. 29, 1807; came to this Co. in 1836; Rep; U. P.; 160 acres, value $8,000; is one of the early settlers of this Co.; living now on the same place where first settled; married Elizabeth A. Carmichael, April 9, 1835, who was born in South Carolina, July 5, 1817; they have had seven children; four sons were in the army, William T., killed at battle of Stone River; Joseph W., living; Abram Y., died from sickness contracted in army; John C., Mrs. Kate Giles, and Mrs. Mary E. Copeland.

ARTHURS JAMES C. Farmer; Sec. 30; P. O. Little York; born in this Co. Nov. 30, 1841; Rep; U. P.; 65 acres, value $3,250; has always lived in this Co.; his father, J. F. Arthurs, among the early settlers here; was in army, 36th I. V. I., Co. C; married Miss Hadassah McCrery, Nov. 16, 1869, who was born in this Co. Oct. 17, 1847; they have one son, Fred Alby, born July 5, 1873.

Arthurs Jno. C. farmer, lives with his father; Sec. 15; P. O. Little York; rep. U. P.

ARTHURS JOSEPH W. Farmer; Sec. 13; P. O. Little York; born in this Co. Sept. 20, 1839; Rep; U. P.; 65 acres, value $3,250; served four years and two months in 36th I. V. I., Co. C; was in twenty-three engagements, commencing at battle of Pea Ridge, June 7, 1862, and closing with battle of Nashville, Dec. 15, 1864; married Miranda M. Hopkins, May 28, 1868, who was born in Richland Co., Ohio, Nov. 28,

1844; they have two children, Etta E., born June 24, 1869, and Lula K., born Feb. 26, 1875.

Atchison D. R. farmer; Sec. 33; P. O. Little York; rep; U. P.; 160 acres; $8,000; Ohio.

ATCHISON REV. J. M. Pastor of Cedar Creek U. P. Church; P. O. Little York; born in Muskingum Co., Ohio, Sept. 1, 1846; came to this Co. in 1872; Rep; graduated at Muskingum College, Ohio, and in Theological Seminary at Zenia, Ohio; married Jennie S. Speer, Oct. 24, 1872, who was born in Muskingum Co., Ohio, Jan. 17, 1850; they have two children, Lula Blanche, born Dec. 7, 1873, and Mary, Sept. 11, 1876.

BAILEY D. B. farm laborer; P. O. Denny; dem; Prot.

Baldwin Alon W. miller; P. O. Denny; rep.

Baldwin Chas. miller and carpenter; P. O. Denny; dem.

Bailey J. O. farmer; P. O. Little York; dem.

Barr Geo. W; retired; P. O. Little York; rep; U. P.

Barr J. T. farmer; Sec. 21; P. O. Little York; rep; U. P.

Barry Wm. farmer, rents; Little York; rep.

Beck Charles W. farmer, with his father; Sec. 11; P. O. Little York; dem; U. P.

BECK HENRY, Farmer; Sec. 11; P. O. Little York; born in Germany, Oct. 18, 1827; emigrated to this country in 1849; Ind; Prot. Epis; 180 acres, value $7,500; lived in Washington Co., N. Y., thirteen years, employed by Rensselear & Saratoga R. R. Co. as Master Car-builder; removed to Ill. in April, 1870; married Christiana Vole, Sept. 12, 1850, who was born Jan. 24, 1824; they have four children, Charles W., John A., Fred T., and Susie S.; one son deceased.

Beck Jno. A. farmer, lives with his father; Sec. 11; P. O. Little York; dem; Prot. Ep.

Bicknell Thomas, laborer; P. O. Alexis; dem; Prot; from England.

BLACKBURN H. W. Carpenter; Sec. 36; P. O. Denny; born in Md., March 2, 1817; Ind; 20 acres, value $800; came to this State in 1830, to this Co. 1852; wife was Matilda Shoemaker, step-daughter of Daniel McNeil; she was born in Chemung Co., N. Y., May 16, 1831; married Feb. 28, 1850; six children, Kit Ida, married Wm. R. Maskrey; Minnie M., married W. A. Baldwin; Guy Carrol, killed by lightning, Aug. 31, 1875; Cora E. and Frank P.; Dan Lee, deceased.

Boyd James, farmer; Sec. 34; P. O. Little York; rep; U. P.; 180 acres; from Ohio.

Bramley Mat. farmer; renter; Sec. 21; P. O. Little York; rep.

BROWN JOSEPH, Farmer; Sec. 2; P. O. Norwood; born in Green Co., Ohio, Nov. 7, 1822; Rep; U. P.; 218 acres, value $10,000; was in 84th Reg. I. V. I. Co. K, three years; married Miss Nancy Gowdy, March 2, 1843, who was born in Clark Co., Ohio, June 17, 1822; they have five children, John G., James A., Wm. S., Ann and Perry; Ann married Zenas Hogue, March 30, 1875; one son, Joseph F.; all living; Z. H. was in 36th I. V. I., Co. K.

Brown Jos. A. farmer; Sec. 12; P. O. Spring Grove; rep; 160 acres.

BROWN THOMAS, farmer; Sec. 12; P. O. Little York; born in Preble Co., Ohio, May 20, 1819; came to this Co. in 1839; Rep; U. P.; 180 acres, value $6,500; living on the place where first settled; married Phœbe Giles, April 1, 1847, who was born in Preble Co., Ohio, Jan. 12, 1822; three children living, Sarah E., John L. and William B.

Brown W. S. farmer; P. O. Norwood; rep; U. P.

Brownlee Jno. farmer; Sec. 17; P. O. Little York; rep; U. P.; 320 acres; from Penn

Brownlee J. S. farmer; Sec. 16; P. O. Little York; rep; U. P.; 530 acres; from Penn.

BROWNLEE NATHANIEL, (deceased) whose portrait appears in this work, was born in Washington Co., Pa., April 11, 1813; and died Aug. 11, 1872; he came to this State and County in 1835; He was a member of the U. P. Church, and gave it a firm and liberal support; he was particularly opposed to Slavery, and was among the first in the Free Soil party, afterward with the Republican party; he married Miss Emily Paine from Painesville, Ohio, Nov. 26, 1846; four children, Emma A., now Mrs. J. C. Kilgore, Clara J., now Mrs. A. P. Hutchinson, Mason C. and Ralph Paine.

BROWNLEE MASON C. Farmer and Stock Raiser; Sec. 16; P. O. Little York; born in this Co. Sept. 22, 1856; Rep; U. P.; 325 acres, value $20,000; personel $4,000; has always lived on his native place.

Brownlee Thomas, farmer; Sec. 17; P. O. Little York; rep; U. P.; 110 acres; Penn.

Burns Edward, farmer; Sec. 5; P. O. Duck Creek; rep; Meth; 160 acres.

Bursem Oliver, farm laborer; P. O. Little York; rep; Luth.

CALDWELL A. F. farmer; Sec. 35; P. O. Denny; 100 acres; rep; U. P.

Caldwell John, farmer, lives with his father; Sec. 27; P. O. Denny; rep; U. P.

Caldwell Rufus, farmer, lives with his father; Sec. 27; P. O. Denny; rep; U. P.

CALDWELL T. J. Farmer and Stock Raiser; Sec. 27; P. O. Denny; born in Green Co., Ohio, March 19, 1820; came to this Co. in 1836; Rep; U. P.; 248 acres, value $12,500; personal $2,000; among the early settlers here; came from Ohio by team; married Miss Mary Allen in April, 1844, from Green Co., Ill., who died July 29, 1868; children, Andrew F., Sarah E., Rufus A., John O., Mary M., Matilda J., and Sherman E., all living; married the second time Miss Matilda J. Bruce, Jan. 3, 1870, daughter of Rev. James C. Bruce, first settled pastor in this Co.; one daughter, Beulah.

Clark Frank, farmer; Sec. 8; P. O. Duck Creek; dem.

Clark C. E. blacksmith; P. O. Little York; Ind; seven children; from Pennsylvania.

Clark James, farmer; Sec. 8; P. O. Duck Creek; dem.

Clark John, farmer; Sec. 7; P. O. Little York; rep.

Clark Thomas, farmer; Sec. 35; P. O. Denny; rep; U. P.; 90 acres, $4,500.

Colver C. S., M.D. farmer; Sec. 20; P. O. Little York; rep; U. P.; 160 acres.

Colver Mark, farmer, lives with his father; Sec. 20; rep; U. P.

Constant Albert B. farmer, lives with his father; Little York; rep.

Constant Enos, farm laborer; Little York; rep.

Constant George, farmer; Little York; rep.

Constant Isaac, farmer; Sec. 19; Little York; rep; 50 acres; from Ohio.

Cook M. farmer; Sec. 21; P. O. Little York; rep; U. P.

Copeland David, carpenter; Sec. 11; P. O. Little York; rep; U.P.; Saratoga Co, N.Y.

Copeland Sheldon, farmer; Sec. 11; P. O. Little York; rep; U. P.; from N. Y.

Crawford S. K., M.D. Sec. 25; P. O. Monmouth; rep; U. P.; 503 acres, $20,000.

Cusack John, farmer; Sec. 14; P. O. Denny; dem; Cath.

CUTHBERT W. L., MD. Physician and Surgeon; Little York; born in New York city, Feb. 17, 1831; rep; land and residence, value $3,000; came to this Co. in 1866; was Assistant Surgeon in 83rd I. V. I.; graduated at Rush Med. College, Chicago, in 1862; was elected Coroner of this Co. in 1868, when upon the death of the Sheriff, succeeded him to that office, and in 1872 was elected Sheriff; married Chloe N. Ball, who was born in Chautauqua Co., N. Y., April 12, 1837; they have four children, DeLaskie M., Georgie A., Frank M. and Nina; one son deceased.

DALY JOHN, farm laborer; P.O. Denny; rep; Prot.

Dalzell John, farmer, lives with his father; P. O. Duck Creek; rep.

DUNN F. J. Farmer; Sec. 13; P.O. Little York; born in Erie Co., Pa., Nov. 25, 1830; came to this Co. in 1857; Rep;

owns 80 acres of land, valued at $5,200; served three years in the Army, in 50th Regt. I. V. I.; married Miss Esther A. McCrery, Jan. 17, 1865, who was born in this Co.; they have two daughters, Zoa Blanche and Mintie Pearl.

DALZELL JOSEPH, Farmer and Stock Raiser; P. O. Duck Creek; born in Miami Co., Ohio, Jan. 1, 1823; came to this Co. in April, 1845; Rep; U. P.; 270 acres, value $13,500; personal, $2,500; has lived on same place twenty-nine years; married Miss Eliza Conner, Sept. 21, 1848, who was born in Washington Co., Pa., July 27, 1830; they have seven children living, Mary A., Emma J., William G., John T., Charles A., Clara A. and Thomas C.

Dalzell Wm. farmer, lives with his father; Sec. 3; P. O. Duck Creek; rep.

Dodson B. S. farmer; P. O. Little York; Ind.

Downey W. farmer; P. O. Little York; dem; Cath.

FINDLEY DAVID, farmer; P. O. Little York; rep; U. P.

Fisher T. A. farmer; Sec. 3; P. O. Duck Creek; dem; from Ohio.

Floyd Richard, farmer; Sec. 14; P. O. Little York; rep; U. P.; 150 acres; Ireland.

Floyd Thomas J. farmer; Sec. 15; P.O. Little York; rep; U. P.; 185 acres; Ireland.

Frazel Warren, farmer; P. O. Denny; rep; Prot; from Ohio.

Friel James, farmer; P. O. Little York; Ind.

Friel John W. farmer; P. O. Little York; rep.

GIBSON DAVID S. farmer, lives with his father; Sec. 27; P. O. Denny; rep.

GIBSON GEORGE, Farmer and Stock Raiser; Sec. 27; P. O. Little York; born in Green Co., O., Jan. 4, 1813; came to this Co. in 1831; Rep; U. P.; 346 acres, value $17,500; personal, $5,000; is one of the early settlers of this Co.; was Assessor for five years; largely interested in feeding stock; married Isabella Martin, March 9, 1835, who was born in Muskingum Co., O., June 14, 1814; they have seven children, four sons and three daughters.

Giles Ed. P. farmer; Sec. 15; P. O. Little York; rep; U. P.

GILES JNO. R. Farmer; Sec. 15; P. O. Little York; born in Warren Co., Ill., Aug. 6, 1846; Rep; U. P.; 150 acres estate, value $7,500; lives on native place; his father, John P. Giles, was one of the early settlers here, in 1833; he died in March, 1861; mother living; was in Army, 47th I. V. I.; holds the office of Township Clerk; married Kate Arthurs, Oct. 3, 1872; they have two children, Frances Bertie, born Oct. 6, 1873, and Helen May, July 15, 1876.

Giles Sarah Mrs. widow of John P. Giles; Sec. 15; P. O. Little York; U. P.

GLOVER WM. M. Farmer; Sec. 22; P. O. Little York; born in Abbeyville Dist., S. C., Nov. 14, 1828; came to this Co. in 1846; Rep; U. P.; 80 acres, value $3,000; married Miss Adaline Conner, Feb. 10, 1853, who was born in Rockbridge Co., Va., Sept. 15, 1857; they have had eight children, four of whom are living, Sarah A., Emma A., Lizzie A. and John Frank; Mr. G. has been Constable for seven years; also served three years in 83rd I. V. I.

Gourley J. B. farmer; Sec. 4; P. O. Duck Creek; rep; Prot.

Gourley Rob't, Sr. retired; Sec.4; P.O. Duck Creek; ind; Presb.

GOURLEY ROBERT, Jr. Farmer and Stock Raiser; P.O. Duck Creek; born in Washington Co., Penn., Sept. 3, 1836; came to this Co. in 1859; Rep; Prot; 470 acres, with brothers, value $20,000; lived in Penn. twenty-three years; his father, Robert Gourley, Sr., was born in Washington Co., Penn., in 1803; has five sons and three daughters living, Alexander, Robert, Jr., John, Thomas R., James B. Ann E., Sarah J. and Catharine.

Graham L. S. farmer; Sec. 16; P. O. Little York; rep; U. P.

Graham L. T. farmer; Sec. 16; P. O. Little York; rep; U. P.

HIRST J. S. blacksmith; Sec. 31; P. O. Little York; rep; Meth.

HANNA O. L. Farmer and Stock Raiser; Secs. 31, and 6 in Hale tp.; P. O. Little York; Rep; Univ; born in this Co., March 14, 1842; has 210 acres of land, value, $10,500; personal, $6,000; holds office of School Director; was in Army, 148th I. V. I.; is now living on native place, where his father, John Hanna, first settled in this Co., and died in the fall of 1862; married Miss Sarah J. Curtis, Sept. 26, 1867, who was from New York; they have three children, Lulu Dell, Clyde L. and Lilian, all living.

Henry E. E., P. M. and Clerk; Little York; rep; U. P.; from Pennsylvania.

Henry S. B. farmer, rents; P. O. Little York; rep; Meth.

Hogue Zenas, farmer; P. O. Duck Creek; rep; U. P.; was in 36th I. V. I.

Hollindrake Jas. farmer; Sec. 6; P. O. Duck Creek; rep.

Hutchinson A. farmer, rents of G. S. Moore; P. O. Little York; rep; U. P.; West Va.

Hutchinson Joseph, farmer, rents; P.O. Little York; rep; U. P.; from Pennsylvania.

IVEY J. J. farmer; Sec. 33; P. O. Little York; rep.

JOENK HANS, shoemaker; Little York; rep; Presb; from Prussia.

Johnson B. L. Secs. 7 and 18; P. O. Little York; 360 acres, value $14,400; Conn.

Jones C. farmer; Sec. 8; P. O. Duck Creek; rep.

Jones Isaac, farmer; P. O. Duck Creek.

Jones John, Sr., farmer; Sec. 8; P. O. Duck Creek; rep; Meth.

Jones John, Jr., farmer; P. O. Duck Creek; rep.

KILGORE GABE, farmer; rents; P. O. Little York; rep; U. P.; from Ohio.

KENDALL A. B. Farmer; Sec. 36; P. O. Denny; born in Greene Co., O., Dec. 14, 1830; came to this Co. in 1831; rep; U. P.; 160 acres, value $5,200; his father, Jas. Kendall, was one of the earliest settlers; came with others from Ohio in 1831; A. B. Kendall married Nancy Turnbull, April 23, 1856, who was born in this Co.; two sons and one daughter; Wm. H., Mary E., John A.; married the second time Almira Furguson, who was born in Penn.; they have three children, Nancy J., David I. and Fanny Belle, all living.

KENDALL W. S. Farmer; Sec 36; P. O. Denny; born in Greene Co., O., Aug. 31, 1827; Rep; U. P.; 160 acres, value $5,200; among the earliest settlers; married Mrs. Virginia Home, April 12, 1870, who was born May 3, 1840; she has one daughter, Nancy E. Home; children —James F., David H., and Lydia I.; all living.

Kirk Alex. C. farmer; Sec. 13; P. O. Monmouth; rep; U. P.; from Ohio.

Kirk Wm. S. farmer; Sec. 13; P. O. Monmouth; rep; U. P.; from Ohio.

Koch Geo. J. wagon-maker; Little York; rep; from Iowa.

LEE MORRIS, farmer; Sec. 24; P. O. Denny; dem; Cath.

Lee Wm. farmer; Sec. 24; P. O. Denny; dem; Cath.

Long Reuben, farmer; laborer; P. O. Denny; rep.

McCLUNG S. H. physician; Little York; Jefferson Med. Col.; rep; Presb.

McCoy Jas. farmer; P. O. Denny; rep; U. P.

McCoy Joseph, farmer; Sec. 32; P. O. Little York; rep; U. P.; 160 acres.

McCoy Thos. farmer, rents; Little York; rep.

McCRACKEN J. R. Farmer and Stock Raiser; Sec. 1; P. O. Norwood; born in Indiana, May 23, 1836; came to this Co. in 1865; Rep; U. P.; 240 acres, value $9,600; was in 77th I. V. I. three years; came to this State in 1852; lived in

Peoria Co. thirteen years; married Margaret E. Walker in 1860; they have four children living, Francis R., Iva, Guy W. and Ralph M.; one daughter deceased.

McCRERY J. C. Farmer; Sec. 11; P. O. Little York; born in S. Carolina, Sept. 13, 1834; came to this Co. in 1836; Rep; E. P.; 80 acres, value $4,500; his father, J. C. McCrery, was one of the early settlers here, an Elder in the church until his death, May 3, 1856; married Lizzie S. Humphrey, in 1858, who was born in this Co. March 24, 1847; they have seven children, Mary M., Stella F., Lizzie A., Sam'l R., John C., Jessie M. and Clara E., all living.

McCrery J. L. Farmer; Sec. 13; P. O. Little Rock; rep; U. P.; 120 acres.

McCRERY S. F. Farmer and Stock Raiser; P. O. Little York; born in S. Carolina, March 16, 1842; came to this Co. in 1836; Rep; U. P.; 325 acres, value $17,800; personal, $6,000; has lived on the same place forty-one years, where his father, J. C. McCrery, first settled, who died here May 3, 1856; married Miss Emma J. Dalzell, Oct. 16, 1872; they have two children, Alice and John Roy.

McElhenny Wm. farmer; P. O. Little York; rep; U. P.

McGregor Jas. H. farmer, rents; Sec. 14; P. O. Denny; rep; U. P.

McINTYRE M. S. Farmer and Stock Raiser; P. O. Duck Creek; born in this Co., May 11, 1857; Rep; Presb; his father owns 257 acres, value $17,000; now living on his native place, where his father first settled in 1852; one brother, W. J.; four sisters—Lizzie; Anna, married N. W. Main; Ellen; and Araminda; married Viola Bullock, from Mercer Co., Ill, Nov. 15, 1876.

McNamarra B. farmer; Sec. 17; P. O. Little York; dem; Cath.

McNamarra Jas. farmer, lives with his father; P. O. Little York; dem; Cath.

McNamarra Wm. farmer, lives with his father; P. O. Little York; dem; Cath.

Mahaffey J. C. harness-maker; Little York; rep; U. P.; from Ohio.

MALEY WASHINGTON, Farmer; Sec. 30; P. O. Little York; born in this Co., Feb. 26, 1835; Rep; Prot; 284 acres, value $9,940; holds office of School Director; is now living on the same place which his father, Thos. Maley, first improved, who died here in 1860; married Mary A. Fisher, who was born in Mercer Co., Ill.; they have three sons, John T., Charles E. and Willard, all living.

Martin David, farmer; Sec. 28; P. O. Little York; rep; U. P.

Martin Findley, farmer; P. O. Little York; rep; U. P.

Martin Hugh, farmer; Sec. 21; P. O. Little York; rep; U. P.; 320 acres, val. $16,000.

MARTIN JOHN, Farmer and Stock Raiser; Sec. 27; P. O. Little York; born in Muskingum Co., O., Sept. 26, 1821; came to this Co. in 1832; Rep; U. P.; 600 acres and orchard 600 trees, value $30,000; personal, $5,000; has held office of School Director for last six years, and is Director in Monmouth National Bank; his father, Hugh Martin, came to this State, Fulton Co., in Fall of 1829; then moved to this Co. in 1832, and first settled on the very place where now is the residence of Mr. Martin, where he has lived constantly for forty-five years; married Miss Mary J. Gibson, Dec. 25, 1862, who was born at Monmouth, Sept. 22, 1834; they have four children, Wm. E., born Sept. 6, 1862; Howard L., Oct. 23, 1865; Sarah E., Dec. 21, 1868; and Frederick A., Sept. 2, 1876.

Maskrey Wm. farmer; Sec. 36; P. O. Denny; Ind; from Pennsylvania.

Matson W. S. farmer; Sec. 3; P. O. Duck Creek; dem; 165 acres; from Ohio.

Monteith Alex. farmer; Sec. 33; P. O. Little York; rep; U. P.; 80 acres; from Penn.

Monteith J. A. student; Sec. 33; P. O. Little York; rep; U. P.; born Warren Co.

Morehead John I. farmer, rents; Sec. 30; P. O. Little York; dem; Meth.

Morehead Lewis, laborer, works for James Boyd; rep.

Moore D. T. laborer; Little York; rep.

MOORE GEO. S. Retired; Sec. 11; P. O. Little York; born in Henry Co., Ky., Sept. 2, 1811; came to this Co. in 1835; Rep; U. P.; 100 acres, value $5,500; moved from Kentucky to Ohio in 1825, where he lived ten years; then came to Illinois in 1835; married Mary Giles, Oct. 23, 1832, who was born March 6, 1808; died April 9, 1861; children, John G., born July 18, 1833; Hugh R., Jan. 18, 1836; James C. and Samuel, both deceased.

MOORE H. R. Farmer; Sec. 13; P. O. Little York; born in this Co. Jan. 17, 1837; Rep; U. P.; 90 acres, value $5,000; has always lived in this Co.; his father one of the early settlers here; married Soretta M. Pyles, Jan. 21, 1858, who was born in Washington Co., Pa., April 26, 1837; they have four children, George C., Ida M., Eva Blanche and Wilbur C., all living.

Moore R. W.; Little York; rep; U. P.

Morrison M. M. farmer; Sec. 34; P. O. Little York; rep; U. P.; 140 acres, value $7,000.

Morrison R. P. merchant; Little York; rep; U. P.; from Ohio.

Muncy M. E.; Little York; rep; U. P.; born in Warren Co.

Munson Isaac laborer, works for O. L. Hanna; P. O. Little York; rep.

Murray John, farm laborer; P. O. Denny; dem; Cath.

NICHOLS JOHN, farmer; Sec. 4; P. O. Little York; rep; U. P.

NICOL WM. J. Farmer and Stock Raiser; Secs. 18 and 19; P. O. Little York; born in Rock Island Co., Ill., Sept. 18, 1846; Ind; 280 acres, value $10,000; has always lived in this State, and in this Co. twenty-four years.

O'LEARY THOS.; Sec. 25; P. O. Spring Grove; dem; Cath.

O'Leary Wm.; Sec. 25; P. O. Spring Grove; dem; Cath.

Osborne Geo. P. farmer; Sec. 24; P. O. Little York; dem; 300 acres.

PAINE B. F. farmer; Sec. 26; P. O. Denny; rep; Ind; 64 acres, value $3,700.

Paine E. A. farmer; Sec. 26; rep; Prot; 140 acres, value $7,000; Lake Co., O.

Paine Geo. A. farmer, lives with his father; Sec. 26; P. O. Denny; rep.

PAINE JOHN E. Farmer and Stock Raiser; Sec. 27; P. O. Denny; born in Painesville, O., Oct. 2, 1824; came to this Co. in 1836; Rep; U. P.; 420 acres, value $21,000; has lived forty years on the same place where his father, Chas. H. Paine, first settled in this Co.; was in 83d I. V. I. three years; married Miss Ann E. Turnbull, March 17, 1860, who was born in this Co., March 13, 1835; nine children living, five sons and four daughters; one son deceased.

PAINE WALTER N. Farmer; Sec. 26; P. O. Denny; born in Lake Co., O., Sept. 21, 1844; Rep; Prot; came to this Co. in 1854; served three years in army, 83d I. V. I.; married Mary Lester, Oct. 3, 1867, who was born in Indiana, April 10, 1846; two children living, Carrie L. and Eliza H.; one son deceased.

Parks Jno. farmer; Sec. 35; P. O. Denny; rep; Prot; 70 acres.

Parkinson John, farmer; Sec. 28; P.O. Little York; rep; U. P.; 164 acres; from Ohio.

Parkinson Wm. farmer, lives with his father; Sec. 28; P.O. Little York; rep; U. P.

Parsons Mrs. A. T., widow; Sec. 33; P. O. Little York; U. P.; 260 acres; from Vt.

Pate Chas. farmer; Sec. 32; P. O. Little York; rep; 10 acres; from Indiana.

Patterson J. R. farmer; Sec. 11; P. O. Little York; rep; U. P.; 80 acres; from Penn.

Payne W. farmer, renter; Sec. 24; P. O. Denny; dem; Cath.

Piper Henry, farmer, rents; P. O. Denny.

Pollock A. P. farmer; Little York; rep.

POLLOCK J. F. Retired; Sec. 28; Little York; born in Nova Scotia, Dec. 5, 1806; came to this Co. in 1831; Rep; Prot; 80 acres, value $6,000; is one of the early settlers here; for many years engaged in the mercantile trade at this place; was first postmaster here, and held the office over twenty years; married Rebecca McFarland, July 30, 1833, who was born in Green Co., Ohio, Nov. 2, 1815; died Aug. 14, 1869; ten children living, Mary J., Margery A., Martha K., Amelia, John S., James F., Jr., William R., Caroline, Arthur P., Eulalia May and Estie L.; one son deceased.

Pollock J. S. harness-maker; Little York; rep; Ind.

Pollock Perry, farmer; Little York; rep; born in this Co.

Pollock W. R. farmer; Little York; rep; born in this Co.

Porter J. Calvin, farmer, lives with his father; Sec. 2; P. O. Alexis; dem; Presb.

Porter J. Doyle, farmer, lives with his father; Sec. 1; P. O. Norwood; rep; Presb.

Porter J. Robb, farmer, lives on his father's place; Sec. 1; P. O. Alexis; 260 acres.

Porter Jas. Lane, farmer, lives with father; Sec. 2; P. O. Alexis; dem; Presb.

PORTER ROBERT, Farmer and Stock Raiser; Sec. 8; P. O. Duck Creek; born in Guernsey Co., Ohio, Feb 27, 1836; came to this Co. in December, 1856; Rep; U. P.; 338 acres, value $16,900; personal, $3,500; held office of Highway Commissioner for three years; married Margaret Gibson, Feb. 13, 1862, who was born in this Co. Dec. 8, 1835; they have five children living, John E., George G., Sarah I., Charlie and Anna B.; one son deceased.

PORTER R. W. Farmer and Stock Raiser; Sec. 1; P. O. Norwood, Mercer Co.; born in Huntingdon Co., Pa., April 9, 1822; Rep; Presb; 220 acres, $11,000; personal, $1,000; lived in Pennsylvania thirty-two years; came to this State and Co. in 1854; has held office of County Supervisor five years, and Township Assessor for nine years; married Miss Ann Doyle in 1847; she died in 1854, in Illinois; five children, James K., William M., Sarah E., Emma J. and J. Doyle; married the second time to Nancy Robb, Jan. 28, 1856, who was born in Penn.; two children, Thomas L. and Anna M., all living.

PORTER WM. Farmer and Stock Raiser; Sec. 2; P. O. Alexis; born in Huntingdon Co., Pa., Nov. 5, 1819; came to this Co. in 1853; Dem; Presb; 373 acres, $15,000; personal, $2,000; has lived in this Co. twenty-four years; has held offices of Road Commissioner, School Director and Justice of Peace for many years; married H. Isabella Lane, March 25, 1845, who was born in Huntingdon Co., Pa., Oct. 15, 1824; they have ten children, Sarah Josephine, Mary Etta, Minnie, James L., J. Calvin, Clara, Ada L., W. Frank, Warren J. and Pearl; all living.

RANNY GILBERT, farmer; Sec. 6; P. O. Duck Creek; Rep.

Ranny N. C. farmer; Sec. 7; P. O. Duck Creek; rep.

Ranny Royal, farmer; Sec. 6; P. O. Duck Creek; rep.

REYNOLDS J. B. Farmer and Stock Raiser; P. O. Little York; born in this Co. Feb. 18, 1838; Dem; U. P.; 190 acres, value $14,500; personal, $3,000; this is his native Co.; his father, Thos. Reynolds, who died June 16, 1870, was among the early settlers of this Co.; mother lives with son, at an advanced age; married Araminta C. McCrery, Feb. 18, 1868, who was born in this Co., June 25, 1849; they have had three children, May Belle, born Jan. 22, 1869; two daughters deceased.

Riley Thos. farmer; Sec. 30; P. O. Little York; dem; Cath; 200 acres.

Roberts H. H. farm laborer; P. O. Denny; rep; Prot.

Robertson J. F. farm laborer; P. O. Denny.

Rockwell A. H. farmer and prop. Rockwell mills; Sec. 35; Denny; rep; Ind; Ohio.

ROCKWELL A. J. Farmer and Stock Raiser; Sec. 35; P. O. Denny; born in Ashtabula Co., Ohio, Jan. 16, 1823; came to this Co. in 1832; Dem; Ind; 235 acres and orchard 500 trees, $17,600; has lived on same place forty-five years; his father, L. P. Rockwell, came here in 1830; built and owned the first mill in this Co.; married Miss Mary J. Craig, March 22, 1846, who was born in Ohio, Jan. 23, 1823, and died Jan. 29, 1848; married the second time, Helen M. Burnett, Feb. 12, 1856, who was born in Washington Co., N. Y., May 23, 1833; six children, four sons and two daughters, Fannie F., John L., James E., Albert J., Jr., Archie M. and Ada G., all living.

Rockwell W. E. farmer, lives with his father; Denny.

Rodgers Nicholas, farmer; Sec. 14; P. O. Little York; rep; U. P.

Romans P. E. laborer; P. O. Denny; dem; Prot; from Kentucky.

Ruse E. farmer; Sec. 24; P. O. Monmouth; rep; Ind; 80 acres.

SANDSTEDT J. E. farm laborer; P. O. Little York; rep; Prot.

Scull Benj. farmer; Sec. 29; P. O. Little York; dem; Ind; from New Jersey.

Scull Ebenezer, farmer; Sec. 29; P. O. Little York; dem; 170 acres; from New Jersey.

Scull Mark, farmer; lives with his father; P. O. Little York.

Seaton J. D. farmer; Sec. 18; P. O. Little York; dem; U.P.; from Scotland.

Shannon Hugh, farmer, rents; P. O. Duck Creek; rep; U. P.

Shannon James, farmer, renter; P. O. Duck Creek; rep; U. P.; from Ireland.

Shepherd Jno. blacksmith; Little York; rep; Ind; from Scotland.

Shoemaker L. G. farmer, rents; Sec. 13; P. O. Little York; rep.

Shunick Thomas, farmer; Sec. 14; P. O. Denny; dem; Cath.

Smith Henry, blacksmith; Little York; dem; from Pennsylvania.

Snell Geo. farmer, lives with his father; Sec. 36; P. O. Denny.

Snell L. farmer; Sec. 36; P. O. Denny; rep; Bapt; 80 acres; from Indiana.

Sterrett D. S. farmer, renter; P. O. Little York; rep; U. P.; from Ohio.

STEWART FRANK, Farmer; Sec. 31; P. O. Little York; born in Chester Co., Penn., Dec. 29, 1828; came to this Co. in 1859; Rep; Adv; 170 acres, value $8,000; married Miss Susan J. Henderson in March, 1859, who was born in Guernsey Co., Ohio; they have nine sons living, John R., Wm. W., Edwin W., Willis B., Louis B., Andrew R., Jesse T. O., Ernest Mac, and Thomas B.; one son deceased.

Stewart Geo. W. farm laborer; P. O. Little York; rep; from Ohio.

Stewart R. C. farmer; Sec. 29; P. O. Little York; rep; U. P.; 112 acres; from Penn.

Stewart Wm. farmer, rents; Little York; rep.

Streeter Wm. farmer, rents; Sec. 10; P. O. Little York; rep; U. P.

THOMPSON MITCHEL, farmer; Sec. 14; P. O. Monmouth; rep; U. P.; 53 acs.

Thompson Martha, widow; Sec. 14; P. O. Monmouth; U. P.; 107 acres; Penn.

VENOY ELIAS, laborer; Sec. 24; P. O. Little York; dem; Prot.

WATSON J. A. farmer, rents; Little York; rep.

Watson Robt. farm laborer; Little York; rep; U. P.

WALLACE T. B. Merchant, firm Wallace & Morrison, General Merchants; Little York; born in this Co., Oct. 21, 1843; Rep; U. P.; 280 acres in estate, value $14,000; his father, Rev. John Wallace, was one of the early settlers here; came in 1833, as a missionary of the Associate Reformed Church, in which he was the first in this region; he died Dec. 20, 1875; his widow living with her only son; T. B. Wallace married Miss Abbie A. Copeland, Jan. 8, 1868, who was born in Washington Co., N. Y., Nov. 12, 1848; they have two children, John C., born Nov. 16, 1868; Roberta Frances, born Feb. 14, 1870.

Wheeland Jas. farmer, rents; P. O. Little York; rep.

Wheeland Jno. farm laborer; P. O. Duck Creek.

Whitchill Cal. farmer; Sec. 10; P. O. Little York; rep; U. P.; from Penn.

Whitchill Jas. farmer; Sec. 10; P. O. Little York; rep; U. P.; from Penn.

Whitchill Thos. retired; Sec. 10; P. O. Little York; rep; U. P.; 160 acres; from Penn.

Wiley R. W. farmer; Sec. 13; P. O. Little York; dem; U. P.; 80 acres.

Wiley S. A. farmer; P. O. Little York; rep.

WRIGHT JOHN A. Farmer; Sec. 16; P. O. Little York; born in Adams Co., O., Nov. 6, 1837; came to this Co. in 1851; Rep; U. P.; served four years in army, in 17th and 83d I. V. I.; married Miss Sarah J. Gowdy, in Oct., 1866, who was born in Greene Co., O.; they have two children, Willie Grant and Fannie May.

YOUNG JOSEPH S. Farmer and Stock Raiser; Secs. 34 and 35; P. O. Denny; born Adams Co., O., Aug. 23, 1835; came to this Co. 1857; Rep; U. P.; owns 120 acres of land, value $7,500; holds office of Highway Commissioner of tp. of Sumner; married Minerva L. Mitchell, Nov. 17, 1863, who was born Sept. 13, 1846, in Warren Co., Ill.; they have six children—Fannie E., Cora J., Chas. M., Della, Mary A. and Bertha G., all living.

ZARR DAVID, farmer, rents; Sec. 9; P. O. Little York; rep.

LITTLE YORK BUSINESS DIRECTORY.

Cuthbert W. L., M. D., Physician and Surgeon.
Wallace & Morrison, Dealers in General Merchandise.

GREENBUSH TOWNSHIP.

ADAMS WILLIS, farmer; P. O. Greenbush; from Kentucky.

Albert David, farmer; Sec. 18; P. O. Greenbush; rep; 12 acres; from Germany.

Almond Thos. weaver; Greenbush; dem; Bapt.

Alvord J. E. physician; Greenbush; rep; Meth; born Illinois.

ALEXANDER W. Farmer; Sec. 34; P. O. Prairie City; born in Ill., Dec. 3, 1852; came to this Co. in 1855; Dem; owns 160 acres land, valued at $9,600; married Carrie Matthews, July 10, 1876; is the son of E. A. Alexander, who lives in McDonough Co., Ill.

Austin Jno. mail carrier; P. O. Greenbush; rep; born Illinois.

BABBET S. J. farm laborer; P. O. Avon.

Barlow J. N. engineer; Greenbush; dem; from New York.

Barnum L. W. rents of Alfred Tompkins; P. O. Avon; dem; from New York.

BEAM H. Farmer; Sec. 16; P. O. Avon; born in Penn., March 22, 1813; came to this Co. in 1851; Rep; Chris; owns 80 acres of land, valued at $5,000; married Nancy Spencer in 1838; seven children, Orlando J., J. O., Rachel A., Mary E., Barbara M., Sarah J., and Addie, who died in 1867; first went to Ohio and lived there 18 years, and then to Illinois, and settled in Warren Co.

Beam Jos. farmer; Sec. 14; P. O. Avon; rep; 40 acres; from Ohio.

Bivens Jno. lives with father on Sec. 14; P. O. Avon; dem.

Bell John, farm hand; P. O. Greenbush.

BIVENS JOSEPH. Farmer; Sec 12; P. O. Avon; born in Penn., Oct. 10, 1810; came to this Co. in 1860; Rep; Meth; owns 105 acres of land, valued at $5,250; married Eliza McEwen; have nine children; Mr. Bivens' farm in 2½ miles from Avon, on the C., B. & Q. R. R.

BOND JOHN C. Retired; Sec. 18; P. O. Greenbush; born in Tenn., Dec. 25, 1799; came to this Co. in 1832; Dem; Old School Bapt; owns 153 acres of land, valued at $7,650; first wife was Polly Grimsley; second wife, Mary Singleton; had five children by first wife and three by second wife, Susanna, William G., Jesse W., Rubie L.; Mr. Bond was the first J. P. in south side of Co.; been County Commissioner and Supervisor for 14 years; was in Black Hawk War, and is a cousin to George Walton, one of the signers of the Declaration of Independence.

Bond J. C. Jr. lives with his grand-father, on Sec. 18; P. O. Greenbush; dem; Cal.

Bowman A. R. rents of W. T. Snapp; Sec. 16; P. O. Greenbush; rep; born Illinois.

Bowman Jno. proprietor Greenbush Mills; Greenbush; rep; Meth; from Penn.

Bright Wm. rents of O. J. Beam; Sec. 15; rep; from Ohio.

Brown Samuel, Sec. 7; P. O. Greenbush; dem; Meth; 25 acres; from Indiana.

Brown William, laborer; P. O. Avon; rep; Cong; from New York.

Buckner A. F. lives with F. G. Snapp; Sec. 7; P. O. Greenbush; rep; from Germany.

Butler John, farmer, rents of John Butler; Sec. 11; P. O. Greenbush; dem.

BUTLER V. W. Justice of the Peace; Greenbush; born in O., Sept. 20, 1825; came to this Co. in 1839; Dem; Chris; owns 160 acres, valued at $9,600; his first wife was Rachel Swain; second wife was Harriet Williams; have seven children, two by first wife and five by last wife, John L., William A., Mary A., Manly E., Ida H., Esta V., and Rachel; is Road Commissioner and Assessor; he owns house and four lots in Greenbush.

Butler W. R. postmaster, keeps restaurant; Greenbush; dem.

CATES RICHARD, cattle trader; Sec. 36; P. O. Prairie City; dem.

CARMADY J. A. Farmer; P. O. Greenbush; born in Mo., Feb. 3, 1853; came to this Co. in 1874; Rep; value of personal property, $1,500; married Fannie Call in 1876.

Chatterton C. farmer; Sec. 25; P. O. Avon; rep; from New York.

Chatterton L. B. farmer; Sec. 24; P. O. Avon; dem; 80 acres.

Claycomb Alf. farmer, renter; P. O. Greenbush; dem.

Clayton C. B. Sec. 7; P. O. Greenbush; dem; 16 acres; from Kentucky.

Clayton S. M. lives on Thomas Wilson's farm; Sec. 36; P. O. Prairie City; dem.

Clore Albert, farmer; P. O. Greenbush; ind.

Clore Wm. farmer; Sec. 5; P. O. Greenbush; Bapt; 83 acres; value $3,320.

Clovis W. A. rents of Judge Lawrence; Sec. 36; P. O. Prairie City; ind.

Coll Mrs. F. N. Sec. 19; P. O. Greenbush; 160 acres; from Germany.

Conley James, rents of Ben Wood; Sec. 30; P. O. Walnut Grove; dem; from Ireland.

Conley John, lives with brother, James Conley; P. O. Walnut Grove; dem.

Coon Jas. farmer; rents of J. A. Butler; dem.

Coon John, P. O. Greenbush; rep; from Indiana.

Coon N. N. rents of J. A. Butler; Sec. 17; P. O. Greenbush; rep; Bapt; from Ind.

Corcoran Jno., Sr., lives on Barney Slocy's farm; Sec. 26; dem; from Ireland.

Corcoran Jno., Jr., lives on Barney Slocy's farm; Sec. 22; dem; born Illinois.

Coursan David, Sec. 18; dem; 15 acres; from Ohio.

Coursan J. T. farm laborer; P. O. Avon; dem.

Coursan Samuel, farmer; Sec. 14; P. O. Avon; rep; Chris; 59 acres; from Ohio.

Crabill Edgar, lives with his father; Sec. 15; P. O. Avon; dem; born Illinois.

Crabill Jas. lives with his father; Sec. 15; P. O. Avon; dem; born Illinois.

Crabill Noah, farmer; Sec. 15; P. O. Avon; dem; Chris; 202 acres; from Ohio.

Crowley Thomas farmer, rents of Barney Slocy; Sec. 26; P. O. Avon; dem.

Cunningham Henry, farmer and mnfr. grape wine; P. O. Avon; rep; 14 acres.

DAMITZ ERNEST, farmer; Sec. 15; P. O. Avon; rep; Presb; 40 acres.

DAMITZ F. W. Farmer; Sec. 14; P. O. Avon; born in Germany, Dec. 1, 1841; came to this Co. in 1847; owns 80 acres of land, valued at $3,200; married Hattie Acton in 1872; have two children, Josephine and Iva L.; went to California in 1862, stayed three years, then came back to Illinois and has lived here since.

Damitz Oscar, lives with his father; Sec. 15; P. O. Avon; rep; Presb; born Illinois.

Darie Daniel, farmer; Sec. 25; P. O. Avon; dem; from New Jersey.

Darneille L. painter; Greenbush; dem; born Illinois.

Darneille Orlando, tax collector; P. O. Greenbush; dem; Meth; born Illinois.

Davis Jas. farmer, lives with his father; Sec. 35; P. O. Prairie City; rep; born Illinois.

DAVIS ROBERT. Farmer and Stock Raiser; Sec. 35; P. O. Prairie City; born in Pennsylvania, Dec. 19, 1819; came to this Co. in 1855; Rep; owns 400 acres of land, valued at $17,600; married Mary Hagerts in April, 1845; have six children, Elizabeth, Susan, Sarah, James, Charley and George.

Davis W. H. farmer; Sec. 12; P. O. Avon; rep; 80 acres; born Illinois.

DECKER A. N. Farmer and School-teacher; P. O. Greenbush; born in New York, Jan. 9, 1849; came to this Co. in 1867; Rep; rents farm of W. McMahill; value of estate $1,500; married Media Starr, July 4, 1875; one child, Royal W.

Delaney Richard, rents of Barney Slocy; P. O. Avon; dem.

Delaney Thos. rents of Barney Slocy; P. O. Avon; dem.

Deltonte N. miner; P. O. Avon; rep; from Ohio.

Dougherty B. A. rents of S. Tompkins; Sec. 25; P. O. Avon; dem.

SPRING GROVE TOWNSHIP

Dougherty Jas. farmer, rents of S. Tompkins; Sec. 25; P. O. Avon; dem.

Dougherty W. rents of S. Tompkins; Sec. 25; dem.

Drake S. H. farmer, rents of Jos. Mears; Sec. 7; P. O. Greenbush; rep; from N. J.

ELLINGER JNO. lives with his father; Sec. 12; P. O. Avon; dem.

Ellinger Jos. lives with his father; Sec. 12; P. O. Avon; dem.

Ellinger Saml. farmer; Sec. 12; P. O. Avon; dem; Univ; 250 acres.

EDOM JNO. Farmer and Stock Raiser; Sec. 24; P. O. Avon; born in England, Dec. 28, 1806; came to this Co. in 1866; Rep; Mis. Bapt; owns 87½ acres land, valued at $5,000; married Emmeline M. Draper in 1838; their union was blessed with twelve children, William E., Sarah L., Almira L., Esther L., Maria J., Martha L., Annis M., Charles B., Dora, Albert K.

Everett Jno. rents of Wilson; Sec. 36; P. O. Prairie City; rep; from Pennsylvania.

FORSHEE G. R. rents of Susan Taft; Sec. 35; P. O. Prairie City; rep; N. J.

Foster Alex. miner; P. O. Avon; dem.

Fouts Jno. rents of Thos. Ennis; Sec. 11; P. O. Avon; rep; New Light.

Franklin Geo. farm laborer; P. O. Prairie City; dem.

Fullerton Henry, farm hand; P. O. Avon; rep; born Illinois.

GAYMAN CHRIS. prop. Mount Rock mill; Sec. 23; P. O. Avon; rep; Chris.

GILLETT O. F. Farmer; Sec. 13; P. O. Avon; born in Butler Co., Ohio. Dec. 14, 1829; came to this Co. in 1853; Rep; owns 40 acres of land, valued at $1,600; married Mary J. Knowlton; nine children; was sergeant in the army, in Co. H, 83d Reg. I. V. I.; served nine months.

Greene Fowler, clerk in store in Prairie City; Ind.

GREEN L. M. Farmer and Stock Raiser; Sec. 21; P. O. Avon; born in Tennessee, June 11, 1814; came to this Co. in 1864; Ind; owns 540 acres land, valued at $32,400; married Nancy O. Abell, Sept. 30, 1840; have five children, John A., William B., Fowler H., Lynn and May; is Supervisor and Road Commissioner, and was Supervisor five years ago.

Greene W. B. lives on his father's farm; Sec. 21; P. O. Avon; lib; Univ.

Griffin W. C. farm laborer; P. O. Greenbush; dem; born Illinois.

HALL WYATT, lives with his father; Sec. 31; P. O. Walnut Grove; rep.

HALL LEONARD. Farmer; Sec. 31; P. O. Walnut Grove; born in New York, Dec. 23, 1819; came to this Co. in 1845; Rep; Meth; owns 130 acres of land, valued

at $8,000; married Susan McMahill in 1853; have six children, William, Wyatt, Warren, Mary, Pliny, Aletha; been Road Commissioner.

Harman A. R. hotel keeper; P. O. Greenbush; rep; Mis. Bapt; from Kentucky.

Harman G. W. carpenter; P. O. Greenbush; rep; Mis. Bapt; from Kentucky.

Harrah J. W. farmer, rents of B. Wood; Sec. 30; P. O. Walnut Grove; ind; Ohio.

Harrah L. M. lives with his father; Sec. 30; P. O. Walnut Grove; dem; born Illinois.

Hartford J. F. farmer and gardener; Sec. 35; P. O. Prairie City; rep; from Penn.

Heinzman Fred, farmer; Sec. 33; P. O. Prairie City; dem; 160 acres; Germany.

Heinzman Jacob, lives with his son-in-law, Jacob Long; Sec. 21; P. O. Prairie City.

Hendricks J. farmer; Sec. 24; P. O. Avon; 40 acres; rep.

HENDRICKS J. M. Farmer and Miner; Sec. 32; P. O. Avon; born in Ind., Feb. 4, 1842; came to this Co. in 1839; Rep; F. W. Bapt; owns 40 acres, valued at $2,400; married Barbara Beam, Aug. 29, 1865; has three children, Alice L., Mary L. and Fannie E.; was in Army in Co. D, 64th Ill. Vol.; held a non-commissioned office for two years.

Hewett A. E., lives with his father; Sec. 29; P. O. Walnut Grove; rep; born Illinois.

Hewett H. H. farmer; Sec. 29; P.O. Youngstown; rep; 320 acres; from Ohio.

Hewett O. L. farmer; Sec. 30; P. O. Walnut Grove; rep; 330 acres; from Ohio.

Hict J. M. farmer and renter; dem; born Ill.

Hilliard C. lives with his son-in-law, Everts; Sec. 36; rep; from Pennsylvania.

Hoff Henry, farmer; Sec. 18; P. O. Greenbush; rep; 35 acres; from Germany.

Hoffman William, farmer; Sec. 18; P. O. Greenbush; rep; 30 acres; from Germany.

Holeman Isaac farmer; Sec. 10; P.O. Avon; dem; 285 acres; from Indiana.

Holeman Uriah, farmer; Sec. 4; P.O. Greenbush; dem; O. S. Bapt; 190 acres.

Holman J. G. farmer, rents Uriah Holeman's farm; dem; from Indiana.

Holman Riley, lives with his father; Sec. 10; P. O. Avon; dem; born Illinois.

Honts Geo. farm laborer; P. O. Greenbush; dem.

Honts J. B. laborer; dem; born Illinois.

Honts Peter, wagon-maker; P.O. Greenbush; dem; from Virginia.

Hutchinson John, lives with J. O. Beam; Sec. 23; Ind.

IRVING S. C. Blacksmith; Greenbush; born in N. J., May 8, 1839; came to this Co. in 1866; Rep; owns 7 town lots, valued at $700; married Ellen Ammerman, May 4, 1859; wife was born June 15, 1835; have six children, Lucy E., Ida N., Emma, Albert E., Sissy, Halley and May; was in Army in Co. A, 30th N. J. Vol.; held the office of School Director; wife's religion, Presb. preferred.

JOHNSON CONDON, lives with his mother; Sec. 19; dem; born Illinois.

Johnson John B. farm hand; P. O. Greenbush; rep; from Sweden.

JOHNSON J. C. Merchant; Greenbush; born in Wisconsin, June 30, 1839; came to this Co. in 1840; Dem; owns 50 acres land, valued at $2,000; married Emily R. Pittman, born May 16, 1861; have four children, Jesse, Newton, Charles and Mabel, who died Oct. 15, 1875; has held the offices of Constable and School Director; was a Lieutenant in Co. H, 83rd Ill. Inf.

JOHNSON MRS. WALTER, lives on Sec. 19; P. O. Greenbush; born in Tenn., Aug. 10, 1819; came to this Co. in 1832; owns 52 acres of land, valued at $2,600; is the widow of Walter Johnson, who died Dec. 13, 1876; eleven children; those living are J. C., J. P., Eva, Zanna P., Carden, Sarah L., Katie C., Anna and Ruby B.

Johnston Fred, farm hand; P.O. Greenbush; from Sweden.

Johnston James, P. O. Greenbush; from Sweden.

KARNES JACOB, farmer; P. O. Greenbush; rep; born Illinois.

Kelly John, Sec. 13; P. O. Avon; dem; 30 acres.

Kelley T. J. lives with his father; P. O. Avon; Sec. 13; dem.

Kelly Mrs. Sec. 13; P. O. Avon; 40 acres; from Ohio.

KELLOUGH C. H. farmer; Sec. 28; P. O. Prairie City; born in Md., March 16, 1834; came to this Co. in 1854; Rep; Presb; owns 120 acres of land, valued at $7,200; married Margaret Holcomb, Dec. 1855; have six children, Martha S., Sarah B., Lura M., Mary E., Anna A. and Minnie E.; has held the office of School Trustee.

KELLOUGH J. M. Farmer and Stock Raiser; Sec. 28; P. O. Prairie City; born in Penn., Feb. 22, 1831; came to this Co. in 1853; Rep; Presb; owns 120 acres of land, valued at $7,200; first wife was Nancy Nicols, married in 1864, and died 1869; second wife was Emily Nicols; had six children, three by first wife and three by last wife; those living are James E., Walter J., Frank W. and Sarah A.

KREIMER JOHN, Farmer and Stock Raiser; Sec. 17; P. O. Greenbush; born in Germany, Dec. 20, 1824; came to this Co. in 1854; Rep; Luth; owns 215 acres land valued at $12,900; married Helen Mens' born in 1858; have six children, Louise C.

Emma, F. William, Bertha, Minnie and Clara; Mr. K. is a tailor by trade; came from Germany to Greenbush, Warren Co.

Kriegh Wm. farmer; Sec. 2; P. O. Greenbush; rep; Bapt; 172 acres.

LAHMAN F. J. lives with his father; Sec. 1; P. O. Avon.

Larkins Patrick, rents of Joshua A. Bullars; Sec. 11; P. O. Avon; dem; Cath.

Layman Jacob, farmer; Sec. 1; P. O. Avon; rep; 100 acres.

Layman Andrew, miner; P. O. Avon; born Illinois.

Link D. S. farmer; Sec. 16; P. O. Greenbush; dem; 65 acres; from Ohio.

Linnman Swan, renter; Sec. 8; P. O. Greenbush; from Sweden.

LLOYD J. R. Farmer; Sec. 11; P. O. Avon; born in Ky., Feb. 16, 1831; came to this Co. in 1834; Dem; owns 204 acres of land, valued at $10,200; married Josephine Park; have two children, Nelly and Rosey; wife was Mrs. Butler; she had one child by first husband, Mary L. Butler.

LOCKWOOD JAMES, Farmer; Sec. 25; P. O. Avon; born in New York, Oct. 13, 1819; came to this Co. in 1845; Rep; Univ; owns 80 acres land, valued at $6,000; married Sarah J. Dunbar in 1841; have two children, Lewis R. and George E.; has been Road Commissioner for six years.

LONG JACOB, Farmer; Sec. 21; P. O. Prairie City; born in Germany, Sept. 9, 1834; came to this Co. in 1858; Dem; owns 95 acres of land, valued at $6,000; married Mary Hinesman; have three children; was in army in Co. H, I. V. I., was under Capt. Bond and Col. Smith; served three years.

LOUK C. W. Farmer; Sec. 35; P. O. Prairie City; born in Ill., May 31, 1839; came to this Co. in 1870; Rep; Meth; owns 47 acres land, valued at $3,290; first wife was T. A. Seal; married in 1860, and died in 1875; second wife was Elizabeth Brink, married 1871; had four children by first wife, William F., Ella D., George E., Mary C., and two by second wife, Eva A. and C. W. Jr.; holds the office of Constable.

McCANN FRANK, lives on Barney Sloey's farm; P. O. Avon.

McCormick John, farmer, rents of Judge Larrence; Sec. 35; P. O. Prairie City; ind.

McFitridge John, farmer, rents of John McKinney, Sr.; Sec. 28; P. O. Prairie City.

McFitridge R. farmer, rents of John McKinney, Sec. 28; P. O. Prairie City; rep; Ire.

McGowan A., lives on his father's farm; Sec. 1; P. O. Avon; rep; 80 acres in Knox Co.

McGOWAN L. Farmer and Stock Raiser; Sec. 1; P. O. Avon; born in Scotland, Sept. 6, 1806; came to this Co. in

WARREN COUNTY : GREENBUSH TOWNSHIP. 249

1846; Rep; Univ; owns 160 acres land, valued at $9,600; married Christina Cummings, 1830; their union was blessed with five children, four born in Scotland, and one in Warren Co.; Mr. McGowan was among the early settlers of Greenbush tp.

McMahill G. W. farmer; Sec. 31; P. O. Walnut Grove; dem; 1,200 acres; from Ky.

McMahill Oscar, farmer; Sec. 31; P. O. Walnut Grove; ind; born Illinois.

McMahill Wm. farmer; Sec. 30; P. O. Walnut Grove; rep; 1,400 acres; from Ky.

Maguire V. B. runs corn-sheller; P.O. Prairie City; dem.

Mark Nels farm hand; P. O. Greenbush; rep; from Sweden.

Mason G. I. painter; P. O. Greenbush; rep; from Connecticut.

Massengale Benj. laborer; P. O. Greenbush; dem; from Ohio.

Mather E. school teacher; Greenbush; lives in Greenbush.

MATTHEWS JAMES, Farmer and Stock Raiser; Sec. 34; P. O. Prairie City; born in Indiana, July 7, 1835; came to this Co. in 1854; Ind; Presb; owns 80 acres land, valued at $5,600; married Georgetta Darneille, Feb. 17, 1871; have two children, Henzie A. and Mary J; is the son of John Matthews, who died in 1870.

Meisbon E. B. farmer; Sec. 20; P. O. Greenbush; ind; 85 acres; from Germany.

Mentzer B. W. school teacher; P. O. Greenbush; rep; Mis. Bapt; from Pennsylvania.

MERRIS B. T. Farmer and Stock Raiser; Sec. 3; P. O. Avon; born in Ill., July 9, 1826; came to this Co. in 1853; Dem; owns 200 acres of land, valued at $12,000; married Mary Crawford, from Ohio, in 1846; their union was blessed with six children, Mary B., Almira, John J., Eliza E., Flora A. and Malissa.

Merris John, lives with his father; Sec. 3; P. O. Avon.

MINGS J. W. Farmer; Sec. 12; P. O. Avon; born in Ill., Sept. 1, 1843; Rep; Meth; owns 200 acres of land, valued at $10,000; married Mary E. Carr, Aug. 6, 1872; have three children, Judd C., Mabel and Orren W.; was in army in Co. D, 64th I. V.; served three years.

Morris John, miner; P. O. Avon; dem.

Morris Mart. farm laborer; dem.

Moulton A. J. farmer; Sec. 16; P. O. Avon; ind; 240 acres; born Illinois.

Moulton T. B. rents of Alfred Simmons; P. O. Avon; dem; born Illinois.

Myers George W. farm hand; P. O. Avon; rep; from Pennsylvania.

NEUBURN JOHN, stone mason; Greenbush; dem; from Ohio.

Nicks J. T. farmer; rep; 160 acres.

OLSON PETER, renter; P. O. Greenbush; rep; from Sweden.

Olson Thomas, farm hand; P. O. Greenbush; from Sweden.

PARK JOHN A. stock dealer; Sec. 7; P. O. Greenbush; dem; 14 acres; from Ky.

Patterson Jno. farmer; Sec. 14; P. O. Avon; rep; 82 acres; from Tennessee.

Pearsall George, farm laborer; P. O. Avon.

Peterson Jno. farmer, rents of Jno. A. Butler; Sec. 8; P. O. Greenbush; Sweden.

Powers C. C. farm laborer; P. O. Greenbush; dem; born Illinois.

REGAN JNO. wagon-maker; Greenbush; dem.

RANDALL WM. Physician and Surgeon; Greenbush; born in Indiana, May 27, 1834; came to this Co. in 1858; Dem; Meth; owns 1,057 acres of land, valued at $53,850; married Caroline Snapp in 1863, who died May 20, 1875; has two children, George S. and Clyde.

RAY J. C. Farmer and Stock Raiser; Sec. 4; P. O. Greenbush; born in Warren Co., Ill., June 22, 1852; Dem; owns 48 acres land, valued at $8,580; married Eliza E. Merris, April 2, 1874; have two children, Marshal B. and Mary E.; Mr. Ray is the grandson of James G. Ray, who settled in this Co. in 1833, in the town of Lenox, where he now lives.

RAY JAMES G. Farmer and Stock Raiser; Sec. 4, P. O. Greenbush; born in Warren Co., Jan. 9, 1851; Dem; Bapt; owns 143 acres land, valued at $8,580; married Almira Merris, Dec. 3, 1874; has one child, James W.; Mr. Ray is the grandson of James G. Ray, who settled in this Co. in 1833, in the town of Lenox, where he now lives.

ROBB JAS. Farmer and Stock Raiser; Sec. 32; P. O. Walnut Grove; born in Ohio, July 20, 1835; came to this Co. in 1859; Rep; owns 163 acres, valued at $9,780; married Elizabeth A. McDonald, March 31, 1859.

Robinson Jas. H. farmer, rents of Lyman Tatts; Sec. 34; P. O. Prairie City; dem.

Rojan Mrs. Alfred; Sec. 7; P. O. Greenbush; 7 acres.

Ross Jos. rents of Riley Simmons; P. O. Greenbush; dem; born Illinois.

Ross Milton, rents of Merris; Sec. 3; P. O. Greenbush; dem; born Illinois.

RUBART NANCY, Farmer and Stock Raiser; Sec. 1; P. O. Avon; born in Pennsylvania, Oct. 27, 1827; came to this Co. in 1852; Chris; owns 303 acres land, valued at $12,120; is the widow of James Rubart, who died Dec. 20, 1872; has six children, Phœbe J., Margaret R., Joseph N., Benjamin W., Albert E., Abram L.;

Mr. R. was in the Black Hawk war; was a mason by trade.
Rullaford Thos. rents of Barney Sloey; dem.

SAILOR ANDREW, farmer; Sec. 23; P. O. Avon; dem; Cath; 60 acres; Ger.

SAILOR SIMON, Farmer; Sec. 23; P. O. Avon; born in Germany, Dec. 8, 1831; came to this Co. in 1857; Dem; Cath; owns 100 acres, valued at $5,000; married Matilda J. Kelly, March 26, 1863; have three children, Thomas, George and William; went to Pike's Peak in 1859; held the office of School Director.

Sands Chas. farmer; works for Dr. Randall.

SANDERS W. H. Farmer; Sec. 22; P. O. Avon; born in New Jersey, March 12, 1842; came to this Co. in 1865; Dem; rents Louis Dean's farm; is unmarried; value of personal property $1,500.

Scudder A. farm laborer; P. O. Walnut Grove; dem; born Illinois.

Shepard John, farm laborer; P. O. Greenbush; rep.

Shinkle G. W. rents of Robert Johnson; P. O. Avon; rep.

Sigler Amos, farmer; Sec. 6; P. O. Greenbush; dem; 190 acres; from Pennsylvania.

Simmons Alfred D., lives with his father; Sec. 8; P. O. Greenbush; dem; born Ill.

SIMMONS ALFRED W. Farmer and Stock Raiser; Sec. 3; P. O. Greenbush; born in Illinois, Nov. 5, 1821; came to this Co. in 1833; Dem; Old School Bapt; owns 277 acres land, valued at $16,620; married Sarah A. Molton, Aug. 26, 1847; has seven children, James H., David R., M. E., William M., Mary L., Rosanna, and Albert; Mr. S. is the son of James Simmons, who came to this State in 1816; has been Road Commissioner.

SIMMONS ANDREW W. Farmer and Stock Raiser; Sec. 8; P. O. Greenbush; born in Kentucky, Sept. 2, 1816; came to this Co. in 1833; Dem; Old School Bapt; owns 469 acres of land, valued at $23,460; married Asenath Brooks, March 2, 1848; have seven children, Thomas F., Albert D., Amanda, James B., Wilson D., Freeman and Roland M.; has held the offices of Supervisor, Justice, Road Commissioner, Assessor, Collector and District Constable.

SIMMONS CHARLES RILEY, Farmer and Stock Raiser; Sec. 4; P. O. Greenbush; born in Madison Co., Ill., Dec. 24, 1825; came to this Co. in 1833; Dem; owns 201 acres land, valued at $12,060; married Martha J. Bair, Jan. 25, 1863; have five children, Lenora E., Nancy V., William J., James A. and Sally; Mr. S. is the son of James Simmons, who came from Kentucky to this Co. in 1816.

SIMMONS F. M. Farmer and Stock Raiser; Sec. 5; P. O. Greenbush; born in Madison Co., Ill., Nov. 10, 1823; came to this Co. in 1833; Dem; Bapt; owns 240 acres land, value $9,500; came to this Co. soon after the Black Hawk war; lived here ever since.

Simmons Henry, lives with his father; Sec. 3; P. O. Greenbush; dem; born Illinois.

Simmons I. M. lives with his father; Sec. 4; P. O. Greenbush; dem.

Simmons Jas. farmer; Sec. 2; P. O. Greenbush; dem; 371 acres.

Simmons J. H. farmer; Sec. 6; P. O. Greenbush; dem; 196 acres; born Illinois.

Simmons J. H. lives with his father; Sec. 3; P. O. Greenbush; dem; is tax payer.

Simmons Thompson, farmer; Sec. 9; P. O. Greenbush; dem; born Warren Co.

Simmons Uriah J. lives with his father; Sec. 4; P. O. Greenbush; dem.

Simmons W. A. lives with his father; Sec. 2; P. O. Greenbush; dem.

Simmons W. J. farmer; Sec. 4; P. O. Greenbush; dem; O. S. Bapt; 257 acres.

Simmons W. R. farmer; Sec. 3; P. O. Greenbush; dem; 201 acres; born Ill.

Simmons Wm. R. lives with his father; Sec. 6; P. O. Greenbush; dem; born Ill.

Slater G. W. lives on Robert Johnson's farm; Sec. 24; P. O. Avon; rep.

Sloey Barnard, lives with his father; P. O. Prairie City.

SLOEY BARNEY, Farmer; Sec. 26; P. O. Avon; born in Ireland, Oct. 23, 1815; came to this Co. in 1840; Dem; Cath; owns 1,000 acres of land, valued at $50,000; married Anna O'Grady, Jan. 26, 1846; ten children, Harry J., W. S., Francis, Susan, James, Thomas B., Helen, Anna, Rose and John M.

Sloey Frank, lives with his father; Sec. 26; P. O. Prairie City.

Sloey Wm. C. lives with his father; P. O. Prairie City.

Smith C. W. farm hand; P. O. Avon; rep; born Illinois.

Smith Henry, carpenter; P. O. Greenbush; dem; Meth; from Indiana.

Smith P. H. farmer, rents of Judge Larrence; Sec. 35; P. O. Prairie City; dem.

Smith S. A. farm laborer; P. O. Prairie City; dem.

Smith William, farmer, rents of Judge Lawrence; Sec. 36; P. O. Prairie City.

Smith Wm. T. works for J. M. Iliet; P. O. Greenbush; dem; Bapt; Warren Co.

Snapp Geo. farmer; Sec. 1; P. O. St. Augustine; dem; New Light; 153 acres.

SNAPP F. G. Retired; lives in Galesburg; born in Kentucky in 1812; came to this Co. in 1833; Rep; owns 1,500 acres of land, valued at $30,000; married Adaline Morse; have seven children, Samuel, George,

Maria, Albert, Caroline, John, Emma and Amanda; his son, John Snapp, was in the Army, in Co. C, 83rd I. V. I.

SNAPP WM. L. Justice of the Peace; Greenbush; born in Ill., Feb. 12, 1842; Dem; Meth; owns 100 acres of land on Sec. 12, valued at $5,000; married Mary E. May, Dec. 19, 1861; have five children, Alice M., Thomas, Wm. L. Jr., Carrie M. and Delos; held the offices of Justice, Town Clerk and Collector.

Snider Peter, farmer; Sec. 5; P. O. Greenbush; dem; 126 acres.

Sparks D. T. Sec. 14; P. O. Avon; dem; 5 acres; from Kentucky.

Spears G. W. Sec. 21; P. O. Avon; rep; 165 acres; born Illinois.

SPURGIN ISRAEL, Farmer and Stock Breeder; Sec. 22; P. O. Prairie City; born in Ky., June 30, 1828; came to this Co. in 1849; Dem; owns 1,240 acres of land, valued at $49,600; married Elizabeth Marshall, July 4, 1849; have seven children living and seven dead; those living are Francis, John, Mary, Henry, Emma, Dora and Elmer; Mr. S. is Director of the First National Bank of Prairie City.

Spurgin John, lives with his father; P. O. Avon; dem.

Spurlock P. farmer, renter; Sec. 36; P. O. Prairie City; 11 acres; from Virginia.

Staley W. S. farmer, renter; P. O. Prairie City; dem.

Stice Oscar, farmer; Sec. 28; P. O. Youngstown; dem; 320 acres.

Stockton C. lives on his mother's farm; Sec. 1; rep; P. O. Avon.

Stockton Mary J. farmer; Sec. 1; P. O. St. Augustine; 90 acres.

Stuckey David, farmer; Sec. 27; P. O. Prairie City; rep; 160 acres; from Penn.

Sweet William, farm hand; P. O. Avon; rep; from Minnesota.

TAFT L. farmer; Sec. 24; dem; 200 acres; from New York.

Taylor Danford, farmer; Sec. 31; ind; 74 acres; from New Hampshire.

Thomas Charles, P. O. Walnut Grove.

TAYLOR GEORGE H. Farmer; Sec. 7; P. O. Greenbush; born in Illinois, July 6, 1851; dem; owns 40 acres of land, valued at $1,600; married Sarah J. Romine, September, 1869; have four children, William H., George H., Mary E., and Lina.

Taylor T. M. miner; P. O. Avon; rep; born Illinois.

Thompson F. W. lives with his father; Sec. 33; P. O. Prairie City; dem; from Ky.

TOMPSON THOMAS W. Farmer; Sec. 33; P. O. Prairie City; born in Ky., Dec. 20, 1815; came to this Co. in 1853; Dem; Cath; owns 120 acres, valued at $7,200; first wife was Miss T. Sheckliff; second wife was Mrs. Edmonds; have had eleven children, J. T., G. W., Joseph, Simeon, Julia A., William, Albert, Frank, James H., Adaline, Alexander E.

Todd John J. laborer; P. O. Greenbush; dem; Bapt; from New Jersey.

VAUGHAN J. T. farmer; Sec. 18; P. O. Greenbush; dem; born Illinois.

VANVEEZER FRANCIS, Farmer; Sec. 10; P. O. Avon; born in New York, Dec. 24, 1818; came to this Co. in 1844; dem; Old School Bapt; owns 80 acres, valued at $4,000; married Amanda Renn; have five children living and two dead; those living are Robert P., Mary E., Priscilla L., Sarah E., and Isaac; was in the Army, in Company H, 83d Ill. Vol.

VAUGHN P. A. Farmer; Sec. 20; P. O. Avon; born in Virginia, March 31, 1810; came to this County in 1837; Dem; Meth; owns 330 acres, valued at $16,500; married Mary Darneille, in 1834; have six children, Elizabeth S., James T., Pathana, Mary Z., George E., Douglas; first came from Virginia to Tennessee, then to Kentucky, and then to Illinois; his son Thomas was in the army.

VAUGHN G. E. Farmer; Sec. 20; P. O. Avon; born in Illinois, July 10, 1852; Dem; Meth; lives on his father's farm; married Josephine Welsh in 1873; have two children, Dora and Charley.

WEAVER CHAS. renter; Sec. 33; P. O. Prairie City; dem; from Kentucky.

Wells B. rents of Mrs. Call; Sec. 19; dem; from Ohio.

Welsh Chas. S. lives with his mother; Sec. 22; P. O. Avon; dem; Meth.

WELSH HESTER A. Farmer; Sec. 22; P. O. Avon; born in New York, Aug. 9, 1818; came to this Co. in 1837; Meth; owns 180 acres of land, valued at $9,000; is the widow of Abram Welsh, who died Dec. 12, 1862; have seven children, Benjamin C., John, William, Oliver C., Josephine, Charles S., Norris S.; his son Wm. was in the Army, in Company H., 83d Ill. Volunteers.

Welsh O. C. farmer, lives with his mother; Sec. 22; P. O. Avon; dem; Meth; N. J.

Welsh Wm. lives on his mother's farm; Sec. 22; P. O. Avon; dem.

West Jno. farmer, rents of Wm. Randall; Sec. 8; P. O. Greenbush; rep; Luth.

West Niles, lives with Jno. West; P. O. Greenbush.

Wetzel Christian, farmer, rents of Stice; Sec. 28; P. O. Walnut Grove; rep; Germany.

Wigert Andrew, farmer; Sec. 8; P. O. Greenbush; rep; Meth; owns 58 acres.

Willard A. J. farm hand; P. O. Greenbush; dem; born Illinois.

Wilson Thos. farmer; Sec. 36; P. O. Prairie City; dem; Presb; owns 320 acres; Penn.

Wingate A. L. farmer; Sec. 8; P. O. Greenbush; rep; Meth; from Germany.

Wingate A. L. lives with his father; Sec. 20; P. O. Avon; dem; born Illinois.

WINGATE JOHN. Farmer; Sec. 20; P. O. Avon; born in Maine, Feb. 1, 1815; came to this Co. in 1838; Dem; owns 250 acres of land, valued at $10,000; married Annis Allen, in 1844; have three children, Arthur L., Ella and Eva; has held the office of Tp. Treasurer for 32 years; been Town Clerk, Assessor and Justice of the Peace.

Wonden H. S. farmer; Sec. 14; P. O. Prairie City; rep; Chris; 70 acres and stone quarry.

WOODS E. W. Farmer and Stock Raiser; Sec. 2; P. O. Avon; born in Madison Co., N. Y., Sept. 16, 1818; came to this Co. in 1842; Rep; Univ; owns 446 acres of land, valued at $22,300; married Rhoda Butler, Jan. 6, 1853; have eight children—Ezra B., William R., Alice A., Olva E., John A., Edwin S., Sarah B., Minnie C.

Woods Ezra, lives with his father; Sec. 2; P. O. Avon; rep.

Woods I. M. farmer; Sec. 24; P. O. Avon; rep; owns 121 acres land; N. Y.

Woods Jno. farmer; P. O. Prairie City; dem; from Pennsylvania.

Woods L. S. lives with his father; Sec. 25; P. O. Avon; rep; born Illinois.

Wren David, Sec. 12; P. O. Avon; dem; Chris; owns 50 acres; from Ohio.

Young G. W. farm laborer; P. O. Greenbush; dem; born Illinois.

Young J. K. P. farm laborer; dem; born Ill.

Young Wm. farmer; Sec. 14; P. O. Avon; dem; owns 43 acres; born in Illinois.

GREENBUSH BUSINESS DIRECTORY.

Butler V. W. Justice of the Peace.
Irving S. C. Blacksmith.
Johnson J. C. Dealer in Dry Goods, Groceries, Drugs and Medicines, Paints, Oils, Putty, Glassware, Hardware, and General Merchandise.
Randall Wm. Physician and Surgeon.
Snapp Wm. L. Justice of the Peace.

POINT PLEASANT TOWNSHIP.

ABBOTT J. farmer; Sec. 33; P. O. Colfax; rep; F. W. Bapt; born Illinois.

Allard David, farmer; Sec. 8; P. O. Roseville; dem; Meth; 240 acres; from N. H.

Allard Frank, farmer, lives with his father, D. Allard; Sec. 8; P. O. Roseville; dem.

Allard Jacob, retired, lives with his son, D. Allard; P. O. Roseville; dem; from N. H.

Almond Geo. farmer, Sec. 34; P. O. Colfax; dem; U. B.; born Illinois.

Almond Jno. W. farmer; Sec. 33; P. O. Colfax; dem; born Illinois.

Almond Newton, farmer; Sec. 36; P. O. Colfax; dem; from Kentucky.

Almond Thos J. farmer; Sec. 34; P. O. Colfax; dem; F. W. Bapt; from Kentucky.

Almond W. S. farmer; Sec. 34; P. O. Colfax; dem; Meth; 320 acres, value $17,230; Va.

Almond Wilson J. postmaster; Sec. 36; P. O. Colfax; dem; F. W. Bapt; from Kentucky.

Almond Z. D. farmer; Sec. 33; P. O. Colfax; dem; F. W. Bapt; from Kentucky.

Andrews Robt. D. farmer; Sec. 14; P. O. Roseville; rep; from Tennessee.

Anstine Newton, farmer; Sec. 25; P. O. Swan Creek; 80 acres, value $4,000; Ill.

BACON JOHN P. farmer; Sec. 36; P. O. Swan Creek; rep; Presb; Ind.

Baldwin Henry, farmer; Sec. 34; P. O. Colfax; rep; 320 acres, value $16,000; Ohio.

Begley James, farmer; Sec. 7; P. O. Raritan; rep; Presb; 99 acres, val. $8,000; Ireland.

Bell David, farmer; Sec. 31; P. O. Sciota; 80 acres, value $4,000; from Pennsylvania.

Boden Andrew, farmer; Sec. 26; P. O. Swan Creek; dem; 80 acres, value $4,000; Ohio.

Booth Burwell, farmer; Sec. 24; P. O. Swan Creek; rep; Meth; 245 acres, val. $12,500.

Booth Furguson, farmer; Sec. 24; P. O. Swan Creek; rep; born Illinois.

Booth John W. farmer; Sec. 23; P. O. Swan Creek; rep; born Illinois.

Booth Wm. farmer; Sec. 23; P. O. Swan Creek; rep; born Illinois.

BOYD CARY J. Farmer and Stock Raiser; Sec. 1; P. O. Roseville; born in Warren Co., July 27, 1848; Dem; Meth; has 133 acres, value $8,000, owned by him and his sister, II. Priscilla Boyd; has been Assessor and Collector of Township; married Nov. 27, 1872, to Miss Victoria Ragon, who was born Oct. 15, 1852; has two children, George E. and Bertha M.

BOYD DRURY B. Farmer; Sec. 2; P. O. Roseville; Dem; born in Greene Co., Ind., Dec. 12, 1839; came to Warren Co. in 1847; was married Sept. 19, 1861, to Miss Harriet Conklin, who was born in Clermont Co., Ohio, Nov. 5, 1843, and came to Illinois in 1850; both members of Meth. church; have two children, Elgie B. and William L.; has 91 acres, Sec. 2, valued at $60, and 80 acres, Sec. 16, valued at $50 per acre.

Boyd Henry, farmer; Sec. 2; P. O. Roseville; dem; 75 acres, value $3,750; Ind.

Boyd John B. farmer; Sec. 1; P. O. Roseville; dem; 80 acres, value $5,000; Ill.

BOYD JOHN J. Farmer; Sec. 10; P. O. Roseville; Dem; was born in Greene Co., Ind., March 25, 1847; was married Feb. 25, 1869, to Miss Emily J. Kirby, who was born in Peoria Co., Ill., Aug. 18, 1851; Mr. B. is a member of the Methodist church, Mrs. B. of the Cumberland Presb; has two children, Albert S. and Phœbe M.; has 160 acres, valued at $50 per acre.

BOYD WM. T. Farmer; Sec. 11; P. O. Roseville; Dem; was born in Greene Co., Ind., Oct. 7, 1845; came to Warren Co. in 1847; was married Oct. 1, 1868, to Miss Susan F. Dean, who was born in Lewiston, Fulton Co., Ill., Sept. 1, 1849; has one child, Jennie May; has 160 acres, valued at $50 per acre; is School Trustee and has held other town offices.

Brady A. H. farmer; Sec. 26; P. O. Good Hope; rep; Chris; from Ohio.

Brooks G. W. farmer; Sec. 28; P. O. Colfax; dem; Bapt; from Pennsylvania.

Bunker Henry, laborer; Sec. 13; P. O. Roseville rep; from Wisconsin.

Bunting John, farmer; Sec. 25; P. O. Swan Creek; dem; from Ohio.

Burk J. W. farmer; Sec. 10; P. O. Swan Creek; rep; from Indiana.

CHAPMAN GILES, farmer; Sec. 14; P. O. Swan Creek; dem; 80 acres; S. C.

Chapman J. P. farmer; Sec. 14; P. O. Swan Creek; dem; from Indiana.

Clark George W. farmer; Sec. 17; P. O. Raritan; rep; from Indiana.

Clark Jamison, farmer; Sec. 12; P. O. Roseville; rep; Meth; from Virginia.

Clark John, farmer; Sec. 17; P. O. Raritan; rep; U. B.; 160 acres, value $6,400; Ohio.

Clark Joel, farmer; Sec. 8; P. O. Roseville; rep; rents 120 acres; from New York.

Coacher Isaac, farmer; Sec. 4; P. O. Roseville; dem; from Indiana.

Cooper Oliver, farmer; Sec. 24; P. O. Swan Creek; dem; born Illinois.

Cooper Thos. W. farmer; Sec. 24; P. O. Swan Creek; dem; 86 acres, value $4,300; Ind.

COOPER THOMAS, Farmer; Sec. 24; P. O. Swan Creek; Dem; born in Hampshire Co., Va., Sept. 1, 1801; came to Ohio in 1805, to Indiana in 1822; married Miss Alezanah Webster, Jan. 4, 1821; she was born Dec. 25, 1801, and died April 28, 1852; had nine children by his first wife, William, Mary, Abagail, James, Massa, Maudana, Thomas W., Emily J., and Deborah; married his second wife, Mrs. Margaret Lewis, April 24, 1853; she has seven children, Edith, Lewis, Stephen W., Oliver, Ada A., Alezana, John H., and Angeline; has 113 acres, valued at $6,000; Mr. and Mrs. Cooper are both members of Christian church; has been Road Commissioner, and held other offices.

Cornell J. T. farmer; Sec. 28; P. O. Colfax; dem; Meth; from Pennsylvania.

Cowgill Joseph, farmer; Sec. 30; P. O. Raritan; rep; U. B.; from Ohio.

Cowgill Newton J. farmer; Sec. 30; P. O. Raritan; rep; from Indiana.

Crosier Henry N. farmer; Sec. 3; P. O. Roseville; rep; Meth; from Vermont.

DAVIS ALBERT, farmer; Sec. 1; P. O. Roseville; dem; from Virginia.

Davis Geo. W. farmer; Sec. 13; P. O. Swan Creek; dem; from Ohio.

Daley G. W. farmer; Sec. 16; P. O. Swan Creek; rep; Bapt; 160 acres, $8,000; Ohio.

DAVIS IRA W. Farmer; Sec. 13; P. O. Swan Creek; Dem; born in Mahoning Co., O., June 13, 1831; came to Warren Co., Oct. 1855; was married in 1852 to Miss Sarah J. Amon, who was born in Mercer Co., Pa., March 11, 1832; have ten children, all living; 160 acres, val. $8,000.

Davis Jas. V. farmer; Sec. 15; P. O. Swan Creek; dem; from Pennsylvania.

Davis Lorenzo K. farmer; Sec. 12; P. O. Roseville; from Virginia.

Davis R. A. farmer; Sec. 15; P. O. Swan Creek; dem; from Pennsylvania.

Dickson Jas. farmer; Sec. 29; P. O. Colfax; dem; Meth; from Kentucky.

Ditch Elias, farmer; Sec. 10; P. O. Roseville; 80 acres; from Indiana.

Ditch Henry, farmer; Sec. 10; P. O. Roseville; rep; 80 acres; from Indiana.

DIXSON ELI Z. Farmer; Sec. 12; P. O. Roseville; Dem; born in Indiana, Jan. 8, 1853; came to Ill. and Warren Co. in 1858; has 80 acres in Sec. 11, also the following: 160 acres in Sec. 2, and 80 acres in Sec. 11, subject to dower; value $60 per acre; he is also a Director of Roseville Union Bank.

DIXSON STEPHEN, Manufacturer of Agricultural Impts. and Farmer; Sec. 1; P. O. Roseville; born in Preble Co., O., Dec. 19, 1813; came to this Co. in 1853; Dem; has three children, all married; has 560 acres, value $34,000; Mr. D. is the inventor of the Dixson Combined Plow and Planter, which is the outgrowth of 40 years' experience in farming.

Duble Wm. farmer, rents of I. Jarred; Sec. 28; P. O. Colfax; dem; Bapt; from Md.

Dunn James, farmer; Sec. 6; P. O. Jackson Corners; dem; born Illinois.

Dunn Lee, farmer; Sec. 6; P. O. Jackson Corners; dem; born Illinois.

E DWARDS RICHARD, farmer; Sec. 22; P. O. Swan Creek; dem; from Indiana.

Elston Alex. farmer; Sec. 1; P. O. Roseville; dem; from Indiana.

Embry W. W. Jr. real estate agt.; Sec. 21; P. O. Swan Creek; rep; from Kentucky.

Ewing G. W. carpenter; Sec. 27; P. O. Colfax; rep; from Pennsylvania.

F ENTON GEORGE, farmer; Sec. 6; P.O. Roseville; rep; Univ; from Ohio.

Flasher John, farmer; Sec. 22; P. O. Colfax; dem; from Pennsylvania.

G REENLEE ROBERT J. farmer; Sec. 17; P. O. Raritan; dem; from Canada.

Guest Joseph E. farmer; Sec. 7; P. O. Raritan; dem; Meth; 50 acres, $3,000; N. J.

Gulic I. V. C. farmer; Sec. 18; P.O. Raritan; rep; Bapt; 20 acres, value $1,500; N. J.

GUNN CHARLES, Farmer; Sec. 15; P. O. Swan Creek; Rep; born in Guernsey Co., Ohio, July 8, 1825; came to Ill. in 1851, and to Warren Co. in 1860; married Oct. 10, 1852, Miss Catharine Frank, who was born in Juniata Co., Penn., June 9, 1833, and came to Ill. in 1843; both members Meth. church; have eight children living, John H., George M., William K., Mary A., Simon F., Ella, Charles B. and Katie M.; has 160 acres, and five acres in Swan tp., valued at $75 per acre.

H ARDISTY CHAS. W. teacher; Sec. 5; P. O. Raritan; dem; Chris; from Mo.

HARRIS ELMER I. Farmer; Sec. 34; P.O. Colfax; Rep; born in Mercer Co., Pa., April 17, 1838; came to this Co. in 1855; married Dec. 3, 1869, to Miss Emma J. Tipton, who was born in Perry Co., O.,

Dec. 15, 1846; both members of Meth. church; have had four children; three living, Rufus Elmer, George Kyle and Claudie, deceased, Freddie Ellsworth; has 160 acres, value $9,600; served three years in 2nd Ill. Vol. Cav.

Higgason Albert, farmer; Sec. 18; P. O. Raritan; dem; Meth; 112½ acres, val. $6,750.

Hindman Thomas W. farmer; Sec. 12; P. O. Roseville; rep; from Indiana.

Hindman Wm. R. farmer; Sec. 12; P. O. Roseville; rep; Cumb. Presb; 125 acres.

Hinman Chas. farmer; Sec. 6; P. O. Jackson Corners; rep; 265 acres, value $3,250; Ill.

HINMAN E. T. Farmer; Sec. 30; P.O. Raritan; Rep; was born in Oneida Co., N. Y., Dec. 21, 1831; came to Warren Co. in 1855; was married June 13, 1855, to Miss Mary E. Reynolds, who was born in Chemung Co., N. Y., July 25, 1833; both members of Meth. church; have four children, Hermon, Henry, Eddie and Susie; has 80 acres, val. $4,000.

Hodges Wm. J. farmer; Sec. 32; P. O. Colfax; rep; from England.

Howard Richard, farmer; Sec. 35; P. O. Colfax; dem; born Illinois.

Howe Bela, farmer; Sec. 36; P. O. Swan Creek; rep; from Indiana.

HUGHEN B. J. Farmer; Sec. 14; P.O. Swan Creek; Dem; born in Greene Co., Ind., Aug. 31, 1825; came to Warren Co. in 1856; was married April 8, 1847, to Miss Mary Boyd, who was also born in Greene Co., Ind., Sept. 9, 1827; Mrs. H. is a member of Cumb. Presb. church; have three children, Elizabeth, Esther A. and Willie; has 85 acres, val $4,250.

Humes Jas. M. farmer; Sec. 4; P. O. Roseville; dem; Meth; 400 acres, $20,000; Va.

Hume Jas. O. Jr. carpenter; Sec. 4; P. O. Roseville; dem; born Illinois.

Hume Wm. farmer; Sec. 4; P. O. Roseville; dem; from Virginia.

Huston James, farmer; Sec. 13; P. O. Roseville; rep; from Ohio.

J ARRED ISRAEL, farmer; Sec. 23; P. O. Swan Creek; dem; 737 acres, val. $37,000.

Johnson B. L. W. farmer; Sec. 33; P.O. Colfax; dem; Meth; from Pennsylvania.

Johnson J. H. farmer; Sec. 34; P. O. Colfax; dem; F. W. Bapt; from Ohio.

Johnson Joseph, farmer; Sec. 13; P.O. Swan Creek; dem; 80 acres, value $5,000; Ill.

Jones W. H. farmer; Sec. 27; P. O. Colfax; dem; born Illinois.

K IRBY G. W. farmer; Sec. 24; P. O. Swan Creek; dem; Chris; 40 acres.

Kritzer Jacob, farmer; Sec. 3; P. O. Roseville; rep; Bapt; has 80 acres; Ohio.

KILLIP THOMAS, Farmer; Sec. 6; P. O. Roseville; Rep; born in Isle of Man,

May 7, 1841; came to America and to Warren Co. in 1860; married Feb. 24, 1866, to Miss Sally A. Sharp, who was born in Adams Co., O., March 22, 1844; have six children, Ellen M., Samuel S., James R., William C., Bohyer I. and Elizabeth A.

King John H. farmer; Sec. 26; P. O. Swan Creek; dem; born Illinois.

King J. M. farmer; Sec. 23; P. O. Swan Creek; dem; has 80 acres, value $4,000.

KING R. T. Farmer; Sec. 25; P. O. Swan Creek; Dem; was born in Washington Co., Tenn., Nov. 28, 1817; came to Illinois in 1835, and to Warren Co. in 1844; was married Nov. 28, 1839, to Miss Martha A. Holden, who was born in Hamilton Co., O., July 2, 1822; have eight children; Mr. K. has been Supervisor and Justice of Peace for 12 years; has always taken an active part in public interests of the tp. and Co.

King Wm. H. farmer; Sec. 23; P. O. Swan Creek; dem; born Illinois.

LAHIFF JNO. farmer; Sec. 34; P.O.Swan Creek; dem; Cath; from Ireland.

Larkins Jas. E. farmer; Sec. 23; P. O. Swan Creek; dem; from Ohio.

Larkins Joshua, farmer; Sec. 23; P. O. Swan Creek; dem.

Larkins Wm. farmer; Sec. 28; P. O. Colfax; dem; born Illinois.

Leary Jno. farmer; Sec. 31; P. O. Sciota; dem; Cath; has 80 acres, value $3,200.

Lee Benny, farmer; Sec. 4; P. O. Roseville; rep; born Illinois.

Lee M. P. farmer; Sec. 4; P. O. Roseville; rep; Bapt; has 335 acres, value $23,400.

LESTER LAMBERT, Farmer; Sec. 12; P. O. Roseville; was born in Greene Co., Ind., Jan. 11, 1839; came to Warren Co. in 1856; was married Oct. 14, 1869, to Miss Mary E. Dixson, who was born in Greene Co., Ind., April 13, 1849, and came to Warren Co. in 1858; Mrs. L. is a member of Cumberland Pres. church; has one child, Minnie J.; Mr. L. has 50 acres in Sec. 12, 160 acres in Sec. 13, and 40 acres in Sec. 14; value, $50 per acre.

Lighter Oliver, farmer; Sec. 25; P. O. Colfax; dem; from Iowa.

Livermore Andrew, farmer; Sec. 4; P. O. Roseville; rep; from Massachusetts.

Livermore Andrew, Jr., farmer; Sec. 16; P. O. Roseville; rep; born Illinois.

Livermore Chas. farmer; Sec. 4; P. O. Roseville; rep; born Illinois.

LIVERMORE DERRICK, Farmer; Sec. 10; P. O. Roseville; was born in Washington Co., O., Aug. 28, 1830, and came to Warren Co. in 1839; married Jan. 8, 1852, to Miss Elizabeth Stephens; she was born in Sangamon Co., Ill., Feb. 15, 1831; have six children, Andrew J., Joshua B., Louisa E. (Mrs. Birdsall), Mary A., Alice E. and Clara E.; has 320 acres, value $19,200.

Livermore Joshua, farmer; Sec. 10; P. O. Roseville; rep; born Illinois.

Livermore Jno. K. farmer; Sec. 5; P. O. Roseville; rep; from Ohio.

Livermore Socrates, farmer; Sec. 4; P. O. Roseville; rep; born Illinois.

Livermore W. T. farmer; Sec. 4; P. O. Roseville; rep; from Ohio.

Lochenour Eden, farmer; Sec. 22; P. O. Swan Creek; rep; from Indiana.

Lochenour Joel, farmer; Sec. 10; P.O. Swan Creek; rep; from Indiana.

Long Henry, farmer; Sec. 29; P. O. Colfax; dem; Chris; from Pennsylvania.

McDONALD FLETCHER L. farmer; Sec. 23; P. O. Swan Creek; dem; Ind.

McCary Anthony, farmer; Sec. 36; P. O. Swan Creek; dem; Cath; has 80 acres.

McCary Jas. farmer; Sec 36; P. O. Swan Creek; dem; Cath; 160 acres, value $8,000.

McCary Thos. farmer; Sec. 35; P. O. Swan Creek; dem; Cath; 80 acres, value $4,000.

McConnell Oren, farmer; Sec. 10; P. O. Roseville; dem; from Canada.

McDermot Frank, farmer; Sec. 31; P. O. Raritan; dem; from Pennsylvania.

McElary M. C. farmer; Sec. 10; P. O. Swan Creek; rep; from Indiana.

McGath Thos. farmer; Sec. 35; P. O. Colfax; dem; from Ireland.

Maberry Chas. farmer; Sec. 24; P. O. Swan Creek; dem; Chris; from Penn.

Manuel Daniel, farmer; Sec. 1; P. O. Roseville; dem; Chris; from Kentucky.

MARSTON F. A. Farmer; Sec. 18; P. O. Raritan; was born in Ashtabula Co., O., May 27, 1835; came to Ill. in 1837, and to Warren Co. in 1866; Rep; Meth; married Dec. 16, 1858, to Miss Mary A. Gorrell, who was born in Tyler Co., W. Va., Dec. 6, 1835; has six children, Francis N., Wilbur H., Mary L., Clara L., Arthur L., and Orrin L.; has 160 acres, value $10,000.

Martin Henry C. farmer; Sec. 24; P. O. Swan Creek; dem; Meth; from Indiana.

Mason Chas. farmer; Sec. 9; P. O. Roseville; dem; has 160 acres, value $8,000; Mo.

MATTESON ANDREW L. Farmer; Sec. 1; P. O. Roseville; born in Bennington Co., Vt., April 16, 1850; came to Ill. in 1867, and to Warren Co. in 1868; married Oct. 28, 1875, to Miss Maggie Dixon, who was born in Warren Co., Oct. 30, 1856; one child.

Matteson L. N. blacksmith; Sec. 1; P. O. Roseville; rep; Bapt; from Vermont.

Means Isaac O. farmer; Sec. 25; P. O. Swan Creek; dem; from Kentucky.

Means Jas. farmer; Sec. 24; P. O. Swan Creek; dem; from Indiana.

MERIDITH DANIEL R. Farmer; Sec. 8; P. O. Raritan; Rep; was born in Rockingham Co., N. C., April 7, 1833; came to Ky. in 1835, to Ill. in 1856, and to Warren Co. in 1862; married Dec. 24, 1861, to Miss Martha A. Delanay, who was born in Lincoln Co., Ky., March 22, 1845; have five children, William L., Ira J., Azro L., Elmer E., and Minnie M.; 80 acres, value $4,000.

Michaels Frederick, retired; Sec. 19; P. O. Raritan; rep; Presb; from Virginia.

Michaels Jas. farmer; Sec. 19; P. O. Raritan; rep; Bapt; 86 acres, value $4,300.

Michaels Wesley N. farmer; Sec. 19; P. O. Raritan; rep; 85 acres, value $4,250.

MOORE F. M. (deceased) Farmer; Sec. 10; P. O. Roseville; born in Somerset Co., N. J., Jan 31, 1832; came to Ill. in 1851, and to Warren Co. in 1857; married Dec. 2, 1857, to Miss Mary E. Curtis, who was born in Baltimore, Md., Oct. 21, 1837; had six children, William V. D., Henry F., Grace, Ulysses G., Francis M. and Mary E.; Mr. Moore died July 20, 1876; heirs have 240 acres, valued at $14,500.

Moore Henry, farmer; Sec. 35; P. O. Swan Creek; dem; from Isle of Man.

Morey C. A. farmer; Sec. 35; P. O. Swan Creek; rep; Chris; from Ohio.

Morey Jno. C. farmer; Sec. 22; P. O. Swan Creek; rep; U. B.; from Ohio.

Morey Peter, farmer; Sec. 35; P. O. Swan Creek; rep; Chris; 80 acres, value $4,000.

Muncy Wm. retired; Sec. 3; P. O. Roseville.; dem; Bapt; from New York.

O'NEAL Isaac, laborer; Sec. 12; P. O. Roseville; dem; from Indiana.

O'Neal J. B. farmer; Sec. 15; P. O. Roseville; dem; Presb; 80 acres, value $4,000.

Onan D. C. farmer; Sec. 15; P. O. Swan Creek; Cath; dem; from Kentucky.

Osborne Andrew, farmer; Sec. 11; P. O. Roseville; rep; from Indiana.

Osborne Daniel, laborer; Sec. 12; P. O. Roseville; rep; from Indiana.

Owen Jacob, farmer; Sec. 11; P. O. Roseville; rep; born Illinois.

Owen James, farmer; Sec. 12; P. O. Roseville; rep; 450 acres, value $27,000; Tenn.

Owen John, farmer; Sec. 12; P. O. Roseville; rep; born Illinois.

Owen Joseph, farmer; Sec. 12; P. O. Roseville; rep; born Illinois.

PARKER JOHN, laborer, Sec. 4; P. O. Roseville; dem; from Missouri.

Pennington Thos. F. farmer; Sec. 21; P. O. Swan Creek; dem; Bapt; 160 acres; Ill.

Philhower Joseph, farmer and plasterer; Sec. 18; P. O. Raritan; rep; Bapt; 105 acres.

PIPER ALVAH. Farmer; Sec. 18; P. O. Raritan; born at Phillipston, Worcester Co., Mass., Feb. 24, 1808; came to Illinois, in 1839, to Warren Co. in 1855; married Nov. 5, 1833, to Miss Elvira Hildreth; she was born July 1, 1811, and died June 17, 1866; has nine children living, Winslow A., Louisa H., Clark H., Sarah M., Edmond W., Maynard B., Mary E., Orestus J., and Josephine C.; has 162 acres, valued at $10,500.

Prather S. H. farmer, rents of D. Rankin; Sec. 20; P. O. Raritan; rep; Meth; Ohio.

QUICK JNO. H. farmer; Sec. 7; P. O. Raritan; rep; 110 acres; from N. J.

RANKIN JAS. A. farmer; Sec. 30; P. O. Raritan; rep; 80 acres, value $4,000.

Rayburn Jesse D. farmer; Sec. 10; P. O. Roseville; rep; from Indiana.

Reede John, farmer; Sec. 8; P. O. Roseville; dem; from Indiana.

Reed John T. farmer; Sec. 22; P. O. Swan Creek; dem; Meth; 160 acres, value $8,000.

Rezner John M. farmer; Sec. 5; P. O. Roseville; dem; born Illinois.

ROSS DANIEL P. Farmer; Sec. 5; P. O. Jackson Corners; Rep; was born in Sussex Co. Del., Oct. 3, 1834; came to Warren Co. in 1850; was married Feb. 23, 1859, to Miss Melinda Newkirk, who was born in Fountain Co., Indiana, Nov. 29, 1838; they have six children living; has 80 acres, valued at $4,000.

Rucker Robert, farmer; Sec. 1; P. O. Roseville; dem; from Tennessee.

SAMPSON B. F., farmer; Sec. 22; P. O. Swan Creek; 160 acres, value $8,000; Ill.

Sargent Robt. farmer; Sec. 7; P. O. Raritan; dem; Cath; 80 acres, value $2,000; Irel'nd.

Schwerdt Sol. farmer; Sec. 16; P. O. Roseville; dem; Luth; from Ohio.

Sefoit Wm. W. farmer; Sec. 27; P. O. Swan Creek; rep; from Indiana.

Sharp James H. farmer; Sec. 16; P. O. Roseville; dem; from Ohio.

Sharp Wm. farmer; Sec. 16; P. O. Roseville; dem; from Ohio.

Smith A. S. farmer; Sec. 9; P. O. Roseville; rep; Spiritualist; 320 acres, value $19,200.

Smith H. D. teacher; Sec. 9; P. O. Roseville; rep; born Illinois.

Smock James C. farmer; Sec. 21; P. O. Colfax; dem; from Penn.

Smock Jonathan C. farmer; Sec. 21; P. O. Colfax; dem; from Penn.

Smock J. C. farmer; Sec. 4; P. O. Roseville; rep; from Penn.

Spiva C. E. farmer; Sec. 22; P. O. Swan Creek; dem; born Illinois.

Stansfield Wm. farmer; Sec. 13; P. O. Roseville; 245 acres, value $14,700; England.

Stevenson Wm. H. farmer; Sec. 13; P. O. Swan Creek; rep; Meth; from Indiana.

Stiles John R. farmer and stock raiser; Sec. 27; P. O. Swan Creek; ind; Meth; Ohio.

Stiles M. L. farmer and stock raiser; Sec. 27; P. O. Swan Creek; ind; Meth; 120 acres.

STRICKLER A. H. Farmer; Sec. 3; P. O. Roseville; Rep; was born in Fayette Co., Penn., Dec. 18, 1829; came to Illinois in 1863; was married to his first wife, Miss Louisa A. Loffus, Oct. 15, 1863; to his second wife, Miss Harriett E. Loffus, Jan. 15, 1868; and to his third wife, Miss Sarah A. Vangilder, Jan. 19, 1871; she was born in Knox Co., Illinois, April 24, 1849; he has five children; has 80 acres, valued at $50 per acre; is Commissioner of Highways, and has held other Town Offices.

Strong John M. farmer; Sec. 5; P. O. Ellison; rep; 152 acres, value $7,600; from Indiana.

Swadley James M. farmer; Sec. 35; P. O. Swan Creek; dem; born Illinois.

TATE THOMAS, farmer; Sec. 22; P. O. Swan Creek; dem; 250 acres, $12,500.

THOMAS DAVID A. Farmer; Sec. 27; P. O. Colfax; was born near Woodstock, Vt., March 18, 1849; came to Wis. in 1849, to Ill. in 1859, and to Warren Co. in 1868; married Mary E. Jones, Sept. 16, 1875; she was born in Fulton Co., Ill., Dec. 28, 1850; has one child, Alvah W.

Thompson Joseph, farmer; Sec. 23; P. O. Swan Creek; dem; from Kentucky.

Tipton William, farmer; Sec. 34; P. O. Colfax; rep; Meth; from Ohio.

TORRANCE CHARLES, Farmer; Sec. 17; P. O. Raritan; Rep; was born in Essex Co., N. Y., Nov. 17, 1834; came to Warren Co. in 1858; married May 18, 1871, to Miss Margaret B. Hindman; she was born in Greene Co., Indiana, Jan. 19, 1844, and came to Warren Co., in 1860; have one child living, Bertha A.; is Commissioner of Highways; has 240 acres, valued at $10,000, and 120 acres in Iowa.

TORRANCE CYRUS B. Farmer; Sec. 16; P. O. Raritan; Rep; born in Essex Co., N. Y., Jan. 10, 1843; came to Warren Co., in 1866; married April 7, 1868, to Miss Mary E. Bockus, who was born in Missisquoi Co., Canada, April 5, 1843, and came to Warren Co. in 1868; both members of Meth. Church; have two children, Frank L., and Gracie A.; Mr. Torrance served one year in 2d N. Y. Harris Light Cav.; was wounded at Appomatox Church, and was present at Lee's surrender; has 80 acres; valued at $4,000.

Torrance Geo. farmer; Sec. 32; P. O. Colfax; rep; U. B.; from New York.

Towler John C. farmer; Sec. 10; P. O. Swan Creek; dem; born Illinois.

Tucker Joseph C. farmer; Sec. 8; P. O. Raritan; dem; 40 acres, value $2,000; Ill.

Tucker Thomas, farmer; Sec. 8; P. O. Raritan; dem; 40 acres, value $2,000; Ill.

Tucker Wm. retired; Sec. 8; P. O. Raritan; dem; Bapt; 80 acres, value $4,000; Va.

Turner Isaac, preacher and farmer; Sec. 33; P. O. Colfax; rep; F. W. Bapt; from Pa.

Turner J. E. farmer; Sec. 21; P. O. Colfax; rep; F. W. Bapt; from Penn.

VANARSDALE JAS. B. farmer; Sec. 7; P. O. Raritan; rep; Reformed; 80 acres.

Vangilder David, farmer; Sec. 22; P. O. Swan Creek; rep; Meth; 160 acres, val. $50.

Vangilder Jas. M. farmer; Sec. 1; P. O. Roseville; rep; Meth; 72 acres, value $5,000.

Vankirk John, farmer; Sec. 36; P. O. Swan Creek; dem; 80 acres, value $4,000; Ky.

Vanvleet Anthony, farmer; Sec. 14; P. O. Swan Creek; rep; Meth; from Ohio.

WAGGY LEMUEL, farmer; Sec. 31; P. O. Raritan; rep; 320 acres; Ohio.

Wagoner G. W. farmer; Sec. 5; P. O. Roseville; rep; from Pennsylvania.

Wallace Rob't, farmer; Sec. 13; P. O. Swan Creek; rep; from New Jersey

Watson James, lives with his father, L. Watson; Sec. 3; P. O. Roseville; rep; Meth.

WATSON JOHN W. Farmer; Sec. 5; P. O. Roseville; Rep; was born in Warren Co., Jan. 26, 1854; was married Nov. 18, 1874, to Miss Eva Smith, who was born in Warren Co., Aug. 15, 1859; have one child, Clifford V., who was born Oct. 27, 1876; has 80 acres, value $4,000.

WATSON LUCIUS, Farmer and Stock Raiser; Sec. 3; P. O. Roseville; born in Albany Co., N. Y., Dec. 2, 1826; came to this Co. in 1835, with his parents; Rep; married April 11, 1850, to Miss George Ann Fort, who was born Jan. 9, 1831, in Warren Co., Ky.; he has seven children, Joseph Washington (dead), John William, James, Louisa Eleanor, Charles Orlin, Jason Lee, and Cora Ida; was first Assessor of the Township; both members of the Meth. Church; has 152 acres on Secs. 3 and 5, 160 acres in Ellison, and 20 acres in Swan Township, valued at $26,500.

Wells Frank I. farmer; Sec. 19; P. O. Raritan; rep; Meth; 84 acres, value $3,000.

Wells Henry S. farmer; Sec. 19; P. O. Raritan; rep; Presb; from Michigan.

West Aquilla, farmer; Sec. 30; P. O. Swan Creek; ind; Meth; born Illinois.

Williams Harvey, farmer; Sec. 21; P. O. Colfax; rep; from Penn.

Williams Henry, farmer; Sec. 21; P. O. Colfax; rep; from Penn.

WILLIAMS JAMES A. Farmer and Broom-maker; Sec. 21; P. O. Colfax born in Crawford Co., Pa., May 10, 1842; came to Warren Co. in 1856; was married Feb. 15, 1872, to Miss Zuretta A. Rockhold, who was born in Fulton Co., Ill., Dec. 6,

1851; both members of Meth. Church; have one child, John F.; has 80 acres, val. $4,000; served seven months in 83d and 61st Ill. Vol. Inf.; Rep.

Wood Buford, farmer; Sec. 31; P. O. Raritan; dem; born Illinois.

Wood Samuel, farmer; Sec. 31; P. O. Raritan; dem; Christ; 160 acres, value $8,000.

Worden Albert, farmer; Sec. 9; P. O. Roseville; rep; from N. Y.

Worrell Weldon; farmer; Sec. 27; P. O. Swan Creek; rep; from Indiana.

Worrell W. W. farmer; Sec. 27; P. O. Swan Creek; rep; from Kentucky.

Worthington Wm. farmer, Sec. 18; P. O. Raritan; rep; Reformed; 105 acres; N. J.

HALE TOWNSHIP.

ABRAMS B. F. farmer; Sec. 29; P. O. Monmouth; rep; U. P.

Allen Chas. E. farmer; Sec. 11; P. O. Monmouth; rep; U. P.

Armstrong L. farmer; Sec. 9; P. O. Monmouth; rep; U. P.

BALDWIN GEO. farmer; Sec. 30; P. O. Monmouth; dem.

Balmer Elizabeth, farmer; Sec. 10; P. O. Monmouth.

Balmer Robert, farmer; Sec. 10; P. O. Monmouth.

Barr Newton, farmer; Sec. 18; P. O. Monmouth; rep; Meth.

BARTON MRS. JANE L. Widow; Sec. 2; P. O. Denny; born in Green Co., O., Feb. 14, 1818; came to this Co. in 1831; U. P.; 90 acres, value $4,500; her husband came here in 1831, from Green Co., O.; he died in 1851; four sons and three daughters, John, William M., Thomas G., James P., Mrs. Mary E. Parks, Mrs. Margaret F. Clark, and Mrs. Mattie A. Paine.

Barton J. P. farmer; Sec. 2; P. O. Denny; rep; U. P.

Barton W. M. farmer; Sec. 2; P. O. Denny; rep; U. P.

Beaton John, farmer; Sec. 6; P. O. Monmouth.

Beuford W. H. H. farmer; Sec. 4; P. O. Monmouth; rep; U. P.

Blodgett E. L. farmer; Sec. 9; P. O. Monmouth; rep.

Brown J. C. farmer; Sec. 30; P. O. Monmouth; rep.

Brown Jas. farmer; Sec. 3; P. O. Monmouth; rep; U. P.

BROWN JOHN, Farmer; Sec. 1; P. O. Monmouth; born in Co. of Tyrone, Ireland, Jan. 10, 1829; came to this Co. in 1855; Rep; U. P.; owns 145 acres land, valued at $7,300; came to this country in 1854; lived in New York City one year; married Margaret Newbanks, May 18, 1848; she was born in 1823; have three children, Jenny, Margaret, and Wm. John.

Byers Jacob, farmer; Sec. 18; P. O. Kirkwood; rep.

Byers John F. farmer; Sec. 7; P. O. Kirkwood; rep.

Byers W. S. farmer; Sec. 36; P. O. Monmouth; rep.

Bullock Wm. farmer; Sec. 1; P. O. Monmouth; dem.

Burke J. H. farmer; Sec. 19; P. O. Kirkwood.

Burns Edward, farmer; Sec. 35; P. O. Monmouth; rep; Meth.

Burns M. V. T. farmer; Sec. 25; P. O. Monmouth; rep; U. P.

Burns Peter, farmer; Sec. 35; P. O. Monmouth; rep; Meth.

Burns W. E. farmer; Sec. 35; P. O. Monmouth; rep; Meth.

CALDWELL F. M. farmer; Sec. 12; P. O. Monmouth; rep; U. P.

Caldwell John, farmer; Sec. 11; P. O. Monmouth; rep; U. P.

Caldwell J. M. farmer; Sec. 12; P. O. Monmouth; rep; U. P.

Caldwell J. R. farmer; Sec. 12; P. O. Monmouth; rep; U. P.

Camble James, farmer; P. O. Monmouth.

Cashman Jerry, farmer, lives on Mrs. Hardin's place; P. O. Monmouth; dem; Cath.

Cavis Frank, farmer; Sec. 19; P. O. Monmouth; rep.

Cavis F. D. farmer; Sec. 19; P. O. Monmouth; rep; U. P.

Cavis O. A. farmer; Sec. 12; P. O. Monmouth.

Chase John, farmer; Sec. 32; P. O. Kirkwood; dem.

Clark Alexander, P. O. Kirkwood.

Clark A. W. farmer; Sec. 16; P. O. Monmouth.

Clark J. L. farmer; Sec. 19; P. O. Monmouth.

Cochran B. J. farmer; Sec. 18; P. O. Monmouth; dem.
Cochran J. S. farmer; Sec. 19; P. O. Kirkwood.
Coddington J. R. farmer; Sec. 13; P. O. Monmouth; rep.
Cooper Henry, farmer; Sec. 7; P. O. Kirkwood; rep.
CUNNINGHAM SAMUEL, Farmer and Stock Raiser; Sec. 16; P. O. Monmouth; born in Penn. in Oct., 1829; came to this Co. in 1855; Rep; U. P.; owns 100 acres of land, valued at $8,000; married Matilda Hill, March 15, 1855; have eight children, Mary, Alice V., Warren, Carrie, Irena, Benjamin, John and James; his wife owns 160 acres of land on Sec. 16; she was born in West Va., Dec. 26, 1835.

Dull C. M. farmer; Sec. 8; P. O. Monmouth; dem.
Darrah C. B. farmer; Sec. 7; P. O. Monmouth; rep.
Davy J. B farmer; Sec. 6; P. O. Monmouth; rep.
Doyle Dennis, farmer; Sec. 29; P. O. Monmouth; dem; Cath.
Dwight John H. farmer; Sec. 25; P. O. Monmouth.

Eckley Martin V. Sec. 28; P. O. Monmouth.
Edwards Wm. farmer; Sec. 34; P. O. Monmouth; rep.

Fierovid Jacob, farmer; Sec. 24; P. O. Monmouth.
Fierovid Wm. farmer; Sec. 35; P. O. Monmouth; dem; Meth.
Findley D. B. farmer; Sec. 9; P. O. Monmouth; dem; U. P.
Findley E. W. farmer; Sec. 10; P. O. Monmouth; dem; U. P.
Findley Wm. H. farmer; Sec. 9; P. O. Monmouth; dem.
Filler Wm. farmer, rents of John Camble; Sec. 6; P. O. Monmouth; rep.
Fleming Harry C. farmer; Sec. 36; P. O. Monmouth; rep.
Fleming Orr, farmer; Sec. 36; P. O. Monmouth; rep.
French Jonathan, farmer; Sec. 25; P. O. Monmouth; rep; U. P.
French Martha C. farmer; Sec. 25; P. O. Monmouth.

Giddings M. A. farmer; Sec. 22; P. O. Monmouth; rep; U. P.
Gilman E. S. farmer; Sec. 6; P. O. Monmouth.
Gevin Wm. B. farmer; Sec. 36; P. O. Monmouth; rep.
Goff C. W. farmer; Sec. 35; P. O. Monmouth; rep.

GOWDY D. C. Farmer; Sec. 22; P. O. Monmouth; born in Clark Co., Ohio, Dec. 27, 1837; came to this Co. in 1851; Rep; U. P.; owns 80 acres land, value $6,000; has held the office of School Director for three years; enlisted in Co. B, I. V., served three years; married Sarah J. Wright, Dec. 15, 1859; she was born in Adams Co. Ohio; have two children, Ellie A. and Fanny Belle.
Gowdy J. C. farmer; Sec. 22; P. O. Monmouth.
Gowdy Jas. S. farmer; Sec. 23; P. O. Monmouth; rep; U. P.
Gowdy Jos. S. farmer; Sec. 23; P. O. Monmouth; rep; U. P.
Gowdy W. C. farmer; Sec. 22; P. O. Monmouth; rep; U. P.
Gowdy W. R. farmer; Sec. 23; P. O. Monmouth; rep.
Graham A. R. farmer; Sec. 3; P. O. Monmouth; dem.
Graham J. A. farmer; Sec. 3; P. O. Monmouth; dem.
Graham J. R. farmer; Sec. 3; P. O. Monmouth; dem; U. P.

Hannah John, farmer; Sec. 28; P. O. Monmouth; dem; Cath.
HAMBURG CHARLES, Farmer; Sec. 31; P. O. Kirkwood; born in Sweden, in 1842; came to this Co. in 1869; Luth; rents farm of Benj. Davis; his wife was Emma Johnson, born in Sweden, Aug. 21, 1844; married in 1864; they have six children, Emily, Helma, Gust., Axle, Ellen and Sarah.
Hardie Jos. farmer; Sec. 24; P. O. Monmouth.
Harsha G. W. farmer; Sec. 10; P. O. Monmouth; rep; U. P.
HARTZELL WILSON S. Farmer; Sec. 13; P. O. Monmouth; born in Belmont Co., Ohio, July 19, 1845; came to this Co. in 1870; Rep; U. P.; rents farm of Mrs. Shaw; married Jessie Robertson, Sept. 7, 1872; she was born in Elgin, Scotland, March 12, 1852; have two children, Ella J. and Fanny B.
Henderson Jos. farmer; Sec. 29; P. O. Monmouth.
Hickman Geo. W. farmer; Sec. 24; P. O. Monmouth; rep; U. P.
Hickman J. B. farmer; Sec. 26; P. O. Monmouth; rep; U. P.
Hill G. W. farmer, works for T. Paxton; Sec. 2; rep.
HILL J. H. Farmer and Stock Raiser; Sec. 34; P. O. Monmouth; born in West Virginia in 1843; came to this Co. in 1875; Rep; U. P.; owns 160 acres of land, valued at $10,000; his wife was E. V. Allen, born in W. Va. in 1845; married in Sept., 1866;

have four children, Laura Bell, Benjamin David, Anna Elizabeth, and Alton Leon.

Hodge Alex. farmer; Sec. 22; P. O. Monmouth; rep; U. P.

Hodge Wm. farmer; Sec. 22; P. O. Monmouth; rep.

Hood James, farmer; Sec. 11; P. O. Monmouth; rep.

Hood J. R. farmer; Sec. 20; P. O. Monmouth; rep.

HOOD WALTER, Farmer and Stock Raiser; Sec. 22; P. O. Monmouth; born in Pennsylvania, July 25, 1837; came to this Co. in 1865; Rep; U. P.; owns 80 acres of land, valued at $8,000; married Sarah Gethmy in 1857; have five children living and two dead; those living are Margaret, Catharine E., Edward E., John, Ralph.

HOORNBEEK JEREMIAH, Farmer and Stock Raiser; Sec. 35; P. O. Monmouth; born in Ulster Co., N. Y., May 3, 1824; came to this Co. in 1855; Dem; Presb; owns 240 acres of land, valued at $17,000; has held the office of School Director for nearly twenty years; married Elizabeth Bruyn, April 2, 1851; have six children, Nathaniel B., Esther, Adelia C., Emmeline D., John W., and Catharine B.

Hoornbeek N. B. lives with his father; Sec. 35; dem.

JAMES E. H. farmer; Sec. 6; P. O. Little York; Luth.

Johnston James, farmer; Sec. 26; P. O. Monmouth; rep.

Johnston Nathaniel, farmer; Sec. 1; P. O. Monmouth.

Junkin Andrew, farmer; Sec. 16; P. O. Monmouth; dem; U. P.

Junkin John B. farmer; Sec. 16; P. O. Monmouth; dem.

Junkin J. L. farmer; Sec. 18; P. O. Kirkwood; dem; U. P.

KELLEY PATRICK A. farmer; Sec. 1; P. O. Monmouth; dem; Cath.

Kinney Terence, farmer; Sec. 35; P. O. Monmouth; dem; Cath.

LACKEY W. S. farmer; Sec. 9; P. O. Monmouth; dem; U. P.

Lee David, farmer; Sec. 17; P. O. Monmouth; dem; Cath.

Lippett C. farmer; Sec. 34; P. O. Monmouth; rep; Bapt.

Lippett T. C. lives with his father; P. O. Monmouth; rep.

Lord H. G. farmer; Sec. 30; P. O. Kirkwood; rep.

LORD W. H. Farmer; Sec. 7; P. O. Monmouth; born in Chenango Co., N. Y., Jan. 18, 1835; came to this Co. in 1853; Rep; Ind; owns 150 acres of land, valued at $7,500; his wife was Mary E. Baker, born in Butler Co., Ohio, Nov. 1, 1835; married June 11, 1857; have two children, Eugene A. and Laura E.

McCAY JAMES, farmer; Sec. 1; P. O. Denny.

McClanahan Chas. lives with his father; Sec. 33; P. O. Monmouth.

McClanahan T. S. farmer; Sec. 28; P. O. Monmouth; rep; U. P.

McClung Chas. farmer; Sec. 29; P. O. Monmouth; rep; Presb.

McClung J. M. farmer; Sec. 29; P. O. Monmouth; rep; Presb.

McClung Wm. P. farmer; Sec. 29; P. O. Monmouth; rep.

McCormick Jacob, farmer; Sec. 20; P. O. Kirkwood; dem.

McCormick R. B. farmer, lives with his father; Sec. 20; P. O. Monmouth; dem.

McCulley Gilbert, farmer; Sec. 3; P. O. Monmouth; rep; U. P.

McGaffin Jas. farmer; Sec. 16; P. O. Monmouth.

McGregor Jno. farmer; Sec. 10; P. O. Monmouth; dem.

McIntyre D. C. farmer; Sec. 13; P. O. Monmouth; rep.

McIntyre David, farmer; Sec. 13; P. O. Monmouth; rep; U. P.

McIntyre Geo. farmer; Sec. 13; P. O. Monmouth; rep.

McKELVEY JAS. N. Farmer; Sec. 13; P. O. Monmouth; born in Pennsylvania, Aug. 13, 1833; came to this Co. in 1858; Rep; U. P.; rents 90 acres of land of his father, value $6,750; has held the office of Township Collector for two years; married Lizzie McMillan, Dec. 22, 1864; have six children, M. Exira, John A., Norris G., Nellie, James M. and Wm. M.

McKelvey Thos. farmer; Sec. 13; P. O. Monmouth; rep.

McKinzir Murdock, farmer; Sec. 7; P. O. Monmouth.

McLaughlin Joseph, farmer; Sec. 25; P. O. Monmouth; rep; U. P.

McLaughlin Newton, Sec. 24; P. O. Monmouth.

Mackey Jas. lives with his father; Sec. 22; P. O. Monmouth.

Mackey Joseph D. lives with his father; Sec. 22; P. O. Monmouth; rep.

Mackey Wm. farmer; Sec. 22; P. O. Monmouth.

Mackey W. Harper, lives with his father; Sec. 22; P. O. Monmouth.

Martin D. M. farmer; Sec. 8; P. O. Kirkwood; rep.

MARTIN JOHN R. Farmer and Stock Raiser; Sec. 33; P. O. Kirkwood; born in

Iroquois Co., Ill., Feb. 23, 1843; came to this Co. in Oct. 1852; Dem; rents farm of 42 acres of J. P. Fierovid; his wife was Mary Foster, born in Alabama in 1842; married Feb. 20, 1865; they have had two children, one living, Eddie, born Aug. 4, 1874, and one deceased, Willie, born Jan. 2, 1867.

Martin Solomon, farmer; Sec. 8; P. O. Kirkwood; rep.

Mason W. Y. farmer; Sec. 24; P. O. Monmouth; rep.

Meisenger Charles, Sec. 16; P. O. Monmouth.

Miller Geo. E. farmer; Sec. 26; P. O. Monmouth; rep; U. P.

Mitchell W. A. farmer; Sec. 3; P. O. Monmouth; rep; U. P.

MONTGOMERY JOHN, Farmer; Sec. 16; P. O. Kirkwood; born in Orange Co., Ind., Aug. 31, 1843; came to this Co. 1865; Rep; Ind; owns 160 acres land, val. $7,200; enlisted in Co. H, 11th Ill. Cav.; served between four and five years; married Sarah J. Davis, March 15, 1860; have three children, Arthur, Evyline and Merton.

MOODY P. H. Farmer and Stock Raiser; ; Sec. 33; P. O. Kirkwood; born in Pa. in 1820; came to this Co. in April, 1856; Dem; Bapt; owns 370 acres of land, valued at $20,000; has held the office of Overseer of Highway, and is now School Director; his wife was Eliza McCormick, born in Pennsylvania in 1825; married in Feb., 1845; they have seven children, Robert, John, Jane, Elizabeth Margaret, Spencer Lee, George F. and Charles Spurgeon.

Moore Rufus W. farmer; Sec. 33; P. O. Monmouth; rep.

Morris Thos. farmer; Sec. 7; P. O. Monmouth; dem; Cath.

Mullahey Peter, farmer; Sec. 5; P. O. Oquawka; dem; Cath.

NASH J. B. farmer; Sec. 16; P. O. Monmouth; rep; U. P.

Nash J. C. farmer; Sec. 15; P.O. Monmouth; rep; U. P.

NASH A. Farmer and Stock Raiser; Sec. 15; P. O. Monmouth; born in Green Co., Ohio, Aug. 1, 1826; came to this Co. in 1832; U. P.; owns 107 acres land, value $10,700; he is one of the oldest settlers in the Co., having lived here 45 years; has held the office of School Director fifteen years; married E. J. French, Nov. 1, 1848; have five children, Mary J., R. W., Emma A., Eddie F. and Wm. G.

Nash Robt. farmer; Sec. 14; P. O. Monmouth; rep; U. P.

Nash W. A. farmer; Sec. 10; P. O. Monmouth; rep; U. P.

Nesbit Jas. C. farmer; Sec. 26; P. O. Monmouth; rep; Presb.

Newlon E. A. farm hand; Sec. 20; P. O. Monmouth; rep.

OLMSTED A. F. farmer; Sec. 30; P.O Monmouth; dem.

Olmsted L. S. retired farmer; Sec. 30; P. O. Monmouth; dem.

Olmsted Newton W. farmer; Sec. 30; P. O. Monmouth; dem.

Olsen James; P.O. Monmouth; from Sweden.

PAINE JAS. farmer; Sec. 28; P.O. Monmouth; rep.

PAIN JAMES, Farmer and Stock Raiser; Sec. 27; P. O. Kirkwood; born in Ireland, Aug. 9, 1836; came to this country in 1845, and to this Co. in 1857; Dem; Cath; owns 80 acres of land, valued at $6,000; his wife was Ann Fitzsimons, born in Ireland in 1839; married April 28, 1861; they have six children, Mary A., Michael, William, Bridget, Thomas and James.

Palmer Geo. W. farmer; Sec. 7; P. O. Kirkwood; rep.

Palmer Wilkinson, farmer; Sec. 18; P. O. Rozetta.

Pape Conrad; farmer, Sec. 33; P. O. Kirkwood; dem; Presb.

Pape John, farmer; Sec. 32; P. O. Kirkwood; dem; Presb.

Patterson J. W. farmer; Sec. 12; P. O. Monmouth; dem.

Patterson R. A. farmer; Sec. 12; P. O. Monmouth; dem; Presb; from Penn.

PATTERSEN SAM'L H. Farmer; Sec. 12; P. O. Monmouth; born in Perry Co., Penn., Nov. 10, 1806; came to this Co. in 1837; Dem; Presb; owns 160 acres of land, valued at $8,000; has held the office of School Director for many years; married Ellen Harper in 1833; have seven children living, Alexander, Samuel L., Ann Elizabeth, Sarah Jane, Wilson, Agnes C. and Bella; one son died in the Army.

Patterson S. L. farmer; Sec. 12; P. O. Monmouth; dem.

Patton J. H. farmer; Sec. 23; P. O. Monmouth; rep.

Patton N T. farmer; Sec. 27; P. O. Monmouth; rep; U. P.

PATTON R. S. Farmer and Stock Raiser; Sec. 23; P. O. Monmouth; born in Ohio in Jan. 1837; came to this Co. in 1860; Rep; U. P.; owns 134 acres of land, valued at $12,060; married Sarah A. Sheppard in 1860; she was born in 1839; have six children; those living are Anna S., George E., John S.; those that are dead are Mary E., Emma A. and Wilbur; holds the office of Township Treasurer, and has been Assessor.

Paston Thomas M. farmer; Sec. 2; P. O. Denny; rep; U. P.; 140 acres, val. $7,000.

Pearson Francis, farmer; Sec. 24; P.O. Monmouth; rep.
Pearson Thos. farmer; Sec. 12; P. O. Monmouth; rep; from Pennsylvania.
Porter R. C. farmer; Sec. 29; P. O. Monmouth.

REIGHTON G. W. farmer; Sec. 24; P. O. Monmouth; dem.
Reynolds J. B. farmer; P. O. Monmouth; rep; U. P.
Reynolds J. W. farmer; Sec. 10; P. O. Monmouth; rep; U. P.
Reynolds W. Y. farmer; Sec. 10; P. O. Monmouth; rep.

RINEHART DAVID W. Farmer and Stock Raiser; Sec. 34; P. O. Monmouth; born in Ulster Co., N. Y., in Oct. 1824; came to this Co. in 1854; Dem; Presb; owns 165 acres, valued at $12,300; holds the offices of Pathmaster and School Director; his wife was Maria Bruyn; she was born in Ulster Co., N. Y., in 1832; married in Dec., 1854; they have eight children, William, Nathaniel, LeFevre, Headley, John, Cornelia, Laura and Chas.

Riggs Henry H. farmer; Sec. 23; P. O. Monmouth; dem.
Rodgers C. M. farmer; Sec. 2; P. O. Monmouth; rep; U. P.
Rodgers J. C. farmer; Sec. 11; P. O. Monmouth; rep; U. P.
Rodgers Jno. lives with his son; Sec. 15; P. O. Monmouth; rep; U. P.
Rodgers Jno. A. lives with his father; Sec. 11; P. O. Monmouth; rep.
Rogers S. A. farmer; Sec. 11; P. O. Monmouth; rep.
Rodgers S. W. farmer; Sec. 2; P. O. Monmouth; rep; U. P.
Rodgers W. A. farmer; Sec. 15; P. O. Monmouth; rep; Presb.
Rodgers W. M. farmer; Sec. 11; P. O. Monmouth; rep; U. P.
Roney Hercules, farmer; Sec. 21; P. O. Monmouth; rep; Presb.
Roney S. W. farmer; Sec. 21; P. O. Monmouth; rep.
Runyan Henry, farmer; Sec. 16; P. O. Monmouth.
Runyan Thos. farmer; Sec. 16; P. O. Monmouth.

SAWIN F. J. farmer; Sec. 19; P. O. Monmouth.
Schweitzer Frederic, farmer; Sec. 1; P. O. Monmouth; dem; 40 acres, value $2,000.

SCHWEITZER JOHN GEO. Farmer; Sec. 1; P. O. Monmouth; born in Germany, May 3, 1828; came to this Co. in 1860; Dem; Luth; owns 41 acres of land, value $2,000; was in the Mexican war, Co. H, 2d N. Y. Vol.; served for eight months; also in the late war, Co. C, I. V. I.; served four and one-half years; is one of the School Directors for present term; married Miss E. Gayer, Dec. 20, 1866; have six children, Jacob, John, Bertha, Christina, Mary Elizabeth and Matilda.

Shafer Geo. farmer; Sec. 1; P. O. Denny; rep.
Shafer John, farmer; Sec. 15; P. O. Monmouth; rep.

SHAW MRS. M. J. Farming; Sec. 13; P. O. Monmouth; born in Ky., April 13, 1836; came to this Co. in 1852; Rep; Chris; owns 185 acres of land, valued at $9,250; was married Nov. 8, 1857, to Clarkson Shaw; have three children, Geo. A., Mary E. and Louie Luella; her husband died Aug. 31, 1869.

Shafer Peter, farmer; Sec. 15; P. O. Monmouth; rep; Presb.
Sloan G. H. farmer; Sec. 13; P. O. Monmouth; dem.
Smiley Mrs. Hannah, Sec. 16; P. O. Monmouth.
Smiley J. S. farmer; Sec. 21; P. O. Monmouth; rep; U. P.
Smiley Robt. W. farmer; Sec. 21; P. O. Monmouth; rep; U. P.
Smiley T. W. farmer; Sec. 21; P. O. Monmouth; rep; U. P.
Smith Adam, farmer; Sec. 16; P. O. Monmouth; rep; U. P.
Smith David, farmer; Sec. 17; P. O. Monmouth.
Smith Jas. farmer; Sec. 6; P. O. Monmouth; rep.
Snooks Elisha, farmer; Sec. 6; P. O. Monmouth; rep.
Spence Geo. farmer; Sec. 20; P. O. Monmouth; rep.
Sperry A. farmer; Sec. 4; P. O. Monmouth.
Sperry Plinn, lives with his father; Sec. 4; P. O. Monmouth; rep.
Sprout John, farmer; Sec. 14; P. O. Monmouth; dem.
Sterrett J. B. farmer; Sec. 3; P. O. Denny; rep; U. P.
Stevenson Calvin, farmer; Sec. 27; P. O. Monmouth; rep; U. P.
Stevenson W. H. farmer; Sec. 25; P. O. Monmouth; rep.
Stevenson W. M. farmer; Sec. 32; P. O. Monmouth.

STEWART A. Farmer and Stock Raiser; Sec. 29; P. O. Monmouth; born in Guernsey Co., O., June 24, 1841; came to this Co. in 1859; Rep; U. P.; owns 80 acres of land, valued at $4,000; is Collector of the tp. and School Director; served three years in the 36th I. V. I. during the late war; his wife was Nancy Jane Hickman; she was born in Perry Co., O., May 25, 1850; married Dec. 31, 1868; they have had three children; Ollie, and Wm. Archibald are living, and Laurietta deceased.

Swain J. F. farmer; Sec. 19; P. O. Monmouth.

TRUMBULL, D. A. farmer; Sec. 3; P. O. Monmouth; rep; U. P.

TORLEY FREDERICK, Farmer and Stock Raiser; Sec. 28; P. O. Monmouth; born in Germany, in 1836; came to this country in 1848; Rep; Meth; owns 168 acres, valued at $8,400; his wife was Barbara Schwab; she was born in Germany, in 1840; married Oct. 2, 1873; they have one child, Frederick Wm.

UNCKLES WM. T. Farmer and Stock Raiser; Sec. 19; P. O. Kirkwood; born in Fulton Co., Pa., Dec. 16, 1841; came to this Co. in 1852; removed to Henderson Co. in 1852; returned to this Co. in 1873; Rep; Meth; owns 96 acres of land, valued at $6,000; holds the office of School Director; served in Co. E, 10th I, V, I, one year, when he was discharged on a certificate of disability from the Surgeon; married Debilla J. Ives, Dec. 28, 1865; she was born in Henderson Co., Ill., Dec. 13, 1848; they have five children living and one dead—Ora M., Mary G., Mabel F., Robert C., Stella M. and Arthur L.

WHITE S. W lives with his father; Sec. 30; P. O. Kirkwood.

WHITE ANDREW, Farmer and Stock Raiser; Sec. 30; P. O. Kirkwood; born in Chester Co., Pa., Aug. 9, 1809; came to this Co. in 1837; Rep; Presb; owns 176 acres of land, value $10,560; married Eliza Andrews, Jan 14, 1841; she died same year; married Lucinda Miller, Oct. 8, 1846; have four children, Samuel W., Charles A., John F. and Mary E.

Williams G. W. farmer; Sec. 27; P. O. Monmouth.

Winebright Geo. farmer; Sec. 18; P. O. Monmouth; rep.

WOODS J. M. Farmer and Stock Raiser; Sec. 32; P. O. Kirkwood; born in Gibson Co., Ind., in 1834; came to this Co. in 1844; Dem; owns 126 acres, valued at $6,300; his wife was Rachel Creswell; she was born in Ohio, July 7, 1832; married March 13, 1856; they have six children, four of whom are living—Hannah N., Mary Jane, David Samuel and Cora Bell.

Woosley Allen S. farmer; Sec. 1; P. O. Monmouth; rep; from Kentucky.

Wright H. L. farmer; Sec. 14; P. O. Monmouth; rep; U. P.

Wright Joseph, farmer; Sec. 28; P. O. Monmouth; rep.

Wright Washington; farmer; Sec. 14; P. O. Monmouth; rep; U. P.

SWAN TOWNSHIP.

ABBOTT CHAS, laborer; Swan Creek; rep; Meth; from Indiana.

Atchison L. B. farmer; Sec. 11; P. O. Greenbush; dem; New Light; 8¼ acres; N. Y.

Acton Elias D. shoemaker; Swan Creek; rep; property worth $600; from Ohio.

Adams John, farmer; Sec. 2; P. O. Roseville; dem; Bapt; 10 acres; from Kentucky.

Adamson M. farmer for C. T. Gossett; Sec. 4; P. O. Roseville; rep; from Iowa.

Adamson Willis, works for L. Perkins; P. O. Roseville; rep; from Iowa.

ADKISON WM. Farmer and Stock Raiser; Secs. 5, 7, 8, 16; P. O. Roseville; born in Breckenridge Co., Ky., Oct. 10, 1830; came to this Co. in 1836; Rep; Chris; owns 530 acres, value $30,000; wife was Lucinda Johnson, born in Christian Co., Ky; married Feb. 24, 1855, in Warren Co., Ill.; twelve children, ten living, Ora, George, Allen, Jane, Seth, Jacob, Fannie, Willie, Orville and Grace.

Albert Henry, farmer; Sec. 14; P. O. Youngstown; dem; rents 140 acres.

Anderson Elias, farmer; Swan Creek; rep; Luth; owns house and lot; from Sweden.

Anderson Oluff, blacksmith; Swan Creek; rep; Luth; from Sweden.

BAIR CALEB, farmer for R. Holeman; Sec. 4; P. O. Roseville; dem; Chris.

Barber Royal B. farmer, with R. R. McKinley; P. O. Youngstown; dem; from Mich.

Barker Marion J. farmer for J. Kepple; P. O. Walnut Grove; dem; from Fulton Co.

Baremore C. M. farmer; Sec. 35; P. O. Walnut Grove; dem; rents 115 acres; Penn.

Baremore John, farmer with C. M. Baremore; P. O. Walnut Grove; dem; Penn.

Baremore Jos. farmer with C. M. Baremore; P. O. Walnut Grove; from Virginia.

Barkland Sylvester, farmer for J. Kepple; P. O. Walnut Grove; dem; Fulton Co.

Barron T. J. wagon-maker; Swan Creek; rep; Meth; property $600; born Illinois.

Beckwith Chas. C. carpenter; Swan Creek; rep; Meth; owns house and lot; Conn.

BECKNER GEO. W. Farmer and Stock Raiser; Sec. 32; P. O. Youngstown; born in Bath Co., Ky., Jan. 13, 1825; came to this Co. Jan., 1852; Dem; Bapt; owns 247 acres, value $12,350; wife was Deborah Vankirk, born Aug. 11, 1826, in Fleming Co., Ky; married March 2, 1848, in Bath Co., Ky; have had eleven children, five living, Miranda A., Robert T., George L., Susan J., Harriet F.; those dead are Mathias W., Abram L., Andrew S., Elizabeth C., Milly A., Mary C.; has been Supervisor, Assessor, Justice of the Peace and School Treasurer.

BECKNER HENRY C. Farmer and Stock Raiser; Sec. 29; P. O Youngstown; born in Bath Co., Ky., March 10, 1849; came to this Co. in 1852; Dem; rents 41 acres; wife was Lydia M. Jones, born in Knox Co., Ill., Dec. 25, 1855; married April 18, 1875, at Maquon, Knox Co; have one child, Oral Winifred.

Beckner R. T. farmer for father, G. W. Beckner; P. O. Youngstown; dem; Warren Co.

Bell Wm. Swan Creek; rep; from New York.

Bliss E. merchant; Swan Creek; rep; Meth; from Vermont.

Bliss E. T. miller; Swan Creek.

Blue F. M. farmer; Sec. 10; P. O. Roseville; dem; 159 acres, value $6,360; from Ind.

Boden Saml. carpenter; Swan Creek; dem; owns house and lot; from Ohio.

Bond Leander H. farmer; Sec. 25; P. O. Walnut Grove; dem; Bapt; rents 160 acres.

BOOTH FRANK, Farmer and Stock Raiser; Sec. 18; P. O. Swan Creek; born in Cabell Co., W. Va., Nov. 7, 1829; came to Knox Co. in 1836, and to this Co. in 1852; Rep; Meth; owns 282½ acres, value $14,125; wife was Martha J. Sargent, born in Morgan Co., Ill., April 3, 1835; married March 23, 1854, at Monmouth, Warren Co; have had seven children; five living, Ira S., Henry T., Allen C., Nola E., Annie L.; those dead, James W. and Nellie M.

Booth Ira S. farmer, with Frank Booth; P. O. Swan Creek; rep; born Swan tp.

Booth Mrs. Lucinda, farmer; Sec. 18; P. O. Swan Creek; 160 acres, val. $8,450; Va.

Booth Washington J. farmer for Mrs. L. Booth; P. O. Swan Creek; dem; Meth.

Booton Jno. coal miner; Sec. 16; P. O. Roseville; rep.

Botts R. L. storekeeper; Swan Creek; ind; Univ; born Illinois.

Bowman Chas. farmer for J. Perkins; P. O. Greenbush; dem; Bapt; born Illinois.

Bozan Richard, works for S. Perkins; P. O. Roseville; dem; Cath; from Ireland.

Bradford Robert, farmer for A.A. Hossington; P. O. Youngstown; rep; from N. Y.

Bradley Robt. works for A. A. Hossington; Sec. 13; P. O. Youngstown; rep.

Brown Daniel, works for S. Perkins; P. O. Roseville; rep; from Indiana.

Buck Henry, farmer; Swan Creek; dem; from Virginia.

Buck Mason, farmer; Swan Creek; dem; Bapt; house and lots, val. $1,000; from Va.

Burk Jas. farmer; Sec. 31; P.O. Swan Creek; rep; Chris; from Indiana.

Burk John, farmer; Sec. 30; P. O. Swan Creek; rep; Chris; rents 80 acres; Indiana.

Burk Wm. lives with Jas. Burk; P. O. Swan Creek; rep; Chris; from Indiana.

CAMPBELL JAS. M. farmer with Matthew Campbell; P. O. Greenbush; dem.

Campbell Matthew, farmer; Sec. 24; P. O. Greenbush; dem; Bapt; rents 76 acres; Pa.

Carr Thomas, farmer; Sec. 3; P. O. Roseville; dem.

CARTER BENJ. C. Farmer and Stock Raiser; Secs. 10-11; P. O. Roseville; born in Caldwell Co., Ky., Aug. 30, 1822; came to this Co. in 1843; Dem; Chris; 39 acres, value $4,500; wife was Mary J. Moulton, born in Decatur Co., Ind.; married Oct. 22, 1854; six children; three living, Margery Ellen, Flora P. and Laura E.; those dead, Mary A., John W. and Jas. W.; Mrs. C. has by former marriage, Susan J., living, and three children dead.

Carter J. R. farmer; Sec. 10; P. O. Roseville; dem; Camp; from Georgia.

Cayton A. J. farmer; Secs. 21-22; P. O. Youngstown; dem; Chris; from Kentucky.

Cayton C. A. lives with A. J. Cayton; P. O. Youngstown; dem; born Illinois.

Chadwick Geo. W. farmer, with A. Crissy; Sec. 2; P. O. Greenbush; dem; Bapt; N.Y.

Chapman J. coal-miner; Sec 16; P. O. Swan Creek; dem.

Chapin Milton, farmer, rents of H. Crissy; Sec. 7; P. O. Greenbush; from Canada.

Chase J. C. farmer, for E. S. Kinney; P. O. Youngstown; rep; from Michigan.

Coghill J. W. farmer, for Jas. Tucker; Sec. 9; dem; Bapt; from Virginia.

Coon David, farmer; Swan Creek; rep; from Kentucky.

Coon John, farmer, for A. A. Hossington; Sec. 13; P. O. Youngstown; rep.

Coon Jno. farmer; Sec. 24; P. O. Greenbush; rep; 3 acres; from Kentucky.

Coon Jno. Jr. farmer; Swan Creek; rep; from Kentucky.

Cooper Michael, farmer, with Isaac Davis; P. O. Roseville; dem; from Missouri.

Cooper Thomas, farmer, with M. F. Blue; P. O. Swan Creek; dem.

Cornell A. A. farmer, with A. B. Sisson; P. O. Swan Creek; rep; Meth; from N. Y.

Courtwright Garner, farmer for J. M. Cunningham; Sec. 3; P. O. Roseville; dem.

Coyl Dennis, farmer, for A. J. Sisson; P.O. Swan Creek; dem; from Ireland.

Crab Jas. M. farmer; Sec. 33; P. O. Youngstown; dem; Chris; 160 acres, value $9,600.

Crab Thos. farmer, for Q. Jared; Sec. 8; P. O. Roseville; dem; from Indiana.

Crawford D. L. farmer; Sec. 35; P. O. Walnut Grove; dem; Meth; 360 acres; Mich.

Crebs C. works on railroad; Youngstown; born McDonough Co.

CRISSY ABRAM, Farmer and Stock Raiser; Sec. 2; P. O. Greenbush; born in Fairfield Co., Conn., Oct. 19, 1795; came to this Co. in Sept. 1847; Rep; Univ; 35 acres, value $2,000; was Justice of Peace and Commissioner of Highways; wife was Harriet E. Conway, born in Saratoga Co., N. Y.; married in Oct. 1865; one child, Emmie May, born Aug. 7, 1868; eight children by former marriage; two sons and three grandsons served in Union Army.

Cunningham G. W. farmer; Sec. 1; Greenbush; dem; New Light; 100 acres; Ind.

Cunningham J. M. farmer; Sec. 3; P. O. Roseville; dem; Bapt; 170 acres; Ind.

Cunningham Jas. farmer; Sec. 27; P. O. Youngstown; dem; rents 160 acres; Ind.

Curry Samuel, farmer; Sec. 3; P. O. Roseville; ind; Meth; 100 acres; from England.

DANIELSON SAM'L, physician; Swan Creek; dem; Meth; from Ohio.

Davis Isaac, farmer; Sec. 11; P. O. Roseville; dem; 92 acres; from Ohio.

Davis John, farmer; Sec. 26; P. O. Youngstown; rents 80 acres.

Davis Wm. farmer, for C. F. Gossett; Sec. 4; P. O. Roseville; from Pennsylvania.

Day Warren, farmer; Sec. 3; P. O. Roseville; dem; Bapt; 120 acres; from Indiana.

Dean Chas. farmer, with M. Dean; P. O. Swan Creek; dem; born Fulton Co.

DEAN MICHAEL, Farmer and Stock Raiser; Sec. 31; P. O. Swan Creek; born in Bath Co. Ky., Nov. 20, 1815; came to this Co. in 1840; dem; owns 125 acres, value $7,500; wife was Susan Cummings, born in Greenock, Scotland, April 8, 1824; married March 10, 1842, at Lewiston, Fulton Co.; have had ten children; eight living, Susan F., Mary, Melissa, Chas. E., Cora L., William W., Bessie and Clara Sybil; those dead, Jas. E. and Jos. W.

Dellague Geo. farmer; Sec. 19; P. O. Swan Creek; born Illinois.

Dewey A. B. wagon-maker; Youngstown; rep; Bapt.

Dewey J. C. wagon-maker; Youngstown; rep; 40 acres.

Ditch John, farmer; Sec. 6; P. O. Roseville; rep; 631½ acres.

Duff Jno. farmer; Sec. 10; P. O. Roseville; dem; 5 acres; from Pennsylvania.

Duncan J. R. farm laborer; Youngstown; dem; Meth; from Missouri.

EDDIE ISAAC, night watch on railroad; Youngstown; rep; Meth from Ohio.

Emerick J. C. farmer, for J. F. Jared; Sec. 8; dem.

Emerick Orris, farmer for E. Jared; Sec. 5; P. O. Roseville; dem; born Illinois.

Emerson Thos. miner for J. Tucker; Sec. 9; from England.

ERBRODT H. C. Harness Shop, Swan Creek; born in Hanover, Prussia, Oct. 4, 1845; came to this County in 1876; Dem; Luth; owns Stock in Store, valued at $500. Mr. Erbrodt is the only Harness Maker within six miles of Swan Creek, and has a stock of first-class goods of every description. Repairing neatly and promptly executed.

FARRAR GEO. farmer, rents 10 acres; Sec. 11; P. O. Roseville; dem; Bapt.

FOLGER H. A., M. D. Druggist; Youngstown; born in Cincinnati, Ohio, Nov. 21, 1835; came to this Co. in April, 1871; Rep; owns property valued at $1,500; wife was Lucy E. Mapes, born Pleasant Mount, Wayne Co., Penn., Dec. 18, 1841; married in Moline, Ill., March 6, 1865; have one child, Alice E., born Jan. 12, 1866; Dr. Folger served as surgeon in 1864, in the 133d Reg. Ill. Vol. Inf.

Freeland Frank B. farmer, for J. P. Reed; P. O. Youngstown.

Fuller Thomas, lives with W. R. Reid; P O. Roseville; rep; from Minn.

GEIMAN J. P. foreman section hands, Youngstown; dem; from Maryland.

Goods Frank, farmer; Sec. 24; P. O. Swan Creek; dem; from Indiana.

GOSSETT C. T. Farmer and Stock Raiser; Sec. 4; P. O. Roseville; born in Jackson Co., Indiana, Jan. 18, 1840; came to this Co. in 1854; Rep; owns property valued at $4,000; served as private for eight months in Co. K, 11th Ill. Cavalry, and was 1st. Lieut. for two years and six months in Companies L and G, 12th Ill. Cavalry; wife was Anna Mahood, born in Butler Co., Penn.; married Jan. 1, 1868; two children, Elizabeth T., born Dec. 16, 1868, and Geo. L., Nov. 6, 1870.

Greer J. Stewart, farmer, rents 200 acres; Sec. 14; P. O. Youngstown; rep; from Ohio.

Grigg Jno. D. farmer; Sec. 32; P. O. Youngstown; rep; 137 acres, value $7,500; Ky.

Grigg Joseph W. lives with J. D. Grigg; P. O. Youngstown; rep; Meth; from Va.

VOTERS AND TAXPAYERS OF

Gutridge M. farmer; Sec. 14; P. O. Roseville; dem; 20 acres.

HAGERTY DENNIS, works for Sol. Perkins; P. O. Roseville; dem; Cath.

Hagerty Michael, works for Sol. Perkins; P. O. Roseville; dem; Cath; from Ireland.

Hall W. L. farmer, rents 160 acres with Geo. J. Lake; Sec. 26; P. O. Youngstown; rep.

Hanks Isaac, farmer; Sec. 34; P. O. Bushnell; 160 acres, value $8,000; from N. Y.

Hanks Joseph, farmer; lives with I. Hanks, P. O. Bushnell; born Warren Co.

Harvey Henry L. farmer, for W. P. Jones; P. O. Youngstown; Bapt; from Iowa.

Helms J. H. laborer, Swan Creek; dem; from Virginia.

Hendrick H. C. farmer for A. Vandiver; P. O. Youngstown; dem; Bapt; from Ky.

Henry H. A. farmer; Secs. 31 and 32; P. O. Swan Creek; rep; Bapt; 400 acres; Ohio.

Herr John E. station agent, Swan Creek; dem; born Illinois.

Hibbs Henry, farmer for Mr. Henry; P. O. Swan Creek; rep; born Illinois.

Higgins J. P. farmer; Sec. 28; P. O. Youngstown; dem; from Kentucky.

Hindman J. S. farmer; Sec. 18; P. O. Roseville; rep; Meth; 100 acres, value $5,000.

Hoisington A. A. farmer; Sec. 13; P. O. Youngstown; rep; 30 acres, value $13,000.

Holden G. W. farmer, rents 40 acres of J. Crabb; Sec. 33; P. O. Youngstown; dem.

Holeman R. A. farmer; Sec. 15; P. O. Youngstown; dem; Bapt; 39 acres; Ind.

Holliday Wm. farmer for G. W. McMahill; P. O. Walnut Grove; dem; Campbelite.

Holmes Wm. farmer, rents 80 acres; Sec. 36; P. O. Walnut Grove; dem; Meth; Iowa.

Huston Reuben, farmer with W. A. Huston; P. O. Swan Creek; rep; born Warren Co.

Huston Robt. M. farmer with W. A. Huston; P. O. Swan Creek; rep; born Warren Co.

HUSTON WM. A. Farmer and Stock Raiser; Sec. 18; P. O. Swan Creek; born in New Castle Co., Del., May 18, 1823; came to Ind. in 1835, and this Co. in 1852; Rep; owns 123 acres, valued at $6,150; wife was Eliza Crabb, born in Wayne Co., Ind. June 17, 1830; married in Wayne Co., Feb. 2, 1849; have had twelve children; ten living; James W., Martha A., Reuben T., Robt. M., John H., Chas. A., Annie E., Susan Paulina, Zoa B., Rosa A.; those dead, Harriet Jane and Isaac M.

JARED FRANK farmer; Sec. 22; P. O. Youngstown; dem.

JARED JAS. F. Farmer and Stock Raiser; Sec. 16; P. O. Roseville; born in Breckenbridge Co., Kentucky, May 20, 1831; came to this Co. in 1856; Dem; 280 acres, valued at $11,200; wife was Margaret A. Kelsey, born in Ill.; married Oct. 5, 1865; seven children, five living, Benj. F., Clarance H., Pearlie, Claudie, and Harry; those dead, Butler and John.

Jared Oscar J. farmer, for T. Jared; Sec 5; P. O. Roseville; born Illinois.

Jared Thos. farmer; Sec. 5; P. O. Roseville; dem; 140 acres; from Kentucky.

Jennings E. farmer; Sec. 23; P. O. Youngstown; dem; Bapt; 140 acres, value $7,000.

Jennings G. S. farmer; P. O. Youngstown; dem; Bapt; property value $300; Illinois.

Johnson A. J. laborer; P. O. Youngstown; from New York.

JOHNSON JOSIAH, Farmer; Sec. 2; P. O. Greenbush; born in Jackson Co., Ohio, July 12, 1837; came to this Co. in 1856; Rep; 129 acres, valued at $6,000; was Town Collector in 1876; wife was Marietta Roberts, born in Warren Co., Ill., married Nov. 26, 1861; seven children, five living, Laura Ellen, Orlan Leon, Amy Gracie, Annie May, and Lottie Pearl; those dead, Herschel B., other unnamed.

Jones Mrs. Alvira, farmer; Sec. 19; P. O. Swan Creek; owns 5 acres.

Jones E. O. farmer, rents 80 acres; Sec. 31; P. O. Swan Creek; dem; from Penn.

Jones F. C. lives with E. O. Jones; P. O. Swan Creek; dem; born Illinois.

Jones P. B. farmer with W. P. Jones; P. O. Youngstown; dem; Bapt; born Illinois.

Jones W. P. farmer; P. O. Youngstown; dem; Bapt; from Kentucky.

KELSEY JOHN, farmer; Sec. 1; P. O. Roseville; dem.

Kelsey Samuel, farmer; Sec. 1; P. O. Greenbush; dem; 26 acres.

Kepple Jacob M. farmer; Sec. 25 & 26; P. O. Walnut Grove; ind; Meth; 240 acres.

Kidder B. H. farmer; Sec. 28; P. O. Youngstown; rep; Bapt; 160 acres, value $8,000.

Kidder H. H. farmer; Sec. 23; P. O. Youngstown; rep; 140 acres, value $7,000; Ill.

Kidder Mrs. M. A. farming; Sec. 28; P. O. Youngstown; 52 acres, value $2,600; Vt.

Kidder N. farmer, lives with Mrs. M. A. Kidder; P. O. Youngstown; rep; 104 acrs.

Kidder W. O. farmer; Sec. 21; P. O. Youngstown; rep; 160 acres, value $8,000; Ill.

KINNEY ELIJAH S. Farmer and Stock Raiser; Sec. 34; P. O. Youngstown; born in Cayuga Co., N. Y., Sep. 13, 1830; came to this Co. in 1857; Dem; owns 160 acres, value $8,000; wife was Elizabeth Agnes McKinley, born in Warren Co. Oct. 2, 1844; married June 24, 1875; one little girl, born Feb 11, 1877; Mr. K., by former wife, had Lillie May and George Washington; Mrs. K., by former husband, Geo. Ewing, Robt. Samuel and Jas. Marvin.

KIRKPATRICK JACOB, Farmer and Stock Raiser; Secs. 6 and 7, and Pt. Pleasant 12; P. O. Roseville; born in Sangamon Co., Ill., Oct. 5, 1828; Rep; owns 540 acres, value $27,000; wife was Hulda Adkinson, born in Swan tp., Warren Co., July 21, 1838; married Dec. 30, 1858, in Swan tp.; have had four children; three living—Henry, Willis, Mary; other unnamed.

LAKE GEO. J. farmer, rents 160 acres; Sec. 26; P. O. Youngstown; rep; Meth.
Lally Thos. shoemaker; Youngstown; dem; from Ireland.
Larkin S. S. farmer; Youngstown; dem; Bapt; property valued at $1,000; Ohio.
Lawson A. W. farmer; Sec. 35; P. O. Bushnell; dem; U. B.; from Tennessee.
Lieurance Abijah, lives with S. Perkins; P. O. Roseville; dem; Chris; from Tenn.
Lieurance C. B. farmer for T. Jared; Sec. 9; dem; from Ohio.
Lieurance Matison, farmer; Sec. 10; P. O. Roseville; dem; Chris; 51 acres; Ohio.
Lilladol Frank, works for Sol. Perkins; P. O. Roseville; rep; Cong; from Sweden.
Linley Levy, farmer for Wm. Adkison; Sec. 7; P. O. Roseville; rep; Cong; Penn.
Lippy Jno. grocery; Swan Creek; rep; owns property valued at $2,000.
Little C. L. farmer for Wm. Thomas; P. O. Youngstown; rep; from Maine.
Louen Wm. miner for J. Tucker; Sec. 9; from England.

McCAMERON JNO, miller; Swan Creek; dem; owns house and lot; Ky.
McCluhan C. W. physician; Swan Creek; rep; Presb; two lots; from Penn.
McCormack Chas. farmer; Sec. 26; P. O. Youngstown; dem; born Ill.
McCoy Jas. farmer; Sec. 36; P. O. Walnut Grove; ind; Meth; born Illinois.
McCoy T. L. farmer with Jas. McCoy; P. O. Walnut Grove; ind; Meth; born Illinois.
McKinley Albert, farmer with father, R. R. McKinley; P. O. Youngstown; dem.
McKinley Jas. farmer for R. R. McKinley; P. O. Youngstown; dem; born Illinois.
McKINLEY ROBT. R. Farmer and Stock Raiser; Secs. 12, 27, 34; P. O. Youngstown; born in Mason Co., Ky., June 29, 1806; came to this Co. in June, 1843; Dem; owns 800 acres, value $40,000; wife was Serena Truitt, born in Flemming Co., Ky., Jan. 15, 1815; married Feb. 10, 1838; have had ten children; seven living, Wm., born March 11, 1843; Elizabeth A., Oct. 2, 1844; Sarah Jane, May 1, 1846; Albert T., Feb. 15, 1850; Jas. E., Feb. 12, 1854; Sodema S., May 2, 1856; Robt. P., Dec. 27, 1859; those dead—Geo., April 28, 1842; Joshua T., Feb. 28, 1848; Rachel T., Feb. 2, 1852.
McKinley Wm. farmer for R. R. McKinley; P. O. Youngstown; dem; born Illinois.
McKinzie Alex. miner; Sec. 16; P. O. Roseville; rep; from Scotland.
McKinzie Daniel, miner for J. Tucker; Sec. 9; P. O. Roseville; from Indiana.
McKinzie Wm. miner for J. Tucker; Sec. 9; P. O. Roseville; from Indiana.
McMahill Matthew, farmer; Sec. 36; P. O. Walnut Grove; rep; born Illinois.
McMullen C. miner for Jas. Tucker; Sec. 9; P. O. Roseville; dem; from Penn.
McMullen Jacob, miner for Jas. Tucker; Sec. 9; P. O. Roseville; dem; born Ill.
MacDonald F. L. farmer for J. Adams; Sec. 2; P. O. Roseville; rep; Chris; Ohio.
Maffins Jos. miner for J. Tucker; Sec. 9; rep; from England.
Manuel Thos. works for S. Perkins; P. O. Roseville; dem; born Kentucky.
Mapes C. W. grocery and dry goods; Youngstown; rep; property valued at $25,000.
Maston, farmer for J. Tucker; Sec. 4; P. O. Roseville; from Canada.
Matthews Jas. farmer rents 80 acres; Sec. 31; P. O. Swan Creek; rep; from Penn.
Mattson Albert N. farmer, rents 30 acres; Sec. 6; P. O. Roseville; rep; from Mass.
Michael Clark, farmer; Sec. 16; dem; Chris; 45 acres; born Illinois.
Michael D. K. farmer; Sec. 17; dem; Chris; 218 acres; from North Carolina.
Michael David H. farmer with D. K. Michael; Sec. 16; dem; Chris.
Michael Perry, farmer; Sec. 17; P. O. Roseville; dem; born Illinois.
Miner W. H. grocery store; Youngstown; dem; stock of goods valued at $1,500; Pa.
Molar Wm. works for S. Perkins; P. O. Roseville; dem.
Morris Cal. farmer; Sec. 1; P. O. Greenbush; rep.
Morris Horatio, farmer; Sec. 35; P. O. Walnut Grove; rep; Campb; 200 acres; Ky.
Morris Horatio, Jr., farmer with H. Morris; P. O. Walnut Grove; Ind; born Ill.
Morris H. A. farmer; Sec. 35; P. O. Walnut Grove; Ind; owns 40 acres, value $2,400.
Morris M. V. farmer; Sec. 1; P. O. Greenbush; rep.
Murrill Wm. farmer; Sec. 15; P. O. Roseville; from Ohio.

NEVINS L. L. farmer; Sec. 28; P. O. Youngstown; ind; Bapt; from Mass.
Nisely Homer, farmer for C. T. Gossett; Sec. 4; P. O. Roseville; dem.

O'HANNAGAN JAS. miner for J. Tucker; Sec. 9; P. O. Roseville; rep.

Oleson Swan, farmer for Jas. Tucker; Sec. 4; P. O. Roseville; Luth; from Sweden.

PATTON J. H. farmer with H. H. Kidder; P. O. Youngstown; dem; N. Y.

Perkins D. R. farmer; Sec. 11; P. O. Roseville; dem; owns 82 acres, value $3,280.

Perkins Isaac, farmer; Sec. 11; P. O. Greenbush; dem; Bapt; 153 acres; born Ill.

Perkins Jno. farmer, with I. Perkins; P. O. Greenbush; dem; born Illinois.

Perkins Solomon, farmer; Sec. 6-7; P. O. Roseville; dem; Chris; 160 acres, $10,000.

Perry Chas. farmer; Sec. 24; P. O. Youngstown; rep; 156 acres, val. $6,240; Europe.

Perry C. W. farmer, with Chas. Perry; P. O. Youngstown, rep; born Illinois.

Perry J. C. farmer; Sec. 30; P. O. Swan Creek; dem; Bapt; 185 acres, val. $9,250.

PERRY LUTHER B. Farmer and Stock Raiser; Sec. 30; P. O. Swan Creek; born in Warren Co., Ill., May 25, 1841; Dem; Meth; owns 50 acres, value $2,500; wife was Sarah Jane Lybarger; born in Knox Co., Ohio, Nov. 20, 1855; married July 4, 1872; have two children, Almina Jane and Orville Luther.

PERRY WM. A. Farmer and Stock Raiser; Sec. 30; P. O. Swan Creek; born Loraine Co., Ohio, Jan. 14, 1834; came to this Co. in 1842; Dem; Chris; owns 127 acres of land, value $6,350; wife was Ann Eliza Vankirk, born Bath Co., Ky., Nov. 22, 1843; married Oct. 27, 1861, in Swan tp., Warren Co.; have had five children, four living, Phœbe N.; Orvilla J.; Mary B., and Walter C.; Loren H. dead.

Peterson Swan, farmer for Jas. Tucker; Sec. 4; P. O. Roseville; from Sweden.

Phillips A. S. farmer; Sec. 33; P. O. Youngstown; ind; Meth; 180 acres, val. $9,000.

Pickard N. W. farmer, with S. Ray; Sec. 10; P. O. Youngstown; rep; Bapt; from Me.

Pittman J. B. farmer; Sec. 24; P. O. Greenbush; dem; Meth; 80 acres; from Ind.

Pittman J. C. farmer; Sec. 13; P. O. Youngstown; rep; Meth; 50 acres; from Indiana.

Prater J. farmer for A. S. Phillips; P. O. Youngstown; dem; Chris; from Ky.

Predmore R. B. farmer; Sec. 33; P. O. Youngstown; 160 acres, val. $8,000; N. J.

RATEKIN E. H. farmer; Sec. 19; P. O. Swan Creek; dem; 105 acres, $6,300.

RATEKIN JOSEPH S. Farmer and Stock Raiser; Sec. 19; P. O. Swan Creek; born in Morgan Co., Ill., March 6, 1835; came to this Co. in Sept., 1835; Dem; owns 360 acres, value $21,600; wife was America Jane Towler, born in Adams Co., Ill., Dec. 12, 1847; married March 31, 1874, at Carthage, Hancock Co., Ill.; have one child, Beulah, born Jan. 6, 1876; two boys by first wife, Lambert L., born March 15, 1860; Sylvester, Aug. 3, 1865.

Ratekin M. P. farmer for J. S. Ratekin; P. O. Swan Creek; born Swan tp.

Ray G. W. farmer for S. Ray; Sec. 10; P. O. Youngstown; dem; from Kentucky.

Ray J. H. farmer, with S. Ray; Sec. 10; P. O. Youngstown; dem; Bapt; from Ky.

Ray J. L. farmer with S. Ray; Sec. 10; P. O. Youngstown; ind; Bapt; born Illinois.

Ray Sarah, farming; Sec. 10; P. O. Youngstown; Bapt; 198½ acres; from Kentucky.

Reed B. A. Sr., farmer; Sec. 25; P. O. Youngstown; dem; Meth; from Kentucky.

Reed B. A. Jr., farmer; Sec. 24; P. O. Youngstown; dem; 50 acres, val. $2,500; Indiana.

Reed B. F. farmer; Sec. 25; P. O. Youngstown; dem; Meth; from Indiana.

Reed J. B. farmer; Sec. 25; P. O. Youngstown; dem; 100 acres; from Indiana.

Reed Wm. B. farmer; Sec. 26 P. O. Youngstown; dem; Meth; 80 acres; from Ind.

Reeves J. A. farmer for J. S. Hindman; P. O. Roseville; dem; from Indiana.

Reid Wm. R. farmer; rents 50 acres; Sec. 7; P. O. Roseville; dem; from Missouri.

Ritchie Lafayette, coal miner; lives on J. Jared's farm; P. O. Roseville; rep.

Roberts Geo. farmer; Sec. 3; P. O. Roseville; rep; 120 acres; born Illinois.

Roberts M. B. storekeeper; Swan Creek; ind; from Ohio.

Roberts Ransom, farmer; Sec. 12; P. O. Greenbush.

Rued Orville, farmer, rents 30 acres; Sec. 10; P. O. Roseville; dem; from Ohio.

Russell J. M. blacksmith; Youngstown; dem; Chris; born McDonough Co.

SANFORD JAS. I. lightning rod peddler; Swan Creek; dem; from New York.

Sansfield Abraham, farmer; Sec. 17; P. O. Roseville; 75 acres from England.

Schomp Jacob, farmer; Sec. 36; P. O. Youngstown; dem; 80 acres; from New Jersey.

Schomp Jno. farmer; Sec. 36; P. O. Youngstown; dem; 80 acres; born Illinois.

Semelroth Phillip, farmer; Sec. 7; P. O. Roseville; rep; 5 acres, val. $250; born Ill.

Shawler Henry, farmer with J. B. Shawler; P. O. Youngstown; dem; born Illinois.

Shawler J. B. farmer; Sec. 22; P. O. Youngstown; dem; Bapt; 160 acres; val. $8,000.

Shawler Wm. farmer, with J. B. Shawler; P. O. Youngstown; dem; born Illinois.

Shoop David, wagon maker; Youngstown; rep; from Pennsylvania.

Shores Geo. farmer, rents 200 acres; Sec. 31; P. O. Swan Creek.

Simmons H. V. farmer, lives on 83 acres of H. Simmons'; Sec. 21; P. O. Youngstown; dem.

Simmons H. W. farmer, lives on 83 acres of H. Simmons'; Sec. 21; P. O. Youngstown.

SIMMONS HEZIKIAH, Farmer and Stock Raiser; Sec. 28; P. O. Youngstown; born in Plymouth Co., Mass., Aug. 21, 1806; came to this Co. in 1838; Dem; owns 540 acres, value $27,000; wife was Zoa Dalie, born in North Bridgewater, Plymouth Co., Mass., Oct. 30, 1802; married Nov. 23, 1830, at North Bridgewater; have had six children, four living, Louis Alden, born March 16, 1833; Zoa Ann, July 18, 1837; Hezikiah Warren, June 17, 1839; Herbert V., Oct. 15, 1841; those dead, Maria Cole, born Feb. 29, 1832; Dan'l W., Dec. 24, 1836; have been Supervisor and Justice Peace.

SISSON A. B. Farmer and Stock Raiser; Sec. 29; P. O. Swan Creek; born in Albany Co., N. Y., Sept. 2, 1813; came to this Co. 1836; Rep; Meth; owns 280 acres, value $14,000; wife was Henrietta Scott, born in Ky., Oct. 22, 1819; married to A. A. Cornell, in Olena, Henderson Co., Aug. 22, 1841; have one child, named Caroline L.; Mr. S. was one of the first settlers in Warren Co.

Sisson A. J. farmer; Sec. 32; P. O. Swan Creek; ind; Meth; 240 acres, val. $12,000.

Sisson M. F. farmer; Sec. 32; P. O. Swan Creek; ind; Meth; from New York.

Sisson R. K. farmer; Sec. 32; P. O. Swan Creek; dem; Meth; 80 acres; from N. Y.

Smalley Mrs. Elizabeth, farm; Sec. 22; P. O. Youngstown; Bapt; 80 acres; born Ill.

Smalley Preston, farmer; Sec. 22; P. O. Youngstown; Bapt; 80 acres, value $4,000.

Smith Chas. R. farmer for P. P. Smith; Sec. 11; P. O. Youngstown; rep; born Illinois.

Smith H. A. farmer for A. J. Cayton; P. O. Youngstown; dem; from Pennsylvania.

Smith J. A. farmer; Sec. 2; P. O. Greenbush; dem; 39 acres; from Indiana.

Smith Peter, works on railroad; P.O. Youngstown; dem; Chris; from Missouri.

SMITH PHINEAS P. Sr., Farmer and Stock Raiser; Sec. 11; P. O. Youngstown; born in Bradford Co., Penn., Sept. 19, 1817; came to this State in 1818, and Co. in 1851; Rep; Univ; 150 acres, value $9,000; his son Charles R. served in Co. C., 138th Ill. Inf.; wife was Mary E. McCormick, born in Tenn.; married Sept. 17, 1840; eight children; living, Marietta, Charles R., Phineas P., Jr., Nancy A., Adelia and Mary E.; those dead, Lucy P. and Jed. W.

Spray Jas. lives with Jno. Lippy; Swan Creek; rep.

Soule E. H. farmer with his father, H. M. Soule; P.O. Youngstown; rep; Bapt; Mass.

Soule H. M. farmer; Sec. 32; P. O. Youngstown; rep; Bapt; 108 acres, $5,400; Mass.

STICE, MRS. ARIXINA SOUTHGATE, Farming; Sec. 29; P.O. Swan Creek; 200 acres, value $10,000; born in Harding Co., Ky., Feb. 3, 1825; came to this Co. in 1829; Bapt; widow of Charles Stice, born in N. C., Feb. 11, 1795; married in Ellison, Warren Co., Jan. 12, 1851; died April 1, 1869; have had three children, all living; Catherine E., David A. and Warren N.; Mr. S. was in the ranger service in the war of 1812, and also in the Black Hawk War.

Stamfield Alex. farmer; Sec. 17; P. O. Roseville; 135 acres; from England.

Stephenson Wm. miner for Jas. Tucker; Sec. 9; P. O. Roseville; rep; from Indiana.

Stewart C. coal-miner; Sec. 16; P. O. Swan Creek; rep.

Stice David A. farmer for Mrs. A. Stice; P.O. Swan Creek; dem; 54 acres, value $2,700.

Stice Geo. farmer for J. J. Jared; Sec. 5; P. O. Roseville; dem; Bapt; born Illinois.

STICE GEO. W. Farmer and Stock Raiser; Sec. 30; P. O. Swan Creek; born in Madison Co., Ill., July 8, 1832; came to this Co. in 1833; Dem; owns 740 acres, value $37,000; wife was Phebe King, born in McDonough Co., Feb. 4, 1841; married Jan. 19, 1860; have had six children; three living, Geo. Franklin, Freeman S., and Sylva A., those dead, Edith, Charles F. and Harry.

Stillwell Daniel, coal miner; Sec. 10; P. O. Roseville.

Stomburg Swan, farmer for R. R. McKinley; P. O. Youngstown; rep; Luth; Sweden.

Swarts Martin, farmer for A. J. Cayton; P. O. Youngstown; rep; from Penn.

TALLY WM. farmer; Sec. 21; P. O. Youngstown; born Illinois.

Tatman Jno. farmer for T. Jared; Sec. 5; P. O. Roseville; rep.

Taylor Geo. farmer for R. Predmore; P. O. Youngstown; rep; from Indiana.

Taylor T. G. carpenter; Sec. 12; P. O. Greenbush; rep; Meth.

Tharp John, farmer for H. Simmons; P. O. Youngstown; Bapt; from New Jersey.

Tharp Wm. farmer; Sec. 36; P. O. Walnut Grove; ind; Meth; rents 40 acres; Mich.

Thomas Chas. farmer; Sec. 23; P.O. Youngstown; rep; 195 acres, value $9,750; Ill.

Thomas E. M. farmer; Sec. 23; P.O. Youngstown; dem; rents 50 acres; born Ill.

Thomas H. R. farmer; Sec. 23; P.O. Youngstown; dem; Bapt; born Illinois.

Thomas W. G. farmer, with Wm. Thomas; P. O. Youngstown; dem; born Illinois.

Thomas Wm. farmer; Sec. 23; P. O. Youngstown; dem; 700 acres; from Vermont.

Thompson Elijah; farmer, with R.B. Thompson; P. O. Swan Creek; dem; Meth; Ohio.

Thompson R. B. farmer, rents 100 acres of Asa Sisson; Sec. 29; P.O. Swan Creek; dem.

Towler Jno. C. farmer for J. S. Ratikin; P.O. Swan Creek; dem; born McDonough Co.

Travis M. coal miner; Sec. 15; P. O. Roseville; dem; from Iowa.

Tucker George, farmer with J. Tucker; Sec. 4; P. O. Roseville; rep; born Illinois.

Tucker Jno. farmer; Swan Creek; rep; born Illinois.

TUCKER JAS. Farmer and Coal Operator; Secs. 4, 9, 20, 16, and Roseville tp. 33; P. O. Roseville; born in Washington Co., Penn., May 15, 1807; came to this Co. in 1835; Rep; Bapt; 1,328 acres, and 526 in Iowa, value $75,000; has been Co. Commissioner and Justice of Peace, and member of Legislature in 1846-7-8; wife was Caroline Johnson, born in Washington Co., Penn., July 9, 1809; five children, Elizabeth, by former marriage; Daniel J., born Aug. 20, 1840; Jas. M., Feb. 24, 1844; John, Nov. 21, 1846; and George, Feb. 22, 1849; Dan'l J. died in Union Army, at Lexington, Mo., Sept. 20, 1861.

UPHOLD HENRY, coal miner, lives on Jas. Jared's farm; P. O. Roseville; rep.

VANDIVER A. farmer; Sec. 15; P. O. Youngstown; dem; Bapt; 300 acres; Ind.

Vandiver Geo. farmer for R. Roberts; Sec. 2; P. O. Roseville; rep; born Illinois.

Vankirk Henry, farmer for G. W. Beckner; P. O. Youngstown; dem; from Kentucky.

Vandiver Jno. farmer; P. O. Greenbush; dem; Bapt; 60 acres.

Vandiver Jno. farmer for J. Vandiver; Sec. 3; P. O. Roseville; dem; born Illinois.

Vandiver L. P. farmer, lives with A. Vandiver; P. O. Youngstown; dem; Bapt; Ill.

Vandiver Wm. farmer for G. Sickman; Sec. 12; P. O. Greenbush; dem.

WALLACE NATHANIEL, farmer for J. Johnson; Sec. 2; P. O. Greenbush.

Walters B. F. farmer; P.O. Swan Creek; rep; Meth; owns house and two lots; Penn.

Watts B. F. farmer; Sec. 35; P. O. Youngstown; dem; 200 acres, $10,000; Madison Co.

Watts Felix, farmer, lives with B. F. Watts; P. O. Youngstown; Rep; from Kentucky.

Weirmoth Robt. farmer; Sec. 23; P. O. Youngstown; dem; 40 acres, $2,000; Eng.

Weirmoth Thos. farmer; Sec. 22; P. O. Youngstown; dem; 40 acres.

Westlake Jno. farmer for H. V. Simmons; P. O. Youngstown.

Westlake Leroy, farmer for G. W Beckner; P. O. Youngstown; dem; from Penn.

Woods Bennet, farmer with D. L. Crawford; P. O. Walnut Grove; dem; Meth.

Woods Wm. M. farmer; Sec. 13; P.O. Greenbush; dem; Bapt; 80 acres, $3,600; Ky.

Worden Avery, farmer; Sec. 6; P. O. Roseville; rep; Cong; 200 acres, $10,000; Conn.

Worden Geo. W. farmer; Sec. 19; P.O. Swan Creek; rep; 95 acres, value $9,500; N. Y.

Worden Jas. farmer; Sec. 5; P. O. Roseville; rep; Cong; 110 acres, $5,500; born Swan tp.

WORDEN JNO. JAY, Farmer and Stock Raiser, also money loaner and notes at discount; Sec. 28; P. O. Youngstown; born in Smyrna, Chenango Co., N. Y., Jan. 10, 1830; came to this Co. in 1845; Bapt; owns 175 acres, val. $10,500; wife was Elizabeth Sargeant Moulton, born Morgan Co., Ill., Jan. 2, 1830; married Feb. 14, 1853, in Swan tp., Warren Co.; have one child, Minnaola; Mr. W. served through Mexican War in Capt. Wyatt. B. Stapp's Ind. Vol. Cav. Co.; made an overland trip to California in 1850 with an ox team; in 1861-2 raised a Co. of Cav. attached to 11th Regt. Ill. Vol., and led his Co. in the actions at Shiloh or Pittsburg Landing.

Worden L. O. farmer for J. D. Grigg; P. O. Swan Creek; rep; from Ohio.

Worden Lycurgus, farmer; Sec. 5; rep; born Illinois.

SWAN CREEK BUSINESS DIRECTORY.

Erbrodt, Henry C. Manufacturer and Dealer in Saddles, Harness, Bridles, Halters, Collars, Whips, &c., best of Stock used, and all work warranted. Prompt attention given to orders.

YOUNGSTOWN.

Folger, H. A., M. D. Physician and Druggist.

John Martin
SUMNER TOWNSHIP

ROSEVILLE TOWNSHIP.

ATKINS H. farmer; P. O. Roseville; rep; from Indiana.

Allen H. S. clerk; Roseville; rep; born Ill.

Allen J. A. farmer, works for J. A. Malcolm; Sec. 25; P. O. Greenbush; dem; from Va.

Allen N. T. pastor M. E. church; Roseville; rep; born Illinois.

Anderson Jno. harness-maker; Roseville; rep; from Sweden.

Anderson M. N. blacksmith; Roseville; rep; Luth; from Sweden.

Anderson P. boot and shoemaker; Roseville; rep; Luth, from Sweden.

Aylesworth H. E. druggist and physician; Roseville; rep; Meth; from N. Y.

Axtell L. C. farmer; Sec. 29; P. O. Roseville; rep; Cong; has 84 acres, value $6,300.

BAILEY E. T. farmer, works for Geo. Grow; Sec. 6; P. O. Lenox; dem.

Baker D. farmer; P. O. Roseville; dem; from Virginia.

BALDWIN GEO. W. drug clerk; Roseville; born in Cayuga Co., N. Y., Sept. 20, 1853; came to this Co. in 1857; single; Rep.

Ballard Wm. laborer; P. O. Roseville; rep; from Kentucky.

Beard A. E. painter; Roseville; rep; from Ohio.

Beckner J. H. farmer, works for T. J. Morris; P O. Berwick; Sec. 11; dem; from Va.

Begges D. M. painter; Roseville; rep; from Ohio.

Bell T. miller; Roseville; rep; from Indiana.

Bird D. brick-mason; Roseville; rep; from England.

Bird G. brick-mason; Roseville; rep; from England.

Bockus G. carpenter; Roseville; rep; Epis; from Vermont.

Bockus W. carpenter; Roseville; rep; from New York.

Bohon T. B. carpenter; Roseville; dem; from Missouri.

Bond L. farmer, rents of J. H. Griggs; Sec. 6; P. O. Lenox; dem; born Illinois.

Bostwick G. L. bookkeeper; Roseville; rep; born Illinois.

BRADLEY THEODORE. Physician and Surgeon; Roseville; born at Hartwick, N. Y., Nov. 4, 1830; married Ellen J. Spencer, Nov. 4, 1855; she was born Sept. 19, 1836, at Middle Haddam, Conn; has three children, Wm. H. born Jan. 18, 1857, Mary A. born April 21, 1863, and Theodore, Jr. born Dec. 25, 1864; settled in Roseville, March 1, 1861.

Bragg J. T. barber; Roseville; dem; born Ill.

Bramhall A. H. mail messenger; P. O. Roseville; rep; from New York.

Brockaw S. H. physician; Roseville; rep; born Illinois.

Brooke W. H. farmer; Sec. 9; P. O. Roseville; dem; 280 acres, value $14,000; born Ill.

Browne A. T. tea agt; Roseville; rep; born Illinois.

Brown J. farmer, works for L. C. Axtell; Sec. 29; P. O. Roseville; rep; from Penn.

Brown J. P. farmer; P. O. Roseville; rep; Meth; from Pennsylvania.

BRUYN ZACHARIAH; Farmer and Stock Raiser; Sec. 9; P. O. Roseville; born in Ulster Co., N. Y., Dec. 30, 1830; came to Co. 1857; wife was Fannie J. Baldwin, born in Cayuga Co., N. Y., Oct. 13, 1840; married July 3, 1870; has six children, Sam'l, John, Elizabeth, Frank, Minnie, Hattie; Dem; has 120 acres, value $7,200.

Buckley W. H. telegraph operator; Roseville; dem; Christian; from Kentucky.

Bushnell E. dairyman; Roseville; rep; from Pennsylvania.

BUTLER JAMES E. Dry Goods Merchant; Roseville; born in town of Greenbush, this Co. Sept. 24, 1856; remained here until 18 years of age, then went to Dallas, Texas, and remained there 2 yrs. then returned to this place; single; Dem.

Byarlay A. painter; Roseville; rep; Baptist; from Tennessee.

Byarlay L. A. photographer; Roseville; rep; Baptist; born Illinois.

CAINE W. G. farmer; Sec. 5; P. O. Lenox; rep; from Isle of Man.

Cady E. C. pastor Bapt. church; Roseville; rep; from Ct.

CALLISTER WM. Farmer and Stock Raiser; Sec. 7; P. O. Roseville; born Isle of Man Oct. 5, 1831, left there and arrived in N. Y. May 4, 1853, then went to Oakland Co., Mich., remained there until 1856, then removed to Peoria Co. Ill., remained there about 11 yrs., and then came to this Co; no family; wife was Miss Jane E. Kane, born in the same place Apl. 19, 1846; married Apl. 30, 1868; both members Meth. church; he served 3 yrs. in the late war in Co. G 77th I. V. I. was imprisoned 18 mos. at Tyler, Texas; has 171 and 71-100 acres, value $11,970; has 160 acres in Green Co., Iowa; Rep.

Campbell E. B. grain buyer; Roseville; rep. from Indiana.

Campbell J. carpenter; Roseville; ind; born Illinois.

Campbell J. B. attorney at law; Roseville; rep. born Illinois.

Capps I. M. farmer; Sec. 15; P. O. Roseville; dem; Bapt; has 270 acres, value $13,500.

Carlson O. butcher; Roseville; Luth; from Sweden.

Carmer S. farmer, rents of Wm. Taylor; Sec. 27; P. O. Roseville; dem; from N. Y.

Carnahan D. S. carpenter; Roseville; rep; from Pennsylvania.

Carr A. farmer; Sec. 26; P. O. Roseville; dem; 160 acres, value $8,000; from Ky.

Carr J. O. farmer; Sec. 13; P. O. Berwick; dem; Chris; 273 acres, value $10,920.

Carr O. farmer; Sec. 13; P. O. Berwick; dem; 135 acres, value $6,750; from Ky.

Carr R. farmer; Sec. 14; P. O. Roseville; dem; 316 acres, value $15,800; born Ill.

Carr W. H. farmer, lives with his father; Sec. 26; P. O. Roseville; dem; born Illinois.

Clark R. B. laborer; P. O. Roseville; rep. from Indiana.

Clark S. P. barber; Roseville; rep; from New York.

Clayton J. C. farmer, rents of R. Carr; Sec. 14; P. O. Roseville; dem; from Kentucky

Clayton J. farmer, rents of A. Lewis; Sec. 16; P. O. Roseville; ind; from Kentucky.

Clem A. J. coal miner; Roseville; rep; from Virginia.

Clemmer J. farmer, rents of P. C. Smith; Sec. 18; P. O. Roseville; dem; from Penn.

Clemmer J. A. farmer, lives with his father; Sec. 18; P. O. Roseville; dem; from Va.

Clinger P. farmer, works for A. Lewis; Sec. 16; P. O. Roseville; ind; from Germany.

Cotes J. W. school teacher; Roseville; rep; Meth; from New York.

Cochler G. W. carpenter; Roseville; rep; from Ohio.

Collins J. farmer; Sec. 23; P. O. Roseville; dem; 164 acres, value $8,200; from Scotl'd.

CONLEE J. W. Agt. St. L., R. I. & C. R. R., branch of the C. B. & Q; Roseville; born in Morgan Co., Ill. Sept. 10, 1847; came to this Co. in 1871; has family two children, J. W., Jr., born Sept. 5, 1872, Mima, Feb. 24, 1874; wife was Miss Sarah E. Buckley, born near Louisville, Ky., Jan. 18, 1851; married Oct. 29, 1871; value of estate $2,000; Dem; is one of the Village Trustees; Bapt; wife is member of the Christian church.

Couch J. N. barber; Roseville; dem; Ill.

Cramer J. farmer, rents of T. J. Morris; Sec. 11; P. O. Berwick; dem; born Illinois.

Creel M. L. carpenter; Roseville; rep; Ill.

Crouch F. W. farmer, works for S. Huston; Sec. 35; P. O. Roseville; rep; from Penn.

DAVENPORT G. R. laborer; P. O. Roseville; rep; Bapt; from Indiana.

Davenport W. C. furniture finisher; Roseville; rep; Bapt; from Indiana.

DAVENPORT JESSE L. Undertaking; Roseville; born in Wayne Co., Ind. Aug. 31, 1832; left there and came to this Co. Sept., 1859; has family four children living, Wm. C., Geo. R., Robt. B. and Sophia; three dead, Arvill, Emma and Elvira A.; wife was Miss Margaret J. Huston, born in New Castle Co., Del., Dec. 27, 1831; married Sept. 4, 1851; value of estate $1,200; rep; all members of Bapt. church.

Davidson W. W. farmer, works for Sarah Gordon; Sec. 32; P. O. Roseville; rep.

DAVIS FRANCIS B. Farmer and Stock Raiser; lives on what is called The Hat Grove Farm; Sec. 19; P. O. Roseville; born in Mercer Co., Penn., Feb. 28, 1834; left there in the spring of 1851, and removed to Mahoning Co. Ohio, remained there one year, thence to Wood Co., Ohio, and remained there until the Fall of 1855, then to the north shore of Lake Superior, Minn., remained there until the Spring of 1858, and then came to this Co; has family of two sons and two daughters, John. C., Vurlinder, Lois R. and Geo. F.; wife was Miss Rebecca Gossett, born in Jackson Co., Ind, Aug. 30, 1831; married Feb. 28, 1860; has 196½ acres, value $11,650; served about three years in the late war, in Co. F 83d I. V. I; Rep; Meth.

Dehart W. farmer; P. O. Roseville; rep; from Pennsylvania.

Dillon W. H. farmer; Sec. 29; P. O. Roseville; rep; Meth; 60 acres, value $4,200.

Dilly F. farmer, lives with his father; Sec. 32; P. O. Roseville; rep; born Illinois.

Dilly J. farmer; Sec. 32; P. O. Roseville; has 65½ acres, value $6,500; rep; Meth.

Dilly I. farmer, lives with his father; Sec. 32; P. O. Roseville; rep; born Illinois.

Dilly S. farmer; Sec. 31; P. O. Roseville; 8½ acres, value $6,800; rep; from Penn.

Dilly T. A. farmer; Sec. 32; P. O. Roseville; 100 acres, value $10,000; rep; Cong; Ill.

DILLY WILLIAM. Retired; Sec. 32; P. O Roseville; born in Mercer Co., Penn., Sept. 8, 1811; left there and came to this Co. and settled on the place he now lives in, March, 1841, there being very few families here when he came; has two sons and four daughters; wife was Miss Mary Axtell, born in the same place, Oct. 24, 1814; both members Cong. church; lives with his son; was Supervisor two years; Rep.

DILLY WM. N. Farmer and Stock Raiser; Sec. 29; P. O. Roseville; born in Roseville tp. this Co., May 28, 1849, being one of the oldest settlers; no family; wife was Miss Eliza Worden, born in Swan tp. this Co. April 4, 1852; married Oct. 2, 1873; both members of the Cong. church; Rep; has 98 acres, value $7,350.

Dixson E. B. prop. Roseville Ag'l Works; Roseville; dem; from Indiana.

Dorris W. farmer, works for P. C. Smith; Sec. 18; P. O. Roseville; dem; from Iowa.

Dundee J. farmer, works for J. V. Mason; Sec. 27; P. O. Roseville; rep; Ireland.

Dunn F. C. farmer, works for D. M. Taliaferro; Sec. 29; P. O. Roseville; rep.

Dye S. blacksmith, rents of L. Gainer; Sec. 5; P. O. Lenox; dem; from Indiana.

EATON J. farmer, rents of J. K. Webster; Sec. 21; P. O. Roseville; rep; Ky.

Eaton J. B. farmer, lives with his father; Sec. 21; P. O. Roseville; rep; from Ky.

ELDRED ARNOLD, Retired; P. O. Roseville; born in Petersburg, Rensselaer Co., N. Y., Feb. 25, 1817; came to this Co. in the fall of 1853, and settled in this tp; has one adopted daughter; wife was Miss Eliza Devoe, born in Martinsburg, Lewis Co., N. Y., Dec. 20, 1831; married Jan. 11, 1857; all members of Bapt. church; has a house and 9 acres where he lives, value of estate $4,000; Rep.

ELDRED S. M. Farmer and Stock Dealer; Roseville; born in Fulton Co., N. Y., Dec. 17, 1828; left there and came to this Co. in May, 1852, and settled in this tp; has family one daughter, May, born Oct. 14, 1866; wife was Miss Sarah Chase, born in Princeville, Peoria Co., Ill., Oct. 4, 1843; married May 12, 1863; Mr. E. has 271 acres on Secs. 17 and 18; value of estate $24,325; was supervisor one term, and is one of the Village Trustees; Rep.

ELDRIDG TRUMAN. Prop. Roseville Steam Flouring Mills; Roseville; born in the town of Hancock, Berkshire Co., Mass., April 24, 1808; left there in the fall of 1838, and came to Warren Co; is the oldest settler in the corporation; has family, one daughter and one adopted daughter; wife was Miss Alma Jones, born in Stephentown, Rensselaer Co., N.

Y., April 2, 1808; married Jan. 12, 1839; both members of the Baptist church; Mr. Eldridg was the first Postmaster in the town; it was then called Hat Grove, afterwards changed to Roseville; Rep.

Elliott J. farmer, rents the Ray farm; Sec. 22; P. O. Roseville; dem; from Ohio.

Emans E. P. general store; Roseville; rep; from Ohio.

Enfield J. farmer; P. O. Roseville; dem; from Indiana.

Everitt J. wagon maker; Roseville; rep; from Indiana.

FEE C. R. bakery and confectionary; Roseville; rep; from Indiana.

Field J. N. farmer, rents of Wm. Atkins; Sec. 33; P. O. Roseville; dem; from Ind.

Fitzgerald B. J. laborer; Roseville; ind; from Ohio.

Fuller A. laborer; P. O. Roseville; rep; Ohio.

Furgeson J. H. carpenter, rents of Peter Watson; Sec. 6; P. O. Lenox; dem; Ohio.

Futhy N. J. laborer; P. O. Roseville; dem; from Pennsylvania.

GAUNT D. farmer, Sec. 21; P. O. Roseville; rep. Meth; 160 acres, value $8,000.

Gaunt L. H. farmer, lives with his father; Sec. 21; P. O. Roseville; born Illinois.

Geiger E. P. farmer; P. O. Roseville; dem; from Pennsylvania.

Gilbert A. police magistrate; Roseville; dem; from New Hampshire.

Gilbert E. B. hotel proprietor; Roseville; dem; from New York.

GORDON JNO. A. Furniture Dealer and Notary Public; Roseville; born in Mercer Co., Penn., Jan. 10, 1835; left there and came to this Co. in 1856, and is among the oldest settlers; no family; wife was Miss Philena Dilly, born in Mercer Co., Penn., Oct. 29, 1834, daughter of Stephen Dilly; married Feb. 7, 1861; was County Surveyor eight years; is Town Clerk, and has held other Town Offices; Rep; Cong; value of estate $5,000.

GORDON MRS. SARAH, Res. Sec. 32; P. O. Roseville; widow of Wm. Gordon, who was born in Mercer Co., Penn., May 10, 1803; came to this Co. and to this town March, 1858, he being one of the oldest settlers; he died May 22, 1875; left a family of five children; Mrs. Gordon's maiden name was Miss Sarah Dilly, born in the same place Feb. 3, 1813; married Oct. 11, 1832; Cong; left an estate of 80 acres, value $5,000.

Gosney A. drayman; Roseville; dem; Mo.

Gassett G. retired; P. O. Roseville; rep; Meth; from North Carolina.

GOSSETT. WM. T. Postmaster; Roseville; born in Jackson Co., Indiana, Sept. 18, 1846; left there with his parent and moved to Pike Co., Ill., in Oct. 1852, and came to this Co. in 1854; no family; wife was Miss M. E. Ward, born in this Co; married June 7, 1876; was Collector two terms; Rep.

Gould J. laborer; Roseville; rep; born Ill.

Gray J. B. sewing machine agent; Roseville; rep; from New York.

GRAY, MRS. LUCY A. Sec. 22; P. O. Roseville; widow of Lawson K. Gray, who was born in Hancock, Hilsborough Co. N. H., June 2, 1830; he came to this Co. in June, 1857; he died Oct. 16, 1868; left family of six children, five now living, Ina L., John K., Julia A., Alice M. and Flora B; Mrs. Gray's maiden name was Miss Lucy A. Dennis, born in same place, March 18, 1831; married March 11, 1852; left an estate of 183 acres, value $9,150; Bapt; Lizzie F., born June 5, 1854, died Aug. 24, 1873.

Griffin C. E. laborer; P. O. Roseville; rep; from Pennsylvania.

Griffin J. laborer; Roseville; rep; born Ill.

Griffin J. A. restaurant; Roseville; rep; Ill.

Grow G. W. farmer; Sec. 6; P. O. Lenox; Ind. 105 acres, value $5,250; from Ohio.

GUNTER, MRS. F. A. Sec. 33; P. O. Roseville; widow of Joseph B. Gunter, who was born in Virginia in 1807; left there and went to Kentucky, and remained there until 1834, then came to this Co., being one of the oldest settlers in the Co; he died in Jan. 1860, leaving a family of eleven children; Mrs. Gunter was Miss F. A. Tally, born in Virginia in 1816; married in 1831; has 190 acres, value $9,500; Bapt.

Gunter G. W. farmer; Sec. 11; P. O. Berwick; dem; 101 acres, value $5,050; Ky.

Gunter H. W. farmer, rents of Mrs. Gunter; Sec. 33; P. O. Roseville; dem; born Ill.

Gunter S. C. carpenter; Roseville; dem; Ill.

GUNTER T. W. Farmer and Stock Raiser; Sec. 33; P. O. Roseville; born in Swan tp. this Co. Feb. 13, 1837; Mr. Gunter is among the first born in that tp; has family of four children living, Geo. W., Lucy May, James B. and Jesse D.; four dead, Mary L., Wm. W., Martha F. and Chas. W.; wife was Miss Lucy A. Honts, born in Johnson Co., Ind., Nov. 20, 1840; married Dec. 6, 1860; both members of the Baptist church; Dem; has 79 acres, value $4,000.

Gunter W. retired, lives on his son's place; Sec. 11; P. O. Berwick; Ind; from Va.

H**AINES** W. C. farmer, works for Mrs. Gray; Sec. 22; P. O. Roseville; rep.

Haldeman W. H. clerk; Roseville; rep; from Ohio.

Hall D. S. retired; P. O. Roseville; rep; value of estate $2,000; from Maine.

Hall H. E. clerk; Roseville; rep; Cong; from Maine.

Hall J. I. farmer, rents of R. B. Woodward; Sec. 30; P. O. Roseville; rep; from Maine.

Hall L. T. farmer; P. O. Roseville; rep; from Maine.

Hamilton E. H. prin. high school; Roseville; rep; Cong; born Illinois.

Hammer H. farmer; P. O. Roseville; rep; from Sweden.

Hampton W. A. physician and surgeon; Roseville; rep; from Ohio.

Harbaugh J. retired farmer; P. O. Roseville; rep; from Pennsylvania.

Harbaugh M. stock buyer; Roseville; rep; born Illinois;

Harris J. M. carpenter; Roseville; dem; from Kentucky.

Harris S. farmer, rents of L. Butler; Sec. 4; P. O. Lenox; dem; born Illinois.

Harris Wm. H. farmer, lives with A. Carr; Sec. 13; P. O. Berwick; dem; from Ky.

Hatley J. E. clerk; Roseville; rep; Ohio.

Hays A. farmer; Sec. 19; Roseville; rep; 171 acres, value $11,970; from New York.

Henderson S. S. farmer; Sec. 8; P. O. Lenox; rep; 152 acres, value $9,120; from Penn.

Hendrickson M. shoemaker; Roseville; rep; from Sweden.

Hepburn E. T. farmer, rents of W. G. Morris; Sec. 14; P. O. Berwick; dem; from Ohio.

Herod F. M. school teacher, rents of R. Holeman; Sec. 32; P. O. Roseville; dem; Ind.

Hickman J. D. manager of Nusbaum's clothing store; Roseville; rep; from Penn.

Hickman T. farmer, rents of Wm. Hiett; Sec. 10; P. O. Berwick; dem; Bapt; from Ky.

Hickman S. farmer, rents of Wyatt Ray; Sec. 3; P. O. Lenox; dem; from Ky.

Hiett J. M. farmer; Sec. 11; P. O. Berwick; 176 acres, value $10,560; dem; Bapt; Ill.

HIETT WILLIAM, Farmer and Stock Raiser; Sec. 10; P. O. Berwick; born in Madison Co., Ky., Dec. 4, 1816; left there with his parents when 3 years of age, and removed to Warren Co., Ky; remained there until 1836, and then came to this Co; is one of the oldest settlers; has family of two sons and two daughters; wife was Aminda Davis, born in Mercer Co., Penn. Feb. 10, 1830; married Jan. 18, 1861; Dem; Bapt; has 410 acres, value $24,600.

Hine Jno. J. blacksmith; Roseville; dem; from Ohio.

Hines J. J. blacksmith; Roseville; dem; from Pennsylvania.

Hobbs D. W. farmer; P. O. Roseville; rep; from Ohio.

HOLEMAN REUBEN, Farmer and Stock Raiser; Sec. 32; P. O. Roseville; born in Jackson Co., Ind., Jan. 20, 1817; came to this Co. in March, 1847; there were very few families when he came; has family of seven sons and one daughter; wife was Miss Susannah Crabb, born in Wayne Co., Ind., Feb. 5, 1825; married Feb. 8, 1844; has been Collector, Road Com. and held other Town offices; Dem; both members of the Christian church; has 437 acres, value $26,220.

Holeman U. farmer, lives with his father; Sec. 32; P. O. Roseville; dem; born Ill.

Hollenberg G. farmer, lives with H. Hollenberg; Sec. 26; P. O. Greenbush; rep.

HOLLENBERG HENRY, Farmer and Stock Raiser; Sec. 26; P. O. Greenbush; born in Prussia, Germany, March 25, 1816; came to the U. S. and to Chicago in 1846; remained there about four years, and then went to California and remained there two years, then came here in 1852; has family of one son and two daughters; wife was Gulina Hatley, born in North Carolina, in 1828; married in 1853; Rep; Luth; has 109½ acres, value $6,540.

HOLLENBERG LOUIS, Retired; P. O. Roseville; born in Prussia, Germany, Nov. 26, 1825; left there and came to the U. S. and to this Co. in Dec., 1854, and is among the oldest settlers; Mr. Hollenberg is a cabinet-maker by trade; he worked at his trade here three years and then went to farming; he has 105 acres on Secs. 25 and 26, value $5,250; has family of one son and one daughter; wife was Miss Charlotte Brown, born in the same place, June 21, 1821 ;married in 1852; Rep.

Hollenberg L., Jr. farmer, works his father's farm; Sec. 25; P. O. Roseville; rep.

Hollenberg L. S. farmer, lives with his father; Sec. 26; P. O. Greenbush; rep; has 80 acres.

Holloway A. farmer, lives with his father; Sec. 29; P. O. Roseville; rep; Penn.

HOLLOWAY JOSEPH, Farmer; Sec. 29; P. O. Roseville; born in Mercer Co., Penn., April 13, 1814; left there and came to this Co. and settled on the place he now lives in Oct., 1859; has family of two sons and one adopted daughter; wife was Miss Elizabeth Axtell, born in the same place, Nov. 13, 1817; married July 14, 1836; both members of the Congregational church; Rep; has 51 acres, value $4,080.

Hoteling F. laborer; P. O. Roseville; rep; born Ill.

Huggett J. wheelwright; Roseville; rep; from Pennsylvania.

Hummel W. S. butcher; Roseville; rep; Bapt; from New Jersey.

Hush F. laborer; P. O. Roseville; rep; from Pennsylvania.

Huston M. C. farmer, lives with M. D. Huston; Sec. 35; P. O. Roseville; dem; Penn.

Huston M. D. farmer; Sec. 35; P. O. Roseville; dem; 160 acres on Sec. 18, val. $8000.

Huston S. farmer; Sec. 35; P. O. Roseville; dem; has 328 acres, value $16,400; Penn.

Hutchinson D. L. shoemaker; Roseville; rep; born Illinois.

JENNINGS F. M. teamster; Roseville; dem; born Illinois.

Johnson A. laborer; P. O. Roseville; rep; from Sweden.

Johnson, Mrs. F; Sec. 12; P. O. Berwick; 138 acres, value $6,900; from Virginia.

Johnson J. farmer, rents of T. J. Morris; Sec. 15; P. O. Berwick; dem; born Illinois.

Johnson P. farmer, works for A. Lewis; Sec. 16; P. O. Roseville; rep; from Sweden.

Johnson T. farmer, works for J. W. Malcolm; Sec. 25; P. O. Roseville; dem; from Ohio.

Johnston A. J. farmer, rents of Jacob Griggs; Sec. 8; P. O. Lenox; dem; from Penn.

Johnston J. M. farmer, rents of J. Griggs; Sec. 8; P. O. Lenox; dem; from Penn.

Jones M. W. farmer; Sec. 11; P. O. Berwick; dem; has 200 acres; from Ky.

KELLY J. C. V. clerk; Roseville; rep; from New Jersey.

Kidd G. laborer; Roseville; rep; from Ky.

Kidd W. laborer; Roseville; rep; from Ky.

King A. hardware merchant; Roseville; rep; from Missouri.

LATHROP J. T. carpenter; Roseville; rep; from Ohio.

Lacey G. farmer, rents of L. Gainer; Sec. 5; P. O. Lenox; dem; from Ireland.

LAPE HIRAM T. Farmer and Stock Raiser; Sec. 7; P. O. Roseville; born in Columbia Co., N. Y., Nov. 16, 1838; left there and came to this Co. in April, 1856, and is among the oldest settlers; has one daughter, Jennie M., born Aug. 26, 1869; wife was Miss Elizabeth Ditch, born in Jackson Co., Ind., Oct. 10, 1843; married Oct. 10, 1865; both members Bapt. church; he served 3 years and 16 days in the late war in Co. C. Engineer Regt. of the West; is Town Constable; Rep; has 140 acres, value $7,800.

Layton P. farmer, works for S. M. Eldrid; Sec. 17; P. O. Roseville; dem; from N. J.

Leacock S. jeweler; Roseville; dem; Meth; born Illinois.

Lee Dr. J. physician and surgeon; Roseville; rep; Cong; from Kentucky.

Lee J. coal miner; Roseville; dem; from England.

Lee T. coal miner; Roseville; dem; from England.

Lee W. H. retired; Roseville; rep; has 515 acres in Ellison tp., value $25,750; Ky.

Lenthard J. laborer; Roseville; dem; from Germany.

LEWIS ALPHEUS, Farmer and Stock Dealer; Sec. 16; P. O. Roseville; born in New Jersey, April 21, 1820; left there Oct. 25, 1837, and located in Berwick tp; is one of the oldest settlers in the Co; has family of three sons and three daughters; wife was Miss Rebecca Cheney, born in Ohio, Feb. 5, 1833; married June 6, 1849; both members of Bapt. church; Mr. Lewis has 960 acres of the best improved land in the Co; value of estate $48,000; is Supervisor, and has held other Town offices; Ind.

Lewis J. C. student, lives with his father; Sec. 16; P. O. Roseville; ind; born Illinois.

Lewis T. farmer; Sec. 35; P. O. Greenbush; dem; Bapt; 157 acres, value $7,850; Ohio.

Lieurance S. T. farmer, rents of I. L. Pratt; Sec. 18; P. O. Roseville; from Ohio.

Lilledahl N. J. farmer; P. O. Roseville; rep; from Sweden.

Little W. J. farmer; Sec. 15; P. O. Roseville; rep; has 120 acres, value $6,000; born Ill.

Long J. T. farmer; Sec.1; P. O. Berwick; dem; 320 acres, value $16,000; from Tenn.

Long W. H. hotel keeper; Roseville; rep; from Pennsylvania.

M^cADAMS JNO. laborer; P. O. Roseville; dem; born Illinois.

McAdams Jos. laborer; P. O. Roseville; dem; born Illinois.

McBride E. clerk; P. O. Roseville; rep; from Indiana.

McCammon G. W. carpenter; Roseville; dem; born Illinois.

McCameron R. teamster; Roseville; dem; from Indiana.

McCammon W. carpenter; Roseville; from Pennsylvania.

McClen J. J. blacksmith; Roseville; rep; from Pennsylvania.

McCurdy J. retired; Roseville; ind; from Pennsylvania.

McCURDY R. W. Farmer and Stock Raiser; Sec. 20; P. O. Roseville; born in McDonough Co., Ill., Oct. 12, 1847; left there when very young, with his parents, and removed to Fulton Co; remained there until the spring of 1865, then came here; has a family of four children, Luella J., Wm. B., Chas. W., and baby not yet named; wife was Miss Lydia A. Pusey, born in Maryland, May 20, 1843; married Jan. 1. 1865; both members of the Meth. church; has 120 acres, value $7,200; Dem.

McElroy W. laborer; P. O. Roseville; rep; from Ohio.

McGrew J. laborer; P. O. Roseville; rep; from Pennsylvania.

McLothlin W. laborer; P. O. Roseville; rep; from Indiana.

McPeake A. C. tinner; Roseville; dem; from Iowa.

McReynolds D. W. farmer; P. O. Roseville; rep; from Ohio.

McReynolds R. L. clerk; Roseville; rep; from Ohio.

Maberry C. farmer; P. O. Roseville; dem; from Indiana.

Mahoney D. farmer; Sec. 27; P. O. Roseville; dem; 75 acres, value $4,000; from Ireland.

MALCOLM J. W. Farmer and Stock Raiser; Sec. 25; P. O. Greenbush; born in St. Jo Co., Mich., April 20, 1840; left there and came to this Co. in 1862; has family of three children, Hattie, Francis and Emma; wife was Miss H. E. Staut, born in Roseville tp., this Co., July 22, 1846; married March 24, 1864; Mr. Malcolm has 760 acres, all under cultivation, value $38,000; Rep; two children dead, Stella and Ella.

Malcomb J. W. farmer; Sec. 25; P. O. Greenbush; rep; 760 acres, value $38,000; Ind.

MALONEY J. B. Harness-maker; Roseville; born in the town of Carlisle, Montgomery Co., Penn., Dec. 16, 1818; left there in 1825 with his parents, and removed to Richland Co., Ohio; remained there about twelve years; came to this State in 1839, and is the oldest in his trade in the Military Tract, who is now following the business; has family of eight children; wife was Miss Rachael Jameson, born in Richmond, Ind; married Jan. 28, 1874, she being his third wife; he served two years and four months in the late war as Sergeant Saddler in the 7th Regt. I. V. C.; Ind.

Maloney J. M. harness-maker; Roseville; dem; born Illinois.

MARSHALL A. A. Farmer; P. O. Roseville; born May 19, 1850, in Batavia, Clermont Co., Ohio; moved to Indiana in 1871; removed to Knox Co., Ill., Oct. 17, 1873, and Warren Co., Ill., in 1874; Rep; Meth. Epis.

Martin G. W. farmer, works for C. E. Mosier; Sec. 23; P. O. Roseville; dem; born Ill.

MASON J. V. Farmer and Stock Raiser; Sec. 27; P. O. Roseville; born in Knox Co., Ill., Nov. 4, 1847; left there and came to this Co. in the Spring of 1868; has one daughter, Eva B., born July 5, 1875; wife was Miss Carrie Young, born in Berwick tp., this Co., May 9, 1847; married Nov. 10, 1870; Rep; has 80 acres, value $4,800.

Mason W. H. farmer; Sec. 26; P. O. Roseville; rep; 80 acres, value $4,800; born Ill.

Maughan J. laborer; P. O. Roseville; dem; from England.

Meacham F. W. farmer and stock raiser; P. O. Roseville; Meth; rep; from Ky.

Meacham O. farmer; P. O. Roseville; rep; Meth; born Illinois.

Meadley N. B. farmer, rents of J. F. Young; Sec. 36; P. O. Roseville; rep; born Ill.

Midgett W. farmer, rents of W. Brooks; Sec. 9; P. O. Roseville; dem; from Missouri.

Miller E. farmer; Sec. 13; P. O. Berwick; dem; 177¾ acres, value $8,850; from Ind.

Mills S. farmer; Sec. 23; P. O. Roseville; dem; 80 acres, value $4,000; Nova Scotia.

Montgomery J. R. farmer, works for S. T. Licurence; Sec. 18; P. O. Roseville; Ky.

Moore J. farmer, works for J. H. Griggs; Sec. 6; P. O. Lenox; rep; Isle of Man.

Moore W. V. D. retired; P. O. Roseville; rep; 255 acres in Pt. Pleasant & Allison tp.

Moreland J. T. machinist; Roseville; rep; from Pennsylvania.

Morford C. retired; Roseville; dem; has 154 acres on Sec. 19, value $9,200; from Penn.

Morris T. J. farmer; Sec. 11; P. O. Berwick; rep; 278 acres, value $13,000; from Penn.

Mosier C. E. farmer; Sec. 23; P. O. Roseville; dem; 320 acres, value $19,200; from N. Y.

Mumford C. C. coal dealer; Roseville; rep; from Kentucky.

NATHAN Wm. laborer; P. O. Roseville; rep; from England.

Nance J. A. farmer; Sec. 10; P. O. Roseville; lives with his father; dem; born Ill.

NANCE J. W. Farmer and Stock Raiser; Sec. 10; P. O. Roseville; born in North Carolina, May 15, 1814; left there with his parents when one year of age, went to Tennessee, and remained there until 1845, and then came to this Co., and is one of the oldest settlers; has been married twice; first wife was Nancy Simmons, born in Warren Co., Ky., Feb. 4, 1815; married May 24, 1836; she died Nov. 13, 1872; has ten children by first wife; living; married again to Harriet E. Brooks, born in Edmundson Co., Ky., Dec. 2, 1823; married Jan. 11, 1874; has 280 acres, value $14,000; Dem; Bapt.

Neal B. farmer; Sec. 25; P. O. Greenbush; lives with his father; rep; from Penn.

Neal R. H. farmer, rents of J. W. Malcolm; Sec. 25; P. O. Greenbush; rep; from Penn.

NEVINS J. R. Farmer and Stock Raiser; Sec. 20; P. O. Roseville; born in Ohio, Grove tp, Mercer Co., Ill., Aug. 21, 1838; came to this Co. Sept. 15, 1868; no family; wife was Miss Elizabeth A. Barnes, born in Wabash Co., Ind., Nov. 19, 1845; married Nov. 29, 1861; has 120 acres, value $9,000; served three years in the late war in Co. D, 83rd Ill. Inf.; served three years as School Director, and is Overseer of Highways; Rep; both members of the Cong. church.

Newburn Jas. L. farmer; Sec. 26; P. O. Roseville; has 100 acres, value $5,000; dem.

NEWBURN THOMAS, Farmer and Stock Raiser, rents farm of his father-in-law; Sec 35; P. O. Roseville; born in Green Co., Penn., Aug. 13, 1836, left there and came to this Co. in 1857; has family six children, Ella, Effie, Martin, Lillie M., Gracie and Nannie; wife was Miss Phebe Pierce, born in this tp Oct. 10, 1845; married Dec. 7, 1862; Dem.

Newburn Wm. broom maker; Roseville; dem. from Penn.

Nicely Geo. W. farmer; Sec. 34; P. O. Roseville; has 136½ acres, value $8,200; dem.

Nicely G. W. Jr. farmer, works for A. Carr; P. O. Roseville; Sec. 26; dem; from Ohio.

Nichols Geo. N. merchant tailor; Roseville; rep; Bapt; from Massachusetts.

Nordgren T. R. wagon maker; Roseville; rep; Luth; from Sweden.

Norwood F. H. farmer, rents of E. Barnes; Sec. 5; P. O. Lenox; dem; from Maine.

OSTRANDER R. H. clerk; Roseville; rep; from Ohio.

OSTRANDER B. R. Lumber and Grain Dealer; Roseville; rep; from Ohio.

PARISH N. teamster; Roseville; rep; from Ohio.

Parrish W. A. farmer, rents of M. B. Ray; Sec. 10; P. O. Berwick; rep; from Ky.

Patch L. D. carpenter; Roseville; dem; from New Hampshire.

Pauley A. J. Sr. retired; Roseville; rep; Meth; from Ohio.

Pauley A. clerk; P. O. Roseville; rep; Meth; born Illinois.

Pauley Geo. W. laborer; P. O. Roseville; rep; born Ill.

Pauley J. L. groceries; P. O. Roseville; rep; Meth; from Ohio.

Peck J. W. Jr. dentist; Roseville; rep; Bapt; from New York.

Pelander C. G. wagon maker; Roseville; rep; from Sweden.

Pennington J. R. Baptist clergyman; Roseville; dem; born Illinois.

Perdue M. laborer; P. O. Roseville; dem; from Vermont.

PERKINS I. H. Farmer and Stock Raiser; Sec. 28; P. O. Roseville; born in Swan tp, this Co., Sept. 29, 1843; has family six children, Evalina, Thornton C., Solomon M., Reuben A., Orville B. and Mary E.; wife was Miss Eliza A. Holeman, born in Johnson Co., Ind., July 2, 1845; married March 2, 1862; has 80 acres, value $5,600; Dem; both members of the Christian church.

Perkins, farmer, rents of A. Lewis; Sec. 16; P. O. Roseville; dem; born Illinois.

Person R. laborer; P. O. Roseville; rep; from Ireland.

Pestle H. laborer; Roseville; dem; from Kentucky.

Pestel H. works for Stephen Pierce; Sec. 36; P. O. Greenbush; rep; from Penn.

Peters Jno. D. laborer; P. O. Roseville; rep; from Indiana.

PETERSON H. C. Farmer and Stock Raiser; Sec. 29; P. O. Roseville; born in Crawford Co., Penn., May 6, 1822; left there and came to McDonough Co., Ill., in the spring of 1855, and remained there until the spring of 1856, then came here; has family seven children, Lucretia, Alice A., Ida, Cordelia, Hiram L., Emma J. and Martha L.; he has been married twice; first wife was Jane Calvin, born in the same place, Sept. 27, 1823; she died in 1851; married again March 15, 1854, to Miss Emily Smith, born in New York; has 185 acres, value $11,100; is Road Commissioner and School Director; Rep; both members of the Meth. church.

Phinister Jno. dry goods merchant; Roseville; rep; from Scotland.

Pierce A. livery stable; Roseville; rep; born Illinois.

Pierce A. G. farmer; Sec. 1; P. O. Berwick; has 370 acres, value, $11,100; rep. from O.

PIERCE CLEMENT. Justice of the Peace; Roseville; born in Rutland Co., Vt., Sept. 24, 1813; left there and removed to Ashtabula Co., Ohio, in 1825; remained there until 1834, and then came to Greenbush, this Co., and is among the oldest settlers; has family three daughters and one son; wife was Miss Nancy Farr, born in Essex Co., N. Y., Jan. 3, 1814, married in March, 1834; value of estate $20,000; rep.

Pierce Geo T. farmer, lives with his father; Sec. 1; P. O. Berwick; rep; born Illinois.

Pierce Stephen, farmer; Sec. 36; P. O. Greenbush; has 198 acres, value $9,800; rep.

Pinckney L. D. dentist; Roseville; rep; from New York.

Powell Jno. hotel keeper; Roseville; rep; from Virginia.

Powell E. E. livery stable; Roseville; rep; from Iowa.

PRATT GEO. E. Lumber Dealer; Roseville; born in Bristol Co., Mass., Aug. 16, 1852; left there and came to this Co. with his parents in 1857; no family; wife was Miss Emma Watson, born in this Co. Jan. 1, 1856; married Aug. 30, 1876; value of estate $1,200; dem; members of the Bapt. church.

PRATT ISAAC L. Farmer and Stock Raiser, Lumber Dealer and Director of Roseville Union Bank; Roseville; born in the town of Easton, Co. of Bristol, Mass.; left there March 29, 1841, arrived here April 24, 1841, and is among the oldest settlers; has family, one son; wife was Miss Harriet W. Drake, from the same place; Married May 16, 1844; she came here in June, 1845; has been Justice of the Peace fifteen years, and held other town offices; has 1,650 acres, most all of which is under cultivation; value of estate, $80,000; Dem.

Pratt J. B. clerk in lumber yard; Roseville; rep; from Massachusetts.

Pratt Mrs. S.; Sec. 19; P. O. Roseville; 37 acres; value $2,960; from Massachusetts.

Pratt Seth F. cashier Roseville Union Bank; Roseville; dem; born Illinois.

RAMBO C. drayman; Roseville; rep; from Indiana.

Ragon Geo. W. bookkeeper; Roseville; rep; born Illinois.

RAGON DR. B. Physician and Surgeon; Roseville; born in Ross Co., Ohio, in 1813; his father moved to the North of Ohio when he was about twelve years old; he commenced studying medicine with Dr. J. Lang when he was about twenty years old; studied with him one year, and finished his study with George W. Sampson, M. D.; at the age of twenty-four commenced practice, July 1837, and married Huldah Mather, Jan. 14, 1837; moved to Greenbush, Ill., 1842; practiced medicine two years, moved to Indiana in 1844, and in the same year moved back to Greenbush; in 1855 attended lectures at the Rush Medical College, Chicago, and graduated at the same place in 1856, and from 1842 to the present time have been in active practice; in 1846 booked from sixty to eighty dollars a day for some time; when he came to Illinois he found Dr. Webster and Dr. Young, two as noble men as ever lived, and well skilled in their profession; Dr. Wright and Dr. Gillmore were practicing in this country.

Ray H. farmer, rents of Wyatt Ray; Sec. 3; P. O. Berwick; dem; from Kentucky.

Ray F. Farmer; Sec. 22; P. O. Roseville; has 120 acres, value $5,400; dem; Bapt.

Ray J. K. farmer; Sec. 22; P. O. Roseville; rep; born Illinois.

Ray R. M. farmer, rents of W. Coats; Sec. 8; P. O. Lenox; dem; from Kentucky.

Ray W. farmer; sec. 3; P. O. Berwick; has 479½ acres, $19,160; dem; from Kentucky.

REED JAMES G. Proprietor Roseville Agricultural Works; Roseville; born in Clarion Co., Penn., Dec. 3, 1831; came to the State in 1855, and to the Co. in 1857, and is among the oldest settlers; has family three sons, Herbert E., Harry H. and Perry B.; wife was Miss Sophia Mayhood, born in Butler Co., Penn., July 18, 1835; married Oct. 11, 1858; is President of the Board of Village Trustees; value of estate $11,000; Rep; Meth.

Rey, Geo. S. farmer; Sec. 19; P. O. Roseville; rep; from Penn.

Rhodes D. ins. agt.; Roseville; rep; from Pennsylvania.

Riggs J. farmer; Sec. 2; P. O. Berwick; has 220 acres, value $11,000; dem; from Tenn.

Rinearson C. painter; Roseville; dem; born Illinois.

Roberts A. farmer; Sec. 35; P. O. Greenbush; 60 acres, value $3,000; rep; born Illinois.

Roberts D. farmer; Sec. 7; P. O. Roseville; 80 acres, value $5,200; rep; from N. Y.

Roberts G. farmer; Sec. 35; Roseville; 61 acres, value $3,050; rep; born Illinois.

Robinson A. S. atty. at law; Roseville; dem; from New Jersey.

Rodenbaugh E. G. farmer, lives with G. S. Rodenbaugh; Sec. 15; P. O. Roseville; rep.

Rodenbaugh G. S. farmer; Sec. 15; P. O. Roseville; 80 acres, value $4,000; rep.

Rodenbaugh H. farmer, lives with G. S. Rodenbaugh; Sec. 15; Roseville; rep.

Rogers A. farmer, rents of W. Coats; Sec. 8; P. O. Lenox; dem; from Ohio.

Rogers F. S. sec. boss; P. O. Roseville; rep; from Ohio.

Romine D. farmer; P. O. Roseville; rep; born Illinois.

Romine W. C. Rev. retired; P. O. Roseville; rep; Christian; from Ohio.

Rose C. L. carpenter; Roseville; rep; from New York.

Rose W. E. painter; Roseville; rep; born Illinois.

Rusher B. harness maker; Roseville; rep; Meth; from Indiana.

Ryan J. laborer; Roseville; dem; born Ill.

Ryan Jno. laborer; Roseville; dem; born Ill.

SAWHILL A. farmer, rents of Seth P. Stern; Sec. 17; P. O. Lenox; rep; from O.

Sawtell Jno. mechanic; Roseville; has 110 acres on Sec. 22; value $5,500; dem.

Saylor H. J. farmer, rents of Stephen Pierce; Sec. 36; P. O. Roseville; born Ill.

SAYLOR J. M. Farmer and Stock Raiser; Sec. 33; P. O. Roseville; born in Columbianna Co., Ohio, Nov. 27, 1823, left there Sept. 12, 1844, and went to Knox Co., Ill.; remained there until 1856, and then came to this Co.; has family three sons and four daughters; wife was Miss Priscilla Mason, born in Stark Co., Ohio, June 7, 1825; married May 13, 1844; has 164 acres, value $9,800; rep; both members of the Christian church.

Saylor W. G. cashier co-operative store; Roseville; rep; born Illinois.

Schroder C. farmer; Sec. 3; P. O. Lenox; has 200 acres, value $10,000; dem; from Geo.

Shanks Wm. laborer; P. O. Roseville; rep; from Ohio.

Sharp J. H. farmer, rents of D. Livermore; Sec. 16; P. O. Roseville; dem; from Ohio.

Sharp W. farmer, lives with his father; Sec. 16; P. O. Roseville; dem; born Illinois.

Shepard G. farmer; P. O. Roseville; dem; from Indiana.

Shepard J. farmer, rents of J. Lathrop; Sec. 34; P. O. Roseville; rep; from Indiana.

Shields D. R. farmer; Sec. 28; P. O. Roseville; rep; born Illinois.

SHIMMONS ROBT. Farmer; Sec. 8; P. O. Lenox; born in the Isle of Man, in Sept. 1829, left there in May, 1850, landed in New York June 27, 1850, came to the State and to La Salle Co. July 9, remained there one year, then removed to Peoria Co. and remained there until 1860; then came here; has family three children, Agnes, Edward and John; wife was Miss Hannah Wilson, from England, born in June 1824; married March 10, 1863; rep.

Shirley H. farmer; Sec. 4; P. O. Lenox; 160 acres, value $8,000; dem; born Illinois.

Shoop W. S. engineer; Roseville; rep; born Illinois.

Simons J. farmer, works for S. H. Tuttle; Sec. 36; P. O. Roseville; rep; born Ill.

Smith B. farmer, rents of C. E. Mosier; Sec. 23; P. O. Roseville; dem; born Illinois.

Smith B. L. farmer, works for R. Carr; Sec. 14; P. O. Roseville; dem; from Ky.

Smith C. K. Jr. prop. Farmers' House Restaurant; Roseville; rep; born Illinois.

Smith Jas. C. farmer; P. O. Roseville; dem; from Kentucky.

Smith J. C. farmer; Sec. 22; P. O. Roseville; has 80 acres on Sec. 13 in Ellison tp; dem.

Smith J. A. J. carpenter; Sec. 11. P. O. Berwick; has 20 acres, value $1,000; dem.

Smith J. W. farmer, works for J. W. Nance; Sec. 10; P. O. Roseville; dem; from Ky.

Smith L. farmer; P. O. Roseville; dem; from Kentucky.

Smith P. C. farmer; Sec. 18; Roseville; 255 acres, value $14,025; rep; from Penn.

Smith S. post office clerk; Roseville; rep; from Minnesota.

Smith Warren, farmer, lives on his father's place; Sec. 29; P. O. Roseville; rep; born Ill.

SMITH WILLIAM, Merchant, Roseville; born in Essex Co., Mass., June 1, 1823; left there and came to this Co. in July 1853, and is among the oldest settlers; has family six children, Emma E., Clara E., Albert, Annie, Lydia and Fred; wife was Miss Abby Nichols, born in the same place, April 20, 1839; married Jan. 10, 1856; has 160 acres in Point Pleasant Tp on Sec. 17; value of estate $12,200; rep.

Smith Wm. P. farmer, rents house of J. Thayer; Sec. 27; P. O. Roseville; rep.

Snively C. carpenter; Roseville; dem; from Ohio.

Sollars C. M. plasterer; Roseville; dem; born Illinois.

Spong J. farmer, rents of A. Hewing; Sec. 4; P. O. Lenox; rep; from Ohio.

Standerford J. W. plasterer; Roseville; rep; from Indiana.

Stafford J. B. farmer, lives with his father; Sec. 17; P. O. Roseville; dem; from Penn.

STAFFORD S. J. Farmer and Stock Raiser; Sec. 17; P. O. Roseville; born in the town of Peru, Clinton Co., N. Y., Aug. 17, 1816, came to this Co. in the fall of 1863; has family five children, James B., Eliza A., Jennie R., Frank and Ida; wife was Miss Jane Black, born in Erie Co., Penn., June 9, 1827; married Feb. 7, 1854; has 80 acres, value $6,400; dem.

Steel J. farmer, rents of Thos. Lewis; Sec. 35; P. O. Greenbush; dem; Bapt; from Iowa;

Stem D. stock dealer; rep; Roseville; from Penn.

Stem C. N. farmer and stock dealer; Roseville; rep; 160 acres on Sec. 28, val. $9,600.

STEM, MRS. MARY A. resides Sec. 32; P. O. Roseville; born in Hunterdon Co., N. J., April 9, 1804; removed to Knox Co., Ohio, in 1845; remained there until 1852, then removed to Canada, and remained until 1855, and then came here; Mrs. Stem has been married four times; married to Frederick Stem March 20, 1871; he died June 8, 1875; her maiden name was Miss Mary A. Wack; Meth; has 40 acres, value $3,200.

STEM M. JUDD, Farmer and Stock Dealer; P. O. Roseville; born in Mercer Co., Penn., June 15, 1844; left there and came to this Co. in 1850; has family of three children, Fred, Gracie E. and Ralph; wife was Miss Lydia Morgan, born in Berry Co., Mich., Dec. 26, 1853; married Oct. 22, 1871; has 225 acres, value of estate $18,000.

STEM SETH P. Farmer and Stock Dealer, and Director of Roseville Union Bank; Roseville; born in Mercer Co., Penn., July 29, 1833; left there and came to this Co. in 1851; has family of two daughters, Elsie L. and Nellie B; wife was Miss Mary J. McDurmott, born in Brooklyn, N. Y., Oct. 31, 1843; married Oct. 9, 1866; she came to this Co. in 1854; both members of the Baptist church; Rep; has 227 acres on Secs. 17 and 20, value of estate $16,000; he served three years in the late war in Co. H. 2d I. V. C.; was Assessor one term, and held other Town offices.

Stephens H. H. farmer, works for H. Lape; Sec. 7; P. O. Roseville; rep; from Ind.

Stewart C. E. farmer, rents of J. McFadden; Sec. 7; P. O. Roseville; dem; from Penn.

Stokes A. farmer, works for H. Shirley; Sec 4; P. O. Lenox; dem; from Kentucky.

Stone A. farmer; P. O. Roseville; rep; from New York.

Stone E. painter; Roseville; rep; N. Y.

Stone S. laborer; P. O. Roseville; rep; Ill.

Suggs J. laborer; P. O. Roseville; rep; Ill.

Sweeny C. farmer; Sec. 4; P. O. Lenox; dem; 80 acres; value $4,000; from Ireland.

Sweeney T. farmer, rents of Jno. Slack; Sec. 4; P. O. Lenox; dem; from Ireland.

TALIAFERRO D. M. physician and surgeon; Sec. 29; Roseville; dem.

Tally G. farmer, works for H. Gunter; Sec. 33; P. O. Roseville; dem; from Ill.

Tally J. W. teaming; Roseville; dem; from Illinois.

Tally J. laborer; Sec. 33; P. O. Roseville; dem; from Illinois.

Tally R. farmer, rents of his father; Sec. 33; P. O. Roseville; dem; from Kentucky.

Tally W. T. farmer; Sec. 33; P. O. Roseville; dem; 89½ acres, value $4,430; Va.

Taylor H. retired; Sec. 33; P. O. Roseville; dem; from Kentucky.

TAYLOR WILLIAM Farmer and Stock Raiser; Sec. 27; P. O. Roseville; born in Perry Co., Ind., Feb. 5, 1827; left there and came to this Co. in April, 1835; he is among the oldest settlers; has family of six sons and four daughters; wife was Miss Mary Underwood, born in Warren Co., N. Y., Aug. 3, 1831; married Jan. 16, 1851; Dem; has 448 acres, value $22,400.

Taylor W. B. farmer; P. O. Roseville; dem; born Illinois.

Taylor W. H. lives with his father; Sec. 27; P. O. Roseville; dem; born Illinois.

THAYER GEORGE, Farmer and Stock Raiser; Sec. 28; P. O. Roseville; born in Lewis Co., N. Y., Aug. 24, 1828; left there in 1840, and came to Knox Co., Ill., remained there about two years, then removed to Hancock Co., remained there about four years, then removed to Racine Co., Wis, remained there about two years, and from there to McDonough Co., and remained there about one year, then went to Lee Co., Iowa, remained there about six months, and then came here; has a family of six children; wife was Miss Genette White, born in New York, in June, 1835; married Aug. 23, 1851; Rep; Bapt; has 165½ acres, value $8,250.

Thompson R. N. financier; Roseville; dem; from Indiana.

Thayer W. farmer, lives with his father; Sec. 28; P. O. Roseville; rep; Bapt; born Ill.

Thompson J. A. engineer; Roseville; dem; from Indiana.

Tiffany M. farmer, rents of S. P. Stem; Sec. 20; P. O. Roseville; rep; from Penn.

Tinder I. R. laborer; P. O. Roseville; dem; from Indiana.

Tinder W. weigh-master; Roseville; dem; from Indiana.

Todd E. J. lives with his father; Sec. 7; P. O. Roseville; rep; born Illinois.

Todd H. A. lives with his father; Sec. 7; P. O. Roseville; rep; born Illinois.

Todd J. A. farmer; Sec. 7; P. O. Roseville; rep; Cong; 80 acres, value $5,000; N. J.

TURNBULL J. C. Farmer and Stock Raiser; P. O. Roseville; born in Montgomery Co., Md., Nov. 18, 1812; left there with his parents and removed to New Albany, Ind, in 1818, remained there three years, then removed to Jackson Co., Ind., remained there until 1865, then came to this Co; has one son living, six children dead; wife was Elizabeth Byraly, born in Jackson Co., Ind., Sept. 23, 1835; married Oct. 19, 1865; both members Bapt. church; Rep; he and his son together have 500 acres, value $28,800.

Turnbull J. C. Jr. farmer; Sec. 21; P. O. Roseville; rep; Bapt; 240 acres; from Ind.

TUTTLE DAVID, Farmer; Sec. 28; P. O. Roseville; born in Green Co., Penn., Oct. 13, 1800; left there and came to this Co. in the Fall of 1850, and is among the oldest settlers; has been married twice; has three children by first wife, Mary, Simeon and Irene; wife was Elizabeth Axtell, born in the same place April 14, 1802; married Feb. 18, 1824; she died Feb. 1853; married again Jan. 24, 1854, to Philena Young, born in Ashtabula Co., Ohio; one daughter, Ruth; Rep; Cong; has 80 acres, value $4,000.

TUTTLE S. H. Farmer and Stock Raiser; Sec. 36; P. O. Roseville, born in Mercer Co., Penn., June 15, 1846; left there with his parents when four years of age, came to this Co; no family; wife was Miss Emma Young, born in this tp, July 8, 1847; married Aug. 11, 1871; both members Meth. church; Rep; served seven months in the late war in Co. I. 61st Ill. Reg't; has 176 acres, value $8,800.

UHL H. clerk; Roseville; rep; from Ohio.

Underwood O. farmer, rents of D. P. Underwood; Sec. 34; P. O. Roseville; dem; Ill.

UNDERWOOD D. P. Farmer and Stock Raiser; Sec. 34; P. O. Roseville; born in Vt., Feb. 8, 1837; left there when very young and came to this State with his parents, and to this Co. when about 15 years of age; has family of four children, Emory, Mayliscie, Pearl and Donnie; wife was Miss Barbara L. Brown, born in Rockingham Co., Va., April 14, 1842; married Sept. 14, 1862; has 132 acres, value $6,600; served six months in the late war in Co. C 83d I. V. I; Ind.

VANDIVER C. farmer, rents of Henry Staat; Sec. 26; P. O. Roseville; dem.

Vandiver W. farmer, works for Jesse Riggs; Sec. 2; P. O. Berwick; dem; born Ill.

WALDRON J. D. dry goods and groceries; Roseville; rep; from N. Y.

Walker M. D. farmer, works for R B. Woodward; Sec. 30; P. O. Roseville; rep; Ill.

WALSH JOHN, Merchant; Roseville; born in Richland Co., town of Belleville, Ohio, Nov. 5, 1835; left there and removed to Randolph Co., Ind., in 1855, remained there four years, then went to Farmington, Fulton Co., Ill., remained there four years,

and then came here; has family of two children; wife was Miss Elizabeth H. Conklin, born in Clermont Co., Ohio, Sept. 18, 1840; married Feb. 24, 1866; served three years in the late war in Co. F., 17th I. V. I; Rep; both members M. E. church.

Warner Geo. farmer, lives with his father; Sec. 28; P. O. Roseville; rep; from Ohio.

Warner G. B. carpenter, rents house of C. N. Stem; Sec. 28; P. O. Roseville; rep.

Waters E. P. harness maker; P. O. Roseville.

Watson Augustus, farmer, rents of J. C. Turnbull, Jr; Sec. 21; Roseville; rep; born Ill.

Watson Geo. retired; P. O. Roseville; rep; Cong; from Connecticut.

Watson Jno. E. farmer, lives with his father; Sec. 6; P. O. Lenox; rep; from England.

WATSON PETER, Farmer and Stock Raiser; Sec. 6; P. O. Lenox; born in the Co. of York, Yorkshire, Eng., Feb. 21, 1824, left there and came to the U. S. Sept. 9, 1857, and arrived in Peoria Co., Ill., Oct. 3, and remained there until March 4, and then came to this Co.; has family two sons, John E. and William H.; wife was Elizabeth Wilson from the same place, born Dec. 1, 1829; married in 1850; has 160 acres, value $8,000; Rep.

Webb J. J. farmer, works for M. W. Jones; Sec. 11; P. O. Berwick; dem; from Ky.

Welch Jno. V. farmer, rents of S. Henderson; Sec. 6; P. O. Lenox; dem; from Ohio.

Welch S. B. cabinet maker; Roseville; rep; Bapt; from Kentucky.

Wells R. L. farmer, rents of R. Crosier; Sec. 19; P. O. Roseville; rep; from Penn.

WELSCH A. L. Farmer and Stock Raiser; Sec. 6; P. O. Lenox; born in Huntington Co., N. J., July 21, 1844, came to this Co. in the fall of 1864; has family three sons, Lyman H., Iziah and Harvey A.; wife was Martha A. Adair, born in Henderson Co., Ill., Sept. 27, 1850; married Feb. 22, 1869; value of estate, $1,500; Dem.

Welsch Wm. farmer, rents of John Wilson; Sec. 6; P. O. Lenox; dem; from Ohio.

White Geo. R. carpenter; Roseville; rep; from Pennsylvania.

Wickersham E. I. merchant; Roseville; rep; Bapt; born Illinois.

Wiley J. P. carpenter; Roseville; dem; from Michigan.

WILLARD JOHN, Bridge Builder; Roseville; born in Greenbush tp, this Co., June 18, 1840, and is among the first born; has family three children, Octavia, Nora and Geo. E.; wife was Miss M. A. Mathews, born in Jefferson Co., Indiana, Sept. 1, 1842; married Aug. 31, 1864; value of estate, $1,060; Dem; Bapt.

Wilson J. coal miner; Roseville; rep; from England.

Woods R. retired, lives with his son; Sec. 19; P. O. Roseville; rep; from Pennsylvania.

WOODS SETH, Farmer and Stock Raiser; Sec. 19; P. O. Roseville; born in Venango Co., Penn., April 11, 1837, left there and came to Pike Co., Ill., in May, 1848,and remained there until March,1851; then came here; has family four children, Herman B., Caleb J., Melvin T. and Robt. R.; has been married twice; first wife, mother of the children, was Miss Zilpah Stem, born in Mercer Co., Penn., Oct. 25, 1845; married Sept. 20, 1865; she died at Hutchinson, Kan., May 15, 1875; he married again May 4, 1876, to Lucy O. Davis, born in Salem, Mass., April 25, 1842; has 86 acres, value $6,880; Rep.

Woodmansee J. L. dry good and groceries; Roseville; rep; from New York.

WOODWARD R. B. Farmer and Stock Raiser, and Director of Roseville Union Bank; Sec. 30; P. O. Roseville; born in Fayette Co., Penn., Oct. 14, 1829, left there March 15, 1853, and arrived here March 31 same year; has family six children living, Mary E., Davis A., Andy D., Seth, Horace H. and Viola A.; three dead, Amey A., Izola J. and George; wife was Miss Sarah A. Work, born in the same place, Jan. 27, 1829; married Dec. 5, 1850; has 450 acres; value of estate $35,000; dem; Davis A. is one of the stockholders in the Roseville Union Bank.

WYATT A. A. Painter; Roseville; born in McDonough Co., Ill., Oct. 13, 1842, came to this Co. in Aug. 1870; no family; wife was Miss Mary J. Sears, born in Tuscarawas Co., Ohio, June 10, 1842; married Sept. 7, 1870; he served 4 yrs. 3 mo. and 17 days in the late war in Co. G 16th Ill. Vet. Vol. Inf.; Rep; both members of the M. E. church.

YOUNG Jno. F. farmer; Sec. 36; P. O. Roseville; has 160 acres, value $8,000.

ROSEVILLE BUSINESS DIRECTORY.

Bradley Theodore, M. D., Physician and Surgeon. Will promptly answer any calls by day or night. Patronage solicited.

Butler J. E. & Co., Dealers in Dry Goods, Notions, etc.

Conlee J. W. Agent St. L., R. I. & C. R. R. branch of the C. B. & Q. R. R.

Davenport J. L. Undertaker and Dealer in Cases and Caskets.

Eldridg Truman, Prop. Roseville Steam Flouring Mills; also Grain Buyer.

Evans & Ostrander, Lumber and Grain Dealers.

Gordon Jno. A. Furniture Dealer, Notary Public and Real Estate Agent.

Maloney J. B. Harness Maker. A great variety of Collars and a big stock of Saddles.

Pauley & Walsh, Dealers in Staple and Fancy Groceries, Crockery, Glassware, Flour and Provisions.

Pierce Clement, Justice of the Peace.

Pratt & Pratt, Dealers in Lumber, Grain, Tile, Shingles, Lath, Sash, Doors, Blinds, Mouldings, Brackets, Pumps, Salt, Lime, Sand, Cement and Plastering Hair, Wagons and Buggies.

Ragon, Dr. B. Physician and Surgeon.

Ragon B. & Son, Dealers in Drugs, Groceries, all kinds of Toilet Articles, Paints, Oils, Varnishes, Window Glass, Putty, Glassware, Queensware, Woodenware, Willowware, Confectionery, Tobacco, Snuff, Cigars, etc.

Reed, Dixson & Bader, Manufacturers and Dealers in Agricultural Implements.

Roseville Union Bank, Pratt, Stem, Worden & Co., Proprietors. Do a general Banking business. Lycurgus Worden, Prest.; Seth F. Pratt, Cashier; Directors, Isaac L. Pratt, Eli Dixson, L. Worden. S. P. Stem, R. B. Woodward, Eli B. Dixson, Seth F. Pratt.

Smith Wm. Merchant.

Willard Jno. Bridge Builder.

Wyatt M. J. Photographer.

KELLY TOWNSHIP.

AMY MRS. ABIGAIL; P. O. Ionia; M. E.; owns house and lot.

Adcock Edmund, student at law school, Chicago; dem; ind; born Illinois.

Adcock G. R. farmer; Sec. 33; P. O. Utah; dem; M. E.; from West Virginia.

Adcock H. J. farmer; Sec. 33; P. O. Utah; dem; ind; 206 acres, value $16,000.

ADCOCK J. W. Farmer; Sec. 27; P. O. Utah; born in Kanawha Co., West Virginia, Jan. 22, 1826, came to Knox Co. in 1830, and to this Co. in 1833; had family seven children, 3 boys and 4 girls; wife was Miss Mary E. McMurtry, born in Indiana, Sept. 26, 1827; married Aug. 30, 1849; 488 acres, value $14,640; is Treasurer Board Trustees; Dem; Chris.

Adcock Mrs. N. H.; Sec. 33; P. O. Utah; 185 acres, value $9,250; Bapt; from W. Va.

ADCOCK R. H. Farmer and Stock Raiser; Sec. 27; P. O. Utah; Born in Kelly tp, West Co., March 16, 1836; family three children; wife was Miss Mary Robertson, born in Knox Co., May 8, 1840; married Jan 8, 1857; 470 acres, value, $14,100; Dem; Ind.

Adcock, Wm. farmer; Sec. 35; P. O. Utah; 240 acres, value, $14,400; dem; ind.

Allen Mrs. A. R.; Sec 30; P. O. Utah; ind; from West Virginia.

Amy Charles, Shanghai; lives with his mother; dem; ind; born Ill.

Anderson J. C. lives with H. N. Hogan; rep; Union; from Rhode Island.

Armstrong George, rents J. Pine's farm; P. O. Ionia; rep; M. E.; from Ireland.

Atchison G. W. renter; Sec. 35; P. O. Utah; dem; Univ; born Illinois.

Armstrong James, farmer; Sec. 28; P. O. Utah; rep; ind; from Ireland.

Armstrong John, rents J. Pine's farm; Sec. 9; P. O. Ionia; rep; M. E.; born Ireland.

Armstrong, Mrs. Martha, Sec. 28; P.O. Utah; 229 acres, value $9,160; Meth; from Ire.

Armstrong Samuel, farmer; Sec. 28; P. O. Utah; rep; ind; from Ireland.

ARNOLD JOHN, Farmer; Sec. 34; P. O. Utah; born in Monroe Co., Ind., Sept. 3, 1825; came to Woodford Co., Ill., in 1830; family seven children, three living; wife was Miss Mary S. Reed, born in Simpson, Ky., Nov. 18, 1822; married Dec. 25, 1845; she came to Sangamon Co. in 1827, and to Knox Co. in 1829; both came to this Co. in 1864; owns 80 acres, valued at $4,000; Dem; Ind; School Director.

Atkins Daniel, rents of Gentry; Sec. 13; P. O. Ionia; dem; ind; from Virginia.

BEARD CHRISTIAN, farmer; Sec. 10; P. O. Ionia; dem; ind; from Indiana.

Beard G. W. farmer; Sec. 10; P. O. Ionia; owns 220 acres, value $15,400; dem; Ind.

Beard R. lives with his father; dem; ind; from Indiana.

Beebe Schuyler, rents of Mrs. Armstrong; Sec. 22; P. O. Ionia; rep; M. E.; from N.Y.

BELLINGER CHAS., Farmer; Sec. 6; P.O. Alexis; born in Somersetshire, Eng., Jan. 1818; came from England to Ohio in 1841, to Knox Co. in 1844, and to this Co. in 1845; while in Knox Co. he bought a year's supply of wheat at 4 cts. per bushel, and in order to get the cash the man threw in a pork barrel extra of corn at the same price; his children are James P., born March 6, 1841; Alfred, Jan. 10, 1843; G. W., Aug. 6, 1844; Louisa G., Feb. 14, 1850; Lucy S., Dec. 25, 1851; Chas. E., April 29, 1854; Fred U., Jan. 18, 1856; children by his second wife, Frank A., June 21, 1867; Albert C., Oct. 5, 1868; his first wife was Sophia Pine, born in Somersetshire, Eng. April 10, 1817; married Dec. 8, 1840; died April 29, 1860; second wife was Catharine A. McCarteny, born in Pennsylvania, April 22, 1840; married Oct. 19, 1865; owns 525 acres; value $4,000; dem; Adv.

Bellinger Charles E. farmer, lives with G. W. Bellinger; P. O. Ionia; dem; born Ill.

BELLINGER GEO. W. Farmer; Sec. 9; P. O. Ionia; born in Geauga Co., Ohio, Aug. 16, 1844; came to this Co. in 1846; Dem; Ind; owns 120 acres, value $6,000; holds the office of Postmaster; wife was Miss Lucinda Holcomb, born in Kelly tp, Nov. 15, 1848; married March 12, 1869; children are Nellie, born Sept. 4, 1870, died Jan. 17, 1875; John, born Nov. 30, 1873, died Aug. 31, 1876; Bennie, born Aug. 10, 1876; he was in the Advent church at the time it was blown down by the tornado, and was buried beneath its ruins; he received but slight bodily injury; he had the roof blown off of his house, stable torn down, and fences demolished generally.

Beswick Alonzo, carpenter; Sec 25; P. O. Utah; owns ten acres, value $1,000; rep.

288   VOTERS AND TAXPAYERS OF

Beswick Theodore, works for Miles; Sec. 25; rep; Ind; born Illinois.
Boozan James, farmer; Sec. 20; P. O. Alexis; owns 190 acres, value $8,000; dem; Cath.
Boozan Michael, farmer; Sec. 18; P. O. Alexis; owns 100 acres, value $5,000; dem.
Boozan P. W. farmer; Sec. 10; P. O. Alexis; owns 80 acres; value $4,000; dem; Cath.
Bratton J. R. rents of Dr. McClanahan; P.O. Alexis; dem; U. P.; from Ohio.
Bride Cornelius, farmer; Sec. 19; P. O. Ionia; owns 124 acres, value $6,000; dem; Cath.
Britt Edward; farmer; Sec. 29; P. O. Utah; owns 80 acres, value $3,200; dem; M. E.
Britt James, farmer; Sec. 29; P. O. Utah; owns 22 acres, value $1,100; dem; Chr'n.
Brown A. G. lives with Wm. Brown; dem; ind; born Illinois.

BROWN JNO. B. Farmer; Sec. 2; P. O. Ionia; born in Dundee, Scotland, in March 1819; came to this Co. in 1853; Rep; M. E.; 138 acres, value $4,500; his wife was Mrs. Lydia Palmer, who was born in Devonshire, Eng., Nov. 2, 1829; married in Sept. 1869; her first husband, Wm. Palmer, was born in England, and died here Dec. 29, 1868; Mr. Brown lived in Knox Co. three years; he visited Scotland in 1873, after an absence of twenty-five years; they have one boy and two girls.

Brown Jno. H. farmer; Sec. 25; P. O. Galesburg; 81 acres, value $4,800; rep; Univ.

BROWN T. M. Farmer; Sec. 12; P. O. Ionia; rep; Univ; 300 acres, value $12,000; he was born in Breckenridge Co., Ky., Nov. 21, 1827; came from Kentucky to Knox Co., Ill., (Henderson) in 1832; lived there eighteen years; has lived here since 1860; wife was Miss Christia A. Vestal, born in Mercer Co., June 14, 1841; married Nov. 11, 1860; two children, Ettie M., born Jan. 27, 1862; Edwin, Jan 29, 1866; holds the office of School Director.

Brown Wm. farmer; Sec. 25; P. O. Galesburg; 108 acres, value $4,400; rep; Univ.
Brown Wm. rents S. Price's farm; P. O. Ionia; rep; M. E.; from North Carolina.
Brown Wm. farmer; Shanghai; P. O. Ionia; rep; Bapt; from North Carolina.
Brown Wilson, lives with A. Lewey; Kelly; rep; Ind; born Illinois.

BRUINGTON THOMAS, Farmer; Sec. 8; P. O. Alexis; born in Breckenridge Co., Ky., May 13, 1807; came to this Co. in 1840; Dem; Ind; 96 acres, value $4,500; holds office of Justice of Peace and Supervisor; first wife was Jane McGlothlin, born Aug. 9, 1809; married June 28, 1828; died Dec. 18, 1849; second wife was Mrs. Anna Goff, born in N. Y., Dec. 6, 1823; married Nov. 30, 1854; children are Sarah Ann, born May 26, 1829, died Oct. 13, 1873, Jas., born Aug. 23, 1831, John M., April 4, 1834, Jane, July 8, 1836, died Aug. 5, 1845, Eliz-

abeth, July 2, 1838, George, Oct. 4, 1840, Thomas, March 1, 1843, Newton, July 16, 1845, Eugene, Nov. 25, 1847; children by second wife, Jno. J., born June 4, 1860, died Aug. 20, 1860, Elmore E., Jan. 26, 1862, Harry T., Feb. 10, 1866, died Nov. 28, 1866, Cassius C., born Kelly tp., Oct. 8, 1855.
Buchanan J. C. renter; Sec. 31; P. O. Gerlaw; ind; Pres; from Indiana.
Bullman Theodore, farmer; Sec. 36; P. O. Galesburg; rep; Pres; 235 acres, val. $11,750.

BUNKER NATHAN, Farmer; Sec. 34; P. O. Utah; born in Armstrong Co., Penn., May 11, 1812; lived in Medina Co; lumbering in Jefferson and Knox Cos., Ill., each ten years; came to this Co. in 1865; Mr. Bunker is of Welsh descent; his grandfather was a soldier in the Revolution; he owned the hill where the battle of that name was fought and the monument erected; wife was Priscilla Halliwell, born in Stark Co., Ohio, Nov. 7, 1816; married at Richfield, Medina Co., Ohio, March 23, 1837; four children, two girls living.

Buttless Joseph, lives with Mr. Ryner; rep; from Connecticut.

CLUTE J. M. farmer; Sec. 23; P. O. Utah; rep; Meth; from New York.
Clute Jas. W. farmer; Sec. 23; P. O. Utah; rep; ind; from New York.

CANE NATHAN, Farmer; Sec. 34; P. O. Utah; born in Ticonderoga, Essex Co., N. Y., Feb. 13, 1825; Rep; Meth; 100 acres, value $5,500; lived in New York and Pennsylvania until about 17 years old; lived in Ohio and Indiana each seven years; came to this Co. Dec. 1, 1856; held the office of School Director; has been Supervisor, Town Collector and Com. Highways; wife was Eunice E. Pebbles, born in Massachusetts, May 23, 1829; married Sept. 10, 1848; seven children, two boys and five girls.

CLARY DANIEL, Farmer; Sec. 3; P. O. Ionia; born in Tipperary Co., Ireland, Nov. 1, 1843; came from Ireland to New York May 15, 1847; lived there nine years; came to Galesburg March 17, 1856; lived there twelve years, and in this Co. since 1868; held the office of Constable two years; Rep; Ind.

Coffey Cornelius; P. O. N. Henderson; dem. Cath; 82 acres, value $3,600; from Ireland.
Cole Alexander, laborer; Sec. 26; P. O. Utah; rep; Ind; from New York.
Cole Amos, teamster; Sec. 26; P. O. Utah; rep; Ind; from New York;
Cole Alfred, laborer; Sec. 26; P. O. Utah; rep; Ind; from New York.
Cole J. H. laborer; Sec. 26; P. O. Utah; rep; Ind; from New York.
Cole Wm. H. Carpenter; Sec. 26; P. O. Utah; rep; Ind; 2½ acres, val. $270; N. Y.

Cowen C. J. lives with Mrs. Kelly; P. O. Utah; rep; Ind; born Illinois.

Cozard A. J. renter; P. O. Utah; rep; Ind.

Cox Wm. H. farmer; Sec. 36; P. O. Utah; rep; Meth; 35 acres, val. $3,500; Ind.

CRIBB T. T. Farmer; Sec. 8; P. O. Alexis; born in Somersetshire, England, Nov. 4, 1844; came to this Co. in 1871; Ind; 156 acres, value $7,500; wife was Mrs E. T. Cheese, born in Somersetshire, England, Dec. 10, 1839; she was married to her first husband, E. T. Cheese, April 19, 1859, who died Dec. 6, 1871, by whom she had four children, Chas. B., born May 18, 1861, J. L., Dec. 13, 1863, Geo. F., Jan. 27, 1867, and E. T., Aug. 25, 1871; married to Mr. Cribb Oct. 7, 1875.

Crosby Frank, lives with Jno. Vestal; P. O. Ionia; dem; Ind; born Illinois.

Crosby John, lives with Wm. Crosby; dem; Ind; born Illinois.

Crosby Wm. farmer; Sec. 12; P. O. Ionia; dem; Ind; 160 acres, value $8,000; Va.

Curtis M. C. farmer; Sec. 2; P. O. Ionia; rep; M. E.; 112½ acres, val. $5,500; Ohio.

DAVIS MARTIN, renter; P. O. Galesburg; rep; Ind; born Ill.

Driffle Joseph, laborer; P. O. Ionia; rep; Ind; from New York.

Duke Frank, works for Geo. Bellinger; dem; Ind; from Indiana.

Duke James, rents of A. Bellinger; P. O. Ionia; dem; Ind; from Indiana.

Duke Jerome, rents of Rucker; P. O. Ionia; dem; Ind; from Indiana.

Dunn G. W. farmer; Sec. 2; P. O. Ionia; rep; Ind; from Indiana.

Dunn Jefferson, lives with R. Dunn; rep; Ind; from Indiana.

Dunn Richardson, farmer; Sec. 11; P. O. Ionia; rep; Ind; 160 acres, value $11,000.

Dunn J. Wm. farmer; Sec. 2, P. O. Ionia; rep; Adv; 80 acres, value $4,800; born Ill.

ENINGER LOUIS, laborer, lives with G. W. Dunn; rep; Ind; from Indiana.

Ennis Isaac F. works for M. S. Reese; ind. in politics and religion; from Indiana.

EDWARDS JOHN, Farmer; Sec. 9; P. O. Ionia; born in Somersetshire, Eng., July 18, 1815; came from England to this country in 1841; traveled in Michigan, New York, Wisconsin and Ohio for about four years; lived here since 1844; wife was Miss Sarah A. Pine, born in Somersetshire, England, March 31, 1824; married March 23, 1845; rep; Meth; 80 acres, value $4,000; nine children, three boys and one girl living.

Ernst W. A. farmer; Sec. 1; P. O. N. Henderson; dem; U. B; 120 acres, val. $3,600.

FEAKE AUGUSTUS, lives with his father; rep; Meth; from Indiana.

Feake John; Sec. 3; P. O. N. Henderson; rep; Meth; 102 acres, value, $5,100; Ind.

Fleming Daniel, laborer, P. O. Ionia, Shanghai; rep; Ind; house and 3 lots, val. $300.

Foster Abram, farmer; Sec. 11; P. O. Ionia; rep; U. B; 160 acres, val. $8,000; England.

Foster Jacob, farmer; Sec. 11; P. O. Ionia; rep; M. E.; 10 acres, val. $600; from Eng.

Foster Joseph, lives with his father; rep; Ind; born Illinois.

Foster Mortimer, lives with his father; rep; Ind; born Illinois.

Foster Richard, farmer; Sec. 4; P. O. Alexis; rep; Pres; 75 acres, val. $3,750; England.

Foster Wm. lives with his father; rep; Ind; from England.

Franklin Albert, Farmer; Sec. 11; P. O. Ionia; dem; Ind; 72½ acres, value $3,775.

Franklin John, farmer; Sec. 11; P. O. Ionia; dem; Ind; 102 acres, value $5,000; Engl'd.

Frantz H. N. farmer; Sec. 17; P. O. Alexis; dem; Ind; from Ohio.

French Jno Y. farmer; Sec. 2; P. O. Ionia; rep; Adv; 80 acres, val $4,000; from Penn

FRYMIRE GEO. H. Farmer; Sec. 36; P. O. Galesburg; born in Monmouth, Warren Co., Ill., Oct. 4, 1840; Dem; Christian; has 200 acres, value $10,000; holds the office of School Director; wife was Miss Amanda J. Gardner, born in Kelly tp., Sept. 9, 1842; married May 15, 1862; six children, Susie, born March 3, 1863, Minnie, Feb. 11, 1865, Ira, Feb. 10, 1867, George, Jan. 18, 1869, Dell, Feb. 28, 1872, Altia, Feb. 12, 1874.

GENTRY E. H., Sen. farmer; Sec. 12; P. O. Ionia; rep; Ind; 107 acres, val. $5,350.

Gentry E. H., Jr. lives with his father; dem; Ind; born Illinois.

GILMORE B. F. Farmer and Stock Raiser; Sec. 3; P. O. Alexis; born in Spring Grove, Warren Co., Ill., March 22, 1837; Dem; Ind; 152 acres, value $9,000; wife was Miss Charlotte Yard, born in Somersetshire, England, March 16, 1843; married Nov. 15, 1860; she came from England to Ohio in 1844, lived there three years, and has lived here since 1847.

Glass Calvin, farmer; Sec. 12; P. O. Ionia; rep; Christian; 90 acres, value $3,600.

Glass Marshall, works the farm of his grandfather; P. O. Ionia; rep; Adv; born Ill.

Glass Seymour, farmer; Sec. 12; P. O. Ionia; rep; Christian; 150 acres, val. $6,000; Ohio.

Graham Wm. retired; Sec. 25; P. O. Utah; rep; Univ; 40 acres, val. $1,600; born Ky.

Graham Wm. D. farmer; Sec. 23; P. O. Utah; rep; Ind; 10 acres, value $500; Ky.

Gregory, Mrs. Anna; Sec. 29; P. O. Utah; Adv; 160 acres, value $6,400; from Penn.

Gregory Asa M. farmer; Sec. 20; P. O. Ionia; ind; Adv; 150 acres, value $6,000; Penn.

Gregory D. C. renter; Sec. 14; P. O. Utah; dem; Adv; born Illinois.

Gregory Davis, lives with his mother; Sec. 29; dem; Adv; born Illinois.

Gregory M. C. farmer; Sec. 20; P. O. Utah; dem; Adv; 120 acres, value $4,800; Penn.

Gregory Porter, lives with his mother; Sec. 29; P. O. Utah; dem; Adv; born Ill.

Gregory Stephen, renter; Sec. 10; P. O. Ionia; dem; Adv; born Illinois.

Gregory Warren, lives with his mother; dem; Adv; born Illinois.

HALL J. M. farmer; Sec. 1; P. O. North Henderson; dem; Ind; from Ohio.

Hall, Mrs. Fansel M.; Sec. 1; ind; 80 acres, value $4,000; born Knox Co., Ill.

Hammond David; Sec. 2; P. O. N. Henderson; rep; U. B.; from Pennsylvania.

Hammond Stephen; Sec. 2; P. O. N. Henderson; dem; U. B.; 80 acres, value $3,600.

Hammond Wm.; P. O. North Henderson; dem; U. B.; from Pennsylvania.

Harshbarger A. lives with J. Vestal; P. O. Ionia; dem; U. B.; born Illinois.

Hawkins J. D. rents of Peace; P. O. Utah; dem; Ind; from Kentucky.

Hayner H. C. farmer; Sec. 24; P. O. Galesburg; rep; Ind; born Illinois.

Hanbrow Richard, farmer; Sec. 3; dem; Ind; 90 acres, value $5,000; from England.

Hibbard H. S. lives with his father; dem; ind; born Illinois.

HIBBARD L. C. Farmer; Sec. 16; P. O. Ionia; born in Erie Co., N. Y., May 20, 1816; came to this Co. in 1840; Dem; Adv; 260 acres, value $13,000; held the office of Postmaster for eight years, and School Director twenty years; wife was Miss Esther Presson, born in Brattleboro, Vt., April 20, 1825; married Feb. 26, 1848; eight children, four boys and two girls living.

Hibbard S. L. lives with his father; dem; ind.

Hicks Thos. B. farmer and minister; Sec. 35; P. O. Utah; dem; Adv; born Illinois.

Hodkiss John, renter; Sec. 25; P. O. Utah; rep; Ind.

HOGAN JOHN R. Sec. 19; P. O. Galesburg; was born in Warren Co., Ill., Oct. 30, 1842; married Eliza Jackson, Feb. 6, 1870; she was born in Westmoreland, Penn., Sept. 2, 1843; they came to this Co. in 1836, and live here about twenty years, and in Knox Co. about fifteen years.

HOGAN H. N. Postmaster Utah; born in Harrison Co., Ind., Dec. 20, 1827; came to this Co. Oct. 1836; Rep; Univ; owns 85 acres, value $4,675; wife's name was Ida A. Thompson, born in Clermont Co., Ohio, Dec. 31, 1841; married Jan. 30, 1862; had eight children, four boys and three girls living; holds offices of Township Clerk and School Director.

HOGAN W. C. Saw Mill; Sec. 19; Henderson tp, Knox Co.; P. O. Galesburg; born in Harrison Co., Indiana, Sept. 17, 1817; Dem; Univ; 40 acres, value $1,200; wife was Martha A. Gormely, born in Ind., March 3, 1819; married Dec. 27, 1841; five children, one boy and two girls living.

House C. B. retired farmer; Shanghai; two houses and six lots, value $500; rep; Ind.

HULSE WM. O. Farmer; Sec. 36; P. O Galesburg; born in Orange Co., Blooming Grove, N. Y., March 16, 1830; came to Ontario, Knox Co., Ill., in 1855, and to this Co. in 1865; Rep; Pres; 200 acres, value $10,000; wife was Harriet Sayre, who was born in Orange Co., N. Y., Nov. 9, 1831; married Dec. 14, 1854; four children, one boy and three girls.

Humphrey Charles, rents C. Pine's farm; P. O. Ionia; dem; Ind; from Pennsylvania.

Humphrey Ira, laborer; Shanghai; dem; Ind; from Pennsylvania.

JUSTICE ST. GEORGE, lives with his father; rep; Ind; from New York.

Jackson Wm. A. farmer; Sec. 1; P. O. North Henderson; dem; Ind; born Illinois.

JACKSON HARRISON, Farmer; Sec. 1; P. O. North Henderson; born in Wayne Co., Indiana, Sept. 27, 1820, and came to this Co. in 1849; Dem; Ind; 139 acres, value $6,950; is School Director; wife was Roxia J. Holcomb, born in Gallipolis, Ohio, Feb. 9, 1821; married Oct. 29, 1840; children are Lucinda, born Aug. 6, 1841; Zephaniah A., Dec. 12, 1842; Nancy M., Jan. 18, 1844, died Feb. 8, 1846; John C., March 18, 1845; William A., November 1, 1846; James R., July 16, 1849; Sarah J., Nov. 22, 1850; Irena E., May 22, 1852; Amond C., July 7th, 1855; Charles H. C., May 29, 1857; Susan M., May 21, 1859. He came to Knox Co. in 1843.

Johnston A. M. rents of B. H. Gardner; Sec. 30; P. O. Gerlaw; Ind; Christian; from Pa.

Johnston Charles A. Sec. 5; P. O. Alexis; rep; Ind; from Sweden.

Johnston F. E. farmer; Sec. 13; P. O. Galesburg; 30 acres, value $1,000; rep; Luth.

Johnston J. P. renter; Sec. 5; P. O. Alexis; rep; Ind; from Sweden.

Johnston R. E. rents of W. J. Miller; Sec. 30; P. O. Gerlaw; dem; Christian.

Jones James, farmer; Sec. 3; P. O. Ionia; 80 acres, value $4,000; dem; Adv; Eng.

Jones J. A. l. farmer; Sec. 6; P. O. Alexis; 160 acres, value $8,000; dem; U. B.

KELLOGG O. N. farmer; Sec. 24; P. O. Utah; 160 acres, value $6,400; rep.

Kelley Harvey, rents of J. Pittard; rep; Ind; from Ohio.

Kelly Milton, renter, rents of J. Pittard; P. O. Utah; rep; M. E.; from Ohio.

Kelly Mrs. Phœbe, Sec. 32; P. O. Utah; 160 acres, value $8,000; dem; M. E.

LARSON S. L. farmer; Sec. 13; P. O. Galesburg; 15 acres; rep; Luth.

Lair W. M. lives with his mother; dem; Ind; born Illinois.

LAIR MRS. SARAH. Sec. 30; P. O. Gerlaw; born in Warren Co., Ky., May 8, 1809, and came to this Co. in 1833; dem; Christian; 192 acres, value $8,000; her husband, Wm. Lair, was born in Kentucky April 9, 1799; married Feb. 1, 1829; died April 7, 1872; nine children, three boys and five girls living.

LAIR T. A. Farmer; Sec. 31; P. O. Gerlaw; born in Warren Co., Ky., May 31, 1831, came to this Co. in 1832, lived in Spring Grove five years, and here since; Ind; Christian; 140 acres, value $7,000; School Director; wife was Miss Margaret Pedigo, born in Kentucky, April 28, 1848; married Jan. 15, 1867.

Landon J. H. farmer; P. O. Utah; 160 acres, value $6,400; rep; Ind; from N. Y.

LANDON J. H. Farmer; Sec. 35; P. O. Utah; born in New York, Feb. 26, 1839, and came to this Co. in 1844; Rep; Ind; 160 acres, value $6,400; wife was Miss Margaret E. Clute, born in N. Y., Sept. 8, 1839; married July 3, 1860; he enlisted Feb. 7, 1865, in the 14th Regt. Co. H I. V. I., was left at Newburn, N. C., for a time, on account of small pox; the Regiment travelled about 7,000 miles, 1,500 on foot; he rejoined it at Washington; was discharged Sept. 16, 1865; children are James T., born April 30, 1861; Charles E., April 25, 1863; William, October 28, 1865; Edgar, November 3, 1867; Millie, March 12, 1870; Llewella, July 19, 1874; his mother, who lives with him, was born in New Hampshire, Oct. 27, 1812; School Director.

Lee John, rents Widow Miller's farm; Sec. 19; P. O. Alexis; dem; Cath; from Ireland.

Lewey Alfred, farmer; Sec. 25; P. O. Galesburg; 119 acres, value $7,795; rep; Ind.

Line Mrs. M. Sec. 17; P. O. Alexis; ⅓ estate of 100 acres; U. B.; from Pennsylvania.

Line Zach. farmer; Sec. 17; P. O. Alexis; owns undivided ⅔ of 100 acres; dem; Ind.

Lyddon Charles, rents C. Bellinger's farm; P. O. Ionia; dem; Ind; born Illinois.

Lyddon George, lives with his mother; Sec. 12; P. O. Ionia; dem; Ind; born Illinois.

Lyddon Mrs. Hannah, Sec. 11; P. O. Ionia; 160 acres, value $7,500; Ind; from Eng.

Lyddon Henry, farmer; Sec. 4; P. O. Ionia; 80 acres, value $4,000; dem; Ind; born Ill.

Lyddon John, Sec. 2; P. O. N. Henderson; 115 acres, value $5,700; dem; M. E.

McDAVID JAMES, laborer; Sec. 26; P.O. Galesburg; rep; Ind; born Illinois.

McGLOTHLIN MRS. ELIZABETH, Sec. 4; P. O. Alexis; Pres; 57 acres, value, $2,850; she was born in Breckenridge Co., Ky., Aug. 8, 1819, and came to this Co. in Oct. 1847; she first married, March 6, 1844, Samuel Squiers, who was born in Kentucky in April, 1814, and died Nov. 20, 1842; her second husband was James McGlothlin, born in Madison Co., Ky., Jan. 21, 1814, and was killed by lightning July 30, 1872; married March 6, 1844; children are Thomas R. Squiers, born in Kentucky April 28, 1837; Albert H., June 26, 1840; John McGlothlin, January 26, 1845, died May 28, 1848; Louisa J., Feb. 7, 1848.

Magrath Henry, farmer; Sec. 28; P. O. Utah; 8 acres, value $400; dem; Cath.

Mahoney Patrick, farmer; Sec. 19; P. O. Alexis; 150 acres, value $6,400; dem; Cath.

Miles Daniel S.; P. O. Ionia; rep; Univ; born Illinois.

Miles E. C. farmer; Sec. 14; P. O. Ionia; rep; Univ; born Illinois.

MILES JNO. M. Farmer; Sec. 13; P.O Galesburg; born in Sangamon Co., Ill., April 13, 1842, and came to this Co. in 1847; Rep; Ind; 61 acres, value $2,085; wife was Miss Margaret E. Hogan, born in Kelly Co., Dec. 23, 1844; married April 11, 1867; three children, one boy living; enlisted Aug. 7, 1862, in the 102nd Regt. Co. B, I. V. I., Capt. Atchison, 20th Army Corps under Sherman; was stationed at Gallatin, Tenn.; discharged for disability June 15, 1863; re-enlisted Feb. 10, 1864, in the 57th Regt. Co. E. I. Veterans, again under Sherman; was in the battles of Atlanta, Resaca, Altoona, Savannah and Bentonville; discharged at the close of the war, July 7, 1865.

Miles Joseph W. farmer; Sec. 14; P. O. Ionia; rep; Univ; born Illinois.

Miller John, farmer; Sec. 19; P. O. Ionia; 120 acres, value $6,000; dem; Ind; born Ill.

MILLER J. A. Farmer; Sec. 1; P. O. Ionia; born in Kelly, Warren Co., Ill., Aug. 1, 1843; Dem; Ind; 120 acres, value $6,000; Roadmaster; wife was Miss Mary E. Gregg, born in Knox Co., Ill., March 18, 1844; married Sept. 29, 1870; Maud, born Sept. 20, 1871; he enlisted Aug. 6, 1862, in 102nd Regt., Co. A, I. V. I., under Brig. Gen. E. A. Ward, afterward under Gen. Payne; was stationed at Gallatin, Tenn., doing garrison duty; was taken sick shortly after enlisting; was detailed as orderly to the Adj. of the Regt.; was discharged on account of continued illness, Jan. 18, 1863.

Miller Louis, lives with widow Miller; dem; Ind; born Kentucky.

Mitchell John, farmer; Sec. 13; P. O. Ionia; 80 acres, value $3,200; dem; Ind; from Ky.

Moneymaker Wm. renter; Sec. 4; P. O. Ionia; dem; Ind; from Virginia.

Moore Jesse, farmer; Sec. 23; P. O. Utah; 20 acres, value $1,000; dem; Ind; from Ky.

Moylen Jno. farmer; Sec. 35; P. O. Utah; 90 acres, value $4,500; dem; Cath.

Moylen Wm. lives with his father; dem; Cath; from New York.

NELSON A. J. laborer; Sec. 13; P. O. Galesburg; house and three acres; rep.

Nelson Newton, farmer; Sec. 32; P. O. Gerlaw; 40 acres, value $800; rep; Ind.

OLEN JOHN, farmer, Sec. 22; P.O.Galesburg; 20 acres, value $600. rep.

PITTARD JAMES, farmer; Sec. 8; 105 acres, value $5,250; rep; M. E.; Eng.

PITTARD A. J. Farmer; Sec. 17; P. O. Alexis; born in Warren Co., Ill., April 10, 1852; Rep; Univ; Personal Property, $1,000; wife was Miss Alma E. Chapin, born in Knox Co., Ill., April 13, 1853; married Nov. 27, 1873; she lived in Mo. about four years, between the age of five and nine; they have one child, George Leroy, born Sept. 24, 1874.

PINE CHARLES, Farmer; Sec. 10; P. O. Ionia; born in Somersetshire, Eng., Sept. 2, 1832; Dem; Ind; 283 acres, value $15,905; holds the offices of Highway Commissioner and School Director; his wife was Miss Jessie C. Yarde, born in Somersetshire, Eng., July 9, 1837; married March 19, 1857; he came to Ohio in 1840, and to this Co. in 1844; she came to Ohio in 1844, and to this Co. in 1847; nine children, five boys and one girl living.

Pratt Chas. renter; Sec. 6; P. O. Alexis; dem; Ind; from Indiana.

Price Jacob, farmer; Sec. 15; P. O. Ionia; 190 acres, value $6,000; rep; U. B.

PRICE HENRY. Farmer; Sec. 15; P. O. Ionia; born in Fayette Co., West Virginia, Feb. 15, 1838, and came to this Co. in 1853; Rep; Ind; 130 acres, value $5,500; his wife was Mrs. Mary Hunt, born in Somersetshire, Eng., May 5, 1840; she was married to her first husband, Alfred Hunt, May 23, 1858; he died April 11, 1874; by whom she had five children,Wm. H.,born March 3, 1859; Alfred G., Aug. 10, 1864; Albert, Jan. 19, 1867; James W., July 4, 1869; Charles, Dec. 27, 1871; to her second husband March 11, 1875; one child, born Dec. 11, 1876.

Price Stuart A., farmer; Sec. 15; P. O. Ionia; 140 acres, value $5,800; rep; Ind.

Pruitt Alfred, farmer, lives with his father; rep; Ind; born Illinois.

PRUITT WILLIS, Farmer; Sec. 25; P. O. Galesburg; born in Henderson Co., Ky., Aug. 31, 1840, and came to this Co. in 1848; Rep; Ind; 80 acres, value $4,000; wife was Miss Jane Moredock, born in Breckenridge Co., Ky., Dec. 24, 1812; married Nov. 19, 1832; nine children, James H., born March 12, 1834, died in Aug. 1848; Mary A., July 1840, died Aug. 3, 1863; Wm. D., Aug. 7, 1843; Chas. N., Feb. 12, 1846, died Oct. 4, 1875; Lucy A., Oct. 15, 1848; Abbie, July 11, 1850; Alfred G., May 16, 1853; Jennie, Jan. 12, 1856; grandson Geo. W. Beswick, Dec. 1, 1862; Wm. D. and Chas. N. enlisted, the first in 1861, the second in 1863, in the 57th Regt. I. V. I.; were with Sherman in his march to the sea, and were in the battles of Corinth, Pittsburgh Landing, Atlanta and Resaca; were mustered out at the close of the war at Louisville, Ky.

Prushafer Fritz, farmer; Sec. 29; 80 acres, value $4,000; rep; Luth; from Germany.

REED JAMES, painter, Shanghai; house and lot; dem; Ind; from Indiana.

Reed Jno. W., lives with James Reed; P. O. Ionia; dem; Ind; from Indiana.

REES M. S. Farmer; Sec. 32; P. O. Gerlaw; born in Kelly tp, Nov. 18, 1838; ind; Ind; 205 acres, value $10,250; Highway Commissioner; wife was Miss Margaret Low, born in Spring Grove, Aug. 31, 1844; married Jan. 16, 1868; three girls; enlisted Aug. 7, 1862, in the 102nd Regt. Co. B, I. V. I., Capt. Atchison 20th Army Corps, first under Dumont, afterward Rosecrans, and finally Sherman; was stationed at Gallatin on garrison duty, with headquarters at Leverne; was at the battles of Resaca, Cassville, New Hope Church, Peach Tree Creek, and at Kenesaw Mt., where they were under fire eighteen days; was with him in his raid through Georgia, and to Washington on foot; discharged June 6, 1865.

Reese Michael, shoemaker and carpenter; P. O. Ionia; rep; New Light; from Penn.

Reese M. D. rents Hayner's farm; Sec. 24; P. O. Ionia; rep; Ind; from Penn.

Reese Stephen, merchant and P. M ; Shanghai; rep; Adv; from Ind.

Rhodes Henry, renter; Sec. 4; P. O. Alexis; dem; Ind; from Kentucky.

Richardson Daniel, farmer; Sec. 6; P. O. Alexis; 66 acres, value, $4,290; rep; U. B.

RICHARDSON HENRY. Farmer; Sec. 6; P. O. Ionia; born in Kentucky, Oct. 21, 1816, and came to this Co. in 1853; Rep; Adventist; 140 acres, value $8,600; wife was Elizabeth Richards, born in Harrison Co., Ind., Oct. 25, 1825; married May 6, 1841; children, Mary J., born Feb. 22, 1842, died Feb. 1, 1844; Eliza, Sept. 12, 1843; Rachel L., July 26, 1845; Wm. S., Oct. 10, 1847; Jacob C. C., Aug. 25, 1849, died July 18, 1850; Sarah C., Oct. 26, 1851; Elizabeth A., Feb. 17, 1854; Henry M., Feb. 5, 1856, died April 9, 1856;

Harmoniah, March 5, 1857, died Sept. 22, 1862; Martha J., Oct. 16, 1859; Harvey G., Feb. 25, 1862, died Oct. 17, 1864; Pliny E., Dec. 13, 1864; Arthur B., Sept. 3, 1867.

Richardson James, farmer; Sec. 16; P. O. Ionia; rep; Adv; born Illinois.

Richardson John, teamster; Sec. 26; P. O. Utah; dem; Ind; from New York.

Richardson Wm. renter; Sec. 16; P. O. Ionia; rep; Adv; from Indiana.

Robison Clark, lives with J. Robinson; rep; Ind; born Illinois.

Robison Garret, farmer; Sec. 31; P. O. Gerlaw; dem; Ind; 169 acres, val. $8,450.

Robison John, farmer; Sec. 31; P. O. Gerlaw; rep; Univ; 185 acres, value $10,175.

Routh David E. laborer; Sec. 3; P. O. Ionia; rep; Ind; born Illinois.

Routh D. S. farmer; Sec. 16; P. O. Ionia; rep; M. E.; 100 acres, value $6,500.

Routh Joseph, lives with widow Amy; Sec. 9; P. O. Ionia; rep; Meth; from Indiana.

ROUTH, MRS. S. A. Sec 3; P. O. Ionia; born in Harrison Co. Ind., June 15, 1827; came to this Co. in 1851; U. B.; owns 76 acres, value $3,800; nine children, three boys and two girls living; Mrs. Routh is the relict of J. C. Routh, who was born in Knox Co., Tenn., April 13, 1825; he enlisted in the 102nd Reg., Co. A, I. V. I., Aug. 6, 1862, under Brig. Gen. Ward; the regiment formed part of the brigade commanded by Gen. Dumont; they were first engaged in pursuit of Bragg, were afterwards stationed at Gallatin, Tenn., as guards over the railroads; was with Sherman in his march to the sea, and at the battle near Resaca; discharged on account of ill health, in Oct., 1864, died Nov. 17, 1864.

Rucker Ambrose, lives with J. Rucker; rep; Adv; from Virginia.

Rucker John, farmer; Sec. 16; P. O. Ionia; ind; Adv; 191 acres, val. $9,750; from Ind.

Ryner James, lives with his father; rep; Ind; born Illinois.

Ryner Spencer, farmer; Sec. 6; P. O. Ionia; rep; Adv; 120 acres, value $6,000; Penn.

Ryner Wm. rents his father's farm; rep; Ind; born Illinois.

Rynehart G. W. laborer; P. O. Utah; rep; Adv; 2½ acres, value $100.

ST. GEORGE JAMES, lives with his father; rep; Ind; from New York.

St. George Robt. renter; Sec. 21; P. O. Utah; rep; Ind; from New York.

SALLEE PHILIP M. Farmer; Sec. 33; P. O. Galesburg; born in Buckingham Co., Va., March 15, 1832; came to this Co. in 1837; Ind; Christian; 175 acres, value $9,000; wife was Miss Paxadine Wallace, born in Cold Brook tp., July 18, 1842; married July 25, 1869; two children, Emma L., born April 16, 1871, and Maggie Frances, Nov. 26, 1876.

Smith Abijah; Sec. 23; P. O. Utah; rep; Ind; from New York.

SMITH ALBERT, Farmer; Sec. 12; P. O. Ionia; born in Sweden, Nov. 5, 1844; came to this Co. in 1853; Rep; Adv; 107 acres, value $6,000; wife was Miss Alice Law, born in Pike Co., Ill., Sept. 20, 1846; married Oct. 1, 1867; four children, one boy, three girls; he enlisted in May, 1864, in the 139th Reg. I. V. I., for 100 days; re-enlisted in the 102nd Reg., Co. B, Capt. Armstrong, 20th Army Corps, under Thomas, afterwards Sherman; was at Chattanooga, Raleigh, and at the battle at Nashville; discharged June 6, 1865.

Smith George, lives with his father; Sec. 23; P. O. Utah; rep; Ind; born Illinois.

Smith Jonas, farmer; Sec. 26; P. O. Utah; rep; Adv; 185 acres, val. $11,100; Indiana.

Smith Lester, lives with Abijah Smith; rep; Ind.

Stacy Mrs. Harriet; Sec. 8; P. O. Alexis; Ind; 140 acres, value $7,000; from England.

Stegall Geo. A. farmer; Sec. 13; P. O. Ionia; rep; Ind; born Galesburg.

Stegall Mrs. Mary; Sec. 13; P. O. Ionia; rep; Adv; 125 acres, value $5,000; Ohio.

Stephens Ammon, works for R. H. Adcock; rep; Ind; from New York.

Stephens Wilson, works for R. H. Adcock; rep; Ind; from New York.

Stephens Henry, engineer; Sec. 22; P. O. Utah; rep; from New York.

Stewart D. B. farmer; Sec. 6; P. O. Alexis; dem; Ind; 151 acres, value $11,325; Penn.

Stodgell James, farmer; Sec. 17; dem; Adv; 279 acres, value $8,370; from England.

Stots Robert, laborer; Sec. 34; P. O Utah; dem; Ind; from Iowa.

Strode Julius, rents of his father; P. O. Ionia; rep; Adv; born Illinois.

Strode W. W. farmer; Sec. 16; P. O. Ionia; rep; Adv; 160 acres, value $8,000; Ky.

STRODE WM. Jr. Farmer; Sec. 13; P. O. Galesburg; born in Kelly tp., Sept. 24, 1849; Rep; Ind; 160 acres, value $4,000; School Director; wife was Miss Angeline M. Wilsey, born in Indiana, Sept. 7, 1857; married Oct. 12, 1873; one child, James L., born Aug. 21, 1874; Jno. Strode was born in Kelly tp., Dec. 21, 1853; wife was Mattie E. Waddel, born in Minnesota, June 3, 1858; married Dec. 18, 1876; no children.

Swanson E. D. farmer; Sec. 12; P. O. Ionia; rep; Luth; 92 acres, $4,500; from Sweden.

Swanson Nels, renter; Sec. 18; P. O. Alexis; rep; from Sweden.

TALBOT GEORGE, farmer; Sec. 17; P. Alexis; rep; M. E.; 190 acres, $12,000.

Terpening David, Sec. 28; P. O. Utah; rep; Ind; 107 acres, value $5,000; from N. Y.

TERPENING CHAS. Farmer; Sec. 35; P. O. Utah; born in Kelly tp., Jan. 31, 1848; Rep; Ind; 40 acres, value $3,000; wife was Mary Armstrong, born in Fermanaugh Co., Ireland, May 4, 1853; married Dec. 10, 1873; one child, Oliver W., born Sept. 27, 1874.

Terpening Geo. farmer; Sec. 28; P. O. Utah; rep; Ind; 106 acres, val. $5,300; from N. Y.

TERPENING J. P. Farmer; Sec. 34; P. O. Utah; born in Clifton Park, Saratoga Co., N. Y., April 12, 1811; came to this Co. March 9, 1836; Rep; M. E.; 320 acres, value $16,000; held the office of Justice of the Peace; wife was Miss Mindwell Smith, born in Clifton Park, Saratoga Co., N. Y., April 2, 1813; married Sept 24, 1835; eight children, six boys and two girls; three of his sons, Harry, Nathan and Wesley, were in the army during the war.

Terpening N. A. farmer; Sec. 34; P. O. Utah; rep; M. E.; born Illinois.

Terpening Samuel, farmer; Sec. 33; P. O. Utah; rep; M. E.; 96 acres, value $4,800.

Thomas Abel, farmer; Sec. 35; P. O. Utah; rep; M. E.; 102 acres, value $4,590; Penn.

Thomas Frank F. attending school at Abington; P. O. Utah. rep; M. E.; born Ill.

Thomas Henry, lives with his father; P. O. Utah; rep; Ind; born Illinois.

Townsend Alex. renter; Sec. 35; P. O. Utah; rep; Ind; house and lot, val. $300; Ind.

Townsend Chas. lives with his father; P. O. Utah; rep; Ind; born Illinois.

VENN CHARLES farmer; Sec. 4; P. O. Ionia; dem; Ind; 127 acres, val. $5,080.

Vestal Alvan, laborer, works for Mr. Franklin; P. O. Ionia; rep; Ind; born Illinois.

VESTAL JOHN, Farmer; Sec. 12; P. O. Ionia; born in Ohio, March 16, 1827; came to this Co. in 1837; Dem; Ind; 70 acres, value $3,000; wife was Miss Lucinda Haishbarger, born in Indiana, March 26, 1831; married Sept. 22, 1851; they first moved to Rock River, but came here shortly after, and have lived here since; three children, Ann, born Aug. 13, 1852, John M., Dec. 15, 1855, and William, Oct. 3, 1860.

WALLACE JNO. D. farmer; Sec. 31; P. O. Gerlaw; dem; Ind; 80 acres, $4,000.

Wallace W. J. T. farmer; Sec. 32; P. O. Gerlaw; dem; Ind; 100 acres, val. $6,000; Ky.

WALLACE WM. C. Farmer; Sec. 33; P. O. Utah; born in Kelly tp., Ill., Oct. 18, 1843; Dem; Christian; 96 acres, value $4,500; wife was Miss Sarah A. Townsend, born in Putnam Co., N. Y., Jan. 26, 1845; married Dec. 19, 1867; three children.

Waight Thos. S. painter; P. O. Ionia; Ind; owns house and lot; from England.

WAIGHT W. F. Physician and Surgeon, Shanghai; P. O. Ionia; born in Wiltshire, England, Jan. 21, 1842; came to this Co. in 1870; Dem; Adv; owns house and lot, value $500; wife was Elizabeth J. House, born in Somersetshire, Eng., March 4, 1845; married March 13, 1867; five children, Beatrice, born May 30, 1868, Annie, Sept. 20, 1869; Frederick J., Nov. 8, 1871, Edith R., Oct. 25, 1873, Mary Ellen, Oct. 21, 1875.

Warner A. H. rents of Pearce; Sec. 20; P. O. Utah; dem; Ind; from Kentucky.

Watson James, laborer, Shanghai; P. O. Ionia; rep; Adv.

Weimer Jacob, farmer; Sec. 16; P. O. Ionia; rep; Ind; from Pennsylvania.

Williams Chester, rents; Sec. 11; P. O. Ionia; dem; Ind; from Indiana.

Williams Jno. farmer; Sec. 23; P. O. Galesburg; rep; Ind; 65 acres, val.$1,950; Wales.

WIXON BRADNER. Farmer; Sec. 18; P. O. Alexis; born in Dutchess Co., N. Y., July 18, 1817; come to this Co. in May, 1840; Rep; Bapt; 400 acres, value $20,000; first wife was Eliza Ann Miller, born in Kentucky, Oct. 19, 1823, died Feb. 24, 1865; second wife, was Mrs. Emeline Clark, born in Massachusetts, Aug. 9, 1827; married Nov. 14, 1867; children are Matilda, born Sept. 16, 1846, died Nov. 27, 1850; Wm. J., July 21, 1851, died April 14, 1862; Harrison, July 28, 1858, died May 8, 1866; John Seward, Feb. 29, 1843, enlisted in 4th Regt., Co. II, Iowa I. V. I, was with Sherman to the sea, died in camp on the route to Savannah, Dec. 3, 1864; Alice M., Aug. 27, 1849; Louisa, March 14, 1853; James E., Sept. 8, 1860; Mary E., Feb. 6, 1863; Franklin E., Jan. 14, 1865; Bradner E., May 4, 1865.

Wixon Edmond, lives with B. Wixon; P. O. Ionia; dem; Ind; born Ill.

Wixon L. W. farmer, lives with his father. Rep; Ind.

YARD ALBERT, Farmer; Sec. 10; P. O. Ionia; born in Somersetshire, Eng., Jan. 3, 1841; came to this Co. in 1847; Dem. to the backbone; Adv; 165 acres, value $1,650; School Director; wife was Miss Elizabeth Lyddon, born in New York, in Sept. 1842; married Sept., 1866; four children, two boys and two girls.

BUSINESS DIRECTORY OF KELLY TOWNSHIP.

Gilmore B. F. Breeder of Thoroughbred Poland China Swine; Sec. 3; P. O. Alexis.

Bunker Nathan, Prop. of the celebrated English Stallion, "Robin Hood," "the Wonderful Lad."

SHANGHAI.

Waight W. F., M. D. Physician, Surgeon and Accoucher.

LENOX TOWNSHIP.

AMEY CHAS. farmer; P. O. Lenox; rep; Lib.

Amey James, farmer; P. O. Lenox, rep; M. E.

AMEY JOSEPH, Farmer; Sec. 28; P. O. Lenox; born in England, May 20, 1820; came to this Co. in 1844; Rep; Meth; owns 283 acres, value $20,000; married to Miss Elizabeth Clark, July 5, 1842; eleven children; had two sons in the army under Generals Curtis and Harding; Ames, the oldest, took part in the battle at Vicksburg; Henry, the youngest, took part in the battle of Ft. Donelson.

Anderson Ben. farmer; Sec. 31; P. O. Lenox; ind; Luth; from Sweden.

Arthers Saml. farmer; P. O. Monmouth; dem.

BAKER J. H. farmer; Sec. 36; dem; Lib; from Virginia.

Barber J. W. farmer; Sec. 30; P. O. Lenox; rep; Meth; 85 acres, value $5,900; Ohio.

BALL JACOB, Farmer; Sec. 23; P. O. Berwick; born in Canada, Sept. 28, 1852; came to this Co. in 1869; Dem; Lib; rents 120 acres, value $7,000; was married to Miss Julia Ann Vantasell, Jan. 16, 1876.

Bates Moses, farmer; P. O. Lenox; dem.

BECKENCAMP FRED, Farmer; Sec. 15; P. O. Monmouth; born in St. Louis, Mo., Jan. 1, 1847; came to this Co. in 1848; Rep; Luth; was married to Miss Mary Miller, 1873; have two children, Henry and Ira.

Boals J. W. farmer; Sec. 11; P. O. Monmouth; dem; Lib; from Pennsylvania.

Boggs Jeff. farmer; Sec. 31; rep; Meth; 80 acres, value $4,000.

Bohlander Peter, farmer; Sec. 16; dem; Cath; 110 acres, value $6,600; Germany.

BOND J. W. Farmer; Sec. 18; P. O. Lenox; born in Ala., Sept. 7, 1825; came to this Co. in 1833; Dem; Lib; owns 120 acres, value $7,000; is Superintendent of Warren County Poor Farm.

Bowles I. I. farmer; Sec. 5; P. O. Monmouth; dem; Lib; 114 acres, val. $7,000; Missouri.

Brannon Thos. farmer; P. O. Lenox; dem; Cath.

BRIDENTHAL J. W. Farmer; Sec. 31; P. O. Lenox; born in Pennsylvania, April 28, 1836; came to this Co. in 1860; Dem; Chris; 605 acres, value $36,000.

Brideson Jas. farmer; Sec. 22; P. O. Lenox; rep; Meth.

Brown M. W. farmer; Sec. 12; P. O. Monmouth; rep; Meth.

Brown Nat. farmer; P. O. Lenox; ind; Meth.

Bryant David, farmer; P. O. Monmouth; rep; Lib.

Burns James, farmer; Sec. 9; dem; Cath; from Ireland.

Butler J. farmer; P.O. Monmouth; dem; Lib.

Butler Polk, farmer; Sec. 32; dem; Lib; 120 acres, value $6,600; from Indiana.

CANNELL EDWARD, farmer; Sec. 28; ind; Lib; 100 acres, val. $6,300; Eng.

Cain Robt. farmer; Sec. 27; P. O. Monmouth; rep; Meth.

CAIN EDWARD, Farmer; Sec. 22; P. O. Lenox; born in Isle of Man, Sept. 4, 1842; came to this Co. in 1861; Rep; M. E; 240 acres, value $14,000; was married to Miss Sarah Jane Gaunt, March 4, 1869; have three children, Anna Jane, Ada Mary, and Oscar Edward.

Capps Asa, farmer; Sec. 27; P. O. Monmouth; dem; 350 acres, value $18,000.

CAPPS T. L. Farmer; Sec. 25; P. O. Monmouth; born in Illinois, June 6, 1843; came to this Co. in 1843; Dem; Bapt; 160 acres, value $9,600; was married to Miss Mary Jewell, Sept. 16, 1866; have three children, daughters.

Capps W. H. farmer; P. O. Monmouth; dem; Bapt.

CHAPMAN JOHN T. Farmer; Sec. 23; P. O. Monmouth; born in Barren Co., Ky., March 13, 1845; came to this Co. in 1857; Dem; Bapt; was married to Miss Laura Jane Ray, Jan. 10, 1875; have one child, George Robert.

Charles Abner, farmer; Sec. 14; P. O. Monmouth; dem; Lib.

Charles Wm. farmer; P. O. Lenox; dem.

COOK JOHN G. Farmer; Sec. 21; P. O. Monmouth; born in Germany, March 22, 1835; came to this Co. in 1856; Rep; U. B; 70 acres, value $4,000; was married to Miss Harriet Jewell in 1858.

Conant A. M. farmer; P. O. Monmouth; dem.

Conant Geo. farmer; P. O. Monmouth; dem.

Cowan R. R. farmer; P. O. Monmouth; rep.

Cowick Jno. farmer; Sec. 34; P. O. Lenox; rep; Lib; 165 acres, value $9,900; Penn.

CRANDALL EMERY, Farmer; Sec. 33; P. O. Lenox; born in Erie Co., Penn., Aug. 8, 1844; came to this Co. in 1860; Rep; Meth; 120 acres, value $8,500; was in 83d Regt. I. V. I., Co. C; was married to Miss Kate Williams, Nov., 1866; have four children.

Crapsey I. F. station agent; rep; Lib; N. Y.

Cunningham Jas. farmer; P. O. Monmouth; rep; Lib.

Currey John, farmer; Sec. 7; P. O. Monmouth; dem; lib; 110 acres, value $5,500.

D AY PHILIP, farmer; P. O. Lenox; dem; Lib; born Illinois.

Dickson J. M. farmer; P. O. Lenox; rep; Presb; 40 acres, value $5,000.

DEWEY I. B. Farmer; Sec. 14; P. O. Monmouth; born in New York, Oct. 12, 1837; came to this Co. in 1869; Rep; Lib; 80 acres, value $5,200; was married to Miss Mary Jane Spong, Feb. 17, 1859; have four children, Deloria, Minnie, Mollie and Emma.

Dunkle David, farmer; P. O. Monmouth; dem; Presb; from Pennsylvania.

DUNN ROBERT, Farmer; Sec. 32; P. O. Lenox; born in Erie Co., Penn., June 4, 1807; Ind; Lib; 160 acres, value, $9,600; came to this Co. Oct. 17, 1857; married Miss Julia Ann Brown, March 7, 1837.

E ATON W. H. farmer; Sec. 29; P. O. Lenox; dem; Lib.

Efaw Wm. farmer; Sec. 20; P. O. Monmouth; rep; U. B; from Ohio.

Ellinger Wm. farmer; Sec. 8; P. O. Monmouth; rep; Meth; from Pennsylvania.

Elliot Robt. farmer; Sec. 34; P. O. Lenox; dem; Bapt; 120 acres, value $7,200; Ohio.

Endeman E. E. farmer; Sec. 3; P. O. Monmouth; dem; Meth; from Germany.

Evans Douglas, farmer; P. O. Lenox; dem.

Evans J. H. farmer; Sec. 29; P. O. Lenox; dem Bapt.

Eversall Geo. farmer; Sec. 21; Monmouth; rep; Lib.

Eversall W. R. farmer; Sec. 21; P. O. Monmouth; rep.

EWAN EVAN, Farmer; Sec. 34; P. O. Lenox; born in Hamilton Co., N. J., Dec. 15, 1824; came to this Co. in 1825; Rep; M. E.; 320 acres, value $19,000; was married to Elizabeth Burk, Oct. 15, 1848; have five children; is Supervisor from Lenox township.

Ewan Jno. farmer and constable; P. O. Lenox; rep; M. E.

F LEAHARTY ROBERT farmer; P. O. Lenox; rep.

G ANOR JOSEPH, farmer; P. O. Lenox; dem; Lib; from Ohio.

Gavin Pat. farmer; P. O. Monmouth; dem; Cath; 174 acres, value $10,000.

Geary J. H. farmer; P. O. Lenox; rep; Lib.

GLENN S. Farmer; Sec. 7; P. O. Monmouth; born in Ohio, July, 1826; came to this Co. in 1855; Rep; Meth; owns 134 acres, value $6,600; was married to Miss Susan McClellan, of Ohio.

Graham Forbes, grocer; P. O. Lenox; ind; from Ohio.

Grooms Sam. farmer; Sec. 21; P. O. Monmouth; rep; U. B.; 120 acres, value $7,000.

H ALY DAVID, farmer; Sec. 15; P. O. Monmouth; dem.

Harris L. M. farmer; P. O. Monmouth; rep; U. B.; from New York.

HARRIS, MRS. E. E. Farmer; Sec. 20; P. O. Monmouth; born in Vermont, April 18, 1821; came to this Co. in 1855; Rep; Univ; 86 acres, value $7,000; has four sons and three daughters living, two children dead; oldest son was in the 33d Regt. I. V. I. during the war; been in the Co. twenty-two years.

Heiflin A. T. farmer; Sec. 20; rep; U. B.; from Georgia.

Heiflin A. T. farmer; Sec. 20; P. O. Lenox; rep; Meth.

Hodson Jno. postmaster; P. O. Lenox; ind; Meth; property valued at $1,000.

HOLGATE HENRY, farmer; Sec. 15; P. O. Monmouth; born in England, March 13, 1846; came to this Co. in 1865; Rep; Lib.

Holgate Jonas, farmer; Sec. 33; rep; U. B.; 240 acres, value $14,400; England.

Hoyt Wm. farmer; P. O. Monmouth; rep; Bapt.

JENKS E. farmer; Sec. 23; P. O. Berwick; rep; Bapt; 80 acres, value $5,000.

JENKS W. B. Farmer; Sec. 23; P. O. Monmouth; born in Illinois, Sept. 19, 1846; came to this Co. in 1846; Rep; Bapt; was married to Miss Carrie Capps, Feb. 7, 1875.

JENKS C. O. Farmer and Stock Raiser; Sec. 23; P. O. Berwick; born in Illinois, Oct. 16, 1853; came to this Co. in 1853; Rep; Bapt; 150 acres, value $9,000; was married to Miss Amanda Smith, of Iowa, Sept. 2, 1875.

JEWELL CHAS. Farmer and Stock Raiser; Sec. 29; P. O. Monmouth; born in Illinois, Dec. 17, 1846; came to this Co. in 1846; Rep; Bapt; 360 acres, value $18,000; was married to Miss Anna M. Townsend, June 26, 1871; has three children, one girl and two boys.

JEWELL DUDLEY, Farmer; Sec. 22; P. O. Monmouth; born in Warren Co., Sept. 7, 1850; came to this Co. in 1850; Rep; Bapt; 80 acres, value $5,000; was married to Miss Sarah M. Jones, Nov. 12, 1874; have one child; Mrs. Jewell is from Pennsylvania; Mr. Jewell intends stocking his farm with a fine breed of Berkshire hogs, also a fine breed of Short-horned cattle.

JEWELL H. L. Farmer; Sec. 24; P. O. Monmouth; born in Illinois, May 19, 1847; came to this Co. in 1847; Rep; Lib; 160 acres, value $8,000; was married to Miss Lydia A. Crandall, Sept. 14, 1871; has three children.

Jewell John, farmer; Sec. 33; P. O. Lenox; dem; U. B; 80 acres, value $4,000; N. Y.

JEWELL W. H. Farmer; Sec. 21; P. O. Monmouth; born in Warren Co., April 12, 1844; Rep; U. B.; 200 acres, value $15,000; was married to Miss E. C. Wonderly; have six children, three sons and three daughters; Mr. Jewell was in the 138th Regt. I. V. I. during the war, under Col. Goodwin, seven months; was honorably discharged; has been Constable, School Director, Tax Collector; is agent for the Double Row Stock Cutter, Seeder and Hay Rake combined; is engaged in fine stock raising; has on hand a fine Bashaw stallion, sired by Green's Bashaw, also a fine Short-horned bull.

Jones K. P. school teacher; Sec. 31; P. O. Lenox; ind; Lib.

KETTERING JOHN, farmer; Sec. 18; P. O. Monmonth; rep; Meth.

Knapp Reuben E. farmer; Sec. 14; P. O. Monmouth; rep; Bapt; 140 acres.

LAMPHERE G. I. farmer; Sec. 19; ind; U. B.; 120 acres, value $6,000; N. Y.

Lehan Ed. clerk; dem; Cath; born Ill.

Lewis Jas. farmer; Sec. 36; P. O. Berwick; rep; Lib; 166 acres, value $8,000; N. J.

Lewis Mrs. J. farmer; Sec. 33; P. O. Lenox; 70 acres, value $4,000.

Luster Dock. doctor; P. O. Lenox; dem; Lib.

McCOMBS GEO. laborer; dem; Lib; from Kentucky.

McCombs W. M. farmer; P. O. Lenox; dem; Lib.

McNally W. M. farmer; Sec. 31; P. O. Monmouth; dem; Lib.

Maginnis John, farmer; Sec. 11; P. O. Monmouth; dem; Meth.

Marsh Jas. farmer; Sec. 33; P. O. Lenox; rep; U. B.; 80 acres, value $4,000; from Pa.

McVEY DANIEL, Farmer; Sec. 10; P. O. Monmouth; born in Ireland, May 8, 1825; came to this Co. in 1853; Lib; was married to Miss Catharine Shimmin Dec. 18, 1856, who is from the Isle of Man; have nine children living.

Martin Andrew, farmer; rep; Luth; from Sweden.

Mattison Colby, farmer; Sec. 36; P. O. Berwick; rep; Bapt; from New York.

Maxwell Wm. J. farmer; Sec. 16, P. O. Monmouth.

Metcalf I. A. farmer; P. O. Lenox; dem; Lib.

Michael H. C. farmer; P. O. Berwick; dem; Lib.

Miller Harrison, farmer; Sec. 17; P. O. Monmouth; rep; U. B.

Miller Henry, farmer; Sec. 15; P. O. Monmouth; rep; U. B.; 80 acres, value $4,500.

Miller J. W. farmer; Sec. 15; P. O. Monmouth; rep; Lib; 80 acs., value $5,000; Va.

Miller Jacob, farmer; Sec. 16; P. O. Monmouth; rep; U. B.; 1,000 acs., val. $50,000.

Miller Jas. C. farmer; P. O. Monmouth; rep; Lib.

Miller Peachey, farmer; P. O. Monmouth; ind; Lib.

Miner J. farmer; Sec. 23; P. O. Cameron; rep; Bapt.

MOREY GEORGE W. Farmer; Sec. 14; P. O. Monmouth; born in Erie Co., Pa., Jan. 18, 1824; came to this Co. in 1841; rep; Lib; 160 acres, value $9,600; was married to Miss Emily Bunnell Sept. 25, 1852; have three children—one girl and two boys; Mr. Morey has been elected Supervisor from his District for two terms.

Morey Wm. F. farmer; rep; Lib; born Ill.

Morford Horton, farmer; Sec. 28; P. O. Lenox; rep; Meth.; from New York

Morris R. A. Mrs. farmer; Lib; 200 acres, value $12,000; born Illinois.

Morris Stephen, farmer; P. O. Monmouth.

Mower Jonas, farmer; Sec. 3; P. O. Monmouth; dem; Luth; from New York.

Murdock Thos. farmer; Sec. 9; P. O. Monmouth; rep; Lib.

Murphey Richard, farmer; Sec. 16; P. O. Monmouth; rep; Chris; 90 acs., $6,000; Ky.

NESBIT ADDISON, farmer; P. O. Monmouth; rep; Presb.

Nesbit John A. farmer; Sec. 11; P. O. Monmouth; rep; Pres; 120 acres, val. $7,200.

Norwood Freeman, lumber merchant; Lenox; dem; Lib; from Maine.

OLSON OLIVER, farmer; P. O. Lenox; rep; Luth; from Sweden.

Olson Peter, farmer; P. O. Lenox; dem; Luth; from Sweden.

OLSON HENRY H., Farmer, Stock Raiser and Renter; Sec. 30; P. O. Lenox; born in Sweden on Jan. 20, 1849; came to this Co. 1869; Rep; Luth; was married to Miss Amelia Nelson Oct. 20, 1875.

PAUL E. Z. farmer; P. O. Monmouth; ind; Lib.

Perry T. P. farmer; Sec. 19; P. O. Monmouth; rep; Lib; 180 acres, value $10,000.

PERRINE D. S., Farmer; Sec. 7; P. O. Lenox; born in Ohio Aug. 27, 1847; came to this Co. in 1858; Dem; Lib; was married to Miss C. T. Carr Feb. 27, 1872.

PHELPS PORTER, Farmer; Sec. 2; P. O. Monmouth; born in Madison Co., New York, April 14, 1804; came to this Co. in 1836; Dem; U. Pres; 300 acres, value $18,000; married Miss Mary Ress March 29, 1826; have six children, two deceased; one of the first settlers in the Co.; lived here 41 years.

Phelps S. D. farmer; Sec. 2; P. O. Monmouth; dem; Lib; from New York.

Pierson Jos. farmer; Sec. 32; P. O. Lenox; ind.

RAY BEDFORD, farmer; P. O. Monmouth; dem; Bapt; 650 acres, $39,000.

Ray H. W. farmer; Sec. 27; P. O. Lenox; dem; Lib.

RAY GARLAND, Farmer; Sec. 35; P. O. Berwick; born in Kentucky in 1798; came to this Co. in 1835 or '36; Dem; U. Bapt; 500 acres, value $40,000; is 79 years of age, and is the oldest settler now living in Warren Co.; he has been here 42 years.

Ray J. C. farmer; P. O. Berwick; dem; Bapt.

Ray I. W. farmer; Sec. 35; P. O. Berwick; dem; U. B.; 150 acres, value $7,500.

Ray Richard Sr., farmer; P. O. Lenox; dem; Bapt.

Ray Richard Jr., farmer; Sec. 29; P. O. Lenox; dem; Bapt; 80 acres, value $5,000.

Ray Robert, farmer; Sec. 29; P. O. Lenox; dem; Lib; 80 acres, value $5,000; from Ky

Ray Warren, farmer; Sec. 29; P. O. Lenox; dem; Bapt; 80 acres, value $5,000; Ky.

RICE TILFORD, Farmer and Stock Raiser; Sec. 27; P. O. Lenox; born in Kentucky, March 1, 1848; came to this Co. in 1869; Dem; Bapt; rents 160 acres of land. Mr. Rice makes a specialty of raising Bronze Turkeys, Bramah Chickens, and Poland China Hogs; also deals in Ky. high grade cattle, having sold over $2,000 in the last three years; married Miss S. E. Ray, daughter of Mr. B. Ray, Dec. 27, 1871.

Rinkney I. W. farmer; P. O. Lenox; dem; U. B.

RITCHIE FRANCIS, Farmer; Sec. 16; P. O. Monmouth; born in Ireland, June 8, 1835; came to this Co. in 1865; Rep; Meth.; was married to Miss Eliza Wilson Sept. 25, 1856; have five children living, two deceased.

Roberson H. C. farmer; P. O. Lenox; Rep; Lib.

ROBERTSON J. W., Farmer; Sec. 32; P. O. Lenox; born in Washington Co., New York, March 4, 1822; came to this Co. in 1843; Rep; Lib; 196 acres, value $12,000; was in the Mexican war, under Gen. Scott, in 1847; was married to Emaline Morgan Jan. 4, 1849; she died in 1868; he was again married, to Miss Jennie E. Clark, Sept. 8, 1871.

Rogers Gordon, farmer; P. O. Lenox; dem; Bapt.

Rosenblad A. farmer; rep; Luth; Denmark.

Russell Jonathan, farmer; P. O. Monmouth; rep; Lib; 160 acres, value $8,000.

Russell Judson, farmer; P. O. Lenox; rep; Lib.

SAYLOR G. M. farmer; Sec. 35; dem; Lib; 170 acres, value $11,000; from Ohio.

Saylor John, farmer; P. O. Lenox; dem; Lib; 80 acres, value $4,500.

Saylor Jos. farmer; Sec. 27; P. O. Lenox; dem; U. B.; 240 acres, value $12,000.

Saylor J. W. farmer; Sec. 34; P. O. Lenox; dem; Bapt; 80 acres, value $5,000.

Schemmerhorn Henry, farmer; Sec. 21; P. O. Monmouth; rep; Meth.; $9,600.

Scurrey Wm. farmer; P. O. Lenox; dem.

Shawler Jacob, farmer; P. O. Cameron; dem; Bapt; 160 acres; value $10,000; Ky.

Shussles John, farmer; Sec. 35; P. O. Berwick; ind; Lib; born Illinois.

Sigafoos Jerome, farmer; P. O. Monmouth; rep.

SIGAFOOS LEVI, Farmer; Sec. 18; P. O. Monmouth; born in New Jersey,

Aug. 6, 1823; came to this Co. in 1853; ind; Lib; 133 acres, value $8,000; was married to Miss Lydia Bennett in March, 1853; have six children.

Smiley D. N. farmer; Sec. 19; P. O. Lenox; dem; U. B.; 80 acres, value $4,000; Ohio.

Smiley Wm. farmer; Sec. 19; P. O. Lenox; ind; U. B.

Smith Chas. farmer; P. O. Berwick; dem; lib.

SMITH D. R. Farmer; Sec. 36; P. O. Berwick; born in Virginia, March 2, 1812; came to this Co. in 1853; dem; Lib; 511 acs, value $35,770; married Miss Elizabeth Keller, Nov. 5, 1835; have seven children living, four daughters and three sons.

Smith Isaac, farmer; Sec. 36; P. O. Berwick; dem; lib; from Virginia.

Smith L. G. farmer; Sec. 30; P. O. Monmouth; rep; Unit; 80 acres, value $5,500.

Smith O. C. farmer; P. O. Monmouth; dem.

Smith T. D. farmer; P. O. Berwick; dem; U. B.; from Virginia.

Smith W. farmer; Sec. 22; P. O. Lenox; dem; Lib; 160 acres, value $10,000; from Va.

Sprout Wm. farmer; Sec. 13; P. O. Monmouth; dem; Meth; 120 acres, val. $7,000.

Sterling Jos. farmer; P. O. Lenox; rep; U. B.

TEAR HENRY, farmer; P. O. Lenox; rep; Meth.

Tere Martha Mrs. Sec. 22; Meth.; 240 acres, value $14,500.

Thomas Tim, farmer, Sec. 23; P. O. Monmouth; rep; Lib; 100 acres, value $5,000.

ULMER HENRY, farmer; Sec. 12; P. O. Monmouth; dem; Lib; from Pa.

VANTASSEL ISAAC, farmer; Sec. 13; P. O. Monmouth; rep; Lib; 120 acres.

Vantassel Wesley, farmer; P. O. Monmouth; rep; Lib.

WALLACE CHAS. farmer; Sec. 16; P. O. Monmouth; rep; Lib; 40 acres. Ky

Webb R. E. farmer; P. O. Lenox; dem; Bapt; from Kentucky.

Weekly F. A. farmer; Sec. 13; P. O. Monmouth; dem; Lib; 120 acres, value $7,200.

Weekley Spangler, farmer; Sec. 13; P. O. Monmouth; dem; Lib; from Pa.

Welsh W. farmer; P. O. Monmouth.

Wilson John H. farmer; Sec. 32; P. O. Lenox; rep; U. B.; from Ohio.

Wilson Oliver P. farmer; P. O. Monmouth; dem; Lib; 160 acres, value $9,600.

Wolfer Andrew, farmer; employed by A. Holgate; dem; Lib; from Germany.

Wonderly D. Y. farmer; Sec. 13; P. O. Monmouth; dem; Lib.

Wonderly John, farmer; Sec. 13; P O Monmouth; dem; Meth; 160 acres; $9,600.

Wonderly J. W. farmer; P. O. Monmouth; dem; Lib.

YOUNG J. L. farmer; Sec. 12; P. O. Monmouth; dem; Lib; 50 acres, val. $3,250.

Young J. M. farmer; Sec. 30; P. O. Lenox; rep; Meth; 167 acres; value $8,300.

ZIMMERMAN M. C. farmer; Sec. 7; 80 acres, value $4,800.

COLDBROOK TOWNSHIP.

ADCOCK J. C. farmer; Sec. 3; P. O. Utah; dem; 125 acres, value $8,125; from Va.

Altman E. R. laborer, lives with Lewis Fair; P. O. Galesburg; rep; from Penn.

Anderson August, rents P. Salle's farm; Sec. 10; P. O. Galesburg; rep; Luth; Sweden.

Anderson John, Sec. 14; rep; Bapt; 32 acres, value $960; from Missouri.

Anderson Peter, rents Rhykerd's; P. O. Cameron; rep; from Sweden.

Aultman Rice, Sec. 12; dem; 240 acres, value $16,400.

Avitt George, lives on James Grace's farm; P. O. Cameron; dem; born Illinois.

BAKNELL GEORGE C. rents H. Leonard's farm; Sec. 9; P. O. Galesburg; rep; Va.

Barnett C. Jr. farmer; Sec. 13; P. O. Galesburg; dem; 127 acres, value $10,160; Ill.

BARNETT J. R. Farmer and Stock Raiser; Sec. 10; P. O. Galesburg; born in Ill., Sept. 22, 1832, and came to this Co. in 1857; Dem; owns 220 acres, value $13,200; married Margaret J. Wallace Dec. 14, 1856; have five children, Emmet T., Alma A., Otis M., Warren J., Selden J.; has been Collector and Supervisor.

Barrett John, laborer; P. O. Cameron; dem; from Kentucky.

Barquest Andrew, farmer; rents H. Bonner's farm; Sec. 15; P. O. Galesburg; rep; Luth.

Barquest A. G. rents G. Claycomb's farm; rep; from Sweden.

Bell John, farmer; Sec. 19; P. O. Monmouth; dem; 30 acres, value $1,500; born Ill.

Blair Sylvester, carpenter; P. O. Cameron; rep; Chris; val. estate $1,000; from Penn.

BLAIR S. J. Carpenter and Dealer in Groceries; Cameron; born in Penn., on April 21, 1836, and came to this Co. in 1870; Dem; Christian; owns town property valued at $1,200; married Martha R. Shinn Dec. 24, 1863; has one child, Hattie, born March 21, 1866; held office of Constable.

Bowers Adam, farmer; Sec. 2; P. O. Utah; dem; M. E.; 260 acres, val. $13,000; Penn.

Bradley Levi, laborer, rents of Nelson Swan; P. O. Monmouth; dem; born Illinois.

BRUINGTON GEORGE, Farmer and Stock Raiser; Sec. 16; P. O. Galesburg; born in Illinois, Oct. 4, 1840; Dem; owns 280 acres, value $16,800; married Mary Wallace June 14, 1862; have four children, Maggie J., born May 30, 1864; Jessie L., Feb. 24, 1866; Arnold, March 13, 1868; Elmer, Aug. 13, 1871.

BRUINGTON JAMES, Farmer and Stock Raiser; Sec. 16; P. O. Galesburg; born in Kentucky, Aug. 23, 1831, and came to this Co. in 1840; Dem; Christian; owns 595 acres, value $29,750; came from Kentucky to Knox Co., Ill., in 1834, then to Warren Co.; married Jemima Wallace June 19, 1853; has eight children, Thomas S., William E., Clara J., Bettey P., Margaret C., Ellen W., Orla Lee and Lilly May; has been Assessor, Road Commissioner and Collector; his son Thomas lives with him.

Bruington T. S. lives with his father; Sec. 16; P. O. Galesburg; dem.

Bruner George, farmer; P. O. Utah; 120 acres, value $7,650; from Kentucky.

Bruner John, lives with his son George; Sec. 4; P. O. Utah; dem; from Kentucky.

CLAYCOMB G. W.; Sec. 17; P. O. Cameron; rep; Univ; 368 acres, val. $22,080.

Cavanaugh Richard, laborer; P. O. Cameron; dem; Cath; from Ireland.

CARLSON JOHN, Farmer and Stock Raiser; Sec 26; P. O. Galesburg; born in Calmer, Sweden, Nov. 26, 1835, and came to this Co. in 1867; Rep; First Luth; rents 220 acres; value of estate $3,000; married Ann S. Johnson, born in Calmer, Sweden; seven children, Carl, August, Amanda, Matilda S., Frank A., Annie E., Fred T. and Alta, who died in 1875; when Mr. Carlson first came to this Co. he worked by the month for eleven months, and then rented a farm, and has lived in Warren Co. ever since.

CLAYCOMB GEORGE W. Retired Farmer; Sec. 17; P. O. Cameron; born in Kentucky, Feb. 4, 1828, and came to this Co. in 1835; Rep; Univ; owns 405 acres, value $24,300; married Sarah A. Goddard, Dec. 17, 1851; she was born April 10, 1834; have four children, three living; Laura E., married to Ph. Shelton Nov. 13, 1871; Albert, born Nov. 7, 1853. died March 6, 1860; Frank E., born May 6, 1857; Alta May, born June 21, 1863; Laura, born Sept. 13, 1852; after Mr. C. came to this Co. he lived with his mother and brother until he arrived at the age of twenty-one.

Clayton J. H. farmer, lives on M. H. Shelton's farm; Sec. 9; P. O. Cameron; dem.

Clayton John, farmer; Sec. 21; P. O. Cameron; dem; Bapt; 83 acres, value $4,150.

Clayton Thomas, farmer, rents John Clayton's farm; P. O. Cameron; dem; from Ky.

Clayton W. H. farmer; Sec. 21; P. O. Cameron; dem; Chris; 145 acres; val $5,800.

Clyborne Wm. L. Jr. farmer, lives on his father's farm; P. O. Galesburg; rep; Mich.

CLYBORN WM. L. Farmer and Stock Raiser; Sec. 24; P. O. Galesburg; born in Va., March 29, 1813; came to this Co. in 1861; Rep; owns 175 acres, value $14,000; married Ruth Thompson, Jan. 18, 1838; have four children, Archibald, William L., Thomas W., Addie; two dead, C. J., and Esquire F.; left Virginia in 1828, and went to Michigan; then came to this Co.; has held the office of Supervisor in Floyd township, and was in the Black Hawk war.

Churchill Ben, farmer; Sec. 10; P. O. Utah; dem; 40 acres, value $2,400; from N. Y.

Churchill C. W. farmer; Sec. 15; P O. Galesburg; dem; 84 acres, value $5,040.

Churchill Earle C. lives with his father; P. O. Galesburg; dem; from New York.

Churchill Henry, farmer; Sec. 10; P. O. Galesburg; dem; 40 acres, value $2,400.

Churchill Leland, lives with his father, C. W. Churchill; dem; P. O. Galesburg.

Churchill L. H. farmer; Sec. 10; P. O. Utah; dem; 80 acres, value $4,800; from N. Y.

Churchill Norton H., lives with his father, C. W.; P. O. Galesburg; dem; from N. Y.

Cone J. D. farmer; Sec. 36; P. O. Galesburg; rep; 200 acres, value $20,000; from Vt.

CONE JNO. Farmer; Sec. 25; P. O. Galesburg; born in Westminster, Vt., Oct. 7, 1797; came to this Co. in 1841; Rep; Bapt; owns 90 acres, value $7,200; married Lucinda Rand in 1821, who was born in Vermont, Dec. 6, 1796; have three children, Leonera L., J. D, and May M.; his farm is five miles west of the city of Galesburg.

Connard N. F. Sec. 34; P. O. Cameron; rep; M. E.; 102 acres, value $6,120; from Ohio.

Cover Wm. M. renter; Sec. 23; P. O. Galesburg; rep; M. E.; from Penn.

Cowan Robt. farmer; Sec. 12; P. O. Galesburg; rep; 80 acres; from Scotland.

Cowan Robert, farmer, Sec. 13; P. O. Galesburg; rep; 80 acres, value $5,000.

Curtiss E. D. farmer, lives on J. McMullin's farm; Sec. 8; P. O. Cameron; dem; Ill.

Curtiss Thomas, laborer; P. O. Cameron; dem; from Kentucky.

DAVIDSON DICK, laborer; P. O. Cameron; dem.

Davidson E. P. farm laborer; P. O. Cameron; dem; Christian; born Illinois.

DAVIDSON W. L. Farmer and Breeder of Hogs; Sec. 29; P. O. Cameron; born in Warren Co., Ill., Feb. 18, 1836; dem; owns 95 acres, value $4,750; he makes a specialty of breeding Poland and China hogs; has one stock hog that cost him $100; it has taken premiums at the Indiana and Ohio State fairs in its class; parties wishing fine stock woud do well to call and examine before purchasing elsewhere; he married Amanda Parker, Feb. 25, 1861; has one child, W. A.

Deweese E. Jr. farmer, rents of William Gardner; P. O. Galesburg; dem; Chris.

Deweese Wm. H. laborer; P. O. Galesburg; dem; from Penn.

Donley Mrs. John, Sec. 14; P. O. Galesburg; Bapt; 40 acres, value $2,000; from Ireland.

DRAKE N. B. Farmer and Stock Raiser; Sec. 13; P. O. Galesburg; born in New York, Dec. 6, 1814; came to this Co. in 1845; Rep; owns 80 acres, value $6,400; married Mary A. Huster, Jan. 1, 1837; has four children, Henry, Hiram, Hattie M., and Emma L.; his farm is 4½ miles west of the city of Galesburg; has been Road Commissioner and School Director.

Dunn M. R. farmer; Sec. 1; P. O. Utah; dem; 100 acres, value $9,600; from Penn.

ELLIS J. M. farmer; Sec. 25; P. O. Galesburg; dem; 213 acres, value, $17,040.

Ellis J. T. farmer; Sec. 25; P. O. Galesburg; dem; 155 acres, value $12,400; born N. Y.

FERRIS GEO. farmer, rents of M. Shelton; P. O. Galesburg; rep; M. E.; N. Y.

Faubl Z. Sec. 27; P. O. Galesburg; rep; Meth; 3 acres, value $150; from Ohio.

FAIR LEWIS, Farmer and Agent for Odell's Eliptic Spring Beds; Sec. 11; P.O. Galesburg; born in Ohio, Oct. 9, 1838, and came to this Co. 1849; has four children, Edwin C., Mary E., Frank L. and Nettie F.; owns 120 acres, value $8,000; married Miss Louisa Altman, Oct. 31, 1860.

Fling M. rents J. Nelson's farm; Sec. 3; P. O. Galesburg; Cath; from Ireland.

Fox Ben, laborer; Cameron; dem.

Fox Samuel, farm laborer; Cameron; dem; from Pennsylvania.

FOX W. A. Farmer; Sec. 20; P. O. Cameron; born in Penn., Aug. 30, 1832; came to this Co. in 1855; Dem; owns 80 acres, value $4,000; married A. J. Pigsley, Sept. 20, 1860; have five children, Cassie, Eliza, Levi, Anna and Bennie; has been Road Commissioner and School Director.

GARDNER JAMES, farmer; Sec. 6; P. O. Monmouth; dem; 155 acres, val. $9,300.

Gardner Walter, lives with his mother; Sec. 7; P. O. Monmouth; dem; born Kentucky.

GARDNER CATHARINE, Farmer; Sec. 7; P. O. Monmouth; born in Barren Co., Ky., April 26, 1801; came to this Co. in 1848; Christian; owns 47 acres, value $2,820; is the widow of Thomas H. Gardner, who died in Ky. in 1846; two years after he died she came to this State; children are James, William, Jefferson, Elizabeth, Walter and Sarah, who died Dec. 6, 1875; Walter lives with his mother; he is married and had two children, one dead.

GARDNER G. W. Farmer and Stock Raiser; Sec. 5; P. O. Galesburg; born in Warren Co., Ill., July 23, 1848; Dem; Christian; owns 155 acres, value $9,300; married Julia Patten, Nov. 28, 1867; have four children, Jessie, born June 24, 1868; Benjamin, March 22, 1870; Lee, June 14, 1873, died Aug. 11, 1875; Lizzie M., Sept. 24, 1876; he is the son of B. H. Gardner, who came from Kentucky in 1832 to Warren Co.

GARDNER WILLIAM M. Farmer and Stock Raiser; Sec. 14; P. O. Galesburg; born in Kentucky, Oct. 5, 1831; came to this Co. in 1848; Dem; owns 245 acres, value $14,700; married Mary E. Hennen, April 8, 1861; four children, Thomas E., Alice M., Frank M. and William H.; he is the son of Thomas H. Gardner, who died in 1847 in Kentucky; his farm is 5½ west and one mile south of the city of Galesburg.

Gates Henry, farmer, lives with his mother; Sec. 6; P. O. Monmouth; dem; born Ill.

Gates Nancy B. Sec. 6; P. O. Gerlaw; rep; Chris; 70 acres, $4,200; from Indiana.

Gates Wilson, farmer, lives with his mother; Sec. 6; P. O. Monmouth; dem; born Ill.

Gifford George, lives with his father; Sec. 6; rep; from New York.

Gifford G. L. farmer; Sec. 6; P.O. Galesburg; rep; 100 acres; value $7,000; born Ky.

Goddard George, retired; P. O. Cameron; rep; Meth; 160 acres, value $9,000.

Graham Charles E., blacksmith; P. O. Utah; rep; born Illinois.

Graham Patrick, laborer; Cameron; dem; Cath; from Ireland.

Graham Sidney, rents Gregg's farm; Sec. 1; P. O. Utah; rep; born Illinois.

GRACE JAMES W. Farmer and Stock Raiser; Sec. 29; P. O. Cameron; born in Indiana, Feb. 10, 1818; came to this Co. in 1840; Rep; owns 677 acres, value $34,000; first wife's name was Sarah E. Lyen; second wife was Aggatha Lyen; third wife's name was Amanda Overman; four children by first wife, Solomon, Percilla, John, and one child unnamed; by second wife five, Mary, Jessie, Franklin, Russell and Betty; by third wife one, Olive; date of first marriage, 1838; second marriage, 1846; third marriage Dec. 3, 1872; number of children ten.

Grace Jesse, fruit farmer; Sec. 28; P. O. Cameron; rep; 54 acres, value $3,240; Ill.

Griffee Charles, farmer; Sec. 29; P. O. Cameron; dem; 42 acres, value $1,600; Ill.

Griffee Daniel, farmer; Sec. 22; P. O. Galesburg; rep; Chris; 100 acres; value $6,000.

Griffee Thomas, lives on his father's farm; Sec. 22; P. O. Galesburg; dem; Chris; Ill.

Griffee Wm. farmer; Sec. 22; P. O. Galesburg; dem; Chris; 215 acres, val. $10,750.

Grounds Harrison, laborer; P. O. Monmouth; dem; Meth; from Kentucky.

HALEY MRS.; Sec. 26; 80 acres, value $500; from Kentucky.

Hartsell J. rents Mrs. Cox's farm; P. O. Utah; dem; from Ohio.

HALL J. D. Farmer and Stock Raiser; Sec. 7; P. O. Monmouth; born in Kentucky, April 5, 1838; came to this Co. in 1846; Ind; Christian; owns 369 acres, value $22,140.

HALL M. W. Farmer and Stock Raiser; Sec. 18; P. O. Monmouth; born in Kentucky, April 30, 1837; came to this Co. in 1846; Ind; Christian; owns 740 acres, value $44,400; married Candis Miller, from Kentucky; has four children, Frank, George, Ada and Ella; been School Director; Mr. Hall is a cattle feeder; feeds on an average 100 cattle and 200 hogs annually.

HARTMAN J. T. Farmer and Stock Raiser; Sec. 12; P. O. Galesburg; born in Indiana, April 21, 1835; came to this Co. in 1856; Dem; owns 80 acres, value $6,400; married Henrietta Freeman, Nov. 27, 1862; three children, Minnie M., Lillie M., Etty J., who died in 1868; has been Collector and Supervisor.

Harte Harvey B. retired; P. O. Cameron; rep; Chris.

Hatchett L., M. D. P. O. Cameron; dem; Chris.

Hawkins E. A. farm laborer; Cameron; dem; Chris; born Illinois.

HEDGEPETH H. S. Farmer; Sec. 27; P. O. Cameron; born in Illinois, Feb. 11, 1845; Dem; owns 160 acres, value $10,200; married Sarah Hart, Sept. 14, 1871; has one child, Olive May, born Oct. 18, 1876.

HEDGEPETH JOEL S. Farmer and Stock Raiser; Sec. 34; P. O. Cameron; born in Virginia, Jan. 21, 1815; came to this Co. in 1840; Dem; owns 500 acres, value $30,000; came to Kentucky at the age of three years; has been Commissioner of Highways and Collector; married Elizabeth Multer, born in Virginia, Aug. 9, 1817; has one child, Holland S; was married in Illinois.

HILLMAN JOSEPH, Farmer and Stock Raiser; Sec. 23; P. O. Galesburg; born in Somersetshire, England, May 11, 1804; came to this Co. in 1875; Rep; Bapt; owns 80 acres, value $5,000; married Anna Hayton, July 4, 1844, and came to America in 1855; have one child, born July 1, 1847; when he first came to America he came to Knox Co., Ill.

HILLS NELSON E. Farmer; Sec. 22; P. O. Galesburg; born in Oneida Co., N. Y., town of Vernon, Sept. 14, 1806; came to this Co. in 1836; Rep; Chris; owns 60 acres, value $3,000; married Elizabeth McFarland, May 14, 1837; six children, William H., Allen R., Jane E., Mary A., Sarah M., Susan A., Allen R., who was in the Rebellion, and was killed in the battle of Vicksburg; William H was with Sherman in the Rebellion.

Holley Charles, butcher; Cameron; value o estate $500; from England.

Holden Adam, farm laborer; P. O. Monmouth; dem.

Holden John, miner; P. O. Monmouth; dem.

Holden Mark, farmer; Sec. 19; P. O. Monmouth; dem; 28 acres, value $1,400; Ill.

Horney J. H. lives with his father, Philip Horney; P. O. Cameron; dem; Meth.

Horney J. T. lives with his father; Sec. 34; P. O. Cameron; dem; born Illinois.

HORNEY JOEL, Farmer and Breeder of Fine Horses and Swine; Sec. 33; P. O. Cameron; born in Warren Co., Ill., Dec. 27, 1849; Dem; married Jennie Lieurance, March 12, 1876; has one child, Archie C., born Dec. 26, 1876; is the son of Philip Horney; lives on his father's farm.

HORNEY PHILIP, Farmer and Fine Stock Breeder; Sec. 34; P. O. Cameron; born in North Carolina, May 4, 1808; came to this Co. in 1835; Dem; owns 460 acres, valued at $30,000; left North Carolina in 1826; came to Schuyler Co., Ill., and then to Warren Co.; there was only one school district in Coldbrook township when he came here; has always voted the Democratic ticket; married Dorcas McKee, Apr. 10, 1834; has seven children, four boys and three girls, William, Jeffrey, Joel T., James H., Elizabeth, Mary and Valeria; has been Justice of the Peace, Supervisor, Overseer of the Poor, School Trustee, and held every other township office except Town Clerk; was Sergeant in the Black Hawk war.

Hudson James, laborer; P. O. Utah; dem.

Hudson John, laborer; P. O. Utah; dem.

JOHNSON MRS. P. O. Cameron; value of estate $500; rep; Bapt.

Johnson Geo. D., laborer; P. O. Cameron; dem; Bapt.

JOHNSON JOHN, Farmer; Sec. 32; P. O. Cameron; born in West Virginia, Nov. 6, 1820; came to this Co. in 1836; Dem; Christian; owns 212 acres, value $12,000; has held the office of School Director; married Amanda F. Whitman, Sept. 18, 1845; have seven children.

Johnson O., P. Sec. 26; O. Utah; 21 acres, value $1,050; rep; from Sweden.

Johnson Peter, farmer; Sec. 24; P. O. Galesburg; 40 acres, value $6,000; rep; Luth.

Johnson Richard, lives with his father, Jno. Johnson, on Sec. 32; P. O. Cameron; dem.

Johnson Swan, rents J. Hall's farm on Sec. 7; P. O. Galesburg; rep; from Sweden.

Jones Albert, lives with his father, M. R. Jones; P. O. Cameron; dem; born Ill.

Jones John M. lives on his father's farm; Sec. 31; P. O. Cameron; dem; Chris.

JONES M. R. Farmer; Sec. 31; P.O. Cameron; born in Kentucky, Nov. 13, 1819; came to this Co. in 1839; Dem; Christian; owns 300 acres of land, valued at $15,000; name of first wife Mary J. Whitman, who died Jan. 18, 1870; second wife was Betsey G. Haley, married April 13, 1870; first wife born in Kentucky, April 23, 1828; birth of second wife, March 8, 1815; had eight children, all by first wife; Mr. Jones has held the office of Commissioner and School Director.

Jones Walter, laborer; P. O. Cameron; dem; Meth; born Illinois.

Julian Mary, Sec. 29; P. O. Cameron; 53 acres, value $2,050; Cath; from France.

KIERNAN FRANCIS, farmer; Sec. 1; P. O. Galesburg; dem; Cath; Ireland.

Kiernan Thos. farmer; Sec. 1; P. O. Utah; dem; Cath; 90 acres, value $5,400; Ill.

KELLY LORIN T. Farmer and Shoemaker; Cameron; born in Vermont, June 10, 1839; came to this Co. in 1856; Rep; Christian; owns 10 acres land, valued at $1,000; married Eliza B. Parker, Oct. 5, 1859; born in Knox Co., May 4, 1840; have two children, Alva E., born May 2, 1861, in Warren Co., Coldbrook tp., and Ora H., born Jan. 27, 1864; held office of Constable.

LANDGREEN G. P. rents Chas. Rocket's farm on Sec. 36; P. O. Galesburg; rep.

Law Amos, farmer; Sec. 22; P. O. Galesburg; dem; 51 acres, value $1,530; Ill.

Law Chas. rents N. Bruner's farm; P. O. Galesburg; dem; born Illinois.

LAW SAMUEL, Farmer and Stock Raiser; Sec. 14; P. O. Galesburg; born in Ireland, July 12, 1818; came to this Co. in 1854; Dem; Meth; owns 130 acres land, valued at $9,800; married Henrietta C. Dean, 1845; have five children, Alice A., Amos, Charles, Mary E., John W.; been Town Clerk and Overseer of the Poor.

Lee F. M. lives with his father on Sec. 32; P. O. Cameron; rep; born Pennsylvania.

Lee S. C. farmer; Sec. 32; P. O. Cameron; rep; 125 acres, value $7,500; from Penn.

LEONARD JNO. L. Farmer and Stock Raiser; Sec. 3; P. O. Galesburg; born in Hamilton Co., N. Y., Sept. 25, 1835; came to this Co. in 1863; Dem; Catholic; owns 80 acres land, valued at $4,800; married Johanna Nash, March 5, 1861; has three children, William, Margaretta, Alice.

Long Calvin A. lives with his father, Daniel Long; Sec. 11; P. O. Galesburg; rep.

Long Daniel farmer; Sec 11; P. O. Galesburg; rep; Luth; 80 acres, value $6,000.

Lowe John H. rents, lives on Eaton's farm; P. O. Cameron; dem; from Kentucky.

Lucas C. farmer; Sec. 10; P. O. Monmouth; rep; from Sweden.

LUCAS JOSIAH CALVIN, Farmer and Stock Raiser; Sec. 18; P. O. Monmouth; born in Warren Co., Ill., July 30, 1832; Dem; owns 807 acres, valued at $48,420; married Miss H. J. Townsend, March 22, 1857; has held the office of Justice of the Peace and School Director; has six children, Berry, Oley A., James L., Jessie, Rose J., Harry C.

Lucas Wm. B. farmer; Sec. 29; P. O. Cameron; dem; 80 acres, value $4,565; Ill.

Ludington H. blacksmith; Cameron; ind; value of estate $1,000; from Pennsylvania.

Lynch David, laborer; P. O. Monmouth; dem; Chris.

Lynch Joseph Jr. carpenter; P. O. Monmouth; dem.

Lyons Joseph, Sr., laborer; Cameron; dem; Chris; value of estate $500; from Ky.

Lyons Marion F. laborer; P. O. Cameron; dem; born Illinois.

LYON WILLIAM, Farmer; Sec. 28; P. O. Cameron; born in Indiana, April 8, 1833; came to this Co. in 1854; Rep; value of estate $2,000; rents Holland Hedgepeth's farm; married Barbara Grace; have four children, Charley, John, George, Ettie; was in army one year.

Lyons C., Jr. farmer, renter, lives on M. R. Jones' farm; P. O. Cameron; dem; Ill.

McCALE THOMAS laborer; P. O. Cameron; dem; Cath; from Ireland.

McCristal James, miner; P. O. Cameron; dem; from Scotland.

McFARLAND B. Farmer and Stock Raiser; Sec. 26; P. O. Galesburg; born in Warren Co., in Coldbrook Tp., Sept. 6, 1831; Dem; owns 220 acres, valued at $13,200; married B. P. Parker, 1855; has four children, Walter E., born March, 1858; Cora L., June, 1863; Carrie L., April, 1874, and Clara F., July, 1856, who died, Nov. 1857; Mr. McFarland's farm is six miles west of the city of Galesburg; is well watered and fenced, and has twenty-five or thirty acres of timber; is considered one of the best stock farms in Warren Co., improvements are second to none.

McFarland Mrs. James, Sec. 26; P. O. Galesburg; Meth; 366 acres, value $25,620; Ky.

McMullin John, farmer; Sec. 17; P. O. Cameron; dem; Chris; 269 acres, value $15,520.

Mafors Wm. C. laborer; P. O. Cameron; dem.

Manson Lewis, rents Lambard's farm; Sec. 12; P. O. Galesburg; rep; Luth; Sweden.

Mardis A. laborer; P. O. Cameron; dem; from Ohio.

Mariam S. A. rents Aaron Bowers' farm; Sec. 36; P. O. Cameron; rep; Meth; from N. Y.

Mecum C. J. lives on his father's farm; Sec. 24; P. O. Galesburg; dem; born Illinois.

Mecum Frank, lives with his father, C. J. Mecum; P. O. Galesburg; dem.

Mecum R. R. farmer; Sec. 36; P. O. Galesburg; dem; 420 acres, value $25,200; Mass.

Miller Chas. R. laborer; P. O. Monmouth; dem; from Kentucky.

Mills Chas. farmer; Sec. 8; P. O. Cameron; rents Calvin Lucas' farm; dem; born Ill.

MILLS WM. Farmer; Cameron; born, Ohio, Nov. 3, 1835; came to this Co. 1851; Dem; Univ; owns 85 acres, value $2,000; has held one or more Township offices ever since 1865; Town Clerk five years, Assessor three years, and Justice of Peace for seven years, and elected for four years more at the last town meeting, also elected Town Clerk; served 6 mos. in the 1st I. V. C. Co. G; was surrendered by Mulligan at battle of Lexington, Mo; afterwards served three years in 9th I. V. C. Co. L; married Lourania Parker, Sept. 16, 1855; have four children living, three boys and one girl; oldest boy 21 years old and married.

Mills Wm. laborer; Sec. 27; P. O. Cameron; dem; from Ohio.

Moites Abijah, farm laborer; dem; from Ohio.

MOORE ALEXANDER, Farmer; P. O. Cameron; born in Kentucky, January, 1811; came to this Co. in 1833; Dem; Christian; owns 95 acres, valued at $5,700; in 1837 went back to Kentucky; in 1844 came back to Warren Co., and has lived here ever since; married Lucy Norris in 1841, who died Nov. 1864; had ten children, five living, Angeline, born 1847; Helen, 1850; Wallace, 1855; Alexander, 1857; Allen, 1859; five deceased, Ann Eliza, died 1850; Alvira, 1867; Victoria, 1869; Jane, 1875; Sarah, 1864; has been Road Commissioner and Overseer of Highways; Wallace lives with his father on Sec. 2.

Moore Geo. farm laborer; P. O. Galesburg; from Kentucky.

Moore Harrison, farmer; Sec. 22; P. O. Cameron; dem; 25 acres, value $750; Ky.

Moore Wallace, lives with Alex. Moore; P. O. Cameron.

Morris Canady, P. O. Monmouth; dem; Chris; born Ill.

Moshier David Sr., farmer; Sec. 7; P. O. Monmouth; rep; Meth; 155 acres, $11,425.

Mitchel Nelson, lives with his father on Sec. 12; P. O. Utah; dem; born in Illinois.

NELSON SAMUEL, lives with his father on Sec. 12; P. O. Galesburg; dem; Ill.

Nelson William H. lives with his father on Sec. 12; P. O. Utah; dem; born in Ill.

NELSON G. J. Farmer and Stock Raiser; Sec. 12; P. O. Utah; born in Indiana, May 22, 1817; came to this Co. in 1848; Dem; owns 472 acres land, valued at $35,680; married Elvira Langdon, 1843; has two children, William H. and Michael; first came to Knox Co. and stayed about three years, and then went to Indiana, and then came to Warren Co., and have lived here ever since.

NELSON WILLIAM J. Farmer and Stock Raiser; Sec. 12; P. O. Utah; born in Jackson Co., Ind., on Oct. 4, 1830; came to this Co. in 1852; Dem; owns 160 acres land, valued at $9,600; married Laura L. Smith, March 17, 1857; has nine children—Amanda M., Elizabeth N., William A., Loretta E., George M., Cora R., James T., Minnie A., Granderson F.

NICOLS GEORGE, Farmer and Stock Raiser; Sec. 13; P. O. Galesburg; born in New York on Nov. 19, 1827; came to this Co. in 1862; Rep; owns 160 acres land, valued at $12,800; married Margaret Moran, April 7, 1852; have three children—Sarah J., Andrew H., Thomas H.; Mr. N. first came to Fulton Co., and then to Knox, and then to Warren Co., Ill.

O'BRIEN RICHARD, lives on George Adcock's farm; rents 80 acres; dem.

Ogden Eugene, farmer; Sec. 19; P. O. Cameron; rep; 150 acres, value $6,200; Ill.

OGDEN RUFUS, Farmer and General Business; P. O. Cameron; born in Oneida Co., New York, on 23d October, 1818;

came to this Co. in 1837; Rep; Bapt; owns 485 acres land, valued at $30,000; married Miss Narcissa C. Wilber, April 25, 1843; have one boy and two girls; Mrs. Ogden was one of the foremost ladies in getting aid for the soldiers during the late war, and many is the box of preserves she sent to the sick and wounded soldiers, whom she loved as well as she did the flag those brave ones fought and died for, and God grant she may reap her reward in Heaven.

Olson Gus, rents H. Bruner's farm; Sec. 4; P. O. Galesburg; rep; from Sweden.

O'Riley William, P. O. Cameron; rep; Meth; from Canada.

PAGE HIRAM, farmer; Sec. 10; P. O. Galesburg; rep; 20 acres, value $1,200.

Page Lyman, laborer; Sec. 2; P. O. Utah; rep; 3 acres, value $400; from New York.

Palmer Mrs. Alfred, P. O. Cameron; Meth; value of estate $500; from Virginia.

Palmer Merrit, farm laborer; P. O. Cameron; rep; Meth; born in Warren Co., Illinois.

Parker Adolph, school teacher; P. O. Cameron; dem; Christian; born in Illinois.

PARKER A. G. Retail Grocer; Cameron; born in Warren Co., Ill., March 28, 1849; dem; owns 5 acres land, valued at $400; married Hulda Jewel, Feb. 12, 1871; three children—Harry, born Nov. 8, 1871; Bertha, born Nov. 23, 1873; Arnold G., born Dec. 19, 1875; wife was born Jan. 20, 1853, in Logan Co., Ohio.

Parker Charles, farmer; P. O. Cameron; dem; Chris; born in Illinois.

PARKER HARVEY, Farmer; Sec. 30; P. O. Cameron; born in Brown Co., Ohio, on Nov. 23, 1805; came to this Co. in 1833; Dem; Univ; owns 70 acres of land, valued at $5,000; been married twice; first wife was Sallie Lyen; second wife, Parmelia H. Miller; has ten children, six of them deceased; Mr. P. was Lieutenant and Major in the army; his son Jacob lives with him.

Parkes J. V. farmer; Sec. 30; dem; 20 acres, value $1,000; born Ill.

Payne C. T. Sec. 27; P. O. Galesburg; rep; 30 acres, value $1,200; from Tennessee.

Pope George, laborer; P. O. Monmouth; dem; Meth; born in Illinois.

Post Chauncey, laborer; P. O. Monmouth; rep; born in Illinois.

Pugh J. S. farm laborer; P. O. Galesburg; dem; Meth; born in Illinois.

RAGLAND J. E. Sec. 18; P. O. Monmouth; dem; 80 acres, value $4,000.

Ragland J. L. farmer; Sec. 18; P. O. Monmouth; dem; 123 acres, value $6,150.

RHYKERD C. A. Farmer; Sec. 35; P. O. Galesburg; born in New York on Dec. 7, 1836; came to this Co. in 1849;

Rep; owns 676 acres land, valued at $40,560; married Anna Ostrom; have three children—Lilly J., Ward and Clark.

Richards H. G. farmer; Sec. 13; P. O. Galesburg; rep; 80 acres, value $5,000; Vt.

RICHARDSON PARIS JR. Farmer and Wagon Maker; Sec. 2; P. O. Utah; born in New York on Sept. 15, 1827; came to this Co. in 1835; Dem; Univ; owns one acre land, valued at $500, and rents 225 acres land; married Barbara Boile, 1850; has six children—Mary E., John P., William D., Lucy M., Malissa E., Charles A., Fred P.; was in army, Company H., 14th Ill., for nine months.

Riley B. F. runs ditching machine; P. O. Cameron; dem; Meth.

Robinson D. D. farmer; Sec. 20; P. O. Cameron; dem; 27 acres, value $1,000; Ill.

ROBINSON MRS. GERILDA Farming; Sec. 29; P. O. Cameron; born in Illinois April 23, 1853; Chris; owns 80 acres of land, valued at $5,000; is the daughter of D. R. Shelton; married D. D. Robinson, Jan. 27, 1869; has four children—Charley, Eddie, Berdine, and Winnie.

Russell G. D. farmer; Sec. 2; rents Terpening's farm; P. O. Utah; rep; Meth; Ohio.

Ryner Harvey, lives with his father; P. O. Galesburg; dem.

Ryner Josiah, farmer; Sec. 2; P. O. Utah; dem; Advent; 500 acres; value $25,000.

SALLEE ADDISON, lives with mother on Sec. 4; P. O. Utah; 1,000 acs. in Iowa.

Sallee J. R. farmer; Sec.4; P. O. Utah; dem; Chris; 133 acres, value $7,780; from Va.

Sallee Mrs. L. N., P. O. Utah; 65 acres, value $4,020; from Kentucky.

SALLEE MINERVA, Farming; Sec. 5; P. O. Utah; born in Warren Co., Sept. 3, 1836; owns 175 acres, valued at $10,500; is the widow of H. A. Sallee; married Nov. 19, 1856; Mr. Sallee was from Virginia; died Oct. 31, 1858; had one child, George M., born March 1, 1858.

Saunders A. G. lives on Hedgepeth's farm; P. O. Cameron; dem; Chris; from Kentucky.

Shelton D. R. farmer; Sec. 32; P. O. Cameron; dem; 180 acres, value $11,000; Ky.

SHELTON JAMES M. Farmer; Sec. 29; P. O. Cameron; born in Warren Co., Ill., on Feb. 2, 1851; Rep; owns 77 acres land, valued at $4,000; married Julia Sales, Feb. 4, 1874; has one child, a girl, Laura M. Shelton.

SHELTON J. D. Farmer and Stock Raiser; Sec. 15; P. O. Galesburg; born in Kentucky on Dec. 9, 1833; came to this Co. in 1837; Ind; Chris; owns 240 acres land, valued at $14,400; married Eliza L. Reece, Sept. 14, 1865; had four children—George V., Mary, John, Orpha M., who died; is a member of the Patrons of Husbandry, of Coldbrook Lodge.

SHELTON S. T. Farmer; Cameron; born in Kentucky, Sept. 6, 1821; came to Warren Co. Nov. 24, 1837; Ind; Chris; owns 540 acres land, valued at $32,400; was member of assembly in 1870, and was enrolling officer for sub-district No. 51, during the war; married Miss Murphy, June 16, 1846; Eugene Clay lives with Shelton.

Shults S. W. farm laborer; P. O. Cameron; dem; from Ohio.

SIMCOCK AARON, Farmer; Sec. 30; P. O. Monmouth; born in Staffordshire, England, Aug., 1834; came to this Co. in 1846; owns 80 acres, valued at $4,800; came from England to Warren Co. in 1855, went back to England in 1856, came back to this Co. 1857, and has lived here ever since; married Ann Ridge, 1855; has two adopted children, Mary J. Rodenscroft and Thomas Rodenscroft; Mr. Simcock is a well-to-do farmer; commenced in the Co. by digging coal; has been school director; went back to England on a visit in 1875.

SIPE JOHN, Retired Farmer; Sec. 9; P. O. Galesburg; born in Pennsylvania on Feb, 20, 1809; came to this Co. in 1845; Dem; Chris; owns 161¾ acres of land, valued at $9,720; left Pennsylvania June 3, 1844; after 21 days travel over the Alleghany mountains, arrived at Mansfield, Ohio, and lived there 11 years, and came to Warren Co., Ill.; married Mary Wise, Nov. 1, 1831; eight children—Mary Jane, born July 10, 1834; Sarah E., April 8, 1836; John T., Jan. 16, 1842; William, Dec. 7, 1842; Francis C., died Feb. 1, 1844; David L., died May 14, 1863; Henry J., of Co. K, 36th Ill., was shot June 27, 1864, aged 25 years, 7 months, 3 days; Eliza A., died in Cal. Feb. 14, 1865, aged 32 years 11 days; been overseer of highways and school director.

Sipe Wm. A. lives with his father on Sec. 9; P. O. Galesburg; dem; Chris; from Ohio.

Smiddy Thomas, farmer; P. O. Utah; dem; Cath; 80 acres, value $4,000; from Ireland.

Smith Albert, farmer; Sec. 14; P. O. Utah; dem; 80 acres, value $4,000; born Illinois.

Smith Joseph, farmer; rents Calvin Lucas' farm; P. O. Galesburg; dem; from Ohio.

Snow G. H. Sec 6; P. O. Galesburg; dem; 25 acres, value $1,500; from Missouri.

Snyder Bennett, farmer; Sec. 2; P. O. Monmouth; rep; Meth; 39 acres, value $2,500.

Sons I. J. farmer; renter; Sec. 25; dem; P. O. Galesburg.

Suver L. G. farmer; Sec. 34; P. O. Cameron; dem; Chris; 123 acres, value $7,380; Ill.

Suver Mrs. Margaret J. Sec. 34; P. O. Cameron; 123 acres, value $7,380; born Ill.

Suver Mrs. Sec. 34; P. O. Cameron; 170 acres, value $10,200; from Kentucky.

TERPENING SMITH, farmer; Sec. 2; P. O. Utah; rep; Meth; 250 acs., $12,500.

Terpening H. renter; lives on Mrs. Armstrong's farm; Sec. 2; P. O. Utah; rep; Ill.

Taylor T. J. Sec. 23; P. O. Galesburg; dem; 90 acres; value $7,200; from Kentucky.

TAYLOR T. J. Farmer and Stock Raiser; Sec. 23; P. O. Galesburg; born in Henry Co., Kentucky, Oct. 22, 1812; came to this Co. 1835; Dem; owns 90 acres land, valued at $5,400; married Edith McFarland in 1838; have five children—Mary J., Sarah, Celestia, Caroline, Anna E., James, who is dead, and Jeremiah was killed in the battle of Franklin, Tenn.; been Road Commissioner and Collector.

Tibbits H. M. farm laborer; P. O. Cameron; dem; from Wisconsin.

Townsend Aaron B. Sec. 8; P. O. Galesburg; dem; 81 acres, value $5,000; from N. Y.

Townsend Wm. A. lives with father; Sec. 8; P. O. Galesburg; dem; from New York.

UNDERWOOD JOHN, farmer; Sec. 25; P. O. Galesburg; rep; Meth; 80 acres.

WADDLE T. rents Davisson's farm; Sec. 6; P. O. Monmouth; born in Illinois.

Washington George, laborer; lives with John Anderson on Sec. 14; P. O. Galesburg.

WALLACE JOHN F. Farmer and Stock Raiser; Sec. 16; P. O. Cameron; born in Warren Co., Ill., March 31, 1846; Dem; Chris; owns 274 acres, valued at $16,840; married Sarah S. Jones, Dec. 19, 1867; have four children—Hugh, Sarah, Frank, Laura; Mr. J. is son of Thomas C. Wallace, who came from Kentucky to Warren Co. in 1832, and died April 9, 1861.

Weeks C. B. farmer; Sec. 2; P. O. Utah; ind; 117 acres, value $8,190; from New York.

Whitman J. T. farmer; Sec. 2; P. O. Cameron; ind; 150 acres; value $8,000; Ky.

Whitman Joseph, lives with his father, J. T. Whitman; P. O. Cameron; ind; born Ill.

WHITMAN W. H. Farmer and Independent Preacher; Sec. 9; P. O. Galesburg; born in Kentucky on March 27, 1824; came to this Co. in November, 1830; ind. in politics and religion; owns 60 acres, valued at $4,500; Mr. H. has worked at the harness and sadlers' trade for 20 years; in 1874 he published a pamphlet of 79 pages, entitled the "Final Destiny of Adam's Race," which contains the religious belief of Mr. Whitman; has three children—Francis M., Washington B. and Henry J.; married Jennie Johnson, Feb. 24, 1846; has been Town Clerk and its Agent for S. C. Adams' Chart of History.

Whitman W. lives with his father; P. O. Galesburg; ind; born in Illinois.

H.R. Gilliland
MERCHANT, ALEXIS, ILL.

Winn U. Z. miner; P. O. Monmouth; dem; from Missouri.

Wilson Andrew, P. O. Monmouth; rep; Chris; 3 acres, value $150.

Wilson Isaac, wagon maker; Cameron; dem; Chris.

WILSON JAMES, Dealer in Coal; Sec. 19; P. O. Monmouth; born in Scotland, Sept. 22, 1834; came to this Co. in 1861; Rep; Church of God; owns 16 acres land, valued at $1,000; married Elizabeth Welsh, Jan. 29, 1866; has five children; came from Scotland in 1854 to the State of Maryland, then to Missouri, and stayed there seven years, then to Warren Co., Ill.

Wilson Mrs. P. O. Cameron; Bapt; value of estate $1,000.

YOUNG CLARENCE, lives with father, L. H. Young; Sec. 7; P. O. Monmouth.

Young Clark, farmer; Sec. 5; P. O. Monmouth; rep; Chris; 101 acs., value $5,050.

Young Geo. L. lives with his father, L. H. Young, on Sec. 7; P. O. Monmouth; rep.

Young H. L. laborer; P. O. Monmouth; dem.

Young L. H. farmer; Sec. 7; P. O. Monmouth; rep; Meth; 203 acres; value $14,210; Con.

COLDBROOK BUSINESS DIRECTORY.

Wilson Jas. Dealer in Coal; bank on Sec. 19; P. O. Cameron.

SPRING GROVE TOWNSHIP.

ALEXANDER J.E. station agent; Alexis; dem; German Ref; from Maryland.

Allingham H. C. farmer; Sec. 36; P. O. Gerlaw; Ind; 172 acres, value $8,600; Ky.

ANDERSON NELS, farmer; Sec. 10; P. O. Alexis; born in Sweden, Feb. 25, 1833; came to this country in 1860; Rep; 75 acres, value $3,750; served in the 43rd Ill. Inf.; wife was Ellen Munson, born in Sweden; married Feb. 5, 1857; seven children, three sons and four daughters; two sons, Edward L. and George W., and three daughters, Hannah, Pearlie and Lulu R. now living.

Armstrong John, farmer; Sec. 24; P. O. Gerlaw; dem; Pres; 264 acres, $50 per acre.

Arthurs Thos. farmer; Sec. 18; P. O. Spring Grove; Ind; U. P.; 80 acres; from N. C.

Ashcraft Al. blacksmith; Alexis; rep; born New York.

Avenell James, farmer; Sec. 31; P. O. Monmouth; rep; U. P.; 160 acres, value $8,000.

BAILEY JACOB, farmer; Sec. 11; P. O. Alexis; rep; from Ohio.

Bailey Jehu, farmer; Sec. 11; P. O. Alexis; rep; Ch. of God; 320 acres; from Penn.

Bates Thomas, farmer for A. Gilmore; Sec. 27; P. O. Gerlaw.

Bell Robt. farmer for B. Donnelly; Sec. 6; P. O. Alexis; rep; from Ireland.

Bellinger Alf. G. farmer; P. O. Alexis; dem; 200 acres, value $8,400; from Ohio.

Bellinger Charles, farmer; Alexis; dem; born England.

Bellinger Eliza, wid; P. O. Alexis; Adv; 116 acres, $25 per acre; from England.

Bellinger Jas. farmer; Sec. 13; P. O. Alexis; dem; Adv; 40 acres; from England.

BENGTSON OLOF, farmer; Sec. 14; P. O. Alexis; born in Sweden Dec. 5, 1823; came to this country in 1853, and Co. in 1854; Rep; Luth; owns 312 acres, value $10,000; wife was Anna Rem, born in Sweden; married May 3, 1859; six children, four boys and two girls; three boys and two girls living.

Black Daniel, farmer for E. Wallace; Sec. 3; P. O. Alexis; rep; from Penn.

Blantin Swan, tailor; Alexis; dem; Luth; from Sweden.

Blanford J. W. saloon keeper; Alexis; dem; $1,000; from Kentucky.

Blayney Henry, livery stable; Alexis; dem; from Ireland.

Blayney J. C. merchant; Alexis; dem; from Ireland.

Blayney M. J. hotel keeper; Alexis; dem. Pres; born West Virginia.

Blayney Robt. livery; Alexis; dem; $400; born Virginia.

Blayney Wm. livery; Alexis; dem; $300; from Ireland.

Boggs Frank A. teacher; Alexis; rep; Pres; born Illinois.

Boggs James, farmer; Sec. 5; P. O. Norwood; dem; Pres; 76 acres in War. Co., 80 in Mer.

Boggs James P. farmer with James Boggs; Sec. 5; P. O. Norwood; dem; from Penn.

Boggs Jos. A. teacher; Sec. 5; P. O. Norwood; dem; Pres; from Penn.

Boggs M. C. doctor; P. O. Gerlaw; rep; Pres; from Penn.

Bogue Peter, grain buyer; Alexis; dem; from New York.

Bollinger M. G. grocer; Alexis; from Penn.

Boozan Richard, farmer for T. Boozan; Sec. 30; P. O. Denny; dem; Cath; from Ireland.

Boozan Thos. Sr. farmer; Sec. 30; P. O. Denny; dem; Cath; 160 acres; Ireland.

Boozan Thos. Jr., farmer for T. Boozan; Sec. 30; P. O. Denny; dem; Cath; from Ireland.

Boozan Thos. farmer; Sec. 10; P. O. Alexis; dem; Cath; 80 acres; Ireland.

Brown James W. rents of Pattison; P. O. Gerlaw; dem; from Kentucky.

Brown W. H. clerk; Alexis; dem; Meth; $500; born Illinois.

Brown Wm. H. Police Magistrate; Alexis.

Brownlee Thos. laborer; P. O. Alexis; dem; from Penn.

Buck A. A. farmer; Sec. 25; P. O. Gerlaw; dem; born Illinois.

Burkholder Jacob, blacksmith; Sec. 4; P. O. Alexis; rep; from Penn

Burns Larry, farmer; Sec. 10; P. O. Alexis; dem; Cath; 80 acres, value $3,600; Ireland.

Butterfield A. V. farmer; Sec. 8; P.O. Alexis; dem; 81 acres, value $3,200; from N. Y.

CALL HENRY, butcher; Alexis; rep; from Ohio.

Campbell J. P. teacher; Sec. 27; P. O. Alexis; dem.

Cannon John, farmer; Sec. 13; P. O. Alexis; dem; Ch. of God; 80 acres, val. $4,000; Ire.

Cannon John S. teacher; Sec. 13; P.O. Alexis; rep; from Penn.

Carmichael Abram, farmer; P. O. Alexis; rep; U. P.

Carmichael Jas. farmer; P. O. Alexis; rep; U. P.; born Illinois.

Carroll Dan, laborer; P. O. Alexis; dem; Cath; from Ireland.

Carroll Thos. laborer; Alexis; dem; Cath; from Ireland.

Carson Harriet, wid. Sec. 34; P. O. Gerlaw; Chris; 270 acres, value $13,500.

Carson Seaton A. farmer; Sec. 3; P. O. Alexis; rep; from Ohio.

Carson Wm. farmer; Sec. 34; P. O. Gerlaw; rep; 130 acres, value $7,000; born Ohio.

Casey John, miner for W. L. Miller; Sec. 13; P. O. Alexis; Ind; Cath; born Ireland.

Caveney Mike, laborer; P. O. Alexis; dem; Cath; $400; born Ireland,

CHAFFEE A. H. M. D; editor and proprietor *Alexis Index*; Alexis; born in La Grange Co., Ind., May 21, 1849; came to this Co. in 1876; Ind; Prot; was in army service, 152d Ind. Infantry; graduated at Eclectic Medical College, Cincinnati, O. in 1867; married Miss Rose Sallady, Aug., 1870, who was from Noble Co., Ind.

Chapman A. A. farmer, Sec. 35; P. O. Gerlaw; rep; 242 acres, value $12.000; N. Y.

CHAPMAN O. G. P. M. and Stationer; Alexis; born in Oswego Co., N. Y., Feb. 26, 1843; came to this Co. in 1867; Rep; owns town property valued at $1,500; is now Postmaster, and has been since Jan. 1871; served three years and four months in the 110th N. Y. Inf.; wife was Adaline Garrett, born in Breckenridge Co., Ky.; married Aug. 19, 1872; one child, Wade, blessed their union.

Churchill B. M. carpenter; Alexis; dem; $200; from New York.

Churchill Dan, wagon maker; Alexis; dem; from New York.

Clark R. J. farmer for A. Rankin; Sec. 32; P. O. Spring Grove; rep; from Indiana.

Claybaugh Matthew, farmer; Sec. 5; P. O. Alexis; rep; U. P.

Cling Noah, farmer for A. Ritchey; Sec. 2; P. O. Alexis; rep; U. B.; from Maryland.

Coffland E. B. farmer for S. Fulton; Sec. 28; P. O. Spring Grove; rep; from Ohio.

Coffland M. L. farmer for R. W. Gerlaw; Sec. 28; P. O. Gerlaw; rep; U. P.; Ohio.

Collins A. M. farmer; Sec. 35; P. O. Gerlaw; dem; Chris; born Illinois.

Collins James, farmer; Sec. 35; P. O. Gerlaw; dem.

Conant H. carpenter; P. O. Alexis; rep; from Ohio.

COOK, WM. Miner and Farmer; Sec. 14; P.O. Alexis; born in England, January 27, 1819; came to this country in 1867; Rep; U. B.; owns 86 acres, valued at $5,000; wife was Jane Kennedy, born in England; married May 3, 1852; one son, William H.

Coulter R. V. farmer; Sec. 10; P. O. Alexis; dem; from Penn.

Cox David, farmer for H. C. Allingham; Sec. 36; P. O. Gerlaw; rep; from Canada.

Croft John, bartender; Alexis; dem; Cath; from Ireland.

Crozier John, farmer; P. O. Spring Grove; rep; U. P.; from New York.

Crozier O. D. farmer; P. O. Gerlaw; rep; U. P.; 80 acres.

Cummings Duncan, farmer for J. H. Frantz; Sec. 27; P. O. Gerlaw; from Canada.

Curtis R. painter; Alexis; rep; born Ill.

DENISON JOHN, farmer for H. R. Gilliland; Sec. 4; P. O. Alexis; dem; Pa.

WARREN COUNTY : SPRING GROVE TOWNSHIP. 311

Dodd Hugh, farmer; Sec. 10; P. O. Alexis; rep; Ch. of God; 120 acres, val. $55 per acre.

Dodge G. B. blacksmith; Alexis; rep; Adv; from New York.

Donnelly Bernard, farmer; Sec. 6; P. O. Alexis; dem; Cath; 24 acres; from Ireland.

Donnelly John, farmer with B. Donnelly; Sec. 6; P. O. Alexis; dem; Cath; Ireland.

Dooland James, farmer with T. Dorland; Sec. 3; P. O. Alexis; rep; from Penn.

Dooland John; teacher, with Thos. Dorland; Sec. 3; P. O. Alexis; rep; Presb; Penn.

Dorland Thos. farmer; Sec. 3; P. O. Alexis; dem; Presb; 80 acres, value $6,000; Penn.

Dowler M. J. farmer with R. Dowler; Sec. 17; dem; U. P.; from Virginia.

Dowler Robt. farmer; Sec. 17; P. O. Spring Grove; dem; 41 acres; from Virginia.

Downey Wm. farmer; Sec. 12; P. O. Alexis; dem; Cath; 60 acres; from Ireland.

Downs R. K. bartender; P. O. Alexis; dem; born Pennsylvania.

Douglas M. L. farmer; Sec. 7; P. O. Alexis; rep; U. P.; from Indiana.

Draney Jno. B. plasterer; P. O. Alexis; rep.

Driffill John, carpenter; P. O. Alexis; dem; from New York.

DUNN ALLEN, Farmer; Sec. 30; P.O. Monmouth; born in Erie Co., Pa., Sept. 13, 1833; Rep; U. P.; 250 acres, value $15,000; personal $2,000; came to this State in 1856, to this Co. in 1867; married Elizabeth J. McKnight, Jan. 15, 1857, who was born in Crawford Co., Pa., Sept. 7, 1832; they have three children living, Alice May, Eva Dale and Harry Emerson; one son and one daughter deceased; was in 102d I.V. I., Co. E.

Dunn Cabel, P. O. Alexis; dem; Bapt; from Ohio.

Dunn Elijah L., P. O. Alexis; dem; from Ohio.

Dunn George S., P. O. Alexis; dem; Bapt; from Ohio.

Dunn James L., P. O. Alexis; dem; from Ohio.

Dunn Marion W., P. O. Alexis; dem; from Ohio.

Dunn Matthias S., P. O. Alexis; dem; from Ohio.

Dunn Thomas, farmer; P. O. Alexis; ind; dem; Bapt; 160 acres; from Ohio.

Dunn Thomas, farmer; Sec. 12; P.O. Alexis; Bapt; 160 acres; from Ohio.

ECKMAN SCOTT, Sec. 18; P. O. Spring Grove; from Maryland.

Edwards Amos, blacksmith; P. O. Alexis; ind.

Elder A. A. merchant; P. O. Gerlaw; rep; U. P.; $1,500; from Ohio.

Elder David, retired farmer; P. O. Alexis; rep; U. P.; from Penn.

Elder D. C. agt; P. O. Alexis; rep; U. P.; from Ohio.

Elder Wm. A. Alexis; rep; U. P.; 160 acres, value $7,000; from Ohio.

Erbeldinger Jacob, farmer; Sec. 15; P. O. Alexis; dem; 40 acres, value $2,000; Ger.

Erbeldinger Willis; farmer; Sec. 15; P. O. Alexis; dem.

Ericson Andrew, grain buyer; P. O. Alexis; rep; from Sweden.

Edwards E. miner; Sec. 15; P. O. Alexis.

Eyre Benjamin, butcher; Alexis; rep; from England.

FINDLEY JOHN A. laborer for R. W. Gerlaw; P. O. Gerlaw; rep; from Miss.

Foster Hamilton, farmer; Sec. 18; P.O. Spring Grove; rep; U. P.; from South Carolina.

FOSTER JOHN A. Farmer; Sec. 18; P. O. Spring Grove; born in Abbeyville, S. C., Nov. 7, 1818; came to this Co. in 1837; Rep; U. P.; 232 acres, value $12,760; came here by team from South Carolina, and was eight weeks on the road; arrived May 18, 1837; married Martha J. Struthers, Oct. 30, 1843; she came from Green Co., Ohio, and died June 7, 1854; children, Elizabeth S., married F. M. McClenahan; Margaret L., married Martin McKee; Nancy J. married Robert Hogue; Mr. F. married the second time Mrs. Rachel W. Mitchell, April 5, 1855; she has one son, John A. Mitchell, M. D.

FORWOOD B. F. Farmer; Sec. 23; P. O. Gerlaw; born in Harford Co., Maryland, Dec. 18, 1816; came to this country in 1838; Dem; owns 160 acres, valued at $9,600; was first Township Clerk; has held office School Treas. since 1846.

FOUST DAVID, Merchant; Gerlaw; born in Franklin Co., Penn., Dec. 29, 1829; came to this country in 1852; Dem; owns town property valued at $4,000; wife was Violet N. Shoemaker, born in Franklin Co., Penn; married Jan. 13, 1859; three sons, John E., Charley W. and David W.

Frank Wm. farmer; Sec. 32; P. O. Spring Grove.

Franklin Henry, merchant; Alexis; rep; Meth; born Illinois.

FRANTZ J. H. Farmer and Stock Raiser; Sec. 22; P. O. Gerlaw; born in Alleghany Co., Maryland, Feb. 20, 1836; came to this Co. in 1857; Rep; owns 237 acres, valued at $1,200; wife was Anne M. Porter, born in Warren Co., Ill.; married Sept. 23, 1860; seven children, four daughters living.

Fulton Jas. W. farmer; Sec. 20; P. O. Spring Grove; dem; 112 acres; born Illinois.

Fulton John W. farmer; Sec. 18; P. O. Spring Grove; rep; 90 acres; born Illinois.

GAMBLE STEPHEN, clerk for Evans & Blayney; P. O. Alexis; dem; Ireland.

GALLOWAY C. Teacher; Alexis; born in Green Co., O., Feb. 29, 1844; came to this Co. in 1853; Rep; Presb; graduated at Monmouth College, Classical course, class of 1870; attended Law Department, Mich. University, term of 1870 and '71; served as clerk in Census Bureau, in Washington, D. C. one year; has been teaching in Public Schools for last five years; married Rebecca A. Wakefield, April 24, 1873, of McVeytown, Pa; they have one child, Horace C.

Gallaugher Chas. farmer for Wm. Gallaugher; Sec. 22; P. O. Gerlaw; rep; Md.

Gallaugher Wm. farmer; Sec. 22; P. O. Gerlaw; rep; 240 acres, at $40 per acre; Scot.

Garvin T. M. printer; P. O. Alexis; rep; from Virginia.

GERLAW R. W. Farmer and Stock Raiser; Sec. 34; P. O. Gerlaw; born in Greene Co., Ohio, March 4, 1817; came to this Co. in 1850; Rep; owns 700 acres, valued at $35,000; wife was Mary J. Black, born in Ohio; married March 16, 1852; five children; one son and three daughters living.

Gillen Mike, miner for Wm. Cook; P. O. Alexis; dem; Cath; 80 acres, $1,500; Ire.

GILLILAND H. R. Merchant; Alexis; born in Huntington Co., Penn., Oct. 22, 1828; came to this Co. in 1852; Dem; Presb; owns 120 acres, worth about $8,000; wife was Rebecca E. Campbell, born in Huntington Co., Penn.; married March 1, 1853; two daughters, Hannah M. and Mary E.

Gilmore C. M. farmer for L. H. Gilmore; Sec. 34; P. O. Gerlaw; dem; Pres; Ill.

GILMORE JAMES T. Farmer and Stock Raiser; Sec. 23; P. O. Gerlaw; born in Jefferson Co., Ohio, June 5, 1823; came to this Co. in 1833; Ind; Chris; owns 410 acres, valued at $20,000; wife was Mary C. Lair, born in Warren Co., Ky.; married Oct. 26, 1848; five children—one son and four daughters; one son, George W., and two daughters, Elizabeth A. and Ella J., are now living.

GILMORE L. H. Farmer and Stock Raiser; Sec. 34; P. O. Gerlaw; born in Jefferson Co., Ohio, April 11, 1830; came to this Co. in 1833; Dem; Presb; 900 acres, valued at $45,000; has held several different offices; is now Supervisor, and has served in that capacity nine terms; wife was S. A. Forwood, born in Harford Co., Maryland; married Nov. 9, 1854; six children, four sons and two daughters, all now living.

Gibson Alex. farmer; Sec. 34; P. O. Gerlaw; rep; Adv; 126 acres, $75 per acre; Ohio.

Glass George, teamster; Alexis; dem; born Illinois.

Godfrey Thos. C. plasterer; Alexis; rep; U. P.; from Ireland.

Goff C. D. laborer; Alexis; rep; born Ill.

Gollagher Michael, laborer; P. O. Alexis; dem; Cath; $400; Ireland.

Graham J. C. furniture dealer; Alexis; rep; U. P.; from Ohio.

Graham Jas. retired farmer; P. O. Alexis; rep; U. P.; town property, $1,500; Penn.

Graham Jos. C. furniture dealer; Alexis; rep; U. P.

Graham W. W. grain and stock buyer; Alexis; dem; $1,500; born Illinois.

Green Harford, printer; Alexis; Rep; Prot; born Bureau Co.

HANNA CRAIG, farmer; Sec. 25; P. O. Gerlaw; 600 acres, value $30,000; Ind.

Hardy B. G. grocer; Alexis; rep; from Ind.

Hardy Wm. miner for J. Simcox; Sec. 11; P. O. Alexis; dem; from England.

Hartwell D. V. farmer for Wm. Hartwell; Sec. 7; P. O. Spring Grove; rep.

Hartwell Wm. farmer; Sec. 7; P. O. Spring Grove; rep; Bapt; 160 acres.

Henderson Robert, miner for W. L. Millar; Sec. 14; P. O. Alexis; rep; U. P.; Ohio.

Hensen Peter P. farmer; Sec. 21; P. O. Spring Grove; Luth; 80 acres, $3,000; Denmark.

HERBERT GEO. Farmer; Sec. 7; P. O. Spring Grove; born in Ohio, Oct. 27, 1848; came to this Co. in 1855, rep; owns 80 acres in Warren Co., and 160 acres in Iowa, valued at $3,600; wife was Rhoda Parker, born in Warren Co., Ill.; married her June, 1871.

Hill J. W. farmer; P. O. Spring Grove; rep; U. P.; 40 acres.

Hogue F. C. merchant; P. O. Gerlaw; rep; U. P.; from Ohio.

Hogue John S. farmer for James McQuiston; Sec. 33; P. O. Gerlaw; rep; U. P.; Ohio.

Hogue Joseph, laborer; P. O. Gerlaw; from Ohio.

Hogue Robert I. farmer; Sec. 33; P. O. Gerlaw; rep; U. P.; 78 acres, $3,500; Ohio.

Hollenbeck Jas. laborer; P. O. Alexis; rep; $400; from New York.

IREY GEORGE, farmer for J. M. Irey; Sec. 23; P. O. Gerlaw; dem; from Penn.

Irey John M. farmer; Sec. 23; P. O. Gerlaw; dem; 80 acres; from Pennsylvania.

INGERSOLL HIRAM, retired; Alexis; born in Courtland Co., N. Y., Feb. 7, 1812; came to this Co. in Sept. 1836; Rep; owns house and lot value, $900, personal $500; settled in Kelly Tp. in Sept. 1836; held offices of Township Clerk and Collector for several terms; married Cecelia E. Potter, Jan. 1, 1846, daughter of Chester Potter, who came here in 1832, the

WARREN COUNTY: SPRING GROVE TOWNSHIP.

first miller, and ground the first grain in this Co.

JOHNSON G. P. laborer; Alexis; Luth; from Sweden.

Johnson Mons. W. shoe-maker; Alexis; dem; Luth; $700; from Sweden.

Johnson Swan I. shoe-maker; Alexis; dem; Meth; from Sweden.

JOHNSON MAJ. CHAS. E. Farmer; Sec. 4; P. O. Alexis; born in New York; came to this Co. in 1860; Rep; owns 95 acres, valued at $7,000; has been Assessor and Collector, and is Village Treasurer; served 3 years and 6 months in 11th Ill. Cavalry.

Johnston J. farmer for Wm. Walker; Sec. 20; P. O. Spring Grove; dem; from Ohio.

Johnston Rufus, pastor U. P. church; P. O. Gerlaw; rep; from Ohio.

Jones Franklin, telegraph operator; Alexis; rep; from New York.

Jones W. H. farmer for David White; P. O. Alexis; dem.

KALSTROM JOHN, laborer; P. O. Gerlaw; from Sweden.

Kindred F. farmer for P. Kindred; Sec. 34; P. O. Gerlaw; dem; born Illinois.

Kindred Jack, farmer for P. Kindred; Sec. 34; P. O. Gerlaw; dem; born Illinois.

Kindred Patterson, farmer for L. H. Gilmore; Sec. 34; P. O. Gerlaw; dem; Ind.

Kindred N. farmer for P. Kindred; P. O. Gerlaw; dem; born Illinois.

Kinkaid J. N. farmer and post-master; P. O. Spring Grove; rep; 48 acs., $40 per acre.

Knox Robert, grocer, Alexis; rep; from Ohio.

LAFFERTY JAMES, laborer; P. O. Alexis; from Ohio.

LAIRD ALLEN. Miller; Alexis; born in Concord, Pa., March 13, 1840; Dem; Prot; owns half interest in Flouring mill, $4,500; served three years and nine months in 45th I. V. I.; came to this State in Spring of 1856; one of proprietors of Oriental Flouring Mills.

Laird J. A. plasterer; Alexis; rep; Meth; from Pennsylvania.

LAIR R. W. Farmer; Sec. 24; P. O. Alexis; born in Warren Co., Ky., May 22, 1829; came to this Co. in 1832; Dem; Chris; owns 167 acres, valued at $10,000; wife was Mary Quinn, born in Ohio; married Jan. 24, 1854; four children, two sons and two daughters; one son dead.

Langhead Samuel, farmer; Sec. 2; P. O. Alexis; rep; U. P.; 120 acres, $6,000; Ire.

Laughlin Dan. farmer; Sec. 17; P. O. Spring Grove; dem; Cath; 160 acres; Ireland.

Lawhead Emmett, teacher; Sec. 33; P. O. Spring Grove; rep; U. P.; from Ohio.

Leonard Silas, clerk; Alexis; from Pennsylvania.

LEONARD STEWART E. Farmer; Sec. 13; P. O. Alexis; born in Perry Co., Penn., March 6, 1854; came to this Co. in 1855; rep; wife was Aggie Gallagher; born in Marion Co., Va.; married Dec. 28, 1876.

Leonard Mrs. S. J. farmer; Sec. 13; P. O. Alexis; Ch. of God; 80 acres.

Lee Edmund, farmer for D. Shunick; P. O. Spring Grove; dem; Cath; from Ireland.

Lee Thomas, farmer for R. Shunick; Sec. 20; P. O. Spring Grove; dem; Cath; Ireland.

Liggett James, farmer for Thomas Arthurs; P. O. Spring Grove; rep; U. P.; Ohio.

Line Henry, laborer; Alexis; dem; from Pennsylvania.

Line W. W. farmer; Sec. 10; P. O. Alexis; dem; 80 acres, value $4,800; from Penn.

Loose Mat, tinner; Alexis; dem; Cath; $1,500; from Germany.

Lord Truman, clerk; Alexis.

Louch George, laborer; Alexis; rep; from England.

Loveridge Herman, butcher; Alexis; rep.

Loveridge James, butcher; Alexis; ind; Meth; 80 acres and town property, $5,000.

Loveridge R. H. painter; Alexis; dem; $250; from England.

LOVERIDGE THOMAS. Merchant and Hotel Keeper; Alexis; born in England, March 6, 1841; came to this country and Co. in 1856; Rep; Meth; owns real and personal property, value $5,000; married Maggie Waddill, Sept. 16, 1868, who was born in Va.; they have three children, Alena, born July 1, 1869, Ray, born Feb. 6, 1871, and May, born April 6, 1875.

Low Lee, farmer; Sec. 27; P. O. Gerlaw; rep; 80 acres, value $4,400; born Illinois.

Loyer John, Alexis; rep; U. B.; Ohio.

McCULLOCH J. H. teacher; Sec. 4; P. O. Alexis; rep; U.P.; born in Illinois.

McCullough W. J. farmer; Sec. 2; P. O. Alexis; rep; from Ohio.

McCullough Wm. R. farmer; Sec. 2; P. O. Alexis; rep; U. P.; from Ohio.

McCartney Chas. F. farmer for I. McCartney; P. O. Alexis; rep; Meth; from Ohio.

McCARTNEY IRVINE. Farmer; Sec. 24; P. O. Alexis; born in Ireland, July 19, 1815; came to this country in 1837, Co. in 1859; Rep; Meth; owns 80 acres, valued at $4,000; wife was Margaret Fyfe, born in Ireland; married May 30, 1834; ten children, four sons and six daughters; two sons, James and Charles F., and three daughters, Eliza J., Catharine A. and Lucy A., are now living.

McCRERY D. H. Farmer and Stock Raiser; Sec. 19; P. O. Spring Grove; born in South Carolina, Aug. 10, 1830; came to this Co. in 1836; Rep; U. P.; 256 acres, value $15,360, personal $3,500; he was with a company of families who emigrated to this State in 1835; married Catharine Struthers, Dec. 27, 1854, who was born in this Co. June 22, 1836; they have eight children, Isa J., Sophronia M., John C., Lizzie A., Myrta B., Celia E., David R and Dwight C.

McCRERY J. H. Farmer; Sec. 19; P. O. Spring Grove; born in this Co. April 20, 1842; Rep; U. P.; 175 acres, value $10,500; has always lived in this Co.; married Elizabeth J. Azdell, Feb. 14, 1867, who was born in Columbiana Co., Ohio, Aug. 23, 1850. They have two children, Samuel L., born Nov. 21, 1867, and Jennie A., Dec. 12, 1869.

McCONNELL ELIZABETH, Widow; Sec. 19; P. O. Monmouth; born in Brown Co., Ohio; came to this Co. in 1854; U. P.; 40 acres, value $2,200; her first husband, Samuel Askren, was from Brown Co., Ohio, died July 2, 1860, from injury received from horse; children, Sarah P. married James Weir, Rebecca J. married James S. Avenall, Martha Luella, Lyman T., all living; Mary E., dead; married the second time Jno. McConnell, Feb. 28, 1867, who died Sept. 25, 1871, from injuries received by horse, in one week.

McCOY AUGUS. Farmer and Stock Raiser; Sec. 27; P. O. Gerlaw; born in Washington Co., Penn, March 13, 1843; came to this Co. in 1854; Dem; owns 250 acres, valued at $11,250; was Town Clerk for 8 years; wife was Lizzie J. Hanna, born in Warren Co., Ill; married Dec. 22, 1870; two daughters, Mary Alice and Ethel Kate.

McFarland Gilbert, farmer; Sec. 3; P. O. Alexis; dem; Ch. of God; from Ohio.

McGee Robert, farmer; Sec. 10; P. O. Alexis; rep; U. P.; 5 acres; from Pennsylvania.

McGrew Jno. H. druggist; Alexis; dem; from Indiana.

McHenry J. farmer for C. B. Winbigler; Sec. 29; P. O. Spring Grove; dem; from Va.

McIntyre Alexander, farmer; Sec. 18; P. O. Spring Grove; rep; U. P.; 10 acres.

McIntyre Hewitt, farmer with J. P. McIntyre; P. O. Spring Grove; U. P.; born Ill.

McIntyre J. P. farmer; Sec. 17; P. O. Spring Grove; rep; 60 acres; from Canada.

McIntyre W. P. farmer with J. P. McIntyre; Sec. 17; P. O. Spring Grove; rep; born Ill.

McKee T. M. farmer; Sec. 21; P. O. Spring Grove; rep; U. P.; 103 acres, $5,000; Ohio.

McKelvie Janet, Sec. 14; P. O. Alexis; 80 acres, value $3,000; from Scotland.

McKELVIE MICHAEL, Farmer; Sec. 14; P. O. Alexis; born in Scotland, Aug. 15, 1844; came to this Co. in 1856; Rep; wife was Marion Peacock, born in Scotland; married March 16, 1868; five children, three sons, Thomas S., John P. and Willie, and two daughters, Annie and Nettie; served about three years in 83d Ill. Inf.

McKirahan Rev. M. F. pastor U. P.; P. O. Alexis; rep; from Ohio.

McKnight D. S. hardware and agr. imps.; Alexis; rep; U. P.; $5,000; from Penn.

McKnight J. A. farmer; P. O. Monmouth; rep; U. P.; 140 acres; from Pennsylvania.

McQuiston James H. farmer; Sec. 33; P. O. Gerlaw; rep; U. P.; 180 acres, val. $10,000.

McQuiston Joseph G. farmer with J. H. McQuiston; Sec. 33; P. O. Gerlaw; rep; U. P.

Martin James, farmer; Sec. 19; P. O. Spring Grove; rep; U. P.; 92 acres, value $5,500.

Martin John, porter; Alexis; rep; Meth; $450; from Germany.

Mayfield I. W. farmer; Sec. 11; P. O. Alexis; rep; Ch. of God; 139 acres; from Ind.

Miller Samuel B. farmer; P. O. Alexis; dem; born Illinois.

MILLER THOMAS M. Farmer and Stock Raiser; Sec. 4; P. O. Alexis; born in Adams Co., O., July 22, 1823; came to this Co. in 1854; rep; U. P.; 320 acres, value $16,000, personal $3,500; married Miss Jane McCutchan, who was born in Adams Co., O., they have ten children, three sons and seven daughters, William O., Mary E., Margaret A., Robert F., Luella J., Emma A., George E., Edith I., Cora A. and Alena A., all living.

Miller Wm. Jasper, farmer for W. J. Miller; Sec. 35; P. O. Gerlaw; dem; born Illinois.

Miller Wm. Jackson, Sr., farmer; Sec. 35; P. O. Gerlaw; dem; 800 acres, $48,000; Ky.

MILLER WM. L. Miner; Sec. 13; P. O. Alexis; born in Scotland, Aug. 27, 1840; came to this Co. in 1873; Rep; owns 13⅔ acres, valued at $900; wife was Annie Morton, born in Scotland; married Oct. 20, 1865; five children, one son and four daughters, all now living.

Mills John, laborer for W. L. Miller; P. O. Alexis; from Scotland.

Mitchell Jno. B. insurance agent; Alexis; dem; from Scotland.

Muir Michael, farmer for Wm. Gallaugher; P. O. Gerlaw; rep; from Scotland.

Muir Thomas, miner for J. Simcox; P. O. Alexis; rep; from Scotland.

Mulnix R. F. farmer; Sec. 10; P. O. Alexis; rep; U. P; 80 acres; born Illinois.

Murphy Jno. H. farmer for R. N. Rogers; P. O. Gerlaw; rep; born Chicago.

N ASH J. O. farmer for Patterson; P. O. Gerlaw; rep; born Illinois.

Nelson Fred. farmer; Sec. 15; P. O. Alexis; 80 acres, value $2,600; from Sweden.

Niles Jerry M.; P. O. Alexis; rep; owns town prop. value $600; from Indiana.
Niles Oscar G. laborer; Sec. 35; P. O. Gerlaw; from Indiana.
Njulin Swen, farmer for S. Palmer; Sec. 15; P. O. Alexis; Luth; from Sweden.
Nolan, Ann widow; Alexis; Cath; $700; from Ireland:
Noonan Patrick, farmer; Sec. 36; P. O. Gerlaw; dem; Cath; 110 acres, value $4,400.
Norcross Isaiah, teacher; Sec. 34; P. O. Gerlaw; dem; Presb; born Illinois.

O'LEARY JAS. farmer; P. O. Alexis; dem; Cath; 60 acres; from Ireland.
Olin John, laborer; P. O. Gerlaw; Luth; from Sweden.
Oliver Robt. farmer; Sec. 3; P. O. Alexis; Ind; 60 acres, value $3,000; from Ireland.
Olson Swan, laborer; P. O. Gerlaw; rep; from Sweden.
Oswalt Jno. carpenter; Alexis; rep; $500; from Ohio.

PALMER SCHUYLER, farmer; Sec. 15; P. O. Alexis; Ind; Bapt; 515 acres.
Parker Geo. farmer, lives with J. Parker; Sec. 30; P. O. Monmouth; rep; Ill.
Parker Jacob, farmer for C. Harding; Sec. 30; P. O. Monmouth; rep; from Canada.
Parker Saml. farmer for Robt. Parker; P. O. Spring Grove; rep; from Maryland.
Patterson C. doctor; Sec. 29; P. O. Spring Grove; rep; U. P.; 10 acres, value $1,000.
Patterson Thos. B. merchant; Alexis; rep; $1,500; born Illinois.
Paul Emily, widow; Alexis; from Virginia.
Pettit David, laborer; Alexis; dem; Campbellite; 10 acres, value $300; from Penn.
Pettit Nathan, drayman; Alexis; rep; $900; from Ohio.
Phelps B. C. farmer for Robt. Holloway; Sec 32; P. O Monmouth; rep; U. P.; Iowa.
Pine Frank J. clerk; Alexis; rep; from Ill.
Peadon Nicholas, miner; P. O. Alexis; Meth; from England.
Pollock J. S. farmer for T. M. McKee; P. O. Spring Grove; rep; born Illinois.
Porter A. A. farmer; Sec. 26; P. O. Gerlaw; dem; 80 acres, value $4,400; born Ill.
Porter F. I. farmer for J. D. Porter, Sec. 5; P. O. Norwood; dem; Presb; from Penn.
Porter J. B. farmer for J. D. Porter; P. O. Alexis; dem; Presb; born Illinois.
Porter J. F. farmer; Sec. 26; P. O. Gerlaw; dem; 280 acres, $50 per acre; born Ill.
Porter J. W. wagon-maker; Alexis; dem; from Pennsylvania.
Porter Jas. D. farmer; Sec. 5; P. O. Alexis; dem; Presb; from Pennsylvania.
Porter Jno. Sr. farmer; Sec. 6; P. O. Alexis; dem; Presb; 80 acres, value $4,000; Penn.
Porter M. C. wagon-maker; Alexis; dem; from Pennsylvania.
Porter Mary, widow; farmer, Sec. 26; P. O. Gerlaw; Advent; 61 acres.
Porter Wm. E. farmer; Sec. 35; P. O. Gerlaw; dem; 88 acres, $75 per acre; Ill.
Porter Wm. L. farmer with Jno. Porter; Sec. 6; P. O. Alexis; dem; Presb; from Penn.
Postlewaite C. W. merchant; Alexis; Ind; $4,000; from Pennsylvania.
Pullen Albert, miner for Wm. Cook; P. O. Alexis; dem; from Indiana.
Pullen John, laborer; Sec. 11; P. O. Alexis; dem; U. B.; from Virginia.

RADER J. E. farmer for H. Sigafoos; Sec. 25; P. O. Gerlaw.
Ragland Robt. farmer; Sec. 36; P. O. Gerlaw; rep; Chris; 53 acres, $65 per acre.
Rhodes J. E. farmer for S. Palmer; P. O. Alexis; dem; from Kentucky.
Richard James, plasterer; Alexis; rep; from England.
Richardson W. F. farmer; P. O. Alexis; rep; Adv; from Indiana.
Rinker Joseph, laborer; Alexis; dem.
RINKER SAMUEL. Farmer; Sec. 11; P. O. Alexis; born in Virginia, Nov. 11, 1826; came to this Co. in 1866; Dem; Bapt; owns 80 acres, valued at $4,000; wife was Rebecca Carder, born in Virginia; married May 27, 1856; three children, one son, John T., and two daughters, Mary V. and Ida B.
RITCHEY A. J. Farmer and Stock Raiser; Sec. 2; P. O. Alexis; born in Indiana, May 17, 1833; came to this Co. in 1854; Dem; United Brethren; owns 315 acres, valued at $15,750; wife was Mary Low, born in Pennsylvania; married Sept. 13, 1855; seven children, one son, Henry, and three daughters, Ida, Emma and Jessie, now living.
Ritchey John T. farmer; Sec. 9; P. O. Spring Grove; rep; U. B.; 160 acres, value $8,000.
Robinson Rowley, farmer for L. A. Green; Sec. 29; P. O. Spring Grove; Ireland.
Robison Irvin F. farmer for C. Lucas; Sec. 36; P. O. Gerlaw; rep; born Illinois.
Rodgers Chas. farmer; P. O. Alexis; dem; Cath; from New York.
Rodgers J. farmer; P. O. Alexis; dem; Cath; from Ireland.
Rogers John H. Dr.; Alexis; dem; Canada.
Rogers R. N. laborer for W. J. Miller; P. O. Gerlaw; dem; from Iowa.
Rohr Anton, miner for Wm. Cook; P. O. Alexis; Cath; from Germany.
Rose Ed. R. farmer; Sec. 25; P. O. Gerlaw; dem; 80 acres; from California.
Rose J. D. farmer for E. R. Rose; Sec. 25; P. O. Gerlaw; from California.

Rowe C. E. Rev. pastor Methodist church; P. O. Alexis; rep; Meth; from Ireland.

ROWE JOHN W. Carpenter; Alexis; born in Franklin Co., Pa., July 5, 1846; came to this Co. in 1866; Rep; U. B.; owns house and lot, value $800; was in army, 21st Pa. Vol., Co. C.; married Angeline Black, Nov. 19, 1867, who was born in Xenia, O., Feb. 28, 1849; they have four children, two boys and two girls.

Rowe Jeremiah, laborer; Alexis; rep; U. B.; $500; from Maryland.

Rowe W. W. farmer for A. J. Ritchey; Sec. 2; P. O. Alexis; rep; U. B.; from Penn.

Ruhey A. J.; Alexis.

Ryan Joseph, assistant road-master; P. O. Alexis; rep;

Ryner James, farmer; P. O. Gerlaw; Chris; 80 acres, value $5,000; from Pennsylvania.

SANTEE GEO. W. miller; Alexis; rep; $1,000; from Pennsylvania.

Sellers Eliza, widow; P. O. Alexis; Adv; $500.

Shaw D. J. farmer; Sec. 11; P. O. Alexis; rep; 280 acres.

Shaw Jas. H. grocer; Alexis; rep; Presb; $3,000.

Shaw Lucinda, farmer; Sec. 4; P. O. Alexis; U. P.; 200 acres; from Ohio.

Shipman H. clerk; Alexis; from New York.

Shunick David, farmer with John Shunick; Sec 14; P. O. Gerlaw; dem; Cath; Irel'd.

Shunick David, farmer; Sec. 31; P. O. Gerlaw; dem; Cath; 240 acres; from Ireland.

Shunnick David, Jr. saloon keeper; Alexis; dem; Cath; $1,000; from Ireland.

Shunick Edmund, farmer; Sec. 12; P. O. Alexis; dem; Cath; 360 acres; Ireland.

Shunick John, farmer; Sec. 14; P. O. Alexis; dem; Cath; 280 acres, $55 per acre; Irel'd.

SHUNICK RICHARD, Farmer and Stock Raiser; Sec. 19; P. O. Spring Grove; born in Ireland in December, 1826; came to this Co. in 1853; Dem; Cath; owns 360 acres, valued at $20,000; wife was Elizabeth O'Neil, born in Ireland; married June 17, 1857; eight children, five sons and two daughters living, one daughter dead.

SIGAFOOS HENRY, Farmer and Stock Raiser; Sec. 33; P. O. Gerlaw; born in Sussex Co., N. J., Aug. 30, 1832; came to this Co. May 7, 1852; Rep; owns 264 acres, valued at $14,500; wife was Flora Shaw, born in Genesee Co., N. Y.; married March 18, 1848; four children, one son and three daughters.

SIMCOX JOHN, Miner and Farmer; Sec. 14; P. O. Alexis; born in England Dec. 27, 1829; came to this Co. in 1856; Rep; Ch. of God; owns 188 acres, valued at $60 per acre; wife was Jennette Mc-

Kelvey, born in Scotland; married April 26, 1858; nine children, three sons and six daughters; eight now living.

Simcox Luke, miner for J. Simcox; Sec. 14; P. O. Alexis; from England.

Simcox Richard, miner for J. Simcox; Sec. 14; P. O. Alexis; from England.

Simpson J. A. farmer; P. O. Alexis; ind; Presb; 7 acres; from Pennsylvania.

Skoogard Jordan, brickmaker; Alexis; rep; U. P.; $1,200; from Denmark.

Smiley Robt. blacksmith; Alexis; dem; from Pennsylvania.

Smith A. N. mason; Alexis; Luth; Norway.

Smith Elias, farmer; Sec. 26; P. O. Gerlaw; dem; 120 acres.

Smith John, farmer; Sec. 21; P. O. Spring Grove; dem; U. P.; 240 acres, val. $9,600.

Smith Rev. O. F. pastor United Brethren; P. O. Alexis; rep; town prop. $800.

Sorensen Andrew C. farmer; Sec. 21; P. O. Spring Grove; Luth; 80 acres, $40 per acre.

Sorensen Fred. farmer for A. C. Sorensen; P. O. Spring Grove; Luth; from Denmark.

Sorensen Martin, farmer; Sec. 30; P. O. Spring Grove; dem; from Denmark.

Sprowl J. A. farmer for J. Sprowl; Sec. 18; P. O. Spring Grove; rep; from Virginia.

Sprowl John, farmer; Sec. 18; P. O. Spring Grove; rep; U. P.; 104 acres; from Va.

Squires Thos. R. gen. col. and ins. agt; Alexis; dem; 80 acres and twn. prop. $7,000.

Stevenson John P. farmer; Sec. 17; P. O. Spring Grove; rep; U. P.; from Ireland.

Stewart Jas. P. O. Alexis; rep; U. P.; town prop. $1,500; from Pennsylvania.

Stewart W. W. farmer with Robt. McGee; P. O. Alexis; rep; from Ohio.

Stinson H. A. teacher; Sec. 6; P. O. Gerlaw; dem; Presb; from Pennsylvania.

Stockdale Wm. clerk for McGrew & Alexander; Alexis; rep; Cong; from Indiana.

Stout C. B. rents of Ryan G. Smith; Sec. 33; P. O. Gerlaw; rep; Chris; from Ohio.

Streeter Wm. farmer, renter; P. O. Little York; rep; U. P.

Swihart I. W. farmer for Craig Hanna; Sec. 25; P. O. Gerlaw; dem; Chris; from Penn.

Swiler Jacob, farmer for R. V. Butterfield; Sec. 8; P. O. Alexis; Ch. of God; Penn.

TALBOT A. G. merchant; Alexis; rep; from New York.

TAYLOR C. H. Photographer; Alexis; born in Oxford, Mass., July 2, 1838; came to this State in 1873, and County in 1875; rep; U. B.; owns Photograph Gallery, value $800; served in army, in 8th Mass. Regt; married Miss Delana Slater, in Nov. 1861, who was born Dec. 25, 1837; Mr. Taylor has followed the business of

[WARREN COUNTY: SPRING GROVE TOWNSHIP. 317

Photography successfully for last eight years.

Theimes Henry, blacksmith; P. O. Gerlaw; rep; from Germany.

Thomas H. H. livery; Alexis; dem; $1,500; from Virginia.

Thompson Ann, widow; P. O. Spring Grove; Meth; 20 acres; from Ohio.

Thompson Geo. farmer; Sec. 28; P. O. Spring Grove; rep; from Pennsylvania.

Thompson John, farmer; Sec. 21; P. O. Gerlaw; rep; U. P.; 87 acres; from Ohio.

Thompson Jane; widow; farmer; Sec. 28; P. O. Spring Grove; 130 acres.

Thompson John B. farmer for J. W. Thompson; Sec. 7; P. O. Norwood; dem; Cath.

Thompson J. W. farmer; Sec. 7; P. O. Norwood; ind; Cath; 260 acres.

Thompson Josiah, farmer; Sec. 20; P. O. Spring Grove; rep; U. P.; 160 acres; Ohio.

Thompson Richard, farmer for J. W. Thompson; Sec. 7; P. O. Norwood; dem; Cath.

Thompson Wm. farmer with J. W. Thompson; Sec. 7; P. O. Norwood; dem; Cath.

Thorn J. D. farmer; Sec. 19; P. O. Spring Grove; rep; U. P.; 60 acres, value $3,000.

Thorn G. W. farmer; Sec. 9; P. O. Spring Grove; rep; from Indiana.

Thorn Thos. M. farmer; Sec. 16; P. O. Alexis; rep; U. P.; 160 acres, value $7,000.

Thorn W. R. farmer; Sec. 9; P. O. Alexis; rep; U. P.; 160 acres, value $8,000; Ind.

Turner Henry B. farmer, with J. B. Turner; Sec. 16; P. O. Spring Grove; rep; Ohio.

Turner Jas. M. farmer, with J. B. Turner; Sec. 16; P. O. Spring Grove; rep; Ohio.

Turner J. B. farmer; Sec. 16; P. O. Alexis; rep; U. P.; 160 acres, value $8,000; S. C.

VANARSDELL JERRY, hotel-keeper; Alexis; dem; Virginia.

Vantyne Jacques, painter; Alexis; dem.

Varce G. H. Rev. pastor United Brethren; P. O. Alexis; rep; from New York.

WALLACE DAVID, farmer for J. M. Irey; P. O. Gerlaw.

Wallace David L. laborer; P. O. Alexis; dem; U. B.; from Penn.

Wallace Emeline, wid. farming; Sec. 3; P. O. Alexis; 80 acres, val. $4,000; Presb; Penn.

Wallace G. W. carpenter; Alexis; rep; U. B.; from Penn.

Wallace M. A. wagon-maker; Alexis; dem; Presb; $2,000; from Pennsylvania.

Wallace M. M. carpenter; Alexis; dem; U. B.; $200; from Pennsylvania.

Wannamaker James, laborer; P. O. Alexis; Luth; from Pennsylvania.

Webb Jno. P. farmer for Mary Campbell; P. O. Norwood; dem; Meth; from Penn.

Webster Frank C. carpenter; Alexis; rep; from New York.

Webster James, farmer; Sec. 27; P. O. Gerlaw; rep; Meth; from Ohio.

Webster Wm. A. farmer; Sec. 27; P. O. Gerlaw; from Ohio.

Whisen J. H. farmer for W. Whisen; P. O. Alexis; dem; Chris; from Pennsylvania.

Whisen J. W. farmer for W. Whisen; P. O. Alexis; ind; Bapt; from Virginia.

Whisen Wm. farmer; Sec. 9; P. O. Alexis; Ind; 60 acres, value $2,500; Virginia.

White David; farmer for D. W. White; P.O. Alexis; from Pennsylvania.

White David W. farmer; Sec. 15; P. O. Alexis; dem; Ch. of God; 200 acres,$6,500.

White H.; P. O. Alexis.

White Joseph, farmer for D. W. White; Sec. 15; P. O. Alexis; dem; from Penn.

Wiley Thos. C. farmer; Sec. 2; P. O. Alexis; ind; Presb; 75 acres, value $5,000; Penn.

WILSON JAMES, Farmer; Sec. 23; P. O. Alexis; born in England, June 19, 1824; came to this Co. in 1860; Dem; Christian; owns 58 acres, valued at $2,700; wife was Elizabeth Brolton; married May 10, 1843; three sons, William H., Enoch J. and James J. W.

Wilson Wm. H. farmer for J. Wilson; Sec. 23; Alexis; dem; Chris; from England.

WINBIGLER C. B. Farmer; Sec. 29; P. O. Spring Grove; born in Indiana, Oct. 10, 1843; came to this Co. in 1859; Rep; owns 155 acres, valued at $10,000.

WINBIGLER JOHN S. Farmer; Sec. 28; P. O. Spring Grove; born in Indiana, Sept. 3, 1841; came to this Co. in 1859; Rep; owns 220 acres, valued at $1,300; wife was Mary L. Small, born in New York; married Feb. 20, 1867; five sons, Edward, Guy, Draper, Roy and Carl; served 4 years in Co. I, 50th Ill. Inf.

Winbigler J. S. farmer; Sec. 28; P.O. Spring Grove; rep; 220 acres; $60 per acre; Ind.

Wixen Ed., laborer; P. O. Alexis.

Wolf Jacob L. harness maker; P. O. Alexis; dem; Presb; from Pennsylvania.

Wood Jas. L. laborer; P. O. Alexis; rep; from New York.

Woolley Chas. W. Jr.; station agt.; Gerlaw; dem; Epis; from Tennessee.

Wray A. B. farmer; Sec. 5; P. O. Norwood; dem; 80 acres, value $4,000; from Penn.

Wray A. L. teacher; Sec. 5; P. O. Norwood; dem; born Ill.

WRAY F. E. Farmer; Sec. 23; P. O. Gerlaw; born in Cuyahoga Co., Ohio, Nov. 25, 1849; came to this Co. in 1856; dem; 84 acres, valued at $4,200.

Wray John W. farmer; Sec. 5; P. O. Alexis; dem; 320 acres, value $16,000; from Penn.

Wray L. H. farmer for J. D. Porter; P. O. Alexis; dem; from Ireland.

Wray R. T. blacksmith; P. O. Alexis; dem; Adv; from Pennsylvania.

Wright J. H. engineer; Alexis; dem; $1,500; from Vermont.

Wright Robert, farmer; Sec. 5; P. O. Alexis; dem; Presb; 80 acres, val. $4,000; Ireland.

YARDE AARON, ret. farmer; P. O. Alexis; dem; Adv; from England.

Yarde C. F. P. grocer; Alexis; dem; born Ill.

Yarde T. C. laborer; Alexis; dem; Adv; $500; from Canada.

YOUNG S. N. Farmer; Sec. 11; P. O. Alexis; born in Medina Co., O., July 23, 1847; came to this County in 1854; Rep; Christian; 40 acres, value $2,000; married Jennie Hall, March 21, 1876, who was born in McDonough Co., Ill., Sept. 9,1853; they have one child, Arthur N., born Jan. 29, 1877.

Young W. W. carpenter; Alexis; rep; from Ohio.

Youngquist A. S. shoemaker; Gerlaw; rep; from Sweden.

ALEXIS BUSINESS DIRECTORY.

Chaffee A. H. Physician and Surgeon, Editor and Proprietor *Alexis Index.*

Chapman O. G. Postmaster; dealer in Books, Stationery, Wall Paper, Notions, etc.

Foust David, Merchant.

Gibson, Postlewaite & Co. Dealers in Dry Goods, Groceries, Clothing, Hats, Caps, Boots, Shoes, etc.

Loveridge T. Prop. "Alexandria House;" best accomodations for the traveling public; good sample rooms for commercial men; livery in connection.

Rowe Jno. W. Carpenter and Builder; specifications furnished when desired.

Santee & Laird, Custom and Merchant Millers; proprietors "Oriental Flouring Mills."

Taylor C. H. Photographer; all work executed in the highest style of art; old pictures enlarged to any size; first-class stock of Frames constantly on hand; friends, take time by the forelock and secure a good, life-like picture of yourself and family before it is too late.

TOMPKINS TOWNSHIP.

ABBEY GEORGE, livery stable; Kirkwood; rep; New York.

Abbey Henry, hotel keeper; Kirkwood; rep; Presb; from New York.

Abbey Horatio, merchant; Kirkwood; rep; from New York.

Abbey J. E. retired; Kirkwood; rep; Presb; from New York.

Abbey Newman, merchant; Kirkwood; rep; Presb; from New Jersey.

Ackerman Jacob, retired farmer; Kirkwood; rep; Presb; from New Jersey.

Ackerman John, Sr., farmer; Sec. 16; P. O. Kirkwood; rep; Meth; 90 acres; N. J.

Adair A. A. professor of music; Kirkwood; dem.

Adams Thomas M. farmer; Sec. 31; P. O. Kirkwood; rep; born Illinois.

Adcock R. J. Sec. 36; P. O. Lenox; rep; Chris.

Allen Ed. B. clerk with M. W. Allen; Kirkwood; rep; from Wisconsin.

Alaman H. C. farmer; Sec. 15; P. O. Kirkwood; rep; from Pennsylvania.

Allen H. W. merchant and shipper; Kirkwood; rep; from Rockford, Ill.

ALLEN MOSES W. Merchant; Kirkwood; born in Northampton, Mass., March 20, 1815; came to Rockford, Ill., in 1837; went to Hortonville, Wis., in 1850; came to this Co. in 1864; Rep; Cong; owns town property valued at $7,000; is Notary Public and Pension Agent; wife was Miss

Minerva C. Fletcher, born at Vergennes, Vt., May 12, 1821; married June 18, 1845, at Rockford, Ill.; has five children.

Allen S. F. travelling agent; Kirkwood; rep; Presb; from Rockton, Ill.

Allen Thomas, farmer; P. O. Kirkwood; ind; from Ohio.

Anderson John, with C. E. Perkins; P. O. Kirkwood; Luth; from Sweden.

Armstrong A. W. physician; Kirkwood; dem; from Tennessee.

Armstrong W. D. dentist; Kirkwood; dem; from Tennessee.

Atkins George, teamster; Kirkwood; rep; from New York.

Atkins John, farmer; Sec. 21; P. O. Kirkwood; rep; 55 acres; from Connecticut.

Atkins William, farmer; Sec. 21; P. O. Kirkwood; rep; from Warren Co.

Austin A. farmer; Lenox; rep; Chris; from Ohio.

BAIN JOHN H. farmer; Kirkwood; rep; from New York.

Baldwin Jacob, farmer; Sec. 17; Kirkwood; Ind; from New York; 83 acres.

Barnes J. E. nurseryman; Kirkwood; rep; Bapt; from New York.

Barnes John, farmer; Sec. 24; P. O. Monmouth; rep; Meth; from Va; 290 acres.

BARNES, CRESWELL & CO. Proprietors of the Young America Nursery, established in 1865; P. O. Kirkwood; have about 80 acres in young trees; it is situated about ¾ mile from Kirkwood Station, of the C., B. & Q. R. R.

BARNES JOHN, Farmer and Stock Raiser; Sec. 24; P. O. Monmouth; born in West Va., Jan. 10, 1820; came to this Co. in 1856; Rep; Lib. Meth; owns 290 acres of land, valued at $17,400; has held the offices of School Director and Overseer of Highways; his wife was Elizabeth Jane Monroe; she was born in Tennessee; they have had nine children, two of whom are dead.

Barnum Chas. L. farmer; Sec 11; P O. Kirkwood; rep; from New York; 40 acres.

BARNUM GEORGE A. Farmer; Sec. 11; P. O. Kirkwood; born in New York, April 20, 1837; came to this Co. in 1844; Rep; Rel. no pref.; owns 40 acres of land, valued at $2,500; served three years in the 83d I. V. I. during the late war; his wife was Cecelia Atkins; she was born in Lewis Co., N. Y., Feb. 12, 1843; married August 11, 1862; they have one child, Nina M.

Barnum Ira, farmer; P. O. Kirkwood; rep; Meth; from New York; 80 acres.

Bassett Chas. E. laborer; Kirkwood; dem; born Illinois.

Barton John L. farmer; Sec. 16; P. O. Kirkwood; Ind; from Indiana.

BEERS THOMAS W. Farmer; Sec. 17; P. O. Kirkwood; born in Bradford Co., Pa., Jan. 15, 1821; came to this Co. in 1850; Dem; owns 80 acres of land, valued at $10,000; was Town Clerk for three years; is Supervisor of the Township; wife was Amy Carr, born in Chemung Co., N. Y., Oct. 31, 1827; married Oct. 24, 1844; has six children.

Benell C. J. section boss; Kirkwood; Luth; from Sweden.

Bennett H. K. farmer; Sec. 19; P. O. Kirkwood; rep; Meth; has 120 acres.

Bennett John, farmer; Kirkwood; rep; Meth; from New York.

Bennett J. M. laborer; Kirkwood; dem; from New York.

Bennett Lorenzo, farmer; Sec. 19; P. O. Kirkwood; rep; 67 acres; from N. Y.

Berry J. C. grocer; Kirkwood; rep; Meth; from Ohio.

Biddle Jonathan, physician; Kirkwood; ind; U. P.; from Pennsylvania.

BILLINGS AMOS B. Farmer; Sec. 11; P. O. Kirkwood; born in Lewis Co., N. Y., Jan. 10, 1811; came to this Co. in 1864; Rep; Meth; owns 160 acres of land, valued at $12,000; wife was Eleanor M. Mott, born in Oneida Co., N. Y., June 3, 1814; married Jan. 15, 1840; has six children.

Billings A. E. farmer, with his father; P. O. Kirkwood; rep; from New York.

Billings Theodore, farmer; Sec. 33; P. O. Kirkwood; rep; from N. Y.; 80 acres.

Billings T. J. farmer; P. O. Kirkwood; rep; from New York; 80 acres.

Billings W. H. farmer; Sec. 12; P. O. Kirkwood; rep; from New York.

Bivens Jonathan, farmer, rents of Oaks; Sec. 20; P. O. Kirkwood; dem; from Indiana.

Black A. H. farmer; Sec. 14; P. O. Kirkwood; rep; from Ohio; 60 acres.

Black James, retired farmer; Kirkwood; rep; from Pennsylvania.

Black John, teamster; Kirkwood; rep; U. P.; from Pennsylvania.

Black Miller, travelling agent; P. O. Kirkwood; rep; U. P.; from Pennsylvania.

Black W. W. laborer; Kirkwook; rep; from Pennsylvania.

Blinn Seymour, laborer; P. O. Kirkwood; dem; Bapt.; from New York.

Blythe D. B. travelling agent; Kirkwood; rep; from Pennsylvania.

Blythe J. C. student; Kirkwood; rep; from Pennsylvania.

Bonner D. L. laborer; Kirkwood; Ind; from Indiana.

Bonner John, laborer; Kirkwood; rep; from Indiana.

Bosler C. harness maker; Kirkwood; dem; Luth; from Germany.
Bosler E. H. harness maker; Kirkwood; Ind; born Henderson Co.
Bosler Edward, harness maker; Kirkwood; dem; born Henderson Co.
Bosler H. E. clerk; Kirkwood; dem; from Germany.
Boston Henry, farmer; Sec. 30; P. O. Kirkwood; dem
Boston Newton M. farmer; Sec. 30; P. O. Kirkwood; rep; Ind.
Bowman A. sewing machine agent; Kirkwood; Ind; from Pennsylvania.
Brace Rev. C. H. minister of Meth. church; Kirkwood; rep; born Stark Co., Ill.
Bradshaw J. G. cabinet-maker; Kirkwood; dem; Bapt; from Kentucky.
Brimhall Rev. S. minister Baptist church; Kirkwood; rep; from New York.
Brooks Edward, stock dealer; Kirkwood; dem; from New Hampshire.
Brooks J. M. farmer; Sec. 32; P. O. Kirkwood; dem; 80 acres; from Kentucky.
Brooks O. F. stock dealer; Kirkwood; dem; from New Hampshire.
Brown C. K. grocer; Kirkwood; rep; Meth; from Henry Co., Ill.
Brown H. S. farmer; Sec. 2; P. O. Monmouth; rep; 80 acres; from Knox Co., Ill.
Brown Otis, grocer; Kirkwood; rep; Presb; from New York.
Brown Willard, restaurant; Kirkwood; rep; from New York.
Brown W. S. reporter; Kirkwood; rep; from Ohio.
Bruyn A. L. farmer; Sec. 3; P. O. Kirkwood; dem; from New York.
Bruyn N. farmer; Sec. 3; P. O. Kirkwood; dem; 280 acres; from New York.
Bryner Geo. farmer; Sec. 33; P. O. Kirkwood; dem; from Pennsylvania.
Bryner Sylvester, laborer; P. O. Kirkwood.
Bryner Milton, laborer; Sec. 33; P. O. Kirkwood; dem; from Pennsylvania.
Bryner Sylvester, laborer; Sec. 33; P. O. Kirkwood; dem; from Pennsylvania.
Burchell Hugh, laborer; Kirkwood; dem; Cath; from England.
Burchell Thos. laborer; Kirkwood; dem; Cath; from England.
Buckley James, painter; Kirkwood; dem; from New York.
Burdsel P. D. farmer; Sec. 33; P. O. Kirkwood; rep; Meth; from Canada.
Burr Oscar, farmer; Sec. 2; P. O. Kirkwood; rep; from Pennsylvania.
BUTE CYRUS, Police Magistrate; Kirkwood; born in Fayette Co., Pa., Sept. 26, 1819; came to this Co. in 1850; Rep; Presb; owns town property valued at $4,000; was chosen Sheriff of the Co. in 1868, and served two years; enlisted Aug. 15, 1862, in the 83rd I. V. I., and served three years; was promoted to the Lieutenancy during the time; was in the battle of Fort Donelson Feb. 3, 1863; wife was Margaret Gibson, born in Fayette Co., Ill., July 16, 1816; married Sept. 16, 1841; has four children.
Butler T. S. farmer; Sec. 26; P. O. Kirkwood; rep; U. P.; 80 acres; from Ind.

CAIN JAMES, farmer; Sec. 12; P. O. Kirkwood; Cath; from Ireland.
Cain John, farmer; Sec. 32; P. O. Kirkwood; dem; 140 acres; from Ireland.
Cain Peter, farmer, with his father; P. O. Kirkwood; dem; from Ireland.
Calahan John, laborer; Kirkwood; rep; Cath; from Ireland.
Calahan Pat. laborer; Kirkwood; dem; Cath; from Ireland.
Camden John C. farm hand; Sec. 13; P. O. Monmouth; dem; from Kentucky.
Campbell John L. mason; Kirkwood; dem; from Indiana.
Campbell W. S. D. farmer; Sec. 24; P. O. Lenox; rep; Presb; from Tennessee.
Carlon B. F. dealer in stone and lime; Kirkwood; dem; Meth; from Pennsylvania.
Carlon George, engineer; Kirkwood; dem; Meth; from Ohio.
Carmichael C. A. clerk; Kirkwood; rep; from Henderson Co., Ill.
Carr Frank, farmer; Sec. 20; P. O. Kirkwood; dem; from New York.
Carr Geo. N. teamster; Kirkwood; rep; from New York.
Carr Mrs. James; widow; Kirkwood; Bapt; from Rhode Island.
Carr Nathan, Sr., farmer; Sec. 20; P. O. Kirkwood; dem; Presb; 120 acres; N. Y.
Carr N. R. farmer; Sec. 20; P. O. Kirkwood; dem; 40 acres; from New York.
Caruthurs J. S. laborer; Kirkwood; rep; Meth.
Caves Benj. shoemaker; Sec. 32; P. O. Kirkwood; rep; from Ohio.
Chapin N. A. merchant; Kirkwood; rep; Univ; from Indiana.
Chapman Charles, carpenter; Kirkwood; rep; Meth; from Sweden.
Clawson E. P. druggist; Kirkwood; dem; Presb; from New Jersey.
Clemens John, teamster; Kirkwood; rep; from Ohio.
Coburn T. L. clerk; Kirkwood; born Ill.
Cole G. O. teamster; Kirkwood; dem; from Pennsylvania.
Colgrove Henry, plasterer; rep; Kirkwood; from Indiana.

WARREN COUNTY: TOMPKINS TOWNSHIP. 321

Collins W. W. farmer; Sec. 5; P. O. Kirkwood; rep; from Ohio.

Conner Patrick, farmer on farm of J. Stack; P. O. Kirkwood; dem; Cath; from Irel'd.

Cook John, carpenter; Kirkwood; rep; Presb; from Germany.

Cowan E. N. farmer; Sec. 35; P. O. Lenox; rep; U. P.; from Indiana.

Cowick L. B. farmer, rents of his father; Sec. 36; P. O. Lenox; rep; Meth; Penn.

Cowick S. R. farmer; Sec. 36; P. O. Kirkwood; rep; from Pennsylvania.

Craig Ed. A. carpenter; Kirkwood; Ind; from Ohio.

Craig John W. gun-maker; Kirkwood; Ind; from Ohio.

Creswell Henry, nurseryman; Kirkwood; Ind; from Ohio.

Creswell Samuel H. farmer, with his father; Kirkwood; Ind; from Henderson Co., Ill.

Crow C. B. teamster; Kirkwood; dem; from Ohio.

Cummings Jas. H. farmer; Kirkwood; rep; from Fulton Co., Ill.

Cummings J. K. merchant; Kirkwood; rep; from Scotland.

Currans J. S. laborer; Kirkwood; dem; from Ohio.

Curtiss J. O. painter; Kirkwood; rep; from Ohio.

DAGNAN HUGH, Kirkwood; dem; from Ireland.

Davidson J. P. clerk with N. & H. Abbey; Kirkwood; rep; from Ohio.

Davidson R. R. carpenter; Kirkwood; rep; from Pennsylvania.

Davis A. farmer; Sec. 31; P. O. Kirkwood; rep; Meth; 80 acres; from Ohio.

Davis B. C. merchant; Kirkwood; rep; from Indiana.

Davis J. M. farmer; Kirkwood; rep; U. P.; Warren Co.

Davis Thomas K. on S. Y. Mason's place; Sec. 24; P. O. Monmouth; dem; Meth; O.

Davis Z. M. farmer; P. O. Kirkwood; rep; 288 acres; from Virginia.

Day A. W. farmer; Sec. 10; P. O. Kirkwood; dem; 160 acres; from Ohio.

Day M. W. farmer; Sec. 10; P. O. Kirkwood; dem; from Ohio.

Dennis John M. farmer; Kirkwood; rep; Bapt; from Pennsylvania.

Dennis Wiley; farmer; Sec. 4; Kirkwood; ind; Bapt; from Pennsylvania.

Dewey James, tailor; Kirkwood; dem; from Kentucky.

Dice George F. carpenter; Kirkwood; rep; from Pennsylvania.

Dickey J. P. carpenter; Kirkwood; dem; Meth; from Pennsylvania.

Doleman E. F. blacksmith; Kirkwood; rep; from Pennsylvania.

Dorris Henry, farmer, rents of D. Phelps; P. O. Lenox; rep; Meth.

Dougherty J. H. laborer; Kirkwood; dem; from Ohio.

Douty L. S. farmer; Sec. 31; P. O. Kirkwood; rep; Presb; from Maine.

Dougherty Z. D. stock dealer; Kirkwood; dem; Bapt; from Ohio.

Drain Andrew, lumber dealer; Kirkwood; rep; born in this Co.

DRAIN WM. F. Lumber Dealer; Kirkwood; born in Ellison, Warren Co., Jan. 28, 1849; Rep; was Collector of Ellison tp. in 1873; was chosen Justice of the Peace in this village in 1876; wife was Almira F. Ray, born in this Co. Dec. 21, 1846; married Feb. 17, 1870; has four children.

Duncan J. W. music teacher; Kirkwood; rep; from Pennsylvania.

EAYRE JOSEPH, clerk with Sofield & Cummings; Kirkwood; rep; from N.J.

Eldredge Delos, farmer; P. O. Kirkwood; dem; born Kendall Co., Ill.

Ervine C. farmer, rents of O. Lamphere; Sec. 35; P. O. Kirkwood; dem; from N. C.

Essex S. B. miller; Kirkwood; rep; from Ohio.

Everett Robert, blacksmith; Kirkwood; rep; Bapt; from Tennessee.

FARIS ISAAC, grain buyer; Kirkwood; rep; U. P.; from Indiana.

Faris J. S. real estate agt.; Kirkwood; rep; Presb; from Virginia.

Farrel Frank, laborer; Kirkwood; dem; from New York.

Field Joseph I. retired farmer; Kirkwood; rep; from Ohio.

Firoved J. P. farmer; Kirkwood; dem; from Pennsylvania.

Firoved J. S. merchant; Kirkwood; dem; Meth; from Pennsylvania.

Fitsimmons M. laborer; Kirkwood; dem; Cath; from Ireland.

Flannigan James, laborer; Sec. 24; P. O. Monmouth; dem; Cath; from Ireland.

Fletcher Chas. S. farmer; P. O. Kirkwood; rep; from Vermont.

Foster Jas. L. retired; Kirkwood; rep; U.P.; from Ohio.

Foster S. C. druggist; Kirkwood; rep; Presb; from Indiana.

Francis J. P. lives with his father; P. O. Kirkwood; rep; U. P.; from Ohio.

Frances John, farmer; Sec. 10; P. O. Kirkwood; rep; U. P.; 160 acres; from Ohio.

Frances James, farmer with his father; P.O. Kirkwood; rep; U. P.; from Ohio.

Frances Samuel, farmer; Sec. 14; P.O. Kirkwood; rep; Meth; from New York.

Frances Wm. farmer; Sec. 3; P. O. Kirkwood; rep; 153 acres; from New York.
Frank Jacob, farmer; Sec. 5; P. O. Kirkwood; dem; Presb; 116 acres; Germany.
Freeland Wm. laborer; Kirkwood; Ind; from Ireland.
Frew J. A. laborer; Kirkwood; rep; U. P.; from Pennsylvania.
Frink L. M. laborer; Kirkwood; dem; from Iowa.

GALBRAITH JAMES, clerk with Chapin, Houlton & Davis; Kirkwood; rep; Pa.
Gamble Robt. merchant; Kirkwood; dem; Presb; from Pennsylvania.
Gamble Wm. merchant; Kirkwood; dem; from Pennsylvania.
Gavin Daniel, farmer; Sec. 13; P. O. Monmouth; dem; Cath; 40 acres; from Ireland.
Gayer J. J. butcher; Kirkwood; dem; from Germany.
Getemy James, farmer; Sec. 3; P. O. Monmouth; rep; U. P. 160 acres; from Penn.
Getemy Robert, farmer with his father; P.O. Monmouth; rep; born Illinois.
Gibson J. K. farmer; Sec. 7; P.O. Kirkwood; dem.
Gibson Robert, laborer; Kirkwood; dem; U.P.; from Warren Co.
Gibson S. L. H. farmer; Sec. 6; Kirkwood; dem; U. P; from Warren Co.
Gilliland David, farmer; Sec. 17; P. O. Kirkwood; dem; from Pennsylvania.
Gilliland Jesse, farmer; Sec. 17; P. O. Kirkwood; dem; from Pennsylvania.
Gilliland Samuel, clerk with W. Stark; Kirkwood; rep; Presb; from Pennsylvania.
Gilmore A. B. with H. Gilmore; P. O. Kirkwood; rep; from Pennsylvania.
Gilmore Edward, farmer; Sec. 17; P. O. Kirkwood.
Gilmore H. merchant; Kirkwood; rep; Meth; from Pennsylvania.
Gilmore J. H. merchant; Kirkwood; rep; from Pennsylvania.
Gilmore L. M. City Marshal; Kirkwood; dem; from Kentucky.
Gilmore William, Kirkwood; dem; born Warren Co.
Gilmore W. Edward, farmer; Sec. 17; P. O. Kirkwood; rep; from Ohio.
Gleason Jackson, laborer; P. O. Kirkwood; rep; from Indiana.
Glover J. S. laborer; Kirkwood; rep; U. P.; from Ohio.
Glover S. C. clerk; Kirkwood; rep; U. P.; from Ohio.
Glover Silas, carpenter; Kirkwood; rep; U. P.; from South Carolina.
Goodwin D. engineer; Kirkwood; dem; from Pennsylvania.
Goodwin Frank, laborer; Kirkwood; dem; from Ohio.
Gordon Cornelius, laborer; Kirkwood; rep; U. P.; from Georgia.
Gordon J. D. carpenter; Kirkwood; rep; U. P.; from Georgia.
Gordon Richard, plasterer; Kirkwood; dem; from Iowa.
Gordon Mathew, harness-maker; Kirkwood; rep; U. P.; from Ohio.
Gordon F. D. harness-maker; Kirkwood; rep; born Warren Co.
Gowdy R. S. retired farmer; Kirkwood; rep; U. P.; from Ohio.
Gray J. A. laborer; Kirkwood; ind; from New York.
Green J. A. teamster; Kirkwood; rep; Meth; from Ohio.
Gregory J. B. painter; Kirkwood; dem; from Pennsylvania.
Groff Thomas, farmer; P. O. Kirkwood; rep; from New York.

HAAG JOHN, baker; Kirkwood; from Germany.
Hall Eldad, farmer; Sec. 29; P. O. Kirkwood; rep; from New York.
Hall Franklin, farmer; Sec. 32; P. O. Kirkwood; dem; from New York.
Hall G. B. farmer, with his father, G. N. Hall; P. O. Kirkwood; rep; from N. Y.
Hall G. N. farmer; Sec. 32; P. O. Kirkwood; rep; Meth; from New York.
Hall Henry, farmer; Sec. 28; P. O. Kirkwood; rep; Meth; from New York.
Hall Jacob, farmer; Sec. 15; P. O. Kirkwood; rep; from Germany.
Hall Oliver, farmer; Sec. 29; P. O. Kirkwood; rep; Meth; from New York.
Hall S. B. retired; Sec. 12; P. O. Kirkwood; rep; from Massachusetts.
Hall Truman, farmer; Sec. 29; P. O. Kirkwood; rep; Meth; from New York.
Hall W. A. farmer; Sec. 12; P. O. Kirkwood; ind; Meth; from New York.
Hall W. B. laborer; Sec. 9; P. O. Kirkwood; rep; Meth; from Ohio.
Hall W. E. farmer; Sec. 16; P. O. Kirkwood; rep; Meth; 79 acres; from New York.
Hardin James, stone cutter; Kirkwood; dem.
Harrington Thomas, cigar-maker; Kirkwood; rep; from Scotland.
Harsha David, farmer; Sec. 2; P. O. Kirkwood; rep; U. P.; 74 acres; from N. Y.
Hasler Chas. cabinet-maker; Kirkwood; rep; from Germany.

HAYES MICHAEL, Farmer and Stock Raiser; Sec. 24; P. O. Monmouth; born in Ireland; came to this country in 1856, and to this Co. in 1863; Dem; Cath; owns 80 acres of land, valued at $4,800; his wife was Hanor Gavin; she was born in the Co. of Cork, Ireland; married in 1861; they have four children, Catharine, John, Thomas and James.

Hayes Samuel, farmer; Kirkwood; rep; from Ohio.

Hayden G. E. teacher, lives with his father; Sec. 12; P. O. Monmouth; rep; Chris.

Hayden Jacob, farmer; Sec. 12; P. O. Monmouth; rep; Chris; 95 acres; from Ohio.

Henry David, barber; Kirkwood; rep; U. P.; from Pennsylvania.

Hess C. merchant; Kirkwood; rep; U. P.; from Pennsylvania.

Hess Joseph, shoemaker; Kirkwood; rep; U. P.; from Ohio.

Hess John, laborer; P. O. Kirkwood; rep; from Pennsylvania.

Hetso Wm. H. laborer; Kirkwood; rep; Presb; from Germany.

Hill Joseph T. farmer; Sec. 28; P. O. Kirkwood; rep; born Illinois.

Hinkley Samuel J. laborer; Kirkwood; dem; from New York.

Hoag Aaron, farmer, Sec. 21; P. O. Kirkwood; rep; Freethinker; 80 acres; Ohio.

Hoag James, Sec. 21; P. O. Kirkwood; rep; born Illinois.

Hoag Wm. H. farmer; Sec. 21; P. O. Kirkwood; rep; from California.

Hogan James, farmer; Sec. 13; P. O. Monmouth; dem; Cath; from Ireland.

Hogue J. C. farmer; Sec. 26; P. O. Kirkwood; rep; U. P.; 121 acres; from Ind.

Hogue J. Henry, laborer; Kirkwood; rep; U. P.; from Indiana.

Hogue J. M. farmer; Sec. 15; P. O. Kirkwood; rep; U. P. from Indiana.

HOGUE S. C. Farmer; Sec. 21; P. O. Kirkwood; born in Gibson Co., Ind., Dec. 3, 1834; came to this Co. in October, 1844; Rep; U. P.; owns 160 acres of land, valued at $9,600; has been Assessor of the township two terms, and now holds the office of Trustee; served three years in the 83d I. V. I. during the late war; his wife was Elizabeth Ward; she was born in Ohio, Feb. 23, 1836; married in 1859; they have one son, J. Elmer Hogue.

Hogue Samuel A. harness-maker; Kirkwood; rep; U. P.; from Indiana.

Hogue Wm. M. farmer; Sec. 15; P. O. Kirkwood; rep; U. P.; from Ind.; 160 acres.

Hollibaugh Edwin, shoemaker; Kirkwood; rep; Bapt; from Ohio.

Holliday John, farmer, rents of N. Carr; Sec. 21; P O. Kirkwood; rep; from Pa.

Holman P. farmer; Sec. 21; P. O. Kirkwood; rep; from New Jersey; 40 acres.

Holmes Samuel, mail carrier; Kirkwood; rep; Meth; from Ohio.

Horton Wm. D. farm hand; Sec. 28; P. O. Kirkwood; rep; from New York.

Hough Jacob, laborer; P. O. Kirkwood; rep; from Ohio.

Hough Joseph, laborer; Kirkwood; rep; from Ohio.

Houlton Chas. A. farmer; Sec. 6; P. O. Kirkwood; rep; from Maine.

Houlton E. R. merchant; Kirkwood; rep; from Maine.

Houlton F. R. merchant; Kirkwood; rep; from Maine.

Howard L. drugs; Kirkwood; ind; Spir; from New York.

Howell J. W. carpenter; Kirkwood; rep; U. P.; from Ohio.

Hulbert C. E. dentist; Kirkwood; rep; born Henderson Co.

Hull Geo. J. farmer; Sec. 11; P. O. Kirkwood; dem; from Georgia.

Hull Geo. farmer; Sec. 12; P. O. Monmouth; dem; Presb; from Ireland.

Huston S. W. farmer; Sec. 23; P. O. Kirkwood; dem; Pres; from Pennsylvania.

IRVINE DAVID, farmer; Sec. 8; P. O. Kirkwood; rep; U. P.; 320 acres; Pa.

Irvine Edward, farmer, lives with his father; P. O. Kirkwood; rep; U. P.; from Pa.

Irvine Jas. P. farmer; Sec. 8; P. O. Kirkwood; rep; 60 acres; from Pa.

Irvine R. D. farmer, lives with his father; Sec. 8; P. O. Kirkwood; ind; U. P.; Pa.

JEFFREY JAMES, blacksmith; Kirkwood; rep; U. P.; from Scotland.

Jeffrey Jas. N. farmer; P. O. Kirkwood; rep; U. P.; from Scotland.

Jenne Chas. farmer; Kirkwood; dem; from New York.

Jenne W. G. farmer; P. O. Kirkwood; dem; from New York.

Johnson Andrew, farm hand; Sec. 10; P. O. Kirkwood; from Denmark.

Johnson A. M. farmer; Sec. 12; P. O. Monmouth; rep; U. P.; 240 acres; from Ohio.

Johnson G. V. laborer; P. O. Kirkwood; rep; from New Jersey.

Johnson T. F. grain dealer; Kirkwood; rep; from New Jersey.

Johnson W. D. retired farmer; Kirkwood; rep; Bapt; from New Jersey.

Johnson W. L. poultry dealer; Kirkwood; rep; born Fulton Co.

Jones Calvin, farmer; Sec. 34; P. O. Kirkwood; rep; 40 acres; from Virginia.

Jones James, livery stable; Kirkwood; dem; from Missouri.

Jones M. T. boarding-house; Kirkwood; dem; Meth; from Missouri.

Jones P. S. farmer; Sec. 32; P. O. Kirkwood; rep; Meth; 80 acres; from Virginia.

Jones Furney, farmer; Sec. 34; P. O. Kirkwood; rep; Meth; from Virginia.

Joos Andrew, shoemaker; Kirkwood; from Switzerland.

KAISER DAVID, laborer; Kirkwood; dem; from Indiana.

Kaiser N. grocer; Kirkwood; ind; Cath; from Germany.

KECK SOLOMON, Farmer; Sec. 23; P. O. Lenox; born in Pennsylvania, in 1840; came to this Co. in 1867; Rep; Meth; owns 90 acres of land, valued at $5,000; has held the office of Overseer of Highways; served in the 133d Regt. Pa. Vol.; wife was Rosanna Renz; she was born in Iowa, in 1839; married in 1868; they have three children, Warren C., Lewis R. and Addie J.

Keener Geo. M. farmer; Sec. 23; P. O. Kirkwood; dem; from Pennsylvania.

KELLOGG GEORGE W. R. R. Agent; Kirkwood; born in Oneida Co., N. Y., July 16, 1837; came to Bureau Co. in 1860; came to this Co. in 1864; Rep; owns town property valued at $2,000; is Trustee of the village; wife was Elizabeth S. Ellinwood, born in Oneida Co., N. Y., Nov. 29, 1837; married Nov. 3, 1863; has one child, Frederick J.

Kness D. K. jeweler; Kirkwood; dem; Meth; born Illinois.

Kness Royal, farmer; Sec. 26; P. O. Lenox; rep; Meth; 80 acres; from Ohio.

Knowland Mrs. C. widow; P. O. Kirkwood; Cath; from Ireland.

Kraus A. L. clothier; Kirkwood; Ind; from Bohemia.

LAMPHERE ALVA, farmer; Sec. 22; P. O. Kirkwood; rep; born Warren Co.

Lamphere Clark, farmer; Sec. 14; P. O. Kirkwood; rep; 80 acres; born Warren Co.

Lamphere G. D. farmer; Sec. 34; P. O. Kirkwood; rep; 200 acres; from New York.

Lamphere Howard, Farmer; Sec. 22; P. O. Kirkwood; rep; born Warren Co.

Lamphere Jesse, farmer; Sec. 36; P. O. Lenox; rep; Meth; 120 acres; from N. Y.

Lamphere Orin, farmer; Sec. 35; P.O.Lenox; rep; Meth; 200 acres; from New York.

Lamphere Oliver, farmer; Sec. 35; Kirkwood; rep; Meth; 160 acres; from N. Y.

Lamphere Mrs. Polly, widow; Sec. 11; P. O. Kirkwood; Univ; 120 acres; from N. Y.

Lamphere Salona, farmer; Sec. 11; P. O. Kirkwood; rep; born Warren Co.

Lamps George, butcher; Kirkwood; dem; from Germany.

Lang William, farm hand with O. Lamphere; P. O. Kirkwood.

Lantz John, laborer; Kirkwood; Ind; from Pennsylvania.

Latimer W. G. farmer; Sec. 28; P. O. Kirkwood; rep; born Sangamon Co.

Laws S. T. laborer; Kirkwood; rep; Presb; from Ohio.

Lawrence Joseph L. farm hand with C. Lampere; P. O. Kirkwood; dem; from N. C.

LEEDHAM WM. H. Editor and Proprietor of the *Kirkwood News*, Kirkwood; born in Washington Co., Ohio, Dec. 17, 1830; went to Henry Co., Iowa, in 1864, and came to this Co. in 1875; Rep; wife was Mary H. Jones; born in Ind., Dec. 4, 1850; married Sept. 27, 1875; has one child.

Leeper Joseph, laborer; Kirkwood; rep; born Warren Co.

Lockwood John M. clerk; Kirkwood; rep; Meth; from Iowa.

Lockwood J. C. merchant; Kirkwood; rep. Meth; from Del.

Long Jacob, wagon-maker; Kirkwood; ind; from Ohio.

Losier David, teamster; Kirkwood; dem; from Pennsylvania.

Losier Rob't G. laborer; Kirkwood; dem; U. P; born Illinois.

Loudon G. R. farmer; Sec. 8; P. O. Kirkwood; dem; R. Presb; from Indiana.

Loudon J. H. farmer; Sec. 8; P. O. Kirkwood; Ind; from Indiana.

Loudon W. F. farmer; Sec. 8; P. O. Kirkwood; dem; R. Pres; 80 acres; from S. C.

Lowther J. F. retired; Kirkwood; dem; Meth; from Ohio.

LOWTHER THOMPSON F. Merchant; Kirkwood; born in Franklin Co. Pa., Jan. 26, 1804; came to Schuyler Co., Ill. in 1835, and to this Co. in 1841; Dem; owns town property valued at $1,800; was chosen Village Trustee for two years; wife was Sarah Black, born in Perry Co., Pa., Sept. 22, 1806; died Feb. 29, 1876; was married June 14, 1825; has six children.

Lowther, W. W. grocer; Kirkwood; ind; U. P.; born Illinois.

Lundin Charles, farm hand of J. M. Irvine; P. O. Kirkwood; rep; Luth; from Sweden.

McCOY, ALEX. H., trader; Kirkwood; rep; from Ohio.

McCoy J. R. farmer; Sec. 16; P. O. Kirkwood; rep; U. P.; half of 82 acres; Ohio.

McCoy J. W. farmer; Sec. 16; P. O. Kirkwood; rep; U. P.; half of 82 acres; Ohio.

McCoy William, farmer; Kirkwood; ind; from Ohio.

McDonald Wm. farmer; Sec. 18; P. O. Kirkwood; dem; from Indiana.

McFarland H. D. miller; Kirkwood; rep; from Pennsylvania.

McFarland James, rents farm of A. Kingsbury; Sec. 2; P. O. Monmouth; dem.

McFarland Patrick, farmer; Sec. 1; P. O. Kirkwood; dem; Cath; from Ireland.

McIntyre Samuel, farmer; Sec. 22; P. O. Kirkwood; rep; born Warren County.
McIntyre Wm. laborer; Kirkwood; rep; from New York.
McLinn J. C. merchant; Kirkwood; rep; from Pennsylvania.
McMahill A. farmer; Sec. 23; P. O. Kirkwood; dem; born Warren Co.
McMahill G. W. farmer; Sec. 2; P. O. Kirkwood; rep; born Warren Co.
McMahill Henry, farm hand; Sec. 10; P. O. Kirkwood; rep; born Warren Co.
McMAHILL T. JEFFERSON, farmer; Sec. 10; P. O. Kirkwood; born in Nicholas Co., Ky., Oct. 20, 1826; came to this County in 1838; Rep; owns 160 acres, valued at $10,000; wife was Maria Vosburgh, born in Lewis Co., N. Y. April 8, 1828; married May 24, 1847; has seven children.
McNight T. C. seller of Osage Fir Hedges; Kirkwood; rep; U. P.; from Pa.
McQuams J. H. miller; Kirkwood; rep; U. P.; from Ohio.
McWilliams S. farmer; Sec. 33; P. O. Kirkwood; dem; Presb; from Ohio.
Main Charles E. watch-maker; Kirkwood; rep; from Ohio.
Marks Matthew, grain dealer; Kirkwood; Ind; from Indiana.
Marks Wm. C. shipper; dem; from Indiana.
Marsh J. P. physician; Kirkwood; rep; from New York.
Martin J. H. farmer; Sec. 10; P. O. Kirkwood; rep; U. P.; from Indiana.
Martin J. L. farmer; Sec. 30; P. O. Kirkwood; rep; U. P. from Indiana.
Martin J. R. farmer, on J. B. Feroved's farm; Sec. 4; P. O. Kirkwood; dem.
Martin W. R. farmer; Sec. 10; P. O. Kirkwood; rep; U. P.; from Warren Co.
Mathews Peter, farmer; Sec. 2; on farm of N. Hardin; rep.
Mayall Rev. James M. Pastor of Meth. (Prot.) Church; Sec. 35; P. O. Lenox; ind.
Merrick F. J. laborer; Kirkwood; rep; N. J.
Merrick W. H. shoemaker; Kirkwood; rep; Meth; from England.
Miller Daniel, stoves and tinware; Kirkwood; rep; from N. Y.
Miller John L. carriage trimmer; rep; from Pennsylvania.
Miller John N. teamster; Kirkwood; rep; from Maryland.
Miller L. E. retired; Kirkwood; dem; Ohio.
Mitchell A. D. laborer; Kirkwood; dem; from Ohio.
Montgomery A. laborer; Kirkwood; rep; from Kentucky.
Moody Robert, farmer; Sec. 4; P. O. Kirkwood; ind; Bapt; from Pa.

Moore M. D. livery stable; Kirkwood; rep; from Vermont.
Moore Marion E. lives with his father; P. O. Kirkwood; rep; born Warren Co.
Moore Robert, farmer; Sec. 15; P. O. Kirkwood; rep; 160 acres; from Ohio.
Moose S. O. farmer; rents of P. D. Birdsel; P. O. Kirkwood; rep; from Pa.
Morris Henry, farmer; Sec. 33; rents of Harding Est.; P. O. Kirkwood; dem; Ohio.
Morris Mrs. P. J. widow; house and lot; Kirkwood; Meth; from N. J.
Mulligan W. M. laborer; Kirkwood; dem; Cath; from Ireland.
Mundorff Peter, farmer; Sec. 16; P. O. Kirkwood; 20 acres; rep; from Pa.
Munshaw Joseph Jr. engineer; Kirkwood; dem; Meth; from Pennsylvania.

NANCE R. H. farmer; Sec. 34; P. O. Kirkwood; dem; born Warren Co.
Nelson A. P., M. D. physician; Kirkwood; rep; U. P.; from Ohio.
Norcross H. R. farmer; Sec. 12; P. O. Monmouth; rep; Presb; 90 acres; from Pa.
Norman Charles, shoemaker; Kirkwood; from Sweden.
Norman G. W. shoemaker; Kirkwood; rep; from Sweden.

OAKES MRS. SETH; wid.; Sec. 18; P. O. Kirkwood; Presb; 305 acres; Penn.
Oakes T. J. barber; Kirkwood; rep; born Illinois.
Oliver Nelson, farm hand; P. O. Kirkwood; rep; Meth; from Sweden.

PADDOCK MERRITT, retired farmer; P. O. Kirkwood; rep; Meth; from N. Y.
Paine Ed. M. tinner; P. O. Kirkwood; rep; from Ohio.
Paine Wm. laborer; Kirkwood; dem; Cath; from Ireland.
Parker S. H. hotel clerk; Kirkwood; dem; from Ohio.
Parks J. W. farmer; Sec. 3; P. O. Kirkwood; rep; U. P.; 9 acres; from Penn.
Peake Marcus M. bridge builder C. B. & Q. R. R.; Kirkwood; rep; from New York.
Pease A. L. clerk with Chapin, Houlton & Davis; Kirkwood; rep; Bapt; from N. Y.
Pease L. coal dealer; Kirkwood; rep; Bapt; from New York.
Pease R. B. painter; Kirkwood; rep; Univ; from New York.
Pease W. W. bookseller; Kirkwood; rep; Lib; from New York.
Perkins Augustus M. farmer; P. O. Kirkwood; dem; born Warren Co.
Pierce Frank, farm hand; rep; from Sweden.
PERKINS CHARLES E. Farmer; Sec. 28; P. O. Kirkwood; born in Frank-

lin Co., Me., July 30, 1832; came to this Co. in 1854; went to Goodhue Co., Minn., in 1855, and returned here in 1863; Rep; Meth; owns 320 acres of land, valued at $20,000; was Commissioner of Highways six years; wife was Mary F. Wornam, born in Warren Co., June 20, 1838; married Feb. 28, 1857; has three children.

Perkins S. D. farmer; P. O. Kirkwood; dem; Univ; from Maine.

Perry M. farmer; Sec. 25; P. O. Lenox; dem; Meth; 70 acres; from New York.

Peterson D. H. blacksmith; Kirkwood; rep; Luth; from Sweden.

Phelps D. P. farmer; Sec. 25; P. O. Monmouth; dem; born Warren Co.

PHELPS DeWITT, Farmer; Sec. 26; P. O. Lenox; born in Steuben Co., N. Y., Jan. 6, 1836; came to this Co. in 1837; was on the Pacific coast five years; Dem; owns 240 acres of land, valued at $15,000; wife was Mary Amanda Lewis, born in Sangamon Co., Ill., July 3, 1838; married Feb. 13, 1872; has two children, Kathrina L. and Mary P.

Porter Geo. T. farm hand.

Porter James, retired; Kirkwood; dem; U. P; from Ireland.

Post J. J. livery stable; Kirkwood; rep; from Pennsylvania.

Powers E. R. dealer in musical instruments; Kirkwood; rep; from Kentucky.

Powers J. H. butcher; Kirkwood; ind; Bapt; born Illinois.

Powers Michael, cigar maker; Kirkwood; dem; from Ireland.

Puntney John, farmer; P. O. Kirkwood; dem; from Indiana.

Puntney J. M. farmer; P. O. Kirkwood; Ind; from Indiana.

Puntney W. J. farmer; P. O. Kirkwood; dem; U. P.; from Indiana.

RANDALL ASAHEL, laborer; P. O. Kirkwood; rep; from New York.

Randall Merchant, carpenter; Kirkwood; dem; from New York.

RANDALL ORLANDO, Farmer; Sec. 16; P. O. Kirkwood; born in Chenango Co., N. Y., Jan. 28, 1827; came to this Co. in 1849; Rep; owns 186 acres land, valued at $12,000; wife was Melissa Hall, born in Oneida Co., N. Y., Jan. 22, 1832; married Sept. 13, 1855; has six children.

Randall Roswell, retired; Kirkwood; rep; Univ; from New Hampshire.

Randall Walter, farmer; Sec. 13; P. O. Monmouth; rep; Meth; from Ohio.

RANKIN CYRUS G. Farmer; Sec. 26; P. O. Monmouth; born in Sullivan Co., Ind., Jan. 30, 1832; came to Henderson Co., Ill., in 1834, and to this Co. in 1873; Rep; U. P.; owns 960 acres of land, valued at $50,000; wife was Martha T. Reynolds, born in Brown Co., Ohio, Oct. 20, 1837; married April 3, 1856; has four children, Elizabeth A., P. Reynolds, E. Addison, and Minnie A.

Rankin Jas., Sr., retired farmer; Kirkwood; rep; U. P.; from Pennsylvania.

Rankin Joseph, grain dealer; Kirkwood; rep; U. P.; from Indiana.

Rankin Thomas, retired farmer; Kirkwood; rep; Meth; from Ohio.

Rapalee Amos, farmer; P. O. Kirkwood; rep; Bapt; born Illinois.

Rapalee Lewis, clothier; Kirkwood; rep; Bapt; from New York.

Ray Geo. F. farmer; Kirkwood; rep; Univ; born Warren Co.

Ray John, retired farmer; Kirkwood; rep; from New Hampshire.

Reddick F. J. stone cutter; Kirkwood; dem; from Germany.

REED GEO. W. Farmer; Kirkwood; born in Warren Co., July 30, 1846; Rep; Lib; owns house and lot valued at $800; enlisted in Co. K, I. V. I., Feb. 14, 1865; served to close of the war; disabled by exposure, so that his health is very poor; married Miss Luella Perkins, of Warren Co., Dec. 4, 1871; one son, Albert Marsh, born Jan. 3, 1874.

Reed Thos. retired farmer; Kirkwood; dem; Presb; from Kentucky.

Rhea S. P. carpenter; Kirkwood; dem; from Tennessee.

Riggs Jas. O. farmer; Sec. 14; P. O. Monmouth; dem; 39 acres; born Warren Co.

Riner Lewis, farmer; Sec. 31; P. O. Kirkwood; rep; Meth; from Ohio.

Roberts Jacob, farmer; Sec. 35; P. O. Lenox; rep; Meth; from New York.

Roberts L. W. farmer; Sec 14; P. O. Kirkwood; rep; Meth; 160 acres; from N. Y.

Roberts W. L. farmer; Kirkwood.

Roman Charles wagon-maker; Kirkwood; from Sweden.

Rowland H. G. farm hand with C. Rankin; P. O. Monmouth; dem; from Penn.

RUSK J. W. Farmer; Sec. 22; P. O. Kirkwood; born in Muskingum Co., Ohio, April 8, 1832; came to this Co. in 1848; Rep; Meth; owns 320 acres of land, valued at $19,000; his wife was Martha J. Tubbs; she was born in Herkimer Co., N. Y., in 1830; married May 27, 1857; they have five children, Hattie R., Mary E., Willard H., Edwin M. and Fannie M.

Rusk Marion D. teamster; Kirkwood; rep; from Ohio.

Russell Geo. J. teamster; Kirkwood; rep; Meth; from Vermont.

SALISBURY ALLEN, grain buyer; Kirkwood; rep; from Ohio.

WARREN COUNTY : TOMPKINS TOWNSHIP. 327

Salisbury S. S. retired farmer; Kirkwood; dem; from New York.

Salter P. L. laborer; P. O. Kirkwood; rep; from New Jersey.

Sample John, laborer; Kirkwood; rep; U. P.; from Ireland.

Sawin Spencer, farmer; P. O. Kirkwood; rep; Meth; born Adams Co., Ills.

Schenberger D. S. farmer; P. O. Kirkwood; Ind; from Pennsylvania.

SCHENBERGER ELIAS, Postmaster; Kirkwood; born in York Co., Pa., Jan. 13, 1846; came to Henderson Co., Ill., 1852; came to this Co. in 1860; Rep; Meth; owns town property valued at $700; has been Postmaster three years; wife was Mary E. Colgrove, born in Hamilton Co., Ohio, May 16, 1847; married Feb. 17, 1870; has one child, Olga C.

Schenberger H. farmer; P. O. Kirkwood; rep; from Pennsylvania.

Schenberger M. B. farmer; P. O. Kirkwood; Ind; from Pennsylvania.

Schenberger M. G. farmer; P. O. Kirkwood; ind; Meth; from Pennsylvania.

Scott T. A. physician; Kirkwood; rep; U.P.; from Scotland.

Seerist Calvin C. attorney-at-law; Kirkwood; rep; Presb; born Henderson Co.

Shawman I. J. farmer; Sec. 30; P. O. Kirkwood; rep; U. P.; from Ohio.

Sheats R. C. farmer; Sec. 2; Kirkwood; dem; Luth; 160 acres; from Ohio.

Sheldon H. F. nurseries; Kirkwood; rep; Bapt; from New York.

Shook John, farmer; Sec. 29; P. O. Kirkwood; rep.

Shotts Jonas, laborer; Kirkwood; rep; from Ohio.

Shotts John, laborer; Kirkwood; rep; from Ohio.

Shotts Peter, laborer; Kirkwood; rep; from Ohio.

Shriner John H. wagon-maker; Kirkwood; rep; from Ohio.

Sloan Jonathan, farmer; Sec. 20; Kirkwood; rep; Meth; 160 acres; from New York.

Smith Albert N. wagon-maker; Kirkwood; rep; from New York.

Smith I. N. carpenter; Kirkwood; ind; from Ohio.

Smith M. L. brakeman on C. B. & Q. R. R.; Kirkwood; rep; from Ohio.

Smith S. C. farmer; P. O. Kirkwood; rep; from Connecticut.

Smith S. H. farmer; Sec. 19; P.O. Kirkwood; rep; 100 acres; from Ohio.

Smith W. J. farmer; Sec. 22; P. O. Kirkwood; rep; Meth; 400 acres; from Ky.

Snyder Anton, with I. Vantuyl; P. O. Kirkwood; dem; Cath; from Germany.

Sofield G. D. laborer; P. O. Kirkwood; rep; from Pennsylvania.

SOFIELD JOHN B. Merchant, and V. Pres. of the First National Bank, Kirkwood; born in Tioga Co., Pa., March 26, 1832; came to this country in 1860; Rep; Univ; owns town property valued at $2,000; was chosen one of the first Trustees of the village; wife was Helen M. Smalley, born in Madison Co., N. Y., Dec. 18, 1838; married Oct. 19, 1859; has one child, Laura A.

Sofield W. J. cigar manufacturer; Kirkwood; rep; from Pennsylvania.

Speakman J. B. farmer; P. O. Monmouth; rep; 80 acres; from Pennsylvania.

Spear Robt. retired farmer; Kirkwood; rep; Presb; from Ohio.

SPENCE WILLIAM, Farmer; Sec. 15; P. O. Kirkwood; born in Warren Co., Ohio, in 1819; came to this Co. in 1854; Rep; Presb; owns 120 acres of land, valued at $8,400; his wife was Hannah Maria Roney; she was born in Pa., May 3, 1835; married Sept. 13, 1855; they have four children living, Newton A., Margaret M., William Lincoln and Eva May.

Stevens A. E. laborer; Kirkwood; dem; Meth; from Ohio.

Staley David, farmer; Sec. 31; P. O. Kirkwood; dem; 160 acres; from Pennsylvania.

Staley Joseph T. farmer; Sec. 31; P. O Kirkwood; dem; 240 acres; from Pennsylvania.

Stark Wm. druggist; Kirkwood; rep; Chris; from Scotland.

Stead Geo. farmer; Kirkwood; dem; from New York.

Stewart C. W. physician; Kirkwood; Ind; from Kentucky.

Stewart Geo. farmer; Sec. 30; P. O. Kirkwood; rep.

Stewart Walter S. painter; Kirkwood; rep; born Adams Co.

Stinemates J. T. Sec. 35; P. O. Lenox; rep; Meth; 100 acres; from Ohio.

Stormont J. T. teamster; Kirkwood; rep; from Indiana.

Stormont W. S. farmer; P. O. Kirkwood; ind; U. P.; 160 acres; from Kentucky.

Strain D. L. farmer, on farm of C. Harden; Kirkwood; rep; Meth; from Penn.

Sullivan M. farmer; Sec. 1; P. O. Monmouth; dem; Cath; 40 acres; from Ireland.

Sweager Samuel, carpenter; Kirkwood; dem; from Pennsylvania.

TALBOT J. O. farmer; Sec. 34; P. O. Kirkwood; rep; Meth; 280 acres; Ind.

Talbott J. S. farmer; P. O. Lenox; rep; 120 acres; from Indiana.

Thomas John F. mason; Kirkwood; rep; from Maryland.

Thompson A. W. teacher; Kirkwood; rep; U. P.; from Ohio.
Thompson David, grain dealer; Kirkwood; rep; U. P.; from Ohio.
Thompson Rev. E. W. minister of Presb. ch.; Kirkwood; rep; from Indiana.
Thompson H. R. farmer; Sec. 13; P. O. Kirkwood; rep; U. P.; from Ohio.
Thompson John, farmer; Sec. 10; P.O. Kirkwood; rep; U. P.; 160 acres; from Ohio.
Thompson J. A. grain dealer; Kirkwood; rep; U. P.; from Iowa.
Thompson John Alex. farmer; Sec. 10; P.O. Kirkwood; rep; U. P.; from Ohio.
Thompson J. F. farmer; Sec. 13; P. O. Kirkwood; rep; U. P.; from Ohio.
THOMSON W. E. Farmer; Sec. 10; P. O. Kirkwood; born in Jefferson Co., Ohio, Feb. 11, 1851; came to this Co. May 22, 1867; Rep; U. P.; rents farm of 160 acres of his father; holds the office of Overseer of Highway; his wife was Maggie Martin; she was born in Warren Co., Ill., July 4, 1857; married Dec. 31, 1874; they have one child, James F.
Thorp M. L. carpenter; Kirkwood; rep; from New York.
Tibbetts L. physician; Kirkwood; dem; from Adams Co., Ill.
Tinkham G. W. farmer; Sec. 19; P. O. Kirkwood; dem; born Warren Co.
TINKHAM JOSEPH, Farmer; Sec. 19; P. O. Kirkwood; born in Windham Co., Vt., March 26, 1812; went to Saratoga Co., N. Y., in 1830, and came to this Co. Nov. 19, 1835; has lived where he now does since 1836; Dem; Chris; owns 320 acres of land, valued at $22,000; was chosen Supervisor for three years, and Township Treasurer for six years; was one of the very first settlers of the county; wife was Ann Robinson, born in Smith Co., Tenn., Dec. 15, 1841; has two children, J. Willard and Mary A.
Tinkham O. B. farmer; Sec. 21; P. O. Kirkwood; dem; 40 acres; born Warren Co.
TINKHAM RANSOM. Retired Farmer; P. O. Kirkwood; born in Windham Co., Vt., July 23, 1815; came to this Co. Nov. 3, 1836; Dem; owns 160 acres of land, valued at $10,000; came to this township when there were but five families, and has resided here nearly all the time since; wife was Cordelia A. Forwood, born in Hartford Co., Md., Aug. 1, 1821; married April 23, 1842; has five children.
Tinkham Willard, farmer; Sec. 20; P. O. Kirkwood; dem; 160 acres; bn. Warren Co.
Tubbs Geo. farmer; Sec. 16; P. O. Kirkwood; rep; Meth; 160 acres; from New York.
Tubbs Henry, banker; Kirkwood; from New York.
Tubbs W. C. clerk; Kirkwood; rep; from New York.

Underhill Samuel, retired farmer; Kirkwood; rep; Meth; from N. Y.
Vandenburg E. mason; Kirkwood; rep; Meth; from New York.
Vanriper A. C. farmer; Kirkwood; dem; Presb; from New Jersey.
Vantuyl Isaac, farmer; Sec. 3; P. O. Kirkwood; rep; 400 acres; from New Jersey.
Vantuyl Michael, farmer; P. O. Kirkwood; rep; Meth; from Ohio.
Vanwinkle A. H. farmer; Sec. 15; P. O. Kirkwood; dem; from Iowa.
Valentine I. H. travelling; Kirkwood; ind; from New York.
Vernoy Alfred, carpenter; Kirkwood; dem; from New York.
Vernoy James W. farmer; Kirkwood; dem; born Warren Co.
Vosburg Jacob, shoemaker; Kirkwood; rep; from Canada.
Vroom Cornelius, laborer; Kirkwood; ind; from New Jersey.
Vroom D. W. laborer; Kirkwood; dem; from New Jersey.
Wade G. W. farmer; Kirkwood; ind; Meth; from Indiana.
Wade James H. barber; Kirkwood; rep; Chris; from Indiana.
Walker A. H. retired farmer; Kirkwood; rep; from New York.
Waters John, merchant; Kirkwood; Epis; from England.
Watson J. H. farmer; Sec. 34; P. O. Kirkwood; rep; Meth; 80 acres; bn. Warren Co.
Waugh James, farm hand; P. O. Kirkwood; dem; from Michigan.
Waystaffe Robert, Sr., farmer; P. O. Monmouth; from Ireland.
Waystaffe Robert, Jr., laborer; Kirkwood; from Ireland.
Weaver Geo. H. carpenter; Kirkwood; dem; from New York.
Weaver John, farm hand with T. W. Beers; P. O. Kirkwood; dem; from New York.
Webb S. John, farmer; Sec. 1; P. O. Monmouth; rep; from Pennsylvania.
Wells Wm. farm hand with C. A. Houlton; P. O. Kirkwood; rep; U. P.
Whiteside John A. cigar-maker; Kirkwood; rep; from New York.
Wilcox Nathan, retired; Kirkwood; rep;
Willett J. E. laborer; Kirkwood; rep; from Kentucky.
Wilson Benj. farmer; Sec. 13; P. O. Monmouth; dem; from Kentucky.
Wise Henry, laborer; Kirkwood; rep; from Pennsylvania.
Wray Mrs. Sarah E. widow; Sec. 7; P. O. Kirkwood; U. P.; from Ohio.

Woods D. C. farmer; Sec. 5; P. O. Kirkwood; dem; 153 acres; from Indiana.

Wood George, farmer; Sec. 9; P. O. Kirkwood; rep; U. P.; from Ohio.

Woods Isaac, farmer; Sec. 4; P. O. Kirkwood; dem; U. P.; born Henderson Co.

Woods J. H. farmer; Sec. 34; Kirkwood; dem; from Indiana.

Woods J. W. retired farmer; P. O. Kirkwood; dem; U. P.; from Tennessee.

Wood Matthew, farmer; Sec. 9; P. O. Kirkwood; rep; U. P.; 110 acres; from Scotl'd.

Woods Mrs. Nancy, widow; Kirkwood; Presb; 11 acres; from Indiana.

Wood Wm. nurseryman; Kirkwood; rep; Meth; from Ohio.

Woods Wm. S laborer; Kirkwood; rep; Bapt; born Illinois.

Wray A. E. farmer; Sec. 7; P. O. Kirkwood; rep; born Warren Co.

Wray Frank M. farmer; Sec. 18; P. O. Kirkwood; rep; born Warren Co.

Wray Josephus S. farmer; Sec. 7; P. O. Kirkwood; rep; 80 acres; from Kentucky.

Wray S. D. farmer; Sec. 7; P. O. Kirkwood; rep; born Warren Co.

YEOMANS A. J. restaurant keeper; Kirkwood; Meth; from New York.

Yeomans W. C. carpenter; Kirkwood; ind; Meth; from New York.

Yoder Wm. tailor; Kirkwood; dem; Luth; from Pennsylvania.

ZIMMERMAN MOSES, Farmer and Stock Raiser; Sec. 12; P. O. Monmouth; born in Cumberland Co., Pa., in 1829; came to this Co. in 1871; Rep; Meth; owns 123 acres of land, valued at $8,500; is overseer of highway; his wife was Agnes Houston; she was born in Cumberland Co., Pa., in 1831; married Sept. 27, 1859; had seven children; six are living.

KIRKWOOD BUSINESS DIRECTORY.

Allen Moses W. Dealer in General Merchandise.

Barnes, Creswell & Co., Props. Young America Nursery, ¾ mile from R. R. Depot.

Bute Cyrus, Police Magistrate.

Drain Bros. Lumber Dealers.

Kellogg Geo. W. Station Agent C. B. & Q. R. R.

Leedham Wm. H. Editor and Proprietor *Kirkwood News*.

Lowther & Gilmore, Dry Goods and Groceries.

Schenberger Elias, Postmaster.

Sofield & Cummings, Hardware, Stoves, and Agricultural Implements.

ELLISON TOWNSHIP.

ABDELL WARREN, farmer, rents of A. M. Irving; Sec. 12; P. O. Roseville.

Adair Jno. farmer, rents of W. Shores; Sec. 3; P. O. Kirkwood; dem; born Illinois.

Adams J. D. farmer, rents of K. Brent, Sr.; Sec. 18; P. O. Ellison; rep; from Ky.

Adams Nelson, farmer, rents of Parker Parrish; Sec. 3; P. O. Kirkwood; rep; N. Y.

ALLARD J. S. Farmer and Stock Raiser; Sec. 10; P. O. Kirkwood; born in Carroll Co., N. H., April 13, 1838; came to this County in the spring of 1856, and is one of the oldest settlers; wife was Miss Fannie Wornom, born in this Co. Feb. 26, 1843; married Aug. 29, 1860; has family five children; living, Clayton A., Blanche, Mertie and Chester; and one dead, Cora; has 160 acres, value $10,000; rep.

Allen Thos. farmer, rents of J. C. Morris; Sec. 9; P. O. Kirkwood; dem; from Ohio.

Appleby Jas. farmer, works for J. A. Pierson; Sec. 17; P. O. Ellison; rep; from Ohio.

BALDWIN JOHN, farmer; Sec. 8; P. O. Ellison; has 80 acres, value $5,000; dem.

Barnett C. R. farmer; Sec. 6; P. O. Kirkwood; 80 acres, value $5,000; rep; Ill.

Barnett Levi, carpenter, P. O. Ellison; dem; from Virginia.

Baxter, Hiram, farmer; Sec. 5; P. O. Ellison; has 45 acres, value $2,925; rep; from N.Y.

Baxter J. C. farmer; Sec. 5; P. O. Ellison; rents of James Gregory; rep; from N. Y.

Beasly J. C. farmer; Sec. 34; P. O. Roseville; 221 acres, value $11,000; rep; Missouri.

Becktel Milford, farmer; Sec. 16; P. O. Ellison; rents of D. C. Brent; rep; from Ohio.

Becktel Wm. farmer; Sec. 10; P. O. Ellison; rep; born Illinois.

Beebe Henry, farmer; P. O. Ellison; rep; born Illinois.

Bell John, farmer, works for J. J. Johnson; Sec. 22; P. O. Roseville; rep; from Ohio.

Birdsall H. A. farmer, rents of H. K. Brent; Sec. 7; P. O. Ellison; rep; from N. Y.

Birdsall Jno. farmer; Sec. 6; P. O. Kirkwood; has 320 acres, value $19,200; rep; Canada.

BIRDSALL WM. Farmer and Stock Raiser; Sec. 6; P. O. Kirkwood; born in Canada, Oct. 21, 1828, and came to this Co. in Sept., 1838; he being one of the oldest settlers in the Co.; has family, five children; Mary married Andrew Oaks, and resides in Mills Co., Iowa; Ella, Celia, Cornelia and Lyman; wife was Miss Jane E. Brazleton, born in Indiana, Sept. 7, 1831; married Jan. 20, 1850; has 201 acres; value $13,065; rep.

Bradford Thos. farmer, works for E. C. Johnston; Sec. 36; P. O. Roseville; dem.

Brazleton Jas. H. School Teacher; Sec. 6; P. O. Kirkwood; rep; from Indiana.

Brazleton Joseph F. farmer; Sec. 6; P. O. Kirkwood; works for C. R. Barnett; rep.

BRENT D. C. farmer and Stock Raiser; Sec. 18; P. O. Ellison; born in Lancaster Co., Va., Oct. 12, 1821; left there with his parents and came to this Co. and to this tp., and settled on the place he now lives, March 14, 1836, and is one of the very oldest settlers in the tp.; has family, six sons and three daughters living; one son and two daughters dead; wife was Miss Jane Brown, born in the same Co., Jan. 1, 1830, married March 7, 1850; rep; Meth.

Brent E. C. farmer; P. O. Ellison; rep; Va.

Brent G. W. farmer; Sec. 18; lives with his father; P. O. Ellison; rep; born Illinois.

BRENT KENNER. Sr. farmer and stock raiser; Sec. 18; P. O. Ellison; born Lancaster Co., Va., March 4, 1796, remained there until the fall of 1835, and arrived here March 14, 1836; Mr. B. as well as being one of the oldest settlers is the oldest man in the tp.; he served about two and one-half years in the war of 1812; he has a family, six sons and four daughters living; two sons and one daughter dead; has been married twice; first wife was Elizabeth Brent, born in the same Co; he married again, to Anne N. Hubbard, born in Lancaster Co., Va., Sept. 26, 1824; married Aug. 27, 1867; has 400 acres, value $20,000; Rep; Meth.

BRENT KENNER, Jr. Farmer and Stock Raiser; Sec. 18; P. O. Ellison; born in Lancaster Co., Va., Oct. 14, 1827; left there and came to this Co. with his parents, March 14, 1836, and is one of the oldest settlers in the tp.; has family, one son and six daughters; three sons and one daughter dead; has been married twice; first wife was Miss Elizabeth V. Simpson, born in Ohio, March 11, 1839; married April 3, 1852; she died March 11, 1866; he married again to Mary A. Dempsey, born in Ohio, March 7, 1846; married Feb. 14, 1870; has 187 acres, value $11,200; Rep; Meth.

BRENT PAUL, Farmer and Stock Raiser; Sec. 8; P. O. Ellison; born in Lancaster Co., Va., June 16, 1831; left there with his parents and came to this Co. in March, 1836, and is one of the very oldest settlers; has family, three sons and four daughters living; two sons and one daughter dead; wife was Phœbe A. Moore, born in Ohio, Oct. 9, 1836; married Aug. 13, 1857; has 200 acres, value, $10,000; Rep; Meth.

BRENT WM. P. Farmer and Stock Raiser; Sec. 17; P. O. Ellison; born in Lancaster Co., Va., Jan. 4, 1820; left there with his parents and arrived here March 14, 1836, and settled on the place he now lives, and has remained here ever since, being one of the very first settlers; has family, four sons and three daughters living; two sons and one daughter dead; wife was Miss Ellen Jamison, born in Henderson Co., Ill., July 1, 1833; married Oct. 8, 1850; has 400 acres, value $20,000; Rep.

Briley C. farmer; P. O. Ellison; dem; Tenn.

Briley John farmer; P. O. Ellison; dem; Meth; born Illinois.

Briley Thos. farmer; P. O. Ellison; dem; born Illinois.

Brook C. farmer; Sec. 16; P. O. Ellison; rep; has 150½ acres, value $11,700; from N. Y.

Brooks E. C. farmer; Sec. 28; P. O. Roseville; rep; 40 acres, value $1,800; born Illinois.

Brooks Geo. farmer; Sec. 16; lives with his father; P. O. Ellison; rep; born Illinois.

Brown Albert, farmer; Sec. 3; lives with his father; P. O. Kirkwood; dem; born Ill.

Brown C. H. farmer; Sec. 3; P. O. Kirkwood; dem; has 80 acres, value $4,800; born Ill.

Brown Geo. farmer; Sec. 3; lives with his father; P. O. Kirkwood; dem; born Ill.

Brown Henry, farmer; Sec. 27; rents of E. Godfrey; P. O. Roseville; dem; from Ind.

Brown Jas. farmer; Sec. 4; P. O. Kirkwood; dem; 240 acres, value, $12,000; from Va.

Brown Wm., Sr. farmer; Sec. 3; P. O. Kirkwood; dem; 40 acres, value $12,400; Va.

Brown Wm., Jr. farmer; Sec. 22; rents of G. Godfrey; P. O. Ellison; dem; from Va.

Brown Wm. L. laborer; P. O. Ellison; dem; from Virginia.

Burch Thos., Sr. farmer; P. O. Roseville; dem; from Ohio.

Burch Thos., Jr. farmer; P. O. Roseville; dem; from Ohio.

Bycroff Wm. farmer; P. O. Jackson Corners; rep; from England.

CALVIN HENRY, farmer, works for E. Mitchell; Sec. 25; P. O. Roseville; rep.

Charter S. L., farmer; P. O. Ellison; dem; Meth; born Illinois.

Clark Merritt, farmer; P. O. Roseville; rep; born Illinois.

Clayton Wm. farmer; P. O. Ellison; dem; born Illinois.

Cochran Jno. farmer; P. O. Ellison; rep; born Illinois.

Cochran Wm. farmer, works for A. P. Loftus; Sec. 34; P. O. Roseville; rep; from Iowa.

Crane S. B. farmer; Sec. 12; P. O. Roseville; dem; has 100 acres, value $8,000; N. J.

Crozier Rodney, farmer; Sec. 36; P. O. Roseville; rep; has 330 acres, value $23,100.

Crozier Warren, farmer, lives with his father; Sec. 36, P. O. Roseville; rep; from Ohio.

DALTON MARION, blacksmith; P. O. Ellison; rep; from Ohio.

Davidson A. H. carpenter; P. O. Ellison; rep; born Illinois.

Dawson F. wagon maker; P. O. Ellison; rep; born Illinois.

Deater Nat. farmer, rents of F. M. Davidson; Sec. 7; P. O. Ellison; dem; from Ind.

Deater Wm. farmer, rents of F. M. Davidson; Sec. 7; P. O. Ellison; dem; from Ind.

Drain C. farmer; P. O. Ellison; rep; born Illinois.

ELMER WM. farmer, works for D. Shalenbarger; Sec. 1; P. O. Lenox Station.

Edwards Wm. L. blacksmith; P. O. Ellison; rep; Meth; born Illinois.

EDWARDS JOHN, Farmer and Stock Raiser; Sec. 5; P. O. Kirkwood; born in Belmont Co., Ohio, May 13, 1835; came to the State in 1853, and to the Co. in 1863, and settled on the place he now lives; family two children, Mary and Elvira; wife was Miss Josephine Johnson, born in Kentucky, in 1839; married Sept. 23, 1863; has 161 acres, value $11,270; served five months in the late war, in Co. B, 71st I. V. I.; Rep.

Eldridge Jas. farmer; Sec. 35; P. O. Roseville; rep; 90 acres, value $5,400; N. Y.

ELDRIDGE N. A. Farmer and Stock Raiser; Sec. 25; P. O. Roseville; born in Berkshire Co., Mass., May 8, 1815; left there in 1838, and moved to Otsego Co., N. Y., and remained there until 1846; then came to this Co.; is one of the oldest settlers; has three children living, Sarah J., James and Florence; two dead, Arlina and Wilson; wife was Miss Nancy Cole, born in the same place, March 19, 1817; married Jan. 6, 1838; has 210 acres, value $11,700; has been Supervisor twelve years, and held other Town Offices; Rep.

Ent Asa, farmer; Sec. 16; P. O. Ellison, rep; 80 acres, value $4,000; from N. J.

Ervin Thos. farmer, works for J. A. Pierson; Sec. 17; rep; from Iowa.

EWING C. O. Farmer and Stock Raiser; Sec. 11; P. O. Lenox Station; born in Madison Co., Ohio, March 4, 1829; came to this Co. in the fall of 1864; has family seven children, Smith, Henry R., William J., Eliza G., Flora A., Elmer G. and Sarah F.; wife was Miss Harriet Moore, born in the same place, Feb. 8, 1826; married Dec. 2, 1852; has 160 acres of land, value $10,000; Rep; both members of the Meth. church.

Ewing Jno. farmer; Sec. 12; P. O. Lenox; rep; 90 acres, value $4,500; from Ohio.

Ewing Smith, farmer; Sec. 10; P. O. Ellison; rep; from Ohio.

FERNALD E. L. farmer, lives with his father; Sec. 13; P. O. Ellison; dem.

Fernald E. W. farmer, rents of E. Brooks; Sec. 15; P. O. Ellison; dem; from N. H.

FLETCHER JAMES M. Farmer and Stock Raiser; Sec. 16; P. O. Ellison; born in Addison Co., Vt., Jan. 4, 1819; left there May 1st, 1835, and went to Lorain Co., Ohio, and remained there until July, 1839; then removed to Knox Co., Ill.; came to this Co. in May, 1845, and has remained here ever since; has family two sons and four daughters living; one son dead; died at Vicksburg, during the war; wife was Miss Mary Frost, born in England, June 30, 1822; married June 18, 1840; has 317 acres of land, value $19,000; Rep.

Foot Sidney, farmer, rents of Wm. Shores; Sec. 13; P. O. Lenox; from Ohio.

Furguson John, farmer; P. O. Ellison; dem; from Ireland.

GALBREATH DANIEL, farmer, lives with his father; Sec. 5; P. O. Ellison.

Galbreath Newton, farmer, lives on his father's place; Sec. 9; P. O. Ellison; dem.

Galbreath Thos. farmer, lives with his father; Sec. 5; P. O. Ellison; dem; from Iowa.

GALBREATH WILLIAM, Sr. Farmer and Stock Raiser; Sec. 5; P. O. Ellison; born in Roane Co., East Tenn., Oct. 22, 1814; left there with his parents, and moved to Morgan Co., Ill., in Dec., 1829; remained there about one year and then went to Adams Co.; came to this Co. in the fall of 1835; is one of the very oldest settlers; has family four sons and six daughters; two sons dead; wife was Sarah

A. Harland, born in Maryland; has 520 acres, value $26,000; Dem; Chris.

Galbreath Wm., Jr. farmer, lives with his father; Sec. 5; P. O. Ellison; dem; Ill.

Garrett Jas. farmer; Sec. 30; P. O. Jackson Corners; rep; 80 acres, value $4,000; Tenn.

Garretson Rev. P. S. pastor of M. E. church; P. O. Ellison; rep; from New Jersey.

George John, farmer, rents of W. R.Rayburn; Sec. 26; P. O. Roseville; dem; Ohio.

Gibson T. H. farmer, rents of J. K..Gibson; Sec. 2; P. O. Kirkwood; rep; from Ohio.

Gilbert B. farmer, rents of Jas. Eldridge; Sec. 35; P. O. Roseville; dem; from N. Y.

Glaze Jno. farmer, rents of W. Rayburn; Sec. 14; Roseville; dem; from Ohio.

Godfrey Burton, farmer; Sec. 27; P. O. Roseville; rep; Meth; 320 acres, value $19,200.

Godfrey Elijah, farmer; Sec. 27; P. O. Roseville; Ind; has 258 acres, value $12,900.

Godfrey E. G. farmer, lives with his father; Sec. 27; P. O. Roseville; rep; Meth; O.

Godfrey J. M. farmer, rents of his father; Sec. 27; P. O. Roseville; rep; Ohio.

Godfrey Jas. farmer; Sec. 21; P. O. Ellison; rep; has 321 acres, value $16,000; Ohio.

Godfrey Jno. farmer, lives with his father; Sec. 21; P. O. Ellison; rep; born Illinois.

Godfrey Jno., Sr. farmer; Sec. 26; P. O. Roseville; rep; 229 acres, value $11,450.

Godfrey Joseph, farmer, lives with his father; Sec. 21; P. O. Ellison; rep; born Ill.

Godfrey Joel B. farmer, rents of Jas. Godfrey; Sec. 21; P. O. Ellison; rep; born Ill.

Golden Oliver, farmer; Sec. 26; P. O. Roseville; rep; Meth; 80 acres, value $4,000.

Goodale B. F. farmer, works for E. Brooks; Sec. 23; P. O. Roseville; rep; from Mich.

Goodwin W. H. farmer, works for J. M. Fletcher; Sec. 21; P. O. Ellison; rep; Vt.

GOULDIN L. L. Farmer and Stock Raiser; Sec. 26; P. O. Roseville; born in Franklin Co., Ohio, Sept. 13, 1851; left there with his parents, and moved to Henderson Co., Ill., in 1857; came to Warren Co. in 1864; has family of one daughter, Minnie Luella, born Oct. 6, 1876; wife was Miss Augusta L. Loftus, born in this Co., June 21, 1856; married Dec. 24, 1874; has 80 acres, value $4,000; Rep; Meth.

Graham C. W. farmer; Sec. 24; P. O. Roseville; rep; 124 acres, value $6,000; Ohio.

Gray Walter, farmer, rents of C. Drain; Sec. 14; P. O. Roseville; from England.

HARBER LEVI M. laborer; P. O. Ellison; dem; born Illinois.

Harbaugh Jas. farmer; Sec. 13; P. O. Roseville; rep; 80 acres, value $4,400; born Ill.

Harris A. farmer; Sec. 22; P. O. Roseville; rep; 10 acres, value $600; born Illinois.

Harris V. K. farmer, rents of D. Hogsett; Sec. 22; P. O. Ellison; rep; born Illinois.

Hawk John, farmer, works for W. Rayburn; Sec. 36; P. O. Roseville; dem; from Ohio.

Hoag L. J. farmer; Sec. 20; P. O. Ellison; rep; 113 acres, value $6,780; born Illinois.

Holloway Edwin, farmer, rents of A. L. Pennoyer; Sec. 24; P. O. Roseville; rep.

Holloway John, laborer; P. O. Ellison; rep; born Illinois.

Holloway Milton, laborer; P. O. Ellison; rep; born Illinois.

Hook E. R. farmer, rents of F. Meacham; Sec. 34; P. O. Roseville; dem; from Ohio.

Hook John, farmer; P. O. Roseville; dem; born Illinois.

Houlton J. F. farmer; Sec. 32; P. O. Jackson Corners; rep; 100 acres, value $8,000; Me.

Houlton Jos., Jr., farmer; Sec. 32; P. O. Jackson Corners; rep; 160 acres, value $8,000.

Houlton Jos., Sr., retired; Sec. 32; P. O. Jackson Corners; rep; from Mass.

Humes John S. farmer; P. O. Roseville; rep; born Ill.

IRVING A. M. Farmer and Stock Raiser; Sec. 12; P. O. Roseville; born in Somerset Co., N. J., March 16, 1834; came to this Co. in October, 1855, and is one of the oldest settlers; has family of six children, Mary Ida, Margaret J., Emma L., Nancy A., Alfred M., and Amanda E; wife was Miss Mary E. McClure, born in McDonough Co., Ill., January 10, 1837; married Dec. 14, 1859; has 376 acres of the best improved land in the tp., value $24,400; both Cong.

JONES A. H. farmer; Sec. 9; P. O. Ellison; rep; 80 acres, value $4,000; Ohio.

Jones E. T. farmer; P. O. Roseville; dem; born Illinois.

Jones Jno. B. farmer; Sec. 1; P. O. Lenox Station; rep; 80 acres, value $4,800; Va.

Jones J. H. farmer, works for J. J. Johnson; Sec. 21; P. O. Roseville; rep; from Ohio.

Jones J. H. farmer, rents of J. Godfrey; Sec. 25; P. O. Roseville; dem; from Ohio.

JAMISON M. V. Farmer and Stock Raiser; Sec. 9; P. O. Ellison; born in Henderson Co., Ill., July 12, 1850; left there and came to this Co. in the fall of 1875; has family of one daughter, Cordelia Josephine, born August 1, 1875; wife was Miss Velina Brent, daughter of Wm. P. Brent, born in this Co. Feb. 12, 1854; married Nov. 22, 1874; has 160 acres, value $8,000; Rep; Presb.

JOHNSON J. J. Farmer and Stock Raiser; Sec. 22; P. O. Roseville; born in Cape May Co., N. J., March 11, 1809; left there when 21 years of age, and went to Madison Co., Ohio; came to this Co. in the fall of 1854; has family of eleven children,

R. W. GERLAW ESQ.
SPRING GROVE TOWNSHIP

six sons and five daughters; has been married twice; first wife was Mary Bryant, who died in October, 1854; married again to Jane Bell, in September, 1856; has 345 acres, value $20,700; has served seven years as Justice of the Peace, and six years as Road Commissioner; Rep.

Johnson J. J. Jr., farmer; Sec. 4; Ellison; 44½ acres, value $2,640; rep; from Ohio.

Johnson Peter, farmer, rents of D. M. Taliaferro; Sec. 11; P. O. Ellison; rep; Sweden.

Johnson Wm. farmer; lives on his father's place; Sec. 22; P. O. Roseville; rep; Ohio.

JOHNSTON E. C. Farmer and Stock Raiser; Sec. 36; P. O. Roseville; born in Green Co., Indiana, Sept. 20, 1830; left there and came to this Co. and settled on the place he now lives in, Oct., 1860; has family of two sons and three daughters, Edward C., Wm. D., Chirena Blanche, Minnie and Estelle; wife was Miss Amanda Andrews, born in Lawrence Co., Tenn. May 19, 1839; married Nov. 26, 1857; Mr. J. has 875 acres, all under cultivation, value $52,500; Dem; Mrs. J. is a member of the Cumberland Presbyterian Church.

KELLY I. A. farmer, rents of D. M. Taliaferro; Sec. 11; P. O. Roseville; rep.

Kane Jno. farmer, lives with his father; Sec. 13; P. O. Roseville; dem; from England.

KANE MICHAEL. Farmer and Stock Raiser; Sec. 13; P. O. Roseville; born in the Co. of Waterford, Ireland, in 1824; left there and came to the United States in June, 1864, and to this Co. in the spring of 1876; has family of five children, John, William, Fannie, Mary, and Edmund; wife was Fannie Stack, from the Co. of Cork, Ireland; married in 1840; has 156 acres, value $7,800; Dem; Cath.

Khron Fred. O. farmer; Sec. 1; P. O. Lenox; 100 acres, value $6,000; dem; from N. Y.

Khron Henry, farmer; Sec. 1; P. O. Lenox, 100 acres, value $6,000; dem; Germany.

Kimball S. H. tinner; P. O. Ellison; rep; from Ohio.

Kimball W. H. farmer, rents of F. M. Davidson; Sec. 7; P. O. Ellison; rep; Ill.

Kirby I. B. farmer; Sec. 34; P. O. Roseville; 187 acres, value $9,350; dem; from Penn.

LEACOCK JACOB, farmer, lives on his father's place; Sec. 5; P. O. Roseville.

Lehman Jacob, farmer; Sec. 1; P. O. Lenox Station; 80 acres, value $5,200; rep; Penn.

Leiter Jacob, farmer; Sec. 12; P. O. Lenox; 54 acres, value $2,700; dem; from Penn.

Livermore A. P. farmer; Sec. 33; P. O. Roseville; 175 acres, value $8,750; rep.

Livermore W. R. farmer, rents of R. Crosier; Sec. 36; P. O. Roseville; rep; born Ill.

LOFFTUS A. J. Farmer and Stock Raiser; Sec. 34; P. O. Roseville; born in Augusta Co., Va., Jan. 16, 1815; left there in Oct., 1823, and moved to Christian Co., Ky., with his parents, and remained there until April, 1837, then came to this Co., and is one of the very oldest settlers; has eight children living, four dead; wife was Lavinia S. Meacham, born in Christian Co., Ky., Feb. 26, 1822; married Dec. 24, 1837; has 311 acres, value $15,550; has served as School Trustee twenty-five years; Rep; Christian.

Lofftus A. P. farmer; Sec. 34; P. O. Roseville; rep; Chris; 80 acres, val. $4,000; Ill.

Lofftus Geo. farmer; Sec. 15; P. O. Roseville; dem; 80 acres, value $4,800; born Illinois.

Lofftus S. D. farmer; Sec. 20; P. O. Ellison; dem; 116 acres, value $5,800; from Va.

Lofftus Wm. farmer; Sec. 20; P. O. Ellison; lives with his father; dem; born Illinois.

Lovett Wm. farmer; Sec. 25; P. O. Roseville; rents of W. H. Lee; rep; from Kentucky.

Lozier James, farmer; Sec. 27; P. O. Roseville; rents of B. Godfrey; rep; Meth; Ill.

McCURDY JOHN, farmer; Sec. 22; P. O. Roseville; rents of D. Hogsett; Ill.

McGlaughlin Andrew, farmer; Sec 24; P. O. Roseville; rents of David Stern; dem; Pa.

McKanna R. A. farmer; P. O. Ellison; rep; Meth; from Ohio.

McMillen David, farmer; Sec. 11; P. O. Kirkwood; rents of J. Greenlee; rep; Can.

McMillen O. J. farmer; Sec. 11; P. O. Kirkwood; rents of J. Greenlee; rep; Canada.

McWilliams J. I. farmer; Sec. 1; P. O. Lenox Station; rep; 80 acres, value $4,800; Ohio.

Madison Stephen, farmer; Sec. 33; P. O. Roseville; rents of J. C. Beasley; rep; O.

MEACHAM A. M. Farmer and Stock Raiser; Sec. 34; P. O. Roseville; born in Sangamon Co., Ill., Dec. 2, 1838; left there when two years of age; came to this Co. and to this tp. with his parents, and has remained here ever since, he being one of the oldest settlers in the town; has family, six children, Albert A., John A., Ziba H., Harman E., Eva M., and Earl; wife was Clarinda M. McMillen, born in Ohio, May 6, 1837; married July 28, 1859; has 120 acres, value $7,200; Rep; Chris.

Meacham Edward, farmer; Sec. 35; P. O. Roseville; rep; 45 acres, value $2,260; Ill.

Meacham Mont. A. farmer; Sec. 29; P. O. Jackson Corners; dem; 98¼ acres, $3,920.

Meacham M. G. farmer; Sec. 32; P. O. Jackson Corners; dem; 125 acs., val. $6,000; Ky.

Means Geo. farmer; Sec. 22; P. O. Roseville; rep; rents of J. J. Johnson; from Ind.

MITCHELL ELIPHALET. Farmer and Stock Raiser; Sec. 25; P. O. Roseville; born in Bristol Co., Mass., Nov. 29, 1817; left there and came to this Co. and this tp. in the spring of 1841, and is among the oldest settlers; has been married twice; first wife was Martha J. Sovereign, born in Upper Canada, Nov. 13, 1829; married June 20, 1845; she died June 14, 1872; has seven sons living and one dead by first wife, Howard A., Ossian K., Morton, Arthur L., S. P., Frank J., and Albert W., one dead, E. L.; married again Oct. 15, 1873, to Mary J. Luster, born in St. Clair Co., Ill., Jan. 17, 1831; second wife has one daughter, Minnie; has 333½ acres, value $23,345; is Supervisor and has been for eight years, and Town Clerk ten years, and held other offices; Rep; Bapt.

Mitchell Robert, farmer; Sec. 27; P. O. Roseville; works for Burton Godfrey; rep; Ind.

Mitchell S. P., farmer; Sec. 25; P. O. Roseville; lives with his father; rep; born Ill.

Moore Enos, farmer; Sec. 30; P. O. Jackson Corners; rents of C. R. Thompson; dem.

Moore Wm. farmer; Sec. 24; P. O. Roseville; rents of J. B. Morford; dem; Isle of Man.

Morris A. K. farmer; Sec. 15; P. O. Ellison; dem; 200 acres, value $12,000; Ohio.

Morris J. C. farmer; Sec. 9; P. O. Kirkwood; dem; 110 acres, value $6,600; from N. J.

Mowder Benj. farmer; Sec. 17; P. O. Ellison; works for Wm. P. Brent; dem; from N. J.

NICHOLS JEFFERSON, farmer; Sec. 32; P. O. Ellison; rep; 5 acs., val. $400.

Nokes David, farmer, lives with his father; Sec. 4; P. O. Ellison; dem; from Ky.

NELSON JOHN, Farmer; Sec. 10; P. O. Ellison; born in Sweden, Sept. 29, 1843; left there and came to the U. S. April 28, 1868, and went to Galesburg, and came to this Co. in March, 1869; single; has 80 acres, value $3,400; Rep; Swedish Luth.

Nokes Wm. farmer, rents of Wm. Spicer; Sec. 4; P. O. Ellison; dem; from Ky.

O'NEAL EDWIN J. farmer, lives with father; Sec. 23; P. O. Roseville; rep.

O'Neal Henry W. farmer, lives with his father; Sec. 23; P. O. Roseville; rep; Ill.

O'Neal John, Sr., farmer; Sec. 23; P. O. Roseville; rep; 130 acres, val. $6,500; Ky.

O'Neal John, Jr., farmer, lives with his father; Sec. 23; P. O. Roseville; rep; Ill.

Oak J. H. farmer; Sec. 9; P. O. Ellison; rep; 40 acres, value $2,000; from Missouri.

OCKERT JOHN, Farmer and Stock Raiser; Sec. 15; P. O. Roseville; born in Baden, Germany, Aug. 27, 1832; left there Nov. 1, 1854; arrived in N. Y. Dec. 17, same year, remained there four weeks, and then came to Knox Co., Ill.; remained there till March, 1858, then came here, and has remained here ever since; has family, five sons and three daughters; wife was Miss Elizabeth Reibold, born in Hessen Darmstadt, Germany, Oct. 26, 1833; married Dec. 22, 1854; has 170 acres, value $8,500; Rep; wife is Meth.

PAINTER ISAAC, farmer; Sec. 22; P. O. Roseville; dem; 105 acs., val. $5,000.

Painter Samuel, farmer; P. O. Ellison; rep; from Iowa.

Pauly R. A. clerk; P. O. Ellison; rep; born Illinois.

Parmenter Chas. farmer, rents of Geo. W. Brent; Sec. 18; P. O. Ellison; dem; Ill.

PARRISH P. R. Farmer and Stock Raiser and Dealer; Sec. 4; P. O. Kirkwood; born in Lafayette, Tippecanoe Co., Ind., Jan. 19, 1833; came to this Co. in the spring of 1862, and settled on this place, and has remained here ever since; Mr. P. has one of the best Stock Farms in the Co., known as the Walnut Grove Farm; he has now 20 head of thoroughbred Short Horn Cattle, and is a breeder of Poland China Hogs; he has Cattle for sale; it would be well to give him a call; has 200 acres, value $18,000; Dem; has family, seven children, four sons and three daughters.

Patch Amasa, farmer; Sec. 30; P. O. Jackson Corners; ind; 90 acres; value $5,400.

Patch Dennis, farmer; Sec. 31; P. O. Jackson Corners; dem; 50 acres, value $3,000; Me.

PATCH E. M. Farmer and Stock Raiser; Sec. 31; P. O. Jackson Corners; born in Carroll Co., N. H., June 10, 1850; came to this Co. with his parents when three years of age; has one son, George, born Sept. 3, 1873; has been married twice; first wife was Ada Merriam, born in Mass.; married March 1, 1872; she died April 14, 1875; married again Feb. 14, to Eva Henderson, from Plymouth, Ill.; has 40 acres, value $3,000; Ind; Meth.

Patch Mayhew, farmer; Sec. 31; P. O. Jackson Corners; Meth; 180 acres, val. $10,800.

Pendarvis J. P. farmer; Sec. 17; P. O. Ellison; rep; 40 acres, value $3,000; born Ill.

PENNOYER A. L. Retired; Sec. 24; P. O. Roseville; born in Fairfield Co., Ct., Oct. 27, 1807; left there and moved to Cincinnati in 1833, and remained there three years, and came to Winchester, Ill., in Dec., 1836, and to this Co. in 1852, and is among the oldest settlers; has family, two children living; wife was Miss Ann Eliza Wyeth, born in Monongahela City, Washington Co., Penn., Feb. 19, 1817, married Dec. 3, 1838; has 200 acres, value $12,000; Rep; was ordained as Minister at Quincy, Ill., in 1837, of the Cong. Church.

Perkins J. B. farmer; Sec. 9; Kirkwood; rents of James Brown.

Peters W. C. farmer; P. O. Roseville; rep; born Illinois.

PIERSON J. A. Postmaster and Merchant; P. O. Ellison; born in Woodsfield, Monroe Co., Ohio, April 8, 1838; left there April 7, 1863, and moved to Tazwell Co., Ill., remained there one year, then went to Davis Co., Mo., remained there one year, then came here; has family, three children living, Cora E., Ollie F. and Virginia B.; one dead, Nancy J.; wife was Miss Nancy Alexander, born in Gibson Co., Ind.; married Aug. 12, 1865; she died May 9, 1873; has 221 acres; value of estate, $16,000; was Supervisor one term, and held other town offices; Rep.

Poniter J. F. farmer; P. O. Ellison; rep; born Illinois.

Prater Andrew, farmer; Sec. 35; P. O. Roseville; rep; works for Ed. Meacham; Ill.

RAYBURN JOS. A. farmer; Sec. 35; P. O. Roseville; rep; lives with mother.

Rayburn Nancy, Sec. 35; P. O. Roseville; Chris; 80 acres, value $5,600; from Ind.

Rayburn U. farmer, lives with his mother; Sec. 35; P. O. Roseville; rep; Illinois.

RAYBURN W. R. Farmer and Stock Raiser; Sec. 36; P. O. Roseville; born in Montgomery Co., Ky., Oct. 18, 1822, and was about four months of age when his parents moved to Ripley Co., Ind., and remained there until the spring of 1855, and then came to this Co.; has family, four sons, George W., Frank S., John and Charley; wife was Miss Sarah A. Roberts, born in Ripley Co., Ind., Nov. 20, 1830; married Nov. 17, 1852; has 561½ acres, value $34,400; was Supervisor two years; Rep.

Reasner James, farmer; Sec. 3; P. O. Kirkwood; rents of P. Parrish; born Illinois.

Reid John, laborer; P. O. Roseville; rep; from Indiana.

Reynolds A. L. farmer; Sec. 25; P. O. Roseville; lives with his father; from Penn.

Reynolds Erastus, farmer; Sec. 25; P. O. Roseville; lives with M. Reynolds; Penn.

Reynolds Madison, farmer; Sec. 25; P. O. Roseville; 80 acres, value $4,000; Penn.

Roberts W. F. farmer, rents the H. Johnson estate; Sec. 22; P. O. Ellison; dem; Ky.

Ross D. C. farmer, rents of J. C. Beasley; Sec. 29; P. O. Jackson Corners; rep; Ind.

Ross H. farmer; Sec. 29; P. O. Ellison; rep; 43 acres, value $1,720; from Ohio.

Ross H. N. farmer; Sec. 23; P. O. Roseville; rep; 80 acres, value $4,000; from Ind.

Ross Henry N. farmer; Sec. 23; P. O. Roseville; rep; 80 acres, value $4,000; Ohio.

Ross John, farmer; Sec. 29; P. O. Ellison; rep; 180 acres, value $9,000; from Del.

Ryder Joshua, farmer; P. O. Ellison; rep; born Illinois.

SANDS B. W. retired; P. O. Ellison; rep; Meth; from Tennessee.

Sands Isaac, laborer; P. O. Ellison; rep; Meth; from Indiana.

SPENCER F. H. Farmer and Stock Raiser; Sec. 24; P. O. Roseville; born in Middlesex Co., Conn., June 26, 1833; left there in May, 1851, and went to Hancock Co., Ill., and came to this Co. in 1858; has family four children, Leeds P., Lillie A., Mary F. and Cora A.; wife was Miss Sarah E. Pennoyer, born in Pike Co., Ill., June 12, 1840; married Oct. 2, 1858; has 84 acres, value $4,200; Rep; wife is Bapt; he served three years in the late war in Co. F., 83rd Ill. Inf.

Sands Jerre, plasterer; Sec. 17; P. O. Ellison; rep; from Indiana.

SANDS O. C. Merchant; Ellison; born in Montgomery Co., Indiana, July 16, 1854; left there and came to this Co. with his parents in 1856; single; Rep.

Salisbury Warren, farmer, works for M. Salisbury; Sec. 4; P. O. Kirkwood; rep.

SALISBURY MARION. Farmer and Stock Raiser; Sec. 4; P. O. Kirkwood; born in Richland Co., Ohio, Aug. 20, 1836; left there when about two years of age with his parents, and came to this Co., and is one of the oldest settlers; has 92 acres, value $5,400; Rep; served three years in the late war, in Co. C, 83rd Ill. Vol.; was Tax Collector one term.

Seabolt J. G. laborer; P. O. Ellison; dem; from Illinois.

Sexton H. F. retired; P. O. Ellison; rep; Meth; from Ohio.

SEYMOUR A. G. Farmer and Stock Raiser; Sec. 2; P. O. Lenox Station; born in Oswego Co., N. Y., Nov. 23, 1835; came to this Co. in the spring of 1860; has family seven children, Florence E., Jessie M., Willard L., Nellie M., Leonard A., Mary G. and Arlina; wife was Miss Mary M. Abdill, born in Carlton, Ohio, Dec. 4, 1837; married Dec. 30, 1863; has 160 acres, value $10,000; was Road Commissioner and School Director; Rep; Mrs. S. is a member of the Meth. Church.

Shearer Jas. farmer; Sec. 17; P. O. Ellison; dem; from North Carolina.

Shelenbarger David, farmer, rents of W. Root; Sec. 1; P. O. Lenox Station; dem.

Shelenbarger Geo. farmer, lives with his son; Sec. 1; P. O. Lenox Station; dem; Penn.

Shingledecker, laborer; P. O. Ellison; rep; from Maryland.

Singley E. M. farmer, rents of Paul Brent; Sec. 8; P. O. Ellison; rep; from Iowa.

Slater Daniel, farmer; Sec. 15; P. O. Ellison; 40 acres, value $2,000; dem; from Ireland.

Slater Dennis, farmer; Sec. 15; P. O. Ellison; 40 acres, value $2,000; dem; from Ireland.

Sloan Wm. C. farmer, works for Isaac Painter; Sec. 22; P. O. Roseville; dem.

SMITH THOMAS. Farmer and Stock Raiser; Sec. 30; P. O. Jackson Corners; born in England, Oct. 22, 1844; came to the U. S. when one and a half years of age; came to this Co. in 1867; has family four children living, Albertie, C. R., Amelia and Nathan; one dead, Catharine; wife was Margaret R. Ganote, born in Clark Co., Indiana, July 17. 1848; married Oct. 18, 1867; has 80 acres, value $4,800; dem; is School Director; Meth.

Sourbeir Chas. blacksmith; P. O. Ellison; rep; born Illinois.

Spicer A. farmer, rents of J. M. Hume; Sec. 33; P. O. Roseville; dem; from Virginia.

Spicer E. farmer, rents of J. M. Hume; Sec. 33; P. O. Roseville; dem; from Virginia.

Spicer Rev. Wm. farmer and preacher; Sec. 4; P. O. Ellison; dem; from Virginia.

Spicer Wm. H. farmer, lives with his father; Sec. 4; P. O. Ellison; dem; from Virginia.

St. Ledger Anthony, farmer, lives with his son; Sec. 15; P. O. Ellison; dem; Ireland.

St. Ledger John, farmer; Sec. 15; P. O. Ellison; dem; 80 acres, value $4,000; Ireland.

Staley Peter, farmer; Sec. 6; P. O. Kirkwood; rep; 80 acres, value $4,500; Penn.

Stewart J. W. farmer, rents of J. M. Fletcher; Sec. 16; P. O. Ellison; rep; born Illinois.

Sutter A. J. farmer; P. O. Kirkwood; dem; from Pennsylvania.

Sutter David, farmer; P.O. Kirkwood; dem; born Illinois.

Sutter Jas. F. farmer; Sec. 4; P. O. Kirkwood; dem; born Illinois.

THOMAS EDWARD, farmer, rents of F. Meacham; Sec. 35; P. O. Roseville; rep.

Thompson C. R. farmer; Sec. 30; P. O. Jackson Corners; dem; 240 acres, val. $12,000.

Thompson J. B. farmer; P. O. Ellison; dem; from Vermont.

Timmons Daniel, farmer, rents the Rayburn Estate; Sec. 31; P. O. Jackson Corners.

Toll Luke, farmer, works for J. C. Beasley; Sec. 34; P. O. Roseville; rep; born Ill.

Townsend W. A. physician and surgeon; rep; Meth; from Ohio.

VAN HORN PETER, farmer, works for Wm. P. Brent; Sec. 17; P. O. Ellison.

Vantuyl M. farmer; Sec. 5; P. O. Kirkwood; rep; 161 acres, value $9,660; from Ohio.

WALKER JOHN, farmer, rents of Geo. Hardin; Sec. 23; P. O. Roseville; rep.

Warner Geo. Sr. farmer; P. O. Roseville; rep; from Ohio.

Warner George Jr. farmer; P. O. Roseville; rep; from Ohio.

Wasson A. farmer; Sec. 28; P. O. Ellison; dem; 196 acres, value $9,800; born Ill.

Wassen Wm. farmer; P. O. Ellison; dem; U. B.; born Illinois.

Wilcox Richard, farmer; Sec. 22; P. O. Ellison; 62½ acres, value $3,720; dem; Ill.

Willard Francis, farmer, rents of Wm. Lee; Sec. 24; P. O. Roseville; dem; born Ill.

Wornum James, farmer, rents of J. Greenlee; Sec. 2; P. O. Kirkwood; rep; born Ill.

Wright Jas. farmer; Sec. 31; P. O. Jackson Corners; rep; from Ohio.

YOHO A. B. farmer, rents of D. Leacock; Sec. 8; P. O. Ellison; dem; from Ohio.

YOHO S. S. farmer; P. O. Ellison; dem; from Missouri.

YOUMANS J. B. Farmer and Stock Raiser; Sec. 1; P. O. Lenox Station; born in Putnam Co., N. Y., July 7, 1824; came to this Co. Oct. 28, 1855; has family four children, Spencer C., Chas. S., Francena and Laura; wife was Miss Abagail Squires, born in the same place Dec. 13, 1828; married Dec. 19, 1850; has 80 acres, value $4,860; rep; Mrs. Y. is a member of the Bapt. church.

Youmans S. C. farmer, lives with his father; Sec. 1; P. O. Lenox Station; rep; N. Y.

ELLISON BUSINESS DIRECTORY.

Pierson J. A., Postmaster and Dealer in Dry Goods, Groceries, Teas, Hardware, Crockery, Hats, Caps, Boots, Shoes, Drugs, Medicines, Paints, Oils, etc.

Sands O. C., Dealer in Dry Goods, Groceries, Hats, Caps, Boots, Shoes, Notions, etc.

FLOYD TOWNSHIP.

ABBOTT JOHNSTON, farmer; P. O. Cameron; dem; born Warren Co.

Abbott Lewis, farmer and lawyer; P. O. Cameron; dem; born Warren Co.

Abbott Paston, farmer; P.O. Cameron; dem; born Warren Co., July 18, 1854.

ABBOTT GREENUP, Farmer; Sec. 11; P. O. Cameron; born in Indiana, July 9, 1813; came to this Co. in 1835; Dem; owns 240 acres of land, valued at $14,400; married April 5, 1837, to Elizabeth Kelley, born in Maryland; has fifteen children, ten boys and five girls, and is one of the oldest settlers in Warren Co.

Allen C. W. rents of T. D. Allen; Sec. 33; P. O. Berwick; rep; Chris; born Illinois.

Allen Harry, harness-maker; P. O. Cameron; dem; from Wisconsin.

ALLEN T. D. Farmer; Sec. 29; P. O. Berwick; born in Oneida Co., N. Y., May 17, 1814; came to this Co. June 18, 1835; Rep; Bapt; owns 444 acres of land, valued at $22,200; married May 16, 1843, to Fidelia Wiswell; born in Townsend, Vt., May 16, 1818; has five children living, Clark W., born Feb. 13, 1844; Clinton D., March 23, 1845, died Dec. 31, 1847; Austin B., Dec. 13, 1848, died Sept. 24, 1865; Laura L., May 6, 1850; Henry E., April 30, 1874; Homer H., May 26, 1858; Jessie L., Jan. 21, 1862.

Andrews Daniel, rents of T. Allen; P. O. Berwick; rep; Chris; born Ill.

Anderson Charles, Sec. 2; P. O. Cameron; rep; Meth; from Sweden.

Ankrom T. S. laborer; P. O. Cameron; rep; Bapt; from Virginia.

Armstrong E. D. rents of John Armstrong; Sec. 34; rep.

Armstrong Geo. lives with J. Armstrong; P. O. Abingdon; rep.

Armstrong John, farmer, rents of J. Armstrong; Sec. 33; P. O. Berwick; rep.

Armstrong John Jr., rents of John Armstrong; Sec. 34; rep; Chris.

ARMSTRONG JOHN, Retired; Sec. 33; P. O. Abingdon; born in Illinois, May 11, 1812; came to this Co. in 1829; Dem; Chris; owns 320 acres of land, valued at $16,000; married first to Eveline Vandeveer, Jan. 16, 1832; she died Dec. 31, 1849; second wife, Norcissa B. Vandeveer, born Feb. 6, 1832; married April 7, 1850; died April 14, 1858; third wife, June Coleman, born May 29, 1824; married Aug. 12, 1858; has had fifteen children, eleven living, seven boys and four girls; the oldest settler in Floyd tp. and Warren Co.

Atkinson Robert, harness-maker; Cameron; dem; Meth; from England.

BAIN J. H. farmer, rents on Sec. 29; P. O. Cameron; rep.

Baker Frederick, laborer; Sec. 34; P. O. Abingdon; rep; born Warren Co.

Beard M. H. laborer for H. Shelden; Berwick; dem; Bapt; from Virginia.

Billingsley H. F. Sec. 20; P. O. Berwick; Ind; 160 acres; from Virginia.

Bishop M. laborer for L. R. Reynolds; Sec. 26; from Kentucky.

Bolan Jno. W. farmer; Sec. 24; P. O. Cameron; rep; Meth; value property $6,000.

Bone C. C. clerk; P. O. Cameron; rep; Meth; from Pennsylvania.

Bone T. W. telegraph operator; Cameron; rep; Meth; from Pennsylvania.

Bowers Aaron, farmer; Sec. 2; P. O. Cameron; Ind; owns 160 acres; Warren Co.

BOYDSTON HON. C. W. Retired; Cameron; born in Greene Co., Penn.,Oct. 17, 1817; came to this Co. in 1854; Rep; Meth; owns 231 acres of land, value $13,860; married first Oct. 3, 1840, to Orpha Evans, born in Penn. in 1820; second marriage Oct. 3, 1858, to Lorretta Underwood, born in Ohio, Dec. 1837; has ten children, five by first wife and five by second wife; has held Supervisor's office four years, and Justice of Peace four years; was elected to 28th Legislature, and re-elected to the 30th Legislature, and is at present at Springfield, Ill.

Bradley D. C. teacher; P. O. Cameron; rep; born Warren Co.

Bradly D. R. farmer; P. O. Cameron; ind; Chris; owns 10 acres.

Bradley Wm. laborer, works for A. Means; Cameron; dem; born Illinois.

BROGAN PETER, Farmer; Sec. 23; P. O. Abingdon; born in Belgian,July 10, 1837; came to this Co. in 1850; Dem; Cath; value of property $500; married to Mary Hay, who was born in Ohio, Feb. 15, 1835; married April 1, 1860; has four children, two girls and two boys.

Brooks J. W. laborer for E. Cable; P. O. Berwick; rep; U. P.

Brugan Peter, farmer; P.O. Abingdon; dem; Cath; from Belgium.

Bryant Wm. H. Sec. 6; P.O. Cameron; dem; from Kentucky.

BURTON JOHN, Farmer; Sec. 11; P. O. Cameron; born in Cambridge, Ohio, June 22, 1835; came to this Co. in 1850;

Dem; owns 141½ acres of land, valued at $1,000; married Eveline Keenan, born in Knox Co., Ill.; married Aug. 23, 1855; had twelve children; seven living, six boys and one girl.

Butler Cyrus, rents of A. S. Harding; Sec. 18; P. O. Cameron; rep; born Illinois.

Butterfield Thomas, Sec. 25; P. O. Abingdon; rep; Meth; 20 acres; from Ohio.

Butterfield Wm. Sec. 25; P. O. Abingdon; rep; Meth; 40 acres; from Ohio.

CABLE C. M. lives with his father; P. O. Berwick; rep; Bapt.

Cable Ezra, farmer and stock raiser; Sec. 19; P. O. Berwick; rep; owns 206 acres.

CABLE GEO. C. Farmer and Stock Raiser; Sec. 19; P. O. Berwick; born in Oneida Co., N. Y., April 1, 1823; came to this Co. in 1855; Rep; Bapt; owns 260 acres of land, valued at $13,000; married Aug. 12, 1859, to Geraldine Matteson, born in Oneida Co., N. Y., July 5, 1830; has eight children, all living.

Cable Wm. H. rents of Henry Cable; Sec. 29; P. O. Berwick; rep; Meth; from N.Y.

CARGILL HENRY, Farmer and Stock Raiser; Sec. 7; P. O. Cameron; born in N. Y., Oct. 27, 1815; came to this Co. in 1857; Dem; Bapt; owns 190 acres of land, value $11,060; married Dec. 29, 1836, to Susan C. Townsend, born in Putnam Co., N. Y., Oct. 11, 1817; had eight children; six living, James T., born Dec. 1, 1837; Sarah M., March 1, 1840; Isaac M., Dec. 5, 1841; Francis M., June 21, 1844; Mary A., Oct. 2, 1846; David E., Aug. 4, 1849; Alice J., Nov. 25, 1851; Wm. H., Jan. 1, 1855, died Sept. 14, 1855; Isaac M. died Feb. 24, 1844.

Clark John C.; P. O. Abingdon; dem; $500; came to this State in 1854.

Clay M. F. farmer; P. O. Cameron; rep; born Warren Co.

Clay Sewell, Sec. 3; P. O. Cameron; rep; Univ; 154 acres, value $9,240.

Clayton Austin, renter; P. O. Cameron; dem; from Kentucky.

Clayton Geo. A.; Sec. 9; P.O. Cameron; ind; 123 acres; from Kentucky.

Clayton J. W. butcher; Cameron; dem; from Kentucky.

Coe Rev. J. W. Methodist minister; P. O. Cameron; rep; from Ohio.

Coursen Wm. farmer; rents of Geo. Harding; P. O. Abingdon; Ind.

Crow Amos; Sec. 25; P. O. Abingdon; rep; Meth; 25 acres.

Cross C. T. Sec. 26; Abingdon; rep; Chris; 60 acres; from New York.

Cross J. C. Sec. 26; P. O. Cameron; rep; 40 acres; from New York.

Cross J. F. Sec. 26; P. O. Abingdon; rep; 40 acres; from New York.

Crosson Clinton, rents of H. Kenan; Cameron; dem; from Ohio.

DANFORD JOS. laborer for I. N. Giddings; P. O. Cameron; rep; from N. H.

Day Ben. rents of N. Gay; dem; from Pennsylvania.

Dell John, blacksmith; P. O. Cameron; rep; Meth; from Canada West.

Devoss F. M. rents of John Short; Sec. 34; P. O. Cameron; rep; from Ohio.

DICKSON DELL, Farmer and Stock Raiser; Sec. 33; P. O. Berwick; born in Illinois, Oct. 18, 1845; came to this Co. in 1845; Rep; personal property $4,500; partner of W. T. Dickson, Breeder of Shorthorn Cattle and Berkshire Hogs, and proprietor of the Aldine herd of Berkshires.

Dickson M. farmer; Sec. 33; P. O. Berwick; rep.

Douglass A. L. school teacher and farmer; Sec. 27; P. O. Abingdon; rep; from Me.

EDWARDS JOHN, retired; P. O. Cameron; rep; Chris; from Kentucky.

Edwards J. W. lawyer; Sec 10; P. O. Cameron; rep; 5 acres land and saw mill.

Enderman Saml. laborer for I. A. Reynolds; P. O. Abingdon; dem; from Pennsylvania.

FAIR DAVID, farmer for W. Wiswell; Sec. 21; Cameron; dem.

Fairchild Wm. farmer, rents of Mrs. Morey; Sec. 20; rep; Bapt; from Canada.

FAMULENER JACOB, Farmer and Stock Raiser; Sec. 12; P. O. Galesburg; born in Ohio, April 9, 1833; came to this Co. in 1857; Rep; owns 250 acres of land, valued at $17,500; married Aug. 30, 1857, to Sarah Jane Warren, born in Ohio, Jan. 26, 1838; has four children, three boys and one girl.

Faning Fritz, Sec. 13; P. O. Galesburg; rep; Meth; came here 1857; Germany.

Freeman J. H. farmer; Sec. 18; P. O. Cameron; rep; Chris; 134 acres.

Freeman R. T., Sr., farmer; Sec. 17; P. O. Cameron; rep; Chris; 320 acres.

Freeman R. T., Jr. Sec: 18; P. O. Cameron; rep; 80 acres; born Illinois.

Footwengler Mrs. Mary, P. O. Cameron; Meth.

Forbes James C. lives on Miss Ella Murphy's farm; P. O. Monmouth; rep.

Forbus Samuel; Sec. 6; P. O. Monmouth; rep; Chris; came to this Co. in 1858.

Forbes Wm. L. lives on Miss Ella Murphy's farm; P. O. Monmouth; rep.

FRANKLIN JAS. H. Farmer; Sec. 34; P. O. Abingdon; born in Kentucky, Sept. 15, 1827; came to this Co. in 1851; Dem; owns 41 acres of land, valued at $2,050; married March 22, 1860, to Anna M. Armstrong, born in this Co., Dec. 4,

WARREN COUNTY: FLOYD TOWNSHIP.   341

1836; has two children living and one dead; William M., and Jennie Franklin.

Fry James, carpenter; P. O. Cameron; dem; from Ohio.

Fulmer Andrew, Sec. 8; P. O. Cameron; dem; Cath; 80 acres; from Ohio.

Furchild Abial, farmer; P. O. Cameron; rep; Bapt.

Furchild Wilford, rents Mrs. Morey's farm; Sec. 20; P. O. Cameron; rep; Bapt.

GARRISON E. V. rents of D. F. Freeman; Sec. 8; P. O. Cameron; dem.

Gay N. farmer; Sec. 6; P. O. Cameron; dem; 80 acres; from Ohio.

Gay Van, retired; P. O. Cameron; dem; 143 acres; came to this Co. in 1857; from Va.

Geunther Henry; Cameron; rep; Luth; came to this Co. in 1862; from Germany.

GEUNTHER JOHN CARL, Farmer; Sec. 10; P.O. Cameron; born in Germany, Sept. 15, 1825; came to this Co. in 1857; Rep; Luth; owns 162 acres of land, valued at $6,720; married May 27, 1851, to Durthan Nader, born in Germany; has four children, two boys and two girls.

Genther Theodore; Cameron; rep; Luth; came to this country in 1857; Germany.

GIDDINGS GEO. Farmer; Sec. 18; P. O. Cameron; born in Warren Co., Ill., March 25, 1847; Rep; married Aug. 6, 1874, to Adelia Smith, born in Cataraugus Co., N. Y., June 11, 1858.

Giddings G. W. farmer, lives with his father; Sec. 29; P. O. Cameron; rep.

Giddings H. C. farmer, lives with his father; Sec. 29; P. O. Cameron; rep.

Giddings J. W. rents Mrs. Richey's farm; Sec. 28; P. O. Berwick; rep; Meth; Penn.

GIDDINGS LEANDER, Farmer; Sec. 8; P. O. Cameron; born in Warren Co., Ill. April 25, 1843; Rep; value of personal property $1,000; married Oct. 8, 1868, to Addie Stafford, born in Erie Co., Penn., Nov. 18, 1847; came to this Co. in 1868; has one child, Rose, born Aug. 21, 1876; served in the late Rebellion, Co. C, 138th Regt. I. V. I., five months.

Giddings M. C.; Sec. 29; P. O. Cameron; rep; Meth; 190 acres; from New York.

Giddings Silas; Sec. 28; P. O. Cameron; rep; 160 acres; from Pensylvania.

Giddings S. C.; Sec. 4; P. O. Cameron; rep; came to this Co. in 1854; from Penn.

Gillett Arthur, rents of I. R. Reynolds; Sec. 26; P. O. Abingdon; rep; from Ohio.

GILLETT IRSON, Farmer; Sec. 34; P. O. Abingdon; born in Ohio, May 18, 1833; came to this Co. in 1856; Dem; Chris; value of property $700; married Dec. 3, 1857, to Mary Blue, born in Warren Co., Ill., March 1, 1842; has eight children living and two dead, six boys and two girls.

Gillett Reuben, rents of I. R. Reynolds; Sec. 26; P. O. Abingdon; rep; from Ohio.

Gillispie Jackson, farmer; Sec. 9; P. O. Cameron; rep; Meth; from Pennsylvania.

Gillispie Robt. farmer; Sec. 9; rep; Meth; from Pennsylvania.

Goddard F. farmer; Sec. 21; P. O. Cameron; rep; Meth; 170 acres, value $9,350.

GODDARD HENRY Farmer; Sec. 11; P. O. Cameron; born in Warren Co. on Nov. 17, 1838; Rep; Meth; owns 280 acres of land, valued at $16,800; married March 7, 1860, to Miss E. B. Morse, who was born in Warren Co. Jan. 11, 1842; has three children, Mary, Chester and Clara; ages 8, 14, and 16.

Goddard Robt. Sec. 12; P. O. Cameron; rep; Meth; owns 208 acres land; born Illinois.

GRIFFEE JOSEPH, Farmer; Sec. 16; P. O. Cameron; born in Illinois, on July 22, 1844; came to this Co. in 1844; Rep; Personal Property valued at $1,500; married to Elizabeth Watters, Dec. 20, 1866, who was born in Huntingdon Co., Penn., Jan. 4, 1844; has five children, two boys and three girls; served in the late Rebellion; two years in Co. "E," 17th Ill. Vol.; rents of G. Goddard.

Graham D. C. farmer; P. O. Cameron; owns 220 acres of land; from Ireland.

Graham James, rents of S. Sheldon; P. O. Cameron; dem; Cath; from Ireland.

HACH, P. I. Sec. 26; P. O. Abingdon; born New York.

Hale Franklin, laborer for I. P. Short; P. O. Cameron; rep; from Ohio.

HALEY H. E. Farmer; Sec. 6; P. O. Cameron; born in Warren Co., Ill., May 8, 1847; Rep; Christian; owns 82½ acres of land, valued at $4,500; married Dec. 12, 1867, to Hulda A. Shelton, born in this Co. March 10, 1851; has three children, Leuella, born Sept. 7, 1868; Jessie, Dec. 2, 1871; Ferressia, Aug. 16, 1875; Mr. Haley served in the late Rebellion in Co. K, 11th Ill. Cavalry, seven months and three days.

Hall Henry H. farmer; Sec. 9; lives with his father; P. O. Cameron; rep; Christian.

Hall T. J. farmer; Sec. 9; P. O. Cameron; rep; owns 20 acres of land; Christian.

Hall Wm. C. Sec. 9; P. O. Cameron; rep; Christian; from Virginia.

Harris Wm. Sec. 3; rents of I. H. Crandell; P. O. Cameron; from Indiana.

Hart Elias, merchant; Cameron, rep; Christ.

Hascall H. B. Sec. 7; rents of H. S. Hascall; P. O. Cameron; rep; Christ.

HASCALL H. S. Farmer; Sec. 7; P. O. Cameron; born in Essex Co., N. Y., Nov. 28, 1811; came to this Co. in 1835; Rep; Christian; owns 120 acres of land, valued $7,800; married Nov. 28, 1839, to Sallie C. Whitman; born in Kentucky,

April 9, 1820; has seven children; Therressia, born Sept. 16, 1840; died June 2, 1870; Charles A., born Nov. 19, 1842; John F., April 16, 1845; Wm. S., Feb. 14, 1848; Burzeal A., Dec. 2, 1850; Harmon B., Aug. 25, 1863; Martha A., April 24, 1856.

Heston Geo. farmer; rep; Meth; from Ind.

High Charles, farmer; P. O. Cameron; dem; born Illinois.

Hill Fred. G. druggist; P. O. Cameron; rep; born Illinois.

Higgins H. C. laborer; P. O. Cameron; ind; from Pennsylvania.

Hill Mrs. Mary, P. O. Cameron; Cath; from Ireland.

Hogg Thomas, rents of E. Adams; P. O. Cameron; rep; from Ohio.

Howard Alonzo, laborer for T. D. Allen; Sec. 29; P. O. Berwick; rep; born Illinois.

Huff S. J. farmer; Sec. 33; P. O. Berwick; rep; owns 92 acres, valued at $4,000.

JOHNSON AMOS. prop. Johnson House; Cameron; dem; born Illinois.

Johnson Lloyd, farmer; rents of Wiswell; P. O. Cameron; dem.

JOHNSON GEO. W. Retired; Sec. 17; P. O. Cameron; born in Vermont, Sept. 6, 1813; came to this Co. in 1844; Dem; Bapt; owns 120 acres, valued at $8,200; married Nancy M. Bonnell, born Oct. 4, 1815; married in Waterford, Erie Co., Pa., 1836; had eleven children, five living; names, James P., Wilson, Lloyd H., Amos, Geo. R.; one of the oldest settlers in Co.

Johnson Perry, prop. Johnson House; Cameron; dem; born Illinois.

Johnson Wilson, rents of G. W. Johnson, farms 120 acres; Sec. 17; P. O. Cameron.

JEWEL ISAAC, Farmer; Sec. 11; P. O. Cameron; born in Warren Co., Illinois, 1854; came to this County in 1874; Dem; Meth; owns five acres of land, valued at $500; married to Alice Burton, born 1857; married Aug. 16, 1874.

KARR JNO. N. rents of R. Karr; Sec. 26; P. O. Abingdon; dem; Meth.

Kelley H. H. grocer; Cameron; rep; Chris; from Vermont.

Kennedy Hugh, laborer, works on S. W. Gale's farm; dem; born Illinois.

Kenan Henry, Sec. 1; P. O. Cameron; dem; owns 340 acres; Meth.

KENAN O. M. Farmer; Sec. 15; P. O. Cameron; born in Sandusky Co., Ohio, on March 27, 1843; came to this County in 1864; Rep; owns 90 acres, valued at $4,500; married Dec. 28, 1869, to Margaret Ickes, born in Bedford Co., Penn., April 26, 1848; has two children; Eugene, born Feb. 9, 1872; Elba, Feb. 20, 1876.

KENT Rev. G. D. Minister of the Baptist Church of Cameron; born in Albany Co., N. Y., June 3, 1830; came to this Co. in 1871; Rep; Bapt; married April 5, 1857, to Carrie A. Bunce, born in Reading, Berkshire Co., England, May 23, 1820; has had five children, all dead.

Kingsbury Thomas, farmer; Sec. 32; P. O. Berwick; rep; 88 acres; Bapt.

Knance Andrew J. farmer, on E. Adams' farm; Sec. 16; P. O. Cameron; rep.

LATHROP E. T. Sec. 25; P. O. Abingdon; dem; 20 acres; Mormon.

Lieurance Stephen, carpenter; Cameron; dem; Christian.

Lister Wm. laborer for O. Kenan; Sec. 15; P. O. Cameron; rep.

Ludington A. R. farmer, lives with G. F. McClure; P. O. Cameron; dem.

McCLURE GEO. Sec. 4; P. O. Cameron; rep; 104 acres; U. P.; from Ireland.

McClure Geo. F. farmer; P. O. Cameron; rep; 101 acres, value $7,075.

McClure, J. W. farmer; Sec. 5; P. O. Cameron; dem; 73 acres, value $5,375.

McCOOL W. H. Farmer and Stock Raiser; Sec. 11; P. O. Cameron; born in Michigan, Dec. 15, 1839; came to this Co. in 1840; Rep; Christian; owns 180 acres, valued at $10,800; married Oct. 17, 1867, to Irene McClure, born in Erie Co., Penn., May 6, 1850; came to this State in 1857; has two children, Carrie L. and Nellie H., aged three and seven years.

McGahey James Albert, farmer; P. O. Cameron; dem; born in Warren County.

McGahey, R. farmer; Sec. 15; P. O. Cameron; dem; Meth; 100 acres, value $5,500.

McCAHEY SAMUEL. Farmer; Sec. 12; P. O. Cameron; born in Kentucky on March 20, 1806; came to this Co. in 1838; Dem; Meth; owns 216 acres of land, valued at $12,960; married to Abigal Bracken, who was born in Bath Co., Ky., Nov. 24, 1815; married May 9, 1833; has eight children: five boys and three girls, and is one of the oldest, as well as the most successful, farmers in Warren Co.

McGAHEY W. H. Farmer; Sec. 3; P. O. Cameron; born in Illinois, on Feb. 12, 1844, in this Co.; Lib; owns 93 acres of land, valued at $5,580; married Oct. 30, 1869, to Maggie Hays, who was born Oct. 30, 1853; has two children—one boy and one girl—aged one and four; Ella and Arthur.

McMahon Chas. laborer for R. McGahey; P. O. Cameron; dem; born Iowa.

McMillion Henry C.; P. O. Galesburg; rep; Meth; born in Virginia, 1856.

Marr Jas. Sec. 24; P. O. Abingdon; dem; Meth; owns 8 acres of land; born in Ky.

Matteson B. P. Sec. 30; P. O. Berwick; rep; Bapt; owns 80 acres; from New York.

NATHANIEL BROWNLEE ESQ.
(DECEASED)
SUMNER TOWNSHIP

MARSH ANDREW K., Farmer; Sec. 18; P. O. Cameron; born in Nova Scotia, on Dec. 9, 1833; came to this Co. 1856; Rep; Bapt; owns 84 acres of land, valued at $4,400; married to Catherine I. Tunnicliff, in Warren Co.; has three children, Mary I., Theopolis, Marrilla M.

MARSH THOMAS, Farmer; Sec. 9; P. O. Cameron; born in Nova Scotia, on Feb. 24, 1837; came to this Co. in 1860; Rep; owns 5 acres of land, valued $1,000; married Sept. 12, 1861, to Harriet Bolin, born in Ohio, Dec. 28, 1841; has ten children, seven living, three dead; two girls and five boys.

MATTESON M. D. Farmer; Sec. 29; P. O. Berwick; Bapt; first wife was born in New York, Oct. 10, 1807; came to this State 1835; married Oct. 10, 1830; died Sept. 29, 1845; was married to Maria L. Davis, born in Mass., Oct. 16, 1811; has six children, all living; two boys and four girls.

MEADOWS M. C. Farmer; Sec. 35; P. O. Abingdon; born in Kentucky, on March 12, 1822; came to this Co. in 1829; Rep; Chris; owns 320 acres of land, valued at $12,800; married Dec. 5, 1844, to Catherine Reynolds; she was born in Indiana, Oct. 9, 1826; has seven children living and one dead, and is one of the oldest settlers in Floyd tp. and Warren Co.

MEANS A. Farmer and Stock Raiser; Sec. 7; P. O. Cameron; born in Kentucky, Sept. 30, 1819; came to this Co. in 1846; dem; Chris; owns 304 acres of land, valued at $16,720; married first to Mary Shelton, born in Kentucky, Oct. 5, 1830; died July, 1859; struck by lightning in her own house; second marriage Dec. 9, 1863, to Cyrena Meadows, born in this Co. Jan. 25, 1837; Mrs. M. was first married to Willis A. Jones, March 12, 1854; have six children.

Means Jas. A. rents of R. C. Robinson; Sec. 22; P. O. Cameron; value property $500.

Means J, D. rents of A. Means; Sec. 8; P. O. Cameron; dem; born Illinois.

MEDHURST JOSEPH. Farmer; Sec. 9; P. O. Cameron; born in England, on Oct. 19, 1823; came to this Co. in 1843; Rep; owns 178 acres of land, valued at $11,570; married July 3, 1861, to Martha Heart, born in Kentucky; married at Monmouth, this Co.; Mr. Medhurst came to Ontario Co., N. Y., in 1828; remained there until 1843; then came to this Co., and has been here ever since; has three children, two girls and one boy.

Merritt Chas. farmer, lives with his mother; Sec. 9; P. O. Cameron; rep.

MERRITT MRS. ELSIE, Farming; Sec. 8; P. O. Cameron; born in Delaware Co., N. Y., on March 28, 1810; came to this Co. in 1869; owns 217 acres of land, valued at $10,850; married Sept 13, 1835, to Wm. Merritt, born in Green Co., N. Y., Sept. 19, 1800, died Oct. 12, 1870; has six children.

Middleton David; Sec. 24; P. O. Abingdon; rep; Meth; owns 30 acres land; Ohio.

Miller Thos. Sec. 19; P. O. Cameron; rep; owns 80 acres of land; from Canada.

Miner Chas. lives with his father; Sec. 2; rep; born Illinois.

Miner Henry, farmer; Sec. 6; rep; owns 89 acres; served in Co. L,9th I.V.I.in late war.

Miner Joshua, farmer, lives with his father; Sec. 3; P. O. Cameron; rep.

Miner Luke, Sec. 3; P. O. Cameron; rep; Bapt; 55 acres; born 1812.

Miner Lafayette; P. O. Cameron; rep; served in the 100-day service; born Illinois.

Moor Allen, Sec. 10; P. O. Cameron; dem; 80 acres; came to this Co. in 1846; Ky

Moor John, bachelor; Sec. 9; P. O. Cameron; dem; born in Ky., April 10, 1818.

MOREY SARAH, Retired; Sec. 20; P. O. Cameron; born in Ky., on Jan. 14, 1839; came to this Co. in 1852; Meth; owns 154 acres of land, valued at $7,700; married March 23, 1856, to Joseph Morey, who died Dec. 17, 1876; who was born March 20, 1857, in Penn.; has four children, two boys and two girls.

Morey W. S. laborer for Butler; P. O. Monmouth; rep; born Illinois.

MURDOCK J. H. Farmer and Stock Raiser; Sec. 31; P. O. Berwick; born in Green Co., Penn., Feb. 10, 1814; came to this Co. in 1854; Rep; Bapt; owns 210 acres of land, valued at $15,750; married Nov. 30, 1837, to Frances Milligan, born in Green Co., Penn., 1815; has seven children living.

Mutter Richard, rents of W. Odell; Sec. 5; came to this Co. four years ago; from Ky.

NEWKIRK J. E. rents of I. Marr; Sec. 24; P. O. Abingdon; dem; Indiana.

Newkirk W. H. Sec. 25; P. O. Abingdon; dem; Meth; owns 20 acres; from Indiana.

NORRIS JOHN M. Farmer and Stock Raiser; Sec. 5; P. O. Cameron; born in Ky., on Feb. 26, 1829; came to this Co. in 1848; Dem; Chris; owns 177½ acres of land, valued at $7,088; married Jan. 22, 1850, to Mary Freeman, born Dec. 18, 1833, died Aug. 22, 1864; married second to Mary A. Goddard, born March 30, 1838; has five children—Eugene, born Oct. 9, 1850, died April 18, 1852; Solonois F., born Jan. 13, 1853; Luella, born March 7, 1855; Eldon C., born Feb.28,1857; Elenora, born Nov. 27, 1858; Elmore H., born May 10, 1861; Laura, born April 30, 1863, died July 26, 1864.

ODELL GABRIEL, farmer; Sec. 5; P. O. Cameron; rep; Bapt.

Ogden F. D. farmer, Sec. 20; P. O. Cameron; rep; Bapt; value property $12,900.

PARKER DAVID, P. O. Cameron; rep; from Iowa.

Parrish Preston, carpenter; P. O. Cameron; rep; Chris; from Kentucky.

Parrish Wm. sawyer; Sec. 10; P. O. Cameron; rep; Meth; owns 5 acrs. and sawmill.

Patrick C. W. P. O. Cameron; dem.

Patterson Alfred, P. O. Cameron; rep; from Canada.

Patterson Irvin, works for R. Goddard; P. O. Cameron; dem; from Ohio.

Perdue Henry, laborer; Sec. 34; P. O. Abingdon; rep; born this Co.

Perdue James E. laborer; Sec. 34; P. O. Abingdon; rep; Chris; born this Co.

Pisten Charlie, rendering dead hogs; Sec. 36; P. O. Abingdon; rep; from Germany.

Porter O. V. farmer; Sec. 30; P. O. Berwick; rep; born Illinois.

PORTER W. B. Farmer and Stock Raiser; Sec. 30; P. O. Berwick; born in Ontario Co., N. Y., on Dec. 17, 1826; came to this Co. in 1848; Rep; owns 247 acres of land, valued at $14,350; married March 9, 1852, to Julia Waggoner, born in Oneida Co., N. Y., Sept. 29, 1834; has four children, Alpha A., born May 25, 1853; Orlando V., Aug. 9, 1855; Miron W., Dec. 20, 1860, and Maud A., Oct. 22, 1874.

RANDALL EDGAR, rents of Rease; P. O. Berwick; rep.

Randall O. T. rents land of I. N. Reece; Sec. 30; P. O. Berwick; rep; from New York.

Reynolds J. A. Sec. 27; P. O. Abingdon; ind; Chris; came to this Co. in 1836; from Ind.

Reynolds John K. Sec. 26; P. O. Abingdon; ind; Chris; from Indiana.

Reynolds M. A. laborer; Cameron; rep; Chris.

Reiley Mrs. M. retired; P. O. Cameron; Meth; from Ireland.

Riggil R. H. clerk; P. O. Cameron; ind; Chris.

Riley Albert, laborer; P. O. Cameron; dem.

Riley B. F., P. O. Cameron; dem; Chris; from Ohio.

Riley Wm. M. laborer; P. O. Cameron; dem.

Riley Wm. T. laborer; P. O. Cameron; dem.

RITCHY MRS. AMELIA, Retired; Sec. 28; P. O. Berwick; born in Solingin, Germany, June 8, 1816; came to this Co. in 1832; Chris; owns 180 acres of land, valued at $9,000; married in Monmouth, June 9, 1834, to Anthony Ritchey, born in France, Oct. 26, 1805, died Oct. 10, 1849; Mrs. R.'s maiden name was Amelia Clanburg; has seven children, two living; Mrs. R. was the first lady married in the City of Monmouth, Ill.; Mr. West performed the ceremony.

Robbins Julia, widow of W. Robbins; Sec. 9; Meth; 3 acres.

Robertson John C. harness maker; Cameron; rep; Meth; from Pennsylvania.

ROBERTSON JOHN R. Farmer; Sec. 27; P. O. Abingdon; born in Warren Co., Ill., on Dec. 23, 1843; Rep; Chris; renter; personal property, value $3,000; married Dec. 27, 1871, to Elizabeth Cox; she was born Feb. 3, 1846, in Warren Co.; has two children, girls, Mary R. and Sarah Linettia Robertson.

Roffey James, Sec. 20; P. O. Cameron; rep; 80 acres; from England.

RUSH R. S. Farmer; Sec. 14; P. O. Cameron; born in Ohio on April 19, 1838; came to this Co. in 1864; Dem; Meth; value of personal property $500; wife's name was Martha A. Cannaday, born in Ill. Aug. 18, 1839; married July 9, 1857; has five children, one boy and four girls.

SILLS WM. rents of Mrs. Sheldon; Sec. 32; P. O. Berwick; rep; from Indiana.

Sigman Frank, lives with his father; Sec. 24; P. O. Berwick; rep.

SIGMAN ISAAC, Farmer; Sec. 24; P. O. Abingdon; born in Ohio Dec. 27, 1811; came to this Co. in 1855; Rep; owns 130 acres of land, valued at $5,200; married first time in 1834; second time April 13, 1848, to Elizabeth Pratt, who was born Jan. 4, 1829; had twenty-one children, seventeen living and four dead.

SHELDON BURR. Farmer and Stock Raiser; Sec. 32; P. O. Berwick; born Nov. 8, 1838, in Warren Co., Ill.; Dem; Bapt; owns 160 acres of land, valued at $8,000; married to Anna Morly, born in Knox Co., Ill. Dec. 10, 1845; has one child, Clarence M. Sheldon, born Jan. 18, 1871.

SHELDON HIRAM, Farmer and Stock Raiser; Sec. 31; P. O. Berwick; born in New York on Nov. 20, 1831; came to this Co. in 1837; Dem; Bapt; owns 652 acres of land, value $37,120; married Jan. 22, 1862, to Emma Aulsworth, born in Ill. April 6, 1841; has four children, all living, W. I., born Oct. 28, 1862; Irena H., Jan. 10, 1865; Donna L., Dec. 5, 1868; C. R., Oct. 28, 1876; Mr. Sheldon is a Stock Broker, and has handled Cattle for the last 20 years.

Sheldon S. M. farmer and stock raiser; Sec. 32; P. O. Berwick; dem; 290 acres; N. Y.

SHELTON JNO. B. Farmer and Stock Raiser; Sec. 5; P. O. Cameron; born in Barren Co., Ky., Dec. 22, 1825; came to this Co. in 1837; Rep; Chris; owns 310 acres of land, value $18,600; married Aug. 9, 1849, Christine I. Whitman; has nine children, John B., born Dec. 25, 1825; Christine I., March 16, 1829; Squire W., June 1, 1850; Theresa E., July 16, 1856; James J., Sept. 15, 1859; Alma J., Jan. 30,

1862, died Feb. 16, 1869; Charlie G., born Aug. 26, 1864; Louise L., Aug. 8, 1867; Jessie B., Feb. 28, 1871.

Shelton Patrick H. farmer; Sec. 9; P. O. Cameron; ind; Chris; born Illinois.

Shelton S. W. farmer, lives with his father; Sec. 5; P. O. Cameron; rep; born this Co.

SHORT AUGUSTINE. Farmer; Sec. 17; P. O. Cameron; born in Floyd tp., Warren Co., Ill., on July 31, 1848; Rep; Meth; value of property $600; married to Euphema Fults, born in Green Co., Ind., Dec. 23, 1856; married Sept. 22, 1875; had one child, dead, aged 4 months and 18 days.

Short J. P. farmer; Sec. 21; P. O. Cameron; rep; Chris; 225 acres, value $11,250.

TAYLOR SANDY, laborer, lives 'on B. C. Robinson's place; P. O. Abingdon.

Thompson Jas. coal digger; P. O. Cameron; rep; Chris; from Kentucky.

TEMPLE THOMAS, M.D., Physician; Cameron; born in Yorkshire, England, July 15, 1821; came to this Co. 1858; Ind; married April 30, 1846, to Mary Ann Galloway, born in Yorkshire, England, June 13, 1822; has nine children, three living.

Tinkham B. L. Sec. 3; P. O. Cameron; 155 acres, value $9,300; born this Co.

Tinkham Benj., Sr., farmer; Sec. 2; P. O. Cameron; rep; Meth; 100 acres, $6,000.

TINKHAM I. N. Farmer; Sec. 2; P. O. Cameron; born in Ill. on May 13, 1843; came to this Co. 1843; Dem; owns 116½ acres of land, valued at $6,990; married Oct. 5, 1865, to Ladema Kenau, who died Dec. 15, 1870; second marriage July 23, 1873, to Maggie Foster, born in Ohio, May 18, 1846; has three children, two boys and one girl, Altha S., Williard, Irie E. Tinkham; served in the late rebellion in the 83d I. V. I., Co. H, two years and eleven months.

Townsend James, P. O. Cameron; dem; Bapt; 81 acres; from New York.

TUNNICLIFF CORNELIUS. Farmer; Sec. 34; P. O. Abingdon; born in Conn. Feb. 8, 1808; came to this Co. in 1836; Rep; Chris; owns 60 acres of land, valued at $2,400; married first wife Aug. 7, 1837, in Tenn.; she died June 1, 1865; married second wife Nov. 9, 1867; has had ten children, five living, four girls and one boy.

VALENTINE ANDREW, farmer; Sec. 10; rep; 10 acres.

Valentine A.; Sec. 12; P. O. Cameron; dem; 20 acres; an old settler.

VAN TASELL DAVID. Farmer; Sec. 9; P. O. Cameron; born in Duchess Co., N. Y., Sept. 11, 1827; came to this Co. in 1857; Rep; Bapt; married in 1854 to Almira Sackett, in N. Y., born 1838; second marriage, June 5, 1870; had two children, both dead; one child by first wife living, Emeretta VanTasell; born Dec., 1854; Mrs. Van Tasell (Mary Miner) first married Jaycox; she owns 260 acres of land on Sec. 7, Floyd tp.; has three children living, Lucy H. Harris, Ida and Ella Jaycox.

Vertreese Lewis, Sec. 3; P. O. Cameron; rep; Chris; came to this Co. 1830; from Ky.

WALDEN MRS. RHOBY, rents of G. F. Harding; Sec. 19; P. O. Cameron.

Waggoner Jay E. lives with his father, Henry Waggoner; P. O. Berwick; rep.

WAGGONER CHAS. W. Farmer; Sec. 30; P. O. Berwick; born in Oneida Co., N. Y., Feb. 8, 1837; came to this Co. in 1851; Rep; Bapt; owns 100 acres of land, value $6,000; married Oct. 21, 1869, to Anna Brown, born in Pickaway Co., Ohio, Dec. 18, 1845; has had two children, one living, Ralph and Chas. Delos Waggoner.

WAGGONER HENRY. Farmer; Sec. 30; P. O. Cameron; born in New York, May 3, 1801; came to this Co. in 1849; rep; Bapt; owns 100 acres of land, valued at $10,000; married first to Orelia Matteson, born in Vermont in 1806; second wife, Esther Sherman, born in Vermont in 1811; has thirteen children, ten living.

Weed A. druggist; P. O. Cameron; rep; from Maine.

Whitman Henry, farmer; Sec. 10; P. O. Cameron; rep; 30 acres; came here 1867.

Wickson Elias, rents of David Van Tasell; P. O. Cameron; rep; Bapt.

Wiggins Benj. F. farmer with C. Wiggins, P. O. Cameron; from New York.

Wiggins C. D. farmer; Sec. 22; P. O. Cameron; rep; Bapt; value property $2,000.

Wiggins Chas. laborer for C. Wiggins; P. O. Cameron; rep; born Illinois.

Wiggins Chauncey, farmer on M. Robinson's land; Sec. 22; P. O. Cameron.

Wilber D. C. Sec. 13; P. O. Abingdon; rep; Meth; born Sept. 3, 1844, came to Ill. 1869.

WILBER GEORGE. Farmer; Sec. 24; P. O. Abingdon, Knox Co.; born in New York State, Sept. 4, 1829; came to this Co. in 1865; Rep; Meth; has 100 acres of land, valued at $3,500; married Nov. 27, 1855, to Delany Howd, born July 20, 1838; had six children, one living.

Wilcher Henry, rents of C. W. Allen; P. O. Berwick; rep; Chris.

Wilson B. Frank, laborer; Sec. 17; P. O. Cameron; dem; from Kentucky.

WISWELL M. M. Retired; Sec. 21; P. O. Cameron; born in Vermont Feb. 1, 1825; came to this Co. in Oct., 1839; Rep; Bapt; owns 349 acres of land, valued at $17,250; married Nov. 19, 1851, to Martha

Sheldon, born Feb. 16, 1833, in N. Y.; has three children; has been Assessor and Collector of this township.

Wood Uriah, Sec. 24; P. O. Abingdon; rep; Meth; 10 acres; from Ohio.

YOUNG G. M. laborer for Hagg; P. O. Cameron; dem; from Kentucky.

Yost Henry, shoemaker; Sec. 9; P. O. Cameron; dem; Bapt.

CAMERON BUSINESS DIRECTORY.

Parkes & Blair, Dealers in Groceries and Agricultural Implements.
Temple Thos. M. D., Physician and Surgeon.

FLOYD TOWNSHIP.

Sheldon Hiram, Dealer in Live Stock; Sec. 31; 1 mile North Berwick P. O.

BERWICK TOWNSHIP.

ALLEN AMBROSE N. farmer, lives with his father; Sec. 4; P. O. Berwick rep.

Allen E. W. farmer; Sec. 4; P. O. Berwick; rep; Bapt; 530 acres; from Ohio.

Andicot Jos. rents of Jas. Miller; Sec. 10; P. O. Abingdon; dem; Chris.

Ayers Abel, wagon-maker; Berwick; dem; from New York.

Ayers A. rents of T. C. Pierce; Sec. 20; P. O. Berwick; dem; from New York.

Ayers A. H. laborer for Theodore Pierce; P. O. Berwick; dem; from New York.

Ayers Jno. A. rents of J. W. Malcom; Sec. 30 P. O. Greenbush; dem; from N. Y.

BABBITT D. rents on Steiss' estate; Sec. 3; P. O. Abingdon; dem.

Babbitt S. I. rents of F. G. Snapp; Sec. 23; St. Augustine; rep; born Illinois.

Beck R. A., P. M. and gen'l merchant; P. O. Berwick; rep; Bapt; from Germany.

Bell John R. rents of Dr. Davis; Sec. 27; P. O. Greenbush; from Iowa.

Benson Henry, farmer, rents of H. F. Trulocks; Sec. 34; P. O. St. Augustine; Luth.

Billingsby D. S. farmer; Sec. 6; P. O. Berwick; dem; 115 acres; from Virginia.

Blood Hiram, farmer; Sec. 24; P. O. Avon; rep; 80 acres; from New York.

Blood Jas. farmer; Sec. 24; P. O. Avon; rep; 40 acres; born Illinois.

Blood Leonard, farmer; Sec. 24; P. O. Avon; rep; 40 acres; born Illinois.

Blood Mrs. Mary, Sec. 24; P. O. Avon; 186 acres; from Maine.

Bowers S. rents of L. Lincoln; Sec. 27; P. O. Avon; rep; Dunkard; from Maryland.

Bowers I. Z. T. laborer on L. Lincoln's farm; Sec. 27; P. O. Abingdon; rep; Md.

Brock W. A. laborer; Sec. 15; P. O. Abingdon; dem; Chris.

Brooks E. B. farmer, renter; P. O. Berwick; rep; Meth.

Brown Thomas, blacksmith; Berwick; dem; from Virginia.

Burns Michael, farmer; Sec. 24; P. O. Abingdon; 40 acres; dem; Cath; Ireland.

CALSON ANGUS, laborer on Lewis' farm; Sec. 19; P. O. Greenbush; Sweden.

Campbell Franklin, farmer; Sec. 8; P. O. Berwick; dem; from Indiana.

Carr Mrs. R. E. Sec. 8; P. O. Berwick; 207 acres; from Ohio.

Clayton J. F. rents of E. W. Allen; Sec. 11; dem; from Kentucky.

Clayton Wm.; gone to Kirkwood.

Clem M. P. O. Berwick, dem; Meth; from Virginia.

Cline S. farmer; Sec. 25; P. O. St. Augustine; 470 acres; dem; Chris; from Ohio.

Couch Rev. C. B. minister; P. O. Berwick; rep; Meth; from Maine.

Courson John, farmer; Sec. 11; P. O. Abingdon; rep; Chris; 220 acres; from Ohio.

Courson John, laborer for S. Reynolds; Sec. 2; P. O. Abingdon.

CORIDON D. DAY, Farmer and Stock Raiser; Sec. 24; P. O. Abingdon;

born in Hanover, N. Y., Sept. 25, 1819; came to this Co. in 1855; Dem; Meth; owns 120 acres of land, valued at $6,000; married first Jan. 1, 1839, to Laurena Louk, born in New York; second marriage, Feb. 19, 1853, to Lucinda Griffin, born in Indiana, July 23, 1829; has eleven children.

Coddington J. farmer; Sec. 15; P. O. Abingdon; 170 acres; rep; Chris; from Ohio.

Crawford P. D. farmer; Sec. 14; P. O. Abingdon; dem; 140 acres; born Illinois.

Crenshaw Joseph, farmer, lives with E. W. Allen; Sec. 4; P. O. Berwick; rep; Bapt.

Crow S. D. laborer; Sec. 2; P. O. Berwick; dem; born Illinois.

Cunningham Jno. rents of D. E. Morse; Sec. 35; P. O. St. Augustine; dem; Cath; Penn.

Cunningham T. rents of Martin Simmons; Sec. 32; P. O. Greenbush; dem; Indiana.

Currier Frank, farmer, rents of N. Carnes; Sec. 6; P. O. Berwick; dem; from Va.

Currier John, farmer, rents of N. Carnes; Sec. 6; P. O. Berwick; dem; from Va.

Currier Noah, carpenter; Sec. 6; P. O. Berwick; dem; 62 acres; from Virginia.

DAY D. R. farmer; Sec. 24; P. O. Abingdon; dem; Chris; undiv. half 160 acres.

Day J. E. farmer; Sec. 24; P. O. Abingdon; dem; undiv. half 160 acres; born Illinois.

Day J. P. carpenter; Berwick; rep; from Ohio.

DAWDY W. H. Farmer; Sec. 11; P. O. Abingdon; born in Illinois, Oct. 2, 1845; came to this Co. in 1872; Dem; owns 320 acres of land, valued at $9,600; married Jan. 3, 1872, to Amanda Howard, born in Kentucky, Oct. 28, 1852; has three children, Della May, born Feb. 1, 1873; Jessie Vernain, May 28, 1874; Daisy, Sept. 10, 1875.

Dickerson N. Y. farmer; Sec. 14; P. O. Abingdon; dem; Chris; 80 acres; from Ky.

Dorsey D. farmer; Sec. 12; P. O. Abingdon; dem; 160 acres; from Virginia.

Douglass H. L. farmer; Sec. 2; P. O. Abingdon; rep; 65 acres.

Duffield D. farmer; Sec. 14; P. O. Abingdon; dem; 80 acres; born Illinois.

Duncan T. M. Sec. 24; P. O. Abingdon; dem; Chris; 160 acres; from Pennsylvania.

ELLINGER JOS. laborer for Jos. Smith; Sec. 24; P. O. Avon; dem; born Ill.

Embree Mrs. C. retired; Sec. 10; P. O. Abingdon; Chris; from Kentucky.

FAIRCHILD F. A. farmer; Sec. 29; P. O. Greenbush; dem; 80 acres; Canada.

Fairchild J. E. rents of Mrs. Baldwin; Sec. 29; P. O. Greenbush; from Canada.

Fairchild J. H. rents of F. Fairchild; Sec. 21; P. O. Greenbush; from Canada.

Fish Geo. W. farmer; Sec. 4; P. O. Berwick; rep; from New York.

Fish Mrs. Lydia, retired; Sec. 4; P. O. Berwick; Presb; 92 acres; from New York.

Fordyce Jno. Sec. 5; P. O. Berwick; rep; 121 acres; from Green Co., Penn.

Foster Elick, rents of James Simmons; Sec. 35; P. O. Avon; dem; born Ill.

GILLASPIE J. H. farmer; Sec. 9; P. O. Abingdon; rep; Chris; owns 40 acres.

GILLASPIE S. G. Farmer; Sec. 15; P. O. Abingdon; born in Ky., Oct. 28, 1828; came to this Co. in 1864; Rep; Chris 25 years; married April 2, 1872, to Millie Glick, born in Berwick tp., Nov. 18, 1849; has three children, Ariel, born Jan. 16, 1873; John H., born Sept. 30, 1875; Jessie Nora, born March 1, 1877; served in Co. A, 14th Ky. Cav. thirteen months, during the late Rebellion; served as private, and received a commission as Second Lieutenant, but did not accept.

Glanden John S. rents of H. Sheldon; Sec. 8; P. O. Berwick; dem; from New York.

Gould W I. rents of Stess' estate; Sec. 3; P. O. Abingdon; rep; Chris.

Gray E. laborer; P. O. Berwick; dem; from Virginia.

Griffin R. M. rents of C. Day; Sec. 24; P. O. Abingdon; dem; born Illinois.

Griffing R. M. G. lives with his father; Sec. 24; P. O. Abingdon; rep; born Illinois.

HARDWICK JESSE, rents; Sec. 14; P. O. Abingdon; rep; Meth; born Ky.

Hatch N. R. farmer; Sec. 10; P. O. Abingdon; rep; Chris; owns 65 acres; Wis.

Hocom Henry, laborer for H. O. Hocom; Sec. 3; dem; Luth; from Sweden.

Hocom P. O. rents of Wm. Simmons; Sec. 31; P. O. Greenbush; dem; Luth; Sweden.

Hollengreen Olaf, rents of Henry Statt; Sec. 19; P. O. Greenbush; from Sweden.

Holman Geo. rents of Meadows; Sec. 3; P. O. Abingdon; dem; from Indiana.

Holmes J. laborer; P. O. Berwick; rep; U. B.; from Ohio.

Holmes M. laborer for T. Pierce; P. O. Berwick; rep; from Ohio.

Holmes Wm. rents of H. Sheldon; P. O. Berwick; rep; from Ohio.

Holtgreen John, laborer for Lewis; Sec. 19; from Sweden.

Houchin J. W. rents of I. G. Ward; Sec. 17; P. O. Berwick; dem; Bapt; from Ky.

House Wm. rents of C. H. Pierce; Sec. 31; P. O. Greenbush; rep; Meth; from Ind.

Howard F. W. laborer for G. W. Howard; Sec. 12; P. O. Abingdon; dem; born Ill.

Howard G. W. farmer; Sec 12; P. O. Abingdon; dem; owns 255 acres; from Ky.

Howard I. L. rents of G. W. Howard; Sec. 12; P. O. Abingdon; dem; born Illinois.

IDEN H. G. rents of Mary Ray; Sec. 23; P. O. Abingdon; rep; from Indiana.
Iden T. I. rents of Thos. Duncan; Sec. 22; P. O. Abingdon; rep; from Ohio.

JEWEL A. Sec. 16; P. O. Abingdon; rep; owns 160 acres of land; born this Co.
Jewel John, Sec. 16; rep; owns 16 acres; born Illinois.
Jenkins Isaac, retired; Sec. 8; P. O. Berwick; rep; Bapt; owns 156 acres; Ohio.
Johnson G. N. rents of S. Barlow; P. O. Greenbush; rep; from Sweden.
Johnson J. J. Sec. 15; P. O. Abingdon; rep; owns 15 acres, stone quarry; from Ohio.
Johnson J. G. Sec. 22; P. O. Abingdon; rep; Luth; owns 160 acres land; from Sweden.
JOHNSON JAMES S. Farmer; Sec. 15; P. O. Abingdon; born in Marion Co., O., Oct. 29, 1855; came to this Co. in 1859; Rep; Chris.
Johnston James, laborer for Lewis; Sec. 19; P. O. Greenbush; from Sweden.
Johnston Olif, rents of Geo. Snapp; Sec. 23; P. O. Abingdon; rep; from Sweden.
Johnston S. I. rents of Dr. Davis; Sec. 27; P. O. Abingdon; from Sweden.
Johnston Swain L. rents of N. H. Pierce; Sec. 23; P. O. Avon; rep; from Sweden.
Jones A. W. farmer; Sec. 17; P. O. Berwick; dem; owns 105 acres land; Ky.

KONKLER LOUIS, rents of Wm. How; Sec. 11; P. O. Abingdon; dem; N. Y.
Konkler W. R. laborer; Sec. 15; P. O. Abingdon; rep; born Illinois.
KARNS PHILIP, Farmer and Stock Raiser; Sec. 32; P. O. Greenbush; born in Baden, Germany, Oct. 22, 1815; came to Ohio in 1828; came to this Co. in 1846; Rep; Luth; owns 489 acres of land, valued at $36,675; married in Lancaster, O., Aug. 20, 1837, to Nancy Ann Ellinger; was born Nov. 15, 1817, in Tarleton, O.; had 11 children; five living; Catherine, born July 3, 1839; Samuel L., Sept. 19, 1840, died Nov. 1, 1874; Margaret Ann, Oct. 27, 1842; John Henry, Aug. 14, 1845, died March 5, 1877; Mary, Feb. 23, 1848, died March 11, 1864; Philip Jacob, Aug. 19, 1854; a son not named, July 31, 1850; Hulda Jane, Aug. 23, 1851, died Feb. 7, 1863; Wm. Riley, March 24, 1857; Josiah C., Nov. 20, 1859, died May 8, 1862; Joseph E., Jan. 5, 1863.
Kirby J. Sec. 7; P. O. Berwick; dem; Bapt; 156 acres land; from Pennsylvania.
Kirby J. H. Sec. 7; P. O. Berwick; dem; Meth; 150 acres land; from Penn.
Kitchem J. R. rents of J. Jenkins; Sec. 8; P. O. Berwick; rep; Bapt; from Penn.

LANDON JOHN, rents of H. Sheldon; Sec. 8; P. O. Berwick; dem; N. J.
Lavine Olaf, rents of Lewis; Sec. 19; from Sweden.
Lewis H. M. farmer and stock raiser; Sec. 19; P. O. Berwick; dem; from N. J.
Lewis J. V. painter; P. O. Berwick; rep; Bapt; born Illinois.
Lewis N. laborer for H. M. Lewis; Sec. 16; P. O. Berwick; dem; Bapt.
Lincoln C. farmer; Sec. 34; P. O. Avon; rep; owns 160 acres land; from N. Y.
Lincoln Dewit, laborer for Wm. Michum; Sec. 34; P. O. Avon; rep; born Ill.
Linn Joseph, rents of Hiram Sheldon; Sec. 6; P. O. Berwick.
Lincoln Levia, farmer; Sec. 27; P. O. Avon; dem; 296 acres; from New York.
Lomax C. T. farmer; Sec. 12; P. O. Abingdon; dem; 80 acres; born Illinois.
Lomax H. J. laborer; Sec. 1; P. O. Abingdon; dem; 5 acres; from Kentucky.
Lomax L. O. rents land of Jessie Cott; Sec. 24; P. O. Abingdon; dem; born Illinois.
Lomax M. F. rents land of Jessie Cott; Sec. 24; P. O. Abingdon; dem; born Illinois.
Lynch E. farmer; Sec. 4; P. O. Berwick; dem; Mass.
Lynch S. farmer; Sec. 4; P. O. Berwick; rep; 180 acres; from New Hampshire.

McCLANIHAN J. M. physician; P. O. Berwick; rep; Presb; from Ohio.
McCone Isaac, laborer for D. L. Billingsly; P. O. Berwick; dem; born Illinois.
McFarlin John, Sec. 25; P. O. St. Augustine; 60 acres; dem; Cath; from Ireland.
McMillion I. D. rents of S. S. Towner; Sec. 12; P. O. Abingdon; rep; W. Va.
Maguire F. P. laborer; Sec. 36; P. O. Avon; dem; Cath; Penn.
Maguire James, farmer; Sec. 36; P. O. Avon; dem; Cath; 160 acres; from Penn.
Maguire J. M. laborer; Sec. 36; P. O. Avon; dem; Cath; Ohio.
Malcolm Chas. O. laborer on his father's farm; Sec. 5; P. O. Berwick; dem; Ind.
Malcolm Otis, retired; Sec. 5; P. O. Berwick; dem; 220 acres; from Canada.
Maltby F. rents of H. M. Lewis; Sec. 18; P. O. Berwick; dem; born Illinois.
Mann James, rents of Jesse Hardwick; Sec. 17; P. O. Berwick; from Kansas.
Mann T. V. farmer; Sec. 29; P. O. Greenbush; dem; 360 acres; from England.
Maple David, farmer, rents of H. F. Trulock; Sec. 36; P. O. St. Augustine; dem; Ohio.
Marshall Geo. laborer for Geo. Robinson; P. O. Berwick; rep; from Ohio.
Mattison N. retired; P. O. Berwick, rep; Bapt; from New York.

Meadows E. farmer; Sec. 3; Ind; Chris; born Illinois.
Meadows E. J. Sec. 3; P. O. Abingdon; dem; Chris; 571½ acres; from Kentucky.
Meadows G. B. farmer; Sec. 1; P. O. Abingdon; dem; Chris; 120 acres; from Ky.
Meadows G. W. rents of Wm. Miller; Sec. 10; P. O. Abingdon; dem; Chris; Illinois.
Meadows T. farmer; Sec. 3; P. O. Abingdon; dem; Chris; 198 acres; born Illinois.
Meadows Wm. H. laborer for Brooks; Sec. 2; dem; born Illinois.
Mecham B. laborer for H. Mecham; Sec. 33; P. O. Greenbush; dem; born Illinois.
Mecham H. farmer; Sec. 33; P. O. Greenbush; dem; 240 acres; from New York.
Mecham John, farmer, rents of H. Mecham; Sec. 33; P. O. Greenbush; dem; N. Y.
Mecham W. rents of Sanders; Sec. 27; P. O. Greenbush; Ind; from New York.
Meguire M. D. laborer; Sec. 36; P. O. Avon; dem; Cath; from Penn.
Miller James, farmer; Sec. 29; P. O. Greenbush; dem; Cath; from Indiana.
Miller John, farmer, Sec. 90; P. O. Greenbush; dem; Cath; Kentucky.
Miller J. W. farmer, rents of H. M. Lewis; Sec. 16; P. O. Berwick; rep; from Canada.
Miller W. D. farmer, rents of John Miller; Sec. 10; P. O. Abingdon; dem; from Ind.
Moon Terry, farmer; Sec. 26; P. O. St. Augustine; dem; Cath; 80 acres; from Ireland.
Moore W. R. farmer, rents of T. Russell; Sec. 16; P. O. Berwick; dem; Bapt; Kentucky.
Morse S. M. farmer; Sec. 13; P. O. Abingdon; rep; 400 acres; born Illinois.
Morse Wm. L. laborer, lives with his father; Sec. 13; rep; born Illinois.
Morse Wm. B. farmer; rents of S. Morse; Sec. 13; rep; Meth; born Illinois.
Murphy Rev. J. H. farmer; Sec. 15; P. O. Abingdon; dem; Chris; 170 acres; Ky.
Murphy M. C. laborer for J. H. Murphy; Sec. 15; P. O. Abingdon; dem; Chris; Ill.

NACE WM. H. farmer, rents of R. A. Sanders; Sec. 27; P. O. Greenbush.
Near J. L. farmer; Sec. 32; P. O. Greenbush; dem; 120 acres; from Maryland.
Nickles D. C. farmer, rents of Mrs. Baldwin; Sec. 29; P. O. Greenbush; from Indiana.

NILE THOMAS, Farmer; Sec. 21; P. O. Greenbush; born in England, April 10, 1850; came to this County in 1877; Dem; Epis; married April 17, 1873, to Salina Gilbert, born June 17, 1852, in England.

PEACOCK H. M. laborer for J. Cunningham; Sec. 3; P. O. St. Augustine; dem.
Peterson S. S. farmer, rents of S. Cline; Sec. 36; P. O. St. Augustine; from Sweden.
Peterson S. S. farmer, rents of H. E. Trulock; Sec. 35; P. O. St. Augustine; Sweden.

PETERSON SWAN, Farmer, rents of Trulock; Sec. 35; P. O. St. Augustine; born in Sweden; came to this Co. in 1876; Rep; Luth; two children, Henry Benson, and Trofos Olson.

Pierce C. H. farmer; Sec. 31; P. O. Greenbush; rep; 160 acres; born Warren Co.
Pile Thomas, farmer, rents of E. Adams; Sec. 21; P. O. Greenbush; dem; Epis; England.
Porter George, farmer, rents of S. Pierce; P. O. Berwick; rep; Meth; New York.
Porter Lewis, laborer for T. C. Pierce; Sec. 20; rep; Bapt; from Indiana.
Powers A. farmer, rents of Mrs. Baldwin; Sec. 28; P. O. Greenbush.
Powers Z. rents of John Miller; Sec. 30; P. O. Greenbush.
Pratt Albert, rents of Wm. Watson; P. O. Abingdon; dem; from New York.
Purdy R. A. farmer; Sec. 10; P. O. Abingdon; rep; Chris; 23 acres; born Ill.
Purdy S. F. farmer; Sec. 10; P. O. Abingdon; rep; 140 acres; from New York.

RAFFERTY F. H. rents of D. Donsey; Sec. 12; P. O. Abingdon; rep.
Randall Asa, farmer; Sec. 21; P. O. Berwick; rep; Bapt; from New York.
Ray A. M. farmer; Sec. 7; P. O. Berwick; dem; 152 acres.
Ray Daniel, rents of Wm. Clure; Sec. 33; P. O. Greenbush; dem; born Illinois.

RAY G. B. Farmer and Stock Raiser; Sec. 19; P. O. Berwick; born in Ky., April 29, 1824; came to this Co. in 1849; Dem; Bapt; owns 500 acres of land, valued at $25,000; married July, 1846, to Mary A. Moore, born in Ky., Nov. 14, 1829; has six children living, two boys and four girls, Martha A., Elizabeth, Wills J., Mary E., Wilburn W., Sarah Jane.

Ray H. L. laborer on O. Ray's farm; Sec. 8; P. O. Berwick; dem.
Ray Irving, laborer; P. O. Berwick; dem; Bapt; from Kentucky.
Ray Ira, laborer on O. Ray's farm; Sec. 8; P. O. Berwick; dem.
Ray J. Wm. blacksmith; P. O. Berwick; dem; Bapt; from Kentucky.
Ray John W. laborer; P. O. Berwick; born Illinois.
Ray O. farmer; Sec. 8; P. O. Berwick; 200 acres; dem; Bapt; from Kentucky.
Ray Wm. John, rents of Wm. Clure; Sec. 33; P. O. Greenbush; dem; born Illinois.
Ray Willis J. son of G. B. Ray; Sec. 19; P. O. Berwick; dem; Bapt; born Illinois.
Reed J. D. rents of J. L. Reynolds; Sec. 9; P. O. Abingdon; rep; born Illinois.
Reynolds S. Sec. 2; P. O. Abingdon; rep; Chris; 200 acres; from South Carolina.

Robertson Isam, farmer; Sec. 9; P. O. Abingdon; dem; 280 acres; from Kentucky.

Robertson I., farmer; Sec. 9; P. O. Abingdon; rep; Chris; 280 acres; from Ky.

Robinson G. H. farmer; Sec. 13; P. O. Abingdon; ind; Presb; from W. Va.

Robinson G. W. farmer; Sec. 5; P. O. Berwick; rep; 166 acres; from New York.

Rodecker G. W. farmer; Sec. 13; P. O. Abingdon; dem; Presb; from Penn.

Rosell B. laborer for I. Fordice; P. O. Berwick; rep; Bapt; from Pennsylvania.

Rosell J. farmer; Sec. 5; P. O. Berwick; rep; Bapt; 103 acres; from Pennsylvania.

SAMPSON H. rents of Laura Rice; Sec. 22; P. O. Abingdon; dem; from Ind.

Sanbury C. rents of John Reynolds; Sec 15; P. O. Abingdon; rep; from Sweden.

SANBURN JOHN H. Farmer; Sec. 1; P. O. Abingdon; born in Knox Co., Ill., Jan. 8, 1848; came to this Co. in 1868; Rep; Presb; owns 160 acres of land, valued at $7,200; married Oct. 10, 1866, to Miss H. E. Harvey, born in Knoxville, Ill., Oct. 30, 1842; has four children; two girls and two boys; served in the late rebellion in Co. D, 1st Ill. Cav., one year; enlisted in Co. A, 77th I. V. I., Aug. 1, 1862; discharged for promotion March 12, 1864; comd. First Lieut. in 76th U. S. C. I. March 12, 1864; promoted to Capt. Sept. 4, 1865; mustered out Dec. 31, 1865.

Scoby C. rents of Jos. Snider; Sec. 3; P. O. Abingdon; rep; Chris; from Ohio.

Sigmon W. M. farmer; Sec. 1; P. O. Abingdon; dem; U. B.; 80 acres; from Ohio.

Smith Cyrus, laborer on J. Foltz's land; Sec. 2; P. O. Abingdon; rep; from Maryland.

Smith J. laborer on H. M. Lewis' farm; Sec. 18; P. O. Berwick; dem; born Illinois.

Smith Joseph, rents of J. W. Vance; Sec. 26; P. O. Avon; dem; Chris.

Smith John, rents of J. Robertson; Sec. 9; P. O. Abingdon; dem; from Missouri.

Spurgin S. A. laborer for Fairchild; Sec. 29; P. O. Greenbush; dem; born Illinois.

Stairs John, miner; Sec. 23.

STAAT HENRY, Farmer and Stock Raiser; Sec. 30; P. O. Greenbush; born in Ill., in Warren Co., Aug. 7, 1842; Dem; owns 908 acres of land, valued at $45,400; married Aug. 12, 1869, to Cordelia C. Bond, born in Ill., June 2, 1850; has four children, two boys and two girls, Oria A., born Oct. 30, 1870; John F., Nov. 24, 1872; Nellie M., Sept. 30, 1874; Lena Staat, May 4, 1876.

Stiles Cassius, laborer on A. P. Randall's farm; Sec. 21; P. O. Greenbush; rep.

Stokes A. laborer for W. Ray; dem; from Kentucky.

Stokes H. laborer; Berwick; dem; Bapt; from Kentucky.

TAYLOR WM. B. rents of Wm. Simmons; P. O. Greenbush; rep; N. Y.

Thomas Louis, rents of F. G. Snapp; Sec. 23; P. O. Avon; rep; born Illinois.

Thompson E. farmer; Sec. 4; P. O. Berwick; rep; Chris; 58 acres; from Sweden.

Tillson J. M. rents of Mrs. Douglass; Sec. 14; P. O. Abingdon; rep; from Sweden.

Trulock H. F. farmer; Sec. 36; P. O. St. Augustine; rep; 490 acres; from Ind.

Trulock Wm. H. student; Sec. 36; P. O. St. Augustine; rep; from Illinois.

WALKER MRS. S. A. farmer; Sec. 15; P. O. Abingdon; 80 acres; born Ill.

Ward J. G. Sec. 17; P. O. Berwick; dem; Bapt; 347 acres; from New York.

Ward Wm. farmer rents of J. G. Ward; Sec. 17; P. O. Berwick; dem; from Penn.

Watson W. J. farmer and blacksmith; Sec. 5; P. O. Berwick; dem; Presb; Scotland.

Webb A. W. laborer; P. O. Berwick; dem; from Kentucky.

White John, rents of John Sanborn; Sec. 1; P. O. Abingdon; dem; born Illinois.

White Jos. laborer for John Courson; Sec. 11; P. O. Abingdon; rep; Meth; Ohio.

Wilcher Henry, Sec 10; P. O. Abingdon; rep; wife owns 80 acres; from Virginia.

WILSHER JOSIAH, Farmer; Sec. 10; P. O. Abingdon; born in Lynchburg, Va., Oct. 14, 1795; came to this Co. in 1833; Rep; wife owns 80 acres of land, valued at $3,200; married first to Sallie Meadows, in Wayne Co., Ky., July 15, 1816; born in North Carolina, May 14, 1793; second marriage to Jane Perdue, July 23, 1874, born May 14, 1804, in Kentucky; has ten children, three sons and seven daughters, P. H., born May 25, 1817; Elizabeth, Feb. 19, 1819; Rebecca, June 21, 1821; John E., Nov. 14, 1822; Ellen, March 16, 1825; Jane, Jan. 7, 1827; Sarah, Jan. 15, 1829; Thomas K., March 12, 1831; Mary, Sept. 15, 1833; Margaret, Sept. 15, 1836.

Wilcher P. H. farmer, Sec. 10; P. O. Abingdon; rep; Chris; from Kentucky.

Wilcher Mrs. S. Sec. 10; P. O. Abingdon; Chris; 30 acres; from Indiana.

Wrenn F. farmer; Sec. 35; P. O. Avon; dem; 122 acres; from Indiana.

Wrenn John, farmer; Sec. 35; P. O. Avon; dem; 122 acres; from Virginia.

Wrenn J. W. farmer; Sec. 35; P. O. Avon; dem; 122 acres; from Ohio.

YATES JOHN; Sec. 8; P. O. Berwick; dem; Bapt; 63 acres; from Ohio.

Young George, rents of A. Simmons; Sec. 34; P. O. Greenbush; dem; born Illinois.

Young Philip, rents of Mrs. Baldwin; Sec. 29; dem; from Missouri.

www.ingramcontent.com/pod-product-compliance
Lightning Source LLC
Chambersburg PA
CBHW030321240426
43673CB00040B/1235